Oxford University Extension Gazette, Volumes 4-5

THE OXFORD
UNIVERSITY EXTENSION
GAZETTE

VOLUME IV

OCTOBER, 1893—SEPTEMBER, 1894

afterwards, counts, as University Extension ?????

Oxford

PUBLISHED FOR THE PROPRIETORS
BY
HORACE HART, PRINTER TO THE UNIVERSITY

Oxford
HORACE HART, PRINTER TO THE UNIVERSITY

INDEX TO VOLUME IV

OXFORD UNIVERSITY

EXTENSION GAZETTE.

VOL. IV. No. 37.] OCTOBER, 1893. [ONE PENNY.

NOTES ON THE WORK.

We very deeply regret to record here the death of the Master of Balliol (Professor Jowett), who was always such a valuable and warm supporter of the University Extension movement.

.·.

University Extension College, Reading. Mr. George Palmer has recently presented to the college, through his son, Mr. Walter Palmer, a cheque for £500, which he desires may be spent in further equipping the college with furniture and scientific apparatus. He adds the request that a portion of it may be devoted to the new Agricultural Department. This is a very thoughtful gift in a form somewhat rare. Many people are willing to erect public buildings, few bear in mind the great expense of fitting them up.

.·.

We are informed that the Duke of Devonshire will preside at the fourth or fifth lecture of Mr. C. E. Mallet's course at Bakewell, and that the Duchess of Devonshire will on the same occasion give the prizes and awards to previously successful candidates. The Bakewell centre is making rapid progress largely through the indefatigable efforts of the local secretary, Miss Martin.

.·.

We regret to say that Dr. Bailey has found himself too unwell to fulfil his lecture engagements during the present Autumn. The effects of the railway accident from which he suffered in the Spring, have not disappeared as completely as was hoped would be the case, and his medical advisers have enjoined absolute rest till Christmas, after which time there is every reason to believe that he will be able to resume his ordinary work.

.·.

University Extension students in all parts of the country will have noticed with pleasure that Mr. E. B. Poulton has been appointed Hope Professor of Zoology in the University of Oxford. Mr. Poulton has for many years been a Delegate of, and for some time was actively employed in lecturing for, the Oxford University Extension.

.·.

The appointment of Mr. Samuel Barnett to a canonry at Bristol is a becoming, though somewhat tardy, acknowledgement of distinguished services to the public interest. Mr. Barnett has the rare but very valuable gift of making scientific and economical methods of investigation into poverty seem more interesting to the benevolent public than cruder methods of ill-considered largesse. By the timely exercise of this gift he has probably prevented the misdirection of tens of thousands of well-meant subscriptions. With the tact of a gifted teacher, he frequently seizes the exact moment at which it is possible to impress some salutary doctrine on the public mind. He has thus become the spokesman of a point of view which seems rarely to be associated with the gift of seasonable and genial utterance. In his work at Bristol Canon Barnett will be aided by the presence of his brother, Mr. Gilmore Barnett, who has for many years taken a leading part in social work in that city.

.·.

By the death of the Rev. Prebendary Cobbold of Ross, University Extension in that town loses a staunch friend. Mr. Cobbold was a Cambridge man, and rowed in the University Eight in 1841 and 1842. After ordination, he proceeded to China, where he served as a Missionary for eleven years, being appointed in 1857 Archdeacon of Mingpo. On his return from China he had a living in Norfolk, but had been Rector of Ross for the twenty years immediately preceding his death.

.·.

Is Nottingham to have a University? Nottingham, it seems, is ambitious of being a University city, and in his closing remarks Professor Burdon-Sanderson, the President of the British Association, is reported to have said, 'that he could not sit down without congratulating Nottingham on the admirable work which it had accomplished in secondary education and in University teaching, and he could only express a hope that, at some not distant date, the town might become the seat of an actual University, discharging all the functions and enjoying all the privileges which appertain to a University.' This remark, which was received with cheers, no doubt points to the federation of University College, Nottingham, with Mason College, Birmingham, in the proposed Midland University to which Mr. Chamberlain has given his support. As we have before stated in these columns, the formation of a Midland University would be a distinct gain to English higher education. The only doubt is whether the federal system of Universities has worked sufficiently well to warrant its reproduction in the Midlands. If the answer to this query is in the negative, then Birmingham will be the sole seat of the Midland University. This being the case, few people would countenance the idea of founding a separate University at Nottingham, which however, is too remote from Leeds, Manchester and Liverpool, to be conveniently admitted as a constituent member of the Victoria University.

.·.

Mr. Tate of Liverpool has, in addition to his previous gifts, munificently contributed £10,000 to the library wing of Manchester College. We are glad to see that Oxford still receives benefactions as generous as those which have aided her work in former generations.

.·.

University Extension Lecturers at the British Association. Several lecturers have taken part in the Nottingham meeting of the British Association. Mr. Price made an interesting speech on Bimetallism. High praise has been given to Dr. Mill's papers on the Clyde Sea Area and on his Survey of the English Lakes, and also to Mr. Dickson's communication on his recent work in the waters which connect the Atlantic and the North Sea. A London Extension lecturer, Mr. Vivian Lewes, delivered one of the popular lectures during the meeting.

1

A Practical piece of University Extension. Record should be made in these columns of an interesting and useful piece of University Extension, undertaken by the Delegates of the Oxford University Press. They have built exclusively for the use of persons employed by the Clarendon Press, a handsome' and commodious Mechanics' Institute and Boys' and Girls' Club, which was opened on September 16 by the Bishop of Oxford. The plot of ground on which the new Institute stands has many interesting associations. It was once the site of the royal palace of Beaumont. It then became the site of a monastery. Next a workhouse was built upon it, and on the demolition of the workhouse, the site was obtained by the late Cardinal Newman, with the object of building upon it a Roman Catholic College. Very little is known of the intention of the Cardinal in this matter, but rumour has it that the plan of promoting the University education of Roman Catholics by establishing a college in Oxford was abandoned with great reluctance and owing to pressure from a quarter which he could not resist. In any case the Cardinal was not able to carry out his fond hope of establishing a college in Oxford, and the piece of ground fell into the hands of the University.

.·.

Technical Education in Kent. The *County Council Times* of Septemer 15 contains an article on Technical Education in Kent, where Mr. Cousins and Mr. Legge, among other Extension lecturers, have been working. The writer declares that the work done has been successful and popular. The Technical Education Committee have, he says, 'the fullest confidence of the Council, who are perfectly satisfied with the results so far attained, some looking forward to still greater achievements in the coming winter months,' as it is felt that the Committee have got beyond the tentative stage of their work and have now learnt the special character of the work to be done, and are better acquainted with the requirements of the county.

.·.

Technical Education in the County Palatine. Mr. J. A. Bennion has issued his report on the work done by the Technical Education Committee in Lancashire during the past year. The report forms a handsome volume, and its many maps and tables, give a complete record of the work done in the county. Mr. Bennion, speaking of the teachers who as exhibitioners of the Council attended the Oxford Summer Meeting in 1892, states clearly his opinion of the value of the work done by them. 'The work done at Oxford,' he writes, 'was solid practical work, the students being required to be in attendance from 9 to 5 daily. . . . There was nothing superficial in any of their work, but all was done, so far as it went, as thoroughly as was possible ; the lecturers and Professors speaking very highly of the character and perseverance of the students.'

.·.

The need of Secondary Education increasingly felt by the Technical Instruction Committees. The report points out that the chief hindrance in the way of technical education is the want of necessary preliminary instruction to enable students to take advantage of technical classes. With regard to this, Mr. Bennion writes that 'it is quite impossible to profit by any science or technical instruction without the necessary preliminary training, and this has been sadly deficient. (This difficulty) will be met by increased efficiency and raising of the standard of exemption in Elementary Schools, and in the establishment of Continuation Schools under the Education Department ; and lastly by the establishment of Secondary Schools, which will complete the link in the existing chain of instruction provided.' It is to be hoped that the practical experience of this difficulty by the Technical Education Committees will lead to the bringing about of such changes as Mr. Bennion suggests in the direction of unifying and completing our educational machinery.

Oxford Co-operators and Civic Education. At the instance of Mr. George Hawkins, the President of the Co-operative Congress of 1893, a Conference was arranged to take place in Oxford on September 30, under the auspices of the Oxford District of the Co-operative Union, in order to discuss the recommendations of the new Continuation School Code, in regard to the teaching of Citizenship, and to consider the aims of the University Extension movement. Delegates from the Oxford Trades' Unions and other workmen's organizations were invited to be present, and Mr. Sadler was asked to contribute an introductory paper. It is hoped that this meeting may increase public interest in the course of twenty-four University Extension lectures, which will be delivered by Mr. Graham Wallas in Oxford, on the Growth of English Institutions in Town and Country.

.·.

Women Pioneer Lecturers. The Association of Women Pioneer Lecturers has published a report of seven months' work. Including rambles in the Museum during the summer, 87 lectures have been delivered since February. The returns given for the average weekly attendance are printed in an incomplete form and not added up in the report, but we regret to notice that the committee of the Association have adopted the misleading practice of adding up the total number of separate admissions and printing this aggregate as the total attendance at the lectures. The committee of the Association make an appeal for funds. As the fees charged by the Association are much lower than those adopted by the organizations for University Extension, we think that their proper course is, before appealing for outside help, to try the effect of slightly increasing the charge for the lectures.

.·.

The Association for the Maintenance of Higher Education in Newport, Isle of Wight, has issued its programme for the Winter Session. Besides containing an attractive outline of the syllabus of the course, the programme gives a concise and lucid summary of the methods of University Extension teaching. The circular, indeed, might well be taken as a model by other local committees. The chairman of the Executive Committee, of which the Rev. John Dendy is Hon. Sec., is Professor Henry Morley, who, as is well known, was a pioneer of University Extension in England.

.·.

Government Grant for University Extension. We observe with pleasure that the weighty influence of the *Journal of Education* supports the scheme for State aid to local organizers of University Extension.

.·.

Mr. Churton Collins is free to accept an invitation to lecture in the neighbourhood of London on alternate Saturdays both before and after Christmas.

The Dates of the Oxford Summer Meeting, and the British Association, 1894.

WE understand that the Oxford Summer Meeting of 1894 will commence on Friday, July 27, and that the First Part will end on Tuesday, August 7. The Oxford Meeting of the British Association, over which the Marquis of Salisbury will preside, will begin on Wednesday, August 8. This arrangement has been made with a view to meeting the convenience of those who desire to be present, both at the First Part of the Oxford Summer Meeting and of the British Association.

The Second Part of the University Extension Meeting will, we understand, commence on August 8, and end on August 24.

UNIVERSITY EXTENSION COLLEGE, READING.

First Annual Report.

THE report of the first year's work of University Extension College, Reading, has just been issued. It is a striking record of energy and progress. After recapitulating the history of the offer of Christ Church, Oxford, which led to the foundation of the College, and summarizing the constitution of the new society, the report states that the Corporation of Reading allows to the College, at a nominal rent, the use of two buildings, the one erected in 1882 for Science and Art teaching, the other an old building principally of the fifteenth century and originally used as the dormitory of the Hospitium of St. John's attached to the great Abbey at Reading. In December last, owing to the increase of the number of students, additional accommodation became necessary, and the Chairman of the Council, Mr. Herbert Sutton, to whom the College is under great obligations, bought the Vicarage of St. Lawrence, which adjoins the Hospitium, at a cost of £4,500. This property Mr. Sutton offers to convey to the College at any time during the next three years for £400. Pending the accumulation of this fund he has let the house to the College at a rent of £120 a year. Thus, the new College enters into the possession of a line of buildings at once picturesque and historic. A fund is now being raised to make some further addition to the College in memory of Mr. W. I. Palmer, and during the last summer considerable improvements have been made in the internal arrangements of the buildings, there having been added a new biological laboratory and theatre, a new physical laboratory and workshop, and a common-room for the teaching staff. Mr. Sutton has generously advanced a sum of £500 towards the cost of these improvements and Mr. George Palmer has made a gift of £500 to be spent in apparatus and furniture, the Report observing 'that his generosity is the more notable because it has taken a form best calculated to meet the immediate difficulties, and to promote the real efficiency of the Institution.'

After reciting certain privileges already acquired by the College, among them being its recognition as one of the public institutions within the meaning of section 10 of the *Science and Art Directory*, the report sums up the teaching which has been given at the College during the first year. Six hundred and fifty-eight students have attended the classes. This number is exclusive of the audiences at the popular and public lectures, whose numbers would, if taken into account, have swollen the aggregate of attendances to 3,581. For the purpose of obtaining the total 658, no student has been counted more than once. The classes of the College were attended by students who came from the following, among other, places outside Reading:—Newbury, Wokingham, Bracknell, Mortimer, Goring, Pangbourne, Maidenhead, Old Windsor and Didcot. This shows that the new College is exerting attractive influence over a wide area. The staff consisted of twenty teachers, of whom nine were University graduates, two of the latter being ladies. The teaching included two courses of Gilchrist lectures, five courses of public lectures on ordinary University Extension lines, and classes in four departments, viz., Natural Science, Art, the Theory of Music, and Teachers' Training.

The great success of the last department is largely attributed to the support which has been received from Mr. West, of the Reading School Board, and Mr. Tremenheere, Her Majesty's Inspector for the district. The report adds that the Education Department has varied its regulations specially for the College and has shown every disposition to favour its work. It is further stated that eleven students, five of whom are ladies, are studying for University degrees and other higher examinations.

The Students' Association has, we are glad to say, maintained its activity under the new conditions. The authorities of the College have consulted the Association as to the choice of lecturers and subjects for the public lectures of next session. 'It is important,' says the Report, 'both in the interests of the students themselves and of the College, that the Association should continue to flourish.'

A prize scheme has not yet been formulated at the College, but the Dean of Christ Church has promised an exhibition of £10 to enable a student to attend the Oxford Summer Meeting next year.

The relations between the College and the Berks County Council are full of promise for the future. In return for an annual grant, the College has agreed to take over from the Berks County Council the technical classes for teachers in elementary schools, which have been conducted hitherto by the Council itself. The scheme provides for a graduated course of instruction extending over three years, some of the more elementary work being done at two outlying centres, Didcot and Newbury, and the remainder at the College itself. The College Council has, in view of this scheme, been strengthened by the addition of three representatives of the technical education committee of the Berks County Council.

The Report makes the still more important announcement that it is proposed to add to the College an agricultural department, such as exists in the Colleges of Bangor, Leeds and Newcastle. Negotiations with this object are still in progress and are evidently in an advanced and favourable state.

In order to secure the College during the first three years of its existence, Mr. Ravenscroft is raising a fund of £2,000. The subscriptions already received amount to £1,381.

Without going into further financial details we may state that the expenditure of the College during the year has amounted to £2,256. Towards this amount the fees from students attending the College classes have furnished £596 2s. 6d., while the receipts at popular and public lectures come to over £255.

The Report of the College and its attractive Calendar for 1893-4, are full of suggestive interest to students of higher education. It is evident that during the next few years many experiments will be made to bring the means of higher education within the reach of a larger number of our population, and those who are made responsible for any larger experiments in this direction will not fail to seek guidance from the University Extension College, Reading.

Work of the kind which is summarized in the Report of the College is not done except when a group of men of great ability are devoting a large part of their energies to a common object. The Report contains an expression of gratitude to many persons who have co-operated for the success of the College. Among these we may here make special mention of the Principal (Mr. Mackinder), of the President (Mr. Herbert Sutton), and of the Secretary (Mr. Wright).

THE OXFORD CONFERENCE ON SECONDARY EDUCATION.

PERHAPS the most representative gathering which has ever met to discuss an educational question, will assemble in Oxford at the invitation of the Vice-Chancellor of the University, on October 10 and 11.

The meeting indeed merits the name of an educational Parliament. The list of delegates shows that every important educational interest and society in the country will be represented. For the first time, we believe, in the history of the English Universities, there will assemble at Oxford officially appointed representatives of the University of Cambridge, of the University of Durham, of the London University, and of the Victoria University. The Education Department, the Charity Commission, and the Science and Art Department will all be represented. The County Councils' Association will send two delegates, and there will also be representatives from ten of the chief County Councils and nine of the chief School Boards in England. The County Boroughs, the City Companies, the Directors of Technical Education, the National Association for promoting Technical Education are all sending delegates. The Head Masters'

Association, the Head Masters' Conference, the Teachers' Guild, the College of Preceptors, the National Union of Teachers, the Private Schools' Association, the Head Masters of Higher Grade Board Schools, and the Girls' Public Day School Company will all be represented. Delegates are coming from the Associated Chamber of Commerce and from the Society of Arts, while the point of view of the working men will be represented by the General Secretary of the Co-operative Union, and the President of the Co-operative Congress. Almost all the local University Colleges, the University Extension Colleges, the chief Training Colleges for Elementary Teachers, and the majority of the Colleges for the University education of women are sending representatives, while among the individual members of the Congress will be the Bishop of London (who is chiefly responsible for the famous report of the Schools' Enquiry Commission), the Dean of St. Paul's, the Dean of Manchester, Sir John Mowbray, Mr. J. G. Talbot, Sir Bernhard Samuelson, Miss Beale, Miss Buss, Mrs. Bryant, and many others who will speak with authority on the questions before the Conference.

The first sitting of the Conference will be devoted to discussing the need of efficient secondary education in England, and the introductory papers will be contributed by the Head Masters of Rugby and Marlborough; by Mr. MacCarthy of Birmingham, who speaks from special experience of second grade schools; by Mrs. Bryant, who writes on schools for girls; by the Clerk of the Manchester School Board, who is one of the chief authorities in England on 'higher grade' Board Schools; by Mr. Draper of Hemel Hempstead, who writes on preparatory schools; and finally by Professor Jebb, M.P., who will discuss the relation between secondary schools and the University.

At the second Session, the administrative problem will be tackled, and papers will be read on the services which could be rendered to secondary education in England by the local authorities, by teachers, and by the Government and the Universities.

Under the first head of the subject, Mr. H. Hobhouse, M.P., will set forth the work which might be done for secondary education by County Councils, and no one is more qualified to write on this subject than he. An equally eminent representative, Mr. L. Stanley, will discuss the contribution which could be made by the School Boards to the organization of secondary education, while the Dean of Manchester, a practical educationalist of wide influence in the North, will represent the views of those who would not assign the care of secondary education either to the County Councils, or to the School Boards, alone.

The services which could be rendered by teachers in the administration of secondary education will be pointed out by Mr. Arthur Sidgwick (President of the Teachers' Guild) and by Mr. Yoxall (General Secretary of the National Union of Teachers), while in the last place the services which could be rendered by the Government and the Universities, will be discussed by the Bishop of London, who speaks on the subject with the weightiest authority. It remains to be said that about 200 representatives are expected to attend the Conference, and that they will be entertained during their visit to Oxford by the Colleges and members of the University. A full report of the proceedings will be subsequently published, and it is likely that what passes at the Conference will have a great influence on subsequent action in regard to secondary education.

BOOK EXCHANGE COLUMN.

THE following books are offered by the Bedford Students' Association for loan or exchange :—

Prof. Seeley's *Life of Stein.* 3 vols.
Lanfrey, *Histoire de Napoléon.* 5 vols.

The above were used in connexion with Mr. Marriott's course on ' Napoleon and Europe since Waterloo,' and books relating to a course on the ' English Citizen, Past and Present,' would be received in exchange.

Address—Miss BLAKE, St. Andrew's Road, Bedford.

SUMMER MEETING AT UPSALA.

IT is interesting to notice how rapidly the idea of holding Summer Meetings in Universities has spread from country to country. This August has seen for the first time a Summer Meeting at the ancient and famous University of Upsala in Sweden. The committee of organization, which consisted of Mr. Harald Hjärne, Professor of History, Mr. J. A. Lundell, Professor of the Slavonic Languages, and Mr. Adolf Noreen, Professor of Norse Languages, issued a well-arranged and interesting series of papers for the guidance of students attending the Meeting. The course opened on Monday, August 14, and lasted a fortnight from that date. Lectures began at 9 o'clock each morning and apparently lasted, with brief intervals, ti.l 2 p.m. Five lectures in a morning for ten days in succession beats the record of our own busiest Summer Meeting. Work began again at 4 p.m. and was continued till 7, scientific excursions being for the most part confined to this portion of the day. A footnote to the time-table informs the student that the following times were appointed for meals; breakfast from 8 till 9, luncheon at 2.30, supper at 8.30. The Upsala Summer Meeting papers contained a map of the town, showing the University buildings, a summary of railway, postal and telegraphic information, and general directions to students.

Among the courses of instruction offered were lectures on the Ancient History of Israel, Buddhism, Scandinavian and Swedish History, Philology, Psychology, and the history of the Reformation. These formed the chief items of the Arts group.

The instruction in science comprised courses on Astronomy, Physiology, Botany and Geology. Admirable syllabuses were issued in the form to which English eyes are now well accustomed. The syllabus issued by Professor Hjärne on ' Sveriges Statsstick ' runs to sixty-four pages. In a future number we hope to be in a positon to give a further account of the Meeting itself.

THE SUMMER MEETING AT PHILADELPHIA.

IF you ask an American as to the progress of any new institution or idea which has been recently imported into his country, he will probably reply to you that ' it has come to stay.' University Extension gives every indication of having come to America to stay. The direct offspring of the English movement, the American Society for the Extension of University Teaching is scarcely three years old, but it is already long past its infant stages; it is a giant growth, recalling that offspring of the gods which sprang full grown from the head of its creator. From its very birth, it seemed to find the soil of the New World congenial to it. Notwithstanding the fact that in almost every State of the Union the machinery for education of every kind has been carried to a higher perfection than we can boast at home, I think I may say in consequence of this very fact, University Extension seems to have come in to complete, perfect, and round off the whole. Nothing struck me so much as the way in which I met University Extension everywhere. In New York State it is identified with the whole system of the State Library—one of the most extensive and perfect library systems in the world. In Chicago it is a department of the University with its special faculty and equal voice in the control of that establishment. In California and Wisconsin it is much the same, and in Pennsylvania it is in the University of that State that the American Society finds its devotees, its lecturers, and in part its home. Ramifications extend or are being extended to Boston in New England, to Virginia and Maryland in the South, even to wild Kentucky in the centre, or ' out west,' as New York or Philadelphia would say. Applications for information come from Toronto in Canada, and from New Orleans in Louisiana, and wherever the work goes it prospers. A highly-educated and essentially reading people find something that they want in the systematic, thorough, regular, and consecutive consideration of great subjects in History, Literature, or Economics, opportunities for culture are offered which they have not found hitherto, and which they greedily welcome.

Last year two lecturers and officers of the American Society came to Oxford to attend the Summer Meeting. Ostensibly they were there in response to an invitation that they would deliver some lectures on that occasion. But silently and unobserved, they were watching every detail of the organization of that great gathering; they were trying to estimate its effects and powers for influence in the future. They were in fact contemplating a Summer Meeting of their own, arranged upon the model of what they saw at Oxford, at Cambridge, and at Edinburgh.

In due course a notice arrived at the office at Oxford to the effect that the American Society had arranged for its first Summer Meeting to take place in July of this year, and asking that a representative of the work in England might if possible be sent over to take part in it.

Faute de mieux I was selected for this purpose, and accordingly I sailed for New York on June 24, arriving in Philadelphia, the headquarters of the American Society, on July 4, the day before the Meeting was fixed to begin. I arrived from New York in the course of the afternoon, and thus I was in two great American cities on Independence Day and travelled a hundred miles by railway into the bargain. There was no doubt much pent-up excitement and burning patriotism in the breast of every devoted and well-constituted American, but it found vent I believe only in the evening, and then chiefly in exclamations of admiration at the fireworks by which the great event was celebrated. Personally I noticed no particular difference between Independence Day and any other, and there was no sort of bustle, confusion and crush at the stations and in the trains such as the unfortunate traveller in England finds upon August Bank Holiday.

I found the officers of the Society at work in their offices just off Chestnut Street, handsome and commodious offices they were, with swing chairs that must of necessity make labour a delight, with desks, fittings, books, papers, which told a tale of hard work, prosperity, and a thriving organization.

I was welcomed by Dr. Devine, the director of the Summer Meeting, who is no stranger to us in England already, and likely I hope to be even better known— by Mr. Lynam Powell, renowned for his energies in the work in the west and for a complete theory of the ideal syllabus—an ideal which he has done much to interpret into a reality. By them I was introduced to Dr. James, the President of the Society, and to Mr. George F. James, the Secretary. The appearance of these gentlemen certainly gave me the impression of 'Youth at the Helm,' and to this impression I was soon able to add that of ' Pleasure at the prow,' for a very short acquaintance with them was sufficient to show that they were all animated in their work by that enthusiasm and high purpose which makes of his labour a man's chief delight.

The reports they gave me of the prospects of the Meeting were bright and encouraging, except that I found myself marked out for a position of honour as extensive as it was unexpected—as far above my merit as my wishes—for I was put down to give the inaugural address when the Meeting opened next evening.

On receipt of this information, I secluded myself as far as possible for twenty-four hours, and at the end of that time I made my way to the University of Pennsylvania in the chapel of which institution the opening meeting was to be held.

The University is a fine stone building, flanked by a library worthy as a structure and by its contents of its surroundings. The chapel is capable of seating over 600 people with ease, and is reached by a handsome stone staircase which sweeps up from the right and from the left to meet upon a spacious landing fronting the chapel doors. It was here I met Mr. Frederick W. Miles, the Treasurer of the Society, a man whose life, devoted to the cares of business, had made the more sensible to the needs and distractions of culture, a rare spirit from whatever point of view regarded, one who was to

be only too soon called upon, under pressure of terrible domestic affliction, to exhibit qualities of fortitude and resignation such as were scarcely to be looked for even by those who knew him well.

I was also introduced to Mr. George Henderson, Chairman of the University Extension Department in the University of Chicago, to Professor de Garmo, who was to begin a course of lectures next day; to Professor Armes from the University of California, and many others, either students, lecturers, or interested in the experiment about to be tried.

In the chapel about 200 people had gathered, the sexes being about equally distributed, and the proceedings began by a short address from Dr. James, explaining the idea of the Summer Meeting, inviting students to enrol their names, and unfolding the programme of the whole proceedings. The inaugural address followed, and when it was ended Mr. Lynam Powell, the director of excursions, informed us of the arrangements he had made. This 'excursion' department was more highly organized than anything else of the kind I had seen or heard of. The idea was similar to that of Mr. Stead's historical pilgrimages, of which full accounts appeared in the *Review of Reviews*. The whole work of the Summer Meeting was to be centred around the American Revolution, and each excursion, of which there were to be four—one on each Saturday during the month—was intended to illustrate in a special manner some feature of the great struggle. Thus on the first Saturday we were to be conducted to ' Independence Hall,' in which a lecture was to be given on the growth of the idea of independence. Such a lecture, delivered under the very roof which covered the signatories of the Declaration in 1776, could not fail to have a peculiarly realistic effect, and bring home to the audience with striking vividness the beginnings of the American nation. Another excursion was to be to the field of Brandywine, another to Germantown, another to Valley Forge. In each case the students were to be under the special conduct of those who were best qualified to dilate upon the local features of those fields and their importance in relation to the history of the war. While on the subject of these excursions, I may say with regard to the last three, which I was unable to join, that I learned before I left America, that they had been an immense success. Hospitality was lavishly bestowed by each locality upon the visitors. It seemed as if each spot thought itself honoured by the concourse of patriotic sons and daughters of America, which flocked to investigate its traditions and its story. The benefit which the whole community must derive in proportion to the interest in the nation's history which each individual exhibits, was recognized to the full, and these excursions were by no means the least valuable features in the Meeting as a whole.

Serious work began at 8.30 the next morning, July 6. At this hour Prof. Mace began his course upon the American Constitution. It was found that about 150 students had enrolled their names, and as the Meeting proceeded this number was increased to over 200. The figures may strike those accustomed to the Oxford gathering as meagre, but when the facts are all considered, the managers must have felt that they had every cause for congratulation. It was the first Meeting of the kind which had ever been held in America. The gathering at Chatauqua must not be put in comparison, for Chatauqua is a summer resort. An immense concourse collects there amid lakes and hills and fresh breezes, as much I suspect for the air and change of scene as for the purposes of serious study. At Philadelphia almost all who enrolled were students, bent upon a month of hard work; in a city where the thermometer stands in the summer at 90° in the shade; a city from which every one in July flies to the sea, in order to escape from a moist and enervating heat which at times is almost unbearable. Oxford is fairly hot at times and always enervating, but Oxford is one of the most beautiful cities in the world, Its venerable buildings; its traditions stretching back to the infancy of our race; its spires and pinnacles, with all the memories which they evoke, make it in a sense the Mecca of England. Simply to visit Oxford and to spend a month there, in that atmosphere where past and present seem to blend to form a keen yet dreamy sense of intellectual voluptuousness, this is in itself sufficient to ensure to our Summer Meetings a numerical success such as no other city but Cambridge could secure ; a success containing perhaps some elements of danger merely by virtue of its being numerical. Philadelphia, rich as she is in associations, cannot rely upon them to attrâct in any large degree. She has to rely upon the enthusiasm of students anxious to extend their range of knowledge, and her first experiment attracted more than 200 of these.

In addition to the courses of lectures which treated of the American War, there were courses on Biology, Geology, Pedagogy, Economics, and such other subjects as form a part of the regular University Extension curriculum. There is no need to refer to them in detail, more especially as owing to the stress of my own work, I was unable to attend more than two or three. In the evenings the regular lecture was sometimes set aside for conferences on the general subject of education and of University Extension, and I shall never forget the pleasure with which I listened to Dr. James' paper on the aims of education, or the lively debate which followed a paper by Dr. Roberts of the London Society on the aims and objects of University Extension. Of all this however I have no space to speak, nor of the pleasant intercourse I had on my way home with Mr. George F. James, who was travelling to England to attend the Summer Meeting at Cambridge. *Vir pietate gravis*, Mr. James bears the weight of less than thirty summers with a lightness and a dignity, which mark him as a leader in high enterprises and, under the Presidential auspicies of his brother, his own secretarial activity and the devotion and ability of Dr. Devine, Mr. Rolfe, Mr. Powell and the others who bear the brunt of the work as lecturers, the American Society cannot fail to fulfil the hopes and expectations which attend it on our side the water no less than on its own.

E. L. S. HORSBURGH.

THE GOVERNMENT GRANT FOR LOCAL COLLEGES.

THE Treasury grant for University Colleges in Great Britain comes up for reconsideration at the end of this year. There is no question whatever that the usefulness of the grant has exceeded the hopes of its most sanguine supporters. It has probably increased the efficiency of higher education in England more than any other single administrative act on the part of the State.

We have always maintained, however, that the Colleges in receipt of the grant should be required to make to Parliament, once in every year, a full report of their operations. The public are interested in the work of the Colleges, and it is in every way expedient to keep public opinion well informed as to the kind of work which the Government grant is making possible. It is satisfactory, therefore, to observe that Mr. Acland intends in future years to publish a full report of the work of each of the local Colleges in receipt of the Government subsidy. As a matter of fact, the Colleges are already required to furnish the Government with the details on which such a report could be based, and Mr. Acland's intention to bring a summary of these several communications under the notice of Parliament will be heartily welcomed on all sides.

The practical question is what shall this local College grant stand at in future years. That it is a popular subsidy there is no doubt. It helps to bring the highest education within the reach of every man and woman in towns where the local Colleges happen to be established. It remains to make the grant still more popular, by allowing a portion of it to be available for the use of the local organizers of University Extension teaching. We hope that steps will be taken to press this matter on the attention of the Government. The fate of University Extension does not depend on Government grants, but a Government grant could enormously increase its efficiency and the thoroughness of its instruction. No higher

education in the world is self-supporting. There is no reason why University Extension should be made the one exception to the rule. Every one who pays taxes contributes his share to the present Local College grant. There is no reason why his enjoyment of the results of that grant should be determined by the accident of his residence. The small towns need higher education at least as much as the large ones, and the arguments which justify Government in aiding the one should impel it also to assist the other.

A CENTRAL BOARD FOR TECHNICAL INSTRUCTION.

(*Communicated.*)

IT is rumoured that the Government contemplates the establishment of a Central Board to advise the County Councils in the administration of the grants for technical and scientific education. There is a great deal to be said for the formation of such an authority. I am not among those who join in the idle cry that the County Councils have wasted their educational funds in foolish experiments. On the contrary, the records show that they have on the whole discharged the new duties, which were suddenly imposed upon them by the allocation of the 'Whiskey Money,' with administrative ability and good sense. It must be remembered that the work of technical education was entrusted to the County Councils almost without notice, and at a time when public opinion, though it had begun to realize the need for technical education, had a very dim idea as to how to meet that need in practice. Under these circumstances much of the work of the County Councils had to be tentative and provisional. Different counties and different districts of the same county vary much in their educational needs and interests.

It will be the work of years to adjust the curriculum and the methods of technical instruction to these various requirements. Time will have to elapse before the teachers, and the technical instruction committees themselves, have fully won the confidence of the less educated part of the population. Much also will have to be learnt through bitter experience as to the practical need of local organization. But the Councils are, with perhaps a few exceptions, working steadily on the right lines. Patience and perseverance are alone required to make the administration of the Technical Instruction Acts not only a national benefit but a conspicuous success.

It is not therefore on the ground of the inaptitude or follies of the County Councils that I write in support of the scheme for the establishment of a Central Advisory Board. My belief is that the County Councils would be materially aided in their work by the suggestions of such a body. There is a need of some means of bringing before the public at regular intervals a concise yet complete statement of the educational work which is being done by the different County Councils. Such a summary ought to be accompanied by authoritative comments and criticism. But the production of such a report cannot be undertaken by any committee, except one possessing the authority of a Government Department.

Moreover the recommendations and the prestige of such a Central Board would strengthen the County Councils against the foes in their own households. We must not blind ourselves to the fact that there exists in every County Council an obscurantist minority which would, if it got the chance, wreck technical education. It is advisable therefore that the friends of technical education should rally their forces and welcome the moral aid which would be given to them in their work by a well-equipped Government Board.

One further reason may be adduced for the scheme. At present it is open to any critic of technical education to urge that the grants are precarious. This uncertainty cuts at the root of the efficiency of the higher grades of educational work. County Councils should be able to depend on the continuance of their educational income. The establishment by Parliament of a Central Board for technical education would be the best guarantee for the permanence of the present grants.

It may seem hardly necessary to lodge a protest against any plan which would hamper the educational freedom of the County Councils. No one who knows the attitude of the chief officials of the Education Department towards these matters will for a moment suspect them of any intention of pressing for harassing state control, but voices may here and there be raised, from those who have not realized the recent changes in educational policy, against what they would call the paralyzing interference of the State. Such critics, however, will agree with us in saying that what we want for technical education is a combination of local freedom of initiative with advice, suggestion and stimulus from headquarters. This, as we understand the matter, is exactly what would be accomplished by the formation of a Central Board.

The silly system of making payment by results is doomed. But the only practical alternative to the system is intelligent, sympathetic and adequate inspection. Where is the staff of inspectors to come from? Without such a staff, the County Councils must either sterilize their local teachers by enforcing payment by results, or they must leave the local teachers to their own devices. A purely local or county inspectorate would fail in prestige, and possibly in detachment of opinion. An inspector should, above all things, be above local bias, and be beyond the reach of local retribution. We need therefore for purposes of technical education a regular staff of qualified and experienced inspectors, representing both local experience and the independent criticism of headquarters. Some of these inspectors might well be local men, but they should represent the State and be appointed by the State. The formation of a Central Board for technical education is the quickest road towards the formation of such a body of inspectors.

We expect that there is a good deal of difficulty in deciding as to which department should undertake the duties of the proposed Central Board. It must of course be affiliated to the Educational Department, and be under the ultimate control of the Vice-President of the Council. But when we ask whether the new duties should be wholly entrusted to any existing department, difficulties begin to crop up. South Kensington is unpopular, as there is a wide-spread feeling that in its management of scientific education, it has missed a great opportunity. And yet it is clear that South Kensington must be represented on any central authority for technical education. Other departments of the State have also a claim for representation. It is essential, for example, that the Board of Agriculture should be strongly represented on any such central authority. It seems probable, therefore, that, if the new Board is formed, it will be of a composite character.

We can imagine one further objection to the whole scheme. Some people have it in their mind that the present technical instruction funds will some day be made available for secondary education. They would therefore prefer to wait until secondary education is organized, before they entrust to any new board the duty of advising the County Councils in their application of the educational funds; for, as they would rightly say, an authority which is competent to direct the expenditure of technical education would not necessarily be qualified to supervise the expenditure on secondary education as well. We hope that this dilatory kind of argument will not receive undue attention. The organization of secondary education will be a long business, and will be much more costly than people at present seem to dare to say. For the supply of a complete system of secondary education, the ' Whiskey Money' will be wholly inadequate. Moreover the whole of it, every penny of it, will be required for an efficient supply of technical and scientific education. Let the whole fund therefore, be definitely set aside for this purpose. Good use can be made of the money, and all of it will be needed. There is no reason in the interests of secondary education to withstand the formation of a Central Board for technical instruction, which would naturally be composed of men experienced in technical, scientific and administrative matters.

X.

THE BRITISH ASSOCIATION AND HIGHER EDUCATION AT NOTTINGHAM.

A SPECIAL feature of the successful meeting of the British Association, which was held in September at Nottingham, has been the part played in the organization by the local University College. Every one has remarked how much the scientific work of the meeting was aided by the use of the lecture rooms of the college, the staff of which has taken a leading part in the local arrangements of the gathering.

Mr. Goldschmidt stated on September 20, that University College, Nottingham, was the outcome of the British Association Meeting at that town in 1866. Put in this form the statement is inaccurate, as the College at Nottingham grew directly out of University Extension work. But there is no doubt that the impetus given to scientific teaching by the British Association in 1866 was one of the factors which led to the remarkable experiment made by the Town Council of Nottingham, in the foundation of University College. It is much to the purpose to remember that the influence of a group of highly-skilled teachers in the town is very marked, both upon local industries and local government. Every now and again on an important occasion like the meeting of the British Association, we see special manifestations of this influence. But as a matter of fact it is always operating and the town is materially and intellectually the richer for its expenditure on higher education. What we should aim at in University Extension is to provide towns, which cannot afford a college equal in equipment to that of Nottingham, with the best attainable substitute for it. Once started on a firm foundation, work of this kind will prosper almost everywhere. There is no reason why, within the next twenty years, England should not be covered with a network of University Extension Colleges, closely federated to the ancient universities. Our aim is to meet the educational needs of the present without losing our hold upon the educational advantages which we have inherited from the past.

IS A ROYAL COMMISSION NEEDED FOR SECONDARY EDUCATION?

THE Provost of Queen's College has a striking letter in the August number of the *Journal of Education*, on the subject of a Royal Commission to inquire into secondary education in England. The *Journal* had pooh-poohed the suggestion that such a Commission was desirable, adding that the objections to such a course had been so fully stated at the Oxford Conference of the Teachers' Guild, that the question need not be re-opened. The Provost disputes this inference from the discussions at the Guild, and endorses the view of Mr. Grubb of Scarborough, ' that great good would come of a full inquiry into existing needs, similar to that instituted by the Schools' Inquiry Commission nearly thirty years ago.' Dr. Magrath concludes, ' I wonder that any one at all conversant with the present confusion of opinion as to the proper aims, methods and possibilities of secondary education, could have any doubt that a rigorous inquiry into these must precede any attempt which is to have the least hope of value or success.' To this the *Journal* replies ' that an inquiry instituted under the direction of the Education Department or the Charity Commission, or the two boards combined, would be sufficient for the purpose.' In our opinion no mere departmental inquiry would have the prestige which is necessary for the successful and searching investigation which circumstances require, nor would it sufficiently attract the attention of the public. We need to impress the public mind with our deficiencies in respect of organization and to secure from the best brains in the country varied suggestions for the cure of those deficiencies. Moreover, the recommendations of the Commission would precede legislation. It is essential that these practical suggestions should emanate from a body directly representing the teachers and business men of the country as well as the administrative ideas of one or two Government Departments.

LETTER TO THE EDITOR.

[We do not hold ourselves responsible for the opinions expressed by our correspondents.]

The Edinburgh Summer Meeting.

DEAR SIR,—It is quite certain that the very frank and vivid account of the Edinburgh Summer Meeting, published in the *Gazette* for September, will be read with great interest by those Extension students who were present. Their own experience will prevent them from attaching too much importance to the defects and shortcomings so plainly set forth by the writer. But perhaps they may feel a little uneasy as to the impression likely to be produced on students who may be readers of the *Gazette*, and who were not present.

In the Memoirs of a Mother-in-law, that misunderstood but excellent lady remarks :—' It is all very well to speak plainly as long as you can do it within four walls, but when it comes to speaking your mind plainly in print, there are a great many things which you have to consider.' A few students from the South who were deeply interested in the Edinburgh Meeting would like to add to the plain-speaking of the report one or two considerations which, in their opinion, should not be omitted, if it is to convey anything like an adequate idea of the value of the Meeting.

Three of these students are themselves occupied in teaching. They cannot speak too highly of Mr. Arthur Thomson's Biological course, and the practical laboratory work done under his guidance, nor of the corresponding Botanical work under Mr. Turnbull. Sections for the microscope were prepared for each individual student, while practical instruction was afterwards given in the processes of preparation and mounting. Few, we think, could fail to respond to the tone of the lectures given by Mr. Thomson ; they were remarkable for lucid expression, for careful discrimination between the history of scientific facts and the history of their interpretation, and yet more for a certain poetic element impossible to define. The objection that to ' understand Weismannism one must get up early,' &c., really does not apply to a course intended primarily for those who were already students of the subject, and who would therefore especially rejoice to hear a gentle and suggestive criticism of well-known modern theories.

After all, the great advantage and refreshment for the student at the Summer Meetings is the coming into direct contact with genuine thinkers—men or women of earnest and thoughtful minds. Such minds reveal themselves in the spoken lecture to an extent which would perhaps surprise the speakers, if they quite knew how much had been conveyed by manner and method.

Even if we cannot to the full share the enthusiasm of such devout disciples as M. Baillache, the Boswell of M. Demolins, we wish cordially and gratefully to bear witness to the great charm of the Edinburgh Meeting.

WESSEX.

THE DISTRICT AND COUNTY ASSOCIATIONS.

THE report of the Lancashire and Cheshire Association for the Extension of University teaching, contains many proofs of the energy with which the Executive Committee of the Association have promoted the interests of the movement. An important conference of the Association took place at Altrincham on September 30, at which Mr. Abbott and Mr. Phythian read interesting papers on subjects connected with University Extension. We hope that it was possible for the leaders of the Association to make satisfactory announcements as to the future attitude of the Lancashire County Council towards University Extension work. A report of the Meeting, at which Mr. C. E. Mallet represented the Oxford Delegacy, will appear in our next issue.

We understand that Mr. Wade has resigned his position as joint Hon. Sec. of the South-Western Association for the Extension of University teaching. Miss Beatrice Vivian, to whom University Extension in the west, and especially in Cornwall, is under heavy obligations, retains her office as Hon. Sec. We have no doubt that the foundation of the University College at Exeter will do much to strengthen the work of the Association in that county.

The Yorkshire Association for the Extension of University teaching has taken the excellent step of forming a scholarship fund for the Summer Meetings. We hope that this fund will be re-opened during the coming session, and that several Yorkshire students will be thereby enabled to attend the Oxford Summer Meeting of 1894.

THE WORK OF THE BOARD OF AGRICULTURE.

PEOPLE are beginning to realize what excellent work is being done for agricultural and technical education by the Board of Agriculture, and its report therefore for 1892-3, which was published a few days ago, is full of interesting reading.

First, the system of Extension lectures has taken a prominent place in the programme of the agricultural instruction. Five of the institutions aided by the Board have been responsible among them for the delivery during the year of 168 courses of University Extension lectures on science and its application to agriculture. This is very satisfactory to us, as the Oxford Delegacy was the first to suggest to the County Councils the advisability of making peripatetic teaching part of their scheme of technical education. The Extension lectures reported by the Board of Agriculture seem to have been as a rule well attended, though in mid-Wales there is some difficulty about language. The Yorkshire College has imitated the Oxford Delegacy in sending out travelling libraries to the centres. The Board reports 'that the diffusion of general knowledge and the promotion of a spirit of intelligent inquiry have been secured by peripatetic lectures and evening classes.'

The next point which strikes us in the Board's report is their policy of strengthening head centres of agricultural instruction. The Extension lectures mentioned above have all been delivered from four colleges subsidized by the Board, viz. University College, Bangor ; Yorkshire College, Leeds ; Durham College of Science, Newcastle ; University College, Aberystwyth. In addition to these four centres the Board mention that a beginning has been made at University College, Nottingham, and ' at Reading by a development of the instruction offered at the University Extension College there, which is worked in connexion with the Oxford Extension Delegacy.' It is clear that the Board are thinking of the University Extension College, Reading, as the best centre of higher agricultural instruction for Berks, Hants, Wilts and Oxon.

In the third place, striking testimony is borne in the Report to the value of short courses of higher instruction offered at some collegiate institutions for the benefit of those who can only spare a brief absence from their practical work. It is exactly the policy which the Oxford Delegacy have maintained in regard to their Summer Meeting, and we are glad to see it endorsed from an entirely different quarter.

But higher teaching of this kind and for the matter of that extension teaching too, especially in small places, cannot be self-supporting. Therefore the grants made by the Board are steadily mounting up. Since 1888-9 the grants have been more than doubled and now stand at £7,425 a year.

In the last place, expenditure on this scale cannot be permitted without adequate and experienced inspection. Three of the County Councils have placed the whole of their agricultural instruction under the inspection of the Board of Agriculture. Several others have taken preliminary steps in the same direction. What is wanted is a combination of local and central inspection, and towards this the Board of Agriculture is certainly showing the way.

A SCHOOLMASTER'S IDEAS ON THE CONTROL OF SECONDARY EDUCATION.

MR. G. D. DAKYNS in a paper on the relation of elementary to secondary education, read to the Head Masters' Association at their summer gathering, claimed that our educational system can be unified without resort to any very heroic measures. To secure unification he proposed a three-fold policy. First, he would set up in every town in the kingdom a practical educational ladder. Among other agencies Mr. Dakyns clearly has in mind University Extension, which is the best means of providing a link between the secondary schools and the University. Mr. Dakyns' second method is the co-ordination of scholastic effort. But you cannot mark out the province and duties of elementary and secondary education until you have set up an authority, which all grades respect. This implies a local authority, say one in each county, and a central department in London. Mr. Dakyns does not seem to see that his own requirements involve the very kind of machinery against which he too hastily protests.

His third suggestion is, that there should be a greater interchange of experience between teachers, and that one grade should have more sympathy with another than is at present the case. This is excellent. It is a truth which should be preached in season and out of season, but how comes Mr. Dakyns to have forgotten the excellent work of the Teachers' Guild, which has existed for years in order to achieve this purpose? All those who sympathize with the aim of the Teachers' Guild and of Mr. Dakyns will welcome the action of the University of Oxford in convening a gathering, representative of every grade of teachers, to discuss the problems connected with the organization of secondary education.

THE PRESIDENT OF MAGDALEN AND SECONDARY EDUCATION.

IN the course of an eloquent address to the Head Masters' Association at Oxford, the President of Magdalen referred to the expected re-organization of secondary education in England.

'There are,' he said, 'two great fundamental questions with regard to secondary education. (1) What should be the curriculum of secondary schools? (2) What should be their government.' On both of these points the President made some timely observations.

In the first place, he pleaded that education should not be too technical, and that too early or too rigorous a specialization should be guarded against. 'The human being,' Mr. Warren said, 'becomes by too great specialization a living tool, which is Aristotle's definition of a slave. Education should be liberal, and, if technical education is to be really worthy of its name, it should be not only technical but educational as well. But it can only be made so by importing into it liberalizing elements and ideas, and by showing the people its relation to wider considerations and to knowledge as a whole.' This side of the question needs emphasis at this particular moment, though the President is undoubtedly right in maintaining that there exists in England at the present moment a great and increasing belief in higher liberal and literary education.

University Extension teaching, so long conducted in almost every town in England, has done yeoman service in gradually changing the public ideal of higher education, but the battle is by no means won yet. The tide is just beginning to turn, and we must lose no opportunity of enforcing and supporting the ideas which the President of Magdalen so well expressed.

Turning to the other part of his subject, the government of secondary schools, the President drew attention to the paramount need of trusting the teachers in administration. 'If,' he remarked, 'you get the right masters and allow them sufficient freedom, they will be able to modify the curriculum in accordance with the needs of the pupil in the school.' We must try to prevent the control of secondary education passing too exclusively into the hands of administrators. Government supervision is excellent, local control is necessary; but to these two indispensable elements in a re-organized system of secondary education we must add a third factor, namely the responsibility and initiative of the teacher. This then is the time that teachers should unite. We have not yet impressed upon the imagination of the country the fact that all teachers belong to one profession. Divided in sections, teachers are weak. Organized as a profession, they might become, within right limits, paramount in the guidance of education.

CONCERNING THE CENTRES.

BAKEWELL.—On Thursday, Sept. 14, a meeting of the Students' Association was held in preparation for an excursion to Chatsworth. Short papers were read by the students on the various authors, sculptors and painters of the eighteenth century, whose works were to be found in the Chatsworth collections. The excursion took place on Saturday, Sept. 16. Special permission was kindly granted by Her Grace the Duchess of Devonshire to enable the students to see whatever might be of interest, in connexion with Mr. Mallet's lectures on 'England in the Eighteenth Century.' The students, numbering forty-two, met at Chatsworth at 12 o'clock, and were received by Mr. and Mrs. Gibson Martin and the Secretary. They then examined, without crowd or hurry, the Duke of Devonshire's valuable art collections. Statues, sculptured by the father of Colley Cibber, were pointed out in the chapel. Carvings by Gibbons, paintings by Reynolds and Kneller, engravings by Hogarth and Bartolozzi, pottery by Wedgwood, illustrated the various developments of art in the eighteenth century. But the chief centre of interest was the library. Placed in glass cases and representing the special period under consideration, were original editions of the writings of Walpole, Bolingbroke, Chesterfield, Burke, Prior, and Gibbon, also of first editions of *The Tatler* and *The Spectator.* The original manuscript of Pope's *Epistle to the Earl of Burlington,* and a contemporary MS. copy of Swift's *History of the Years* 1711 and 1712, corrected and annotated by Swift himself. While among the books of general interest were Claude's *Liber Veritatis,* Henry VII's *Book of Prayers,* and several Caxtons. After a primitive lunch and a stroll of nearly two hours in the grounds, the whole party reassembled at Edensor, where they were entertained at tea by Mr. and Mrs. Gibson Martin. The Bakewell Students' Association is greatly indebted to the Duchess of Devonshire for the kind interest she is taking in their work, and for the facilities she granted them, by means of which the excursion was not only interesting but also thoroughly stimulating and instructive.

LEOMINSTER.—Miss J. D. Montgomery of Exeter kindly paid a visit to this centre on Sept. 11, and gave an excellent lecture in the Town Hall, on the advantages offered to all classes by the Extension lectures and the Summer Meetings at Oxford and Cambridge. It was much to be regretted that there was not a larger attendance, but the fine weather still tempts every one to spend their evenings out of doors. The chair was taken by the Rev. G. Whitehouse, who contrasted the time when education was locked up in monasteries with the wide-spread beneficial influence among all classes which it now seeks to achieve. Miss Montgomery showed that by means of the Extension movement the Universities were now in touch with the national life. In this they were returning to their original ideal, when in the early enthusiasm of their rise, their work was not confined to any age, class or sex. The sense of interests and aims in common which was specially felt at the Summer Meetings was dwelt upon, and the further advantages of these gatherings impressed by a number of excellent lantern slides of some of the most characteristic views of Oxford and Cambridge.

THE FUTURE OF SOUTH KENSINGTON.

A SIGNIFICANT conversation took place in the House of Lords on September 8. The Bishop of Salisbury asked the Lord President of the Council whether the Science and Art Department would reconsider the exclusive system of payment by results of examination, in view of the effects of that system and the general dissatisfaction of science teachers with it, and would adopt that in use in the Education Department of fixed grants for scholars properly attending and instructed, supplemented by a system of rewards for those who show special merit.

The Earl of Kimberley replied as follows:—

'The aid of the Department is not granted exclusively on a system of payment by results of examination. A capitation

not exceeding one penny per lecture, or sixpence for the course of ten; printed syllabuses of the course being supplied to the audience at a cost not exceeding one penny per copy.

In the event of less than fifty lectures being given, the amount of grant to be reduced in proportion.

SIR WILLIAM HART DYKE, M.P., ON THE POSITION OF TEACHERS.

SIR WILLIAM HART DYKE made some very sensible remarks on October 21 at a meeting held under the auspices of the National Union of Teachers. He remarked that 'Upon entering on his duties at the Education Office he was at once convinced that there was something wrong in their educational system as regarded the relations between the teachers and the Department. He found incessant friction, hard language, and strong minutes, the result of which was most undesirable. He came to the conclusion that no system could be good where such constant friction arose, and set himself the task of accomplishing some improvement. A good many difficulties presented themselves, but ultimately he was enabled to relieve teachers from the bonds by which they had been fettered, and gave them elbow-room, as it were, in their work. He gave them a freedom of classification and other advantages which he believed had made the teachers' task pleasanter and easier of performance, at the same time producing something like a revolution in this direction.'

Sir William Hart Dyke further pointed out the extreme importance of paying good teachers well for their work, and there is no doubt that a good instrument in education is cheap at the price. It is encouraging to see that the representative speakers on both sides of the House of Commons agree in thinking that teachers in elementary schools should have a larger freedom of initiative. Is it not reasonable to urge that they should enjoy the same liberty and administrative freedom which is at present given to teachers in secondary schools, and that the latter should share with the former the special training in educational methods which has done so much to increase the efficiency of teachers in elementary schools? In fact, what we have to work for is the unity of the teaching profession—not a sham unity of mere bowing and politeness, but a real unity based on constant interchange of experience, on associated effort, and as far as possible, on the possession of an identical University training.

UNIVERSITY EXTENSION IN AUSTRALIA.

THE *Melbourne University Extension Journal* has just completed its first year of issue. Two Students' Associations have been formed in connexion with the Melbourne branch of the movement, and one of them has met with remarkable success. We are glad to see that the leaders urge upon all the local centres the desirability of forming Students' Associations. There is every sign that University Extension in Victoria has a bright future before it.

The University Extension Board of the Sydney University report a falling off in the attendance at the lectures. It is possible that commercial depression has something to do with this decline, which we trust will be only temporary. Six courses have already been sanctioned for the present session, one being on Economics, one (by a lady lecturer) on Roman History, one on Victorian Literature, one on Mineralogy, and two on Physiography. The Board has seventeen lecturers on the Staff, four being Professors of, and three more directly connected with, the University.

Professor Scott, an old Oxford man, who is Chairman of the Sydney University Extension Board, visited Brisbane in May, and helped to start the Extension movement in Queensland. The Queensland Council decided to work in connexion with the Sydney Board, and a course has been sanctioned in Brisbane under their joint auspices.

We hear also that Tasmania is following the lead of Victoria and of New South Wales, and the *Melbourne University Extension Journal* remarks that 'the prospects of University Extension are widening so rapidly that very soon we may be within reach of an Australasian System.'

ARRANGEMENTS FOR 1893-4.

Autumn, 1893.

Centre.	No. of Lectures in Course.	Subject of Course.	Lecturer.	Course begins.	Course ends.
UNIVERSITY EXTENSION COLLEGE, READING (afternoon)	12	The Homeric Poems	J. CHURTON COLLINS, M.A.	S. Sept. 30	Dec. 9
TODMORDEN (evening)	6	Puritan Revolution	Rev. W. H. SHAW, M.A.	M. Sept. 25	Dec. 4
PRESTWICH (evening) ...	6	Making of England	„ „ ...	M. Oct. 2	Dec. 11
MANCHESTER, ANCOATS (even.)	6	Making of England	„ „ ...	W. Sept. 27	Dec. 6
OLDHAM (evening)	6	Making of England	„ „ ...	W. Oct. 4	Dec. 13
CHESTER (afternoon)	6	Making of England	„ „ ...	F. Sept. 29	Dec. 8
HYDE (evening)	6	Making of England	„ „ ...	F. Oct. 6	Dec. 15
BIRMINGHAM, SEVERN ST. (evening)	6	Making of England	„ „ ...	T. Oct. 3	Dec. 12
WIGAN (afternoon)	6	Age of Elizabeth	„ „ ...	W. Sept. 27	Dec. 6
RIPON (evening)	6	Age of Elizabeth	„ „ ...	T. Sept. 26	Dec. 5
RIPON (afternoon)	6	Florence	„ „ ...	T. Sept. 26	Dec. 5
CHEETHAM (evening) ...	6	Florence	„ „ ...	F. Sept. 29	Dec. 8
KENDAL (afternoon) ...	6	Florence	„ „ ...	M. Oct. 2	Dec. 11
BOLTON (afternoon)	6	Venice	„ „ ...	Th. Oct. 5	Dec. 14
BOLTON (evening)	6	Making of England	„ „ ...	Th. Oct. 5	Dec. 14
LANCASTER (afternoon) ...	6	Venice	„ „ ...	Th. Sept. 28	Dec. 7
LANCASTER (evening) ...	6	Representative Englishmen ...	„ „ ...	Th. Sept. 28	Dec. 7
STAFFORD (afternoon) ...	6	Venice	„ „ ...	T. Oct. 3	Dec. 12
HODDESDON (afternoon) ...	12	Louis XIV and Frederick the Great	J. A. R. MARRIOTT, M.A.	T. Sept. 26	Dec. 19
BANBURY (evening) ...	6	English Colonies	„ „ ...	F. Oct. 6	Dec. 15
CLEVEDON (afternoon) ...	6	Europe since Waterloo ...	„ „ ...	Th. Oct. 5	Dec. 14
WELLS (evening)	6	England in the 18th Century ...	„ „ ...	Th. Oct. 5	Dec. 14
ROMSEY (afternoon)	6	Historical Plays of Shakespeare...	„ „ ...	W. Sept. 27	Dec. 6
WINCHESTER (afternoon) ...	6	The Tudors	„ „ ...	Th. Sept. 28	Dec. 7
LYMINGTON (afternoon) ...	6	Europe since Waterloo	„ „ ...	F. Sept. 29	Dec. 8
WESTON-SUPER-MARE (even.)	12	English Novelists	„ „ ...	W. Oct. 4	Dec. 13
ST. MICHAEL'S HALL, BRIGHTON (morning)	6	The Tudors	„ „ ...	W. Oct. 4	Dec. 13

Centre.	No. of Lectures in Course.	Subject of Course.	Lecturer.	Course begins.	Course ends.
EDGBASTON (afternoon)	12	Growth of Polit. System of Europe	H. J. MACKINDER, M.A.	Th. Oct. 12	Dec. 19
BRIGHTON (afternoon)	6	English Painters	D. S. MACCOLL, M.A.	W. Nov. 1	Dec. 6
TUNBRIDGE WELLS (afternoon)	10	Literature of Cavaliers & Puritans	F. S. BOAS, M.A.	T. Oct. 10	Dec. 12
HARROGATE (evening)	12	Shakespeare	,, ,,	Th. Sept. 28	Dec. 14
PETERBOROUGH (evening)	12	Victorian Poets	,, ,,	F. Sept. 29	Dec. 8
ILKLEY (afternoon)	6	Tennyson	,, ,,	Th. Sept. 28	Dec. 7
RUGBY (evening)	6	Tennyson	,, ,,	F. Oct. 6	Dec. 15
BAKEWELL (evening)	6	England in the 18th Century	C. E. MALLET, B.A.	M. Sept. 25	Dec. 4
BURNLEY (evening)	12	England in the 18th Century	,, ,,	Th. Sept. 28	Dec. 7
TAMWORTH (afternoon)	10	The Stuarts	,, ,,	T. Sept. 26	Dec. 5
TAMWORTH (evening)	10	The Stuarts	,, ,,	T. Sept. 26	Dec. 5
OTLEY (evening)	6	The Tudors	,, ,,	M. Oct. 2	Dec. 11
MATLOCK (afternoon)	6	The Tudors	,, ,,	W. Sept. 27	Dec. 6
WAKEFIELD (evening)	6	French Revolution	,, ,,	T. Oct. 3	Dec. 12
BURY (evening)	12	French Revolution	,, ,,	W. Oct. 4	Dec. 13
SETTLE (evening)	6	Irish History	,, ,,	F. Sept. 29	Dec. 8
BATH (afternoon)	12	England in the 18th Century	,, ,,	Th. Oct. 5	Dec. 14
BATH (evening)	12	English Prose Writers	,, ,,	Th. Oct. 5	Dec. 14
ILKLEY (afternoon)	6	Browning	Rev. C. G. LANG, M.A.	Th. Oct. 5	Dec. 14
BRADFORD (evening)	6	Victorian Poets	,, ,,	Th. Oct. 5	Dec. 14
HUDDERSFIELD (evening)	6	Industrial Revolution	,, ,,	Th. Sept. 21	Jan. 25
STAFFORD (evening)	6	Light	G. J. BURCH, B.A.	T. Sept. 26	Dec. 5
CANTERBURY (afternoon)	6	Physiography	,, ,,	T. Oct. 3	Dec. 12
CANTERBURY (evening)	6	Electricity	,, ,,	T. Oct. 3	Dec. 12
BIRMINGHAM MIDLAND INSTITUTE (evening)	12	Commercial Geography	H. R. MILL, D.Sc.	F. Sept. 29	Dec. 15
BARNSTAPLE (evening)	9 or 12	Design	C. R. ASHBEE, M.A.	M. Oct. 9	Dec. 18
NEWBURY (afternoon)	6	Architecture	,, ,,	Th. Oct. 5	Dec. 14
HEREFORD (evening)	6	Development of the Drama	R. W. BOND, M.A.	M. Oct. 23	Nov. 27
RYDE (afternoon)	12	Shakespeare	,, ,,	F. Oct. 6	Dec. 15
WINDSOR (afternoon)	6	Gothic Architecture	F. BOND, M.A.	Th. Sept. 28	Dec. 7
SOUTHAMPTON (evening)	6	Physical Geography	,, ,,	Th. Oct. 5	Dec. 14
BRIGHTON (evening)	12	Commercial Geography	,, ,,	F. Sept. 29	Dec. 15
TRURO (evening)	8	Social England Series, Pt. II.	K. D. COTES, M.A.	M. Sept. 25	Nov. 23
ST. AUSTELL (evening)	6	Social England Series, Pt. I.	,, ,,	T. Sept. 26	Oct. 31
BODMIN (evening)	6	Social England Series, Pt. I.	,, ,,	W. Sept. 27	Nov. 1
FALMOUTH (evening)	6	Relation of History to Painting, Part II.	,, ,,	Th. Sept. 28	Nov. 2
PENZANCE (afternoon)	6	Social England Series, Pt. I.	,, ,,	F. Sept. 29	Nov. 3
CAMBORNE (evening)	6	Social England Series, Pt. I.	,, ,,	F. Sept. 29	Nov. 3
SWANSEA (evening)	6	Social Life in England at different Periods	W. A. S. HEWINS, M.A.	T. Oct. 3	Dec. 12
LLANELLY (evening)	6	Social Life in England at different Periods	,, ,,	M. Oct. 2	Dec. 11
GRIMSBY (evening)	6	Economic Aspects of Social Questions of to-day	,, ,,	T. Oct. 10	Dec. 19
LEAMINGTON (evening)	6	Problems of Poverty, Part I.	J. A. HOBSON, M.A.	F. Oct. 6	Dec. 15
TEAN (afternoon)	6	Problems of Poverty, Part II.	,, ,,	S. Oct. 7	Dec. 16
ACCRINGTON (evening)	6	Problems of Poverty, Part I.	,, ,,	M. Oct. 9	Dec. 18
KNOWLE (afternoon)	6	Novelists of the 19th Century	,, ,,	T. Oct. 10	Dec. 19
REIGATE (afternoon)	12	The Renaissance	E. L. S. HORSBURGH, B.A.	F. Oct. 13	Dec. 22
WEST BRIGHTON (afternoon)	12	The Renaissance	,, ,,	Th. Oct. 12	Dec. 21
RAMSGATE (afternoon)	12	French Revolution	,, ,,	S. Sept. 30	Dec. 9
HEBDEN BRIDGE (evening)	6	French Revolution	,, ,,	S. Oct. 7	Dec. 16
BOURNEMOUTH (afternoon)	12	Literature of the 18th Century	,, ,,	F. Oct. 6	Dec. 15
BOURNEMOUTH (evening)	6	Epochs in English History	,, ,,	Th. Oct. 5	Dec. 14
WINSLOW (evening)	6	Expansion of England	,, ,,	M. Oct. 2	Dec. 11
GLOUCESTER (evening)	6	Story of the English Parliament	,, ,,	M. Oct. 9	Dec. 18
CIRENCESTER (afternoon)	6	Literature of the 18th Century	,, ,,	M. Oct. 9.	Dec. 18
SOUTHAMPTON (evening)	6	History of Tudor Period	,, ,,	F. Oct. 6	Dec. 15
LEWES (evening)	12	Studies from the Georges	,, ,,	Th. Oct. 12	Dec. 21
LITTLE BERKHAMPSTEAD (aft.)	6	Early Stuarts	Miss LACEY	Th. Sept 28	Dec. 7
HALIFAX (evening)	12	Architecture	J. E. PHYTHIAN	Th. Oct. 5	Dec. 14
BRISTOL (University Coll.) (aft.)	6	Architecture	Rev. G. H. WEST, D.D.	W. Oct. 4	Dec. 13
BRIDPORT (evening)	12	Architecture	,, ,,	T. Oct. 3	Dec. 12
BEDFORD (afternoon)	12	The English Citizen	GRAHAM WALLAS, M.A.	T. Oct. 3	Dec. 12
OXFORD (evening)	24	Growth of English Institutions	,, ,,	Th. Oct. 19	Dec. 7
CARLISLE (afternoon)	6	Tennyson	Miss WOOLLEY	W. Oct. 4	Dec. 13
*PUCKLECHURCH (evening)	6	Geology	A. B. BADGER, M.A.	Not fixed	Not fixed
GRANGE (evening)	6	Outlines of Geology	C. CARUS-WILSON, F.G.S.	M. Oct. 2	Dec. 11
ULVERSTON (evening)	6	Outlines of Geology	,, ,,	T. Oct. 3	Dec. 12
LOUTH (evening)	6	Outlines of Geology	,, ,,	Th. Oct. 5	Dec. 14
WHITEHAVEN (evening)	6	Physiography	,, ,,	T. Oct. 10	Dec. 19
STROUD (afternoon)	12	Electricity	A. H. FISON, D.Sc.	T. Oct. 17	Dec. 12
STROUD (evening)	12	Electricity	,, ,,	T. Oct. 17	Dec. 12
VENTNOR (evening)	12	Astronomy	,, ,,	T. Oct. 10	Dec. 19
NEWPORT, I.W. (evening)	12	Astronomy	,, ,,	W. Oct. 11	Dec. 20
TUNBRIDGE WELLS (evening)	8	Laws of Health	T. M. LEGGE, M.A., M.B.	T. Oct. 10	Nov. 28
AMBLESIDE (evening)	6	Forces of Nature	J. W. McPHERSON, B.A.	T. Oct. 3	Dec. 12
GARSTANG (evening)	6	Astronomy	W. E. PLUMMER, M.A.	T. Oct. 10	Dec. 19
KESWICK (evening)	6	Astronomy	,, ,,	M. Oct. 9	Dec. 18
Kent County Council five courses each of	10	Chemistry	H. H. COUSINS, M.A.	Oct.	Dec.
four courses each of	10	Hygiene	T. LEGGE, M.B.	Oct.	Dec.

Centre.	No. of Lectures in Course.	Subject of Course.	Lecturer.	Course begins.	Course ends.
Surrey County Council					
nine courses	24, 12, 6	Chemistry	A. D. HALL, M.A. ...	Sept.	Dec.
two courses	24	Chemistry	H. GORDON, M.A. ...	Sept.	Dec.
Somerset County Council					
seven courses...	12, 6	Beginnings and Prevention of Disease	C. H. WADE, M.A. ...	Oct.	Dec.
nine courses...	12, 6	Soils, Plants, and Animals ...	H. E. NIBLETT, B.A....	Oct.	Dec.

Spring 1894.

Centre.	No. of Lectures in Course.	Subject of Course.	Lecturer.	Course begins.	Course ends.
†UNIVERSITY EXTENSION COLLEGE, READING (afternoon)	12	The Homeric Poems	J. CHURTON COLLINS, M.A.	S. Not fixed	Not fixed
ASHTON-UNDER-LYNE (aft.) ...	6	Not fixed	Rev. W. H. SHAW, M.A.	T. Jan. 16	Mar. 27
ASHTON-UNDER-LYNE (even.)	6	Not fixed	,, ,, ...	T. Jan. 16	Mar. 27
*STROUD (afternoon)	6	Not fixed	,, ,, ...	M. Jan. 22	Apr. 2
GLOUCESTER (evening) ...	6	English Social Reformers ...	,, ,, ...	M. Jan. 22	Apr. 2
BIRMINGHAM, SEVERN STREET (evening)	6	Not fixed	,, ,, ...	T. Jan. 23	Apr. 3
CHELTENHAM (afternoon) ...	6	Not fixed	,, ,, ...	W. Jan. 24	Apr. 4
SWINDON (evening)	6	Puritan Revolution	,, ,, ...	W. Jan. 24	Apr. 4
NEWBURY (afternoon) ..	6	Florence	,, ,, ...	Th. Jan. 25	Apr. 5
TUNBRIDGE WELLS (afternoon)	10	Florence and Venice ...	,, ,, ...	F. Jan. 19	Mar. 30
BRIGHTON (evening)	12	Making of England	,, ,, ...	F. Jan. 19	Apr. 6
WINDSOR (afternoon)	6	Venice	,, ,, ...	Th. Jan. 18	Not fixed
CHESTER (afternoon)	6	Not fixed	J. A. R. MARRIOTT, M.A.	W. Jan. 17	Mar. 28
CHESTER (evening)	6	Not fixed	,, ,, ...	T. Jan. 16	Mar. 27
WALLASEY (evening)	6	Not fixed	,, ,, ...	W. Jan. 17	Mar. 28
BRADFORD (evening)	6	Europe since Waterloo	,, ,, ...	Th. Jan. 18	Mar. 29
MALVERN (afternoon) ...	6	Historical Plays of Shakespeare...	,, ,, ...	W. Feb. 7	Not fixed
†EDGBASTON (afternoon) ...	12	Growth of Polit. System of Europe	H. J. MACKINDER, M.A.	T. Jan. 16	Mar. 27
†PETERBOROUGH (evening)	12	Victorian Poets	F. S. BOAS, M.A.	F. Jan. 19	Mar. 30
VENTNOR (afternoon)	6	Tennyson	,, ,, ...	Not fixed	Not fixed
MIDHURST (afternoon) ...	6	The Two Pitts	C. E. MALLET, B.A. ...	M. Jan. 15	Mar. 26
GRANGE (evening)	6	English Prose Writers ...	,, ,, ...	M. Jan. 22	Apr. 2
†TAMWORTH (afternoon) ...	10	The Stuarts	,, ,, ...	T. Jan. 16	Feb. 27
†TAMWORTH (evening) ...	10	The Stuarts	,, ,, ...	T. Jan. 16	Feb. 27
WHITEHAVEN (evening) ...	6	French Revolution	,, ,, ...	T. Jan. 23	Apr. 3
†BURY (evening)	12	French Revolution	,, ,, ...	W. Jan. 24	Apr. 4
†BURNLEY (evening)	12	England in the 18th Century ...	,, ,, ...	Th. Jan. 25	Apr. 5
†BATH (afternoon)	12	England in the 18th Century ...	,, ,, ...	Th. Jan. 18	Mar. 29
†BATH (evening)	12	English Prose Writers ...	,, ,, ...	Th. Jan. 18	Mar. 29
†WEST BRIGHTON (evening)...	6	Tennyson	Rev. J. G. BAILEY, LL.D.	Th. Jan. 11	Mar. 22
KEIGHLEY (evening)	6	Wordsworth, Shelley, Keats ...	,, ,, ...	M. Jan. 15	Mar. 26
SALE (evening)	6	Shakespeare	,, ,, ...	T. Jan. 16	Mar. 27
ROCHDALE (evening) ...	6	Shakespeare	,, ,, ...	W. Jan. 17	Mar. 28
†BARNSTAPLE (evening) ...	9 or 12	Design	C. R. ASHBEE, M.A. ...	M. Not fixed	Not fixed
†RYDE (afternoon)	12	Shakespeare	R. W. BOND, M.A. ...	Th. Jan. 11	Mar. 22
ROCHDALE (evening)	6	Social Questions of To-day ...	W. A S. HEWINS, M.A.	Th. Jan. 18	Mar. 29
†WEST BRIGHTON (afternoon)	12	The Renaissance	E. L. S. HORSBURGH, B.A.	Th. Jan. 18	Mar. 29
†REIGATE (afternoon)... ...	12	The Renaissance	,, ,, ...	F. Jan. 19	Mar. 30
†RAMSGATE (afternoon) ...	12	French Revolution	,, ,, ...	S. Jan. 20	Mar. 31
BOURNEMOUTH (afternoon) ...	12	Literature of the 18th Century ...	,, ,, ...	F. Jan. 12	Apr. 6
LEOMINSTER (afternoon) ...	6	Rise of Parliament	,, ,, ...	M. Jan. 15	Not fixed
HEREFORD (evening)	6	The Renaissance	,, ,, ...	M. Jan. 15	Not fixed
MAIDENHEAD (afternoon) ...	6	The Renaissance	,, ,, ...	Th. Jan. 11	Mar. 22
ABERGAVENNY (evening) ...	6	Italian Renaissance	,, ,, ...	M. Jan. 22	Apr. 2
†LEWES (evening)	12	Studies from the Georges ...	,, ,, ...	Th. Jan. 18	Mar. 29
†HALIFAX (evening)	12	Architecture	J. E. PHYTHIAN ...	Th. Not fixed	Not fixed
†OXFORD (evening)	24	Growth of English Institutions ...	GRAHAM WALLAS, M.A.	Th. Jan. 18	May
†BEDFORD (afternoon)... ...	12	The English Citizen	,, ,, ...	T. Jan. 16	Mar. 27
†BRIDPORT (evening)	12	Architecture	Rev. G. H. WEST, D.D.	T. Jan. 23	Apr. 3
†VENTNOR (evening)	12	Astronomy...	A. H. FISON, D.Sc. ...	T. Jan. 9	Mar. 20
†NEWPORT (evening)	12	Astronomy...	,, ,, ...	W. Jan. 10	Mar. 21
†STROUD (afternoon)	12	Electricity	,, ,, ...	T. Jan. 16	Apr. 10
†STROUD (evening)	12	Electricity	,, ,, ...	T. Jan. 16	Apr. 10
CLEVEDON (afternoon)... ...	6	Astronomy...	,, ,, ...	W. Jan 17	Mar. 28
WARRINGTON (evening) ...	6	Astronomy...	W. E. PLUMMER, M.A.	Th. Feb. 1	Apr. 12
ILKLEY (evening)	6	Astronomy...	,, ,, ...	Th. Jan. 25	Apr. 5
Kent County Council					
five courses each of	10	Chemistry	H. H. COUSINS, M.A.	Jan.	Apr.
†**Surrey County Council** ...					
eight courses	24, 12, 6	Chemistry	A. D. HALL, M.A. ...	Jan.	Apr.
two courses	24	Chemistry	H. GORDON, M.A. ...	Jan.	Apr.
Somerset County Council					
5 courses each of	12	Not fixed	C. H. WADE, M.A. ...	Jan.	Apr.
5 courses each of	12	Not fixed	H. SESSIONS,	Jan.	Apr.

* Arrangements not yet completed.   † Continued from Autumn 1893.

Other courses in process of arrangement.

Note.— Application for Courses and all information as to fees, &c., can be obtained from The Secretary, University Extension Office, Examination Schools, Oxford.

OXFORD UNIVERSITY

EXTENSION GAZETTE.

Vol. IV. No. 39.]   December, 1893.   [One Penny.

N.B.—Local Organizers of Oxford University Extension Lectures are invited to send to the Secretary, Extension Office, Examination Schools, Oxford, copies of any journals containing notices of, or references to, Extension work.

NOTES ON THE WORK.

The Vice-Chancellor and Proctors have appointed Mr. Philip Lyttelton Gell, M.A., Balliol College, Secretary of the Delegates of the University Press, to be a Delegate for the Extension of Teaching beyond the limits of the University, in place of Sir William Markby, D.C.L., Fellow of Balliol College, resigned.

.·.

The New University for Wales. The Queen has just approved the charter of the new University for Wales. The Statutes have now to be prepared, but it is expected that the University will begin its work early next summer. It will be a federal University with three constituent Colleges, viz. those already established at Bangor, Cardiff and Aberystwyth.

.·.

Mr. Acland on South Kensington. In a blinding snowstorm on November 18 Mr. A. H. D. Acland laid the foundation stone of the new Municipal Technical School at Birmingham. In the evening he delivered one of the weightiest speeches which have been delivered on education for some time. In the course of it he said 'There are four lines of Wordsworth which I sometimes repeat to myself as I pay my weekly visits to South Kensington—

Enough of Science and of Art,
Close up these barren leaves;
Come forth and bring with you a heart,
That watches and receives.

All I can do is to try to hope that I may be the head of the Science and Art Department and yet retain a heart which tries to watch and receive.' Mr. Acland also made an important statement as to the future policy of the Science and Art Department. He pointed out that the machinery which he had to carry on at Whitehall and South Kensington had to adapt itself both to the largest city and the smallest village. It was therefore extremely difficult to find a way by which the Departments could be elastic in their methods, and, while almost withdrawing their minute inspection from the large centres, yet keep up the stimulus which was necessary in the small ones. This is the crucial difficulty in educational administration, and it can only be met by making large exceptions to necessary rules in favour of the cities and institutions which the Departments can trust.

.·.

Colonies, Political and Educational. Mr. Lecky, in his discourse at the Imperial Institute on November 20, pointed out the decline of the theory that England should loosen the bands which unite her to her Colonies. There is, as he remarked, a growing feeling that Colonies and the Motherland derive reciprocal advantage from their position in a great Empire. Exactly the same change of feeling has been taking place in regard to educational work. Twenty years ago the ruling idea was that, though the Universities should seek to establish intellectual settlements in the big towns, they should quickly cut off connexion between themselves and those new foundations, leaving the latter to an independent and separate destiny. Nowadays, however, this idea is being supplanted by the view that we should aim at forming a number of University Extension Colleges, federated with one another through a common tie to the ancient Universities.

.·.

We are glad to notice a further recognition of the mutual benefits that University Extension and County Technical Instruction Committees may derive from working in concert. At Truro, on November 7, the County Council of Cornwall unanimously accepted the motion of Mr. Ray recommending the Technical Instruction Committee to take into consideration the University Extension movement with a view to assisting it financially or otherwise. We hope the committee will act on the advice of their Council, as owing to many peculiar difficulties, distance and the like, the Cornish centres have at present no slight trouble in carrying on their work ; and the mere fact that they have arranged courses year by year for the past seven years is sufficient proof of their ability to profit by whatever help they may receive from the County Council.

.·.

School Boards and Secondary Education. The federation of educational forces seems to be the order of the day. On September 30, the Association of School Boards held its first meeting in London under the chairmanship of the Dean of Manchester. One hundred and thirty School Boards were represented at this most influential assembly, and there is no doubt that, through the agency of the new Association, the School Board interest will assert itself with largely increased force. Mr. C. H. Wyatt, the Clerk of the Manchester School Board, who read an important paper at the Oxford Conference, is Hon. Sec. of the Association. A motion urging the Government 'to appoint at the earliest moment a Royal Commission to inquire into the question of secondary and intermediate education in England' was unanimously adopted.

.·.

Another instance of the same tendency towards federation has occurred during the past month. The Technical Institutions in the country have decided to form an Association. This gathering of forces really means that people expect a Royal Commission on Secondary Education.

.·.

It is stated in the *University Correspondent* that of the recently successful Queen's Scholars, five are entering the Oxford, and six the Cambridge University Day Training College.

1

The Rev. H. D. Rawnsley of Keswick, who has for many years taken great interest in University Extension, has been appointed Honorary Canon of Carlisle.

.·.

The *Schoolmaster* of November 18 contains a highly appreciative account of the work which Mr. Kekewich, the Secretary of the Education Department, has done for the teachers engaged in elementary schools. All those who know what Mr. Kekewich has done for education in England will welcome this cordial recognition of his labours.

.·.

| Local Scholarships for the Summer Meeting. | Beyond the formation of the Scholarship fund to enable deserving and needy Extension students to attend the Summer Meeting, the Delegates have always urged on local committees the desirability of raising a local fund for the purpose of offering one or more scholarships to their own students with the |

same object. We are therefore glad to learn that already two centres, Ryde and Bradford, have announced their intention of each offering one scholarship of £10 for competition among their own students, to enable the holder to attend the Oxford Summer Meeting in 1894. Such an announcement affords the best possible proof of the vigour and enthusiasm of a local committee, and will, we hope, be followed by others of a like nature.

.·.

Readers of the 'Prelude' will remember the lines in which Wordsworth describes his rooms, 'a nook obscure,' in St. John's College, Cambridge. They were above the College kitchen whence came

A humming sound, less tunable than bees
But hardly less industrious ; with shrill notes
Of sharp command and scolding intermixed.

During last Vacation these rooms were destroyed, the floor being knocked out in order to give more ventilation to the kitchen. A correspondent, writing to the *Westminster Gazette* of November 14 to deplore the destruction of an interesting chamber, remarks that comparatively little is done at Oxford or Cambridge to keep a record of the rooms occupied in their undergraduate days by men who afterwards became famous. To this stricture one exception at least should be made—viz. Queen's College, Oxford, where the names of subsequently famous occupants are painted up over the doors of many of the rooms.

.·.

| Government Grant for Local Organizers. | There has been during the past month a good deal of correspondence in the newspapers upon the claim of the local organizers of University Extension to share in the Parliamentary |

Grant now given to the University Colleges of Great Britain. The correspondence began with a letter in *The Journal of Education,* which was followed by communications to *The Times* from Prof. Jebb, M.P., Dr. Percival (Headmaster of Rugby), Professor Case, the President of Magdalen College, Mr. J. G. Talbot, M.P., and Mr. James Stuart, M.P. *The Times* in a leading article gave a faint support to the scheme. The claims of the local organizers were very emphatically endorsed in leading articles in the *Manchester Guardian* and the *Yorkshire Herald,* as well as in editorial notes in the *Yorkshire Post.* Correspondence on the same subject has appeared in the *Newcastle Daily Chronicle, Birmingham Post, Birmingham Gazette,* the *Guardian,* and *Western Morning News.*

.·.

It is said that the facts about secondary education in England, which have been collected by a committee representing the Education Department, the Charity Commission, and the Science and Art Department, will shortly be laid before Parliament in the form of a report.

The official verbatim report of the Oxford Conference on Secondary Education has now been published with an index and appendices. It can be obtained from the Clarendon Press Depository, High Street, Oxford, and its price is one shilling net, or 1s. 3d. free by post.

.·.

At Bradford on November 8 a boy was carrying to the station two cylinders, charged respectively with compressed coal-gas and oxygen for use in the magic lantern, when the latter fell from his shoulders, exploded, and nearly blew his head off. At the inquest it transpired that the metal, of which the cylinder was made, was too brittle, and had not been annealed. The accident should warn those who make use of the lantern to be careful how they pack their gas-cylinders for transport.

.·.

| | A warning. |

Dr. Edwin Abbott has put out a scathing paper on the subject of the dismissal of Professor Aldis by the Council of University College, Auckland, New Zealand. The charges which he brings against the Council are so serious that, without satisfying himself in regard to them, no one could with propriety become a candidate for the vacant post or assist the Council in filling it. Dr. Abbott's address is Wellside, Well Walk, Hampstead.

.·.

'There are only two rules for good manners. One is to think of other people. The other is not to think of yourself.' This saying of the late Master of Balliol is quoted by Archdeacon Wilson in an address on 'the Duties of a Citizen,' which he gave last month to the boys of the Manchester Grammar School. The Archdeacon divided his subject under the three heads—livelihood, public service, and the cultivation of character—the three things at which a citizen has to aim. 'But,' he concluded, 'without religion, the earning of a livelihood may be drudgery, public service a sphere for petty ambition, and culture a mere dilettantism.'

.·.

| | Victoria University Extension. |

The lately published list of Extension lectures that are being delivered during the present session, under the auspices of the Victoria University, contains several points of interest. Some fifty-three courses have been arranged, and, of these, fifty are on scientific subjects and three on arts subjects. The vast preponderance of the former is due no doubt to the fact that no fewer than thirty-four courses are delivered under arrangement with the Yorkshire County Councils. Eighteen courses of lectures are being given in Lancashire and Cheshire, and of these fifteen are on various scientific subjects, Greek Archaeology, Roman Britain, and the Age of Elizabeth being the courses on the arts subjects. The rapid growth in the number of science courses points most clearly to the danger of the endowment of one branch of knowledge to the prejudice of the other, and is a strong argument in favour of making uniform State grants towards the teaching of both the arts and the sciences.

.·.

| | University Extension and Continuation Schools. |

The Education Department has addressed to the Inspectors of Schools an important letter on Evening Continuation Schools, defining the position which the latter should take in the general scheme of public education. The circular contains the following passage :—'These schools should be in a true sense Continuation Schools, that is to say, they should be schools which continue and carry forward the education given in the Day Elementary Schools. They should be so constituted as to offer to scholars leaving the Day Elementary Schools facilities for continuing their education, and should not, either as regards the age or social class of the scholars or the subject of instruction, be divided from these day schools by any palpable barrier or interval. They should not consist of mere isolated classes, nor should the instruction given in them be of a too advanced or too highly special-ized a character. . . . As instances of such may be mentioned, Science and Art classes, which may properly receive grants from the Science and Art Department; technical classes aided by the various County Councils, and classes of various kinds in connexion with the Extension lectures of the different Universities.' We take the last sentence to mean that a couple of Uni-versity Extension courses alone should not be regarded as constituting a Continuation School. But it is clear from the Code itself that the Department is anxious that lectures, like those given under the University Extension, should, where practicable, be made part of the programme of these schools. Thus, in the explana-tory memorandum prefixed to the Code, the fifth clause suggests that 'encouragement might be given to capable lecturers to deliver, from time to time, short lectures with illustrations in connexion with some of the subjects in the school time-table.'

.·.

We hear from Professor Rein that it is proposed to arrange the following Extension courses in Jena in August 1894, (1) a course in Natural Science for teachers in Higher Grade Schools, (2) a course in German in Pedagogy for English teachers, (3) a course in Pedagogy, History and Literature for German teachers, (4) a course in Political Economy.

.·.

University Extension grows apace in Aus-
University Extension in Australia. tralia. From the *Melbourne University Extension Journal* we learn that not only Victoria and New South Wales, the latter under a new and specially appointed Board, but also Queensland and Tasmania have now established Extension lectures. It would seem that the difficulties of organization are much the same in Australia as elsewhere. The New South Wales courses consist of ten weekly lectures, shorter courses of six lectures being allowed only by special arrangement, whereas the Editor of the above-named paper argues in favour of fortnightly lectures and offers the opinion that two related courses of six lectures are possibly better than one course of twelve. The longer course tempts the lecturer to try to cover too much ground as it suggests a wider and more compre-hensive handling than is possible in a shorter course; hence in two six-lecture courses two branches of a subject may be treated with greater thoroughness and more care-ful detail. There can be no doubt, too, that fortnightly lectures afford more time for the effective working of Students' Associations and enable busy people to prepare more carefully for both lectures and classes.

.·.

On November 1 the American Univer-
A Welcome to the U. E. Bulletin. sity Extension Society published the first number of their monthly *Bulletin*. This new journal, which pays us the compli-ment of close resemblance, is to be a record of current University Extension work, while the Society's monthly magazine *University Extension* will be devoted to the discussion of 'the many pressing peda-gogical problems peculiar to the work of carrying on our system of Extension courses.' The first number of the *Bulletin* is attractive and well arranged, and we heartily welcome it into the field of University Extension journal-ism. Among its articles is one on the possibilities of Extension work among the foreign population in America, containing a suggestion that, where necessary, the lectures should be delivered in Italian, German or Hebrew.

.·.

Attention is called to the announcement of the Scholar-ship Competition which is this year made three months earlier than usual.

Christmas Holidays. — The University Extension Office will be closed as usual between Christmas and New Year's Day.

THE DUKE OF DEVONSHIRE ON UNIVERSITY EXTENSION.

ON Nov. 6 the Duke of Devonshire, who is Chancellor of the University of Cambridge, presided at one of the lectures of the course of Oxford University Extension lectures which Mr. C. E. Mallet of Balliol College is now delivering at Bakewell. This is the sixth course which has been given at this centre, and the third in a sequence of historical study which was begun in 1891. On the invitation of the local Committee, of which Miss Martin is the Hon. Sec., the Duke of Devonshire consented to take the chair at the fourth lecture of Mr. Mallet's course on England in the Eighteenth Century. The subject of the lecture was the Revolt of the American Colonies. After the lecture, the Duchess of Devonshire distributed the prizes and awards gained in connexion with the pre-vious course. The proceedings were exceedingly success-ful, and the local interest in University Extension, though already great, will be increased by the address of the Duke of Devonshire, part of which we print below.

On taking the chair the Duke said—

I hope that the presence of the Duchess and myself to-night may not prove to be any disturbing element in the very useful proceedings in which you are engaged, and in which we are going to take part this evening. Many of you who are present here this evening have been, I believe, now for some years going through a course of what are called University Extension lec-tures, and some no doubt are entering upon that course for the first time. You have had the advantage not only of hearing lectures upon some questions of historical or material importance, but you have also had an opportunity of studying and furthering that subject in the classes by means of oral discussion and explanation by the teachers; and some of you, as we shall find to-night, have been willing to submit the results of that course of instruction which you have been going through to the test of examination. Now I am quite certain in what you have been doing, and what you are going to do, you have been much more usefully engaged than you would be if I were to take up much of your time by asking you to listen to what must be, to what would be, but a perfunctory discourse upon the subject of education in general. The Duchess and I have only come here this evening with the object of showing that we take some interest in this movement, and to give proof, some small proof, that we take an interest, not only in the material prosperity and well-being of this district—of which I hope that my family and I myself have already been able to give some proof—but also to show that we are equally interested in the intellectual improve-ments of the inhabitants of the district. Now, ladies and gentle-men, this University Extension movement is a movement of a national character, in which each local centre is called upon to take a part. It is a movement which has been going on for some considerable time. I was scarcely aware until the other day, I scarcely recollected how long the movement had been started, until I was reminded by a paper which I happened accidentally to find, that not only has it been going on for some considerable period, but that it is a very long time ago since I myself took a very humble share in promoting it. In the year 1875, eighteen years ago, I am sorry to say, I was asked to take part in a meeting in the neighbouring town of Nottingham for the purpose of promoting this movement, and so very naturally I must have consulted my father, who then had the honour, as I have now, of being Chancellor of the University of Cambridge. I must have consulted my father as to the view which he took of this movement, for I happened the other day quite accidentally to come across a letter which evidently had reference to that occasion, and in which he gave some of his views upon the subject. I think as he was so well known, and I might say universally respected in this district, it may be interesting to you to know what the views were at the beginning, but not quite at the commencement of this movement, of one who occupied the distinguished post of Chancellor of the University of Cam-bridge. I can't read to you his exact words, because the letter

2

which he wrote to me was framed rather in the form of notes than in consecutive writing. He said to me : It is highly satisfactory to me as a Cambridge man—and he referred in the first instance to the great reforms—to hear of the great revolution which has been made in the educational arrangements and the course of study in the Universities. He said it was highly satisfactory to him as a Cambridge man that Cambridge had framed and had established this system of so-called University Extension. There were something like 350 Fellows of the University, and it was highly creditable that some of the more energetic of those Fellows had found a wider field for the exercise of their abilities by undertaking lecturing and teaching in populous districts. Lectures were often of interest, but it was questionable whether by themselves they were of much permanent good. It was necessary, if permanent results were to follow, that those who attended them should be encouraged and assisted in studying the subjects methodically. He strongly approved of the proposed change in the character of the teaching, by which it was to assume more of a tuitional character. That, the Duke proceeding, said, was the spirit in which this movement started eighteen years ago; and I don't think it would be difficult to show you that the work has been carried out by the Universities exactly in the same spirit. At the Summer Meeting held at Cambridge during the present year, Dr. Jebb, Professor of Greek, delivered the inaugural lectures on the work of the Universities, and he referred, as my father has done, to the great change which has come over the whole spirit of the teaching at the Universities, and he (Dr. Jebb) pointed out the fact that during the last thirty years a change has been passing over the relations of the ancient Universities and the country, and said that they were no longer the only seats of learning but that colleges for intellectual teaching were being spread throughout the land. He referred to the policy which, in former times, actuated the Universities and led them to discourage any attempt to convey higher teaching and higher instruction in any other places than their own seats of learning, but it is gratifying to know that during the last twenty-five or thirty years the doors of the Universities have been open to those against whom they were formerly closed. As nature creates brotherhoods of families, so in like manner there can be created a fraternity in learning. I have endeavoured to point out to you what has been the spirit in which this movement has been fostered by the University of Cambridge. You, I know, are affiliated with the University of Oxford, but I have not the smallest doubt that precisely the same spirit which has animated the authorities at Cambridge has animated the authorities here. I do not know whether the progress of this movement has entirely reached the extent anticipated by those who founded it. It is difficult to judge on such matters from mere figures. So far as I understand from the figures to which I have access, the number of students who have availed themselves of the course of lectures under the University of Oxford exceeds the number who have taken similar advantage of the classes held under Cambridge University. I understand that during last year, according to the returns that are accessible, no fewer than 28,000 students took advantage of the Oxford University Extension lectures, whilst the average number of students under the Cambridge Extension scheme was 19,000. I do not know whether these figures were arrived at by exactly the same process of computation, but, at all events, they show, whether or not those figures are as large as were expected, that access has been given to higher education to a very large number of persons who, in the absence of these efforts of the Universities, would never have had the opportunity of acquiring it. In the last few years another movement has been in progress which has had a certain effect upon the University Extension movement. Attention has been very strongly called to the necessity of extending in the country what is called technical education. That is a movement in which I have taken some part, and upon which I hold very strong opinions. The object of that movement is twofold : First, to direct elementary education into more practical directions; and it aims at the education of the hand and the eye of the scholar, as well as the brain, and to induce those who are receiving a course of elementary education

to exercise the faculties of observation and of reason, as well as to cultivate the faculty of memory. Its second object has been to continue longer the educational process beyond the years of school attendance, and to give the means to large numbers of people of this country to obtain some knowledge of those sciences and some acquaintance with those arts which form the foundation of our industrial work. I have taken some part in promoting this movement, and I have very strong opinions on its importance. I believe it is a matter of national importance. I believe that upon the practical acquaintance which our industrial classes might obtain of the sciences and arts, which enter at the present day so largely into every industrial process—on the amount of intelligence and practical acquaintance depend not only the continuance and maintenance of our industrial prosperity, but perhaps of our very existence in the world at all. For these reasons I am not in the smallest degree inclined to retract anything I have said on this question. It is a movement which must necessarily have exercised some influence upon the University Extension movement. The attention which has been called to our scientific and artistic requirements has necessarily created a large demand for lectures upon science, and that demand it has only been possible to satisfy to some extent at the expense of the literary and historical subjects in which interest has been begun to be roused. I should very much regret if anything should occur to diminish that interest which has been roused in subjects of a literary and historical character. It may be true that these subjects are not of such pressing immediate national importance as those on the scientific side. It may be true that instruction upon literary, historical, or philosophical subjects does not offer to the students the same means of turning their knowledge to account as does instruction in science and art, but at the same time it is none the less true that it is only through literary instruction that the highest enjoyment can be obtained—the privilege of communication, through the use of books, with the greatest and noblest minds which have existed in former years, or may exist in our time, is the highest privilege given to human creatures to enjoy. In the times in which we live some tolerably complete and intelligent appreciation of the facts of history is a matter of no small national importance. It is the duty of every one of us to take a greater or less, wider or narrower, part in the control of the affairs of the nation, but we cannot do this intelligently unless we have some knowledge of the great deeds and sacrifices made by our forefathers in the past, and at the same time some conception of the errors and mistakes which were at times mingled with those great and noble deeds. The course of lectures which you have been taking part in, has given you some insight into the history of your own country. You are this evening to listen to a lecture on the subject of the revolt of the American Colonies. You have in former lectures studied the history of your country during the reign of the Stuarts, and you have been able to form some conception of the events and courses which have made England and its Constitution and its people what they are. You are this evening to listen to a lecture from which you will learn something relating to one of the greatest, perhaps the greatest, mistake which has ever been made by our country, since she became a Constitution. I have no doubt that you will find in this course which you are now going through not only much that is mentally interesting to every one of you, but also much that will prove instructive and valuable to every one who is called upon, either directly or indirectly, to take any part in the future government and control of the nation.

Mr. C. E. Mallet, B.A., then delivered a lecture dealing with the history of the revolt of the American colonies, a subject which he dealt with exhaustively. He concluded by remarking that the history of that revolution assured the British nation that the proper way to ensure the continuance of the bond between the colonies and the mother nation was to treat them fairly, and give them that due freedom which they required.

The Duke of Devonshire then proposed a vote of thanks to Mr. Mallet for his lecture, which he described as a most brilliant one, and one which showed that the lessons of history ought not to be forgotten. The lecture showed that through mismanagement the States of America were lost to this empire. That page of our history was not, however, one upon which we ought to look back with shame or disgrace, but it showed mistakes which ought not to be repeated in these modern times. They could not reproach their ancestors with being actuated by any feeling of ill-will towards those colonies, but they had made a mistake for which the people of this generation had had to suffer. He trusted the lesson would not be lost, and it was also satisfactory to know that it was not possible for such a mistake to be repeated in these days.

Mr. S. Taylor Whitehead then proposed, and Mr. Groome seconded, a vote of thanks to the Duke and Duchess, Mr. Whitehead remarking that the success of the Bakewell centre had been largely due to their determination to have courses of lectures arranged in sequence. Mr. Mallet supported the resolution in an eloquent speech.

In reply to the vote of thanks, the Duke of Devonshire remarked that ' Something had been said about the importance of securing a good class of lecturers, and he would tell them that the authorities both at Oxford and Cambridge considered this of great importance, and also the selection of energetic local secretaries and committees. As for the recognition of this movement by the State, about which something had also been said, he was not prepared to express any opinion, but he might say that there was no nation in which higher education had been self-supporting. He did not know why the system of University education should be self-supporting any more than any other system. This, however, was a question upon which they might hear something more before they were very much older.

NOTES ON UNIVERSITY EXTENSION IN AMERICA.

Extension in the Southern States.

Mr. W. P. Trent, writing in *University Extension* for November, maintains that the Southern States are ripe for University Extension work. He says the South is dull. There are few public libraries and not many enterprising booksellers, and the popular lecture has never been acclimatised in that part of America. We fear that Mr. Trent is too sanguine. Much educational work has to be done before the ground is ready for University Extension, and it seems clear, by his own showing, that in the South this preparation has not yet been undertaken.

Supplementary class work at Milwaukee.

Some Extension courses at Milwaukee have been followed by additional classes for further work. The leaders of these classes have given their services. Professor Ely's course on Socialism, for example, was followed by a six months' class in Political Economy under the guidance of the Superintendent of the People's Institute. The most successful of the supplementary classes was that conducted by Mr. Mapel after a course by Professor Freeman on English Literature. This class consisted of fifty pupils and lasted for three months. We may note that exactly the same experiment is being tried in conjunction with Mr. Graham Wallas's course on the English Institutions.

Extension in Colorado.

Writing in *University Extension*, Mr. Gardner does not hold out very hopeful prospects for University Extension in Colorado. He thinks the people there are indifferent; the 'Silver Barons' do not care for culture; the farmers are short of ready money; and the miners are hard hit by the silver crisis. They work so hard in Colorado, and live in such a rarified atmosphere, that when they have done their day's work they cannot stand the wear and tear of an evening lecture. Moreover, it appears that the people of Colorado think that education does not pay and that University men are the foes of the people.' So Mr. Gardner is not hopeful.

At Knox College in Illinois the management has strengthened its own curriculum and increased its popularity with the public by arranging several courses of University Extension lectures, which are open both to the students of the College and to the residents in the neighbourhood.

The excellent magazine of the American Society, *University Extension*, has changed its cover—much (in our judgement) for the worse. It contains an essay by Mr. Edwards, of Newcastle-on-Tyne, in which the writer strongly advocates the class teaching being taken before, instead of after, the lecture. His arguments are not very strong. The chief of them is that, if the class is held after the lecture, the students are prevented from profiting by the lecturer's discourse because the difficulties raised by the previous lecture have not been cleared away from their minds. There is something in this, but less than Mr. Edwards thinks. He also does not take into account the unwisdom of tiring the lecturer before he gives his lecture. However there is a good deal to be said on both sides.

Mr. Harris on University Extension in England.

The U.S. Commissioner for Education, the Hon. W. T. Harris, has just issued another of his well-known reports. The two volumes of the new issue include a short sketch of University Extension in England. The writer says Cambridge cares for the high standard of its Extension work, while Oxford is anxious to extend the influence of the University. This is misleading. Oxford, at any rate, cares for both.

University Extension in the State of New York.

The University of the State of New York is a federation, somewhat miscellaneous in its nature, of scattered colleges and schools. Napoleonic, rather than English or German, in its constitution, it has a closer resemblance to the University of London, as the latter was in its early days, than to any other of our English institutions. It comprises 396 schools and academies, 32 colleges of arts and science, and 50 technical and professional schools. These contained last May as many as 63,691 students, of whom 33,962 were men. The administrative centre of the University is at Albany, where, under the energetic and resourceful direction of Mr. Melvil Dewey, its well-organized library has its home. Since 1891 the Regents, who form the Governing Body of the University, have established a system of Extension teaching which 'includes all agencies supplementary to the regular schools and colleges for the diffusion of education throughout the State.' Reports reach us that the Extension work of the University is becoming more generally known and appreciated throughout the wide area of the State of New York. Fourteen courses seem to have been arranged for the winter as well as some additional classes. At Rochester a course on 'Roman Life,' illustrated by the lantern, is being so largely attended that the lectures are now given in a larger hall than was originally chosen for the purpose. The Secretary of the University is compiling a list of Summer Schools with statistics showing in each case the cost of tickets and the curriculum of study. It is also reported that some of the travelling libraries are now being sent out in boxes similar to those used in our Oxford work. The lists of lecturers are explained as being ' merely convenient summaries of available teachers with information to enable each center to use its own judgment as to who is best adapted to its work.' After each lecturer's name is printed a figure showing the number of years he has spent in lecturing or teaching. These range from 27 to 0. But no list of towns is given showing where the lecturer has lectured and the name of the local secretary of the committee under whose auspices the lectures were delivered. Until this information is furnished the list—as a guide to local organizers— will be incomplete.

THE EDUCATIONAL LADDER.

THOSE who have talked glibly about the educational ladder have not always thought out with care the real bearing of their schemes. Up to a certain point there is agreement on all hands in the matter, because everybody desires the children of genius to meet with opportunities for the development and use of their powers. As Mr. Ruskin said, 'we must leave no Giotto lost among the hill shepherds.' But what if our plans, besides catching children of genius, push into unaccustomed and uncongenial spheres young people of precocious but mediocre ability? What if the chief outcome of our scholarship systems is to fill with vague unattainable ambitions the minds of a number of boys and girls physically unfit for the long strain of hothouse forcing which their education so often involves? What if we are simply spoiling the future of many who, but for the artificial incentives of our educational system, would have become good workmen, happier in the mastery of a craft, than in the possession of aptitudes of which the supply already exceeds the effective demand? Such are some of the questions which are being asked about schemes of educational reform, and it is well that we should look the difficulties clearly in the face, and not gloze them over with smooth sayings.

It used once to be comfortably believed that genius always found its way to the top and triumphed over every obstacle, growing in the process only the more robust. But is it not more likely to have been the fact that for one humbly born child of genius that found scope and opportunity, many were done to death in the struggle for recognition and livelihood? Those who survived the terrible struggle, were in a sense the strongest, and, though they lost in the battle something of freshness and simplicity and hope, they doubtless gained something too—self-dependence, austerity, acquaintance with suffering and a sense of the pathos of things. The rest, however, went under and were perhaps wasted. Now any scheme, which may be devised to save genius, must be made available for many who do not possess genius. And there is a type of ability which, though not commanding or particularly fruitful, is peculiarly responsive to bounties and educational incitements. Often at the expense of other and more solid parts of character, it develops itself according to the fashion which happens at the time to obtain recognition and reward. Were the stimulus and inducements absent, its normal development would take another and healthier direction. But the educational ladder tempts it up into a range of interests and effort which is really beyond its strength. And thus, besides drawing out the children of genius, we get a crop of rather weedy characters which would have developed more healthily in obscurer places if we had left them to themselves.

Are we then, because of this, to abandon all our schemes for the encouragement of rare ability? This is the point of the controversy which is now beginning, and to this if possible we must find a straight answer.

Perhaps the mischief will in the longrun cure itself. Gradually it may be found out that few lives are more unhappy than that of the youth of poor abilities who has been pushed into an uncongenial surrounding. The world cannot afford to pay good wages for poor work. And good wages alone can recoup the outlay which has to be made in a prolonged education. Just as now it is the fashion for ambitious parents to try to cultivate all their children for a grade of work suitable only for those of special promise, so it will gradually become a commonplace of parental prudence to avoid the danger of so educating their children as to swell the ranks of what has been called the intellectual proletariate.

The chief source of difficulty is that social glamour surrounds certain kinds of work, for the reason that these have been the normal occupations of the wealthier classes. Slowly however we may hope that a better judgement will prevail, and that people will begin to realize that all good work is equally honourable; that in occupations there is no 'first or last'; that satisfaction is gained by doing something well, rather than by doing one sort of thing instead of another; that the motive of the work rather than its nature, its thoroughness and excellence rather than its particular form and character, make it praiseworthy and noble. And this view of the matter will be strengthened by the growing tendency to give an honourable place in public education to the training and exercise of the hand.

But we are not yet at the end of the problem. The fact remains that to a large number of people, whatever their ability, literary interests in their wider sense have a great fascination. This is felt by many who are not sufficiently gifted to earn their living in a literary, as opposed to an industrial, employment. It arises from the great importance of the studies involved, from the inevitable attraction which they will always exercise, though with differing degrees of force, on any minds which are susceptible to a sense of their beauty and wide reaching importance. At present, however, enjoyment of these interests is very largely confined to those whose daily avocations are somewhat in keeping with them. What therefore we have to do is to bring within the reach of men and women in every rank of life, and in every employment, wisely ordered opportunities for obtaining such culture as they are capable of profiting by. This done, we shall have removed the real inducement which tempts so many away from their more appropriate occupations, and which so often leads parents to give a wrong twist to the education of their children. If a man felt that his son, whether a workman or not, would still be able all through his life to come within reach of the intellectual interests which he dimly and truly perceives to be among the highest aims of life, he would be less anxious to force his son into a line of training which is at present the only avenue to the attainment of this aim. In other words, must we not seek to establish a system of higher adult education adjusted to the different needs of different kinds of people, but inspired throughout its range with a high ideal and with the contempt for the second rate which is the mark which really distinguishes a liberal education?

THE LATE MASTER OF BALLIOL ON SECONDARY EDUCATION.

THE following remarks on the duty of the State towards Secondary Education were made by Professor Jowett in a speech which he delivered at a luncheon in Balliol College Hall on April 21, 1887, at the close of a Conference on University Extension. His words have a direct bearing on matters now under discussion, but the report of them has been for some time out of print.

Beyond the establishment of University Extension classes or the foundation of Colleges, there is still a wider question, but one already within the horizon of practical politics. This question, which I now venture to raise, is whether Secondary Education shall be supported by the State? I know that this is a subject about which the opinions even of the most liberal persons are very much divided. Now that the Conference is over, let me say a few words about it. I would urge that no principle of political economy prevents a government from doing for its subjects what it can do for them, and what they cannot do for themselves; and that the expense of the higher education is far beyond the means of what may be termed the lower half of the middle class. It is often said that we should make good use of existing endowments first and then come to the Public Exchequer. I do not agree in this view, because existing endowments are inadequate for the purpose, and the transference of them from one place to another is not entirely just, and is always met with an indignant opposition. It is easy to see that if we trust to existing endowments, the progress of higher education among the middle classes will be retarded for a century. So much for the question of principle. As for the probability of such a measure being passed at no very distant date I would ask you to remember that very nearly every civilized country in the world, France, Germany, Switzerland, America already provides education, both primary and secondary, either free of cost or at a very trifling cost, for all their citizens; and what has already become well established in other countries is likely in a very short period to be adopted in our own. That has been our universal experience. May I remind you also that statesmen such as Mr. Chamberlain, Mr. Morley, or Mr. Mundella, who represent the statesmen of the future, and who are likely to exercise a great influence on public affairs, are in favour of giving the greatest facilities for education and the utmost extension to it? Lastly, let me ask you to consider that secondary education is as important as primary, because although the number of persons affected by it are not one-fifteenth or one-twentieth of the whole population, the influence of each individual upon society is so very much greater. Whatever may be the natural commercial disadvantages of this country compared with other countries, it is possible that they might be much more than compensated by the spread of education. I will ask you to excuse my offering these speculations in such a hasty manner for your consideration. They are quite outside the purposes of the Conference, though connected with it. Whether any large scheme of secondary education is adopted by the State or not, the University Extension lectures are the best preparation for it. They prove the need of it, and though their twenty thousand students are not much more than one in a thousand of the whole population of England, still to a considerable extent they supply the need of education which is felt by every man who desires to have it, and in the degree in which he is able to receive it.

MEMORIAL FROM THE UNIVERSITY OF OXFORD ON SECONDARY EDUCATION.

THE seal of the University has been affixed to the following document, which may be regarded as the outcome of the Conference on Secondary Education held in Oxford in October :—

To the Right Honourable WILLIAM EWART GLADSTONE, *Member of Parliament, First Lord of the Treasury, &c., &c.*

The Memorial of the Chancellor, Masters and Scholars of the University of Oxford, sheweth—

That during the late and present Sessions of Parliament Bills have been prepared and laid before the House of Commons for giving to certain bodies great powers with reference to the provision, organization, and control of Secondary Education within the kingdom.

That on the tenth and eleventh of October last past a Conference was held in Oxford, which was attended by representatives from a large number of the chief Educational Bodies in England.

That in the proceedings of this Conference it appeared that great diversity of opinion, much imperfect knowledge, and some confusion and perplexity existed with reference to the matters incident to such organization of Secondary Education as was contemplated in the aforesaid Bills.

That in view of the far-reaching importance of this subject it is desirable that no settlement of the matters at issue be made save with fuller consideration of the subject, in detail and in general, with more exact knowledge, and with greater concurrence of opinion.

That your Memorialists accordingly desire that before any legislation on the subject is proposed a Commission be appointed under the authority either of Her Majesty the Queen or of the High Court of Parliament to inquire into the present state of Secondary Education within the kingdom, the further needs of Her Majesty's subjects in this respect, and the best means whereby those needs may be met.

In witness whereof your Memorialists have affixed their Common Seal to this Memorial in their House of Convocation on the fourteenth day of November in the year of our Lord one thousand eight hundred and ninety-three.

In acknowledging receipt of the memorial, Mr. Gladstone says that it shall receive 'his most anxious consideration.'

CONTEMPORARY CRITICISM.

'. . . See them once on the other side
Your good men and your bad men every one,
Oft would you rub your eyes and change your names.'
The Ring and the Book.

'The History of University Extension is the history of a sham. That it stimulates certain of the earnest middle class to a knowledge of history we do not deny. That it makes a pleasant diversion with its magic lanterns in the dull life of the London suburbs, or of the dreary Midlands, is also obvious. But to assert that it takes the University on tour to the provinces is to deceive the people, and to arrogate to yourself the accomplishment of a work beyond the power of mortal man. The University extender is a familiar type. He is not chosen for his scholarship, nor for any quality that would confer upon him the distinctions of an Academy. He must be eloquent and of an imposing presence. His business is not to teach but to "hold his audience." (That is the actual phrase used by the organizers.) He is generally a curate *manqué*, that is to say, he would have adorned a pulpit had not the superficial scruples of fashion stood in his way. Commonly he has won his spurs at the Union, and takes the light of learning into the country while he is waiting for an empty woolsack. But his very existence is a negation of the University's ideal. How shall he inculcate habits of thoroughness, whose knowledge on every conceivable subject is slender? How shall he instruct bank-clerks and shop-girls (even if he be lucky enough to win so appropriate an audience) in the art of the Periclean age, when these bank-clerks and shop-girls have not got beyond Landseer and the Pictures of the Year? . . . . In fact, University Extension has all along aimed at the impossible. You cannot make a silk purse out of a sow's ear, and it is idle to fish for scholars in the kitchen. A little knowledge is worse than dangerous—it is immoral; and though *post hoc* is not always *propter hoc*, there was no Jack the Ripper before there was a Toynbee Hall, before sham learning stalked in Whitechapel.' — *National Observer*, Nov. 11, 1893.

'University Extension lectures as far as they diffuse at once knowledge and a taste for knowledge, and furnish their students with some test for distinguishing between real knowledge and the smattering half knowledge, which is not much better than ignorance, give an ample return for the great pains which have been taken about them, and they fully justify all that has been said in their praise. They are doing their part in the educational work of the country, and we recognize with gratitude what they have done already and their purposes of future work.'—*Times* (Leading Article), Nov. 20, 1893.

'No educational development of recent years has so conspicuously exceeded the expectations of those who discerned its possibility as that energetic popularization of University culture known as University Extension. The conception which animates it is that there is an education of citizens which can be thorough and inspiring, and yet accessible to busy and hard-working people. The lecturers of the movement have proved in some 400 centres that this is an absolutely practical ideal, and not at all a visionary one. They have almost everywhere had a welcome which has kept their zeal aflame, and convinced them that the scheme of operations upon which they work is capable of being freely and widely enlarged.'—The *Yorkshire Post*, November, '93.

'University Extension is very valuable in itself, and I have great sympathy with it.'—THE CHANCELLOR OF THE EXCHEQUER, Nov. 22, 1893.

PROFESSOR GEDDES ON UNIVERSITY SYSTEMS.

IN the October *Fortnightly*, Professor Geddes has a suggestive article on ' University Systems Past and Present '; and the appearance of such an essay is in itself a sign of the academic revival which he speaks of as increasingly conspicuous both in the Old World and in the New. But its contents are rather rhetorical than scientific in that they are thrown into the form of too sharp an antithesis between the modern French and the modern German ideals of University organization. That the two ideals are in a sense antagonistic is a commonplace ; but in real life the two systems are not as sharply contrasted as Professor Geddes would have us believe. He pourtrays the Napoleonic University of France as the type of all that is orderly, mechanical and bureaucratic in method and organization. Symmetrical, uniform, precise, it produces functionaries rather than cultivated men. It is impartial, it is methodical, it is open to all comers, but it is also wanting in variety, mechanical, sterile. For the German ideal of education, however, Professor Geddes has as much praise as he has blame for the French. It recognizes all departments of serious study as equal in academic rank. It insists on original research as the best means of securing originality among teachers and students. It has superseded the barren test of examination by the more fruitful method of the thesis. What its studies lack in polish, they gain in intrinsic value. Its scholars may not be elegant, but they are at all events original. By the operations of its system, a student becomes a master of his subject, not an amateur and dilettante. It has made the German Universities the greatest in the world.

Such in outline is Professor Geddes' view of the situation. According to him, our English attempts at academic organization fluctuate between the French ideal and the German. While we were in bondage to the French, we founded the University of London, and set up that Frankenstein of an Examining Board. But now, he says, it is towards Germany that academic reformers are looking. ' The new American Universities are wholly German in their type, their aims, and ideals ; if Scottish University reformers are to have their way at all, it will be in the direction of Germanization ; and the new University of London will satisfy most of its projectors in proportion as it becomes a German University instead of a Napoleonic one.' To us, however, it appears that Professor Geddes has greatly exaggerated the intellectual pre-eminence of the German Universities, and has at least as seriously underrated the educational efficiency of the French. The fact remains that the German style remains the laughing stock of Europe, and that the French are the envy of the world for the incomparable lucidity and elegance of their diction. Nor is it by any means certain that the new stir of academic revival has shown itself with as great force in the German as in the French or English Universities. The scientific value, again, of the thesis, which the German system produces in such large numbers, is open to grave dispute. Still graver is the objection to the German system that it sets before the student a false ideal of excessive specialism. Most people would prefer that the young graduate, instead of being one who knows more about a tiny part of one subject than any of his contemporaries, should be a widely cultivated man, well-practised in using his intellectual weapons, impressed with the sense of his own ignorance and shortcomings, but at the same time able to take a broad view of the various departments of human knowledge and to perceive the connexions which link each with the rest.

But far more important than this is it to insist that the highest aim of all education is not to increase a man's knowledge so much as to strengthen and develop his character. So far as its work lies in the training of undergraduates, the business of the University is not so much to turn out learned men, as to teach men how to learn and how to act. It would be a great misfortune if it ever came to be regarded as the sole function of a University to produce professional students. When a man has graduated, the choice of occupation lies before him. Some men are fitted by nature for scholarship, others for action. It is not the business of the University to depreciate the life of action in comparison with the life of study, but to equip men for either destiny according to their natural gifts. This the English Universities have never failed to do, and one reason why they have so well discharged this duty is that they have always insisted on an element in education which tends to be overlooked both in the French and German systems. This is the element of residence under tutorial care in an atmosphere charged with the high traditions of an ancient place of learning.

Professor Geddes' indiscriminate laudation of the German system and his too rhetorical criticism of the French, will provoke reprisals. We are far, however, from desiring to speak disrespectfully either of the German or the French ideal of University education. The world would be poorer without either of them. The fact is that the ideal University life of the future must comprise three elements—the intellectual freedom of the German Universities, the intellectual drill of the French, the ethical discipline of the English. No country has ever yet reached its own ideal of University training. The ideal of each, even if fully attained, would be incomplete. The aim of University reformers should be as far as possible to blend together into one system the different virtues for which the French, the German, and the English Universities have separately, though often unconsciously, striven.

The Beginnings of University Life.

ON November 3, Mr. Wells, one of the Oxford University Extension Delegates, gave at the invitation of the students, the Inaugural Lecture for the session at the Glasgow Dialectic Society, one of the largest students' Unions in Scotland. He took for his subject the ' Beginnings of University Life.' After sketching the educational condition of Europe in the Dark Ages, which followed the overthrow of the Roman Empire, and the invasions of the Northern barbarians, and referring to the educational progress under Charlemagne, he pointed out the causes of the educational revival which marked the eleventh and twelfth centuries, and of which the ultimate outcome was the formation of Universities. He then described in some detail the growth of the two typical Universities of Bologna and of Paris. The former was an association of students, banded together to secure those privileges which, as aliens in Bologna, they could not obtain from the ordinary laws of the city. Mr. Wells caused great amusement by the extracts which he read from Mr. Rashdall's forthcoming book (the proofs of which had been most kindly lent to him), describing the tyranny exercised by the students over the Professors, who, as being generally citizens of Bologna, were outside the University and its privileges. At Paris, on the other hand, the University had grown up out of the association of the Masters, banded together to protect themselves against the oppression of the Chancellor, the representative of the Cathedral, in the schools of which the University had gradually developed.

After referring to the different position of the Chancellor at Oxford, in which city he was the head champion of the scholars, not their oppressor, he briefly sketched the character of the mediaeval curriculum, pointing out how the idea of a fixed sequence of studies had gradually grown up, and how the modern conception of a degree, being given simply as the result of an examination, was entirely absent. In concluding Mr. Wells dwelt upon the three great lessons to be drawn from mediaeval Universities :—(1) their independence. They owed their origin to themselves ; they were not founded by kings or popes, as was later the case, and as used to be asserted by uncritical historians about all Universities, early and late alike ; (2) the importance of the personal influence of the teacher ; (3) their loyalty to truth and religion, however opposed they were to ecclesiastical domination.

In replying to the vote of thanks, proposed by the President of the Dialectic, Mr. Horn, Mr. Wells answered two or three questions as to the early history of Oxford, and urged on the students the importance of making history live, by using the survivals of the past so frequent everywhere, but especially in university towns. In this way history and antiquarianism might be made to supplement each other ; the present was better understood and its problems could be better met, if we understood and sympathized with the past.

LETTERS TO THE EDITOR.

[*We do not hold ourselves responsible for the opinions expressed by our correspondents.*]

Are Audiences of Ladies worth while?

DEAR SIR,—May I be allowed a little space for a few remarks on a letter signed ' L. Steuart,' which appeared in the November number of the *Oxford University Extension Gazette.* I am entirely at one with your correspondent in his ' plea for the serious criticism by lecturers of paper-work done by students,' in all cases where that serious criticism is not already given. He however, implies that lecturers withhold this serious criticism because the ' young lady students,' of whom University Extension, audiences are largely composed, do not like it. Now I think Mr. Steuart (for I cannot imagine that the letter is written from a lady's point of view) must have been very unfortunate in his experiences of Extension students. The course of events in this centre, where we have an overwhelming proportion of lady students, leads me to the conclusion that, while doubtless amongst the thousands of ladies attracted by University Extension lectures, there are some, possibly many, who prefer as criticism of their paper-work sweetness rather than light, yet hat at the heart of every flourishing centre there is a body of earnest students, very often mostly ladies, who do not care for unlimited sugar-plums, and who do appreciate honest and serious criticism. The mere fact of a change of lecturer, with a consequent change of manner and method, may sometimes produce at first a slight falling off in the paper-work ; but if the lecture makes it felt that he is honestly endeavouring to teach, the tide will soon flow back, and high water-mark be again reached.

From the point of view from which I look at University Extension, the tone of Mr. Steuart's letter seems to me singularly unfortunate. In his closing paragraph he talks about a class of students ' for whom University Extension is *not* primarily intended.' Now with the exception of the comparatively small number of people who are both able and willing to go to the Universities themselves, I should have said that such a class of students was unknown. University Extension surely comes as a healer of the breach, a closer of the gaps, between the various sections of society. In its lecture halls it knows no classes but its own ; it does not inquire whether its students are drawn from the upper ten thousand, or the submerged tenth, whether they are men, or whether they are women, only if they are earnest seekers after knowledge.

Some centres may from the first have been fortunate enough to draw support from, and to fill their lecture halls with, people of all classes ; but in very many others, as here, this is not the case, and the local organizers can certainly not afford to speak contemptuously of their lady students. For five years this has been a fairly flourishing centre, and we have only just succeeded in getting any number of working class students to attend our lectures, or to believe that we wish for their support and co-operation. We should not have been able to arrive at this stage, we should have died out altogether in five months, not five years, if it had not been for the steady enthusiastic work, the unfailing help which our lady supporters have given us. We should not only have had no funds wherewith to pay our lecturers, but these latter if they had come without fees, would have found themselves in the still more unfortunate position of having no students of any class to teach. I should imagine that, in the south of England centres at least, our experience has not been singular. Apologizing for the length of my letter,

I remain, Sir, Yours truly,

Bournemouth.　　　　　　　　　CATHARINE PUNCH.

'Young Ladies' and University Extension.

DEAR SIR,—Many opinions have been expressed in your columns as to the classes of people that we should try to bring within reach of University Extension, but hitherto no one has so emphatically stated, as in last month's *Gazette*, that there was one class for whom they were *not* primarily intended.

It seems hardly in keeping with the movement on all sides for the higher education of women, that ' young ladies' should be excluded from what is, in many cases, their only chance of culture apart from private study.

Looking back on the history of the Extension movement—in the early days at least—did not the majority of the students, and earnest ones too, come from this despised class, and have not many of the most active secretaries been drawn from its ranks ?

If they were so deplorably silly as your correspondent L. Steuart implies, would they not still more need the training that comes from University Extension lectures, and the helps that gather round them ?

Yours truly,

Peterborough.　　　　　　　　　KATE E. COLMAN.

Criticism of Paper Work.

DEAR SIR,—I am glad to see that this most important question has been once more raised in your columns. ' Even young ladies ' have sometimes a true thirst for knowledge and are earnest Extension students, and it is most disappointing and disheartening to such, after spending much time and thought in reading for and writing their papers, to have them returned with such scanty criticism as ' good,' ' fair,' scrawled (evidently in the train) in the margin. A true student wants all the criticism and help he can get from the lecturer, and surely it is not necessary to pander to those who take offence, unless their work is commended, and whose object in attending lectures and writing papers is most assuredly not to *learn.*

Yours faithfully,

London,　　　　　　　　　C. HELEN SCOTT.
November 2, 1893.

DEAR SIR,—Your correspondent in the November issue of the *Gazette* touches on a tough problem. Without thorough and frank criticism of the contents, I venture to think paper work loses half its use, and University Extension work a considerable fraction of its characteristic value. Probably want of time may make it almost impossible for the busier lecturers to follow each paper offered them at all closely, and may explain the curious phenomenon that, in this department of their work, first magnitude stars sometimes shine less brightly than those of inferior brilliancy.

Might not the difficulty your correspondent refers to be partly overcome, if a common understanding obtained among the lecturers that no terms of mere courtesy, and no general commendation apart from criticism, should be employed? Any verbal praise awarded should be of such a nature as itself to operate as criticism. Compliments should mean that a paper was beneath anything better. The marks assigned would show the comparative merit of each essay. The danger of diminishing the number of papers must be risked by the lecturers, if the aim of training men and women to think is not to be exchanged for that of providing unemployed ladies of various ages with a pleasing and innocuous means of getting through some of their leisure time.

Yours truly,

AN EXTENSION STUDENT AND SECRETARY.

BOOK EXCHANGE COLUMN.

THE Bedford Students' Association offers—

Lanfrey, *Vie de Napoléon,* 5 vols.,

for loan or exchange. Address :—Miss BLAKE, St. Andrew's Road, Bedford.

GOVERNMENT GRANT
TO UNIVERSITY COLLEGES.

A POSSE of Principals waited on Sir William Harcourt at the Treasury on November 21 to ask for a continuance and increase of the Parliamentary Grant to the University Colleges. Much the best report of the proceedings is that given by the *Manchester Guardian* of November 22. Mr. James Stuart introduced the deputation and Principal Ward of Owens College, Manchester, made a weighty speech in support of the views of the deputation. He stated that, at the eleven University Colleges in receipt of the grant, there are now 4,600 day students in Arts, Science and Law. The evening classes comprise another 7,000. He added that 'the annual subscriptions of the localities have as a rule been stimulated rather than diminished by the receipt of a Government Grant.' Dr. Ward further pointed out that the recent developments in English education have thrown a great strain on the resources of the Colleges. For example, the University training of teachers for elementary schools has necessitated increased outlay on the part of those institutions. 'The operation of the Technical Instruction Grants,' added Dr. Ward, 'while giving the Colleges scholarships and exhibitions, has not relieved their finances, and has even at times proved suggestive of new expenditure.' The speaker further pointed out 'that the strong impulse given to technical instruction in the Colleges has made it more difficult to maintain that due balance between technical studies and that higher scientific and literary instruction, which it is of the very essence of the character of the University Colleges to preserve.' In conclusion he pointed out that, while the Parliamentary Grant to three University Colleges in Wales is £13,500 a year, ten English Colleges and one Scotch College only receive £15,000 a year among them.

The Chancellor of the Exchequer in reply let it be understood that he meant to renew the grants, but not to increase them. No one can find fault with this decision, though many will regret it on the ground that the present is a crisis in the educational development of England. It is unlucky that this crisis has been coincident with mercantile depression. In his speech Sir William Harcourt laid stress on three points which deserve attention.

(1) The towns where the Colleges are situate, should, he thought, make a municipal contribution to meet the Government Grant. This it seems to us is sound policy, and might be made a *sine qua non.* We may point out that such municipal aid is already given at Reading to the University Extension College.

(2) 'The Government,' he considered, 'were bound to satisfy themselves as to the way in which the subsidized institutions were conducted, and that the grant was in all respects worthily dealt with.' He added 'that of course any means taken to ascertain those circumstances would be used in a manner most agreeable to the institutions themselves.' He was sure that 'the Colleges would not resent the Government satisfying itself that public money was being spent to the greatest possible advantage.' This again is sound policy, provided that the inspection leaves the Colleges free to develop their own educational ideas and serves rather as an act of audit and of observation than as an occasion for dictation or interference. Indeed a closer connexion between the Government and the Colleges will be reciprocally advantageous. It will keep the Government acquainted with the work and the needs of the Colleges, and the Colleges in a healthy kind of relation to the movements of public opinion.

(3) Sir William Harcourt's third principle was that grants of public money should be devoted to purposes accessible to any class of the community without distinction of religious opinions. The Government apparently means no portion of the Grant to go to support any professorship, in filling which regard was had to the religious opinions of its candidates. The application of this principle seems to us to raise difficulties which are by no means to be settled by any off-hand judgement. No doubt, however, the subject will receive full consideration.

CONCERNING THE CENTRES.

BEDFORD.—The third and fourth lectures of Mr. Graham Wallas' course have greatly added to its interest, for the 'Town' and 'County' are subjects which have a direct bearing on the everyday life of the English citizen. One result of gaining such comprehensive views as to the gradual development of municipal institutions is to re-awaken local patriotism where it is dormant. Our two last students' meetings have been remarkable for several able papers (by Mr. Rowland Hill, Mr R. Steele, Mr. Henderson, and others) on 'Parochial and Municipal History,' compiled after much careful investigation and inquiry. The early association of Bedford with Oxford is a fact that has been prominently brought forward from the town records, which show that the charter of the former was framed on the model of that of the University city As it appears that these are now the only two Oxford centres at which the 'English Citizen' course is being delivered, it would be an advantage to Bedford if the old ties could be revived in the form of some interchange of students' papers, according to a plan which is already adopted by some south of England centres.—E. BLAKE.

BODMIN.—The first series of lectures in connexion with this centre was concluded on Wednesday, November 1. The Extension movement was initiated in the centre in the autumn of 1892, by Mr. K. D. Cotes, who visited the town at the close of his lecture session in Cornwall, and delivered a specimen lecture. This led to the formation of a strong local committee who succeeded in raising an ample guarantee fund for the cost of the course, and Mr. Cotes was invited to lecture on 'English Social Life (Anglo-Saxon and Medieval England).' The course has proved thoroughly successful. The interest in the lectures has steadily increased, and an average attendance of seventy has been registered. At the conclusion of the last lecture, a very hearty vote of thanks was awarded to Mr. Cotes, and in the course of some interesting speeches, it was strongly urged that it was desirable, if the best results of University Extension work were to be secured, to follow up the same branch of study, or one nearly allied to it, next year. Allusion was also made to the possibility of securing some portion of the 'Whiskey' money, in aid of Extension work in Cornwall; and there seemed good ground for hoping that, in co-operation with the Science and Art Department in the County, it might be possible to establish a College at Truro, on the lines of the University Extension Colleges at Reading and Exeter.—J. J. FARRELL, *Hon. Sec.*

BRIGHTON.—Mr. MacColl's lectures on the English Painters are thoroughly successful. The Town Council have renewed their grant of £50 towards the expenses of the Committee's work during the present year.

CAMBORNE.—We have just concluded our eighth annual course. This year Mr. Kenelm D. Cotes has revisited us, in common with the other Cornish centres, and we have had six lectures on 'English Social Life,' Part I. The attendance at the lectures has been very steady, in spite of many counter-attractions. Mr. Cotes has had a large audience out-side the lecture-room, for the lectures have been very fully reported in the *Cornish Post,* and by this means have attracted quite abnormal attention, being generally considered one of the most interesting History courses ever given. The lectures have been illustrated throughout by limelight. We have been glad to welcome four students (ladies) from the neighbouring town of Redruth, who have shown an unflagging interest in the work, never missing lectures or students' meetings, in spite of late hours and bad weather. The work of the Students' Association has been regular and constant, having scarcely ceased since Mr. Cotes' lectures last year. This is largely due to his unfailing interest in the class, and to the energy and ability of Miss E. S. Budge, the Hon. Sec. to the Students' Association, to whom all the students feel very grateful for her unwearied efforts. About fourteen will attend the Examination, which will take place Nov. 30.—BEATRICE VIVIAN, *Hon. Sec.*

The *Cornish Post* of Oct. 13 writes as follows of Mr. Cotes' lectures :—' There probably have never been any lectures given on History of a more interesting nature than those which are being given by Mr. Kenelm D. Cotes, M.A., of Oxford. Last week we gave and this week we have given long reports of those lectures ; but mere reports do not convey any idea of the pleasure and profit it is to hear the lecturer himself actually discoursing.'

FALMOUTH.—A series of lectures by K. D. Cotes, M.A., has just ended. The subject dealt with—' The Relation of History to Painting '—was entirely new to the majority of the students and those attending the lectures. From the first lecture to the concluding one on Venice, Mr. Cotes succeeded in arousing the utmost interest in his audience. The historical side of the course was naturally most exhaustively dealt with, but its relation to Art and the gradual growth of art from the rude hieroglyphics and wall paintings of the ancient nations to the world-known painters of Florence and Venice were skilfully traced. Whether tracing the ideal age of Pericles or the practical Philistinism of the Romans, or again comparing Athens with Florence and Rome with Venetian policy, Mr. Cotes equally pleased his audience, and the students owe him particular thanks for special instruction in a difficult subject.—JANETTE CLIFT, *Hon. Sec.*

GLOUCESTER.—Mr. Horsburgh's lectures on the ' Growth of Parliament' continue to attract crowded audiences in the Southgate Lecture Hall. At the second lecture of the course, the lecturer read a letter he had received suggesting the desirability of the city papers publishing full reports of the lectures for the benefit of those who are unable to take good notes We are glad to see that the *Gloucestershire Chronicle* continues to give a careful report and summary of the course.

HARROGATE.—Mr. Boas' lectures on Shakespeare have been much enjoyed and, for Harrogate, the attendance has been very good.—Z. JENNINGS, *Hon. Sec.*

HEBDEN BRIDGE.—The course of lectures arranged by the Committee of the Hebden Bridge Manufacturing Society, which is being delivered by Mr. E. L. S. Horsburgh on the ' French Revolution,' has begun successfully. The lectures are to be illustrated by lantern slides, but owing to the non-arrival of the slides the first of the series was given without illustration. The lectures are being delivered in the Co-operative Hall, and Mr. J. Craven presided at the first lecture.

HUDDERSFIELD.—During the long interval which unavoidably occurs between the third and fourth lectures of Mr. Lang's course, four fortnightly lectures have been arranged by the educational committee of the Industrial Society and the Technical School. These lectures are to be delivered by local sympathizers of Extension work, and Mr. George Thomson gave the first of the series on ' Some Aspects of the New Industrial Revolution and its Prophet,' on the last Thursday in October, Mr. James Broadbent, President of the Industrial Society, being in the chair.

HYDE.—Mr. Shaw's lectures on the ' Making of England' promise to be even more successful than those on the ' Age of Elizabeth,' delivered by the same lecturer last year. The lectures are illustrated by lantern slides, and have been very well attended.

LEAMINGTON.—Mr. J. A. Hobson is giving us this Autumn the first part of his lectures on ' Problems of Poverty.' It is the first time that any subject touching on the industrio-social question has been attempted here, and that an opportunity has been given to workmen, by the issue of a limited number of course tickets at 1s. 6d. each (the ordinary price is 6s.), to attend Extension lectures. We regarded the new departure as rather a leap in the dark, and were anxious for the result. But now that we are two-thirds through the course, and find that probably we shall at least clear expenses, we may venture on congratulating ourselves on having alighted on our feet. We have had other courses more numerously attended, but none which have excited more interest among those who do attend, or drawn from so wide a social area, including as it does workmen, business men, and young ladies' schools. We disseminated the artisans tickets in the orthodox way through the workmen's own associations, but only about thirty were bought, all, or nearly all, through the Trades' Council, and the adherents of the Pleasant Sunday Afternoon movement. The after-class is a distinct success. Most of the workmen stop for it, and there have never been less than forty present, i. e. about a third of the audience at the lectures. A town-councillor, a poor-law inspector, a trades-union secretary, a bank-manager, and several professional men and prominent tradesmen have on different occasions joined in the discussion at these classes. The committee has felt encouraged to arrange for the delivery of the second part of Mr. Hobson's course during the Spring. A member of the local Trades' Council has just joined its ranks. The local papers publish summaries of the lectures, to which one paper gives a brief *résumé* of the discussion in the after-class.— C. H. d' E. LEPPINGTON, *Hon. Sec.*

LOUTH.—On Thursday evening, November 2, Mr. Cecil Carus-Wilson continued his course of lectures on the ' Outlines of Geology' to a large and appreciative audience. A class was held at the end of the lecture.

OXFORD.—The course of twenty-four lectures by Mr. Graham Wallas on ' The English Citizen, Past and Present,' has begun very successfully. The lectures are delivered weekly in the hall of the Y.M.C.A., and are attended this term by about 190 people, nearly all of whom stay for the class after the lecture, and between thirty and forty of whom are writing the weekly papers. The tutorial class on Saturdays, conducted by Mr. Ambrose Bennett, is also well attended, about forty students being present each week. The course has been arranged in accordance with the regulation of the Education Department, which allows marks in the Queen's Scholarship Examination to candidates who shall present certificates awarded after examination on this course of twenty-four University Extension lectures. We learn that four

hend teachers of elementary schools, twelve assistant teachers, and eleven pupil teachers, are attending the course. The local committee contains representatives of every kind of educational work in the University and the city. This is the first course of Extension lectures that has been given in Oxford for some years, and we are very glad to be able to record the successful revival of the centre.

PETERBOROUGH.—We are thoroughly enjoying Mr. Boas' lectures; the amount of paper-work is disappointing, but the lecturer seems to think the quality pretty fair.—K. COLMAN, *Hon. Sec.*

ROMSEY.—The course of Shaksperian lectures which is being delivered in this centre by Mr. Marriott is proving a great success. The subject on Nov. 8 was Richard II, and the lecturer's skilful treatment of it gained for him a delighted audience.— E. PHILLIPS.

SWANSEA.—The *Cambrian* contains an interesting account of Mr. Hewins' second lecture at Swansea, which is said to have been very interesting and lucid. The lecturer recommended the formation of a Students' Association, and after the lecture the names of those who were anxious to join were received. Before the class some beautiful slides illustrating the lecture were thrown on the screen.

TAVISTOCK.—A well-attended meeting was held in the Town Hall on November 8, when Mr. Kenelm D. Cotes, M.A., University Extension lecturer, kindly gave an eloquent and interesting lecture on Oxford, illustrated by beautiful lime-light photographs. The Rev. D. P. Alford, M.A., Vicar of Tavistock, took the chair, and at the conclusion of the lecture a vote of thanks was proposed by the Rev. F. J. Bryant, D.D., Rector of St. Peters', Tavistock. The Rev. W. H. David, M.A., Headmaster of Kelly College, seconded by Colonel Jacob, Indian Staff Corps, moved that ' this meeting being anxious to secure for Tavistock three courses of Extension lectures, six in each course, to be spread over three winter sessions, pledges itself to raise the necessary funds by all available means.' The motion was carried unanimously, and several promises of support were received by the secretary in the room We may therefore hope to hear of the revival of lectures, on a more permanent basis, at this centre after Christmas.—GRACE JOHNSTONE, *Loc. Sec.*

TODMORDEN.—Large audiences have assembled in the Co-operative Hall, Dale Street, to hear the Rev. Hudson Shaw's lectures on the ' Puritan Revolution.' The subjects of the lectures are Pym and Hampden, Hyde, Fairfax and Cromwell.

WHITEHAVEN.—The Oxford Extension lectures at this centre have hitherto been carried on in connexion with the Whitehaven Scientific Association, and the subjects have been solely of a historical character. But this year two new departures from the old method of procedure have been introduced. The work is now done under the joint auspices of the Whitehaven Scientific Association and of the Young Men's Christian Association, and a scientific subject, viz., Physiography, has been selected for one of the courses of lectures. A grant in aid has also been given by the Cumberland County Council, and the Committee of Management have therefore been enabled to reduce the charge for admission to the lectures to 1s. for the course of six lectures, so that the advantages of the University Extension teaching are now placed within the reach of all classes. The members of the two Associations are admitted free on production of member's ticket. More than 2,500 handbills have been distributed by a house to house visitation, and the sale of admission tickets has been actively prosecuted amongst the labouring classes, thus bringing the lectures prominently before the inhabitants of the town. The course of six lectures on Physiography by Mr. C. Carus-Wilson commenced on October 10 and the exertions of the committee have been well rewarded, while the selection of a science subject has been popular in a very marked manner. The number of persons present have been much greater than at any of the previous courses given at this centre. Three lectures, or half of the course, have now been delivered, and large audiences have been maintained throughout, the number varying from 400 at the first lecture to 300 at the third lecture, while from 90 to 60 remained to the class held after each lecture. Mr. Carus-Wilson's lectures are clear, lucid, and attractive, and his treatment of the portions of the subject already dealt with, such as, ' The World in Space,' ' The Chemistry of Nature,' and ' The Atmosphere,' together with the lantern views and the experiments illustrating the lectures, has tended greatly to increase the popularity of the Oxford Extension work in the locality as exemplified by the increased attendance already mentioned, and augurs well for the continued success of the remainder of the course. In order to give a further impetus to real work, especially amongst the junior students, the committee have under consideration a proposal to provide a £10 Scholarship to enable a student from the Whitehaven centre to attend the Oxford Summer Meeting, 1894.—R. RUSSELL, *Hon. Sec.*

UNIVERSITY EXTENSION COLLEGE, READING.

ON October 30, at the invitation of the Mayor and Mrs J. Wessley Martin, a large and thoroughly representative gathering of people assembled at a Conversazione in the Town Hall 'to meet the Council and Staff of the University Extension College.' Among those present, in addition to members of the College, were the Warden of Radley College, the Mayors of Abingdon, Basingstoke, Henley, Wallingford, Newbury, and Wokingham, Sir John Mowbray, M.P., Captain Abney (Director of the Science Division of the Science and Art Department, South Kensington), the Headmasters of Reading and Newbury Schools, and Mr. J. Wells. The Governing Body of Christ Church was represented by Mr. Hassall (the Senior Proctor), Mr. Stewart, the Rev. T. B. Strong and Mr. M. E. Sadler.

The Conversazione was in every respect most successful; during the course of the evening the Silchester Museum was thrown open to the guests, and an organ recital was given by Mr. Tirbutt, the lecturer on Music at the University Extension College. At 9 o'clock the guests assembled in the large hall, and the Mayor in welcoming them touched on the work of the College during the past year, which had been marked by rapid development and unqualified success, and for that reason he had invited his fellow townsmen and other friends to meet the staff of the College, which he believed had instituted a good educational work, and one which would tell its own tale and reap its own reward in days to come. Mr. H. J. Mackinder (Principal of the College) then explained what had been done during the past year. He acknowledged most gratefully the loyal support of the people of Reading, of the Berks County Council, and of the Staff of the College. Even in their first thirteen months of existence they could show that some success had been achieved in return for the liberality and help which had been given them. In the May Examination of the Science and Art Department they had taken one first class honours in Chemistry, and in the Art Examination had gained three 'excellents.' Of 23 candidates sent in for the Queen's Scholarship Examination 17 had succeeded, 5 in the first, 8 in the second, and 4 in the third class. Two of the first class were in the first hundred of the five thousand successful candidates.

Sir John Mowbray, after expressing regret at the unavoidable absence of the Dean of Christ Church, declared that as one who for twenty-five years had represented the University of Oxford, he could state on behalf of the University how cordially they sanctioned, and how warmly they thanked the town of Reading for, the great effort it had made in the work of University Extension; and on his own behalf as an Honorary Student of Christ Church he was proud of the share that House had taken in the work. The speaker added that it was sixty years ago since he had matriculated in the University of Oxford, and he had watched with the greatest interest the growth of the University within and without its own walls. It had been the aim and object of all University reformers, of all shades of opinion, and especially of the two pioneers of the movement, Mr. William Sewell and Dr. Pusey, that the Universities of the nation should be made more accessible to the people, and that, if the people could not resort to the University, the University should go to them. Reading would, it seemed to him, realize what many had for thirty-five years thought to be a dream, and to an extent beyond what the most fond promoters of the College could have ventured to hope. Referring to the manner in which various bodies had co-operated for the success of the work, Sir John said that 'he was pleased to see so many distinguished men upon the platform, including one Proctor of the University, the Junior Censor of Christ Church, four members of the Governing Body of Christ Church, and also the head of the Science and Art Department. They had the Town Council of Reading, the School Board, all the Church and other schools combining; and the University of Oxford, the great House of Christ Church, the Science and Art Department, the Board of Agriculture, and the County Council, all show-

ing their interest in that movement, which further had the support of the two great families who had given Reading a world-wide reputation, who, with every family connected with the professions, the trades, and the industries of the place had been nobly working for the same end.' He was sure the Mayor felt it a great privilege to entertain those visitors, and he had done so with a large-hearted spirit and most courteous hospitality which they thoroughly appreciated.'

The Chairman of the Council (Mr. Herbert Sutton) proposed a vote of thanks to the Mayor, which was seconded by Captain Abney, who remarked that in the Reading College they had a happy combination of University Extension with the Science and Art teaching of South Kensington. This was the first time the experiment had been tried, and he regarded it with hope, believing that only by that co-operation could true science teaching be carried through the country. The experiment was of great interest not only to Reading itself, but to England at large.

.·.

The Mayor of Reading, speaking at the second of an interesting course of public lectures, which are being delivered by Mr. H. J. Mackinder in the large Town Hall, said that he had the honour, as Mayor of the town, to preside at an important meeting of the Town Council, when the Council by a majority of three to one resolved to vote £600 to the University Extension College.

.·.

We are heartily glad to see that the municipal interest at the University Extension College is aroused at Reading. It is of fundamental importance that higher education should not be exclusive in England. On this point Mr. Mackinder made an excellent speech at a recent dinner of the Oddfellows at Reading. Mr. Mackinder, in proposing 'Floreat Radingensis,' remarked that—

Some might say that the reason for the State aiding primary education was because it was compulsory, but that reason could not be advanced for aiding technical education. The State was aiding technical education because not only did each one educate himself for the purpose of doing himself good, but because each one was a portion of the nation; because it was dangerous for those around us to go about uneducated in the same way that it was dangerous for a person with some disease to walk the streets; because, as education had gone up, the criminal statistics had gone down; because this nation was fighting to maintain its industrial position; and because other nations were devoting the public funds with no stinted hand to the education of the working classes. If England was to hold her own she must follow their example of these other countries and keep alongside of them. It was not for a selfish end merely that each educated himself. It was their duty to help the nation, and therefore, though technical and higher education was not compulsory, the State wisely stepped in, because the State recognized that those whom they assisted were educating themselves not for themselves but for the country at large. He was especially glad to have the opportunity of saying these things, because in Reading in connexion with the University Extension College they were anxious that this institution should not go the way of so many educational institutions, which, though founded in the first instance for all classes, had in the end become the property of one class. He was anxious that the College should be the property of the entire town of Reading and do good to all classes. Mr. Mackinder thanked the Corporation through the Mayor for the recent grant of £600 to the College out of the Customs and Excise duties, and also Mr. George Palmer for his generous gift of £500 for furniture. Further he expressed his thanks to those who had given help in organizing the Gilchrist lectures, and this year the popular lectures which were taking their place.

.·.

One of the great institutions at Reading is the Reading School, over which, in former years, the celebrated

Dr. Valpy presided. Every three years, under the will of Archbishop Laud, this school is visited by the Vice-Chancellor of the University of Oxford, the President of St. John's College, and the Warden of All Souls. At the luncheon which is customary on this occasion, Mr. Guilding made an interesting speech upon the connexion between Reading and Oxford. His concluding remarks were as follows :—

> The latest, but not the least, benefit to Reading by this connexion with the University of Oxford was that experiment recently tried by Christ Church, Oxford, in the foundation of a University Extension College. He called it an experiment, but owing to the energy of its able and accomplished Principal, Mr. Mackinder, it was no longer an experiment but an assured success.

.·.

The public lectures on historical and literary subjects arranged by the University Extension College, Reading, and delivered by various well-known lecturers after the pattern of the Gilchrist lectures, seem already to prove the wisdom of the experiment of attempting for these subjects what has been so long done for science. The last lecture, the fourth of the series, was delivered by Mr. J. H. Rose, M.A., of Christ's College, Cambridge, and a well-known lecturer to the Syndicate, the subject of the lecture being 'Travelling, past and present.' The College is to be congratulated on its wisdom in drawing its lecturers from Cambridge as well as from Oxford. Although from geographical position it must largely depend for its regular teachers upon the nearer University, it can afford for its more public and popular lectures to have the best it can get from both Universities without distinction.

OPENING OF ST. HILDA'S, OXFORD.

THE new Ladies' Hall at St. Hilda's, which was opened at the beginning of the Term with seven residents, was formally inaugurated by the Bishop of Oxford on Monday, November 6. The Principal of the Cheltenham Ladies' College and a considerable number of the staff were present. After a short service in the chapel, the Bishop of Oxford addressed the students, dwelling particularly on the danger of excessive specialization, which sometimes causes men to lose sight of the correlation of all knowledge—of the fact that 'truth is one and indivisible.'

The Dean of Winchester, Chairman of the Cheltenham Ladies' College, thanked the Bishop for the kind interest he had shown in St. Hilda's, and spoke of the charm of life in Oxford, and the pleasant recollections of their University and the strong affection for it of Oxford men ; he explained the special objects of this Hall,—viz. to afford the students the opportunity of continuing their studies, without necessarily taking examinations, and said it was desired rather to make it a post-graduate College. He explained that it was also open to teachers, who might profit by the opportunities of culture which the University affords, but for whom it would be an unprofitable expenditure of time to study for examination. He spoke of the good example set by the existing Ladies' Halls, and the prudence which had made it impossible for the voice of scandal to utter a word. He urged the students to keep before them a high ideal, and made a graceful allusion to the rainbow, which appeared just as the proceedings began.

At the conclusion the Lady Principal (Mrs. Burrows) and the Principal of the Cheltenham Ladies' College entertained their guests and a considerable number of Oxford friends at afternoon tea ; the Cheltenham party returned home by a special train, the Great Western having made this extraordinary concession in consequence of the large number of passengers—about 150.

The total number of residents is to be eighteen. There are at present seven in residence, and others are already entered for January.

HOW A NORTH COUNTRY CENTRE WAS ESTABLISHED.

By Miss E. M. Dowson, *Hon. Sec.* at Hyde.

I HAVE been asked to give a short account of the way in which a centre in the North of England has been started.

It was first ascertained what lecturer would be able to come ; then all the wealthiest people of the neighbourhood were asked how much they would give to start the movement, and about ten guarantors were found. This was done before any meeting was held. At a meeting of the chief representatives of the town it was decided what course of lectures should be given, and a committee and officers were elected. The committee priced the tickets at 5s. for the supporters, and 6d. for the working people, for the course of six lectures, the 6d. tickets being well distributed.

A great many were sold by mill-owners to the men in their employment, and posters were put up in the mills ; 3,000 hand-bills were printed and distributed throughout the town by small boys, and given out from shop-counters. The lectures were well advertised both before and during the course. It has been impossible to get quite such large subscriptions the second year, so a greater number have been asked to support the movement, and many have promised an annual subscription of 5s. A Postal Directory of the neighbourhood was found an indispensable help in doing this. Now that the lectures have a reputation it is not difficult to find subscribers of 5s., and probably, next year, no one need buy more tickets than they really want.

In a manufacturing district such as the one of which I am speaking, it is really necessary to have very cheap tickets for the working people, as trade is often bad. Any trouble incurred in getting support is repaid by seeing the number and quality of the audience at each lecture. The working men of the district have been found the keenest and most attentive listeners.

ANNUAL MEETING OF THE LONDON UNIVERSITY EXTENSION SOCIETY.

THE London Society held its annual meeting on Saturday, November 18. There was a large attendance of distinguished people, but the speeches did not contain anything of special interest. Among those present were Sir Richard Webster, Rev. J. E. C. Welldon (Headmaster of Harrow), Mr. G. W. Kekewich (Secretary of the Education Department), Canon Barnett, Mr. Alfred Milner, Mr. Diggle (Chairman of the London School Board), and Mr. Goschen, who was in the chair. Mr. Goschen in his introductory remarks congratulated the Society on its success in securing continuous study at the centres. On this point he quoted some remarkable figures. Out of 139 courses arranged by the London Society during last session, 86 were in educational sequence. Referring to the delightful speech which Lord Rosebery had made a few days before on the growth of municipal interest in London, Mr. Goschen gave his testimony that educational interest had equally grown in the metropolis. Mr. Welldon subsequently gave an address, which the *Times* chaffed in its leading article, as the speaker seemed to imply that both Mr. Darwin and Dr. Pusey would both have been better for attending University Extension lectures. But it appears from a later correction that Mr. Welldon was misreported.

.·.

The report of the London Society has recently been issued. It marks a satisfactory advance. One hundred and thirty courses have been delivered, 13,374 students entered for them, and 1,355 certificates were awarded. Of the courses, fifty-five were on different branches of Natural and Physical Science, and eighty-four were on Arts. The latter figure is made up as follows :—thirty-nine courses were on Literature, twenty-three on History, nine on Economics, six on Architecture and Art, and seven on Philosophy.

COUNTY COUNCILS AND SECONDARY EDUCATION.

A PAMPHLET bearing the title *Secondary Education under the County Councils* has been published by Mr. Macan, the energetic Organizing Secretary of the Surrey County Council. The gist of this pointed and readable essay is summed up in three of his propositions as follows :—

(1) 'Let the County Councils leave all the work in which the Educational Department has a hand to the control of the Elementary School Authorities, stipulating only that they keep within due limits of age, methods, and curriculum.'

(2) 'The County Councils have no wish to assist or interfere with the great public schools or other schools, such as Uppingham, Haileybury, Cheltenham, Wellington, &c., of a similar character. Expensive boarding schools can be safely allowed to support themselves as at present.'

(3) 'Existing schools should be strengthened in their staff and buildings, and especially in the teaching and apparatus of their modern sides. No interference with their general work should be contemplated, but a small representation of the County Council on the governing body should be insisted upon, in order to see, *inter alia*, that masters are properly remunerated and children taught with a view to industrial and not social progress.'

What seems to us the chief defect of Mr. Macan's essay is that it is too largely influenced by the tacit assumption that what Secondary Education chiefly wants is more money. We doubt if this is the case. What are needed above all things are guidance, inspection, and correlation. Funds may in some cases be wanted as well, but the financial needs are trivial compared with the need of regulation and advice. In Secondary Education we do not so much want new sources of income as measures which will secure the present funds being wisely spent. This is the reason why there is such a strong and growing feeling in favour of the establishment of new educational authorities, so constituted as to secure for the country a wise and liberal policy in the direction and furtherance of Secondary Education.

Again, Mr. Macan's definition of Secondary Education seems to imply some want of perception of the fact that each grade of education is necessarily connected with other grades, and should be viewed, not as a thing apart, but as a section of a great whole. This makes it necessary that the educational authorities should represent the interests and experience of the various grades of education as well as the tax-payers and the great organs of local government. There is no question that County Councils will have an honourable place in the direction of Secondary Education, but a candid perusal of Mr. Macan's pamphlet will make most of its readers doubt whether it would be expedient to entrust to the County Councils the sole oversight of such an important matter.

THE 'SPECTATOR' ON POPULAR EDUCATION.

LORD HERSCHELL'S speech at the opening of Hymer's College at Hull provided the *Spectator* of November 4 with the text for an interesting article on education. The writer, though he thinks that we are right to persevere in our educational work, does not take a very sanguine view as to the immediate and tangible benefits which will follow from it. He thinks, for example, that the diffusion of elementary education is turning out 'thousands of children of the same monotonous type and with the same dreary attainments of superficial and often useless knowledge.' This probably means that the *Spectator* would sympathize with those who are anxious to give larger freedom of initiative to the teachers in elementary schools. If the results of our present system of primary education are monotonous, this is partly due to the restrictions we have placed upon the originality of the teachers. In another part of the article the view is advanced that genius is never repressed by unfavourable surroundings. 'In its very essence, genius is of the nature of a spiritual force that triumphs over all obstacles and draws nutriment and strength from the difficulties with which it has to contend.' Surely this is a very bold assumption. Is it not more reasonable to believe that, though genius frequently does force its way to the front against adverse conditions, it is often (especially when found in modest natures) suppressed and crushed in the struggle? The *Spectator* admits that this is the case with the lower kinds of capacity which we call talent in contradistinction to genius. Is it not likely that the same is true of genius itself? With a third contention of the writer there will be much cordial agreement. He says in popular education that 'we have thought too exclusively of the discipline of the intellect, of acquiring a more certain amount of book learning, or of passing through a curriculum at school.' This, he says, is the narrow and sterile view of educational work. 'The worth of any educational system is determined far more by the moral, than by the intellectual, discipline which it imparts.' In other words, the highest aim of education is, not attainment but, character.

A HOLIDAY COURSE IN JENA.

YET another Summer Meeting came into existence this year, the English-German course held at Jena in August.

It is an attractive idea for the English teacher to reside for a while in a continental University town, to speak the language, to attend lectures, to visit schools, and to exchange ideas with native teachers. Professor Rein of the Jena University, Mr. J. J. Findlay and other friends made arrangements this year for English teachers to attend a four weeks' course of lectures in Jena, the aims being firstly to learn the language, and secondly to see German methods of teaching. There were twenty-three English teachers present. We were a fairly representative company, including a Cambridge graduate, a High School mistress, two Elementary teachers, four lecturers in Day Training and University Colleges, two medical students, two teachers from America, two private governesses, and three head teachers of private schools.

The Fortbildungskurse an der Universität Jena für Lehrer Deutschlands, Oesterreichs und der Schweiz was held this year in August instead of Michaelmas, and some forty teachers from all parts of Germany came to Jena chiefly for the Natural Science lectures. This course was open to English men, and some of them took advantage of it ; but according to German custom women were excluded. Professor Rein declared his intention of admitting women to his lectures on Herbarlian Pedagogics, which were held in the Gymnasium—not the University —and some five women attended.

After an Introductory Meeting and a welcome from Professor Rein we were assigned to our classes.

The Elementary courses consisted of twenty-four lectures. Herr Oberlehrer Scholz lectured to beginners in the language on Jena, its surroundings, the Battle of Jena, Schiller in Jena, Luther in Jena, and Goethe in Jena ; the Erl König and the celebration of the Sedantag.

Doctor Noack conducted a more advanced course of Elementary German. He began with a more detailed account of Jena and its surroundings, and went on to a sketch of Germany and its constitution. This class read a German play and discussed the literature of Schiller and Goethe.

Herr Scholz's class was especially interesting from a Pedagogical point of view. His instruction was entirely in German, and he succeeded in making his students understand, speak, and write German. A discussion on the Teaching of Modern Languages dealt mainly with the methods adopted by Herr Scholz in his Elementary course.

In connexion with the lectures were walks and excursions with Herr Scholz and Dr. Noack to places of literary and historic interest.

Thus Herr Scholz took his class to the Battlefield

of Jena, to the Schiller Garten, and the Statue of the Erl König before he introduced these subjects in class. Doctor Noack conducted a party to Weimar and visited the Museum, the Schiller Haus, the Grethe Haus, and the Ducal Palace.

Visits to schools were also arranged, and interested teachers visited the Bürgerschule, the Stoysche Erziehungs-Anstalt, and Direktor Trüpers Pädagogische Heil-Anstalt in Jena, while those who were sufficiently interested visited schools and Training Colleges in Leipsic, Berlin, Eisenach, and Erfurt. Kindergartens were also visited, and Froebel's School-house at Blankenburg.

At the end of the course a provisional committee was formed to carry out arrangements for repeating the course next year, and also for extending operations into France.

Miss Dodd, Day Training Department, Owens College, Manchester, will be glad to send a report and announcements for next year to Teachers who desire further information.

C. I. DODD,
Member of Committee of Modern Language Holiday Courses.

The following is the Programme issued for 1894 :—
MODERN LANGUAGE HOLIDAY COURSES, 1894.
First Announcement.

PROVISIONAL COMMITTEE.—Miss C. I. Dodd, Day Training Department, Owens College, Manchester; Mr. J. J. Findlay, M.A., Rugby (*Hon. Secretary*); Mr. R. A. Jones, B.A., Queen's College, Oxford (*Hon. Treasurer*); Mr. R. L. Lancelot, The New School, Abbotsholme; Miss. M. F. Pease, Day Training Department, University College, Bristol; Miss H. M. Richards, Principal of the Stamford Hill High School (Abney Park College, N.); Professor Spencer, University College of N. Wales, Bangor; Miss Tooke, The Girls' High School, Sheffield.

The courses offered are of two kinds :—

(*a*) Elementary, for those who have little or no previous acquaintance with the *spoken* language. The instruction will be conducted by experienced teachers, who will speak very slowly and clearly, but will *only employ the foreign language itself as the medium of instruction.* The students will be expected to take their part in question and answer.

In these courses a lesson lasting 1½ hours will be given each morning, and the Instructor will occasionally meet the class for informal conversation in the afternoon or evening.

(*b*) Advanced, for those who can already follow a lecture in the foreign tongue. Lecture courses upon the Literature or History of the country, or upon other branches of Arts or Science, will be organized, according to the wishes of students who elect to take Advanced courses.

The other arrangements, described in § 4 of the Report, will, as far as possible, be repeated and improved upon. Opportunity will also be given for the discussion of Modern Language Teaching (see § 5 of Report).

I. GERMANY. *At Jena* i/Thür., a small University town, delightfully situated in the neighbourhood of the Thüringer Wald (for further details see Report).

(1) An Elementary course, for three weeks, commencing on or about July 16.

(2) Elementary and Advanced courses for three weeks, commencing on or about August 4.

The Advanced courses will include lectures (in connexion with the Fortbildungskurse—see Report § 4 c) on Pädagogik, Schulhygiene, Physiologische Psychologie, and on all branches of Natural Science, with practical work. Lectures on German History, Literature and Philology will be also arranged for, if a sufficient number of entries are forthcoming.

II. FRANCE. *At Caen*, a small town with a University Faculty, pleasantly situated on the Orne, about nine miles from the sea-shore of Normandy, with frequent train-service to several small bathing resorts. Caen itself and the country around (Bayeux, Cherbourg, &c.) contain much that is of historic interest to Englishmen.

(1) An Elementary course, for two weeks, commencing early in April, so as to fall within the Easter vacation of secondary schools, *for those who have not been previously to France, and have not acquired conversational French.*

(2) Elementary and Advanced courses, similar to those at Jena, commencing July 16 and August 4.

It is hoped that many students will be able to commence at Caen in the Spring and resume their work in the Summer, since the cost of travelling from England is so small.

FEES and TRAVELLING. The fees (including entrance fee) will range (according to the length of the course taken) between £1 10s. and £3.

Residence (board and lodging) costs per week between 25s. and 30s.

A monthly second class return ticket costs, according to route—

From London to Jena between £4 10s. and £6.
From London to Caen between £2 and £2 10s.

Note :—The present Circular will be reprinted early in the Spring, with further details and with entrance forms.

Treasurer's address :—R. A. JONES, Esq., Queen's College, Oxford.

Secretary's address :—J. J. FINDLAY, Esq., Rugby.

In order to assist the Committee in making their arrangements, students *who think it likely* that they will attend are requested to fill in a printed form, and forward it, either to the Secretary or to some other member of the Committee, as soon as possible.

NON-COLLEGIATE STUDENTS AT OXFORD.

THE Delegacy of Non-Collegiate Students at Oxford has issued its report for 1892 and 1893. From this we learn that 210 undergraduates and 243 graduates were on the books of the Delegacy on July 31 last. This shows a steady increase of undergraduates since the year 1890. The Delegacy has now completed twenty-five years of its existence, and a brief review of its history shows that during this period 2,279 persons have become Non-Collegiate students. It is stated that £60 per annum will meet all the necessary University expenses of Non-Collegiate students, who have to pay some additional fees for practical work. The report, which is full of interesting information, points out that the Delegates are willing to admit without examination students in any special branch of study who do not desire to pass through the Arts courses and can show evidence of fitness for their special subject. Under this provision, which should be more widely known than at present appears to be the case, seventeen students have been admitted during the past year. The report records that the present number of names on the books of the Delegacy is the largest which has ever yet been reached, and contains expressions of gratitude to Mrs. Shute for her gift of £2,500, which has been conveyed to the University to be held in trust for the benefit of Non-Collegiate students. It is interesting to note that during the last twenty-five years, Non-Collegiate students have obtained nine University prizes, fourteen University Scholarships, four University Exhibitions, as well as twenty-four scholarships and fifty-five exhibitions at different Colleges and Halls.

SCHOLARSHIPS FOR THE OXFORD SUMMER MEETING, 1894.

AMOUNT OF FUND TO DATE, £168.

A FUND, to which subscriptions amounting to £168 have already been promised, has been opened for the provision of scholarships to enable students from local centres to attend the Summer Meeting, which will be held in Oxford, from July 27 to August 24, 1894.

The Scholarships will be awarded after an Essay competition, and will be of two values—£10 and £5. Holders of the former must attend the whole Meeting; those of the latter may, if they prefer, attend either the First or Second Part only. Part I lasts from July 27 to Aug. 7; Part II from Aug. 8 to 24.

Conditions of Award.

The Scholarships will be awarded on or about July 2, 1894, for English Essays on subjects drawn from English Literature, English History, Natural Science, and Political Economy.

A. *Competition for Scholarships.*

The Scholarships will be awarded in three divisions :—

(*a*) Open to all Oxford University Extension Students *who need the assistance of the Scholarships* in order to study in Oxford, according to the intention of the donors.

(*b*) Open to all Elementary School Teachers (men or women), who are also Oxford University Extension Students.

(*c*) Open to all working men and women, who are also Oxford University Extension Students.

To qualify themselves for election to a Scholarship—

(1) All competitors must be recommended by their Local Committee as suitable candidates.

(2) Competitors in *divisions* (*a*) and (*b*) must, in order to qualify, obtain *distinction* in an examination on a course of Oxford University Extension Lectures delivered between January 1893 and June 1894.

(3) Competitors in *division* (*c*) must pass an examination on a course of Oxford University Extension Lectures delivered between the same dates.

The Delegates, however, reserve to themselves the right of rejecting the name of any candidate; and, unless compositions of sufficient merit are sent in, do not bind themselves to award Scholarships in any or all of the following four subjects.

B. *Competition for Prizes.*

A limited number of Prizes, of the value of £1, will be awarded in the same competition without any limitation as to the means of the competitors. Candidates for this branch of the competition must qualify as regards examinations, like the competitors in *divisions* (*a*) and (*b*).

SUBJECTS.

(1) *History* (one only to be selected).

(i) The Norman Conquest as a fresh departure in our History.

(ii) The Foreign Policy of the Stuarts.

(iii) The Political Views of Bolingbroke and Burke.

(2) *Literature* (one only to be selected).

(i) Show in detail what is meant by the influence of one literature on another.

(ii) Compare the works of any two great poets in regard to what you consider the principal aims of poetry.

(iii) Discuss the legitimate use of the Supernatural in Drama and Fiction.

(3) *Political Economy* (one only to be selected).

(i) What economical effects may be expected to follow from the spread of co operation ?

(ii) What circumstances in modern times have given increased importance to currency questions ?

(iii) Can any form of State-action be devised for the relief of the unemployed ?

(4) *Science* (one only to be selected).

(i) Practical Science Teaching in Schools.

(ii) Weather Charts and Forecasts.

(iii) The Nitrogen of the Farm.

REGULATIONS.

1. Each candidate may write an essay *on one subject only*, but may select one from any of the above four groups.

2. All compositions must reach the Delegacy [addressed—The Secretary, University Extension Office, Examination Schools, Oxford] on or before Monday, June 4, 1894 ; must each bear the writer's full name and address, with a note saying whether the writer is competing for a Scholarship or a Prize, or both, and, if

the former, in which division (*a*, *b*. or *c*, see above) ; must be written on foolscap paper, and on one side of the paper only ; must state, at the top of the first page, the writer's occupation ; and must be accompanied by a certificate of qualification from his or her Local Committee in the following form :—

'On behalf of the members of the Local Committee acting in concert with the Oxford University Delegates for the establishment of Lectures and Teaching at   , I certify that *A. B.* is in all respects a suitable person for election to a University Extension   , according to the regulations.

Signed on behalf of the Committee,

Secretary.'

3. Candidates are not debarred from the consultation of standard works, quotation from which should be notified in the margin.

4. The names of the unsuccessful competitors will not be divulged by the Delegates, and all compositions may be obtained from them after the announcement of the result of the competition.

5. Successful candidates will be informed by the Delegacy of the result of the competition.

6. The students elected to the Scholarships will be required to visit Oxford during the Summer Meeting of University Extension Students, 1894.

7. Holders of Scholarships of £10 are expected to reside in Oxford during the whole Meeting. If they are unable to do so, they may resign half their Scholarship, retaining, however, the position on the list of scholars to which the excellence of their essay entitled them.

8. The Programme of the Summer Meeting will be published at Easter and copies (7*d.* each post free) can then be obtained on application to the Secretary, University Extension Office, Oxford.

Contributions to the Scholarship fund should be sent to the Secretary, University Extension Office, Oxford.

¹ *State whether Scholarship or Prize, or both.*

BOOKS ON OUR TABLE.

British Commerce and Colonies. (From Elizabeth to Victoria.) By H. de B. GIBBINS, M.A. London, Methuen & Co. (University Extension Series.) Crown 8vo, pp. viii, 136. Price 2*s. 6d.*

This little volume gives a clear and succinct account of the growth and development of English trade and colonization from Elizabethan times. Especially interesting are the chapters on the Conquest of India. A list of British possessions, together with the dates of their acquisition, forms a fitting conclusion to the volume.

In a subsequent edition of this handbook, a somewhat confusing printer's error, which appears on pp. 120-121, where the footnote to a reference in the text of p. 120 appears on p. 121, might be rectified with advantage.

Agricultural Botany. By M. C. POTTER, M.A., F.L.S., Professor of Botany in the Durham College of Science, Newcastle-on-Tyne. London, Methuen & Co. (University Extension Series.) Crown 8vo, pp. xi, 250. Price 3*s. 6d.*

The Intermediate Text-Book of English History. Vol. II (1485-1603). By C. S. FEARENSIDE, M.A. Oxon. London, Univ. Corr. Coll. Press. Crown 8vo, pp. xvi, 336 : with Map and Appendices. Price 3*s. 6d.*

This book contains a clear and intelligent account of the Tudor period. The information in it is full and accurate, and the writer has wisely not attempted to economize space by omitting all mention of the great movements intellectual, social, and political, which play so important a part in sixteenth-century history. Hence Mr. Fearenside has written a book which is really better than a 'cram' book, though sadly marred for educational purposes by frequent use of slang and colloquial phrases.

London University Guide and Univ. Corr. Coll. Calendar, 1893-4. London, Univ. Corr. Coll. Press. Crown 8vo, pp. xvi, 215. Price 1*s.*

A useful Guide for students preparing for the London University Examinations.

OXFORD UNIVERSITY

EXTENSION GAZETTE.

Vol. IV. No. 40.]   JANUARY, 1894.   [One Penny.

N.B.—Local Organizers of Oxford University Extension Lectures are invited to send to the Secretary, Extension Office, Examination Schools, Oxford, copies of any journals containing notices of, or references to, Extension work.

THE PIONEER OF UNIVERSITY EXTENSION TEACHING.

(With portrait of the Rev. W. Sewell.)

THE first man to suggest the extension of University teaching to the great towns was the Rev. William Sewell of Exeter College, Oxford. From Mr. Joseph Foster's excellent *Alumni Oxonienses*, it appears that Mr. Sewell was the second son of Mr. Thomas Sewell of Newport, Isle of Wight. He matriculated as a member of Merton College on Nov. 4, 1822, aged eighteen, was Postmaster (or Scholar) of Merton for five years, took the degree of B.A. in 1827 and became Fellow of Exeter College in the same year. For twenty-two years (1831-53) he was Tutor of that college, serving the further offices of librarian (1833), sub-rector (1835), divinity reader (1835), and dean (1839). For five years (1836-41) he was Whyte's Professor of Moral Philosophy in the University of Oxford, and for eight years (1852-60) he was Warden of St. Peter's College, Radley.

THE REV. W. SEWELL.
(From a Photograph by Hills and Saunders.)

Among his other writings, he published in 1850 an essay entitled *Suggestions for the Extension of University Teaching*[1], which contains a forecast, so curiously explicit, of the University Extension system, that we make no apology for reprinting some of its rare pages.

The writer thus states the general object of his scheme. 'The diminution of the expense of education—its extension

[1] *Suggestions for the Extension of the University, addressed to the Rev. the Vice-Chancellor.* By WILLIAM SEWELL, B.D. (Baxter, Oxford, 1850.)

in the best form—that form which the Universities alone are capable of supplying—its expansion to its utmost limits, so that it may embrace the whole kingdom, not even excluding the most distant colonies if possible—these are objects of general concern, for which it is the duty of the Universities themselves to provide to the utmost of their power.'

'A plan,' he continues, 'suggests itself for consideration which upon the whole appears to combine the advantages required with the least amount of objection. Though it may be impossible to bring the masses requiring education to the University, may it not be possible to carry the University to them?

'The University possesses a large amount of available resources and machinery ... These resources, consisting partly of pecuniary means and partly and principally of men of high talents and endowments, ... may be made instrumental in planting the seeds of Academical Institutions throughout the country, by establishing Professorships, Lectureships, and Examinations ... in the most important places in the kingdom. For instance, at first and by way of experiment, Professorships and Lectureships might be founded, say at Manchester and Birmingham, the great centres of the manufacturing districts, and in the midst of the densest population. *The institution of these Professorships and Lectures would be strictly analogous to the original foundation of the Universities themselves.* ... In order to facilitate the immediate commencement of such a system, without involving the necessity of costly buildings, communication might be opened with the proper authorities of the places mentioned, who would no doubt gladly provide the requisite accommodation for the delivery of Lectures, holding Examinations, &c.

'By degrees the system might be extended through the whole country, and similar institutions might be planted in the principal towns in convenient districts, such as Norwich, Exeter, Leeds, Canterbury, Newcastle, &c. Cambridge would, of course, take its due share of the work. The nucleus of a University being thus formed in each place, the same laws which have developed by degrees the institutions of Oxford might be expected, in some proportion at least, to create a Collegiate and Tutorial system subordinate to it. A plan of this kind would immediately open a wide field of occupation for Fellows of Colleges. ... It would extend the benefits of University instruction to the utmost possible limits. It would reduce the expense to the lowest point. ... The cycle of instruction itself would embrace the various subjects comprehended in the University Examinations. ... Probably five or six Professors would be necessary at first for each locality. ... The suitable income for each may be estimated at not less than £500 a year. ... The opportunity of holding such Professorships would be an inducement to men of talent to devote themselves to particular branches of literature at the Universities. ... Lastly, by originating such a comprehensive scheme, the Universities would become, as they ought to be, the great centres and springs of education throughout the country, and would command the sympathy and affection of the nation at large, without sacrificing or compromising any principle which they are bound to maintain.'

1

NOTES AND COMMENTS.

Jowett
Memorial
Fund.

Worthy testimony was borne to the labours of the late Master of Balliol at the great meeting at London which met on December 2, to consider how to perpetuate Professor Jowett's memory and carry forward his work. The Speaker of the House of Commons dwelt on the late Master's universal sympathy; the Marquis of Salisbury, on the extraordinary simplicity, honesty and purity of his will and motives; Mr. Asquith, on the absorption of his mind in the fortunes of his college and of its members; the Lord Chief Justice, on the uplifting influence of his counsel; and Dr. Martineau, on his deep interest in University Extension. It was decided that, in addition to placing a memorial of the late Master in Balliol College Chapel or some other convenient place, those present should raise a fund to be applied under the direction of trustees to maintain, strengthen and extend the educational work of Balliol College. The Honorary Secretaries of the fund are Hon. G. N. Curzon, M.P., House of Commons, London, and Mr. P. Lyttelton Gell, Langley Lodge, near Oxford.

.·.

Mr. H. Llewellyn Smith, Commissioner for Labour, has been elected by the Delegacy an Honorary Member of the staff of the Oxford University Extension. Mr. Llewellyn Smith was for several years an Oxford Extension lecturer and Secretary of the National Association for promoting Technical and Secondary Education.

.·.

The Technical Instruction Committee of the Oxfordshire County Council have appointed Mr. P. Elford as their organizing Secretary. Mr. Elford, who is a Fellow of St. John's College, is well known as an Oxford University Extension lecturer, and as a member of the staff of the University Extension College, Reading.

.·.

In the Department of Liberal Arts (Group 149, Education) at the Chicago Exhibition, an award has been given for the books, papers, photographs and drawings illustrative of the history and method of the University Extension system, exhibited by the Oxford University Extension Delegacy.

.·.

Scholarships
for 1894.

Copies of the Scholarship Regulations for 1894 can be obtained free of charge on application to the Secretary, University Extension Office, Oxford.

ROYAL COMMISSION ON SECONDARY EDUCATION.

Letter of the Prime Minister to the Vice-Chancellor.

10 DOWNING STREET, WHITEHALL,
Dec. 6, 1893.

MY DEAR SIR,

I have already sent a formal acknowledgement of the receipt of the Memorial of the University relating to Secondary Education.

I have now the pleasure to inform you that Her Majesty's Government proposes to advise the appointment of a Royal Commission to consider certain questions in connexion with Secondary Education. It is with much satisfaction that I find we are following the path marked out by the Memorial of the University.

I remain, my dear Sir,
Faithfully yours,
W. E. GLADSTONE.

Rev. the Vice-Chancellor of the University
of Oxford, &c., &c.

TEACHING CITIZENSHIP.

CRAM is often due to want of time. A teacher, generally from praiseworthy motives, sometimes from ignoble ones, tries to squeeze into the curriculum of his school a subject which he has not himself the leisure to teach nutritiously. Overdriven with other duties, he finds himself prevented from acquiring that large knowledge of the new subject which would alone enable him to become deeply interested in its problems. He forms no ideas of his own on the issues raised by it. He fails to appreciate the varying shades of certainty which give it fascination and interest. And so he buys a compendium or two, and serves out to his scholars slices of other people's pemmican. The chief result of the process is, not a freshening of the intellectual interests of himself or of his pupils, but an added burden to the memory of both of them, a new piece of cram. The remedy for the mischief is to relieve the overworked teacher either of other duties or of this new one, and, if the latter, to find some one who has leisure to teach the subject in such a way as to convey the stimulus of his own delight in it to the minds of his hearers, and who has a mind so free from preoccupation as to enable him to handle his subject freshly, suggestively, and with a just sense of the different value and certitude of the various parts of it.

The finer the subject the more to be regretted is flatness in teaching it. No manual, for example, is so contemptible as the cram-book in philosophy. It is therefore to be hoped that citizenship will not be crammed in evening schools for the sake of a penny per head per hour. But there is some danger of this happening, and the following words, contributed by Mr. Dyer to the *Co-operative News* of Dec. 9, deserve attention.

Although the introduction of the syllabus of the 'Life and Duties of the Citizen' into the new Code for Evening Continuation Schools is to be welcomed as a great advance from an educational point of view, it is not altogether unattended with danger. In every department of education at the present time the tendency is to isolate the different subjects, and present them in such a manner as to make them convenient for examination purposes. We have for instance science, which is taught in a very unscientific manner because its relations to other departments are not shown, and the brains of the scholars are simply packed with facts and figures which have little or no educative value, and which simply act as so much dead weight and destroy all traces of originality in those who are subjected to the treatment. In the same way there is a tendency to present cut and dry statements of fact or descriptions of legislative or administrative machinery as sufficient lessons in civic duty. It is not at all likely, if this is all that is done, that it will have much effect on the scholars, or that the instruction will do anything to improve social and economic conditions, which after all is the main object which should be kept in view.

If it were possible it might be better to dispense altogether with the use of special text-books in the teaching of the duties and responsibilities of citizenship, and trust to well-informed and enthusiastic teachers to present the subject in such a manner as would rouse a desire on the part of the scholars to do all in their power to serve their country, and at the same time be useful in educating their minds, and not simply loading them with useless lumber. A great deal of the science which is possible in schools should be conveyed, not so much in the shape of formal lectures, but as object lessons and illustrations of all the other work of the classes, and even in these the social bearings of the subjects should never be overlooked. In the same way the whole object of the work of the schools should be to fit for the life and duties of the citizen, and not simply to prepare for examinations; and it is possible for intelligent teachers to convey a great deal of useful information regarding social and civic duties in almost every subject which is taken up in the school. For instance, history should not be a mere collection of dates and facts about events of comparatively little importance, but should be treated in such a manner as to show the growth of our national institutions, and their effects on the social and economic conditions of the people, while geography should be largely a combination of elementary science with simple lessons in social and political economy. In this way it would be possible to show the bearings of physical and natural science on many of the problems of a social nature with which we are at present confronted, and the ultimate solution of which is only possible on scientific lines. Our legislators in the future must not be mere empirists or opportunists, but must be qualified to take into account all the factors of the problems with which they are expected to deal, and hence the necessity for the new subject of the 'Life and Duties of the Citizen' being taken up in a scientific and intelligent manner.

UNIVERSITY EXTENSION IN A GLOUCESTERSHIRE VILLAGE.

THIS winter, for the first time, the small mining village of Pucklechurch near Bristol had a regular course of Extension lectures in connexion with the Oxford Delegacy. The local committee, consisting of the School Board, reinforced by ten other persons interested in the work, issued a circular explaining the object of the lectures and the arrangements made in regard to them, from which we extract the following paragraphs:—

University Extension is the name given to a great work which the English Universities have been doing for some years past. That work is for the good of those many men and women dwelling in the small towns and villages of England, who cannot afford to become University graduates, but who have a healthy relish for higher education. The Extension work takes a twofold form. First, local centres are established where students are aided by lecture, class and examination; secondly, Summer Meetings are held at the Universities, where students are cordially welcomed by the authorities, taught by lectures in great variety, and gladdened intellectually and socially by their residence in those beautiful and historic homes of learning. Oxford is the University which most attracts the dwellers in the Western Counties, and to which, therefore, a Gloucestershire village becomes naturally associated.

Pucklechurch is one of the smallest centres which that University as yet possesses, and it was formed in the following way. In 1891, a parishioner attended the Oxford Summer Meeting, and on his return he enlisted the interest of others in the Extension movement. At the Summer Meeting of 1892, he appeared again, accompanied by three of his fellow-parishioners. The presence of four men from one village, all working in the same coal mine, favourably impressed many of the University lecturers, amongst whom was Mr. A. B. Badger, M.A., of New College. This favour was much increased by a visit to Pucklechurch made by that gentleman in the autumn of 1892, which resulted in his giving two courses of lectures on Geology in the winter of 1892–3. Lectures were entirely gratuitous, and even the travelling expenses of the first course were made up from the University Extension Fund. Both the room and the magic lantern were kindly lent for the occasion.

The School Board having secured a grant from the County Council, and kindly help through the medium of the Oxford University Extension Delegacy, arrangements have been made for a course of lectures on Geology by Mr. Badger during the coming winter, which is to be preceded by an introductory lecture on 'Technical Instruction and the Practical Uses of Geology.'

The lectures will be delivered in the Parish Schoolroom, on Thursday evenings at 7 o'clock. A magic lantern will be used for illustration.

One hundred parishioners, it is hoped, will attend these lectures with regularity, and it is also hoped that at least twenty of them will be enrolled in Mr. Badger's class for special study of the subject.

The first lecture is free. Tickets for the course of six lectures can be had 1s. each, from any member of the committee. The charge for a single lecture is 3d. Any surplus will go to clear off 13s. 7d., last year's deficiency, and then to buy a magic lantern for the future good of the parish.

LETTERS TO THE EDITOR.

[We do not hold ourselves responsible for the opinions expressed by our correspondents.]

The Criticism of Paper Work.

DEAR SIR,—I have often admired the prudence of my fellow-lecturers in abstaining from the controversies started from time to time in your columns; controversies in which their own action was directly involved, and on which they were in some respects best qualified to pronounce. I have admired, and, till now, imitated. Were I anything like a 'first magnitude star,' I should be compelled to imitate still; for contribution to such discussions might then be still more imprudent, and would, moreover, be impossible to so busy a person. Even a star of quite 'inferior brilliancy' risks somewhat by shedding a single ray of his 'light' on these troubled waters. If he may be guilty of such a vulgarism and such a mixture of metaphor, he'd much better 'sit tight' and say nothing. But even an asteroid has his rare inclination for a shine.

The answers to Mr. (?) L. Steuart's letter are devoted in part to maintaining what he never, perhaps, intended seriously to dispute—that young ladies are fit and natural recipients of University Extension teaching. Miss Punch must certainly be right in supposing that, without their help and attendance, lectures in the South of England at any rate could not have been kept up: and lecturers, who have had such constant reason to be grateful for the cordial reception and kind hospitality extended to them, must have been as constantly surprised at the devoted efforts continued, quite gratuitously, through session after session by the various Local Secretaries, nearly half of whom are ladies.

The point of Mr. Steuart's letter seems to be that in one centre there appears to be a ratio between the number of papers written and the amount of praise bestowed by the lecturer. The fact is in accord with human nature as we know it; yet there can be few, and those only the younger and less active-minded, who do not know that fair criticism is better worth having than indiscriminate praise. The implication which Mr. Steuart founds on his fact, that lecturers do not criticize freely for fear of consequences to themselves, is more serious; but, I should say, extremely questionable. It is contradicted by one of the two instances referred to in his letter. Probably the most popular of our body have little need to fear such consequences; and I question whether any of us pay the slightest heed to them. I very certainly do not. The chief reason for the paucity or brevity of the criticisms offered is, of course, the want of time.

A man in full work, giving his nine to twelve lectures a week in different parts of the country, will have only his mornings free for paper-work, and many of these will be spent in the train. The circumstances of railway-travelling are not the most favourable to mental concentration, and render writing to any extent impossible. At most his time for paper-work in each day will amount to some three to four hours, say four. If each of his 12 audiences sends him 12 papers a lecture—many send in very little paper-work, but many send in far more than the average I have taken—he will have 24 papers to look through in 240 minutes. Is it so easy, in the 10 minutes he can give to each, to read some half-dozen closely-written foolscap sheets, to score what is wrong, to collect mentally the total contents and assign the paper to its proper class, or, it may be, to weigh accurately its precise value as compared with its competitors? How *can* the 'criticism' written on each paper be other than the briefest, especially if, with a view to watching the student's progress, he makes a brief note in some private memorandum-book to assist his memory among the scores of students with whom he has to deal? Even this cursory performance of his functions supposes perpetual health, the habits of a machine, a memory so perfect as to be able, without reading, to answer chance questions on details, and a vitality that will bring him up fresh and smiling to audience after audience.

He can gain time of course by taking fewer lectures, i.e. by diminishing his income; and undoubtedly lecturers do refuse

2

work that they might possibly take: but those who know what are the maximum profits accruing to our most successful men, and realize by what arduous toil they are earned, will not think them overpaid. Extension work would hardly attract or retain men of high degree or abilities, were its emoluments less than at present.

Lecturers in less demand can, no doubt, give rather more time. It is no uncommon thing with me to spend an hour apiece on some three or four of the best and longest papers from a single centre. Many are so well and thoughtfully written as to demand a long time for their full and fair consideration, especially if they are to be placed in a scale of relative merit. I confess there have been moments when, on the arrival of some additional enthusiastic reams, I could have wished that the Prince of Denmark, for instance, had acted in a more simple and straightforward fashion. But I dare say others of the less pressed among my fellow-lecturers spend as much time as I do. Perhaps I work more slowly than the rest. Or it may be that I get longer papers, because I set too many questions—I believe their suggestion, whether all are treated by the student or not, to be a necessary and important adjunct to the work, and, if read over beforehand, to render the lecture more useful. But much of the time I spend on papers is spent, not from a sense of obligation, but because all hurried or half-work is painful. Within certain limits I think fuller treatment may be expected of the less popular lecturer: yet, if he cannot earn more than £50-60 a year by lecturing, he has surely the fullest right to reserve the majority of his time for quite other work. Generally speaking, I think that the demand for full written individual criticism is one that cannot be supplied, except under the special circumstances of personal private tuition at high fees.

In practice, no doubt, there is great variety. Not all papers receive, or deserve, the same treatment. From an abstract point of view all may claim an equal share of the lecturer's time: actually, it is difficult to avoid allotting a preponderance to the better papers, which are usually the longest, and the work of the most enthusiastic students, who have laboured hardest to secure and maintain the lectures. If some papers are of twelve or fifteen sheets (I have had twenty), some are of only two. if some are full of thought and reading, others are simply foolish. Many are written by quite young girls at school, who can hardly yet express themselves correctly. I am far from saying that it is not advantageous to them to attend the lectures, and the effort to write will no doubt be of service to them; but it is not, I think, to be expected of the lecturer that he shall assume the functions of the English master at the academy to which these young ladies are attached. Our work aims at a University standard, and does better to disclaim at once the tasks of the elementary teacher. Even in the case of the best work, remarks on composition will be more or less incidental.

And in his special sphere his treatment will vary much. Not all papers call for criticism. Some are simply correct answers to plain questions of fact, or exact reproductions of arguments used in the lecture, which it was very desirable that the student should write, but which, if correctly done, call for no remark. In cases where the argument has been only partially grasped, how can the lecturer inscribe all that has been omitted in each paper? If in a word or two he can indicate the omissions, he does so; and thus refers the student's memory to those parts of the lecture which have been forgotten. And is it not the case that the same omissions, the same misapprehensions, occur in several papers? The lecturer notes this, sees how it may be due to his too concise, or possibly confused, presentment of the matter, and tries to remedy it in the following class by a clearer explanation, or even by dictating some brief note slowly enough to be taken down *verbatim* by all who will. This collective criticism is the right economy of time: yet how many students would acknowledge that the lecturer who does this is doing his work better than he who fills the blank spaces of his papers with the same remarks repeated in case after case?

And let it be said that those brief interjections, 'good,' 'fair,' 'v. g.,' 'it,' &c., to which one of your correspondents refers, are very far from useless. Even if only one such expression of praise were employed by a lecturer, it would be educative by comparison with the passages from which it was withheld. These brief remarks derive their chief utility from the *place where they are put*. Accompanied by a line drawn along that portion of the MS to which they refer, they answer the student's possible doubt as to the validity of an argument, the applicability of an instance, the choice of a phrase; and, by distinguishing between different parts of his work, help to give precision to his standard of value. To exhibit the grounds for these interjectional notes in each paper would take an amount of time which I have tried to show it would be impossible to expend: yet this alone would fully satisfy the student. In many cases, where I feel it is most requisite and will be most useful, I do try to exhibit my grounds; but I could not do so in all, nor perhaps, were I very busy, in any.

I fear, Sir, I have been too long. I hope I have been fair. The points I have tried to put are no doubt recognized at Oxford, and among lecturers; but I think they are hardly realized among those friendly critics who write in your columns. I have thought that they might be urged most fittingly by one who, while quite in touch with the work, and of fifteen years' educational experience, is yet outside that circle of busiest lecturers to whom this correspondence chiefly applies.

I am, Sir, yours faithfully,

R. WARWICK BOND, M.A.

London: *Dec.* 4.

.·.

Audiences of Ladies.

DEAR SIR,—Will you kindly allow me space to explain a remark in my letter on ' Criticism of Paper Work,' which has, I fear, been misunderstood by one of your correspondents, in the December issue of the *Oxford University Extension Gazette?*

In that letter I spoke of certain students as belonging to a class ' for whom University Extension is *not* primarily intended.' Now, my classification of students is not based on social distinctions, far from it; but I do rank ladies among those who (given the will and the means) can obtain their teaching at the University itself.

The existence of Somerville, Lady Margaret, and St. Hilda's Halls at Oxford, and of Girton and Newnham at Cambridge, surely bears out this view of the case.

I am, Sir,

Your obedient servant,

L. STEUART.

Dec. 8, 1893.

PUPIL TEACHERS' UNIVERSITY SCHOLAR-SHIP COMMITTEE.

THIS committee has issued its first annual report from which it appears that during last year it raised sufficient funds to grant five scholarships, of £25 a year each, to selected Queen's scholars. The object of the Committee is to enable Queen's scholars to get their training at a University before entering on their work in the elementary schools. The Committee, of which Canon Barnett is chairman, includes the Rector of Exeter, the Headmaster of Rugby, and Mr. A. J. Mundella, M.P. The hon. sec. is Mr. T. S. Widdowson, 27 Eastfield Road, Walthamstow. Of the five scholars this year, four went to Cambridge and one to Oxford. At Oxford the holder of the scholarship has passed Responsions, having acquired the necessary knowledge of Greek since coming up to the University. The chief difficulty which prevents other pupil teachers from enjoying the advantages of a University training, is the want of the necessary funds. These funds the Committee are anxious to collect, and we heartily wish them success in their efforts.

REPORTS FROM THE CENTRES.

BURY.—We find Mr. Mallet a most able and interesting lecturer. The course is greatly enjoyed by all who go to it. But I am sorry to say that we have again failed to reach the working men. The number of papers is very good.—E. ROTH-WELL, *Hon. Sec.*

CLEVEDON.—The Hon. Sec. (Miss Woodward) writes that Mr. Marriot's lectures on 'Europe since Waterloo' have been much enjoyed by an audience of between seventy and eighty persons.

HEREFORD.—During the autumn a particularly interesting series of lectures has been given by Mr. R. Warwick Bond at this centre, on 'The Development of the Drama and Shakespeare.' The course ended on Nov. 27 with a most eloquent lecture on King Lear. The attendance was much larger than has been the case at Hereford for some years, and great interest was shown all through by the audience, many of whom have expressed the hope that Mr. Bond will again visit the centre. A great number stayed for the classes, but unfortunately very few papers were sent up. This is the first course held since the formation of the University Extension Society, which numbers between fifty and sixty members. Mr. E. L. S. Horsburgh will give a course on 'The Renaissance in Italy' in the Spring Session.—M. E. BULL, *Hon. Sec.*

ILKLEY.—Several persons interested in Extension work gave a very successful concert on Dec. 2 in aid of the funds of the committee. The attendance was good, so that Mr. Haines was enabled to announce that the debt of £10 would be about extinguished. Among those who kindly consented to take part in the concert were Mrs. Howson, Miss Lund, Miss Sayers, Mr. P. N. Lee, Mr. Leopold Ahrons, Mr. Mammatt, Mr. Haines, Mr J. K. Empsall, and Mr. C. Carus-Wilson, who recently lectured at the centre.

LITTLE BERKHAMPSTEAD.—A course of six lectures on 'The Early Stuarts,' by Miss Lacey, has just been concluded here. Miss Lacey has been successful in arousing and stimulating the interest of her audience in this period of our history. The discussions held at the class after each lecture have been by no means the least important feature of the work done here.— E. STEUART.

MATLOCK.—Mr. Mallet's most interesting course of lectures on 'The Tudors' was concluded on Dec. 6. After the lecture the Rev. F. R. Bellamy proposed, and Mr. Gladwin Turbut, J.P. seconded, a most cordial vote of thanks to Mr Mallet, who in response expressed the hope that the success of the course would encourage the centre to continue the good work it had done so well in the past. On the motion of Mr. G. H. Brown and the Rev. W. H. Arkwright, a hearty vote of thanks to the secretary, Mrs. Gwilliam, was passed, to whose skilful organization and untiring work much of the present success is due.

OTLEY.—We concluded our annual course of Extension lectures on December 11, bidding Mr. Mallet a very regretful good-bye. The subject has been 'The Tudor Period,' and he has invested it with a charm and interest that will not soon be forgotten. The number of the audience has been well maintained, and the lectures listened to with keenest attention. We have been glad to note a goodly number of working men in regular attendance, and at the close of the last lecture one of them, on behalf of his fellows, spoke in warm terms of the interest and profit they had derived from Mr. Mallet's stirring addresses. The paper-work has not been so satisfactory as it ought to have been, but the committee hopes in the event of further historical lectures being given that students will contribute in greater numbers. The travelling library has been thoroughly well used, which is a sure sign of interest, and we look back upon the season's work as having materially enhanced the interest in the Extension movement in Otley.—JANETTE DUNCAN, *Hon. Sec.*

STROUD.—It is reported that the audience attending Dr. Fison's evening lectures is the largest that has ever been brought together by the local University Extension Committee. The attendance at the afternoon lectures, says the *Stroud Journal*, is not so encouraging.

TRURO.—A course of eight lectures on 'English Social Life' was given by Mr. Kenelm D. Cotes at this centre between Monday, September 25, and Thursday, November 9. The first two lectures were on 'The Mediaeval Period,' and the last six on 'The New Era, and the New World.' By the permission of the mayor, the lectures were given in the Town Hall. The attendance was good, and the class was almost equal in number to the audience. Through the kindness of Mr. W. G. N. Earthy, six of the lectures were illustrated by lantern views. The chair was taken on successive evenings by Archdeacon Cornish, Chancellor R. M. Paul, Canon Bourke, Rector of Truro, Mr. J. H. Bawden, Treasurer of the University Extension Committee, Rev. Owen Davis, Minister of St. Mary's Wesleyan Chapel, Truro, Canon

Donaldson, Precentor of the Cathedral, Rev. T. F. Maddrell, Head Master of the Truro Grammar School, and Canon Worledge, Chancellor of the Cathedral. The lectures were most attentively listened to, and excited much interest. The Students' Association organized by Miss L. Paull met regularly under the direction of Canon Donaldson. At the close of the lectures, a hearty vote of thanks was given to Mr. Cotes on the motion of Mr. J. H. Bawden, seconded by Canon J. H. Moore. A very successful conversazione was organized by the Students' Association on November 11, at which Canon Donaldson and Mr. Cotes contributed readings, and several ladies and gentlemen sang and played. The sale of tickets for the conversazione defrayed, to a large extent, some deficit on the account of the Extension lectures. It is hoped that the Cornwall County Council may be induced to make a grant in aid of the Extension lectures. A petition to the Technical Instruction Committee of the County Council is in circulation, and has been influentially and numerously signed with a view to the attainment of this object.—A. J. WORLLEDGE, *Hon. Sec.*

TUNBRIDGE WELLS.—Our autumn series of lectures here have been thoroughly successful. Mr. Boas's course in the afternoon on 'Cavalier and Puritan Literature' has proved very interesting, and it is satisfactory that, though it has not attracted quite one of our largest audiences, it has called forth more and better work from the students than we often get here. The evening course by Mr. Legge on 'The Laws of Health' has been an extremely useful one, and his literally 'world-wide' experience has added to the interest of the lectures. The audience has not been quite so large as usual, about 100 on an average, but the attendance has been very regular, and about twenty-five students have been writing papers.—LAURA F. JONES, *Hon. Sec.*

ULVERSTON.—On Tuesday, Dec. 12, our second half-course on 'Geology' by Mr. Carus-Wilson was concluded. Notwithstanding the excellence of the lectures, we cannot unhappily report that the Oxford Extension movement has grown materially in influence at this centre. our numbers compared with last session in point of fact showing a falling off. Although the subject was chosen to meet what the committee considered a specific want in a mining district and placed the fees at a low level, a very small number of working miners presented an appearance. The attendance averaging about forty-five was very regular, the interest well sustained, and the paper-work good. The committee are in favour next year of a historical or literary subject, but the limitation of the powers of the County Council, which may grant aid towards the teaching of so-called 'technical' subjects only, is an obstacle.—E. G. TOSH, *Hon. Sec.*

WELLS, SOMERSET.—The last lecture on 'England in the Eighteenth Century' was given on Tuesday, Dec. 19, and we are once more experiencing the mingled feelings of joy and grief which accompany the conclusion of a successful course—joy, that all is well over ; but grief, that it *is* over. When I wrote last we were in some anxiety lest the centre should in any way suffer from the accidental delay caused by the lecturer's illness : the only ill effect has been that many students who have attended the lectures regularly, including last week's which should have been the sixth, were prevented, through illness and other causes, from being present last night. We have every reason to congratulate ourselves upon the term's work. There is no need to praise the lecturer—Mr. Marriott on English history is well known ; as was said yesterday, 'he has given us a masterly summary of a most interesting period,' and he has been appreciated. The average attendance has been 112 ; the audience has contained more clerks, shop assistants, &c., than hitherto ; has in fact been more widely representative. The meetings of the Students' Association have been held alternately with the lectures, and have been open to all students during the course. Thanks to the association the fortnightly essays written for the lecturer have improved both in quantity and quality. We feel at the present moment very hopeful respecting future prospects of University Extension in our little city, though we know that 'work, work, work,' must still be the motto of the organizers.—M. A. G. LIVETT, *Hon. Sec.*

WEST BRIGHTON.—The first part of Mr. Horsburgh's course on the 'Renaissance in Italy and England,' given in the Hove Town Hall, has proved successful. The room has been well filled, and a large number of students do paper-work. The subject is felt to be one of great interest, treated ably and with much clearness by the lecturer. The lectures have met with some very delightful illustration owing to the kindness of Mr North, lecturer for the County Council, who has lent on two occasions a number of valuable specimens of early printing and manuscripts, which were exhibited under glass-cases in an adjoining room at the conclusion of the lecture. Amongst the collection were facsimiles of some of Caxton's productions, as well as an original specimen of Wynkyn de Wode, Caxton's apprentice and successor; several productions of Aldus, and other Italian and German printers of the same period ; an early edition of Machiavelli ; a page of the first folio edition of Shakespeare; an original of the 'Biblica Pauperum,' and a valuable specimen of the 'Prayer Book,' which in the reign of Henry VIII was condemned to be burnt along with its possessor as popish, sharing a similar fate in the reign of Queen Mary on directly opposite grounds. These and several other interesting specimens of a like nature were much appreciated by the audience. The course recommences on Thursday, January 18.—M. F. BASDEN. *Hon. Sec.*

WINDSOR.—Mr. F. Bond's course of lectures on 'English Ecclesiastical Architecture' has been successful. The lectures have aroused a keen interest among the students, and there seems likelihood that this interest will lead many of them to continue independently their study of Gothic architecture.

WINSLOW.—Mr. E. L. S. Horsburgh's course of six lectures on 'The Expansion of England' was concluded on Monday, Dec. 11, to the regret of many who have found the subject most interesting, Mr. Horsburgh's treatment of it being clear and helpful. It is true that the largeness of subject has forced the lecturer to sacrifice something of vividness and picturesqueness in detail and incident, in order to present a clear birds-eye view of each phase of expansion. This was done most successfully, and we would recommend any centre choosing this subject to ask for twelve lectures, if they can possibly arrange for them, in order to gain the fuller treatment which we are confident would add to the value of this interesting course. Ten students have qualified for examination. The lecturer's criticisms on the paper-work of the centre have been careful and helpful, and he has spared no pains to make points clear to the more serious students. —A. L. NEWCOMBE, *Hon. Sec.*

OXFORD AS AN INTERNATIONAL CENTRE FOR HIGHER STUDY.

THERE are many signs that Oxford may again become, as she was in the middle ages, a meeting-place for students of all nationalities. In the thirteenth and fourteenth centuries, one of the proverbs of social life recalled the common associations of University training enjoyed by men from widely different parts of Europe. The words ' nos fuimus simul in Galandia '—' we were once comrades in the Rue Galande' (the quarter of Paris in which the University was situated)—often used to pass between comrades when Germans, Italians, Frenchmen and Englishmen found themselves thrown together in military or diplomatic enterprise. And it would seem that one of the results of the afferent power of railways and quick steamships, will be the revival in the great Universities of this international life which, in Oxford at all events, has been for so many centuries interrupted.

From America a large number of students—several thousands at least—go every year to study at the German Universities. There is no reason why some of them could not come to Oxford. Blood is thicker than water, and it would be a great advantage if the young men of the English-speaking folk, destined to wield influence in so many different parts of the world, could look back to common associations of University life. Here and in America the Universities are over-spilling into journalism. Of all forms of University Extension, this is at the present moment the most significant. It is not a small matter that the young American 'College men,' who are devoting themselves to the direction of great newspapers, should carry with them into public life German ideals of politics and study. Excellent as these latter are, salutary as they are as an element in our conceptions of learned and political life, it would be to the general advantage if English ideals were to enjoy equal opportunities of general diffusion.

It is by some greatly desired that graduate study should become a more leading feature of Oxford life. Paramount among the varied duties of a University is the encouragement and direction of learned research. Nothing would give such a stimulus to the best interests of learning in Oxford as the presence of a large number of students, all of them bent on carrying forward to a higher point the studies which they had severally begun as undergraduates in their different Universities.

There are those who think that a comparatively small change in our arrangements would draw to us a sufficient number of young graduates from American and foreign Universities. It has been suggested that courses of graduate study should be organized by the University, and that the details of these arrangements should be clearly printed in a programme and circulated among the Universities of America and the Continent. Others add to this proposal the further suggestion that the Colleges, as distinct from the University, should also enter the arrangement, and that each of our foundations should seek to promote a personal connexion between itself and students from one or other distant University. The latter would then find less difficulty than they do at present in obtaining the information as to rooms, residence, and tuition, which they naturally desire to obtain whilst forming their plans for graduate study. Each College, again, might make a practice of recognizing the graduates from some chosen University as being, during their period of residence, among its own B.A.s. It might (for example) admit them to the B.A.'s table at its Hall dinner, assign them seats in its Chapel, and show to them the other forms of consideration, which count for so much in the happiness of University life.

Others, however, feel that the offer of courses of instruction, even when coupled with College recognition, would not be enough. They maintain that any young graduate who might undertake a course of higher study would require at the close of it some diploma or certificate from those in whose tutorial or professorial care he had been. It is pointed out, however, that an informal letter from an Oxford Professor would be comparatively valueless as a diploma when compared with the degree of Doctor given by the German Universities. Many, therefore, are inclined to think that it is desirable to establish a new degree as part of the arrangements for the encouragement of graduate study in Oxford. Such a course of study and degree would naturally be confined to persons of whose competence the University was satisfied. The amount of residence required for the degree, the question whether it would be a doctorate or not, the nature of the preliminary test to be imposed on all candidates for the honour, are at present matters for discussion. It is noteworthy, however, that the question is exciting so much interest in many different parts of the University.

HEALTH MISSIONERS.

THE Bucks County Council has made an attempt to bring the knowledge of the laws of health to the homes of the people. The Council's method of carrying out this project was suggested in a letter from Miss Florence Nightingale, who, in a touching letter recently printed, urged upon it the sore need of bringing such knowledge home to mothers in country villages. A class of ladies attended a course of lectures carefully prepared for this purpose by Mr. De'Ath, Medical Officer of Health for the Buckingham District, and of those who passed a satisfactory examination, four were employed by the County Council as Health Missioners. Their duty has been two-fold, viz., to give simple addresses to the women of the villages on what is essential for the healthy lives of themselves and of their families, and to go, when invited, to the villagers' houses in order to speak privately to the mothers of families on matters of health, which can be more easily and effectually treated in this way. The Technical Instruction Committee of the County Council feel that teaching on the laws of health is best given by those who, by sympathy and friendship, can win their way into the homes of the people. Perverse habits and unhealthy ways of life have been customary for generations, and a change in these conditions, to which sickness and disease are often directly traceable, can only be brought about by tact and personal influence, accompanied by clear and pointed teaching. In the report of the County Council an interesting letter is published from Mr. Dale, the Rector of Radclive, as to the way in which these lectures have been received. Mr. Dale says that the courses were clearly, simply, and pleasantly delivered, and he finds that the lecturers' hints are being put into practice, that cottage bedroom windows are much more regularly opened since the lectures were given, and that the cleaning of house walls is becoming much more common. A Health Missioner's diary for the month of June (which by an error is made a day too long) appears in the Council's report. The journal shows that the teacher in question visited ten villages, some of them three times ; that the audiences at the lectures varied from three to twenty-four ; and that 186 different cottages were personally visited at the request of the occupiers. The details of the scheme are given in a pamphlet called *Health at Home*, and printed by Mr. French of Winslow, Bucks, This interesting little paper contains two letters by Miss Nightingale.

BOOKS ON OUR TABLE.

French Wars of Religion. By EDWARD ARMSTRONG, M.A., Fellow of Queen's College, Oxford. London, Percival & Co.

Many students who heard Mr. Armstrong's lectures at the last Oxford Summer Meeting, and still more who did not, will be glad to know that they can. possess them in a permanent form. Nor can there be any doubt that the lectures have gained much from expansion and publication. It has been objected by some critics that the lectures, though admirable in themselves, were unsuited to the audience to whom they were originally addressed. The criticism, however, seems to us to be unfair both to Mr. Armstrong and to his auditors. These discourses were addressed avowedly to the select aristocracy of the Extension students. They were intended not for novices, but for the advanced students who had prepared themselves by years of careful study. By no others, we readily admit, could they have been fully appreciated. But that there are present at every Summer Meeting mo-e than a handful of such students is known to every one who has any knowledge of the Extension movement. To our thinking Mr. Armstrong paid a delicate and well-deserved compliment to those students by the delivery of lectures which presuppose unquestionably a considerable amount of preparatory training.

As to the intrinsic value of this little volume there can hardly be two opinions. Already, as we are glad to notice, it has found a place among the 'authorities' prescribed or rather 'suggested' to the candidates in the Final Honour School of Modern History. The compliment is not undeserved, for Mr. Armstrong deals in a masterly way with a period of extraordinary difficulty and complexity. Not to novices alone has

the period of the 'Wars of Religion in France' appeared to be one of almost fatally deterrent difficulty. Faint-hearted students, however, will find in Mr. Armstrong a thoroughly reliable and trustworthy guide.

Mr. Armstrong deals almost exclusively with the political aspects of the religious wars in France; the first lecture being devoted to the Huguenots, the second to the Catholic League, and the third to the position of the Crown in the struggle. Of the three, the last lecture—on the Crown—seems to us the clearest and best. But they are all admirable alike in conception and execution, and may be commended almost without reserve to our historical students.

The Earl of Auckland. By Captain L. J. TROTTER. ('Rulers of India' Series.) Oxford, Clarendon Press, 1893. Crown 8vo, pp. 220. Price 2s. 6d.

It is one of the best features of the laudable attempt of the Delegates of the Clarendon Press to popularize the knowledge of Indian history that the crimes and errors of British rule are as truthfully recorded as the triumphs of British valour and the wisdom of British statesmanship. The career of Lord Auckland as Governor-General is a monument of misfortune and wrong-doing, of fatuous policy and merited failure. It is relieved by deeds of heroism and devotion, but it is at best a sordid story of unjustifiable aggression. Captain Trotter does not attempt to disguise the immorality of the policy which he records ; he does his best to tell a plain unvarnished tale. But the volume is perhaps the least successful of the series.

Guelphs and Ghibellines. A Short History of Mediaeval Italy from 1250—1409. By OSCAR BROWNING, London, Methuen & Co. Crown 8vo, pp. ix, 213, Price 5s.

Dante's Divine Comedy : The Inferno or Hell. Translated by GEORGE MUSGRAVE, M.A., St. John's Coll., Oxford. London, Swan Sonnenschein & Co. 8vo, pp. xxiv, 247.

London Intermediate Arts Directory. No. VI. With the Calendar for 1892-3, and with Solutions to the Papers set in July, 1893. London, Univ. Corr. Coll. Press. Price 1s. 6d. net.

London Intermediate Science and Preliminary Science Directory. No. IV. Containing the Papers set in July, 1893, with Solutions. London, Univ. Corr. Coll. Press, Price 2s. 6d. net.

ARRANGEMENTS FOR 1894.

Spring 1894.

Centre.	No. of Lectures in Course.	Subject of Course.	Lecturer.	Course begins.	Course ends.
†UNIVERSITY EXTENSION COLLEGE, READING	12	Physical Geography	H. J. MACKINDER, M.A.	W. Jan. 17	Mar. 14
,, ,,	12	Homeric Poems	J. CHURTON COLLINS, M.A.	S. Feb. 3	Mar. 14
,, ,,	12	English History. 18th Century ...	W. M. CHILDS, B.A. ...	F. Jan. 19	Mar. 16
,, ,,	24	Chemistry	G. J. BURCH, M.A. ...	Th. Jan. 18	Apr. 12
,, ,,	24	Electricity	,, ,, ...	Th. Jan. 18	Apr. 12
,, ,,	24	Biology	B. J. AUSTIN, F L S. ...	T. Jan. 23	Apr. 17
,, ,,	24	Chemistry	G. J. BURCH, M.A ...	S. Jan. 20	Apr. 14
,, *Newbury Sub-Centre*	24	Botany	B. J. AUSTIN, F.L.S. ...	S. Jan. 20	Apr. 14
,, ,,	24	Chemistry	P. ELFORD, M.A. ...	S. Jan 20	Apr. 14
,, *Didcot Sub-Centre*	24	Botany	Miss E. C. POLLARD, B.Sc.	S. Jan. 20	Apr. 14
,, ,,	24	Chemistry	P. ELFORD, M.A. ...	S. Jan. 20	Apr. 14
,, ,,	24	Botany	A. A. LINTERN, B.Sc.	S. Jan. 20	Apr. 14
EASTBOURNE (afternoon) ...	6	Not fixed	J. CHURTON COLLINS, M.A.	S. Jan. 27	Apr. 7
ASHTON-UNDER-LYNE (aft.) ...	6	Age of Elizabeth	Rev. W. H. SHAW, M.A.	T. Jan. 16	Mar. 27
ASHTON-UNDER-LYNE (even)	6	Making of England ...	,, ,, ...	T. Jan. 16	Mar. 27
GLOUCESTER (evening) ...	6	English Social Reformers ...	,, ,, ...	M. Jan. 22	Apr. 2
BIRMINGHAM, SEVERN STREET (evening)	6	Florence and Venice	,, ,, ...	T. Jan. 23	Apr. 3

† Continued from Autumn Session.

Centre.	No. of Lectures in Course.	Subject of Course.	Lecturer.	Course begins.	Course ends.
SWINDON (evening)	6	Puritan Revolution	Rev. W. H. SHAW, M.A.	W Jan. 24	Apr. 4
NEWBURY (afternoon)	6	Florence	,, ,,	Th. Jan. 25	Apr. 5
TUNBRIDGE WELLS (afternoon)	10	Florence and Venice	,, ,,	F. Jan. 26	Apr. 6
BRIGHTON (evening)	12	Florence and Venice	,, ,,	F. Jan. 19	Apr. 6
WINDSOR (afternoon)	6	Venice	,, ,,	Th. Jan. 18	Mar. 15
CHELTENHAM (afternoon)	6	Social Reformers	,, ,,	W. Jan. 31	Apr. 4
CHESTER (afternoon)	6	Age of Louis XIV	J. A. R. MARRIOTT, M.A.	W. Jan. 17	Mar. 28
CHESTER (evening)	6	Cavaliers and Roundheads	,, ,,	T. Jan. 16	Mar. 27
WALLASEY (evening)	6	Historical Plays of Shakespeare	,, ,,	W. Jan. 17	Mar. 28
BRADFORD (evening)	6	Europe since Waterloo	,, ,,	Th. Jan. 18	Mar. 29
MALVERN (afternoon)	6	Historical Plays of Shakespeare	,, ,,	W. Feb. 7	Apr. 11
EVESHAM (evening)	6	Cavaliers and Roundheads	,, ,,	W. Jan. 24	Apr. 4
WARE (afternoon)	6	Age of Anne	,, ,,	F. Not fixed	Not fixed
ROSS (afternoon)	6	Age of Louis XIV	,, ,,	T. Jan 23	Apr. 3
†EDGBASTON (afternoon)	12	Growth of Polit. System of Europe	H J. MACKINDER, M.A.	T. Jan. 16	Mar. 27
†PETERBOROUGH (evening)	12	Victorian Poets	F. S. BOAS, M.A.	F. Jan. 19	Mar. 30
FOLKESTONE (afternoon)	10	Victorian Poets	,, ,,	M. Jan. 29	Apr. 2
VENTNOR (afternoon)	6	Tennyson	,, ,,	T. Jan. 16	Mar. 27
MIDHURST (afternoon)	6	The Two Pitts	C E. MALLET, B.A	M. Jan. 15	Mar. 26
FROME (afternoon)	6	The Two Pitts	,, ,,	F. Jan. 19	Mar. 30
FROME (evening)	6	The Two Pitts	,, ,,	F. Jan. 19	Mar. 30
GRANGE (evening)	6	English Prose Writers	,, ,,	M. Jan. 22	Apr. 2
†TAMWORTH (afternoon)	10	The Stuarts	,, ,,	T. Jan. 16	Feb. 27
†TAMWORTH (evening)	10	The Stuarts	,, ,,	T. Jan. 16	Feb. 27
WHITEHAVEN (evening)	6	French Revolution	,, ,,	T. Jan. 23	Apr. 3
†BURY (evening)	12	French Revolution	,, ,,	W. Jan. 24	Apr 4
GRIMSBY (evening)	6	French Revolution	,, ,,	F. Feb. 9	Apr. 20
†BURNLEY (evening)	12	England in the 18th Century	,, ,,	Th. Jan. 25	Apr. 5
†BATH (afternoon)	12	England in the 18th Century	,, ,,	Th. Jan. 18	Mar. 29
†BATH (evening)	12	English Prose Writers	,, ,,	Th. Jan. 18	Mar. 29
DEVIZES (evening)	6 or 8	Shakespeare	Rev. J. G. BAILEY, LL.D.	M. Jan. 22	Not fixed
KEIGHLEY (evening)	6	Wordsworth, Shelley, Keats	,, ,,	M. Jan. 15	Not fixed
SALE (evening)	6	Shakespeare	,, ,,	T. Jan. 16	Not fixed
ROCHDALE (afternoon)	6	Shakespeare	,, ,,	W. Jan. 17	Not fixed
TUNBRIDGE WELLS (evening)	8	Regions, Races, and Resources	H. R. MILL, D.Sc.	T. Jan. 16	Mar. 6
†BARNSTAPLE (evening)	12	Design	C. R. ASHBEE, M.A.	M. Not fixed	Not fixed
†RYDE (afternoon)	12	Shakespeare	R. W. BOND. M.A.	Th. Jan. 11	Mar. 29
WEST BRIGHTON (evening)	6	Trade, Adventure, and Discovery	K. D. COTES, M A	Th. Jan. 25	Apr. 5
ROCHDALE (evening)	6	Social Questions of To-day	W. A. S. HEWINS, M.A.	Th. Jan. 18	Mar. 22
†LEAMINGTON (evening)	12	Problems of Poverty	J. A. HOBSON, M.A.	F. Feb. 2	Apr. 13
WEST BROMWICH (evening)	6	Problems of Poverty	,, ,,	T. Mar. 13	Apr. 17
†WEST BRIGHTON (afternoon)	12	The Renaissance	E. L. S. HORSBURGH, B.A.	Th. Jan. 18	Mar. 29
†REIGATE (afternoon)	12	The Renaissance	,, ,,	F. Jan. 19	Mar. 30
†RAMSGATE (afternoon)	12	French Revolution	,, ,,	S. Jan. 20	Mar. 31
†BOURNEMOUTH (afternoon)	12	Literature of the 18th Century	,, ,,	F. Jan. 12	Apr. 6
BOURNEMOUTH (evening)		Studies from the 18th and 19th Centuries	,, ,,	Th. Jan. 11	Apr. 5
†SOUTHAMPTON (evening)	12	The Tudors	,, ,,	F. Feb. 9	Apr. 20
LEOMINSTER (afternoon)	6	Rise of Parliament	,, ,,	M. Jan. 15	Not fixed
HEREFORD (evening)	6	Italian Renaissance	,, ,,	M. Jan. 15	Not fixed
MAIDENHEAD (afternoon)	6	The Renaissance	,, ,,	Th. Jan. 11	Mar. 22
ABERGAVENNY (evening)	6	Italian Renaissance	,, ,,	M. Jan. 22	Apr. 2
†LEWES (evening)	12	Studies from the Georges	,, ,,	Th. Jan. 18	Mar. 29
†HALIFAX (evening)	12	Architecture	J. E. PHYTHIAN	Th. Jan. 25	Mar. 29
†OXFORD (evening)	24	The English Citizen	GRAHAM WALLAS, M.A.	Th. Jan. 18	June 14
†BEDFORD (afternoon)	12	The English Citizen	,, ,,	T. Jan. 16	Mar. 27
†BRIDPORT (evening)	12	Architecture	Rev. G. H. WEST, D.D.	T. Jan. 23	Apr. 3
†VENTNOR (evening)	12	Astronomy	A. H. FISON, D.Sc	T. Jan. 9	Mar. 20
†NEWPORT (evening)	12	Astronomy	,, ,,	W. Jan. 10	Mar. 21
†STROUD (afternoon)	12	Electricity	,, ,,	T. Jan. 16	Apr. 10
†STROUD (evening)	12	Electricity	,, ,,	T. Jan. 16	Apr. 10
CLEVEDON (afternoon)	6	Astronomy	,, ,,	W. Jan 31	Apr. 11
WARRINGTON (evening)	6	Astronomy	W. E PLUMMER, M.A.	F. Feb. 2	Apr. 13
Kent County Council five courses each of	10	Chemistry	H. H. COUSINS, M.A.	Jan.	Apr.
†Surrey County Council six courses	24, 12, 6	Chemistry	A. D. HALL, M A.	Jan.	Apr.
two courses	24	Chemistry	H. GORDON, M.A.	Jan.	Apr.
Somerset County Council 5 courses each of	12	Hygiene	C. H. WADE, M.A.	Jan.	Apr.
5 courses each of	12	Farm Animals	H. SESSIONS	Jan.	Apr.

Other courses in process of arrangement.

† Continued from Autumn 1893.

Note.—Application for Courses and all information as to fees, &c., can be obtained from The Secretary, University Extension Office, Examination Schools, Oxford.

INFORMATION TO CONTRIBUTORS.

All communications should be addressed to the Editor, OXFORD UNIVERSITY EXTENSION GAZETTE, University Press, Oxford.

All matter intended for insertion in the February issue should reach him not later than January 20.

Contributions should be written on one side of the paper only, and must be accompanied by his name of the writer not necessarily for publication.

N.B.—*All orders should carefully specify the full title,* OXFORD UNIVERSITY EXTENSION GAZETTE.

OXFORD UNIVERSITY

EXTENSION GAZETTE.

Vol. IV. No. 41.] FEBRUARY, 1894. [ONE PENNY.

N.B.—Local Organizers of Oxford University Extension Lectures are invited to send to the Secretary, Extension Office, Examination Schools, Oxford, copies of any journals containing notices of, or references to, Extension work.

NOTES AND COMMENTS.

Correlation of Examination Standards. An important step has been taken in English University Extension by the establishment of a joint committee, representative of the Universities of Oxford, Cambridge, and Victoria, and of the London University Extension Society, charged with the duty of correlating the standards of award adopted by the four University Extension authorities in England. The duties of the joint committee, which will be laborious, cannot well be completed within a twelvemonth, but many will hope that the formation of the committee is one step towards the unification of the certificates of the whole English University Extension movement. An arrangement by which every University Extension certificate should run in the name of the four authorities, would be a simple and effective means of unifying the system, without depriving the country of the advantage accruing from the liberty and emulation of its several branches.

.˙.

The Grant to the New University for Wales. In spite of commercial distress and manifold pressure on the Treasury, the Chancellor of the Exchequer has wisely decided to begin a grant, at the rate of three thousand a year, to start the new University of Wales on what we hope will be a prosperous career. Few things can in the long-run contribute more to national welfare than an intense and liberal University life. It is of good omen that both of the great parties in England are at one in their desire to further the extension of University influence. We in Oxford may also feel special gratification at the deserved tribute of thanks, which was paid by the representative deputation from Wales to Mr. Arthur Acland for his great services to the higher education of the Principality.

.˙.

An Excellent Suggestion. No one quite knows what to do with the historic site of Christ's Hospital. In the *Times* of January 18, Dr. R. D. Roberts made the admirable proposal that it should be used for the new Gresham University. It would be well that a site so intimately associated with literature should be saved for educational work.

.˙.

Mr. Acland on the Training of Teachers in Secondary Schools. Speaking on January 8 at Westminster, the Vice-President of the Council laid great emphasis on the importance of training University men for work in secondary schools. He strongly endorsed what has been from time to time said in these columns as to the desirability of such training being offered in Oxford. It will be interesting to him and other friends of educational training to know, that the University Extension Delegacy have decided to make a course of practical instruction in the science and art of education one of the chief features of their next Summer Meeting.

We hear that the Council of the London University Extension Society contemplate holding a conference of representatives of the authorities and centres of the four branches of the University Extension movement in England. Such a conference would be of the highest importance and value, and no doubt would be attended by a large number of influential delegates.

.˙.

We understand that Professor Tout, late Fellow of Pembroke College, Oxford, has succeeded Professor Milnes Marshall as Secretary of the Victoria University Extension. Mr. Tout is Professor of History at Owens College.

.˙.

Changes at South Kensington. The appointment by Mr. Acland of twelve permanent Inspectors under the Science and Art Department presages large changes in the administration of South Kensington grants. Many regulations, necessary enough under present conditions, can be swept away when once the Department has the means of becoming personally acquainted with the teachers' work; and it is probable that Captain Abney and his twelve Inspectors will bring about a silent revolution in Science and Art teaching all over the country. We are pleased to see that a former Oxford University Extension lecturer, Mr. F. Pullinger, of C. C. C., has been chosen to fill one of the newly created and responsible posts, and it is stated that the same honour was offered to one of our present lecturers who was, however, unable to accept it.

.˙.

At a Conference on Technical Education at Claydon House on December 13, the President of Magdalen College made an interesting speech on the attitude of the University towards Technical Education. While regarding the advancement of science and the preparation of teachers as the chief function of the University, he thought it possible that more should be done for technical education at the University than has been hitherto attempted.

.˙.

At a meeting of the Somerset County Council on January 2, it was reported that Mr. Niblett's Oxford University Extension lectures had been very successful, the audiences at almost all the centres having consisted chiefly of farmers and others engaged on the soil.

.˙.

International Centres of Higher Study. From many quarters come indications that the Universities are gradually beginning to resume, under changed conditions, the international place which they held in the Middle Ages. An article in the *Contemporary Review* for December last, on 'The Strasburg Commemoration,' attempts to depict the possibilities which lie before such a University as that of Strasburg, when regarded as one of the centres of the higher education of young men from the different countries of Europe and America.

1

Mr. G. F. James, who has devoted much energy and vigour to University Extension in the United States, has resigned his position of secretary to the American Society for the Extension of University Teaching. It is to be hoped that Mr. James' severance from the work will only be a temporary one, and that after he returns from Europe, whither he is coming for purposes of research and study, he will again take up the cause of Extension, which can ill-afford to lose the services of so able a worker. It will be in the memory of many that only last summer Mr. James was in England, and visited both the Cambridge and Edinburgh Summer Meetings.

.˙.

University Extension in Belgium. We learn from the *Revue Universitaire* of Brussels that University Extension is succeeding in Belgium beyond the most sanguine hopes of its supporters. It is being carried on in the right spirit and on wise lines. ' Pour être efficace, l'œuvre doit être largement conçue, sans aucune préoccupation de parti. Instrument de diffusion scientifique, elle ne peut être une arme servant à la propagande politique.' Eleven courses have been arranged at seven centres—Brussels. Liege, Ixelles, La Louvière, Malines, Tournai and Verviers. The subjects are, with one exception, economic or historical.

.˙.

An Educational Clearing-house. The editor of *University Extension*, the organ of the American Society, happily describes the Summer Meeting as ' The Educators' Clearing-house Association.' Not only do these meetings, it is claimed, lead to increasing exchange in plans, ideas, and methods of education, but they provide stated and convenient times and places where persons can meet to discuss and see the working out of various educational theories. There is, indeed, no doubt that the Summer Meetings both in this country and in America have done much to form opinion in matters of education, and the novelty of the experiment backed by its undoubted success has won the attention and the presence of many with whom we should not otherwise have been able to exchange views. England and America, after mutual visits of lecturers and organizers, have learnt much from one another in their attempts to work out the problems connected with Extension work ; and this alone would justify the writer above-mentioned in describing the Summer Meeting as ' International.' This year Greece and Switzerland sent delegates to the Edinburgh Summer Meeting, and Russia, we are told, sent a commissioner to Cambridge to inquire into Extension methods with a view to their introduction into Russia.

.˙.

During the Christmas vacation Mr. J. Wells, Fellow and Tutor of Wadham College, very kindly delivered a number of lectures on Oxford in aid of the funds of various centres in the north of England. He lectured at Keighley, Harrogate, Rawtenstall and Oldham, and our thanks are due to him for the services he has thus rendered to the movement. Under the title of ' University Extension and the English Central Government,' he has also contributed to the *University Extension Bulletin* (Philadelphia) of December 8, an interesting survey of the relations between the Extension movement, the County Councils and the Education Department. Mr. Wells concludes as follows :—' At present those who believe in education here are in high hopes. It has ceased to be a party subject (except on one unlucky subject, that of secular schools). It has warm supporters everywhere, who are prepared to make sacrifices. The Government is willing to help, and to relax the iron hand of the " payment by results system." The teachers are willing to be helped. There are many difficulties to be faced, but we believe they will be surmounted by loyal co-operation and systematic belief in England's old traditions, supplemented by the new methods of modern life.'

.˙.

Mr. Danks, who was formerly an Oxford University Extension lecturer, has been asked to accept the Bishopric of Wellington (N. Z.)

It has been decided to hold a Conference of local organizers at Bournemouth during next April. The members of the Bournemouth Committee and others will entertain the delegates. The Oxford Delegacy will be represented in the discussions. The Conference will probably last one whole day and parts of two others. The chief object will be to discuss the possibility of combination between the centres in the Bournemouth district.

Forthcoming Conference at Bournemouth.

.˙.

It was stated at the concluding lecture of Mr. Hudson Shaw's course of lectures at Oldham on the ' Making of England,' that the audience this year had been the largest Extension audience on the continent of Europe. Without vouching for the accuracy of this statement, we think that the large numbers of students who attended the lectures, and who were almost wholly working men, prove very conclusively that it is possible to interest the artisan classes of the North in the educational work of the Extension movement.

.˙.

Mr. H. Dyke Acland has written an interesting essay on the Petrology of the Herefordshire Beacon. In this he acknowledges the instruction he has received from various teachers, including Professor A. H. Green. He also states that in his geological study he owes much to Mr. Carus Wilson's University Extension lectures on Geology.

.˙.

Cambridge, following the lead of Oxford, will provide in the second fortnight of July 1894 theological lectures for the clergy on the lines of those which proved so acceptable in Oxford last summer. The Rev. A. Caldecott, 45 Chesterton Road, Cambridge, will act as Secretary. The Board of Management is a strong one and the Archbishops and Bishops strongly approve of the scheme.

Long Vacation Lectures in Theology for Clergymen.

.˙.

In a valuable article published in *Nature* (Dec. 21, 1893) on ' the progress of Technical Education,' Mr. Gregory points out that ' the work of the Berkshire Technical Instruction Committee has been greatly facilitated by the establishment of the University Extension College at Reading.' The establishment of University Extension Colleges at strong centres is certainly an admirable plan,' the writer concludes, ' and County Councils would do well to assist in their foundation and adequate equipment.'

County Councils and University Extension Colleges.

.˙.

Mansfield House University Settlement in East London has now completed the third year of its existence and the annual *Report* just issued naturally takes stock of the work that has already been done. The growth of the many clubs, classes, and societies connected with the House shows that the early enthusiasm of the residents has not in any degree lessened, nor the need for such settlements in East London diminished. Although the work of the residents is chiefly social, something has been done during the past year for education, but, as is pointed out in the *Report*, the first efforts of the Settlement have been superseded by University Extension lectures and Evening Continuation Schools. For the former the hall of Mansfield House is lent to the West Ham Corporation, and in addition to the latter a most promising class of teachers and others for the London University Matriculation Examination meets at the Settlement four evenings a week.

Mansfield House.

.˙.

We congratulate Mr. Austen Keen on his appointment as joint organizing Secretary for the county and borough of Cambridge. Mr. Keen has for some time acted as Secretary to the Huddersfield Technical School, and for University Extension in that town.

DEATH OF PROFESSOR MILNES MARSHALL.

Secretary of the Victoria University Extension.

THE New Year opened with the sad intelligence that University Extension had lost one of its most distinguished advocates and organizers by the fatal fall of Dr. Milnes Marshall on Scawfell on New Year's Eve. A practised and cautious climber, Professor Milnes Marshall met his death on a part of the mountain which is ordinarily free from danger, and at a time when his party were resting towards the close of their day's expedition. The accident took place at the foot of the Lord's Rake, while Dr. Marshall was looking for a place from which to take a photograph. The exact cause of the fatality remains a mystery, and the jury, which sat on January 2, at Wastdale Head, returned a verdict of accidental death.

Dr. Marshall, who was in .his forty-third year, was the son of a well-known Birmingham engineer. A Fellow of St. John's College, Cambridge, he had worked since 1879 as Professor of Zoology at the Owens College, and so brilliant were his services to biological study, that an American who came to London to inquire into the English teaching of Biology, was told by a leading savant, 'We can do nothing half so good for you as to send you to Marshall's laboratory at Manchester.'

It is characteristic of the time that this distinguished man of science divided his thought between questions of research and problems of University administration. He had the insight to perceive that the present is a time of critical reorganization of University studies, and that the future of academic life in England will be influenced for decades by the decisions which are now being reached. So far therefore from isolating himself in his laboratory and regarding any time as wasted that was not given to the advancement of pure science, Professor Marshall gave unstinted thought to the matters of policy connected with the new Victoria University, and was one of the small group of men who secured for it a leading place in the educational institutions of the country.

Professor Marshall however saw that the work of University organization lay not only within the walls of a college, but in that field of outside effort which goes by the loose name of University Extension. He understood that, if universities are to be made and kept strong, if they are to retain their old influence, to gain a firm grip on the respect and affections of the masses of the people, and themselves to win first-hand knowledge of public needs, they must send out as their missionaries and representatives men of power and enthusiasm, who will familiarize the nation with the principal aims, methods and results of University work. Professor Marshall therefore made University Extension work a large part of his academic duty, and for many years served as Secretary to the Victoria University Extension. His death is a great blow to the whole movement.

We print below a contribution from a Manchester correspondent who was brought into intimate acquaintance with the late Professor.

The three weeks that have elapsed since the fatal 31st of December have not made it much easier to realize Dr. Marshall's death. Of all the men I ever knew he was the most *alive*. It seems only the other day that I heard him say in his room at Owens College, just after his return from his last holiday in the Alps, 'I came back to do some work, but it's no use: I find I can't work : *I'm too well!*' He looked then as if he had vital energy enough for a whole staff of professors : and indeed he threw more enthusiasm than most men distribute over all their occupations into each of the many interests with which his life was crowded.

The part which the Victoria University has taken in University Extension work was largely due to his initiative, and it remained under his direction throughout. In addition to the work of his Professorship, of various Examinerships, of authorship and research, he found time to discharge the duties of University Extension secretary for his University, and to deliver three or four courses in each winter himself. He was an ideal lecturer and an ideal teacher; he had the power of interesting large audiences and of stimulating individual students. Those who heard his last course at Kersal, on 'The Darwinian Theory,' added to their admiration for his powers a new admiration for his character, his perfect frankness coupled with delicate tact. There had been some apprehensions that the subject might wound tender susceptibilities; but Dr. Marshall, whilst never shirking any question, avoided this danger completely. He thoroughly enjoyed lecturing to a large audience ; he found it 'refreshing,' he would say, after his day's work at the college. It is only right to add, however, that he held somewhat strong views, as a teacher, on the inadvisability of making Extension lecturing an independent career. He thought the temptation to the professional lecturer to weaken the quality of his lectures gradually, instead of improving them, was so strong that it was very difficult for him to grow intellectually.

Dr. Marshall's zeal for his adopted University and natural anxiety to safeguard its interests in every possible way made him at one time somewhat jealous of the intrusion of any other University into the local area served by Victoria lecturers. He afterwards abandoned this position, and threw himself heart and soul into the formation of the Lancashire and Cheshire Association as the medium for obtaining the best Extension teaching for the district without friction between the three Universities engaged in the work. During the past two years he has presided at almost every meeting of the Executive Committee of the Association, and in many other ways at the cost of much personal inconvenience, he has furthered its interests. In this, as indeed in every other department of his work, his unfailing cheerfulness, his promptitude, resourcefulness, tact and courtesy won for him the love as well as the admiration of those whose privilege it was to labour with or under him.

THE OXFORD SUMMER MEETING, 1894.

THE first part of the Summer Meeting will begin on Friday, July 27, and will end on Tuesday, August 7. The second part will begin on Wednesday, August 8, and end on Friday, August 24. The lectures during the first part will be chiefly given in the Examination Schools, but, in consequence of the meeting of the British Association which will be concurrent with the second part of the Summer Meeting, the lectures after August 7 will be delivered in other rooms, including the Divinity School and Convocation House, which have been specially granted by the Vice-Chancellor for this purpose.

The chief sequence of lectures will deal with the history, literature, art and economics of Europe in the seventeenth century. It is understood that the number of alternative lectures will be reduced and the number of classes largely increased. It is believed that this step forward in the direction of thorough study will be appreciated by the students.

Among the novel features of this year's Meeting will be a course of instruction, specially designed for teachers, on the Life and Duties of the Citizen. It has also been decided to make philosophical teaching a noteworthy part of the Oxford Meeting, and this year the course will begin with lectures probably on Logic and others on Psychology.

Another new feature will be a course of practical instruction in Art, which will be kindly undertaken by Mr. Alexander Macdonald, the Ruskin Teacher of Drawing.

It is known to many of our readers that the Delegates are about to publish a new set of regulations recognizing class teaching in Greek and other languages. The students attending these classes will not be allowed to obtain certificates in recognition of their work, unless they have attended a course of University Extension lectures on the history, literature, philosophy or art of the nation, whose language they are studying. As however it will be difficult in many centres for committees to arrange courses of lectures in Greek subjects, it has

2

been decided to arrange at the Summer Meeting a full course of lectures on Greek Literature, with classes and examination. Individual students from small centres will thus have an opportunity of obtaining this part of the qualification for a certificate in Greek language.

There will be also, as in former years, ample provision of scientific teaching. By permission of the Delegates of the Museum and the kindness of Dr. Odling and Mr. Fisher, practical courses will be given in the chemical laboratories. Professor Green will superintend a course on field work in Geology. There will also be a practical course of instruction in Hygiene under the care of Dr. Wade, and probably courses in two or three other sciences as well.

Special interest will be taken in the decision of the Delegacy to institute a course of lectures and practical instruction in the science and art of education. Much thought is now being given to the training of teachers, and it is believed that a course of study, under the direction of a group of men who have devoted much of their life to the study of educational science, will, though it cannot pretend to be more than a beginning, suggest fruitful thoughts and subjects for useful discussion to those who are either themselves engaged in teaching or are interested in educational progress.

The arrangements for the Meeting are now far advanced, and further announcements will be made month by month in these columns and, by the courtesy of the Editor, in the *University Extension Journal.* The Programme of the Meeting will be published in April, and the list of lodging-houses is already at press. By an arrangement between the University Extension Delegates and the authorities of the British Association, the first part of the Summer Meeting and the assembly of the British Association will not overlap. Any student however who wishes to stay on for the latter gathering after the first part of the Summer Meeting, will be able to do so without waste of time.

The number of tickets issued for the first part of the Meeting will be limited to one thousand, and for the first three weeks after the publication of the Programme the sale of tickets will be confined to those who are or have been University Extension students, and have attended lectures authorized by any one of the four branches of the movement. A certain number of tickets, however, will be reserved, at any rate till June, for the convenience of students from the Continent and America.

A SUMMER SCHOOL OF LIBRARY SCIENCE.

At the meeting of the Library Association held in Paris in 1892, Mr. J. J. Ogle read an interesting paper in support of a scheme for a Summer School of Library Science. His plan was based on the Extension Summer Meetings, Mr. Dewey's Library School at Albany and the Oxford Summer School of Theology. It sketched a programme of three days' library study so arranged as to meet the needs of persons engaged in library administration. At the Liverpool meeting of the Library Association last December the matter was pushed further and the first Summer School for Library Assistants was announced to take place in London in July.

.·.

The programme of work of the Summer School included a visit to the British Museum, with an address by Dr. Garnett, and explanations of the system of classification used in the Museum, followed by a visit to the book-binding department. On the other days visits were paid to various libraries in London, among others, to the Guildhall, St. Martin's, and Chelsea Public Libraries, and special facilities were given to the students in order that they might learn something of the technical arts with which their profession is concerned. Visits were accordingly paid to the Type-foundry of Sir Chas. Reed and Sons, to Messrs. Blades' Printing Office and to Zachnsdorf Book-binding Atelier. The meeting was decidedly successful, being attended by forty-five students, and it is hoped to arrange for a second meeting next year.

MR. BRYCE ON GRADUATE STUDY IN OXFORD.

IN the course of his valedictory lecture[1] given in June last, on his retirement from the Professorship of Civil Law in the University of Oxford, Mr. Bryce spoke at some length on the means which could be taken to encourage at Oxford higher courses of graduate study. Coming from so distinguished a member of the University, these words deserve the careful attention of those in whose hands rests the direction of the policy of Oxford.

As Homer occasionally invests a dying warrior with prophetic gifts, one who is on the eve of departure may be permitted to give expression to some of the aspirations that have long filled his mind when he has thought of what Oxford might achieve. She seems at present to be too exclusively occupied not only with the giving of a general liberal education (to the disparagement of professional studies), but also with her regular curriculum and those who follow it, to the neglect of those others, now comparatively few, but capable of almost indefinite increase, who desire not so much to follow a regular course or secure a degree as to obtain special training in some department of learning. Have we not, in our English love of competition and our tendency to reduce everything to a palpable concrete result, allowed the examination system to grow too powerful, till it has become the master instead of the servant of teaching and has distracted our attention from the primary duty of a University? It is not any revolutionary change one would desire to see. Such changes are seldom either easy or salutary; while as regards the college system, I find much to regret in those serious inroads upon the social life and corporate character of the colleges for which the last Commission is responsible. The reform chiefly needed is a reform that would neither injure the colleges nor affect the character of the University as a seat of general liberal education. Rather let us return to the older conception of Oxford as a place to which every one who desired instruction might come, knowing that as she took all knowledge for her province she would provide him with whatever instruction he required. The abundance and the cheapness of literature have not diminished, perhaps they have even stimulated, the demand for the best oral teaching, while the recent establishment of so many prosperous colleges in the great towns, the spread of University Extension lectures, the growth of Science schools, have immensely increased the number of young men who would come hither for a year or more to obtain such teaching were they sure of finding it. What is the present position? We have professors, many of whom, eminent as they are, cannot secure proper classes, because the undergraduates are occupied, under the guidance of the college teachers, in preparing for degree examinations. For the teaching of some important branches, especially in natural and in economic science, we possess no adequate staff. We have been outstripped not only by Germany but also by the United States, in the provision of what the Americans call Post-Graduate courses, a provision which even our present poverty need not hinder us from making, were but a reasonable system of fees introduced and revenues husbanded that are now unprofitably spent. Both the new University teachers whom we might create and the present professors to whom our system refuses hearers would be only too happy to give those courses, if the students could be found and the requisite arrangements made. The men who would attend the courses exist, some of them within, many more without, the University. Those without do not come, because we have not offered the courses: and to provide for both sets we must remodel our existing arrangements, which contemplate only the normal undergraduate who arrives at nineteen, is examined, and departs at twenty-two or twenty-three, and take no account of those who desire neither examinations nor degrees, but simply to perfect themselves in some department of science or learning. Were such courses offered, and were those antiquated arrangements altered, we might soon expect a large afflux of students, not from

[1] *Legal Studies in the University of Oxford.* London : Macmillan. 1s. net.

England only, but from far beyond the bounds of England. Perhaps we in Oxford have scarcely yet realized the magnificent position our University holds, as not only the oldest and the most externally beautiful and sumptuous place of education in the English-speaking world, but as a place whose name and fame exert a wonderful power over the imagination of the English peoples beyond the sea, many of whose youth would gladly flock hither did we encourage them to do so by arrangements suited to their needs! For those among the studious youth of the United States and Canada who desire to follow out their special s'udies, I can safely say from what I have seen of Canada and the United States that did Oxford and Cambridge provide what the Universities of Germany provide, and were it as easy to enter here and choose the subject one seeks to study as it is in the Universities of Germany, it is to Oxford and Cambridge rather than to Germany that most of them would resort: nor could the value be over-estimated of such a tie as their membership here would create between the ancient mother and the scattered children, soon to be stronger than their mother, but still looking to her as the hallowed well-spring of their life.

THE OXFORD CONFERENCE OF THE NATIONAL UNION OF TEACHERS.

Arrangements of the Committee of Welcome.

WE are glad to be able to announce that the Easter Conference of the National Union of Teachers, which is to be held this year in Oxford, will receive a very hearty welcome from the University. It is understood that the Vice-Chancellor and Proctors will, at the opening ceremony on Easter Monday, convey to the Conference an expression of the cordial goodwill of the University towards the work of the Union. The sessions of the Conference will be held in the Examination Schools, which have been lent by the University for the purpose. In order that more personal hospitality may be shown to the members of the Conference, there has been formed in the University a Committee of Welcome, comprising more than one hundred well-known names, among which are those of the Vice-Chancellor and Proctors, the Dean of Christ Church, the Provost of Queen's, the Warden of New College, the Warden of All Souls, the President of Magdalen, the Principal of Brasenose, the Master of University, the Rector of Exeter, the Master of Pembroke, the Provost of Worcester, the Warden of Keble, and the Principal of St. Mary Hall, the Censor of Non-Collegiate students, the Archdeacon of Oxford; Canons Ince, Bright, Driver and Moberly; Professors Sir Henry Acland, Max Müller, Odling, Pelham, Dicey, A. H. Green, and Poulton; Sir William Markby, Sir John Conroy, Mr. T. Raleigh, Mr. Alfred Robinson, Mr. Arthur Sidgwick, Mr. W. Warde Fowler, Mr. York Powell, Mr. D. G. Ritchie: the Principals of Pusey House, Wycliffe Hall, Mansfield College, and Manchester College; the Chairman of the Oxford School Board, H. M. Inspector of Schools of the district, the Diocesan Inspector of Schools; the Principals of Somerville, Lady Margaret, and St. Hugh's Halls; Mrs. T. H. Green, Mrs. Arnold Toynbee and Miss Beard, as well as a large number of other representatives of the University and City. The Secretaries of the Committee are Messrs. Wells, Gerrans, Matheson and Sadler. By the invitation of the Committee of Welcome, the members of the Conference will be entertained on March 28 at a conversazione in the University Museum, which has been lent for the purpose. The Conference dinner will take place on March 27 in the Hall of Christ Church, by permission of the Governing Body. On Friday, March 30, the members of the Conference will be invited to join parties, which will be conducted by resident members of the University to the chief places of interest in the City and the colleges. The attendance at the Conference is expected to be very large and the majority of the thousand persons, who will probably attend it, will be accommodated with lodgings in the City, but we are glad to state that over two hundred of the

teachers will be offered accommodation in certain of the colleges, viz. Balliol, Oriel, New College, Brasenose, St. John's, University and Worcester, as well as at St. Mary Hall and at Somerville Hall, St. Hugh's and Lady Margaret Halls. It is understood that members of the University will be invited by the National Union of Teachers to take part in one of the Sessions of the Conference, at which a paper will be read by Mr. Arthur Sidgwick on an educational subject.

The welcome which is thus being extended to the National Union of Teachers is one of many signs of the increasing appreciation of the unity of the whole teaching profession. We hope that the Conference will be thoroughly successful, and that the members in looking back on their Oxford meeting will associate it with the most pleasant recollections of a hearty welcome.

UNIVERSITY EXTENSION COLLEGE, READING.

PROFESSOR DOUGLAS GILCHRIST, late of University College, Bangor, has been appointed Instructor in Agriculture at the University Extension College, Reading.

.·.

With the express approval and promised assistance of the Board of Agriculture, the Council of the University Extension College propose holding a class of an advanced character for Dairy Teachers, specially designed for those who attended the short course at Bangor, in February last. The class will extend over eight weeks—from Monday, January 22, to Saturday, March 17. No fees for tuition will be demanded from those who attended the Bangor Class, but they will be required to pay for their board and lodging (unless this is defrayed by the County Council, or Society, or other Local Body, in whose employ they may be). It is estimated that the cost of board and lodging in Reading need not exceed £1 a week. An Examination will be held at the end of the course, and certificates will be awarded. The course of instruction will consist of lectures and practical laboratory work in the following subjects:—

(1) Agriculture and Dairying, by Mr. D. A. Gilchrist; B.Sc. Edin., and P. H. Foulkes, B.Sc. Edin.

(2) Chemistry and Bacteriology as applied to Dairy Work; by Mr. F. G. Lloyd, F.C.S., F.I.C., and Mr. G. J. Burch, M.A, Oxon.

(3) Anatomy and Physiology as applied to Dairy Work, by Mr. B. J. Austin, F.L.S., and Miss E. C. Pollard, B.Sc. Lond.

A few other lectures may be arranged on subjects interesting to Dairy Teachers. In addition to those members of the Bangor Class who may desire to attend this continuation class, a limited number of other students may be admitted on payment of a fee of £4 4s., provided that they can give satisfactory evidence of having had such previous training as will fit them to receive full benefit from the advanced course now proposed. A list of lodgings will be forwarded on application to the Secretary of the University Extension College, Reading.

.·.

At the end of Mr. Churton Collins' Autumn course of lectures on the Homeric Age, a conversational meeting was held in the Abbey Gate room, which was attended by the lecturer and members of the Students' Association and their friends.

GRADUATE SCHOOLS AT THE ENGLISH UNIVERSITIES.

WITHIN the last few days, another sign has appeared of the strong interest which is being taken in schemes for the encouragement of graduate study at Oxford and Cambridge. Dr. Lawrence, in a letter addressed to the resident members of the Senate of the University of Cambridge, writes as follows:—

With our magnificent libraries and our wealth of treasures in art and science and literature we possess unrivalled facilities for carrying on graduate work, if some of those whose world-wide reputation in science and scholarship is at once the strength and the pride of our University could be induced to undertake it. Not only would many of the best of our own *alumni* gladly avail themselves of the advantages offered, but Cambridge wou'd rapidly attract a large portion of those American students who now complete their training in German Universities. In order to secure them we should be obliged either to alter in some measure our system of granting the higher degrees, or to offer new degrees, such as the Mastership and Doctorate of Philosophy, to those who, after graduating here or elsewhere, came to Cambridge to pass through one of our Graduate Schools. There are some among us who would welcome the prospect of being allowed to teach without constant reference to the schedules of a scheme of examinations and would regard with equanimity the destruction of the idea, engendered by our present system, that the end of education is a high place in a Tripos. To them I commend the project I have indicated, in the hope that, if it bears their scrutiny, they will endeavour to carry it into effect.

UNIVERSITY EXTENSION AND COUNTY COUNCIL GRANTS.

CONSIDERED WITH REFERENCE TO EDUCATIONAL WORK AMONGST CO-OPERATORS.

THE Co-operators of the Calderdale Conference met in conference at Hebden Bridge on Saturday, December 30 last, in order to discuss the above subject. Two students at the Hebden Bridge centre, both of them workers at the Hebden Bridge Fustian Manufacturing Co-operative Society, submitted an interesting paper, extracts from which are given below. It is well known how deep an interest is taken in University Extension at Hebden Bridge, and we hope that the discussion of Messrs. Fielding and Halstead's paper may increase the number of centres in the Calderdale district.

INTRODUCTION.

The previous paper read some time ago in this beautiful hall, was an appeal to working men *as students* ; the present one is an appeal to working men organized as co-operators, to adopt University Extension lectures as a permanent part of their educational programme.

OBJECTS AND AIMS OF UNIVERSITY EXTENSION.

Some of the well-known objects and aims of University Extension may be cited at the outset with advantage and interest. Briefly they are these : (*a*) To extend its benefits to talented and well-conditioned persons, however born, provided they shall be prepared to benefit by its education ; and this not because they are poor as objects of pity, but because they show talent, and industry, and willingness and desire to improve themselves, and because they ought not to be shut out from advantages open to other persons with whom they might perhaps compete successfully. (*b*) To keep abreast of the times by supplying the literary, philosophical, and scientific yearnings of the ever-increasing number of the population, by sending the best lecturers on these subjects to any town or village where such demand for education exists, and where the hearty co-operation of local societies and institutions, like the Nutclough Fustian, Hebden Bridge Industrial, and other societies (organizers) are willing to bear their fair share of the necessary labour and expenses. (*c*) By the help which such local organizers can render when acting in concert with them, on account of their intimate knowledge of the requirements of the districts, to adapt the lectures and teaching to such requirements as far as possible, and thus bring the University to the people when it is impossible for the people to go to the University. (*d*) By means of its central organization or central offices to give the best and most matured advice to the local centres as to the best methods of working the system, by carrying out its manifold details with punctuality, accuracy, and method, so as to meet any new wants and emergencies, and throw light on the best ways of overcoming any difficulties which might arise and impede further progress.

Helped in this way, our local educational efforts become centres of stimulus and guidance to every young man and young woman, and at the same time retain the intellectual sympathy, interest, and help of the older people. This is the great ideal of the University Extension movement, whose complete system, now briefly reviewed, is calculated to utilize much of the immense expenditure on education now unhappily running to waste. These are a few of the objects and aims of University Extension, which, if appreciated and used, are eminently qualified to give a healthy, liberal tone to school education, as a preparation for the busy occupations of social, agricultural, and commercial life, no less than for literary and scientific pursuits.

CLAIMS OF UNIVERSITY EXTENSION TO THE SYMPATHY OF CO-OPERATORS.

It is very desirable, therefore, that such a large industrial organization as is represented by co-operators should be in sympathetic touch with the large educational establishments of the nation. If, as co-operators, we will but follow in the footsteps of our first great teachers and leaders—Maurice, Kingsley, Neale, Hughes, and others, we shall not allow greed of gain and love of 'divi' to bring our whole movement into ridicule and contempt ; but keeping their high ideals before us, we shall seek to uplift the worker, and to benefit our neighbours in every possible way, and let reason and conscientiousness triumph over selfishness, and give to learning and leisure their due help and place.

THE GREAT INFLUENCE OF MEN OF CULTURE.

A slight contact with men such as I have mentioned, and with the world of culture, which helped to make them the benefactors of their race, will enable us to understand the larger purposes of their work, and strengthen our fidelity to their noble ideals, as we seek to set them forth in practical effort in our co-operative life. A few words concerning these purposes and ideals might be given. The root principles of our co-operative life were summarized by Maurice as follows :—(1) ' Human society is a brotherhood, and not a collection of warring atoms. (2) That true workers should be fellow workers, not rivals. (3) That a principle of justice and not selfishness should regulate exchange.' In order to fully grasp these principles, we shall have to have an intellectual and moral education higher than what we get from contact with a world of industry based on competitive principles. This we can find in their various co-operative writings, in which the most successful systems of working them out in daily practice are clearly and fully shown. (See *Manual for Co-operators, Co-operative News, Working Men Co-operators* and the Co-operative Union's publications.) These ideals and modes of working cannot be achieved ' so long as the societies in our Co-operative Union—faithless to the principles to which they are pledged—permit their greatest Wholesale centre to deal with the claims of labour as if it were an ordinary joint-stock company, by distributing the profits of production according to the wealth of the recipients measured by their purchases, instead of according to the energy manifested in their productive work.' That our working men may understand the far-reaching importance of this principle of co-operation, they will have to get something of the wider view of economic problems of our day, and catch something of the deep moral earnestness and sympathy that characterized those heralds of a nobler industrial life.

Happily this touch with cultured influence has already begun to affect the every-day lives of the men and women of this district, and we feel that we have better desires, higher aspirations, and nobler purposes for which to live, and we see our way to make all these desires and purposes real practical blessings to us, now that a number of University men have been amongst us and shown us the way.

PROOFS OF THIS HIGHER INFLUENCE.

We see proof of this on every hand—in the demand for a higher class of ' paper' work at our mutual improvement classes —in a growing demand for reading rooms with journalism with less of a partisan bias than those to which we have been accustomed—in connexion with our Sunday schools. We see the change, too, in a more definite form, in the rise of a literary society, which its organizers avow sprang directly from University Extension lectures given in this town.

THE BENEFITS OPEN TO THE CALDERDALE DISTRICT.

What University Extension has done for Hebden Bridge and district by co-operative organization and the devoted zeal of a few enthusiastic educationists, which almost every district contains, it can do for the entirety of this Calderdale district.

That co-operators as a section of the working class need the much discussed secondary education, everyone who has had any experience of Extension work as a student knows; but one way of making the bulk of the people realize the need of this most readily is to give them some examples of the higher ideals of culture insisted on by the great academic institutions of our land. We shall be great losers if this influence be removed from our midst, either from indifference, want of financial aid, or any other cause.

THE FINANCIAL DIFFICULTY,

however, is perhaps the greatest with which we have to contend; comparatively slight with large and wealthy societies, but great with small ones. Both these might combine with other educational bodies—school boards, Sunday and day schools, mechanics' institutes, &c.—and thus bring the expenses down to the lowest point, and at the same time widen the influence, consolidate local effort, and lessen individual labour.

COUNTY COUNCIL GRANTS CONSIDERED.

This brings us to the second part of our subject—County Council grants considered with reference to educational work amongst co-operators. The assistance from this source is considerable, and may be applied to local educational purposes.

*　　*　　*　　*　　*　　*　　*

THE TECHNICAL INSTRUCTION ACT

of 1891 enables the County Council, where necessary, to aid the provision of technical instruction given in institutions ; to provide, or assist in providing, scholarships; and pay, or assist in paying, school fees; and in distributing funds in aid of technical and manual instruction. For this purpose the County Council, as well as the other local authorities referred to in the Act, may levy a rate in their respective districts, of not more than a penny in the pound in any one year.

*　　*　　*　　*　　*　　*　　*

PRESSING APPEAL TO CO-OPERATORS TO TAKE FULL ADVANTAGE OF SUCH ASSISTANCE.

Let us, in conclusion, now appeal to you as co-operators, to take this question of University Extension into your earnest consideration. We have to remember that we are committed to other matters in our co-operative life than extensive shopkeeping, making of large dividends, and accumulating share capital. Co-operation is, in the first place, no doubt, an economic movement, and as such needs careful attention amid the cut-throat competition of to-day. But to grapple with a gigantic competitive system in a broad spirit, and in an efficient manner, we shall require the advantages of a broad-minded education. Besides being an economic movement, co-operation is an educational one, and viewed in this aspect of our work, we are called on to be true to the great ideals of the movement. If we are 'a State within a State,' we shall have to gain the broad and large outlook of statesmanship on the problems of our great system of social and economic life. We have seen that with the funds at our disposal for educational purposes, and by combination with other educational institutions, and with the assistance from public funds, the financial difficulties can be minimized to a great extent.

The next requisites to ensure success as far as organizing Extension work in our several localities is concerned, is the getting hold of a few educational-minded people, and arousing their interest in the movement, and gaining their hearty co-operation in the work. For these we might look among the active members of our Sunday schools, leaders of our mutual improvement classes, and working men's clubs, and the cultured minds of our wealthier classes. If our different localities should not prove during the first session of Extension lectures to be teeming with enthusiastic and capable students, we need not give up in despair. If we can secure only a few of such, they may prove centres of intellectual ferment, and the little leaven be used for leavening the whole lump. If we do nothing more we shall let into the midst of our provincial districts a little of broader intellectual daylight that shall show life to be good for other and nobler things than ' the gospel of getting on.' One of the great obstacles to the spread of higher education is persistent belief of the majority of our people that unless knowledge in some way affects our incomes it is not worth the trouble of acquiring. What we particularly need is to break up this notion and create a sympathy with and desire for knowledge, because it broadens life, heightens pleasure, and puts us in communication with the best that has been said and thought and known. These things may seem far remote from co-operation as some of us have known it in actual practice, but yet for all that one may say that until co-operators have taken some such large and comprehensive view of their function in their day and generation, they have not grasped the full meaning of their own work, or got on the right track for fulfilling its noblest destinies.

SAMUEL FIELDING.
ROBERT HALSTEAD.

The reading of the paper was followed by a discussion during which delegates from Hebden Bridge, Heptonstall, Walsden, Todmorden and Brighouse spoke. Mr. Joseph Greenwood, the Secretary of the Conference, testified to the great appreciation of University Extension lectures at Hebden Bridge. At the invitation of the Conference Mr. Sadler delivered an address on the aims of University Extension and the powers of the County Councils in furthering this branch of educational work.

In replying to a vote of thanks to the writers of the paper, Mr. Halstead said that University Extension had been such a great boon to himself that he was a perfect enthusiast on its behalf. After the Conference, the delegates present were entertained at tea by the Nutclough Co-operative Society.

Oxford University Extension lectures have now been delivered at Hebden Bridge for seven years in succession, and it is gratifying to see that the movement in the town and neighbourhood seems to grow stronger year by year.

PROPOSED INTERNATIONAL UNIVERSITY EXTENSION CONGRESS AT CAMBRIDGE.

THIS year the local lecture side of the University Extension movement comes of age. It is twenty-one years since the Cambridge Senate adopted the report of a special syndicate in favour of sending out University lecturers to large towns. In honour of this event, the well-known lecturer, Dr. Lawrence, in a striking letter addressed to the resident members of the University, that of Cambridge, makes the following proposal.

I venture to suggest that the twenty-first anniversary of the sending forth of the first lecturers should be commemorated by a great International University Extension Congress to be held in Cambridge in the summer of the present year. It should be a conference of experts. Every University and Society doing University Extension work should be invited to send a certain number of delegates, and special invitations should be forwarded to prominent friends of the movement. The questions I have indicated and many others should be thoroughly discussed. Great benefit would accrue to the cause of higher education on both sides of the Atlantic from an exchange of views between English and American Extensionists; and the presence of Continental and Colonial representatives would increase the advantages to be derived from a comparison of experiences and a discussion of difficulties. Much light would be thrown by the Congress upon the problems which await solution in the immediate future, and the feeling of solidarity and sense of brotherhood among the workers in the University Extension cause would be greatly increased by it. Cambridge would take the place which historically belongs to her in the front of the movement, and would gain from the deliberations of the Congress valuable information to guide her in making those changes that are necessary for its well-being and progress.

If the 'majority' of University Extension is celebrated by such a Congress as Dr. Lawrence suggests, we gladly recognize the fact that Cambridge is the right place to hold it. Nor do we think that such a gathering would render the proposed conference in London unnecessary. The latter would be national, the former international, in its character. It is unlikely that an assembly of representatives from many different counties would be able to contribute much in the way of detailed suggestion as to the improvement of our methods of organization; but their presence and deliberations might well excite an interest which would not be without its effect on the prosperity and development of the English branch of the movement.

LETTERS TO THE EDITOR.

[*We do not hold ourselves responsible for the opinions expressed by our correspondents.*]

Wanted.—More Information.

SIR,—I agree with Mr. Warwick Bond, as to the prudence of lecturers in abstaining from controversy in your columns. But I think it would be of service if they now and then gave their experience on the more important questions, which their year's work led them to believe might be useful if embodied in a paper.

Whether or not it was advisable to print the papers, it is obvious that if the Extension Office, which has its hands pretty full at all times, could undertake in addition an intelligence department, it would be of considerable use.

For instance, I should like a good deal of information, which it would not be very difficult to procure.

(1) How many papers were written after each lecture, and their aggregate length?

(2) How many of the writers qualified, and for what reason were the rest disqualified?

(3) How many of those qualified entered for examination?

(4) The proportion of (a) papers, (b) qualified candidates, (c) passes to the numbers of the audience.

(5) Whether audiences tend to fall off or not towards the end of the course (for this the average number attending each lecture must be given).

From these facts could be drawn conclusions as to the relative value of six and twelve lecture courses, of the meaning of a 'strong centre' or a 'weak centre,' and this might suggest whether attendance or class-work, or paper-work, or examination, were each or all necessary for the former. Perhaps it would be well to quote instances of the best centres.

But the subject that has lately occupied most of my time is County Council aid. Through the unwearied patience of the Office, and the kindness of local secretaries, I have got some of the facts I wanted, but there has not been that keen enjoyment of the work, which is supposed to make effort its own reward. The information was necessary, but it would have been more gratifying if the trouble had fallen to the lot of some one else. There is first the question of procuring the Technical Education Act, and next ascertaining its interpretation. It distinctly contemplates a commercial as well as an industrial education; and it is well to know what subjects besides science, for Extension courses, have already received a County Council grant; farther, what subjects have already been recognized by the Science and Art Department; and farther still, what subjects they might reasonably be asked to place upon the list.

Some centres might consider it advisable to have a footing in Institutes or Public Libraries; on one of these points there are already precedents: how does the experiment work?

County Councils, too, desire to have statistics laid before them: they ask where the work has been successful, especially in villages: whether other counties have subsidized Extension, and to what extent, and under what conditions.

It is also put with extreme and exasperating brevity, 'What scheme would you suggest for making use of a grant, if it was given you?' It is exasperating, because of course the question means that you should support your contention by facts, numbered and tabulated, and not by rhetoric.

But it appears to me there is a point of still greater importance, and one that follows on all the rest. A great many centres are receiving grants; might it not be well if those near one another took steps to combine? Imposing buildings are not necessary to secure efficient teaching, or the organization and combination of various educational agencies.

A College in its primary sense signifies students and teachers, nor is it necessary that it should be for one town only, it may serve for two or three or even for a whole county. But to attempt to secure this with any chance of success, or indeed to be convinced that it is desirable to make the attempt, it is necessary to be able to answer yet another difficult and complex question, difficult and complex because the facts are not ordinarily attainable, 'What is the precise value of an Extension College?'

The questions suggested in this letter, and I think some others, might be answered in pamphlet form, if the material was once collected, and if there was a centre at which it was known all information would be welcome. On some points a form resembling the census paper, would discover a great deal of good material. Perhaps some local secretary will give the latter suggestion a trial in the Students' Association?

Yours faithfully,

Jan. 22, 1894.   K. D. COTES.

Celebrities and their College Rooms at the Universities.

DEAR SIR,—As a visitor to both Oxford and Cambridge Summer Meetings of 1891, 1892, and 1893, I have been much struck with the difficulty there is in ascertaining where to find the rooms in the Colleges that have been occupied by our celebrated men. The desire to do so is surely a natural one. Let me give an instance. While attending a course of lectures on Thackeray at Cambridge this summer, I inquired in vain as to the situation of his rooms at Trinity College; there was uncertainty also about those of Hallam and Tennyson. The doubt was even suggested whether Tennyson had had rooms in College at all, but had not lodged in Sidney Sussex Street. At St. John's College the same thing happened with regard to Wordsworth's rooms; they were unknown by the tutor of whom the question was asked. He pointed out the window of Kirke White's room, and I might say, in passing, who now cares for Kirke White? At Queen's College for a wonder, the gate porter *did* know the Erasmus tower. I cite these instances because they are fresh in my memory; but the same thing is to be observed in the Oxford Colleges.

Does it not seem a pity that small tablets should not be placed over the doors, or at least a book of record kept at the porters' lodges? Many students come up to the Universities full of reverence for the great names that are associated throughout generations with their history; and it has a curiously chilling effect to find those names apparently less-cherished there than could have been thought possible. Surely it is not *only* a sentimental wish to see with one's own eyes the walls that have surrounded the great thinkers, poets, or writers of our own and past days? To be able to say 'here he must have stood—on this he must have looked!' One can even imagine that to a young fellow coming up for the first time to College, and finding himself inhabiting the same rooms where has dwelt some scholar of world-wide fame, it would act as an incentive to intellectual effort and noble living. But men, possibly, are not so open to such influences as women would be.

It can hardly be a question of expense with College authorities that they do not follow the Kyrle Society's example in London. Our great men are not so numerous. Can it be that Alma Mater is not so proud of her best sons as we should expect? Will she not do this honour to men who are *her* honour? Whether long dead, or still living, such men are our national possession, our national pride; and it should therefore be of national interest to cherish all that may help to keep alive in our memories their noble thoughts, their great deeds.

I am, Sir,

Yours truly,

A Summer Meeting Student.

.˙.

A Workman's View of University Extension.

Sir,—I notice in the *Gazette* for November a record of the work done in Bedford, both before and during the present course of lectures; and as the first six lectures have now been given, I should like to give my own impressions as to their usefulness to myself personally, and also to my brother artisans, who have been good enough to give me their opinion. And first, I wish to say, that in Mr. Graham Wallas we have a lecturer who is all that can be desired, never dry or uninteresting, which is a very important point to us working men, who have to be early risers, and who are not yet in possession of an eight hour day.

The lectures themselves have been very interesting and also very useful, especially to some of us who are trying to be of some use to our fellow working men, and we feel that it is a great privilege that we should be able to enjoy advantages in the way of mental culture, which our fathers never dreamed of.

The time has come when we may aspire to positions of trust on our public bodies, but it is manifest that we shall need the help of the University lectures, and classes, if we are to fit ourselves for these positions. But if we working men are to attend either lectures or classes, they must not be held in the afternoon; and I am glad that evening meetings have been adopted by the Bedford centre, and also a number of books lent by friends interested in the movement, although I regret that personally I have not been able to make so much use of them as I should have liked, owing to the fact that my hands are already full of other work. Still I have found them very useful, and hope that others of my class may have been able to give more time to them than I have found it possible to do. Some of my friends think that the number of working men, who have attended the lectures, has been quite as large as could be expected, but in my opinion there is great need of improvement in this direction.

J. Hull,

Member of the Bedford Board of Guardians.

36 Russell Street, Bedford.

REDUCED RAILWAY FARES FOR STUDENTS.

In Mr. Bennion's Report is an interesting record of negotiations between the Technical Education Committee of the Lancashire County Council and the various Lancashire Railway Companies, with the object of obtaining reduced railway fares for students. It appears that the only reduction hitherto granted by the companies to students is the issue of contract tickets to scholars and apprentices under eighteen years of age, at one-half the ordinary rate. In view of the fact that the London, Brighton and South Coast, and the London, Chatham and Dover Railway Companies give considerable advantages to students attending the Crystal Palace Schools of Art, Science and Literature, a deputation of the committee was present at the General Conference of Railway Managers in Feb. 1892, to urge that similar concessions should be made by other companies. It is to be regretted, however, that at the next meeting of the Managers' Conference it was considered 'undesirable to agree to the propositions made' by the Technical Education Committee. Is it altogether vain to hope that before long the railway companies will reconsider their decision, and offer special facilities not only to bona fide students, but to lecturers and other travelling teachers? If so, the difficulties in the way of organizing technical instruction and Extension lectures will be materially lessened, and it is hardly likely that the companies will suffer financial loss by their concession.

UNIVERSITY EXTENSION IN CORNWALL.

Important Action of the County Council.

During the last few months an important petition has been widely circulated in Cornwall and has been endorsed by many of the leading residents in the County. The petition runs as follows:—

To the Chairman and Members of The Technical Instruction Committee of the Cornwall County Council.

Gentlemen,—We, the undersigned, respectfully request to lay the following points before your Committee—

I. The Oxford University Extension movement has been at work in Cornwall for seven years.

II. During this time (*a*) 2,689 students have attended the lectures. (*b*) The classes held after the lectures have been well attended. This year, 1893, in some cases the whole of the audience, and in all cases a very large proportion stayed to the classes. (*c*) The pass standard of examinations is the same as that required of students at the Universities who enter for the degrees, and the 'distinction' is equivalent to the Oxford standard for honours in the College examinations. The Examiners appointed by the University are for the most part those who sit in the honour schools at Oxford. Mr. Lodge (the examiner for five Cornish centres in 1892) reported (1890-1), '*In awarding distinction I have looked for a standard of knowledge and ability that would do credit to a candidate in the honour schools of the University.*' A large number of candidates have passed, and many with distinction; e.g. in 1892, 52 candidates entered from Cornwall; 4 failed, 34 passed, and 14 passed with distinction.

III. A great feature of the work are the Students' Associations, which are guilds of Extension students working together before, during, and after the lectures, under the presidency of some one from the district most qualified to direct them. To take a most encouraging instance. The Camborne Students' Association, after the lectures in the Autumn of 1892 met 20 times, reading papers on the following subjects [1], in pursuance of the course of study laid down in the lectures, 'The Making of the English Empire.' An August 11 they prepared for the ensuing course, 'The History of English Social Life,' by reading and discussing papers, &c. The papers read were:—(1) The life and customs of our Anglo-Saxon Forefathers; (2) Invasion of Britain contrasted with the invasions of the rest of the Empire; (3) Home Life of the Early English; (4) Bede; (5) Norman Conquest; (6) Feudal System; (7) Growth of the English Parliament; (8) Origin and Development of the University of Oxford; (9) Domesday Book; (10) Coming of the Friars; (11) Chaucer; (12) Wycliffe. The association numbers 50 members (half of whom are honorary), and the members attending the meeting immediately preceding the first lecture was 36, and the average number attending in preparation for the lectures was 25.

IV. The lecturer prepares a printed syllabus, showing the course of the lectures, and gives a list of books he recommends, with prices and publishers. At the end of the lectures a class is held, and questions are set. In the intervals between the lectures, the Students' Association meets to discuss the questions; the lecturer corrects and marks the papers, and those passages and answers which he marks 'good' are read out at the next Students' Association, and papers are interchanged, not only between the members, but between one centre and another. The number of papers in the Autumn of 1892 was about 60 a week.

The secretaries of the South-Western Association would represent—(1) That long courses of lectures would be far more advantageous, but that they cannot be given owing to paucity of funds. (2) That the subject has to be varied each year, so as to secure popularity rather than continuity of study. (3) That the lecturer constantly changes, so that the relations that should exist of friendly interest between lecturer and student are broken as soon as formed. (4) That lectures have to be held in inconvenient rooms (to quote cases in the Autumn of 1893):—(*a*) With sometimes political meetings overhead. (*b*) With

[1] See *Extension Gazette*, April 1893.

rinking or singing in an adjacent hall. (*c*) In rooms too small to accommodate the audience, and with no tables for taking notes. (*d*) That there is no place fixed where the lecturer can meet his students the day after the lecture, and give them the minute instruction, which is unsuitable for a popular lecture.

V. That the subjects of University Extension lectures comprise many of those permitted by the Technical Instruction Acts, viz. ,—(*a*) for general audiences, Commercial Geography, History of Commerce, Economic and Industrial History, Physiography, Chemistry, Botany, Geology, Astronomy, Laws of Health, Art, and Architecture. (*b*) For special audiences, the application of the various sciences to industrial occupations, e. g. Chemistry in its relation to Agriculture, Geology in relation to Mining, &c. A special course of lectures for Cornwall, it is suggested, might be ' Mining, as it affects civilization and population, and in its economic aspect at the present time.'

VI. That lectures on such subjects have already been given, and others arranged for, by the County Councils of Kent, Surrey, and Somerset, and that individual centres have received subsidies from the County Councils of Lancashire, Berkshire, Yorkshire (East and West Riding), Gloucestershire, &c.

VII. That we believe a grant in aid from the County Council would result in the immediate establishment of fresh centres in the County.

We, therefore, respectfully request your Committee to consider the possibility of assisting the University Extension Association with a grant for their work, and also would suggest that an Extension College, as e. g. at Reading, for the whole of Cornwall, with its headquarters where the Council thought most convenient, in connexion with Science and Art, and with subbranches in other towns would be a means of drawing more closely together all the educational advantages of Cornwall, and bringing them in touch with the Universities. We would venture to quote the precedents of Reading and Exeter.

(*Signed*)

J. J. FARRELL, Hon. Sec. Bodmin Centre.
BEATRICE VIVIAN, Hon. Sec. Camborne Centre and Hon. Sec. South-Western Association.
JANETTE CLIFT, Hon. Sec. Falmouth Centre.
Mrs. C. L COWLARD and H. THOMPSON, Hon. Secs. Launceston Centre.
JOHN B. CORNISH, Hon. Sec Penzance Centre.
JOHN STONA, *late* Hon. Sec. Redruth Centre.
MEDLAND STOCKER. Hon. Sec. St. Austell Centre.
A. J. WORLLEDGE, Hon. Sec. Truro Centre.
KENELM D. COTES, M.A., Oxford University Extension Lecturer (Cornwall District, 1892 and 1893).

Among those who have appended their signatures to the petition, as showing their sympathy with its requests, are the Bishop of Truro, the Archdeacons of Cornwall and of Bodmin, and twenty-two others of the leading Clergymen and Nonconformist Ministers in Cornwall ; Mr. Leonard Courtney, Mr. T. P. Bolitho, Mr. Conybeare, Mr. Owen, Mr. Williams and Mr. Cavendish-Bentinck, who are all members for Cornish constituencies ; Lord Robartes, Lord Kingsale, and thirty-four other members of the County Council ; Lord St. Germans, and fifty-four other magistrates ; representative members of the leading county societies, including Mr. Howard Fox of Falmouth and others ; leading representatives of the Science and Art classes at Camborne, Falmouth, and Penzance ; thirty-two leading members of educational institutions in the county, as well as a number of others.

We have never seen a more numerously signed or representative petition to a public body in support of University Extension work, and thanks are due to Mr. K. D. Cotes, on whom has devolved the greater part of the labour of procuring the signatures.

On Thursday, January 18, the Technical Instruction Committee of the County Council met at Truro and considered the petition. The following report of the proceedings appears in the *Western Morning News* :—

The Chairman said they must give very careful consideration to a memorial so influentially signed as this was, and must be prepared to pay considerable deference to the views expressed

therein. At the same time they should be very cautious before they adopted all its recommendations. They had had some experience in Cornwall of the University Extension movement, and while considerable advantage had been gained, the result was not completely satisfactory in every place. Unless they were careful they might repeat the mistakes apparently made by other counties in relation to this work. He had a letter from the Devon Technical Education Committee. In that county they entered most heartily into the adoption of the scheme in 1891, and employed lecturers at a very large cost. In fact, about seventy courses of lectures were delivered in that year all over Devonshire. The result was not satisfactory, for it was not considered that the instruction given by the lecturers was suitable for the industrial classes, whose education in the rural neighbourhoods is not of a very high standard. A letter from the organizing secretary of the Somersetshire committee was a little more encouraging, but the experience there showed that six courses were more successful than the twelve course lectures. As to the last clause of the memorial, he was afraid they could not entertain the idea of a college. They were situated differently to Reading, where there were plenty of liberal subscribers to such an object. There were other ways of assisting the movement— by employing a lecturer entirely, or subsidizing the various centres, and, perhaps, they would hardly find which was best adapted for the county until they had tried one or the other.

Mr. G. J. Smith would like an expression of opinion as regards the utilization of the opportunities afforded by these courses on the part of the artisan industrial population. While it was not specifically stipulated that the fund was to be employed for the benefit of one particular class, yet it was their desire to help those who most required help. He believed there was widespread uncertainty as to what extent these advantages were embraced. In the Camborne district, owing to the initiative of the late Mr. Basset, a considerable number of miners had attended.

Mr. Vivian said many miners and others had attended the Camborne classes, mainly owing, perhaps, to the inducement of prizes offered by Mr. Basset and other gentlemen.

Mr. Grylls said their object should be to help those who could not help themselves. By educating these classes they would be conferring benefit on the country generally.—Mr. Dobell favoured the dissemination of information among the industrial classes more particularly.—Mr. Ray thought that perhaps the fee charged at the lectures had prevented many from attending.

The Chairman thought if they were to make grants to centres as to which they were satisfied that a fair proportion of cost would be contributed therefrom they could encourage the movement without incurring any serious risk.—Mr. Davis wanted to know whether the areas of the centres would be extended consequent upon the granting the subsidies.—The Chairman : Inasmuch as the centres themselves would contribute a larger sum than we, they would decide that.—Mr. Smith said that to subsidize existing centres was obviously the easiest way out of the difficulty. But they must be sure, if possible, that the money they gave was expended in additional effort.

On the motion of Mr. Ray, seconded by Mr. Vivian, it was resolved ' That this committee recommends that a sum not exceeding £250 be devoted during the ensuing year for the purpose of assisting the University Extension movement in the county, and that a sub-committee be appointed to consult with the Oxford University Delegacy and local committees as to the best way of carrying out the scheme, subject to the approval of this committee and the Council.'—This was carried.

The same journal the next day commented on the proceedings of the Technical Instruction Committee in the following terms :—

On Thursday the Committee received an important memorial with reference to University Extension. It was most influentially supported. The signatories included all the members of Parliament for the county, over thirty members of the County Council, the Bishop, and numerous ministers of all denominations, besides many other chief residents of the county. The petitioners requested the County Council to assist the University Extension movement by grants of money, and a further suggestion was made that an Extension College should be established, as has been done at Reading. The committee would have shown very considerable want of wisdom had they at once adopted all these suggestions. University Extension in the West of England has not yet proved that conspicuous success which would justify the Council in at present founding an Extension College. The idea is one for the future. Its adoption must depend upon the results of more tentative efforts. The Committee acted, we doubt not, in accordance with the wishes of most educated people in Cornwall, when they decided to grant £250 during the present year for the assistance of the University Extension movement in the county. A year hence it will be possible to judge whether this movement merits further support from the county funds. We should be sorry to say that in the past the movement in Cornwall has not met with any success, in reference to the Camborne district such a statement would certainly be contrary to the facts. In some quarters the results have been most encouraging. It must be admitted, however, that it is too early yet to form a definite and ultimate decision such as would have justified the committee in committing the Council to any large expenditure. The memorialists have every reason to be satisfied with the action of the committee, who have provided them with considerable assistance wherewith to develop their work. Their influentially supported suggestion that an Extension College should be established is on record, and can be revived at any future date when the success of University Extension is thought to justify its adoption. When that time comes we trust the success of the movement will be justly measured. It is impossible to accurately gauge the most lasting results by mere figures. The effects of the wide dissemination of knowledge and the promotion of thought are too subtle to be confined within mere statistical statements. Provided those who attend the lectures possess the facility for assimilating knowledge, the indirect results must be incalculable. Their horizon will be widened, a healthy thirst for knowledge created, and self-improvement, from being a lesser martyrdom to the necessities of the time, will become an actual pleasure. It is in its indirect influence that most may be expected from the University Extension movement, and its organizers will be unfairly dealt with if the success of their work is judged solely, or even mainly, by the results shown by the examinations.

A NORWEGIAN ACCOUNT OF UNIVERSITY EXTENSION.

(*Contributed by Miss Olga Hassel of Laurvik.*)

PROFESSOR Dr. J. Mourley Vold's pamphlet on University Extension is grounded on his own impressions formed during his sojourn in England in the summer of 1892, together with what he has learned from books and papers on the subject. Among the latter are: *The Student's Handbook to the University and Colleges of Oxford*, 11th ed., Oxford 1891; *Oxford and Oxford Life* (J. Wells editor), London 1892, and *The Oxford University Extension Gazette*. The writer begins his pamphlet by discussing the relations between the Norwegians and the English. What is it that gives a little people like the Norwegians a right to exist in the history of the world? It is that it should carry out the task that rests on the little peoples. First, that it try to develop its national gifts to the highest possible perfection, so that these will be of significance for the culture of other people. Secondly, that its people adopt all that is best from other nations, thus forming a rallying point for the culture of the world, and, if possible, lead it a step further. Isolation is more dangerous to a small nation than to a great one. We cannot build up Norwegian culture by shutting ourselves up in a mountain parish. We are not following the intellectual work of our time, especially that which is being done in England, as fully as we should. We are indebted to Germany for almost the whole of our culture, education, religion, and literature; English is not understood by all cultivated people, and English books are rare with us. Many of our authors are influenced in their

style by Germany and France, and there is among the young literary men an attempt at paradox and brilliancy, which often sounds artificial to Norwegian ears. The short, straightforward, energetic style, which hits the right nail on the head, is very seldom seen with us. The writer goes on to regret that so few Norwegians travel in England, and that it is only a minority who know the modern English authors even by name. He replies to the Norwegian objections of travelling in England point by point. He did not find the food so impossible, nor the draughts from doors and windows so unbearable, and the fog was not seen a single day for two and a half months, not even during the three weeks he stayed in London. He did not think the English inaccessible to foreigners. Certainly, like the philosopher Lotze, they seemed to regard it as their first duty to their neighbour to let him pass undisturbed, but on closer acquaintance with them they are all that is amiable. 'Don't think,' he says, 'that they are only dry matter-of-fact people, and that it is useless to go to England to improve in intelligence. It is only a Norwegian misconception. The English peculiarity is their desire to bring theory into practice, so that the practical life becomes law-directed and intelligent, and to bring practice into theory. The English understand the art of knitting together life and theory. If private and public education can be learned, then England is one of the first places to go to. Their ideals are the Norwegian ideals—love of home, of nature, of individual, social, and political liberty. At the same time the German culture ought of course in future to be of great significance to us. The Germans' depth of thought and feeling gives them a great power in intellectual life even if their often complicated and diffuse style perplex some and terrify others. We must learn from all nations, but our intellectual connexion with England should be more intense. The Englishmen's clear practical style seasoned with humour, their thorough life of culture, ought to be of great importance for us.'

Then the professor gives a survey of the organization and method of the Universities of Oxford and Cambridge. He prizes the ideal thought, the impartial judgement, the tolerant perception of opposite opinions and the noble life, which, besides scientific education, the English University system strives to inculcate. 'Even if the English University system,' he says, 'is not so well fitted to create learned men in the special sense of the word (students of history, for instance, are not accustomed to the reading of manuscript, great theses are seldom composed by the students), and granting that England has not produced the infinity of learned special theses, which overflow Germany (many of them of significance, but to be sure, some also of rather small scientific value), yet, on the other hand, England is also, as far as I can understand, free from a proletariat of breadless academics, of superfluous students, unsuccessful in the struggle for existence.'

After treating of the Universities, Dr. Vold gives a splendid view of the University Extension, its past, present, and future. 'I don't think,' he urges, 'that the popularizing of science for a great multitude needs to be superficial. The versatile method of the University Extension system seems to me to embrace a certain guarantee for thoroughness, and besides—what is not the least result of the movement—University Extension is of vital social importance, it has an elevating effect on the working classes, and causes them to work together with others of their fellow-citizens for ideal aims. They feel themselves one part of a great culture-society.' Then he treats more fully of the Oxford University Extension. He gives a report and general review of the fifth Summer Meeting in Oxford, with which he was much pleased. After referring to many of the lecturers and other workers engaged in the meeting, he says: 'If you ask me for my general impression of the meeting, I can only exclaim: What attention, what enthusiasm during the lectures, what energy in the work, what interest, humour, and tolerance in discussions, what gaiety in the conversations and on the excursions. Briefly; what life, what health and vivacity! I should be tempted to compare the meeting with an old Greek festival.'

~ORTS FROM THE CENTRES.

ASHTON-UNDER-LYNE.—The attendance at the first lectures of the first courses of Oxford Extension lectures given in this town since 1886 was excellent. The subject of the afternoon lectures is the 'Age of Elizabeth,' that of the evening course the 'Making of England.'

BEDFORD.—At the end of the Autumn half-course of lectures, our local committee had to face financial difficulties in the form of a probable deficit to be met next Easter, owing to the low price fixed for tickets for the 'English Citizen' course. Happily our prospects have now been improved by a donation of £10 kindly sent by the Duke of Bedford to our treasurer; and also by the hope of valuable results from a public meeting and social gathering of students and others to be held at 8 p.m. on Saturday, January 27. Mr. Sadler and Mr. Graham Wallas, our lecturer, have kindly promised to speak that evening on the subject of 'University Extension' in general, and its special value in the education of the citizen. The Mayor of Bedford has consented to preside during the first part of the meeting, and after 9 p.m. its character will be 'social,' and a musical programme is being arranged, chiefly by the exertions of members of the Students' Association and their friends. Our first lecture for the Spring term was given on Tuesday, Jan. 20.—E. BLAKE, *Hon. Sec. of Students' Association.*

BOURNEMOUTH.—The report of this centre for last year has recently been issued, and it is noteworthy that the attempt of the committee to interest the working people of Bournemouth in the lectures has been successful owing largely to the co-operation of the Trades' Council with the committee. The evening lectures were delivered in the east end of the town, the average attendance was more than doubled; at one lecture the audience numbering 160. Both the afternoon and evening courses have recommenced successfully.

CARLISLE.—A very successful course of six afternoon lectures was given at this centre in the autumn term by Miss H. M. Woolley. The lectures were well delivered, and were full of thought and originality—those on 'Maud,' 'In Memoriam,' and the 'Dramas' being especially enjoyed. The audience showed its appreciation of Miss Woolley's ability by asking the committee to arrange for an extra lecture, which was numerously attended and listened to with the greatest interest. In the Spring term an evening course of six lectures on 'Electricity' will be given by Mr. H. J. R. Murray, M.A.—M. J. FERGUSON, *Hon. Sec.*

CLEVEDON.—At the conclusion of Mr. Marriott's course on 'Europe since Waterloo' a vote of thanks was accorded to him, the proposer remarking that the lectures had been greatly valued for their clearness and force. The students had been stimulated to read history, which was the chief object of the lectures.

EDGBASTON.— Our centre has been highly favoured this season, for besides enjoying the privilege of an exceptionally interesting course of lectures from Mr. Mackinder on the 'Growth of European Nations,' Mr. Sadler kindly responded to the invitation of the Ladies' Association for Useful Work, and gave a lecture on Oxford, on January 8, at the Central Hall. The chair was taken by Mr. W. Kenrick, M.P., and many members of the Edgbaston and Birmingham centres were present, all ticket-holders for the adult schools lecture course being invited to attend the lecture, free of charge. The inclemency of the weather prevented the audience being as large as it should have been, and unfortunately no representative of Mason College, or the Midland Institute, was able to be present, owing to other engagements and absence from home. Mr. Mackinder's afternoon course recommenced on Tuesday, Jan. 16, when, after a masterly description of the differences in the Eastern and Western Empire, he proceeded to review the part played by the Saracens in European history, and traced some of the causes which have resulted in the legacy to the modern world of the unhappy 'Eastern Question.' The Students' Association, which was formed last year, on Mr. Marriott's suggestion, is becoming a valuable adjunct to the lectures, and has been the means of drawing together a large band of young students. The essays, this season, more than keep up in number and quality the former level reached at this centre.—PHŒBE TIMMINS, *Hon. Sec.*

EVESHAM.—A very successful conversazione was held here, on January 10, to inaugurate Mr. Marriott's course of lectures. During the proceedings the chairman of the lecture committee, Mr. William Smith, gave an address, in which he referred to the great services which had been rendered to the cause of higher education by the lamented Mr. Herbert New. A most interesting address was subsequently delivered by Mr. Marriott on the history and aims of the University Extension movement. He gave a comprehensive survey of University history during the last hundred years, and showed the relations to one another of the different parts of the University Extension movement.

GRIMSBY.—The University Extension movement has been

attempted here before and good work has been done, but owing to the expense of weekly lectures it was given up. The course, just ended, on 'Economics and Social Questions,' with Mr. Hewins as lecturer, has been a success in every way; the audiences have been larger. Mr. Hewins has done admirably, and the committee have very nearly made ends meet. Discussions on the previous lectures have been held in the intervening weeks; these have helped more than anything to develop the aims of the movement. The prospects for the next course are bright.

ILKLEY (Evening).—At the close of our last course of lectures there remained a deficit of £32; we obtained £22 by donations, and finding a difficulty in raising the remainder, Mr. Carus-Wilson, who has given two courses of lectures at this centre, suggested that a concert should be given in aid of the funds The committee was in some doubt as to the financial result; but on Mr. Carus-Wilson kindly offering to come over and to take part himself, the suggestion was adopted, and the concert took place on December 2; and with the assistance of local friends interested in the work it was a complete success, and the debt is entirely cleared off. We regret that owing to the adverse decision of the W. R. County Council the proposed course of lectures on 'Astronomy' will not be given; the committee however hope to resume the work at an early date.—F. BROADBENT MUFF, *Hon. Local Sec.*

ILKLEY (afternoon).—We had a course of six lectures on Tennyson by Mr. Boas, and six on Browning by Mr. Lang, in the autumn of 1893. An examination was held on Dec. 18, when ten students sat and all passed, four with distinction. The lectures have been thoroughly enjoyed by an average audience of 160, and the committee wish they could report a greater number of writers for the weekly essays. Ten is a very small number out of 160, but we hope the lecturers do not think they see all the results of their work in the few papers sent in. We know that many are deeply interested and read thoughtfully who never come under the lecturer's notice at all, and the influence of their work is far more wide-spreading than they can have any idea of from what they actually see. It seems rather strange that both the lecturer and the examiner reported more favourably of the work done on Browning's poems than that on Tennyson's. But the reason is not far to seek. The students thought they had some tough work before them in Browning, and dived into him with considerable zeal. The reading of Tennyson was regarded as a recreation in the alternate weeks, and they only skimmed the surface instead of searching the hidden depths. It is not necessary for us to say a word about our lecturers; they are too well known and highly valued to need any commendation from us. We feel we have been a highly-favoured centre.—EMILY DALE, *Hon. Sec.*

LOUTH.—On December 14 Mr. C. Carus-Wilson concluded a most excellent series of six fortnightly lectures on 'Geology.' The local committee had some doubts as to the probable popularity of the subject, but the good average attendance at the lectures and the great interest shown in the subject most fully justified their selection. The success of the course was undoubtedly due to the great ability and fluency of the lecturer. The lectures were rendered (if possible) more attractive by the lime-light lantern slides which were exceedingly good, the lantern being most efficiently manipulated by Mr. S. F. Clarke. The number of papers written during the course was regrettably small, but it is highly gratifying to be able to report that all the students who entered for the examination passed—three 'with distinction' and four 'satisfying the examiner,' and the report of the examiner was also very satisfactory. The local committee offered a scholarship of £3 for adults, and a similar one for those under 21 years of age, to enable the student gaining the scholarship to attend the Oxford Summer Meeting; also three prizes, open to all students, of books to the value of £1, 15s., and 10s. Those who had the pleasure of attending the lectures look forward to the Autumn of this year, when it is hoped that Mr. Carus-Wilson will be able to arrange to take the second part of his syllabus on 'Geology,' and also to arrange for several excursions in the district, which is by no means devoid of interest to geological students. The local committee have arranged for a course of six fortnightly lectures by Mr. F. S. Boas on 'Tennyson,' to commence on January 23 —PHILIP ALLISON, *Hon. Sec.*

OXFORD.—At the invitation of Mr. and Mrs. J. Estlin Carpenter and Miss M. S. Beard, a large number of the students who have been attending lectures at this centre and others interested in the movement, assembled at Manchester College on Friday, January 12, to meet Mr. Graham Wallas and the local committee. There was a large gathering representing all sides of educational work in the City and University. During the evening short speeches were delivered by Mr. Wallas, Mr. Wells, Mr. Burch, Mr. Sadler, and Mr. Estlin Carpenter, the latter suggesting that a Students' Association should be formed in connexion with the centre. A most enjoyable evening was spent, music being contributed by Miss Liddell and Mr. Ely. At the first lecture of Mr. Graham Wallas's course on the following Thursday, it was unanimously agreed to form a Students' Association.

PRESTWICH.—The committee are glad to find that in this centre at the end of five years work, there is no diminution in the numbers of our audiences. In 1888, when University Extension was a novelty in this district, we sold 195 tickets; now in 1893 we have sold 222 tickets, in spite of two other centres having sprung up close at hand. This is most encouraging, although our financial position continues to be bad. The lectures have only paid the expenses once, in 1889, and we have come to the conclusion that they cannot be made to pay here. However, we shall continue them with the help of subscriptions.—HENRY W. FRESTON, *Hon. Sec.*

RIPON.—At the end of Mr. Hudson Shaw's course on ' Florentine History,' the Dean of Ripon, who presided, expressed the great delight with which he and the rest of the audience had listened to Mr. Shaw's valuable and inspiring lectures.

WELLINGTON (Somerset).—Mr. Niblett's course of lectures on Soils, Plants, and Animals, has been attended by a small but most interested audience, almost exclusively farmers and gardeners, nearly all of whom attended the whole course.

WEST BRIGHTON.—On Wednesday, January 10, a meeting was held in the banqueting room of the Hove Town Hall to inaugurate the first course of *Evening* Extension lectures in this centre, Mr. Sadler visiting us for this purpose. The room, which is somewhat limited in size, was crowded to overflowing with an audience of over 300 persons, many only finding standing room. The chair was taken by Mr. Fisher, who opened the meeting, and who was followed by two local speakers, Mr. H. R. Knipe, a prominent member of the County Council, and Mr. James Kelly, a working man. Mr. Sadler then gave an address on Oxford, illustrated by lantern slides. He sketched the history of Oxford and of the University with reference to its great men, and some of the religious and educational movements which have proceeded from it, and concluded by alluding to the aims of University Extension teaching, and the lines of study which would be followed at the forthcoming Summer Meeting. The large majority of the audience consisted of persons who had not attended afternoon courses; and as the aim of the meeting was to arouse an interest amongst a new class, we regard this as a hopeful sign, and trust that a large number of fresh students may be added through the evening course.—M. F. BASDEN, *Hon. Sec.*

. ' .

From copies of the local newspapers forwarded to us, we learn that at—

CHARD.—The popularity of Dr. Wade's lectures has been proved by the large and regular attendance during the course, and by the hearty vote of thanks to the lecturer, proposed by the Rev. C. F. Wimberley and Mr. Young. General regret was expressed that there seemed little prospect of further lectures from Dr. Wade at the present.

ILMINSTER.—The average number of persons who attended Dr. Wade's lectures during the past term has been 63. Although perhaps more persons might have been expected to be present, the lectures were followed with the greatest interest, and hopes were expressed that the lecturer will again visit Ilminster next year.

TAUNTON.—Dr. C. H. Wade's lectures on the ' Beginnings and Prevention of Disease,' which have been delivered in connexion with the Technical Instruction Committee of the County Council, have proved full of interest and value. The attendance was not so large as might have been expected, but those who were present learnt much from the clear and attractive style of the lecturer. The lectures are to be continued in the Spring.

THE EXTENSION OF UNIVERSITY TEACHING AMONG WORKING-MEN'S SOCIETIES.

WE have pleasure in stating that the Oxford Delegacy has received an offer of £100 to encourage University Extension teaching in connexion with the societies of working-men. During the last month a further contribution of £10 has been received for the same purpose, and the fund, which includes the subscriptions paid at the Summer Meeting of 1892, now stands at £127. The question how to make the best use of this fund is now receiving the attention of the Delegacy.

WILL DEMOCRACY DESTROY UNIVERSITIES?

' THE danger,' says Professor Laurie, in an article entitled ' The University and the People ; and the University of the Future,' which is published in the Co-operative Wholesale Societies' Annual for 1894, ' to which the Universities of the future are exposed is interference with their liberty of thought and government on the part of the democracy. Slow to apprehend remote issues, and swayed by the impulse of the moment, the people may be intolerant of abstract study, and may also resent teaching which runs counter to their own temporary convictions and supposed interests. To obviate this, we can only look to the general diffusion of education, and to the action of the Universities themselves in casting aside all narrow conceptions of their duties to the public.'

Almost at the very time that this article made its appearance, Mr. Fletcher, the editor of the *Daily Chronicle*, which may be regarded as the organ of advanced democracy in England, told a large gathering of London teachers that ' no teacher need regret the growing power of democracy, because democrats believe in education, favour education, insist upon education, and hold the educator in the honour to which he is entitled.' It is satisfactory that in England the most active leaders of the democratic movement are among the warmest friends of higher education. The suspicion indeed that democracy might be hostile to education seems to have grown, partly out of contempt for popular ignorance and the form of government which the multitude is supposed to affect ; and secondly, from the undoubted fact that the Democratic, as distinguished from the Republican, party in America has certainly grudged expenditure on higher teaching. But it is probable that a fundamental change has come over popular ideas in regard to education during the last ten years. It is now a common-place to admit that the economic welfare of an individual very largely depends on his or her intellectual and moral qualities, and that the latter are influenced not a little by the environment in which the childhood of the individual was spent. In other words, in each human character there is a wide range of potentialities for good and evil, and which of these are to be educed depends very largely on the particular kind of training received by the child. It would appear therefore that democracy is likely to be profuse in its expenditure on education, provided that the latter is made accessible on reasonable terms to all who are fully qualified to profit by it.

Pains however must be taken to familiarize the people with the work of the organs of higher education. Unless we assiduously set ourselves to work to prove that the Universities are necessary to the continuance and development of higher knowledge, and that the latter is the necessary matrix for further technical and industrial discoveries and social improvements, we cannot expect the masses of the people to understand by the light of nature that of all forms of government a democracy has most to gain from higher education, and most to lose by its neglect.

It seems to us therefore that Professor Laurie is wise in his argument that the Universities should maintain their connexion with the life of the people by the system of University Extension teaching. He says ' that in this way, the University of the future will extend its benefits and consequent influence, while its Extension work by bringing the Universities into contact with the people will stimulate their vitality.'

University Extension, accordingly, is one of the means by which public opinion can be familiarized with the real drift, value, and social import of the higher ranges of University work. We ourselves have no doubt that the alliance between the Universities and the masses of the people, which is the brightest mark of Oxford history in the thirteenth and fourteenth centuries, was no accident, but arose from mutual perception of reciprocal need. The people need the Universities because the latter widen for them the horizon of knowledge, of freedom, and of power. The Universities need the people because no great literary or scientific work can be done except that which is inspired by an unselfish motive, and in many departments of human learning no fruitful or accurate work can be accomplished without intimate acquaintance with the needs and conditions of common life.

We conclude, therefore, that the Universities have nothing to fear from democracy, provided that they are true to the ideal of plain living and high thinking; that they include in their curriculum of studies the whole range of subjects with which contemporary thought is seriously grappling; and that they vigorously familiarize the public mind with the aims and methods of University work by means of an elastic system of University Extension teaching.

UNIVERSITY EXTENSION IN THE ISLE OF WIGHT.

Liberal Guarantee of £200.

IT is announced that a resident in the Isle of Wight has generously guaranteed £200 in order to secure combination of effort and continuity of work in the centres for University Extension teaching in the Isle of Wight. The guarantee has already resulted in an influential meeting of delegates from the three centres in the Isle of Wight, at which it was agreed that steps should be taken to form a joint committee to promote unity of effort. We hope that the labours of this joint committee may result not only in the strengthening of the existing centres, but in the formation of new ones; in the provision of special teaching for the more advanced students at each centre; and in the offer of scholarships to enable students to avail themselves of the educational advantages of the Summer Meetings.

THE UNITY OF THE TEACHING PROFESSION.

THE following passages which appeared in a recent article in the *Schoolmaster*, will be of interest to many workers in University Extension :—

The master-current in educational matters to-day makes for professional unity, to a degree never seen before in the history of Education in England and Wales. It is worth while to contemplate awhile this unifying and solidifying movement; it is worth while for even the youngest and most infallible among us, and it is equally worth while for the oldest and most stagnatory (so to speak). And calm observers of both classes must agree that the prevailing drift runs in the direction of completer unity, and towards the obliteration of the sandbanks that have raised between teachers sharp distinctions and separative bars There are backward swirls, no doubt; but the tide is rising towards its flood, and ' Mrs. Partington' will oppose her mop in vain.

For many a year the various classes of teachers in this country misunderstood each other. Some of them thought that the others could not teach, and did not even care to know how to teach; others of them thought that the teachers who knew how to teach knew little or nothing of the subjects they taught. The teacher in holy orders looked askance at the layman teacher; often the grammar-schoolmaster regarded the 'elementary' schoolmaster as a good deal of an ignoramus and not a little of a boor. These kindly feelings were reciprocated in one way or another, and the result was disunion, mutual jealousy, and a want of that professional feeling which had so long ago united the professors of medicine or of law. Chaotic disorganization of education, public and private, furthered this state of things, and retained the profession at loggerheads. Serene and apart in their Olympus sate the dignitaries of the Universities, and only a little lower were enstalled the masters of the great Public Schools, by Act of Parliament so-called. Aiding and abetting this disunion and misunderstanding was that lack of public interest and appreciation in educational matters which England and Wales manifested for so long. It would be too long a story now to tell how this condition of things began to be, and continued to be, affected for the

better; it is sufficient to say that signs are plentiful that ' the old order changeth.' A floating straw will show when the tide begins to turn, and there can be no doubt that the straws are floating forward now.

We are not yet in the full flow of the current. There are still dignitaries of the higher education who sedulously hold aloof from this movement, and there are teachers in humbler schools who do not yet recognize the movement as they should do in its meaning and its force. The educational Rome will not be built in a day, but the materials are accumulated, and the foundations are being ' well and truly laid.' The master-current in the educational world of the present time is shown by the growth of a mutual esteem and a desire for co-operation which exist among the more statesman-like and philosophic leading teachers in every branch of the work. Contact and acquaintance have brought about a truer appreciation. . The stand-off attitude and suspicious scrutiny with which various classes of the profession were wont so long to regard each other, are passing away. What has been described as 'a supercilious attitude on the one part, and a supersensitive feeling on the other,' is gradually dying out from among us. It is possible, now-a-days, to say ' us' of the teachers in every efficient kind of college and school. Things have moved so rapidly during the past fifteen months, that, although there are still many teachers in each class of educational institution who maintain the old separative feeling, these no longer represent the majority or the better portions of the profession. *Rapport et rapprochement* have more than begun to exist. One sees them in the catholic polity of the Teachers' Guild; one sees them in the public action or utterances of . . . One sees them also in articles published in the educational press, and not least, we venture to claim, in the articles which we ourselves have addressed to the consideration of the question. One saw them in the Conference of Educational Authorities which recently met at Oxford. One sees them, again, in the friendly reception which Oxford is to give to the primary teachers who assemble in the beautiful city of ' dreaming spires' next Easter. One sees them, again, in the discussions which have taken place, here, there, and everywhere, concerning the State and Municipal Organization of Secondary Education.

A WARNING FROM AUSTRALIA.

THE old controversy of the six-lecture versus the twelve-lecture course is raging in Australia. In the columns of our contemporary, the *Melbourne University Extension Journal*, it has become in part mixed up with a secondary dispute, the chief point of which is contained in the following sentence appearing in its December issue: ' It was only when the University of Oxford declared for the shorter course of six lectures, as against the longer courses upon which Cambridge insisted, that University Extension entered upon its real prosperity.'

For venturing upon this statement our Melbourne contemporary has got into hot water but, as we think, unjustly. It appears to us beyond dispute that the revival of the Oxford branch of the movement was at any rate a powerful cause of the marked growth of public interest in University Extension which has taken place between the year 1888 and the present time. We are far from arrogating to ourselves the sole credit for this increase of the public importance of the work. But the policy of short courses was an essential feature of the new departure from Oxford. It was essential because, without it, Oxford could never have spread the work into the large number of towns which had been previously untouched by the system. And the increased magnitude of the operations of the movement, the simple fact that it began to influence so largely an increased part of English life, were among the chief reasons why it came to enjoy so much larger a measure of public support as to enable it to claim, from the first, financial recognition from the County Councils.

But the Melbourne *Journal* proceeds to deal at greater length with the more important question of principle, which underlies the dispute about short courses. So suggestive a comment on a matter of fundamental importance to University Extension deserves careful consideration on our part, and we therefore print it *in extenso*.

The real question at issue is dealt with by a certain trite saying about a half-loaf. Our English critics hardly appreciate the necessity there is in Australia of *creating* an audience. We have no Gilchrist Trust, with its admirable series of lectures, familiarizing our public with the methods and scope of lecture teaching. All that has been known in Australia, until the advent of University Extension, was the single lecture, generally of a popular and amusing, rather than directly instructive, character. The taste for this form of amusement, and the consequent confusion of educational lectures in series with disconnected lectures whose aim is simple to amuse, we have still to combat. It is one of our difficulties; and peculiarly the difficulty which confronts us in dealing with the working classes. Our public is still timid, and at the outset absolutely refused to commit itself to an experiment on so large a scale as a course of twelve lectures. But that feeling is passing away; and, thanks to the system we have followed,—wisely followed as we still venture to think,—there is a steady growth in the number of those who, familiar now with what lectures, and Extension lectures in particular, involve, are increasingly desirous of a more protracted and more detailed study of a single subject. This is markedly shown in some of the reports from local centres during the year. In a new country education must start well down in the scale, otherwise it would be a mere top-dressing of ground which had never been broken in.

While we therefore have to bend all our energies to make our tuition more thorough, avoiding a popular superficiality, one of the dangers which seems to us to threaten University Extension in England is of the opposite character. It is the danger of scholasticism. System is replacing the old missionary spirit with which Extension began. Twenty years have borne their fruit. A class of students has been brought together who will find their natural home, not in the Extension lecture-room, but in the so-called Extension College. University Extension is even becoming a cheap road to a University degree; its examinations and certificates are to be accepted in lieu of those of the Education Department. All this is excellent in its way. But having lifted one section of the community into a position where they can care for themselves, University Extension must resume its missionary dress, and seek in a lower grade for another class to be lifted. It must go back to the people.

Even in a centre which has been some time established there are still two classes in the audience, neither of whom can be favoured to the exclusion or neglect of the other. It has always been the boast of University Extension that it is catholic in method and in spirit; it offers something for all, not for one sex, or one age, or one temper; and if we rightly understand its scope, its moral strength rests on the bringing into contact of various types of intellectual life and aspiration such as may be found in a general audience. There are those, especially among the younger members of a centre, who may be called 'earnest students,' of whom 'sustained and strenuous work' may be expected, and in whose case the greater the effort demanded in the direction of continuous study the closer will be their attachment to a system of education which offers them facilities for such continuous study. But there is another and even larger class of those who, having gone through in earlier life an educational discipline are left with an educational hunger, which is but another example of 'functional survival.' They have their business, their profession, and in this find sufficient satisfaction of the need for 'sustained and strenuous work'; they have not time for the '*serious*' study' (if we are to use terms in their strictness) of fresh subjects in science, art, or literature. They are attracted to Extension lectures by the prospect of new mental stimuli, of fresh modes of thought and life; they ask, not schooling so much, as suggestiveness and the guidance which can be given by one who has made a speciality of what to them is a pleasant study. Are we to give such a class stones for bread? University Extension is not a method of cram; it is destructive in that it clears away the growth of false reasoning and erring effort; it is constructive less as teaching facts than as teaching principles.

In spite of the old saying that onlookers see most of the game, we are inclined to think that our friends in Melbourne are alarmed without due cause as to the present tendency of the University Extension movement in England. The foundation of the University Extension College at Reading, the development of the work in London and at Exeter, the action of the Education Department in offering to recognize certain certificates, the long discussions which have been lately taking place as to the institution of new certificates and the recognition of affiliated centres, have all no doubt combined to fill the pages of the journals of the University Extension movement with new matter bearing rather on the more highly organized part of the system than on its missionary enterprise. But, for all that, the proportion of highly organized centres, though increasing, is still small, and the great body of the movement still remains in the preparative stage in which stimulus and missionary effort count for more than consolidation and material equipment. But the University Extension movement comprises, both elements. It will be a poor result of all our work if it simply ossifies into a second-rate University system. Equally disappointing on the other hand will it be if years of missionary enthusiasm do not result at centre after centre in permanent foundations and in highly organized effort. In other words, the twelve-lecture system and the six-lecture system are complementary parts of one great whole and are not mutual exclusive policies.

UNIVERSITY EXTENSION IN RHODE ISLAND.

THE President of Brown University has recently issued a report of the progress of Extension work in Providence and other parts of Rhode Island. Dr. Andrews writes in cordial terms of the success of this branch of University work. The number of students, now standing at nineteen hundred, shows a 'substantial and unexpected increase.' Thirty-six courses have been delivered during the year. Teachers, and especially women teachers, constituted a large proportion of the classes, though many business men were also present, as well as young people, who, having been unable to carry their regular education beyond the High School, welcome the system which brings some part of University teaching within their reach. The most popular courses are those in History, English and American literature, Social Science, Botany and Biology. It is believed that this year the city of Pawtucket will start a number of concurrent courses, and require all teachers in the public schools to attend them, and to pass the required examinations. If this step is taken at Pawtucket, it is believed that it will lead to further developments in the public education of the State. Professor Andrews also makes an urgent appeal for the endowment of the University Extension, and pays a deserved tribute to the skill and energy with which Professor Munro has directed the Brown University Extension.

Professor Munro in his own report makes it clear that the average size of the audiences has largely increased during the past year. This is significant, because Brown University has hitherto laid stress on the fact that its Extension work has chiefly been carried on in small classes. Indeed the authorities of Brown University have almost formed the right wing of the University Extension movement in consistently deprecating the educational value of appeals to large audiences. It would seem however that a process of assimilation is taking place between the Brown University Extension and the other branches of the movement. This is as it should be, because the University Extension system must necessarily contain some centres at which large audiences are a sign of educational success, and others at which the regular attendance of small classes is all that can be hoped for. It is satisfactory to note that a sincere desire for study has pervaded nearly all the centres where Brown University Extension work has been carried on.

Professor Munro declares that 'except in the Laboratory courses, the examination is not likely to play a very conspicuous part in University Extension in America. The members of the Laboratory courses are for the most part men and women who are accustomed to examinations. For them the set of questions has no terrors. The same class of people, mostly teachers, take the examinations in the Lecture courses, and almost always pass them with great credit. But the great American public has no desire again to undergo these afflictions of student days. It is quite willing to work, but it does not care to be examined upon that work. Moreover, if examinations were required, it would not be wi.ling to do the work. Examinations therefore do not measure the success of the movement. The large demand made upon the public libraries everywhere, the larger sales of the booksellers, the "class work" do. With these latter tests we are quite satisfied. Examinations can never play the same part here that they do in the English system. Our English cousins are apparently animated by an enthusiasm over "pass cards" that finds no counterpart in the American breast.'

That there is much truth in these remarks every one will admit. It is the indirect, rather than the direct, results of University Extension that are educationally most significant. In fact, if examinations and certificates became, we will not say the *raison d'être* but, the main cause of interest in University Extension, the chief value of the movement as a source of educational stimulus would have been lost. But Professor Munro overlooks the fact that a considerable proportion of the students who in England do best in the examinations, undergo this test, not from any desire to possess a certificate, but because they wish, by the only means in their power, to give practical proof of the standard of attainment reached at University Extension centres. So long as we are challenged to produce examination results in proof of the thoroughness of our Extension work, so long must it be pressed as a matter of duty on the best students to enter for examinations which to them personally are as unnecessary as distasteful. And it is more satisfactory to such students to feel that the standard of the examinations is difficult than if it were an easy matter to obtain distinction in them.

BOOKS ON OUR TABLE.

Meteorology. The Elements of Weather and Climate. By H. N. DICKSON, F.R.S.E., F.R.Met.Soc. London, Methuen & Co. (University Extension Series.) Crown 8vo, pp. viii, 192. Price 2s. 6d.

In this work Mr. Dickson has given us a capital introduction to meteorology: he starts from the general fund of weather-lore possessed by most people, and developing this in a scientific manner, leads by easy, yet clear and definite, steps to a consideration of modern meteorological methods and results, finally leaving the student in the position to make immediate practical use of his knowledge, or to build further on a sure foundation.

The Vault of Heaven. Elementary Physical Astronomy. By R. A. GREGORY, F.R.A.S. London, Methuen & Co. (University Extension Series.) Crown 8vo, pp. xii, 188. Price 2s. 6d.

This is a popular account of the chief and latest results of physical and descriptive Astronomy: it will be found attractive by the beginner, while the leavening of tables of astronomical statistics and of lists of standard works will be very useful to the student who wishes to go more deeply into the subject.

London B.A. Directory. No. IV, 1893. With Solutions to Exam. Papers. London, Univ. Corr. Coll. Press. Price 2s. 6d. net.

London Matriculation Directory. No. XV, January, 1894. With Solutions to the Examination Papers set. London, Univ. Corr. Coll. Press. Price 1s. net.

LECTURERS' RESERVE FUND.

SUBSCRIPTIONS AND DONATIONS FOR 1893-4 RECEIVED UP TO JANUARY 18, 1894.

	£	s.	d.
M. F.	5	0	0
L. F.	3	0	0
Miss Woolston	5	0	0
Miss A. Walton	2	0	0
Miss Prangley	1	1	0
Miss Edwards	1	1	0
Mrs. Lelacheur	1	0	0
Miss Goldie	1	0	0
Miss Hills	1	0	0
Miss Brassey	1	1	0
The Misses Partridge	1	0	0
The Misses Harris	1	0	0
The Misses Jones	1	10	0
Mrs. R. Crompton Jones	0	10	0
Mrs. Gibson Martin	0	10	0
Miss E. A. Slack	0	10	0
Mrs. Le Lacheur Edwards	0	10	0
Miss D. Cowley	0	10	0
Miss Tetley	0	10	0
Mrs. Reid	0	5	0
Miss McClure	0	5	0
Miss Borlase	0	5	0
Miss Williams	0	10	0
Miss M. E. Coultate	0	10	0
Miss Sharp	0	10	0
Miss Cook	0	5	0
Miss Lund	0	5	0
Miss Fletcher	0	10	0
Sir John Conroy	0	10	0
Miss Banister	0	10	0
Miss Harlow	0	10	0
Miss Prideaux	0	10	0
Miss Cecil	0	5	0
Miss Davy	0	10	0
Miss Wilson	0	10	0
Miss Bentley	0	10	0
The Misses Nicholson	0	15	0
Miss Purton	0	10	0
Miss S. M. Scott	0	10	6
Miss M. S. Beard	0	10	0
The Misses Whidborne	10	0	0
Mr. and Mrs. M. E. Sadler	11	0	0

SCHOLARSHIPS FOR THE OXFORD SUMMER MEETING, 1894.

A FUND has been opened for the provision of Scholarships for the Oxford Summer Meeting of 1894.

	£	s.	d.
The Marquis of Ripon, K.G.	50	0	0
The Secretary's Scholarships (being residue of the fund subscribed by students at the Oxford Summer Meeting, 1892)	47	9	6
Dr. E. B. Tylor, F.R.S.	10	0	0
Professor Poulton, F.R.S.	10	0	0
Rev. E. F. Sampson, Censor of Christ Church	10	0	0
Mr. J. E. Marsh	10	0	0
The late Rev. E. Massie	5	0	0
Professor Percy Gardner	5	0	0
Mr. W. M. Acworth	3	0	0
Mr. R. Ward	0	10	0
Mr. M. E. Sadler	10	0	0
Miss M. B. K. Davies	1	0	0
Miss K. Major and friends (for working-class centres)	5	0	0
Rev. W. H. Shaw	5	0	0
Mr. C. E. Mallet	1	1	0

OXFORD UNIVERSITY

EXTENSION GAZETTE.

VOL. IV. No. 42.]   MARCH, 1894.   [ONE PENNY.

N.B.—Local Organizers of Oxford University Extension Lectures are invited to send to the Secretary, Extension Office, Examination Schools, Oxford, copies of any journals containing notices of, or references to, Extension work.

NOTES AND COMMENTS.

In the *Gazette* of last month we printed the names of some of the residents who had joined the Committee of Welcome for the Easter meeting of the National Union of Teachers in Oxford. In addition to the list then given, the committee includes Mrs. A. H. Johnson and Mrs. Poole, the Hon. Secretary and Hon. Treasurer, respectively, of the Association for the Education of Women in Oxford, Mr. Lyttelton Gell, Mr. Stewart, the Rev. E. F. Sampson, Rev. J. H. Maude, Rev. T. H. Grose, Rev. W. H. Hutton, and Rev. Ll. J. M. Bebb.

⁂

The Education of Women in Oxford.
From the Annual Report of the Association for promoting the education of women in Oxford, we are glad to see that the work which the Association has done so much to further, is steadily making headway. The number of students attending during the last twelve months college courses, and the lectures provided by the Association is the largest on record.

⁂

The announcement of the appointment of Mr. Arthur Sidgwick to a Readership in Greek in the University of Oxford will give much pleasure not only to the many students who have attended his lectures in Oxford, but also to those more widely scattered who have known Mr. Sidgwick in his official capacity as a member of the Extension Delegacy, or have listened to his lectures at the Summer Meetings.

⁂

Co-operators and University Extension.
In his report on the Oldham centre, Mr. Hudson Shaw writes as follows:— 'Nothing could exceed the generosity and thoughtfulness which the Oldham Industrial Co-operative Society displays towards the Extension cause. Books are bought for the use of students, a meeting-room provided, and every encouragement given by the secretary (Mr. Spencer) and his colleagues. For seven years this society has borne the whole financial burden of the work, without the slightest outside help, and one cannot help wondering how long it will be before the State recognizes that the training of its citizens in History is as important, and as worthy of assistance, as the teaching of Botany and Zoology.'

⁂

The Co-operative Union have offered six scholarships to enable students to attend this year's Summer Meeting in Oxford.

⁂

A pleasant instance of the harmony that exists between the County Councils and University Extension occurred a few days ago at Bakewell, where Mr. George Fletcher delivered two lectures on Electricity in aid of the funds of the Bakewell University Extension Association and Technical Education Committee.

⁂

Mr. E. L. S. Horsburgh has been appointed a staff lecturer.

There is a bright February number of *The Bournemouth Students' Association Gazette*. Miss L. M. Roberts of St. Hilda's contributes a vivacious account of a week's work in Oxford. The Association is trying to collect two scholarships for the Summer Meeting. Of the £10 needed, £4 has been subscribed.

⁂

Mr. Edward T. Devine has been elected secretary of the American Society for the Extension of University Teaching, in place of Mr. George F. James.

⁂

Mr. Melvil Dewey writes as follows of the Extension work of the University of the State of New York:— 'Gratifying as is the steady growth of Extension courses, the main work of the department lies in founding new free libraries, scattering travelling libraries throughout the state, and in various ways guiding and stimulating reading of the best books. Forty-one new libraries have already been chartered by the University, and about 100 travelling libraries are in use, while new ones are being added as rapidly as the work of selection, cataloguing, annotating, finding lists, &c., can be satisfactorily done.'

THE GRESHAM UNIVERSITY COMMISSION.

Issue of the Report.

THE report of the Gresham University Commissioners (Lords Cowper, Reay and Playfair, Sir W. S. Savory, Professors Humphry, Ramsay, Burdon Sanderson and Henry Sidgwick, Canon Browne, Messrs. Rendall, Anstie and Palmer) was published on Feb. 24. The unauthorized summary which appeared—no one knows how—about a fortnight ago in the columns of the *Times* had prepared us for the chief proposals of the Commissioners, but gave no idea of the significant character of the document in which they have stated the outcome of their consideration of the draft charter for the proposed Gresham University in London. It is not too much to say that no more important paper on academic policy has appeared since the report of the last Oxford University Commission.

At the same time it must be admitted that a perusal of it leaves the reader in great doubt as to the practicability of the Commissioners' scheme. But great allowances must be made for them. They have had to deal with a complicated problem in a transitional stage of public opinion. They have therefore approached their difficulties in the spirit of compromise. Compromise is apparent in every paragraph of their report, in the elaborate qualifications of their language, in the balance of their arguments, in the fact that, though all the Commissioners sign the report, two of them (including possibly the most influential member) explicitly state the grounds of their profound dissent from the fundamental principle on which it is framed. In fact, the unanimity of the report indicates no real argument among the Commissioners. It only masks a difference of opinion, which is all the more important because it strictly corresponds to a similar cleavage of thought dividing those who are among the heartiest

1

well-wishers of the movement for a teaching University in London.

The Commissioners, in short, have attempted to combine in one institution the functions of a teaching University with those of the existing University of London. This is trying to mix oil and water. To the one degree of B.A., two avenues are to open—the one for external, the other for internal, students. If, by the ingenuity of the Senate and the Academic Council, the examinations for resident and non-resident undergraduates can be assimilated, so much the more hope for the success of the Commissioners' scheme. But if they cannot (and, that they cannot, is evidently more than a suspicion in the mind of the Commissioners), the Academic Council (a small body of fifteen representatives of the Faculties) is to arrange for the holding of the examinations for the *internal* students and to have a significant right of comment on the Senate's action in appointing the examiners of them, while the Senate (an unwieldy body of sixty-six representatives, an amalgam of Crown and Government nominees, elective members, and the spokesmen of seventeen heterogeneous institutions and public bodies) is to appoint a Standing Board for the superintendence of the examination of the *external* students and itself to nominate their examiners.

In other words, a student in Firth College, Sheffield, may still read for a London University degree. But he will come under the supervision of an entirely different Board from that which will advise on the examination of a student at University College, London. Both will probably have to undergo different examinations, but both will, if successful, receive exactly the same degree. The herrings and the pilchards, to use Mr. Huxley's phrase, are to bear the same brand.

Now if there is anything in academic residence, as we in Oxford have always maintained, and as it seems the world in general is beginning to admit, in what way is the education of a student resident in Sheffield, and attending a prescribed course of study at Firth College, likely to fall short of that of a student living in Shepherd's Bush and attending a prescribed course of study at (say) the Guildhall School of Music? *Mutatis mutandis*, each of them will have enjoyed as much or as little of what the Commissioners call the advantages of 'residence' as the other. But, according to the Commissioners' scheme, the youth who lives in Shepherd's Bush will have the privilege of entering for one kind of examination which is refused to his competitor from Sheffield. In so far as this privilege is a real one (and that it is coveted is proved by the very appointment of the Commission), this limitation imposes a hardship on the Sheffield lad without any real justification in principle and on no better ground than that of mere convenience of geographical division. Now such a hardship must inevitably lead to agitation for degree giving powers on the part of those Colleges outside London, which have not yet been federated as Universities, or to the permanent and unfair depression of their fortunes. If attendance at certain classes within what happens to be the area of the City and County of London is to qualify for admission to examinations judiciously adapted to the teaching received, why should not attendance at similar classes in the West Riding of Yorkshire entitle to equivalent privileges, when the degree which is ultimately conferred on the youth from Sheffield is to be exactly the same as that conferred on his competitor from Shepherd's Bush?

But this is not the greatest anomaly proposed by the Commission. Assuming that 'residence' has a virtue of its own (and in his dissentient note Bishop Barry well describes this somewhat indefinite quality), the youth who 'resides,' say at University College, Nottingham, is getting more of this kind of advantage out of his College course, than *ceteris paribus* a poor lad who is grinding for his examination in his spare hours in a lonely garret at Bawtry. Yet for both of these the Commissioners prescribe the same scheme of University examination. Both, in the eyes of the new University, are to be 'external students' because neither of them lives within the County or City of London.

Yet both are to receive the same degree as the internal students. Now, if 'residence' is valuable in itself, ought

not a degree to signify either that the candidate has 'resided' or that he has merely passed examinations? An Oxford or Cambridge degree implies residence. The London degree in future may imply it, but not necessarily so. Two different articles are to be marked with the same brand. But how will the 'resident' or 'internal' students like this? Will they not inevitably agitate for a special degree? Would it not be better from the first to recognize this and to make no attempt to combine the new teaching University with the existing University of London? If adopted, will not this confusion of resident and non-resident students under the style of one degree weaken the position of those who sympathize with Oxford and Cambridge in regarding residence as an essential part of the complete academic training? Shall we not here have a corresponding agitation to give the same degree to resident and non-resident students? Or, if the reverse of this happens, will not (to quote the weighty words of Professor Henry Sidgwick's dissentient note) 'the new Teaching University be unfairly handicapped in its competition with the other Universities of Great Britain, through being unable to give its students the ordinary and recognized attestation that they have gone through the course of training with profit? It will be forced to allow them to be confounded with a different class of students, who will not have subjected themselves to its training but will have merely passed its examinations. . . . If a University is in a healthy condition, its training has a value not expressed in the marks which it enables its students to obtain in examination; and I think it hard that a new University should be singled out to be deprived of the power of representing their value by its degrees.'

This cleavage of interest will almost inevitably weaken the new University, if ever it is founded as the Commissioners propose. And the balance of the suggested constitution is no less precarious. The small academic Council, representing the teaching and resident side of the University, will have much more power of swift, effective and united action than the swollen Senate of sixty-six heterogeneous nominees, which is politely called the supreme Governing Body of the University. Yet in the Senate will linger the powerful tradition of the existing University of London. Such a constitution must, it would appear, lead to internal weakness and indecision, possibly to eventual separation.

As for the rest, the Commissioners heartily commend University Extension; recommend the appointment of a Standing Board for its oversight and direction: and advise the University to accept work done under the superintendence of this Board as an equivalent for such part of the regular courses of the University as may be determined by the Senate, on the report of the Academic Council, to be of correspondent value. In other words, 'residence' may, if the Council of fifteen so decree, be interpreted to mean attendance at a certain number of University Extension courses within the London area. But it is doubtful whether the Academic Council, if constituted as proposed, will see its way to granting much recognition of this kind. The Council of fifteen is likely to take a rather rigid view of what constitutes desirable 'residence.'

The proposed University will apparently be a 'mixed' one, and there will be nothing to prevent the lady head of Bedford College from becoming Vice-Chancellor. The smaller details of administration and organization are to be worked out by an executive Commission with statutory powers. Generous recognition is offered to applied, as well as to pure, science. There are to be six Faculties, Arts, Science, Medicine, Law, Music, and Theological Science, and degrees in the last-named subject will not be confined to members of the Church of England. The Commissioners try to sweep within the net of the new University the Inns of Court, ten of the London Schools of Medicine, six London Theological Colleges, and four London Colleges of Music. The Polytechnics are left outside. It is hoped that something may be made of the Gresham Lectures, but the name 'Gresham' apparently drops out of the title of the new University. The Training Colleges are excluded, but lectures on educational science are suggested for them. Courses of 'post-graduate' study are foreshadowed. And, with two exceptions no institutions outside the County or City of London are to be admitted as Schools of the University at which 'residence' is to count. But these exceptions are significant. They are the Theological Colleges at Cheshunt and Richmond. This recommendation will lead to jealousies, and is likely to cause the gradual extension of the area within which residence is recognized. Finally, the Commissioners evidently anticipate that the execution of their scheme will entail large subsidies from the public funds.

The whole report deserves the most careful attention from all who are in any way interested in University matters. It is published by Eyre and Spottiswoode and costs sixpence.

THE UNIVERSITY EXTENSION COLLEGE, READING.

THE following influentially signed Memorial has been sent to the Treasury urging the desirability of making grants to the University Extension College at Reading; a similar application being also made on behalf of the University Extension College, Exeter :—

We, the undersigned, respectfully urge on the Chancellor of the Exchequer the desirability of small annual grants being made by Parliament to the local Colleges at Reading and Exeter known respectively as the University Extension College, Reading, and the Exeter Technical and University Extension College. These institutions are of a novel type, and although they differ considerably in details of organization they both endeavour to do for smaller centres of population what is done in larger places by the local University Colleges. The enclosed brief statements show that they have already met with considerable initial success, and have been well supported both by students and by subscribers. At present, however, their financial resources depend largely on grants from local authorities, which, though liberal in amount, are limited in their application to scientific and technical subjects. We believe it to be important that these institutions should, from the first, be placed in a position to offer a well-balanced curriculum, for as they grow they will almost certainly become models for similar institutions in other parts of the country. As efforts to solve the question of higher education in the smaller cities and towns their adequate maintenance becomes a question of national importance. Therefore we venture to ask for small grants even in the next financial year.

Herbert Sutton, Chairman of Council, University Extension College, Reading; John Messer, Deputy Chairman of Council, University Extension College, Reading; Richard Benyon, High Steward of Reading; Charles G. Field, Mayor of Reading and Chairman of Trustees of Reading School; George William Palmer, M.P. for Reading; Francis Pierrepont Barnard, M.A., Head Master of Reading School; J. Henry Wilson, Chairman of the School Board for Reading and of the Kendrick (Reading) Middle Schools; Nicholas T. Garry, M.A., Chairman of (Reading) Church Schools Council; J. M. Guilding, President of the Reading Literary and Scientific Society; S. C. Saxby, President of the Reading and District Teachers' Association; George Fraser, Chairman of the Reading Amalgamated Friendly and Trade Societies; Thomas Macbeth, Chairman of the Reading Trades and Labour Council; David Rose, President of the Reading Co-operative Society; William George Mount, Chairman of the Berks County Council, M.P. for South Berks; Wm. H. Dunn, Chairman of the Technical Education Committee of the Berks County Council; Philip Wroughton, M.P. for North Berks; B. Samuelson, Bart., Chairman of the Technical Education Committee of the Oxfordshire County Council, M.P. for North Oxon; Edmond Firzmaurice, Chairman of the Technical Education Committee of the Wilts County Council; F. A. Layton, Mayor of Windsor; Joseph Elliott, Mayor of Newbury; S. Morland, Mayor of Abingdon; John May, Mayor of Basingstoke; J. Weyman, Mayor of Henley-on-Thames; Sidney Payne, Mayor of Wallingford; William Barnard Mower, Mayor of Wokingham;

William Withnall, Mayor of Maidenhead; John R. Mowbray, P.C., Bart., M.P. for the University of Oxford; John G. Talbot, M.P. for the University of Oxford; James Stuart, M.P., Chairman of Universities Joint Board London University Extension Society; H. L. W. Lawson, M.P., of Taplow, Bucks, Member of the Council, London University Extension Society; George Palmer, of the Acacias, Reading, Berks, Alderman, formerly M.P. for Reading; C. T. Murdoch, of Buckhurst, Wokingham, Berks, formerly M.P. for Reading; Charles Morley, of Padworth House, Berks, Hon. Secretary of the Royal College of Music.

The signatures of the Right Hon. Lord Wantage, Lord Lieutenant of Berks, and of the Hon. Frank Parker, M.P. for South Oxfordshire, were received too late for insertion in the petition.

We understand that in reply it is stated that, as the Government have not seen their way to increase the amount of the Parliamentary Grant available for distribution among the University Colleges, it is not possible to make any grant to the University Extension Colleges.

.·.

Dr. Shettle, of Reading, has kindly presented to the Council of the College £50 to provide scientific apparatus for the newly erected Physical Laboratory.

SUMMER SCHOOL OF THEOLOGY AT MANSFIELD COLLEGE.

WE are glad to hear that the Council of Mansfield College has decided to hold a Second Summer School in July, 1894. It is announced that 'As before, the course of instruction has been designed to meet the wants of men who feel that the ordinary work of the ministry has not allowed them to keep abreast of the later inquiries and discussions in the field of Theology in its various branches. The School will be open on the same terms to ministers of all denominations, and will extend from Monday evening, July 16, to Saturday, July 28. On Sunday, July 22, special services will be held in Mansfield College Chapel, when the preachers will be Rev. George A. Gordon, D.D., Pastor of the Old South Church, Boston, U.S.A., and Rev. John Watson, M.A., of Sefton Park Presbyterian Church, Liverpool. The uniform charge of £2 10s. will be made for the tickets, which will include admission to all lectures and meetings, and dinner in Hall, which will be provided daily at 7 p.m. Application for tickets should be made *at once*, but they will not be issued until Monday, May 14. With the tickets will be sent a Map of Oxford, and a list of suitable lodgings at moderate rates, from which members of the School will make their own selection, and arrange directly with those who let the lodgings. The Council believes from past experience that the whole cost, inclusive of ticket for lectures and dinners, lodgings, and partial board, &c., need not exceed £5. All communications should be addressed to Mr. NORMAN H. SMITH, M.A., Mansfield College, Oxford.

The following provisional programme has been issued :—

Philosophical and Systematic Theology.

Andrew Seth, M.A., Professor of Logic and Metaphysics in the University of Edinburgh : 'Modern Philosophy and Theism' (3 lectures). Rev. A. M. Fairbairn, D.D., Principal of Mansfield College : 'The Philosophy of Religion' (3 lectures). Rev. D. W. Simon, D D., Principal of the United Yorkshire College, Bradford : 'Cosmological Implications of the Christian Redemption' (3 lectures). Rev. H. E. Ryle, B.D., Hulsean Professor of Divinity in the University of Cambridge: 'The influence of Modern Studies upon our conception of Inspiration' (3 lectures).

Old Testament Theology.

Rev. George Adam Smith, D.D., Professor of Hebrew in the Free Church College, Glasgow : 'The Beginnings of Hebrew Prophecy' (3 lectures). Rev. James Robertson, D.D, Professor of Oriental Languages in the University of Glasgow: 'The book of Joel: a study in Exegesis, Criticism, and Prophecy' (3 lectures).

2

Rev. Canon T. K. Cheyne, Oriel Professor of Interpretation of Holy Scripture, Oxford : ' The Book of Psalms ' (3 lectures.)

New Testament Theology.

Rev. W. Sanday, D.D., Ireland Professor of Exegesis, Oxford : ' Some characteristics of the Apostolic Age ' (3 lectures). J. Massie, M.A., Professor of New Testament Greek and Exegesis, Mansfield College : ' The Present State of New Testament Criticism ' (Concluded) (3 lectures).

Apologetic Theology.

Rev. A. B. Bruce, D.D., Professor of New Testament Exegesis, Free Church College, Glasgow : ' The Historical Foundations of Christianity : their trustworthiness and their religious value ' (4 lectures).

Church History.

Rev. James Orr, D.D., Professor of Church History, United Presbyterian College, Edinburgh : ' Neglected Factors in the study of the Early Progress of Christianity ' (3 lectures).

Pastoral Theology.

Rev. John Watson, M.A., of Sefton Park, Liverpool : Lecture I.—' The Genesis of a Sermon.' Lecture II.—' The Machinery of a Congregation.'

SPECIAL LECTURERS :—

J. G. McKendrick, M.D., F.R.S., Professor of Physiology in the University of Glasgow : ' The Limitation of the Senses ' (1 lecture). A. Macalister, M.D., F.R.S., Professor of Anatomy in the University of Cambridge : ' The Physical Reactions of Mental Emotions ' (1 lecture).

PREPARATIVE READING FOR THE SUMMER MEETING OF 1894.

[*An asterisk is prefixed to the more important books.*]

A. ENGLISH HISTORY AND LITERATURE OF THE SEVENTEENTH CENTURY.

(i) *Elementary Books.*

*Gardiner, *Student's History of England.* Part II. (Longmans, 4s.)
Or Green, *Short History of the English People.* (Macmillan, 8s. 6d.)
Gardiner, *Puritan Revolution.* (Longmans, 2s. 6d.)

(ii) *Advanced Books* (for Reference).

*Gardiner, *History of England*, 1603—1642. 10 vols. (Longmans, £3.)
*Gardiner, *History of the Great Civil War*, 1642—1649. 4 vols. (Longmans, £1 4s.)
Guizot, *Commonwealth of England.* (Bentley, out of print.)
Or Godwin, *History of the Commonwealth of England.* 4 vols. (out of print.)
Ranke, *History of England in the Seventeenth Century* (especially for the reigns of Charles II and James II.) 6 vols. (Clarendon Press, £3 3s.)

(iii) *General Books.*

Wakeman, *The Church and the Puritans* (Epochs of Church History). (Longmans, 2s. 6d.)
Browning, *Life of Strafford.* (Kegan, Paul & Co.) Or in Forster's *Eminent British Statesmen*, vol. ii.
Life of Nicholas Ferrar. (Longmans, 3s. 6d.)
*Clarendon, *History of the Great Rebellion.* (Clarendon Press.) Many Editions. (Read especially Books i—viii.)
Pepys, *Diary* (National Library). 5 vols. (Cassell, 3d. each.)
*Carlyle, *Letters and Speeches of Oliver Cromwell.* 5 vols. (Chapman & Hall, 5s.)
Burnet, *History of His Own Times.* (Many Editions.)
Memoirs of Col. Hutchinson. Ed. by C. H. Firth. 2 vols. (Nimmo, £2 2s.) (Or Bell, 3s. 6d.)

(iv) *Literature.*

Taine, *History of English Literature.* 2 vols. (Chatto & Windus, 15s.)
Herbert, *Poems.* (Nisbet, 1s.)

Herrick, *Hesperides* (Universal Library). (Routledge, 1s.)
*Pattison, *Milton* (Eng. Men of Letters). (Macmillan, 1s.)
Saintsbury, *Dryden* (Eng. Men of Letters). (Macmillan, 1s.)
Milton, *Poems.* (Macmillan, 3s. 6d.)
Milton, *Selected Prose Works.* (Kegan, Paul & Co., 6s.)
Dryden, *Political Poems.* (Clarendon Press, 3s. 6d.)
Browne, *Religio Medici.* (Macmillan, 2s. 6d.)
Bunyan, *Pilgrim's Progress.* (Macmillan, 2s. 6d.)

(v) *Colonial, &c.*

Payne, *European Colonies.* (Macmillan, 4s. 6d.)
*Thwaites, *The Colonies* (Epochs of American History) 1492—1750. (Longmans, 2s. 6d.)
Hewins, *English Trade and Finance in the Seventeenth Century.* (Methuen, 2s. 6d.)
Fiske, *Beginnings of New England.* (Macmillan, 7s. 6d.)

B. FOREIGN HISTORY AND LITERATURE.

(i) *History.*

*Gardiner, *Thirty Years' War.* (Longmans, 2s. 6d.)
Airy, *The Restoration and Louis XIV.* (Longmans, 2s. 6d.)
*Kitchin, *History of France*, vol. iii. (Clarendon Press, 10s. 6d.)
Or *Lavallée, *Histoire des Français*, vol. iii. (Charpentier, Paris, 3s. 6d.)
Stephen, *Lectures on the History of France*, vol. ii. (Out of print.)
Perkins, *France under Richelieu and Mazarin.* 2 vols. (Macmillan, out of print.)
Voltaire, *Siècle de Louis XIV* (translated, but out of print.)
*Wakeman, *Europe, Period V.* 1598–1715. Rivington & Co.

(ii) *Literature.*

Pascal, *Thoughts* (translated). (Longmans, 2s. 6d.)
Molière, *Plays* (translated, a selection). (Bell, 1s.)
[*The list of books recommended in other subjects will be printed in the April Number.*]

SCHOOLS OF CITIZENSHIP IN SCANDINAVIA.

A Successful System of Adult Education.

[*Reprinted by permission from Miss E. Healey's Report on* ' *The Educational Systems of Sweden, Norway, and Denmark* ' ; *published by the authority of the Gilchrist Trustees*, 1892.]

' HIGH Schools for the People '—' Folkehöjskoler '—are peculiarly Scandinavian institutions. The first idea of such schools originated in Denmark, and was due to a religious-political movement initiated by Bishop Grundtvig. His ideal was a national ' People's School,' in which the mother-tongue should be used as the instrument of education—not the dead languages, which were foreign to national life and character ; Scandinavian history and poetry were to be the chief means of instructing the pupils in the affairs and interests of their own country. Such a school should appeal to young men, should prepare them for their work as citizens, and lead them to appreciate the special characteristics and needs of the Northern nations. Grundtvig's ideas appeared at a favourable time, as many peasant farmers in Slesvig took up with zeal the plan for such a school, in which they hoped to find a safeguard against German influence and an aid to future national security. The first school was opened in 1844 in South Jutland ; but the most important of the earlier ' People's High Schools ' was that started in 1850 by Kristen Kold in a small house on the island of Funen. In order to awaken and expand the minds of his pupils, he read with them Ingemann's romances, which treat of early Danish history, and also told them stories from the history of the world. The number of his pupils quickly increased. An account of a visit paid to the school says that though the teaching dealt mainly with historical subjects, yet questions of everyday life were not neglected. The school was so arranged that the teachers lived together with the scholars in a frugal style.

*   *   *   *   *   *

Kold's example was followed by other schools, and he may be

Printed names of Towns show
UNIVERSITY
EXTENSION CENTRES
ON THE OXFORD LIST
1893-4.

George Philip & Son 32 Fleet St E.C.

said to have had a large share in the widespread development of the Danish 'People's High School.' It was, however, about twenty years from the opening of the first school before Grundtvig and Kold's school plans made much advance in Denmark; but after the disastrous war with Germany in 1864 came a time of rapid and powerful growth of the 'Folkehöjskoler'; and twenty years later again there were in Denmark more than seventy such schools, with over 4,500 pupils yearly, most of them from the country districts.

In the impetus which Kold gave to these schools lay, of course, the danger that men who lacked his great knowledge of human nature, as well as his natural gifts and experience of life, might use the same means and methods but in a mechanical manner, and therefore without awakening the minds of the pupils or attaining any satisfactory result. Fortunately, however, Kold's successors on the whole possessed originality, and also perceived that it was not possible to remain at the point where he began, as the pupils themselves compelled advance through their growing desire for knowledge. The schools have thus gone forward in instruction, while retaining their aim of uplifting and ennobling. One of their advocates justly says that to speak of the development of spiritual life and intellectual power, without giving increased knowledge, is a contradiction; awakened intelligence craves for food, and the pupils must have material on which to exercise their abilities.

A marked religious element is perceptible in the schools, and their aim is first and foremost to render those who go to them patriotic and Christian. At the same time the teachers endeavour to give practical knowledge of the kind which shall be most useful in after life. This is more prominent in the Swedish high schools for the people. The primary object of the Danish schools is spiritual development and widening of interests, not the imparting of facts.

In Askov a successful effort has been made to partly carry out Grundtvig's idea of a democratic university which should be a centre for a comprehensive, thorough and national work of instruction without degenerating into an establishment for awarding offices by examination. The subjects taught to young men are:—Bible History; General History; Scandinavian History; Geography; Physics; Constitution and Laws of Denmark; Language and Literature; Book-keeping; Slöjd; Singing and Gymnastics. In addition, at Askov a few pupils have had lessons in foreign languages, Icelandic, German and English.

Instruction to young men takes place in the winter, and the course lasts about six months. Many pupils return a second year, even a third or fourth, according to the degree of education they wish for; and, as far as possible, they are taught whatever they most wish.

The wider development of the school in Askov is the more useful, inasmuch as previously there was no place where young men who desired to become teachers in the 'People's High Schools' or 'free schools' (where the parents of the pupils select the teacher) but could not afford to study at the university could find suitable instruction. Askov is also visited by a great many persons who, after taking a course at the school, return to their former occupations, and by some who only seek intellectual stimulus and enlightenment.

In summer, courses of instruction are held for young girls and women. These last three months. Lectures are given in Religion; History, especially Scandinavian; Geography; Literature; and a short series on Hygiene. The other subjects taught are:—Drawing; Writing; Arithmetic; Needlework of all kinds; and Gymnastics. During the needlework some interesting book is read aloud. At the beginning and end of each lecture some more or less appropriate song, usually religious or patriotic, is sung by the pupils.

Two characteristic features of these schools are that the pupils have much liberty, and that social demarcations disappear in the school. Very many of the girls attending the schools are domestic servants, daughters of peasants, who have worked for years in order to save sufficient money to enable them to spend two or three months at a school. The very poorest often receive grants from the State or from their own parish. It is by these that the school-time is most appreciated, as a time for rest, for thought, and for self-improvement after many years of hard manual work with scanty leisure and few opportunities for learning.

The school at Vallekilde, which is a high school of the type desired by Grundtvig, is favourably situated in the midst of an agricultural population and several miles from any town. There are several buildings—a whole colony, in fact—which form the school. Some of them are the houses of the teachers; others contain the pupils' rooms; and in a third set different parts of the school-work are carried on. One large room is used for Slöjd classes during the winter, and for hand-weaving in summer. There is a technical school for painters, carpenters and builders who attend the winter course; a museum containing specimens of all fishes caught off the Danish coasts, nets and other apparatus for fishing, &c., as there is also a special section for fishermen and sailors in winter. The largest building is that where the head-master lives and where the class-rooms are. The walls of the lecture-rooms and gymnasium are hung with pictures, some of them fine oil paintings by well-known Danish artists; and the rooms are large, lofty, well-arranged, and lighted by several windows, from which pleasant views are seen of the garden and the wide fertile plain beyond. The course this summer was attended by more than 150 pupils, most of them from the working-class. The cost for board, lodging and instruction is £1 14s. a month. One shilling a month is paid into a sick-fund, and in case of illness the patient is free from all expense for doctor, medicine, nursing, &c.; a small hospital is attached to the school. Lessons in weaving are an extra—3s. 6d. for the whole course. In a little church, which also forms part of the colony, service is held every Sunday by ministers who come from neighbouring villages. The principal event of the day is the head-master's lecture, which is simple yet impressive. These lectures treat very often of religion, occasionally of historical events or moral questions; but in whatever he says there is always something which appeals directly to the souls of the hearers.

From Denmark the plan of the Grundtvig 'People's High School' has been introduced into Norway, where there are now about twelve such schools. One point in which the Danish and Norwegian 'People's High Schools' differ from the Swedish is that the former are quite private, belong to the head-master, and the pupils board and lodge at the school; they receive a relatively inconsiderable grant from the State, usually less than £55 yearly. These grants enable a number of poor young men and women to attend the schools.

The first Swedish high schools for the people were opened in 1868. With one exception they are maintained by the fees of the pupils, supplemented by aid from the State and local authorities. The head-master is, as a rule, completely independent, though he does not own the school. This is obviously most important in questions of organization and instruction.

The oldest and one of the best known 'People's High Schools' is at 'Hvilan,' between Malmö and Lund.

This summer the number of girls and young women for the three months' course was seventy-two, eighteen of whom attended a dairy class for those who had already had at least one year's practical experience. The fees are £2 for three months' tuition. The pupils arrange for their own board and lodging, and live, generally two or three together, in the houses near the school. The State grant is, at the highest, £112 to schools with a one-year's course for young men, and £167 to schools with a two-years' course, Agriculture being studied during the second year.

'Hvilan' is surrounded by a large garden; the school buildings are not so extensive as those at Vallekilde, as the number of pupils is less and they do not live at the school. The chief class-room is long and well lighted by ten windows opening on to the garden. There is a platform at one end, and the walls are covered with portraits of famous people and pictures. The gymnasium is large, and fitted with the usual apparatus for Ling's gymnastics. In it there are seven hand-looms, and all the hand-weaving is done there. It is also used for assemblies, meetings and public lectures, and contains a rostrum and piano. The girls here, as at Vallekilde, seem to thoroughly enjoy the school-life, and it must be of great service to them in developing intelligence, increasing knowledge, giving skilfulness in handiwork, which is taught more thoroughly and systematically here than in the Danish school, and showing them how to make it beautiful as well as useful. The school hours are long; morning prayer is held before the first lesson, at 7.30 A.M. At 8.30 there is an interval of half-an-hour for breakfast; lessons begin again at 9, and go on, with short breaks of five minutes between every two classes, till 1 o'clock. At 2 hand-work is begun; this lasts till 5 every day, except Saturday, which is a half-holiday. At 5 o'clock some book is read aloud, and from 6 to 7 a singing class is held. For dairy pupils lessons begin two mornings a week at 6.45 A.M., and on four evenings there is a lecture from 7 to 8. The instruction is theoretical only.

The Swedish 'People's High Schools' have not had such an influx of pupils as the Danish ones, because there have been no stirring political disturbances, or widespread religious movement such as the Grundtvigian, to arouse national feeling. The Danes are also a more prosperous and wealthy nation than the Swedes, which no doubt has had some effect on the growth of the Danish schools. In Sweden the people have always enjoyed freedom and have seen their rights and privileges considerably increased without effort on their part. To impart increased education as a citizen and member of a community was the object for which these schools were begun in Sweden, but through Danish influence came also the desire to work for the development of the soul in all possible ways. It is stated that the Swedish teachers have learnt from the Danish to associate with their pupils in a free and natural manner as comrades, and in their lessons to employ spoken words, simple and popular, to awake the interest of the scholars in God and Fatherland.

The Swedish schools have from the first endeavoured to give *practical* knowledge, in which the work of the Danish schools among girls seems decidedly deficient.

In Sweden the mother-tongue and Natural Science (especially Hygiene) have equal shares in the lesson time. At 'Hvilan' lessons and lectures were given in Northern history and geography, hygiene, domestic economy, gymnastics, general history and geography, Swedish grammar and composition, handiwork, physics, chemistry, arithmetic, and singing. Here, as at Vallekilde, an hour each day is devoted to gymnastics, which has been found to be most beneficial, especially to those pupils who had led a sedentary life or suffered from weakness and anaemia. Written home-work is also given, which is never done at Vallekilde. There the girls spend most of their leisure time in doing fancy work, which they are allowed to do in the lectures also. This appears to a visitor a distinct mistake, as frequently the girls' thoughts and attention are much more taken up by their embroidery than by the subject treated of, in spite of the fact that the lectures are delivered in the most vivid and impressive, sometimes eloquent manner imaginable.

* * * * * *

Discussions concerning subjects of general interest often take place in these schools; the pupils thereby become not only accustomed to think of such things, but also to express their opinions with sense and moderation. These meetings are usually held in the evenings, after the ordinary school lessons are over. In the Swedish schools there is no special religious instruction, but the day's work is always begun with prayer and hymn. Public lectures at the 'high schools' are generally attended by a great number of people who enjoy meeting together now and then, and hearing a good lecture. It is not the topics of everyday life which draw the largest audiences. For example, a few years ago a course of lectures on Domestic Economy was delivered, in a thickly populated country district, to less than 100 listeners, while at the same time several hundred persons assembled at the 'People's High School' to hear lectures on religious, ethical, biographical, or historical subjects.

The organization and methods employed are peculiar to the 'high schools for the people,' as the object of such schools is different from that of schools for children. No entrance examination is required, for the desire of a man or woman to attend the

school is a proof of his fitness. There is no examination on leaving, as the pupils do not go to school in order to take an examination, or, after the end of the course, to choose new ways in life for themselves. They visit the school voluntarily, and afterwards go back quietly to their former employment at home or in the service of others. The 'People's High School' is distinguished by its freedom from formalism and by the full play it gives to the teacher's personality, more than any other kind of school; it does not try to shape its pupils to the same type; it calls forth unrestrained intercourse between teacher and pupil and becomes a home for the pupils which they enter with pleasure and leave with regret.

Unions of old pupils are formed in connexion with very many of the 'People's High Schools,' and 'summer meetings' of the members are held sometimes. These often last several days, and the time is filled with lectures, discussion of educational and social questions, and pleasant friendly gatherings.

Similar schools have been started among the Scandinavian settlers in the United States, in Finland, and in Iceland. The hope has been expressed by a Swedish writer that 'People's High Schools' may some day be established in other European countries when the burden of compulsory military service is removed or lightened for the youth of those States.

REPORTS FROM THE CENTRES.

ABERGAVENNY.—On February 17, the annual entertainment in connexion with the Oxford Extension movement was held in the Town Hall. A beautiful collection of photographs of Italian subjects illustrating the Renaissance in Italy were shown by lime-light, and an explanatory lecture was given by Mr. Phythian, who had most kindly consented to assist the local committee in this way. The lecturer dealt mainly with the artistic and architectural side of the Renaissance, showing in a clear and interesting manner the return to classic ideals.

BATH.—We learn from the *Bath Chronicle* that on the occasion of the eighth lecture of Mr. Mallet's course on ' English Prose Writers,' the large room of the Literary Institution was full.

BEDFORD.—The beginning of the Spring course at this centre was marked by a visit from Mr. Sadler, who was present at a public meeting and social gathering, held on Jan. 27. He gave an address on the origin, growth, and future development of University Extension, as the outcome of a more active sympathy between the Universities and national life, characteristic of the last half-century. This was followed by a speech from our present lecturer, Mr. Graham Wallas, who graphically set forth the historic continuity and importance of English town life; and put before us a high ideal of patriotism and citizenship, as the result to be attained from true education. Mr. Sadler in his concluding words had already shown that the acquisition and application of knowledge was not to 'end at the age of three-and-twenty, but might be continued like a golden thread all through human life.' In spite of unfavourable weather the town was quite full, and the audience (of about 250) was a fairly representative one. Additional importance and value was given to the meeting by the presidency of the mayor of Bedford, and by the presence of the two head-masters and two head-mistresses, representing the Boys' Grammar and Modern Schools, and the High School and Girls' Modern School. Our former connexion with Cambridge (as a local lecture centre) was also recalled and emphasized by the kindly interest shown in our present work by Dr. T. J. Lawrence (our first Extension lecturer eighteen years ago), who gave a short but encouraging address, in seconding a vote of thanks to the speakers, proposed by Mr. J. S. Phillpotts. The audience was sympathetic and deeply interested. The artisans of Bedford were well represented.—MISS E. BLAKE, *Hon. Sec.*

CARLISLE.—Mr. Murray's course on Electricity began with a good attendance. The lecturer drew attention to the Students' Association, and urged his hearers to join it.

CHELTENHAM.—The beginning of the present session marks a somewhat critical point in the history of University Extension in this town, as at the end of last session the former committee resigned, and it seemed as if, for a time at least, the work here was at an end. After a short delay, however, a new committee was formed, who entered on their work with some anxiety, but resolved to do their utmost to prevent such a collapse, and their efforts have been completely successful. They were fortunate enough—owing to an arrangement previously made—to secure the Rev. W. Hudson Shaw as lecturer, and they chose his course on 'English Social Reformers' as the subject. The result has been most encouraging. Both of the lectures already delivered have been attended by large and appreciative audiences, and the interest in the course seems growing. About forty have given in their names as 'students' to attend the classes and write the papers.—F. H. CRAWLEY, *Hon. Sec.*

EVESHAM.—The revival of the University Extension lectures in this town has been attended, it is gratifying to learn, with marked success. The Council of the Evesham Institute, feeling that it was a serious loss to the educational resources of the neighbourhood that these lectures should altogether cease, determined to assume the responsibility of arranging for another course and the lecture committee of that body have had the matter in hand. The committee were fortunate enough to be able to engage Mr. J. A. R. Marriott to lecture upon the Stuart Monarchy and the Puritan Revolution or 'Cavaliers and Round-heads' as the course is entitled. The popularity of the lecturer in Evesham and the selection of one of the most interesting and eventful periods of English History as the subject, have brought an average attendance of about 200 to the lectures, and the result is highly encouraging to the organizers, who will now in all probability make a course of Extension lectures a permanent part of their season's work.—W. GILL SMITH. *Hon. Sec.*

SALE.—As an introduction to the Lent term an afternoon meeting of Extension students and friends was held at this centre on January 2, at which Mr. M. E. Sadler gave an address in favour of Students' Associations. It was hoped that this meeting would draw the students together, such a long interval having elapsed during Dr. Bailey's serious illness, which caused the most unfortunate interruption to the delightful course of Shakespearian lectures which was being given by him. So far he has lectured on Julius Caesar, Hamlet and King Lear; the attendance is good, and the paper-work keeps up to a high standard, although fewer students are writing than in 1893.—CAROLINE M. TAYLOR. *Hon. Sec. Sale Students' Association.*

WELLS.—In their annual report the committee record their sense of the value of the Students' Association, which has been of great assistance to students in directing and systematizing their work. They also report with pleasure that there was a larger attendance in 1893 than heretofore of teachers in schools, shop assistants, artisans, &c., with a good proportion of men. It is much to be hoped that the citizens will continue thus to make increasing use of this scheme for the higher education of all classes. They continue: 'There are two further points to which attention must be drawn. (1) In former years many persons more or less wealthy subscribed, partly for their own benefit, but also, and perhaps chiefly, for the benefit of others. In 1893 this class of supporters fell off; they thought probably that the lectures, being so popular, were now self-supporting, and that their money was no longer needed. The committee venture to remind them that this can never be the case in so small a city as Wells, if the price of tickets is to be low enough to admit their poorer neighbours. The cause of higher education may surely claim support on public grounds, quite apart from the individual pleasure and benefit to be derived from particular courses of lectures. (2) Mentioned last year, is the importance of being able to depend upon the *regular* support of the sub-scribers. The expenses of each course have to be guaranteed beforehand, and much embarrassment and anxiety are caused to the committee by its being a matter of pure speculation whether or not the necessary money will be forthcoming. So late as one week before the first lecture in October, the local secretary had received so few subscriptions that a considerable adverse balance was feared. This most unsatisfactory 'hand to mouth' condition would be remedied if persons would apply for tickets *as soon as* the forthcoming course is announced. The Very Rev. the Dean, Mrs. Welsh, and one or two other friends give yearly subscriptions in January, receiving full value in tickets—an example which might be followed (where possible) with great advantage to the stability and permanence of the scheme.'

WEST BRIGHTON.—The first course of *evening* lectures at this centre commenced on January 25, the subject being 'The Making of the English Empire,' illustrated by lantern slides, the lecturer being Mr. Kenelm D. Cotes, M.A. The two lectures already given have been attended by an audience of about 140, many of whom stayed for the after-class.—M. F. BASDEN, *Hon. Sec.*

Notice to Correspondents.—Owing to pressure on our limited space the following articles will appear in our next number—viz.: *In Quest of Nature: Proposed Continental Centres: Reduced Railway Fares for Students.*

ARRANGEMENTS FOR 1894.
Spring 1894.

Centre.	No. of Lectures in Course.	Subject of Course.	Lecturer.	Course begins.	Course ends.
†UNIVERSITY EXTENSION COLLEGE, READING	12	Physical Geography	H. J. MACKINDER, M.A.	W. Jan. 17	Mar. 14
,, ,,	12	Homeric Poems	J. CHURTON COLLINS, M.A.	S. Feb. 3	Mar. 14
,, ,,	12	English History, 18th Century ...	W. M. CHILDS, B.A. ...	F. Jan. 19	Mar. 16
,, ,,	24	Chemistry	G. J. BURCH, M.A. ...	Th. Jan. 18	Apr. 12
,, ,,	24	Electricity	,, ,,	Th. Jan. 18	Apr. 12
,, ,,	24	Biology	B. J. AUSTIN, F.L.S. ...	T. Jan. 23	Apr. 17
,, ,,	24	Chemistry	G. J. BURCH, M.A. ...	S. Jan. 20	Apr. 14
,, ,,	24	Botany	B. J. AUSTIN, F.L.S. ...	S. Jan. 20	Apr. 14
,, ,, *Newbury Sub-Centre*	24	Chemistry	P. ELFORD, M.A. ...	S. Jan. 20	Apr. 14
,, ,,	24	Botany	Miss E. C. POLLARD, B.Sc.	S. Jan. 20	Apr. 14
,, ,, *Didcot Sub-Centre*	24	Chemistry	P. ELFORD, M.A. ...	S. Jan. 20	Apr. 14
,, ,,	24	Botany	A. A. LINTERN, B.Sc.	S. Jan. 20	Apr. 14
EASTBOURNE (afternoon) ...	6	Elizabethan Literature ...	J. CHURTON COLLINS, M.A.	S. Feb. 10	Apr. 21
ASHTON-UNDER-LYNE (aft.) ...	6	Age of Elizabeth	Rev. W. H. SHAW, M.A.	T. Jan. 16	Mar. 27
ASHTON-UNDER-LYNE (even.)	6	Making of England	,, ,, ...	T. Jan. 16	Mar. 27
GLOUCESTER (evening) ...	6	English Social Reformers ...	,, ,, ...	M. Jan. 22	Apr. 2
BIRMINGHAM, SEVERN STREET (evening)	6	Florence and Venice	,, ,, ...	T. Jan. 23	Apr. 3
SWINDON (evening)	6	Puritan Revolution ...	,, ,, ...	W. Jan. 24	Apr. 4
NEWBURY (afternoon) ...	6	Florence	,, ,, ...	Th. Jan. 25	Apr. 5
TUNBRIDGE WELLS (afternoon)	10	Florence and Venice	,, ,, ...	F. Jan. 26	Apr. 6
BRIGHTON (evening)	12	Florence and Venice ...	,, ,, ...	F. Jan. 19	Apr. 6
WINDSOR (afternoon) ...	6	Venice	,, ,, ...	Th. Jan. 18	Mar. 15
TEDDINGTON (afternoon) ...	6	Venice	,, ,, ...	W. Feb. 28	May 9
CHELTENHAM (afternoon) ...	6	Social Reformers	,, ,, ...	W. Jan. 31	Apr. 4
CHESTER (afternoon) ...	6	Age of Louis XIV ...	J. A. R. MARRIOTT, M.A.	W. Jan. 31	Not fixed
CHESTER (evening) ...	6	Cavaliers and Roundheads ...	,, ,, ...	T. Jan. 30	Not fixed
BRIGHTON (St. Michael's Hall) (afternoon)	6	The Stuarts	,, ,, ...	F. Jan. 26	Not fixed

† Continued from Autumn Session.

Centre.	No. of Lectures in Course.	Subject of Course.	Lecturer.	Course begins.	Course ends.
WALLASEY (evening)	6	Historical Plays of Shakespeare ...	J. A. R. MARRIOTT, M.A.	W. Jan. 31	Not fixed
BRADFORD (evening) ...	6	Europe since Waterloo	„ „ ...	Th. Feb. 1	Not fixed
MALVERN (afternoon) ...	6	Historical Plays of Shakespeare...	„ „ ...	W. Feb. 7	Apr. 11
EVESHAM (evening) ...		Cavaliers and Roundheads ...	„ „ ...	W. Jan. 24	Apr. 4
WARE (afternoon)	6	Age of Anne	„ „ ...	F. Jan. 19	Mar. 30
ROSS (afternoon) ...	6	Age of Louis XIV.	„ „ ...	T. Jan. 23	Apr. 3
CHELTENHAM COLLEGE (aft.)	6	English History 1399-1509 ...	„ „ ...	Th. May 10	June 14
†EDGBASTON (afternoon) ...	12	Growth of Polit. System of Europe	H. J. MACKINDER, M.A.	T. Jan. 16	Mar. 27
†PETERBOROUGH (evening) ...	12	Victorian Poets	F. S. BOAS, M.A.	F. Jan. 19	Mar. 30
FOLKESTONE (afternoon) ...	12	Victorian Poets	„ „ ...	M. Jan. 29	Apr. 2
VENTNOR (afternoon) ...	10	Tennyson	„ „ ...	T. Jan. 16	Mar. 27
LOUTH (evening) ...	6	Tennyson	„ „ ...	T. Jan. 23	April 3
MIDHURST (afternoon) ...	6	The Two Pitts	C. E. MALLET, B.A.	M. Jan. 15	Mar. 26
FROME (afternoon) ...	6	The Two Pitts	„ „ ...	F. Jan. 19	Mar. 30
FROME (evening) ...	6	The Two Pitts	„ „ ...	F. Jan. 19	Mar. 30
GRANGE (evening) ...	6	English Prose Writers ...	„ „ ...	M. Jan. 22	Apr. 2
†TAMWORTH (afternoon) ...	10	The Stuarts	„ „ ...	T. Jan. 16	Feb. 27
†TAMWORTH (evening) ...	10	The Stuarts	„ „ ...	T. Jan. 23	Feb. 27
WHITEHAVEN (evening) ...	6	French Revolution ...	„ „ ...	T. Jan. 16	Apr. 3
†BURY (evening) ...	12	French Revolution ...	„ „ ...	W. Jan. 24	Apr. 4
GRIMSBY (evening) ...	6	French Revolution ...	„ „ ...	F. Feb. 9	Apr. 20
†BURNLEY (evening) ...	12	England in the 18th Century ...	„ „ ...	Th. Jan. 25	Apr. 5
†BATH (afternoon) ...	12	England in the 18th Century ...	„ „ ...	Th. Feb. 1	Apr. 12
†BATH (evening) ...	12	English Prose Writers ...	„ „ ...	Th. Feb. 1	Apr. 12
DEVIZES (evening) ...	6	Shakespeare	Rev. J. G. BAILEY, LL.D.	M. Jan. 22	Apr. 2
KEIGHLEY (evening) ...	6	Wordsworth, Shelley, Keats ...	„ „ ...	M. Jan. 15	Not fixed
SALE (evening)	6	Shakespeare	„ „ ...	T. Jan. 16	Not fixed
ROCHDALE (afternoon) ...	6	Shakespeare	„ „ ...	W. Jan. 17	Not fixed
TUNBRIDGE WELLS (evening)...	8	Regions, Races, and Resources ...	H. R. MILL, D.Sc.	T. Jan. 16	Mar. 6
†BARNSTAPLE (evening) ...	12	Design	C. R. ASHBEE, M.A. ...	M. Jan. 8	Mar. 19
†RYDE (afternoon) ...	12	Shakespeare	R. W. BOND, M.A. ...	Th. Jan. 11	Mar. 29
WEST BRIGHTON (evening) ...	6	Trade, Adventure, and Discovery	K. D. COTES, M.A. ...	Th. Jan. 25	Apr. 5
TAVISTOCK (afternoon) ...	6	Shakespeare's England ...	„ „ ...	M. Feb. 26	Apr. 2
ROCHDALE (evening) ...	6	Social Questions of To-day ...	W. A. S. HEWINS, M.A.	Th. Jan. 18	Mar. 29
†LEAMINGTON (evening) ...	12	Problems of Poverty ...	J. A. HOBSON, M.A. ...	F. Feb. 2	Apr. 13
WEST BROMWICH (evening) ...	6	Problems of Poverty ...	„ „ ...	T. Mar. 13	Apr. 24
†WEST BRIGHTON (afternoon)	12	The Renaissance	E. L. S. HORSBURGH, B.A.	Th. Jan. 18	Mar. 29
†REIGATE (afternoon) ...	12	The Renaissance	„ „ ...	F. Jan. 19	Mar. 30
†RAMSGATE (evening) ...	12	French Revolution ...	„ „ ...	S. Jan. 20	Mar. 31
†BOURNEMOUTH (afternoon) ...	12	Literature of the 18th Century ...	„ „ ...	F. Jan. 12	Apr. 6
BOURNEMOUTH (evening) ...	6	Studies from the 18th and 19th Centuries	„ „ ...	Th. Jan. 11	Apr. 5
†SOUTHAMPTON (evening) ...	12	The Tudors	„ „ ...	F. Feb. 9	Apr. 20
LEOMINSTER (afternoon) ...	6	Rise of Parliament ...	„ „ ...	M. Jan. 15	Not fixed
HEREFORD (evening) ...	6	Italian Renaissance ...	„ „ ...	M. Jan. 15	Not fixed
MAIDENHEAD (afternoon) ...	6	Italian Renaissance ...	„ „ ...	Th. Jan. 11	Mar. 22
ABERGAVENNY (evening) ...	6	Italian Renaissance ...	„ „ ...	M. Jan. 22	Apr. 2
†LEWES (evening)	12	Studies from the Georges ...	„ „ ...	Th. Jan. 18	Mar. 29
†HALIFAX (evening) ...	12	Architecture	J. E. PHYTHIAN ...	Th. Jan. 25	Mar. 29
†OXFORD (evening) ...	24	The English Citizen ...	GRAHAM WALLAS, M.A.	Th. Jan. 18	June 14
†BEDFORD (afternoon)... ...	12	The English Citizen ...	„ „ ...	T. Jan. 16	Mar. 27
†BRIDPORT (evening) ...	12	Architecture	Rev. G. H. WEST, D.D.	T. Jan. 23	Apr. 3
†VENTNOR (evening) ...	12	Astronomy...	A. H. FISON, D.Sc. ...	T. Jan. 9	Mar. 20
†NEWPORT (evening) ...	12	Astronomy...	„ „ ...	W. Jan. 10	Mar. 21
†STROUD (afternoon) ...	12	Electricity	„ „ ...	T. Jan. 16	Apr. 10
†STROUD (evening) ...	12	Electricity	„ „ ...	T. Jan. 16	Apr. 10
CARLISLE (evening) ...	6	Astronomy...	„ „ ...	W. Jan. 31	Apr. 11
CARLISLE (evening) ...	6	Electricity	H. J. R. MURRAY, B.A.	W. Feb. 7	May 14
WARRINGTON (evening) ...	6	Astronomy...	W. E. PLUMMER, M.A.	F. Feb. 2	Apr. 13
Kent County Council five courses each of	10	Chemistry	H. H. COUSINS, M.A.	Jan.	Apr.
†Surrey County Council six courses	24, 12, 6	Chemistry	A. D. HALL, M.A. ...	Jan.	Apr.
two courses	24	Chemistry	H. GORDON, M.A. ...	Jan.	Apr.
Somerset County Council 5 courses each of	12	Hygiene	C. H. WADE, M.A. ...	Jan.	Apr.
5 courses each of	12	Farm Animals	H. SESSIONS ...	Jan.	Apr.

Other courses in process of arrangement.

† Continued from Autumn 1893.

Note.—Application for Courses and all information as to fees, &c., can be obtained from The Secretary, University Extension Office, Examination Schools, Oxford.

INFORMATION TO CONTRIBUTORS.

All communications should be addressed to the Editor, OXFORD UNIVERSITY EXTENSION GAZETTE, *University Press, Oxford.*

All matter intended for insertion in the April issue should reach him not later than March 20.

Contributions should be written on one side of the paper only, and must be accompanied by the name of the writer (not necessarily for publication).

N.B.—*All orders should carefully specify the full title,* OXFORD UNIVERSITY EXTENSION GAZETTE.

OXFORD UNIVERSITY

EXTENSION GAZETTE.

Vol. IV. No. 43.] APRIL, 1894. [ONE PENNY.

N.B.—Local Organizers of Oxford University Extension Lectures are invited to send to the Secretary, Extension Office, Examination Schools, Oxford, copies of any journals containing notices of, or references to, Extension work.

NOTES AND COMMENTS.

It is proposed that Mr. Gladstone should be the first Chancellor of the University of Wales.

．・．

County Council Aid to Economic Lectures. The Lancashire County Council has aided, to the extent of half the entire cost, the course of Oxford University Extension Lectures on Problems of Poverty, recently delivered by Mr. J. A. Hobson in connexion with the Educational Department of the Accrington and Church Co-operative Society. This statesmanlike action on the part of the Lancashire County Council will meet with general approval. The episode is indeed from every point of view satisfactory. This is what has happened. A society of workmen decided to arrange a course of University lectures on some of the most serious economic problems of our time. The lectures were largely attended and stimulated their hearers to serious reading and careful discussion. Finally, the public authority of the county agreed to help those who had been willing to help themselves, and now contributes half the expense of the experiment. These are significant facts. They mean that we are gradually beginning to recognize the duty of the community in regard to the education of its citizens. Why should the State aid instruction in botany, but refuse to help the teaching of history? No satisfactory answer has been, or can be given, to this question. In fact the present situation is anomalous and absurd. But such action as that of the Lancashire County Council will help us through the difficulty. When the local authorities once begin to teach economics, they will soon want to teach history as well. And probably nothing would be more popular or more useful. Democratic institutions make it necessary to extend the higher education of the people.

．・．

A significant Report. One of the lecturers writes as follows about a Yorkshire centre:—'—— was one of the centres tempted by the Technical Education Act to abandon historical and literary courses for science. After two years' trial (and failure) the committee have returned to Oxford, declaring that far more interest is taken by working men in the non-scientific subjects.' What this means is, not that scientific teaching is unnecessary, but that it is now provided with profusion, and that there is consequently a felt need for teaching in the humanities as well. We want a well-balanced policy in public education. It would be a great misfortune if reaction resulted from a surfeit of science.

．・．

The Lancashire and Cheshire Association for the Extension of University Teaching will meet at Owens College on Saturday, April 7, at 3 p.m.

．・．

In the Ninth Report of the Technical Education Committee of the Kent County Council recently issued, it is remarked that the attendance at science lectures has not been as good as might be expected. It is stated that 'only small audiences have presented themselves, and it is to be feared that the interest taken by the rural population in this subject is of a somewhat discouraging character.'

．・．

We learn with pleasure that Mr. H. H. Cousins, who has for some time been lecturing for the Oxford Extension Delegacy in connexion with the County Council in Kent, has been appointed by the County Council to conduct experiments on the prevention and cure of Hop-mould during the summer. The work is to be carried on at three stations, where plots of ground will be allotted for the practical testing of 'preventives'; and in addition communications will be established with prominent hop-growers at fifteen other places, so that on notice of the outbreak of mould Mr. Cousins may at once be able to make experiments on the diseased plant in its own district. We understand that the object of the experiments is to find some better and cheaper remedy than the present one of sprinkling sulphur on the plant. We wish Mr. Cousins all success in his investigations.

．・．

A Correction. In the article entitled 'A Norwegian Account of University Extension' (contributed by Miss Olga Hassel of Laurvik, Norway), which appeared on page 63 of our February issue, the words 'The *versatile* method of the University Extension system . . .,' &c., should read 'The *comprehensive* method of the University Extension system . . .,' &c.

SUMMER MEETING NOTES.

The *Programme* of the Summer Meeting is now ready and can be obtained from the University Extension Office, price 7*d.* post free. It contains a list of lodgings, a synopsis of the courses, and much other detailed information. The programme shows which lectures will be given in Part I, but the time-table will not be published till May 15, as the exact date of some of the lectures cannot at present be determined. A copy of the time-table, when published, will be sent to every purchaser of the programme.

．・．

The Right Hon. James Bryce, M.P., author of the *Holy Roman Empire*, and the *American Commonwealth*, has been asked, and has consented (if his engagements permit), to deliver the Inaugural Lecture. The subject will be 'The Worth of the Study of Ancient Literature to our Time.'

．・．

In the course on Education, the lectures on Teachers' Training will be delivered by Mr. H. Courthope Bowen, M.A. There will be a practice class and criticism lessons.

．・．

The Essex County Council has voted £15 to the Saffron Walden Technical Instruction Committee for the purpose of sending scholars to the Summer Meeting.

1

Hughes had rendered to the co-operative movement, and the form of the memorial chosen was that of a scholarship at Oriel College, where Mr. Hughes was an undergraduate. The first co-operative scholar elected on the Hughes Foundation was Mr. Broadbent of Lewes, who, after taking his degree from Oriel, entered upon a course of study at Manchester College, Oxford. About six months ago he was appointed minister of the Unitarian Church at Cheltenham, where he suddenly died about the middle of April. His beautiful character and simple goodness endeared him to all who knew him.

.·.

We should feel obliged if those of our readers who have any spare copies of No. 1, vol. i, of the *Gazette* for disposal, would kindly forward them to the ' Publisher, *University Extension Gazette*, University Press, Oxford.' Copies of this early number are urgently needed for making a complete file of the *Gazette* for the Chicago Public Library.

SUMMER MEETING NOTES.

We are glad to be able to announce that Dr. John Fiske of Cambridge, Massachusetts, has just accepted the invitation of the Delegacy to deliver three lectures at the Summer Meeting on 'The Pilgrim Fathers and the Planting of New England.' English students of the seventeenth century will welcome this opportunity of hearing Dr. Fiske's lectures on a subject upon which he speaks with unrivalled authority. The course will be given on August 13, 14 and 15.

.·.

University Extension students will hear with pleasure that the Secretary of the American Society for the Extension of University Teaching, Dr. Edward T. Devine, will give a course of six lectures on Economics at the Summer Meeting. The titles of the lectures of the course will probably be :—

(1) Introduction to the Ricardian Economics.
(2) Introduction to the Economics of Walker.
(3) Introduction to the ' New Economics.'
(4) The Increase of Wealth.
(5) The Increase of Wages.
(6) The Relation of Economics to Social Reform.

The title of the lectures of Dr. Devine's course may be modified hereafter, but the above outline will indicate the interesting topics with which he proposes to deal.

.·.

We have pleasure in announcing that Mr. D. G. Ritchie, Fellow of Jesus College, the well-known author of *Darwinism and Politics* and other works on Philosophy and Economics, will deliver four lectures at the Summer Meeting on Descartes, Spinoza, and Locke, as typical figures of the seventeenth century. The course will consist of four lectures, on August 8, 9, 10 and 11; one being devoted to Locke's place in general philosophy, and another to his work as a political philosopher. This course marks a new departure at the Summer Meeting, and it is possible that it will be followed next year by a longer course on some branch of philosophical study.

.·.

A marked feature of the Meeting will be the delivery of lectures by leading representatives of the sister branches of the University Extension movement. Mr. Arthur Berry from Cambridge, Dr. Devine and, it is hoped, Mr. Rolfe from the American Society, will contribute interesting lectures to the programme. The work of the Science and Art Department of South Kensington will be represented by Captain Abney, C.B., F.R.S. General regret will be felt that Dr. R. D. Roberts was unable to accept the invitation of the Delegacy to take part in the Meeting.

UNIVERSITY EXTENSION
CONFERENCE AT BOURNEMOUTH.

THE characteristic feature of the machinery of University Extension has been from the first the co-operation between local activity and the central authority. Hitherto it has been the latter which has taken the initiative in summoning conferences in which the principles of the work could be emphasized and details discussed; but it is obvious that for these to have their full use, they need to be specially held for different parts of England; hence it was a happy idea on the part of the Bournemouth local committee to call together a conference of the centres in some of the southern counties. The idea has been fully justified by the result.

The conference met on the morning of Tuesday, April 17; there were present representatives from a considerable number of Hants, Wilts, Dorset, and E. Somerset centres, besides Mr. Mackinder, Mr. Marriott and Mr. Wells, from the central delegacy at Oxford, and Mr. Horsburgh, who has been lecturing at Bournemouth during the last session. The proceedings began with a discussion of 'Students' Associations,' which was well maintained and useful; this part of the work has been so marked a success at Bournemouth that representatives of other centres were fortunate in being able to hear something on the spot of the methods and the spirit prevailing there. In the afternoon the subject was 'The Amalgamation of the various Educational Committees of a large Town.' Mr. Mackinder spoke first on ' Work at Reading '; unfortunately it would be impossible to do more here than give the barest outlines of his interesting account of Oxford's most highly developed centre, and these are already familiar to the readers of the *University Extension Gazette*; but the happy blending of principles and details which marked the speech will not be soon forgotten by those who had the good fortune to hear it. After many questions had been asked of and answered by Mr. Mackinder, Mr. Perkins of Southampton read a paper on 'The Relation of University Extension to the Elementary Schools.' In this he gave a most interesting account of the new departure just taken by the School Board at Southampton in sending their pupil teachers to Mr. Horsburgh's course of Extension lectures on history: it was too early to speak much of results, but two may be mentioned—that the centre for the first time has a balance on the right side, and that the lecturer reports the most marked improvement in the style of the answers of the teachers who do papers for him (it is stipulated by the Board that the papers *must* be done, but Mr. Perkins seemed inclined to think that this compulsion was a mistake). A most interesting short discussion followed, due especially to the question of the chairman, who happily putting himself in the room of the unlearned, asked as to the educational results of University Extension work; the replies given, especially by Mr. Horsburgh, Mr. Mackinder and Mr. Marriott, were very striking. Mr. Whitting then read a paper on ' Local Aspects of Amalgamation': as the Secretary, and largely the founder, of the ' Bournemouth Central Council of Education,' he naturally spoke especially of its constitution and prospects: it consists of thirty-five members, twenty-four elected by nineteen different societies, and eleven co-opted. The paper was full of suggestion as to possible improvements in educational machinery, due to centralization and co-operation.

In the evening there was a public meeting in the gymnasium of the Shaftesbury Hall. Unfortunately the room was not full, there being only about 150 present, but it made up in appreciation for any lack of quantity. The Mayor presided, and introduced first Mr. Mackinder: it is to be hoped that the latter's speech may be reproduced in some form. It set forth the real ideal of University Extension as a national movement: it was in this light that its past history was described and its possible developments sketched. Mr. Mackinder sees in University Extension a part, and a very important part, of the machinery by which the English democracy is to be educated to the duties which have now been devolved upon it. The speech must be described as having been really eloquent, and was brilliantly successful. Mr. Herbert Burrows, of the Social Democratic Federation, spoke next; it was rather a pity that his most interesting and excellent speech was largely taken up with emphasizing his own position as a democrat and a socialist: the result was that he did little more in his speech of three-quarters of an hour than reinforce from a different point of view the principles laid down by Mr. Mackinder. Mr. Wells and Mr. Marriott spoke shortly, the former on the various classes in an Extension audience, the latter on the harmony of University Extension with the spirit in which Universities had been first founded. The meeting ended soon after ten, with a vote of thanks to the Mayor, moved by Mr. Leveson Scarth, the President of the local committee.

On Wednesday morning the subject for discussion was the 'Combination of Centres.' Mr. Marriott and Mr. Horsburgh urged this from the side of practical necessity, and Mr. Mackinder from that of the statesmanship for the future. The two former pointed out the greatly-increased expense, the wear and tear on the lecturer (Mr. Marriott had in the last five or six years travelled over 50,000 miles to deliver over 1,500 lectures), and the greater efficiency in teaching which can be secured if a lecturer is able to spend some time with his students out of the lecture-room, instead of being always in the train or hurrying to catch one. The latter laid stress on the need for combinations of two kinds: on the one hand there must be groups of three or four centres, who would form a 'lecture unit,' working together for practical purposes; such a unit had been formed by the three centres already existing in the Isle of Wight: on the other hand there must be larger 'Federations' representing whole districts, which could assist in organizing lecture units, but which would find their work especially in representing the claims of University Extension in the coming reorganization of Secondary Education in England. The practical outcome of the meeting was two resolutions: one resolving on the formation of a Southern Counties Federation for Berks, Hants, Wilts, and Dorset, and appointing a committee to carry out this arrangement, and especially to organize a similar conference to the present one next year (it was hoped that it might be held in Reading); the second urging on local centres and the central executive that it was most desirable that neighbouring centres should unite and work together. How difficult this last is, however desirable, was well seen in the afternoon, when a business meeting of delegates was held with a view to arranging circuits in the southern district: the different needs of different localities, special preferences, the awkwardness of railway communication and other such points, made the task of arrangement apparently almost hopeless; but something practical was done in the arrangement of two circuits for lecturers, and still more a beginning was made in the most necessary work of getting all to realize at once the need for, and the difficulties in, combination. The afternoon concluded with a discussion on the question of Prizes in University Extension work. Mr. Horsburgh moved the abolition of these, Mr. Wells defended them; the debate was well sustained, but no division was taken.

The Conference ended with a Conversazione in the Havergal Hall, which looked exceedingly pretty. Most of the proceedings were social, but Mr. Scarth towards the close announced the results of the recent examinations, and admirably summed up the results of the Conference, while a vote of thanks was moved to the Bournemouth Committee by Mr. Horsburgh and Miss Bussell of Bridport. The latter pointed out admirably in a charming short speech the advantages to local secretaries of such meetings as these, where difficulties can be smoothed away at once which correspondence is powerless to touch. The vote of thanks was acknowledged by Miss Punch: though she dwelt specially on the assistance given her by others, yet it was fitting that she should have the last word in a Conference which has owed so much to her untiring energy, her kind thoughtfulness, and her fertility of resource.

J. W.

RESULTS OF THE BOURNEMOUTH CONFERENCE.

IT is to be hoped that the Conference held at Bournemouth on April 17 and 18, may be the first of a new type of meeting, from which the University Extension movement may gather fresh strength. We have been accustomed to Conferences held at Oxford, Cambridge, and other great centres, and to isolated meetings either for business or stimulus in the local centres. At Bournemouth we have now had a Conference consisting of a series of sittings for business, culminating in a public meeting for stimulus. There can be no question that the effect on the locality of the cumulative action of such a Conference is far greater than that of an isolated meeting, and the time has probably come when the University Extension movement might usefully follow the example set by the Trades Unions, the Friendly Societies, and various religious associations, and by holding Conferences of the Bournemouth pattern annually in various local centres, make each of them in turn conscious of its participation in a national movement. On all hands it was admitted that the main result of the late Conference was to give a new sense of dignity and power to the Extension workers of Bournemouth and the neighbouring towns.

With a view to securing the repetition of such Conferences, at any rate in one portion of the country, a Southern Counties Federation has been formed, based on the triangle of towns—Bournemouth, Reading, Bath, and upon the railways connecting them. This Federation will not attempt to fol ow the example of the Federal Associations already existing in other parts of the country, in the effort to bring about the co operation of centres for the employment of the same lecturers. That is a difficult duty which, if it is to be successfully accomplished, will have to be left to much smaller bodies. The Southern Counties Federation will for the present limit itself to the holding of an annual Conference within the district, for the discussion more especially of the larger issues involved in the work. For the rest, it will aim only at the perfecting of an organization whereby it may act with decision and authority, whenever, amid the coming changes, University Extension ought to assert itself in the State, as a force to be reckoned with in re-arrangements and compromises. Next year's Conference will probably be held at Reading.

H. J. MACKINDER.

A BELGIAN VIEW OF THE OXFORD SUMMER MEETING.

THE following announcement of the forthcoming Summer Meeting in Oxford is taken from *La Flandre Libérale*, and is of interest as giving a foreign view of the value of the work done in connexion with English University Extension:—

L'UNIVERSITY EXTENSION EN ANGLETERRE.—Tous nos lecteurs connaissent l'œuvre de l'*University Extension*, qu'une heureuse initiative a transportée, dans ses traits généraux, en Belgique il y a quelques mois à peine. Ses promoteurs ne se bornent pas, en Angleterre, à l'établissement de véritables Universités populaires, ouvertes à tous, dans les centres populeux du pays. Ils organisent de plus chaque année, à Oxford et à Cambridge, des meetings d'été, où se réunissent les étudiants des autres locaux affiliés aux deux Universités. Le programme du sixième Summer Meeting d'Oxford vient de paraître; il se réunira du 27 juillet au 24 août. James Bryce, le membre bien connu des Communes, lira l'adresse inaugurale. De nombreux cours y seront donnés sur l'histoire, la littérature au XVIIe siècle, les devoirs du citoyen, les poèmes homériques, l'astronomie, l'anthropologie, la géologie, l'hygiène, la chimie, l'économie politique, l'histoire d'Oxford, &c. La cotisation de chaque participant est fixée à 1 livre 10 shillings, soit 35 francs. Des bourses d'un import total de 177 livres seront mises au concours. Ainsi tous les ans, pendant un mois, la jeune Université démocratique vient dans les palais gothiques, les halls majestueux, les antiques chapelles, les riches bibliothèques et les parcs séculaires des collèges d'Oxford, prendre la place de la vieille Université aristocratique d'Angleterre.

2

SOUTH-EASTERN AGRICULTURAL COLLEGE AT WYE.

Appointment of Mr. A. D. Hall as Principal.

WE are glad to announce that Mr. A. D. Hall, M.A., one of the lecturers of the Oxford University Extension Delegacy who has been working for the Surrey County Council, has been elected Principal of the South-Eastern Agricultural College at Wye, near Ashford, in Kent. This recognition of Mr. Hall's ability and distinguished services to educational work will be welcomed by all University Extension students, and the more so as almost the whole body of University Extension lecturers engaged by the counties of Surrey and Kent have also been placed upon the staff of the College.

In the *Technical World* of Oct. 7, 1893, there appeared an excellent summary of the scheme for the establishment of the South-Eastern Agricultural College, an undertaking which owes much to the proposals originally made by Mr. H. Macan, Organizing Secretary of the Surrey County Council.

The following note of Mr. Hall's appointment appeared in a recent issue of the *County Council Times* :—

The Governors of the South-Eastern Agricultural College, Wye, have elected Mr. A. D. Hall, M.A., F.C.S., as Principal. Mr. Hall's election was proposed by Sir H. E. Roscoe, M.P., seconded by Professor Liveing. The four candidates selected to appear before the Governors were Mr. Hall; Dr. Munro, Professor of Chemistry at Downham; Mr. C. M. Aikman, Professor of Chemistry, Glasgow Veterinary College; and Mr. James Clark, Lecturer on Agricultural Chemistry, Yorkshire College, Leeds. Mr. Hall is twenty-nine years of age. He was educated at the Manchester Grammar School, was elected to a science scholarship at Balliol College, Oxford, in 1881, and obtained a First Class in the Final Honour Schools (Chemistry) in 1884. After a year's further work at Oxford under Professor H. B. Dixon he became the first science master at Blairlodge School, N.B., where he organized the teaching and saw to the fitting of the lecture-rooms, workshops, &c. At the opening of the Hulme Grammar School, Manchester, he was invited to become science master, and again had to make all arrangements necessary to the equipment of the laboratories and the inauguration of the science teaching. In 1888 he was appointed senior science master at King Edward's High School, Birmingham, when the Science Department was just entering into new lecture-rooms and laboratories. He has published two courses of laboratory work that he developed during his stay in Birmingham—*Exercises in Practical Chemistry*, 1890, and *Exercises in Heat*, 1893. Three years ago he was invited to lecture for the Oxford University Extension Delegates, and since then he has been lecturing in agricultural chemistry, &c., for the County Council of Surrey. The basis on which Mr. Hall proposes to work may be gathered from the following extract from his application to the Governors for the appointment :—'Whilst loyally carrying out the policy of the Governors, it would be my desire, if elected Principal, to develop the work of the College on the following lines—(1) To so organize and supervise the scientific teaching that it should never become academic and out of touch with agriculture; since the object of the College is not to train chemists or teachers, but working farmers sufficiently acquainted with the method and results of acquired science to be able to read a technical communication, and judge for themselves how far it is applicable to their own circumstances; (2) To carry on by the help of the students themselves a routine series of field experiments on manuring, cropping, treatment against disease, &c.; to disseminate the results as widely as possible, and so make the College an intelligence department for the two counties; (3) To perfect a system of dairy work adapted to the poor grass lands of Kent and Surrey, and to arrange instruction in the after treatment of milk, sterilization, humanizing, &c., on a commercial scale; (4) To organize a system of book-keeping for the fields and stock used by the College, and to make every pupil thoroughly familiar with the routine of this side of farming; (5) To give special attention to the arrangement of short time courses in dairy work, horticulture, and other practical subjects, to meet the needs of older students, elementary teachers, and others attending lectures within the counties.'

UNIVERSITY EXTENSION CONGRESS, LONDON, 1894.

THE following paper has been issued by the London University Extension Society :—

'It has been decided by the Council of the London Society for the Extension of University Teaching to hold in London in the month of June a University Extension Congress. In the initiation and arrangement of this Congress the Universities of Oxford and Cambridge are cordially co-operating with the Council. There are several reasons which render the present year opportune for such a gathering. In the first place, the University Extension movement attains its majority, the first course of lectures having been arranged by the University of Cambridge in the autumn of 1873. In the second place, the report of the Gresham University Commission has outlined a comprehensive scheme for the establishment of a Teaching University for London, and in that scheme University Extension work has a defined place. In view of the anticipated establishment of a Teaching University on the lines laid down in the Report of the Royal Commission, it is important to sum up and present the educational results of the twenty-one years' work in University Extension, and to consider, in the light of past experience, practical proposals and a general policy for the future of the whole movement. The rapid spread of the University Extension movement into English-speaking countries beyond the seas, and the establishment of work on somewhat similar lines in several countries on the continent of Europe, render a gathering of those actively engaged in promoting this work in the various areas where it has been taken up a matter of real moment. This remarkable expansion of the movement makes it specially important to indicate the direction of possible advance, and to consider carefully the nature of, and the remedies for, the difficulties and dangers which experience has shown are likely to be encountered.

'It is proposed to invite to the Congress (1) Representatives from the central organizations conducting University Extension work in the United Kingdom, the Colonies, America, and the various European countries where it is being carried on; (2) Representatives from all local centres in the United Kingdom; and (3) Lecturers and educational experts interested in the University Extension movement.

'The Congress, which will meet in the Lecture-Theatre of the University of London, will include three Sessions, to be held on Friday afternoon, June 22, and Saturday morning and afternoon, June 23. The Marquess of Salisbury, Chancellor of the University of Cambridge, and Lord Herschell, Chancellor of the University of London, will preside at the three Sessions respectively.

'The subjects for discussion will be :—

1. The means of preserving and further developing the educational character of University Extension work, and the relation of the more popular to the more strictly educational side of the movement.

2. The essentials of efficient central and local organization, and the relation, educational and financial, of the University Extension movement to the State and to local authorities.

3. The educational possibilities of University Extension work and methods in relation to regular University studies and University degrees.

'These subjects will be considered beforehand by a Committee or Committees of experts, who will present reports and formulate the resolutions to be submitted for discussion to the Congress. The Council hope to be able to make arrangements to offer hospitality to representatives who may desire it.'

THE PRESIDENT OF MAGDALEN AT THE TEACHERS' GUILD.

Interesting Address on Secondary Education.

THIS year's Conference of the Teachers' Guild was held at Bath, and on Tuesday, April 17, the President of Magdalen delivered his presidential address. For the following summary of it we are indebted to the *Schoolmaster*:—

Starting out with the statement that the past year had been full of educational events and gatherings, Mr. Warren said the fact had come home to them very much in Oxford. Oxford, since the Guild met there a year since, had been the scene of several notable conferences. The members of the Guild were with them at Easter; in July the Head Masters' Association held their meetings in his own college; in October came the great Secondary Education Conference; and only the other day they had the pleasant and successful meeting of their friends of the N. U. T.

The Secondary Education Conference resulted, as they knew, in the appointment of a Royal Commission upon Secondary Education, a step of which he most heartily and thoroughly approved. There were some bold spirits who were anxious to push ahead: ' Legislate first, and you'll find out the requirement afterwards, or as you go along,' was what they said. Some of these bold spirits were, he was glad to say, upon the Royal Commission, and his belief was, they would find the problem not nearly so simple as they imagined. The constitution of the Commission would not, of course, satisfy all parties. With the complaint which had found a voice in Parliament, that the private schools were not sufficiently represented, he had some sympathy; but the Teachers' Guild as such had no cause to complain. It was represented by its chairman, and he was glad to think they had, or would have at their meetings, a gentleman whose experience and proved sagacity peculiarly fitted him to be on the Commission—Dr. Wormell, head master of the Cowper Street Central School.

What the result of the Royal Commission's report would be they must wait to see. Its immediate effect was rather to suspend their thoughts, if not their practical activities, in one direction, that of organization. Of organization their thoughts had been for a long time past only too full. But while the Royal Commission were sitting, while they were finding out the facts and deciding what to propose, they might, he thought, take the opportunity—it was this he proposed to ask them to do—to consider what was and would remain the duty of the teachers under any organization which could be devised.

They were going to make another great effort to organize education, and to organize it on democratic lines, and in the interests of the democracy, that was to say, of the community at large. The object proposed was to provide Secondary Education for all parts of the country. What was the ideal to be aimed at and what could teachers do to aid in its realization? Was the ideal to produce equality? Was equality desirable? And could education produce it? What did the democracy expect, what ought they to expect to get from this better, more generally diffused, and accessible higher education? What could education do for the people?

He addressed those who were experts in education, and the Teachers' Guild ought to be under no illusions. There were not a few illusions about education, and the democracy were liable to

be deceived by them. The democracy expected to be, and their friends told them that they would be, the better off for education. He personally thought so, or he should not be there. But what did they mean by being better off? Did they mean having more money, better or more smart clothes, a higher station or rank in life? Was this what education was to bring to the masses? It was certainly what some people thought and said. There was no phrase more common and current than that of the ladder of education which was to conduct from the gutter to the university, or from the bench in the elementary school to the woolsack.

To aspire to the woolsack was a noble ambition, but there was only one woolsack, and with all the education in the world every one could not enjoy it. To aspire to go to the university was also a noble aspiration, but the true educational ladder was that whereby, in the poet's noble phrase, men might rise on stepping-stones of their dead selves to higher things. There was a meaning in the desire for material advancement, and a reason in the belief that education conduced to it. He would be the last to deny this. He recognized most fully the nobility and the justice of the ideal that every single human unit born into the world should have the help of education provided for it equally, that it should be readily and universally accessible.

He believed firmly that by universal education, and by universal education alone, could the general sum of wealth available for distribution among the human race be increased, and he thought it was possible that the distribution of it might be much more equalized than it was at present, only care must be exercised in equalizing the distribution not to destroy the incentive to production. They must introduce, perhaps by education too, other, perhaps higher, motives to take the place of those which now stimulated men to production. It was certain, he thought, that in the production of wealth men must ever play very different and, in a sense, very unequal parts. It was supposed sometimes that the state of nature was a state of equality, and that inequality was artificial. They had been misled by comparing the educated rich in days when the poor were uneducated with the uneducated poor. The language of Gray's immortal Elegy had been taken with prosaic literalness and applied to every village.

It had been supposed that in every churchyard, sleeping among the rude forefathers of the hamlet, were to be found not one but many village Hampdens, mute inglorious Miltons, and Cromwells guiltless of their country's blood, and some people talked as though it needed only the institution of free education, and he supposed they might add now the Parish Council, to make genius for letters and affairs as common in every village as the blackberries on the hedgerows. He believed this to be largely an illusion. Real genius was rare, exceedingly rare. All the education in the world would not create it, and he believed that want of higher education did not often retard it.

If the genius was taught to read, and if he had the necessary moral qualities, he believed he would generally show himself and rise to the top. The divinely-gifted man would, he was convinced, not find it very difficult to burst his fates' invidious bar, and to grasp the skirts of happy chance. What was possible for Bunyan and Burns, Stephenson and Davy, Faraday, Wolsey, and Marlborough, was always possible. It was want, not of education, but of real genius and force of character, that arrested the progress at various stages short of the highest achievement.

Nowhere, he thought teachers would agree with him, was the survival of the fittest more conspicuously true than in the field of education. Some people imagined that the result of education would be to make all the same, that every one, to use their phrase, would be put through the mill and come out shaped to the regulation pattern. Heaven forbid that such should be the result of education. If so it was the result of bad, not of good education. They were apt at times to think that education consisted not in bringing out but in putting in. They talked of forming a character, or, in somewhat ambiguous language, of licking a boy into shape, as though the teacher had absolute control over an inert and plastic material. He likened education to the action of the shower upon the seed and upon the bud, and went on to show that the function of the teacher, if not literally the unconscious function of the summer rain, was at least that of the gardener.

As the latter in his garden so the teacher in his seminary might select and weed, might graft and prune, might water, feed, and train the plant ; he might, indeed, do much, but there was a limit. He might force and distort, produce double flowers, the scented peony, possibly some day the blue rose, but he could not change the rose into the lily, or make the acorn grow into anything but the oak. Nature herself was often the best educator, and the unmitigated struggle for existence would sometimes produce the toughest vitality. To be let alone was sometimes the condition most needed for growth, and so schools sunk in idleness, and even in morality, had at times produced the rarest and fairest flowers of scholarship or character. Sometimes the most opposite persons, the most contradictory, had succeeded in education. He asked them to read or consider the lives of or personalities of some of the great teachers—and here truth, as well as partiality, prompted him to add the name of Dunn. Mr. Warren went on to explain that there was a science of education as well as a science of medicine, and the first thing a teacher should set himself to know was the constitution of the pupil, what qualities and capacities were in him, and which and how should they be brought out. They must have, in other words, some idea of the perfect character first, perhaps absolutely ; and secondly, as attainable under the general conditions imposed upon them.

Now there was no doubt the ideal of a perfectly healthy human nature with every faculty developed, in just proportion to this and to this alone perfect and ideal education would correspond. Absolutely it was not within their ken ; they might believe, perhaps, that it was the ideal to which in the ultimate survival of the fittest natural selection in a divine order of the universe was tending, but as yet they were only tending and straining after it ; the reaching and realization of it was part of the far-off haven to which they deemed or dreamed the whole creation moved. In fact, they could not reach it alone ; they must reach it, if at all, altogether. This was what the ancients saw so clearly when they said that such an ideal could only be realized in a perfect society, or that, as they put it, the good man was relative to the good State. But the State was not perfect, society around us was far from perfect, and in the imperfection of society the fact with which they were met was that at one end the characters they had to deal with came to them imperfect, warpe¹, distorted, starved, stunted, biased ; and at the other they were obliged to prepare them for conditions by no means favourable to or compatible with absolute health.

Here lay their problem—the problem of education. What compromise were they to make, and how were they to determine its conditions? They must, he thought, form as clear and high a conception of the ideal as possible. Perfect society, as Plato said, might not be for earth at all, or not for earth in our time, but the pattern of it was ever kept in heaven, and he who desired might behold it, and beholding it might order his own life. Especially was it the duty and the inspiration of the educator to have some outline of the heavenly pattern before him, to have, to speak in more ordinary language, if not the absolute, the high ideal before him as an attainable possibility. It was not for them to think merely what would make the most successful man either in examinations now or in life afterwards, but what would make the best man.

Practically the question was determined for them by practical considerations. It was to some extent the old question between a liberal and a technical education. It was the duty of the educator to fit the pupil not only to get his bread but for life in all its fulness ; and it would be their duty as teachers all the more in the organized system of the future. There were the broad common duties, as there were the common capacities of the human being ; the great cardinal virtues, moral and intellectual must be inculcated upon all. In these let them seek to produce equality and similarity, but for the rest he would say to democracy, seek equality not in similarity but in diversity, and to the teacher, cultivate for healthy individuality! It was the profound criticism of Goethe upon our present system of education that it awakened desires when it ought to cultivate tastes. It should be their

object to preach to their pupils the doctrine of being rather than getting, to teach them the true principle of a true democracy, that all honest occupations were in kind and essentially equally honourable.

As he had explained, they wanted a science of education just as they wanted a science of medicine. The ordinary practitioner did not, perhaps, often add much by his observation and record to the science of medicine, but now and again the scientific and diligent practitioner was found who added something. The teacher, he thought, added even less, but was this necessarily so?

Might not this be just one of the most useful functions of the Teachers' Guild to collect and to compare, to sift and to record educational experience, and to make teaching thus a science and a fine art. The numbers of pupils were, he knew, the difficulty, and a difficulty which it might be feared democratic organization would increase rather than diminish. Its temptation would be to economize, to spread education thin, to suit the average, and to force every one into what suited the average, producing only that kind of education which was a proof and result of bad education, and not of good. For there were, it seemed to him, several ways in which education might produce equality, but they were all bad. It might stunt and starve faculty, that was perhaps the least likely way ; it might misdirect it and put it on the wrong tack, and in so doing it might irritate and exasperate the character ; or what was a more insidious danger, might persuade it unconsciously into what was not its true line.

Bad education might thus prove more destructive to genius than little education or even almost no education. It might produce an equality, but the equality of a dead level. True equality would come about in a very different and more legitimate way when each did what he was best fitted to do, and when there was a generally diffused sense that all good work was practically equal. There was a danger in freedom of education, but there was as much, nay, more danger, in a want of freedom. The danger of the old system, or want of system, was the danger of educational quackery, of neglect, but the danger of the future was monotony. He hoped the new system which the Royal Commission, and legislation which might follow, would establish, would provide enough teachers to do justice to the number of pupils. He hoped also it would give a free hand and an assured status to those it did provide. He hoped that the curriculum would have some elasticity, and that the kind of mistake made in elementary education by the system of payment by results would not be repeated in the higher field.

For, after all, it must be not to any system but to the men who taught and worked under it, that they must look to make it a living reality, and not a mechanical routine, and to give them those conditions which were the conditions of a healthy and advancing society, the conditions namely, not of a dead level of uniformity, but of an equal, fair, and free development of individual function.

Among the other notable features of the Conference was a spirited address by Mr. T. W. Dunn of Bath College, on the dangers of any State interference with Education. An important point this, and one that it is well to bear in mind. Mr. Storr contributed an excellent paper on the State organization of Secondary Education, and Mr. Graham Wallas a characteristic and valuable paper on training in citizenship.

REVIEW.

Philip's Systematic Atlas : Physical and Political. By E. G. RAVENSTEIN, F.R.G.S. London, George Philip & Son, 1894. Price 15s. net.

Admirably adapted to its purpose and specially well fitted for the use of University Extension Students is the *Systematic Atlas*, which Messrs. Philip and Son have just published under the editorship of Messrs. J. Scott Keltie, H. J. Mackinder, and E. G. Ravenstein. It is handy in form, convenient in plan and full of wisely ordered information. Its price brings it within the reach of every student, and it is wonderful that at so small a charge the publishers are able to provide such a variety of clear, well-coloured and suggestive maps.

YORKSHIRE ASSOCIATION FOR THE EXTENSION OF UNIVERSITY TEACHING.

THE annual conference of the Association was held at Leeds on Saturday afternoon, April 21. Seven Oxford centres were represented — Bradford, Halifax, Hebden Bridge, Ilkley, Settle, Thornton and Wakefield — and about the same number of Cambridge centres. Mr. E. J. Wilson of Hull was in the chair, and after a statement of accounts from the Hon. Treasurer, which showed the Association to be in a satisfactory financial position, the meeting proceeded to the election of officers for the ensuing year, Mr. E. J. Wilson of Hull and Miss Snowdon of Ilkley being re-elected Hon. Secretaries, and Miss Thompson of Scarborough Hon. Treasurer.

The question of the continuation of the Yorkshire Scholarship Fund to enable Yorkshire students to attend the Summer Meetings, was next brought forward, and it was decided, after some discussion as to the method of award, to continue the present system, by which the scholarships are given to those students who, being otherwise eligible, gain the highest marks in the examinations held during the previous winter. The advisability of printing an annual report of the work of the Association was also discussed, and the secretary was instructed to prepare a short report and ask for its insertion in the *University Extension Gazette* and *Journal.*

Miss Thompson of Scarborough made some interesting suggestions with regard to missionary work, more of which she thought the associated centres might well undertake, and it was decided to leave the matter in the hands of the district sub-committees, with a special recommendation to them to do all they could to help in the organization of courses in connexion with school boards.

Mr. Wilson suggested that the Association might get together a fund and engage a resident lecturer for the winter, something on the plan worked out by Mr. Grant in his article on Provincial Organization in the April number of the *University Extension Journal,* but the idea being quite new to most of those present, consideration of it was postponed with the understanding that a definite scheme would be proposed next year.

It was decided that the next meeting of the Association should be held at York. The rest of the time at the disposal of the conference was taken up with the making of arrangements for lectures for the winter of 1894-95.

Annual Meeting of the Lancashire and Cheshire Association for the Extension of University Teaching.

THE annual meeting of the Lancashire and Cheshire Association was held on Saturday, April 7, at 3.30 p.m., at the rooms of the Owens College Union, Oxford Street, Manchester, Mr. J. E. Phythian in the chair. About thirty delegates from local centres were present.

The Chairman, in opening the proceedings of the conference, referred to the loss which the University Extension movement had sustained by the death of Professor Marshall, one of their most enthusiastic supporters in the north of England.

Mr. J. H. Fowler, Hon. Sec. of the Association, then read the annual report. The report dealt largely with the relations of the Association to the Lancashire County Council. The committee regretted that the County Council had determined to withdraw its subsidy from the Association and spend £500 on University Extension lectures under its own control. The two centres in Lancashire that deserved pecuniary support above all others, because they had arranged for continuity of teaching in subjects that attracted only bona fide students and no outside audience whatsoever — Earlestown, where engineering lectures had been given with most encouraging results, and Woolton, where a mutual improvement society of gardeners had for several years been studying botany — had been compelled to suspend operations through the refusal of the County Council to pay more than half of the total expense. Under such circumstances as these the committee were reluctantly forced to the conclusion, that until some radical change was effected in the administration of the Technical Instruction Department, any attempt at harmonious co-operation would be doomed to disappointment. The report went on to note with regret the losses sustained during the past year in the deaths of the Earl of Derby, the first president of the Association, and of Professor Marshall, to whom more than to any one else the Association owed its origin. The Rt. Hon. James Bryce, M.P., Chancellor of the Duchy of Lancaster, had accepted the vacant Presidency: and the Association had now to congratulate itself on the appointment of its new President to the head of the Commission on Secondary Education. Lastly, the curtailment of operations on the scientific and technical sides left the Association more free to devote its energies to the equally important task of fostering literary and historical teaching. The committee were convinced that there were many localities in the two counties in which the establishment of University lectures in those subjects was possible as well as desirable, and were most anxious that the coming year should witness decided progress in that direction. They considered also that the example set at Liverpool, where a course of twenty-four lectures on 'Milton and his Times' had been arranged with the co-operation of the School Board, was one which might with advantage be followed in other parts of the district.

The report being adopted, financial and other business was transacted : after which the conference proceeded to the discussion of the following subjects :—

(1) The work of the Association with regard to School Boards, together with the condition of the existing centres.

(2) The National Home Reading Union as an auxiliary to University Extension.

(1) The first subject was introduced by Professor Tout, Secretary to the Victoria University Extension Committee. In advocating co-operation between large town centres and the School Boards, he instanced the recent action of the Liverpool Board, which had arranged the course of lectures referred to in the report for the benefit of pupil teachers entering for the Queen's Scholarships. The course was extremely well attended by 300 or 400 pupil teachers, and of these 200 would probably offer themselves for examination. What was done at Liverpool should also be done in Manchester, Salford, Stockport, Bolton, and other large towns. There were great difficulties in the way of the better education of the pupil teacher, and very few humanizing influences were brought to bear on him. They had heard that the Association had been obliged to contract its scientific and technical operations ; but it would not be all loss if their comparative leisure enabled them to concentrate themselves on that side of education which had never got any grant from County Councils.

Mr. Arthur Berry (Secretary to the Cambridge Syndicate) said that Professor Tout had shown what could be done by local effort. While the subjects for which it was, possible at present to get recognition from the Education Department were rather limited, it was always possible to arrange valuable courses for pupil teachers within these limits. In many cases the pupil teacher picked up the knowledge for his examination in such spare time as the head teacher could give to teaching him. Many School Boards were now arranging central classes for pupil teachers in the ordinary subjects of the Queen's Scholarship Examinations, in order to lighten the increasingly heavy task of the certificated teachers. The Association would do well to use its influence with School Boards in this direction.

Mr. Broadbent (Bolton) described how in his town such central classes had been in existence for many years — the pupil teachers being practically half-timers, teaching half the day and receiving instruction for the other half.

The Rev. A. H. Fish said that at Chester they had organized very successful courses of free lectures in the evenings in connexion with the Free Libraries Committee of the Corporation.

The Chairman advocated that steps should be taken to establish similar lectures in Manchester. Hitherto it had been thought that the Corporation were not allowed to spend money upon lectures under the Free Libraries Act.

Mr. de Burgh (Oxford) expressed Mr. Sadler's regret at not being able to attend the Conference. In the South they were always told that if they wanted to see successful Extension courses among workmen they should go to the large towns of the North of England. He believed there was much truth in that; but large audiences were not all that was necessary. They must also have method and continuity in the courses arranged. He described how in East London they had been trying to arrange three - year courses in history, literature, and science respectively, with the idea that any one who kept up attendance for that time would obtain a thorough mastery of his subject, and would find University Extension take the place of University education in those branches of learning. The importance of continuity of study could not be too strongly enforced.

(2) Professor Flux then introduced the question of the National Home Reading Union as an aid to University Extension. Here was another organization which was working on the same lines as themselves. In weak centres where financial difficulties prevented the development of Extension work, much might be done by the formation of reading circles. Again, such reading circles could form a basis for building up Extension centres. The Union commended itself to him, as a lecturer, because it culti- vated a habit of reading among students, and he urged local secretaries of centres to make themselves acquainted with its methods and organization.

The Chairman said that he had been on the committee formed with a view of starting reading circles in Man- chester, but they had encountered difficulties through the number of existing educational institutions. He expected that the Union would be more successful in smaller towns. The business of the conference then closed with votes of thanks to the Chairman for presiding and to the Owens College Union for the use of the room. After the pro- ceedings had ended those present adjourned for refresh- ment, and the conference separated about half-past five.

The Relation of University Extension to the Elementary Teachers.

[*A Paper read at the Bournemouth Conference* by W. FRANK PERKINS (*Hon. Sec.* Southampton).]

UNIVERSITY Extension has done great things in assisting the education of nearly every class of society; but, so far as I know, little or nothing has been attempted among the masses of our elementary school teachers, a most deserving and enthusiastic class, who seem eager to avail themselves of any additional means of higher education that may be within their reach, but whose aspirations have been thwarted and their ambitions cramped in great measure by the nature of their environment.

Without attempting in this short paper to deal with the whole question of the education of our public elementary teachers, perhaps it may at the outset be desirable to explain to those who have no practical knowledge of the subject, that the elemen- tary teacher is for many years of his or her life the much harassed creature of code and examination. Recruited in a very large degree from the highest standards of the elementary schools, the embryo teacher passes in turn through the successive develop- mental phases of Candidate, Pupil Teacher, Ex Pupil Teacher, Assistant Teacher, Certificated Assistant, Certificated and Trained Assistant, to reach in a few instances the highest attainable development, viz. the Head Teacher. Most of these successive stages are only entered by the narrow door of examination, and accordingly the whole of the young teacher's spare time is or should be occupied in preparing for these successive examina- tions. Now it so happens that as regards these examinations the position of the youthful teacher is unique. For whereas the young man preparing for the Army, the Navy, the Bar, or any of

the occupations of life to which examination-certificates are a passport, is in nearly every case allowed to devote the whole of his time to the adequate preparation for these examinations, the unfortunate elementary teacher is compelled to work some six hours a day for five days in the week at the ordinary business of teaching, the spare time at his disposal being considered to be sufficiently ample for the purpose of preparation for examination. What should we say of the hardship endured by an under- graduate, a law or medical student who had to give up six hours a day to working at the *practice* of his future profession, in order to earn his daily bread? It will therefore be readily understood that the time at the disposal of our younger teachers, until they have earned their final certificates, is extremely limited, and consequently they are disposed to look askance at any en- croachment upon that spare time, and to ask the very natural and pertinent question, 'Will it pay?' when new subjects of study or new means of acquiring knowledge are offered them. Moreover, having once got into the habit of regarding everything educational from the 'Will it pay?' point of view, the teachers, as soon as they have passed all their examinations, are inclined, in practice, although not in theory, of course, to consider that their education is finished, and having no further monetary advantage to gain for themselves by additional study, they are inclined to rest on their oars, and not to study for study's sake. There is every excuse for this mental attitude of indifference on the part of teachers   The iron limits of strictly construed codes ; the official severity of the Education Department, the Inspector and the voluntary or board managers, all help to extinguish in the teacher's breast that love for knowledge for its own sake to which it is the mission of University Extension to minister. Further, the daily contact with minds so infinitely less expanded than their own, and the humdrum routine of the three Rs, all tend to dull their educational appetite. And finally the teachers for the most part have scarcely ever known the pleasure of that high intellectual stimulus and companionship which only the Universities can give.

It will I think be clear that in the elementary teacher there is material, although unpromising, of which an Extension student may be made. For while on the one hand we have to contend with the 'Will it pay?' habit of mind, on the other hand we have to deal with a disciplined and receptive intellect, accus- tomed to select, classify, and assimilate facts, and to state them clearly ; accustomed also to student-like habits of work. As Bacon says, 'Reading maketh a full man ; conference a ready man ; and writing an exact man'; and my experience of elemen- tary teachers is that they have quite their fair share of each of these forms of intellectual equipment.

How then are we to get hold of the elementary teacher? The answer to this question depends primarily on certain facts which must carefully be considered. First of all, it must always be remembered that as regards pupil teachers in Elementary Schools, the Managers, i.e. either the Committee of Management in the case of a Voluntary School, or the School Board, or such managers as they may depute, in the case of a Board School, are responsible for their education. Art. 34 of the code says—' The Managers are bound to see that the pupil teachers are properly instructed during the engagement.' In practice this instruction is given partly or entirely by the Head Teacher, under whose control the pupil teacher is placed; and partly or entirely by specially appointed teachers, the pupil teachers attending a certain number of pupil teachers' classes. It will therefore be under- stood that the pupil teachers are bound to attend such classes and means of instruction as the managers may provide for them : but no other class of teacher is under such control.

Secondly it must be remembered that University Extension lectures are recognized by the code as suitable instruction for pupil teachers. By Art. 51 the Vice-Chancellor's certificate qualifies for recognition as an Assistant Teacher, and by a note to Sched. V, marks towards the Queen's Scholarship Examination are gained by teachers who can produce University Extension certificates of a certain kind. Quite irrespectively therefore of any educational advantage accruing to teachers attending University

Extension lectures, there is attached to them a purely monetary advantage, which local committees must be careful to advertise.

Now it seems to me that almost the best way to attract the elementary teachers to our lectures is to prove to them by circular and in conversation that they will directly benefit by attending the courses. I am of opinion that if members of our local committees would arrange among themselves to canvass all the elementary teachers in their respective districts, putting the facts plainly before them, and inviting them to attend the first lecture of each course, the result would be distinctly remunerative. Be it understood that many courses of lectures are unsuitable, as not of any special bearing on the education of an elementary teacher. History and Geography are, I think, the most acceptable subjects for courses. Further, short courses wont attract teachers so readily as long ones. They will attend two courses of twelve lectures each, in sequence, because these are the courses recognized by the Department; but they regard with disfavour the sweet sips at miscellaneous knowledge afforded by the six lecture courses on English literature, followed by six lectures on Astronomy, and six on Greek Mythology, which forms the staple of not a few centres. Moreover, time, place and price must be carefully considered. The lectures must not be too late in the evening, for many of the pupil teachers are little more than children. The spot selected should be as near as practicable to the centre of the school district, and accessible by train, tram, and 'buss. And the admission must be fixed very low, for, remember, we are catering for a class of students which is but poorly paid.

Perhaps in conclusion I may be allowed to give a concrete illustration of the successful working of University Extension among teachers, taken from the experience of my own centre, Southampton.

Ever since courses of University Extension lectures have been given in Southampton they have been attended by a *few* elementary teachers, but the great mass of teachers have been indifferent to them. Two years ago we made application to the Southampton School Board to take tickets for such of their teachers as cared to attend the lectures. Unfortunately, however, the course arranged was on the English Novelists, and the Board did not consider it to be of sufficient educational value to send their teachers to it. A compromise of tickets at half price was offered us, but declined. Last summer, the alterations in the code, to which I have already alluded, were, thanks I suppose to Mr. Acland, first formulated. My local committee agreed to another application to the Board being made, and this time we obtained the unanimous support of the Board, which undertook not only to provide tickets for any of its teachers who were willing to attend the lectures, but also to recognize the lectures as suitable instruction in History for all the pupil teachers under its control. Accordingly the course was attended not only by a good many head and assistant teachers, but also by all or nearly all the pupil teachers.

We had the good fortune to secure in Mr. Horsburgh, a lecturer who not only is a master of his subject but is also keenly interested in this new departure, and has shown the greatest sympathy with the teachers of all grades. Four half-courses, each of six lectures, have been arranged in sequence, the period of study extending from Henry VII to Elizabeth; the lectures have been arranged to occupy the autumns and springs of two years, six being before and six after Christmas in each year. Friday evening at 8 has been the day and hour selected; Friday is undoubtedly the most suitable day, but I am not quite certain that half-past seven would not be a more suitable hour for the pupil teachers.

As to the results—first of all I must admit that there has been a falling off in the attendance of the ordinary audience: this is explainable I think on three grounds. Many people are disinclined to commit themselves to courses of twelve lectures; many people are not interested in Mediaeval English History; many people who are willing and eager to attend lectures before Christmas, are considerably less keen after Christmas. On the other hand, the attendance of teachers has been most satisfactory. You

will understand that the *pupil* teachers have no option in the matter; but as regards the other teachers, those who have taken tickets have attended, so far as I can judge, remarkably well.

Of the work done Mr. Horsburgh is far better able to speak than I; but I believe that, having regard to the many difficulties in the way of young teachers, he is satisfied with their attention and progress. One difficulty we have had to face. In order that the teachers, who take advantage of the privilege of free attendance at these lectures, shall not regard them merely as an amusement, the School Board has laid down as a condition of the acceptance of a ticket, that the teacher attends the classes and writes the papers. The pupil teachers also are required to attend classes and to write papers. This at first gave rise to some little discontent. Teachers of all grades have very little spare time, and pupil teachers urge that already they are overworked: moreover the principle of compulsion has never been associated with the Extension lecture system, and I have been extremely sorry to find that this action of the Board has been regarded by some few teachers as oppressive. However, although a member of the Board, I do not feel justified as local secretary in either defending or condemning its action. So far as the local committee is concerned, the classes and paper work are as usual perfectly voluntary, and any difference that may have arisen is between the Board and its teachers.

It is clear that a public body like a School Board can be of immense assistance to a centre in swelling the number of students, and consequently the funds. And accordingly it is comparatively easy for friendly relations to be established between the centre and the Board School teachers. But no such facility exists in the case of the voluntary school teachers. Managers of voluntary schools are so hard pressed for funds that they are very unwilling to spend more money on their teachers' education than they are compelled; and therefore I am afraid that it is hopeless ever to expect a great influx of voluntary school teachers. But as regards the voluntary teachers in the neighbourhood of my own centre I am glad to say that some have been stimulated to attend our lectures by the knowledge of the advantages gained by the Board teachers; and my local committee has met them half-way by the offer of a specially reduced entrance fee. I have great hope of further interest being aroused among them.

I have purposely in this paper avoided any reference to the enormous advantage that Extension lectures offer to elementary teachers. I feel that any attempt to dilate on the direct and indirect value from an educational point of view of our system and methods of teaching would be a waste of time, when addressing an audience of experts. But I am satisfied that although many of our more experienced teachers are already enthusiastic Extension students, there still remains a great work to be accomplished in convincing the rank and file of the elementary teachers of the supreme benefits which University Extension brings within their reach.

REPORTS FROM THE CENTRES.

BAKEWELL.—Monthly meetings are being held here by the Students' Association for continued study in connexion with Mr. Mallet's last course of lectures on ' England in the Eighteenth Century.' The second meeting was held on Thursday, April 12. The subject for discussion was ' The Scientific Discoveries of the Eighteenth Century.' The following papers were read. ' The Scientific Discoveries of Murdoch, Priestley, Volta and Franklin,' by Dr. Evans. ' Fahrenheit and his Thermometer,' by Mr. Wragg. ' The Geological Theories of Werner and Hutton,' by Miss K. Martin. The next meeting will be held on May 3; the subject being ' Ireland in the Eighteenth Century.'

BANBURY.—At the annual meeting of those interested in University Extension work, it was stated that the committee had not only succeeded in wiping out the deficit of last year, but had accumulated a balance of over £15. Next winter it is hoped to arrange for two courses of lectures; one before, one after Christmas. A hope was expressed that these would be attended by a large number of artisans and teachers, and that the students would show the desire to use to the utmost the educational opportunities provided by the lectures by the writing of essays for the lecturers.

BATH.—On April 12 Mr. C. E. Mallet's course of twelve fortnightly lectures on English Prose Writers was brought to a conclusion. This is the first occasion on which a continuous course of six lectures before and six lectures after Christmas has been tried here: and though the experiment has in some degree proved a success, a certain failing of interest became apparent towards the end of the course. To those really interested in the subject the entire course has been a treat: but the general public (to whom this and every other centre must look for financial support) perhaps expected more literature and less history.

BEDFORD.—The 'English Citizen' course proved the most successful yet delivered at this centre, for the interest in the subject, awakened last autumn, increased during the spring term, when the average attendance rose to 170, nearly one-fourth of this number being artisans. Some of the latter regularly attended the Students' Meetings, and one of their number being a member of the Board of Guardians was able to contribute the result of his practical experience to discussions on the Poor Law. Papers on that subject, as well as on Education, and Justice and Police, were read on different occasions by students having special knowledge of each department of citizen life. Although eight candidates only sat for the final examination, this number very inadequately represented the educational value of the course, as a means of developing general interest in local and national institutions. After the last lecture, on April 10, a vote of thanks to Mr. Graham Wallas, moved by Dr. T. J. Lawrence (lecturer to the Cambridge Syndicate) and seconded by Archdeacon Michell, was carried with acclamation. In reply the lecturer gave a brief address describing some of the most valuable characteristics of University Extension work. Dr. Lawrence had previously shown the necessity of steady support to the movement, thus enforcing an appeal for annual subscriptions made by the local committee with the object of forming a society whose members will feel personally interested in the cause. During the first half of next term five lectures on Dante and the Divina Commedia are to be given for the benefit of the Students' Association, by the kindness of the Rev. Alban Wright. A slight outline of the subject was given on March 29, in a preliminary exhibition of lantern-slides from Gustave Doré's engravings of scenes from the Purgatorio and Paradiso, prepared by Messrs. Cassell, and shown for the first time on this occasion.

BRADFORD.—The *Bradford Observer* of April 3 commented as follows on the closing lecture of Mr. Marriott's course:— 'There was quite an ardent leave-taking between Mr. J. A. R. Marriott, M.A., and the Bradford Philosophical Society at the close of his last lecture. The lecturer himself confessed to having enjoyed the delivery of his lectures before such an appreciative audience, and no doubt it was because his heart was in the work that he made himself so persuasive and stimulating. The lecturer is palpably touched with a human interest in his subject. At the outset he proposed to trace the segregation of European States since Waterloo on the basis of nationalities, and all through the course it was clear that the victories of the peoples over the dynastic diplomatists were to him not merely matters of scientific curiosity, but events for exultation and enthusiasm. Particularly fine was the concluding lecture on "The Unification of Italy"— quite a notable exhibition of literary eloquence.'

BRIDPORT.—The Rev. G. H. West, D.D., ended the course of twelve lectures on Architecture, which he has given at the centre, on April 3. The course has been well attended, although there has been a diminution in the numbers since Christmas, while marked interest has been taken in the subject, and a very large percentage of the audience has always remained for the class. Dr. West remarked that one of the pleasantest features of the work had been the keen interest and intelligence shown by some of the working men students. A hearty vote of thanks was given to the lecturer, and special stress was laid on the very careful and able manner in which the papers of the students had been corrected. —KATHERINE C. BUSSELL, *Hon. Local Sec.*

GLOUCESTER.—After the last of Mr. Shaw's lectures on English Social Reformers, a hearty vote of thanks to the lecturer was passed on the motion of Mr. Seekings and Mr. Fell; and a strong wish was expressed that Mr. Shaw should lecture again next autumn. A motion proposed by Dr. Oscar Clarke urging the City Council to pass a resolution, which is shortly to be moved, in favour of adopting the Public Libraries Act, was seconded by Mr. Rowles and carried unanimously.

LEAMINGTON.—Under the title of 'Social and Industrial Problems,' Mr. J. A. Hobson has just concluded Part II of his 'Problems of Poverty,' in continuation of Part I, given during the autumn. The issue of cheap artisans' tickets for shop assistants and school teachers, who, however, from some obscure cause or other did not avail themselves of this facility to the extent we had hoped for. As usual in this town, the average attendance was less than in the autumn, being fifty-five. It is the first time we ... twelve lecture course, and the result is hardly encouraging ... financial point of view. On the other hand,

the strong feeling manifested in favour of continuing the course during the spring term, the large proportion of the audience which habitually stayed for the after-class, and the length and vigour of the discussions showed that if the interest aroused was not general it certainly was keen. There can be no doubt that the course has stimulated the thoughtful study of social questions among persons of both sexes and of very various positions in life. There is reason to believe that Mr. Hobson's teaching has fired at least one lady student with the ambition to become a Guardian of the Poor.—C. H. d'E. LEPPINGTON, *Hon. Local Sec.*

LOUTH.—On April 3 Mr. F. S. Boas completed a course of six fortnightly lectures on 'Tennyson,' and the local committee have on the whole reason to congratulate themselves upon the success attending the course. It was the first course on Literature at the centre, and therefore somewhat of an experiment; but, thanks to the able and interesting manner in which the lecturer treated the subject, there was a satisfactory attendance at the lectures, and a large number remained for the class after each lecture. The number of papers written varied from time to time, but were always too few. It is to be regretted that only four students entered for the examination, but this need not discourage us, as it appears to be a weak point at other centres, and it seems hard to find a remedy.—PHILIP ALLISON, *Hon. (local) Sec.*

RAMSGATE.—The course given this winter was most successful. The average attendance has increased to 117 at the lectures and fifty-seven at the class. The last lecture was given on March 31. A vote of thanks to the lecturer, Mr. Horsburgh, was proposed by the Rev. H. C. V. Snowden, who said that he knew he was only expressing the feelings of all present in asking Mr. Horsburgh to accept their warmest thanks for his services. His lectures on the French Revolution had been full of the deepest interest, and they had been universally appreciated. Mr. Raven, in seconding the resolution, said that it was encouraging to feel that now that they had come to their sixth year, the Oxford University Extension movement in Ramsgate stood on a firmer basis than ever; not only had numbers increased, but the intelligent interest of the students had become more marked. There were, however, two classes of persons whom he should like to see reached in future years. They were first, those who considered that their education was 'finished,' that they had learnt all that it was necessary for them to know; and secondly, those who for the sake of convenience he would call 'contractionists,' as opposed to 'extensionists,' who set their faces against the movement altogether. He called upon all the students to institute a campaign against these two classes of people before the next course began. Mr. Horsburgh, in returning thanks, said that it gave him great pleasure to be able to congratulate the Ramsgate centre on its flourishing condition. He had never met a specimen of the interesting race of 'contractionists,' alluded to by Mr. Raven, and he sincerely hoped that they might be induced to attend the lectures, as their opinions would probably give rise to many interesting discussions. As to those who looked upon their education as finished, he could only say he had no sympathy with the doctrine of finality in education, for education in its true sense went on to the last day of our lives. The vote of thanks was heartily responded to.

REIGATE.—Our lectures on 'The Renaissance in Italy and England' have been more appreciated than any previous course. The attendance was extremely satisfactory, and kept up well through the autumn and spring. The committee feel very grateful to Mr. Horsburgh for the valuable help that he has given to this centre, and the interest that has been aroused by his lectures for the last three sessions.—FRANCIS J. BAKER, *Hon Sec.*

SOUTHAMPTON.—The good attendance at Mr. Bond's last lecture on March 15, delivered in the Hartley Hall, shows that the subject of the course, Commercial Geography, has proved attractive. Mr. Ellaby introduced the lecturer, who gave an interesting account of the trade, commerce, and manufactures of Germany. The use of illustrations, by lantern slides, has added much to the popularity and value of the lectures.

[*Reports unavoidably held over:*—Swindon, Tavistock, West Brighton, Whitehaven.]

INFORMATION TO CONTRIBUTORS.

All communications should be addressed to the Editor, OXFORD UNIVERSITY EXTENSION GAZETTE, *University Press, Oxford.*

All matter intended for insertion in the June issue should reach him not later than May 20.

Contributions should be written on one side of the paper only, and must be accompanied by the name of the writer (not necessarily for publication).

N.B.—*All orders should carefully specify the full title,* OXFORD UNIVERSITY EXTENSION GAZETTE.

Advt.]

THE GRINDELWALD CONFERENCE, 1894.

Dr. Lunn's Forecast of the Arrangements.

Dover-Calais-Paris route adopted.

IN an interesting interview with Dr. Lunn, which appeared recently in *The St. James' Budget*, Dr. Lunn said, ' It was on a Norwegian tour organized by the Polytechnic that I first conceived the notion of organizing a holiday in which the enjoyment of travel should be combined with a little intellectual refreshment. My first attempt in this direction was to induce clergymen of various denominations to spend a holiday together. Accordingly I organized my first winter party to Grindelwald.

'This tour answered so well that from Grindelwald I wrote to Earl Nelson, the President of the Home Re-Union Society, and to the Bishop of Ripon, asking them to support me in my efforts to form a Conference for the promotion of Christian Re-union. I had enthusiastic replies from them, and in the end I arranged the first Re-union Conference. This was held at Grindelwald early in 1892, and was attended by 950 people of all denominations, who had a twelve days' holiday for ten guineas, inclusive of everything.'

The fact that within two years over three thousand persons have availed themselves of Dr. Lunn's arrangements for combining the advantages of a Continental

holiday with the other attractions of these gatherings, proves how wisely the recreative and intellectual elements in the Conference are adjusted to each other. The days are devoted to mountaineering and other excursions, and the evenings, which are ordinarily felt to be so tedious by the Swiss traveller, are rendered the most interesting part of the day by addresses, lectures, and discussions, some of which have already had an historic importance.

The Character of the 1894 Conference.

Several questions from different quarters having reached him, Dr. Lunn has answered them at length. In reply to the question, What will be the character of the 1894 Conference? Dr. Lunn says, ' My intention this year is to somewhat widen the scope of the Conference. I am anxious that the strong religious character of these gatherings should be maintained, and that their influence for Christian unity should, if possible, be intensified. At the same time, I have endeavoured this year to give a distinctly educational character to the latter part of the Conference, approximating it as far as is possible under European conditions, to the excellent organization developed by my friend, Bishop Vincent, at Chautauqua. Keeping the first

two objects in view, I have divided the Conference into five sections. The first section will last a fortnight, commencing on June 30, and terminating on July 14, and the programme will be entirely devotional in character. I have not yet arranged the programme for this gathering, but am hoping that it may be possible for some evangelical leaders in the Church of England to assist in this part of the programme, together with some well-known representatives of other evangelical denominations.'

The Social Problems Section.

' The next fortnight will be devoted to the consideration of social problems, work amongst the slums of the large towns, the best way to use the Press for the purposes of the Christian Church, the right attitude of the Church with respect to amusements, and other similar questions will be fully considered.

' Mr. Stead has promised to be present at this section, and to give an address on Social Problems at Chicago, and their lessons to Englishmen. The Rev. Dr. Newman Hall, whose attitude is clearly defined on the question, will give an address on the subject of theatre-going. Professor H. C. Shuttleworth will also speak on the same question. The Rev. Dr. Mackennal will speak on Home Missionary Problems. The Rev. A. R. Buckland, editor of *The Record*, will deal with the attitude of the Press in relation to religion in England, and several other important questions will be discussed by representative speakers.'

The Re-union and Church Problems Section.

' The first fortnight in August will be devoted to Re-union and other ecclesiastical problems. My programme for this fortnight is still in embryo, but I hope to make it thoroughly representative of all the great denominations, and I have every reason to believe that the meetings will be even more important than those which have preceded them in 1892 and 1893.

' During this fortnight I intend myself to give a paper on " The Truth about Hindu Idolatry, and The Way to Grapple With It." I am making most elaborate investigations into the exact facts of the case, with the assistance of a number of Indian missionaries, and I hope to be able to lay before the Conference such information as will command the attention of the whole Christian Church at home.

' As at Grindelwald, one day of each week of this fortnight will be entirely given up to the discussion of Re-union. Up to the present the High Church party have been conspicuous by their absence at our gatherings, with the solitary and notable exception of Canon Hammond. I am glad to say, however, that this year I have assurances from some eminent representatives of the Anglo-Catholic movement that they will be well represented.

The Young People's Month.

' My friend Mr. Atkins has arranged the programme for this month in the Conference, for the special benefit of the readers of *The Young Man* and *The Young Woman*. It is always difficult, in the height of the holiday season, to continue the discussion of the graver questions with which we deal in the earlier weeks of the Conference. This section of our gatherings will, however, have a very considerable educational and scientific value. Sir Benjamin Ward Richardson will be the President of this section, and will open the section with an address on " How to Make the Most of Life." Sir Robert Ball will lecture on " The Great Ice Age." Mr. Edmund Gosse, Professor Carus Wilson, and many other excellent lecturers will take part in the proceedings.'

Switzerland: Its History and Politics.

' The last section of the Conference will commence on September 8, and will be in many respects the most interesting of the whole series. Mr. Joseph King, of Hampstead, who has taken a great interest in Switzerland, has assisted me in arranging this section, and we are securing lectures on Swiss Institutions by a number of leading statesmen and Swiss authorities who are conversant with our own language. Addresses will be given on "The Referendum," "Religion and the State," "Switzerland in Relation to International Peace," and the "Swiss Alcohol Monopoly."

'On the conclusion of this week's programme there will be a pilgrimage to some of the most interesting places in Swiss History—the scene of William Tell's exp'oits, the Meadow of Rütli, where the three Swiss patriots swore to free Switzerland from the Austrian yoke, and other scenes of historic interest. Perhaps the most interesting feature of the pilgrimage will consist of some patriotic representations by Swiss peasants of great events in their national history. I am indebted for this idea to Mr. W. T. Stead, who, during his stay at Lucerne last summer, urged me to complete the educational side of the Conference in this manner. He suggested that as at Ober-Ammergau the peasants gave their wonderful representation of the greatest event in Christian history, so patriotic Swiss peasants might reproduce in some village hall a few of the many thrilling incidents of their national life. The peasants of Hochdorf—a village near Lucerne—I found on inquiry have regularly during the winter months thus cultivated the virtue of patriotism, and I have accordingly arranged with them to give our pilgrims an unpublished patriotic play written by an able Swiss pastor, also some extracts from Schiller's *Wilhelm Tell*, and tableaux vivants of " The Three Men of Rütli," " Arnold von Winkelried," and other Swiss heroes.'

The Travelling Arrangements.

'With each year's experience, I have been able to make more and more successful arrangements for the travelling and hotel accommodation. The original sum of ten guineas will be adhered to for the regular tour, and this sum will include a second class ticket to Grindelwald by Dover and Calais with the right to return over the Brunig Pass and by Lucerne through Paris, a week's accommodation at Grindelwald, and three days at Lucerne. Those who do not wish to stay at Lucerne can substitute a walk over the great Scheidegg Pass, hotel accommodation for the night at Meiringen, a walk over the Grimsel Pass and hotel accommodation at the Rhone Glacier Hotel, a walk over the Furka Pass, hotel accommodation at Andermatt, and then returning home by the Lake of Lucerne.

' I have also arranged a series of extensions by which travellers may economically prolong their holiday, and include in it the following places :—

(1) An extension to the Italian Lakes, Venice, and the chief towns of North Italy.

(2) An extension to the St. Gothard, and thence to Zermatt for the Matterhorn, and Chamonix for Mont Blanc, returning home by the Lake of Geneva.

(3) An extension to Zurich, Constance, and the Falls of the Rhine, and

(4) An extension to the Engadine, which will also include part of the Italian Lakes.'

The Financial Side of the Conference.

' I should like to take this opportunity (says Dr. Lunn) to say a word or two with reference to the financial side of the Conference. Some most absurd statements have appeared in the Press with reference to this question. Of course it will be manifest to every one that if the Conference had not been organized very carefully on strict financial lines, a very heavy loss might have been incurred, but any one who knows anything about Swiss travel will know that after paying the heavy advertising expenses of the Conference, the expenses of the speakers, and the cost of a large staff of secretaries, there cannot be much margin on the sum of ten guineas charged. Last year I had all my accounts carefully audited by Messrs. T.

Leman and Co., Chartered Accountants of 99 Gresham Street, E.C., and the balance-sheet shows that there was a margin of just about 2*s.* on each member, after paying all expenses, the net balance being £162 7*s.* 11*d.*, and I may further add that I made no charge for my own personal supervision in this statement of accounts. This sum of £162 7*s.* 11*d.* I have placed at the service of the Archdeacon of London, in order to secure the presence of a fuller representation of members of the Anglican Communion at the Conference of 1894. By this means I hope to more adequately balance the representation in the Re-union discussions of the Established Church and Nonconformity.'

The Arrangements for Booking.

' It only remains for me to add that any who wish to avail themselves of the advantages of the Conference arrangements should lose no time in securing their places. The accommodation in Grindelwald is strictly limited, and already I have had very many applications, so that it is clearly evident that some hundreds of those who wish to be present will be disappointed this year. Parties will leave London every Tuesday from June 5 to September 11, and every Friday from June 29 to September 14. The booking fee of one guinea, by cheque, payable to Henry S. Lunn, crossed London and County Banking Company, Oxford Street Branch, specifying the date selected, should be sent at once to my secretary, Mr. T. H. Bishop, 5 Endsleigh Gardens, London, N.W. All inquiries, whether personal or by post, should also be addressed to Mr. Bishop.

THE GRINDELWALD CONFERENCE, 1894.

A Unique Twelve Days' Holiday for Ten Guineas.

[All announcements are made subject to necessary modifications.]

THE FOLLOWING FOUR TOURS ARE TEN GUINEAS EACH :—

Tour 1.—Berne, Grindelwald, Lake Brienz, the Brunig Pass, and Lucerne.

Tour 2.—Berne, Grindelwald, Meiringen, the Brunig Pass, and the Stanserhorn.

Tour 3.—Berne, Grindelwald, Meiringen, the Brunig Pass, Goeschenen, and the Lake of Lucerne.

Tour 4.—Berne, Grindelwald, the Scheidegg Pass, Meiringen, the Grimsel Pass, the Rhone Glacier, Goeschenen, and the St. Gothard.

The sum of Ten Guineas includes Second Class Return Ticket, outward via Berne, and homeward via the Brunig Pass and Lucerne. Meals on the outward journey, a week's hotel accommodation at Grindelwald, and either three days' hotel accommodation at Lucerne, or in tours 2, 3 and 4, hotel accommodation at any place in the itinerary.

SPECIAL EXTENSIONS STARTING FROM GRINDELWALD.

The Tickets to be taken in London.

Extension A.—Grindelwald, Lake Brienz, Meiringen, the Brunig Pass, Lake of Lucerne, the St. Gothard Railway, the Italian Lakes. Milan, Axenstein or Axenfels, and Strassburg or Brussels. *Eight days tour after leaving Grindelwald,* £5 *extra.*

Extension A 1.—Milan to Venice, return, and two days at Venice. £2 5*s. additional to* A.

Extension A 2.—Milan, Genoa, Pisa, Florence, Bologna, and Venice. *Seven days' tour from Milan.* £6 6*s. additional to* A.

Extension B.—Grindelwald, Lake Brienz, Meiringen, Brunig Pass, Lake of Lucerne, the St. Gothard Railway, Goeschenen, Rhone Glacier, Zermatt and the Matterhorn, Chamonix and Mont Blanc, Lausanne, Strassburg or Brussels. *Eleven days' tour after leaving Grindelwald.* £7 7*s. extra.*

Extension C.—Berne, Grindelwald, Lake Brienz, Meiringen, Brunig Pass, Zurich, Schaffhausen and the Falls of the Rhine, Basle, Strassburg or Brussels. *Four days' tour after leaving Grindelwald.* £2 2*s. extra.*

Apply to the Secretary, 5 Endsleigh Gardens, London, N.W.

[*Advt.*

OXFORD UNIVERSITY

EXTENSION GAZETTE.

VOL. IV. No. 45.]　　　　　　　　　JUNE, 1894.　　　　　　　　　[ONE PENNY.

N.B.—Local Organizers of Oxford University Extension Lectures are invited to send to the Secretary, Extension Office, Examination Schools, Oxford, copies of any journals containing notices of, or references to, Extension work.

NOTES AND COMMENTS.

Chicago Exhibition, 1893. Award to the Oxford University Extension.

It is officially announced that in Group 149 (Primary, Secondary and Superior Education) a medal and diploma have been awarded to the Oxford University Extension Delegacy. Nineteen awards in all have have been made to British exhibitors in this section. Among these are the Science and Art Department (South Kensington); the School Boards for London and Glasgow ; the White-chapel Craft School ; and the High Schools of Sheffield and Blackheath.

Mr. Hugh Gordon, Oxford University Extension lecturer, has been appointed Inspector of Schools and Classes under the Science and Art Department.

Death of Professor Henry Morley.

We deeply regret to record the death at Carisbrooke, Isle of Wight, of Professor Henry Morley, who during the course of a long and busy life, was an unfailing friend of popular education. It was largely due to him that the treasury of English literature has been thrown open, by means of cheap reprints, to the poorest student in England. He was years ago the indefatigable pioneer of peripatetic teaching, and, long before the Universities recognized the system, Professor Henry Morley had established what we should now call University Extension classes in many of the chief towns of England. In the closing years of his honoured life, he was one of the most active members of the University Extension Committee at Newport, I.W., close to which town he lived. Through his influence, seconded by that of Mr. Dendy, whose sudden death we recorded in our last issue, he was instrumental in making the Newport centre a model of efficiency and organization. Those whose good fortune it was to know him can never forget the kindness of his heart, the unselfish enthusiasm of his nature, his absolute freedom from vanity or ostentation.

Modern Benefactions.

The age of benefactors has not gone by. Mr. Longstaff, a former Scholar, has given to New College the sum of £1,000 to be awarded in exhibitions 'as a reward for excellence in any subjects recognized in the Honour Schools of the University, preferably to the sons of professional men in actual need of pecuniary assistance.' Almost at the same time it was announced that University College, Liverpool, has received from Mr. George Holt the sum of £10,000 for the endowment of the Chair of Pathology ; from the Earl of Derby an endowment for the Chair of Anatomy : and from Mr. Henry Tate, a promise of books, the value of which will amount approximately to £5,500. With regard to the last gift, it seems that Mr. Tate visited University College in the course of last summer and, remarking on the naked appearance of some of the library shelves, invited the preparation of a list of the standard works needed by the various departments of the College, and with the guidance of this list made his gift to the library. But while welcoming large gifts, let us not forget that it is on the steady stream of smaller but not less liberal benefactions from donors of more limited means, that the prosperity of great institutions most depends.

The death of Bishop Smythies.

One of the bravest ventures in which Oxford and Cambridge men are now engaged—the Universities' Mission in Central Africa—has lost a leader by the death of Bishop Smythies at sea, on his way home from Zanzibar to Aden, on May 7. This is not the place to speak at length of the Bishop's undaunted hope, of his unfaltering devotion to a great cause. But the work in which his strength was spent is one of the noblest achievements of the English Universities. They can do no greater thing than raise up men like Charles Alan Smythies.

The English Literature School at Oxford.

Two important amendments have been made in the Statute respecting the new Honour School of English Language and Literature at Oxford. The first requires the candidates to show knowledge of the history, and especially the social history, of England during the period of English literature which he offers. The second aims at securing that the candidates should be prepared for their work in English literature by previous study of the classics. It will be remembered that, in earlier discussions of the question, Mr. Churton Collins emphasized the importance to the students of English literature of acquaintance with the classical writers.

Oxford Lecturers at the Royal Society's Conversazione.

At a conversazione of the Royal Society on May 2 Professor Poulton gave a brilliant lecture, with lantern illustrations, on the ' Influence of Environment on Caterpillars.' Dr. H. R. Mill exhibited a new map of the English lake basins and Mr. H. N. Dickson, in a series of isothermal charts, showed the distribution of temperature in the sea between Scotland and Faröe as observed by him last August.

We understand that most of the Extension lecturers who have lately been employed in Kent have been appointed to the staff of the Wye College, and that the Technical Education Committee of the Kent County Council have decided to discontinue the direct organization of science lectures for the villages.

1

The Oxfordshire County Council and Technical Education.
There being a deficiency in the receipts of the Oxford County Council, the opportunity was taken at the quarterly meeting on May 9 of proposing that £2,000 of the money derived from the Customs and Excise duties should be devoted to the reduction of the rates instead of to technical education. Sir William Markby, Chairman of the Finance Committee of the County Council and formerly a member of the University Extension Delegacy, made a powerful speech against the proposal, and in favour of the policy of the Technical Instruction Committee. After a long debate, the attack on technical education was repulsed by 28 votes to 16, six other members of the Council being present, but not voting. Among the recommendations of the Technical Instruction Committee, which were ultimately adopted, was a renewal of the grant of £75 to the Reading University Extension College.

.·.

The present method of assigning to the County Councils funds which the State intends, but does not specifically vote, for technical education is highly unsatisfactory. It renders the educational work of the Councils precarious, and their policy uncertain. It tempts those councillors who are not interested in educational work to watch for convenient opportunities of transferring part of the Customs and Excise funds to the relief of the rates. And it obscures the certain fact that these funds will not continue to be paid to the County Councils if the latter cease to spend them in educational undertakings. The grants to each County Council should be made permanent ; their employment in educational work clearly prescribed ; and their expenditure entrusted to a special Board, armed with executive authority, and composed partly of members of the Council, and partly of persons selected for their educational experience and ability. The necessity of referring all their educational proposals to the arbitrament of a mixed, and in some respects hostile, assembly must not only embarrass each Technical Instruction Committee, but must injure the quality of their work by affecting from its first inception every scheme which they propose.

.·.

An interesting meeting was held at the Palace, Wells, on May 6, by kind invitation of the Bishop, for the purpose of distributing the certificates and prizes to the successful students in connexion with Dr. Wade's and Mr. Marriott's courses. Very wisely the meeting was made to serve several educational purposes. Mr Goodford explained the work of the County Council in regard to the technical education, and it may be said in passing that there are few County Councils in England, which can show a better record for ability and administrative success in their educational work. At a later stage, Canon Church gave details of the progress of the Higher Religious Education Society, and finally the Dean, seconded by Dr. Livett, emphasized the need of a historical museum in Wells. Few men in England have shown greater insight into the aims and best methods of higher popular education than the Bishop of Bath and Wells. As Lord Arthur Hervey, he addressed in 1855 to the members of the University of Cambridge a pamphlet which contained in embryo much of what has in later times practically monopolized the phrase ‘ University Extension.’

.·.

Education by Conferences on Education.
In order to promote a better understanding of the needs and desires of various London trades with regard to technical education, a series of public conferences are being held in London between representatives of the principal London industries, of the trade unions, of the London Chamber of Commerce and the London Trades Council, and of the Technical Education Board of the London County Council. With careful organization these gatherings should do much good. They promote mutual understanding and friendly acquaintance between the various bodies on whose co-operation the successful development of technical instruction depends. But conferences give scope to the cranks, and, to judge from the *Technical World*, there are persons engaged in technical instruction in London whose knowledge and judgment are too light ballast for their impetuosity.

.·.

Lord Herschell on the work of the University of London.
On May 9 Lord Herschell spoke for the first time in his capacity of Chancellor of the University of London. He justly claimed that the University has during the last fifty years done a great educational work not only in London, but throughout the whole British Empire. Oxford especially owes much to the vigour of the University of London. For the movement, which produced the younger University, did not spend itself without accomplishing the reform of the older seats of learning through the Universities' Commissions, which were the direct outcome of the same propaganda which had previously established the University in the metropolis. It was, moreover, the one-sided zeal of the London University reformers that called forth John Henry Newman's unrivalled analysis of the true functions of a University. And his arguments in favour of retaining residence as an essential part of academic organization are even now bearing fruit in the controversy which promises to end in the reconstitution of the London University itself.

.·.

We are glad to notice that the large and influential committee, including the Vice-Chancellor of the Victoria University and the Principals of Owens College and the Yorkshire College, which was formed to consider the erection of some suitable memorial to the late Professor Milnes Marshall, have decided that the maintenance and development of his very valuable library is the most appropriate form of perpetuating his memory and continuing his work. The library, generously presented to Owens College by Prof. Marshall's family, contains most valuable monographs and periodicals in zoological science, and it is proposed by means of endowment to ensure its being kept up to the level of advancing science. It is also proposed to institute a gold medal for athletics, which shall be competed for yearly by the college students. Both these proposals are, it is thought, such as the Professor would himself have approved. Subscriptions may be sent to the chairman of the committee, Mr. E. Donner, Oak Mount, Fallowfield, Manchester.

.·.

The Home Reading Union at Salisbury.
Salisbury was a good place to choose for the Summer assembly of the Home Reading Union in the last week of June. And the list of lecturers is highly attractive. Mr. York Powell will speak on Saxon and Scandinavian England ; Mrs. Brownlow on Early English Music ; Mr. Jebb on Tennyson ; the Dean of Salisbury on Browning ; and Sir Robert Ball on Recent Discoveries about the Sun. Mr. Wells will lecture about Oxford, and General Pitt Rivers will meet the party at Rushmore. This programme marks a great advance on arrangements for the previous assemblies of the National Home Reading Union.

.·.

A Modern ‘Pilgrimage.’
A party of American and English ‘ pilgrims ’ have visited this month London, Oxford, Cambridge, Peterborough, Ely, Bedford and Stratford-on-Avon. At each place distinguished teachers have met them and given an address on its historical associations. Thus the Bishop addressed the party at Peterborough on the days of Hereward ; Mr. Edmund Gosse lectured at Stratford ; Mr. Bryce and Mr. Walter Besant in London. It was a good idea to arrange this excursion, but a pity to spoil it by a silly name.

A correspondent to the *Student*, Mr. Howson, suggests that 50 or 100 Extension students should spend a week in London, Devonshire, North Wales or the Lakes, or even in Paris, Norway, Switzerland or on the Rhine. It will be interesting to see whether anything comes of this new form of co-operative touring.

•.•

The name University Extension vexes the spirit of an 'old student,' who writes to the same organ. He thinks the word University Extension is too formidable a title. To the abbreviated form 'Extension lectures' he strongly objects, and always shudders on hearing it. His own suggestion is that we should talk about Oxford lectures and Cambridge lectures instead. The Oxford undergraduate calls them stretchers.

•.•

The Study of Political Science in Switzerland.

An interesting course of lectures will be delivered in Switzerland between September 10 and 19, its object being to set forth some of the lessons in political science which the constitution of Switzerland offers to Europe. Among the subjects to be dealt with by lecturers are 'The Swiss Laws respecting the Sale of intoxicants,' by Herr W. Milliet, the Director of the Swiss Alcohol Monopoly ; 'The Endowment of Religion by the State,' 'The Educational System of Switzerland,' 'The Communal System of Self-Government,' and 'Swiss Neutrality.' At the conclusion of the course of lectures, the visitors will be taken to various places of historic interest in the country. The arrangements for the visit are being made by Dr. Lunn, 5 Endsleigh Gardens, N.W.

•.•

Rightly or wrongly it is a common charge against higher education that it leaves young women ignorant of the details of household management. Those who sympathize with this criticism will be glad to hear that a residential school of household and domestic training has been started in a bracing air and in the midst of attractive scenery near Malvern. The aim of the school is to supplement general education by thorough instruction in all that a mistress of a house should not only know, but be able practically to carry out. Instruction will be given in cookery and all domestic work, in elementary hygiene, in laundry-work, and, if desired, in dress-making. Among those ladies who approve of the scheme are Mrs. Garrett Anderson, M.D., Mrs. Henry Sidgwick of Newnham College, Cambridge, and Miss Maitland, the Principal of Somerville Hall, Oxford. The school is to open on June 1 of this year, and will be under the direction of Mrs. Buck and Miss Brander, both of whom are connected with the North Midland School of Cookery. Further information can be obtained from Mrs. Buck, Birstall Holt, Leicester.

•.•

Mr. E. L. S. Horsburgh writes as follows concerning the lectures delivered by him at Southampton during the past winter :—

'The Autumn course on the Oxford Reformers attracted a large audience of over 250, and it was determined to proceed in sequence, and accordingly after Christmas a course of six lectures was given on the early Tudors. The audience was not so large, but still was fairly well maintained. The work at Southampton has been of a peculiarly interesting character because the Southampton School Board subsidized the lectures, and the audience was as a consequence largely composed of teachers in the elementary schools of the town, and also because an attempt is being made to cover a definite period of English history in consecutive courses of lectures, thus securing sequence and thoroughness. The twelve lectures already given carry the subject of the Tudor Monarchy from 1485 to 1558 ; twelve more it is hoped will be given on the Age of Elizabeth. The results, so far, I consider excellent. The history of the experiment has been excellently given by Mr. Perkins, the Hon. Secretary, in the May number of the *Extension Gazette*, and it only remains for me to say that the work done by the students (I have sixty names of students on the register) has been thoroughly sound and progressive.'

Armand Colin et Cie have just published a bright and well informed description of English secondary education from the pen of M. Max Leclerc. The title of the book is *L'éducation des classes moyennes et dirigeantes en Angleterre*. Its chief object is to suggest some answer to the question, How is it that, although its organization of secondary education is confessedly chaotic, England is nevertheless the centre of an active movement in natural science and in literature as well as of unceasing enterprise in industry and trade? To arm himself for his inquiry, M. Leclerc paid more than one visit to England and inspected typical varieties of secondary schools. Eton, Harrow and Marlborough; University College School, Dulwich, and the Middle Class School in Cowper Street; the educational provision of Birmingham, Liverpool, Manchester, Bradford, Leeds and Bristol; the secondary schools of Somerset and Devonshire were all visited by him and are on the whole well described. M. Leclerc also reviews the history of English education; the main characteristics of English training in the home, the school and the playing field; the action of the Universities through the Joint Board and the Local Examination and Extension Delegacies; the work of the Local Colleges; the functions of the Charity Commission and the Science and Art Department; the movement for technical instruction; and the working of the Intermediate Education Act in Wales. His conclusions are twofold. Let us give them in his own words. This is the first. 'Entre l'abstention presque complète de l'État anglais et la tyrannie tracassière et absorbante de l'État français, il y a place pour une autre conception, celle de l'État modérateur, tantôt auxiliaire, tantôt propulseur.' And this is the second. 'Les maîtres anglais sont avant tout des éducateurs; ils n'ont jamais oublié qu'ils avaient à former des hommes.' Private enterprise must be blended with, corrected and aided by, State supervision; the aim of education is, not mere attainment, but character; these are the maxims which M. Leclerc would impress upon his readers in both countries. And his deductions are commended in an admirable preface, written by M. Émile Boutmy, the Director of the École Libre des Sciences Politique. In M. Leclerc's volume, M. Boutmy believes that he finds the clue to the puzzle of English education, 'la clef de cette contradiction apparente: des écoles plus que médiocres et en regard une admirable efflorescence littéraire, une prodigieuse expansion industrielle et scientifique.'

A French review of Secondary Education in England.

•.•

A despatch from Copenhagen declares that the Icelandic Parliament has passed a resolution in favour of establishing a University at Reikavik. At present every pupil who passes the final examination at the Latin School in Reikavik (some six or eight boys doing this in each year), is given free board and lodging in the Icelandic College at Copenhagen, together with an allowance of about £2 10s. a month. This period of academic study in Denmark is doubtless a benefit to the Icelandic youth. He sees something of the world outside his own remote island, and carries home with him new ideas and a higher standard of intellectual attainment. The establishment, however, of a University at Reikavik would mean that these youths would complete their education in Iceland itself. Such an arrangement would provincialise the culture of the young Icelanders. Nor, would one think, could Iceland, even with financial aid from Denmark, support a worthy University in Reikavik. At the same time we greatly sympathize with those Icelanders who wish to see a national movement for higher education in their own country. Iceland has great traditions, literary, political, and historical, and at present these are in danger of being weakened by the removal of her cleverest youths, at a most impressionable age, to a foreign country. What seems to be wanted is a system which should supply Reikavik with opportunities of higher education, while maintaining the present connexion with Copenhagen. Could not this be accomplished by a scheme of University Extension ? For each winter two or three teachers might

University Extension for Iceland.

2

be sent from Denmark in order to conduct University classes and to deliver lectures in Reikavik. In this way the services of Icelandic graduates might be employed to enlarge the intellectual opportunities of their fellow-countrymen, and to provide academic teaching for those who at present cannot win scholarships to Copenhagen.

.˙.

What seems to be a change of fundamental importance in the attitude of the University of Chicago towards its Extension system, is announced in the editorial notes of *University Extension* (Philadelphia) for May. It is there stated that 'in future no University credit will be given to lecture-study courses as such.' This rather obscure and technically-worded sentence apparently implies that the University of Chicago has withdrawn from University Extension students the privileges, which they have previously enjoyed, in respect of obtaining credit in their university course for work done at the local centres. If our interpretation of the change is correct, the University of Chicago has adopted the position generally accepted in Oxford, viz. that while the University should do all in its power to encourage and help forward University Extension work, no remission of residence for the degree course should be made in the case of those students who have obtained certificates at a local centre. We hope, however, in an early number to put our readers in possession of the exact facts.

.˙.

Summer Meeting of Economists. The *University Extension Bulletin* of May 10 contains an interesting account of the Summer Meeting of Economists to be held in July in Philadelphia. The object of the meeting is rather the instruction of teachers than that of elementary students, and it is proposed to arrange courses of lectures to be delivered by well-known economists. The lectures will last about three hours a day for four weeks, and opportunities will be afforded for discussion and informal teaching in the subject. It is hoped that in this way much will be done to increase the general understanding of the more recent additions that have been made to our knowledge of economics.

.˙.

The United States Bureau of Education has issued the report of the Committee on Secondary School studies, appointed by the National Educational Association. The report deals with the question of the educational value of different curricula in secondary schools, and Mr. W. T. Harris, the United States Commissioner for Education, states that 'in this respect he considers it the most important document ever published in America.'

.˙.

The *Providence Journal* (U. S. A.) reports an interesting lecture delivered in Providence (Rhode Island) on the University of Oxford by Dr. Buckham, President of the University of Vermont, who, it will be remembered, was present at the Oxford Summer Meeting of 1892. Dr. Buckham laid stress on the great movements which had been associated with the name of Oxford, and spoke with especial regard of the School of Biblical learning, which 'for the English speaking world has its centre in Oxford.'

.˙.

The May number of *University Extension* contains an enthusiastic article on Mr. Churton Collins. The article is full of hearty and deserved admiration, but we suspect that our colleague would himself have preferred a more reticent panegyric.

UNIVERSITY EXTENSION IN THE MIDDLE AGES.

By Mr. ANDREW G. LITTLE, M.A.; author of *The Grey Friars in Oxford*.

THE object of this article is to show that in the thirteenth century there grew up an educational system in England, which may, without playing with words, be described as 'University Extension'—that is, the dissemination of knowledge over the country, from the Universities outwards, by means of lectures.

The mention of the thirteenth century will at once show us where to look for the originators of the plan. Like the rise of painting, the study of physical science, the reform of the Church, the growth of the Universities —like almost every intellectual and moral movement of the thirteenth century—the movement for the spread of higher education was called into being and carried out by the Mendicant Friars. Of the four great Mendicant Orders, the Dominicans, Franciscans, Carmelites, and Austin Friars, we shall be concerned mainly with the Franciscans (or Grey Friars, or Friars Minors), first because their system resembled our University Extension more closely than that of the Dominicans, secondly because they had greater influence in England than any other Order, and thirdly because more is known about them than about the other Orders in this country.

A better way of putting it would be that even less is known about the other Orders than about the Franciscans. A word of warning about the state of the materials for the history of the Grey Friars is necessary. It would hardly be an exaggeration to say that the whole number of Franciscan records now existing in England, whether in print or manuscript—i.e. of official or semi-official documents issued by the Order or any part of it—could be counted on one's fingers. This being so, it will hardly surprise any one that references to the University Extension are few and far between. Enough however, in my opinion, remains to prove that it existed; and there are probably other notices of it, scattered up and down mediaeval chronicles and records, which may in time be brought to light.

Let us now bring together a few of these scattered references. The most important statement on the subject is contained in the Chronicle of Thomas Eccleston. Eccleston wrote his Chronicle about the year 1260, or a little later, having been occupied twenty-five years in collecting materials. He was himself a Franciscan, had been a student in the Minorite convent at Oxford, and knew personally all the leading English friars in the middle of the thirteenth century. Thus he had the best possible opportunities of knowing the history of his Order, and he honestly tried to tell the truth; a more trustworthy authority than Eccleston could hardly be desired. The passage relating to our subject runs as follows: 'The gift of wisdom so overflowed in the English province, that before the deposition of Friar William of Nottingham (1251), there were thirty lecturers in England who solemnly disputed, and three or four who lectured without disputation. For he had assigned in the Universities, for every convent, students who were to succeed to the lecturers on their death or removal.' The point of the passage has hitherto been missed. The late Mr. Brewer, in editing Eccleston's Chronicle in the Rolls Series, wrote such a brilliant preface, that few people have thought it worth their while to examine the text. But the preface contains a few inaccuracies, pne of them occurs in Mr. Brewer's translation or paraphrase of the passage in question. Instead of the last sentence, 'For he had assigned,' &c., Mr. Brewer translates: 'and a regular succession of them (i. e. lecturers) was provided in the Universities.' This, to say the least, does not make Eccleston's meaning clear. His point is that men were educated at the Universities, in order that they might be sent as lecturers to the various convents ; 'a regular succession of lecturers for each convent was provided in the Universities.' Here then, within about five-and-twenty years of the coming of the friars, we have the system in full working order—more than thirty University lecturers established at various 'centres.' These 'centres,' being the houses of the friars, were of course situated in the chief towns; Eccleston expressly mentions several of them—namely, London, Canterbury, Hereford, Leicester and Bristol; there was also a lectureship at Norwich in 1250; and in the fourteenth century London, York, Norwich, Newcastle, Stamford, Coventry and Exeter are mentioned as the most flourishing, or at any rate the most honourable, places of study outside the Universities[1].

The next question to consider is, how were these lecturers appointed? At first, there is no doubt, they were nominated by the Provincial Minister, or head of the English branch of the Franciscan Order. Actual instances of such nominations may be found in the pages of Eccleston, and it was clearly the intention of William of Nottingham with his 'successions of lecturers in the Universities'; the local 'centres' were to have little to say in the matter. But all through the early history of the Franciscans there is a strong tendency from despotic to popular government. At first the General Minister or 'General' appointed the Provincial Ministers, and so on all through the various grades; but this did not last long. A few years after the death of St. Francis, the appointment of the 'wardens' of the convents was taken away from the 'custodian' (the officer next above the wardens) and given to the convent; in other words, election from below took the place of nomination from above. A similar change was effected in the case of lecturers. William of Nottingham was Provincial Minister from 1240 to 1251, and before his deposition the local 'centres' had begun to assert themselves. They did not exactly choose their lecturer, but they petitioned the Provincial Chapter, or assembly of delegates of the friars, to send down to them as lecturer some particular man, whom they named. This became the usual method of appointment. We may take a somewhat late instance—from the end of the fourteenth or beginning of the fifteenth century. The friars of Hereford desired to secure John David, a Cambridge man, and afterwards Provincial Minister, as their lecturer for the ensuing year. Friar John was probably quite willing to come; his name points to a Welsh origin, and Hereford may well have been his native place. The only authority to be reckoned with would therefore be the Provincial Chapter. The convent sent two delegates thither to represent their views, and obtained a letter of recommendation from a local dignitary, John Prophet, dean of Hereford. Two letters of his to the Provincial Chapter on this subject, referring to different years, are extant in Harleian MS. 431 in the British Museum. I give here a translation of the second letter.

'Venerable and religious men, most dear in Christ. . . . Whereas my predecessors, the deans and Chapter of Hereford, are known to be in part founders of the house of your brethren in Hereford, and whereas the convent there desires and aspires, as I am informed, to have Friar John David as their lecturer and regent (of their schools) during the ensuing year, I have thought fit to beseech your reverences by these presents, that you will, at the instance of these my prayers, if it be your pleasure, depute the same Friar John to the said Convent as their lecturer and regent, that they may in this respect obtain the ends of their desire; knowing for certain that the aforesaid Convent has greater confidence of making advance under him than under any one else, as I am informed. Therefore take thought, if it please you, in this your reverend Provincial Chapter, that under an acceptable teacher the disciples of this most eminent profession may heap up the fruit also of scholastic discipline. And may the Ruler of all things prosperous keep in prosperity your venerable assembly for the government and rule of your religion.'

This letter illustrates the influence of the locality on the appointment of a lecturer; it shows that the lecturer resided for one year at least[2] in the convent to which he was assigned; and it proves that the 'Extension' system of the thirteenth century was still at work in 1400.

[1] See MS. Canonic. Misc. 75, fol. 78, in the Bodleian Library.
[2] Lecturers were usually appointed for one year in the first instance, then reappointed for two more years: so that the normal term of residence was three years.

But, to be honest, is not all this very dull and disappointing? Is it not an abuse of language to call a private arrangement between a set of begging friars 'University Extension'? Granting then for the moment that only the friars were affected, let us realize what that meant. What part did the friars play in England during the first hundred years of their residence in this country? They were the thinkers of the age and the teachers of the people; they preached, when the clergy were silent, and helped by their sermons to create English prose; they healed the sick; they visited the houses

'Where the infectious pestilence did reign.'

Surely an organization which gave to every one of these men, who had any intellectual gifts, the best instruction in all the learning of the time, was no little thing: surely the 'University Extension' of the Middle Ages conferred a great boon on England, and was of immense importance in history, even if it touched directly only the Begging Friars.

But was it confined to them? This question suggests another: what classes can have had the intellectual interests and the preliminary training necessary to enable them to understand and appreciate a University education? We are at present assuming (what as yet has not been proved) that the lecturers were not elementary teachers, but teachers of the more advanced branches of knowledge. If we pass in review the various grades into which English society was divided in the thirteenth and fourteenth centuries, we shall, I think, be led to the conclusion that there were only two classes of men, to any considerable proportion of whom a University education could appeal—namely (1) the monks, and (2) the secular clergy.

(1) For more than thirty years, i.e. from before 1285 to 1314, the office of lecturer to the monks of Christchurch, Canterbury, was filled by Franciscan Friars, first by Friar R. of Wydeheye, then by Friar Robert of Fulham. In 1314 the monks parted with Fulham and gave him a testimonial, a copy of which is still preserved in a MS. in the University Library at Cambridge (MS. E e V. 31, f. 156, b). It is a letter from the Prior and Chapter of Christchurch to the Provincial Minister and friars of the English province. After a polite and unnecessary preface, according to the fashion of mediaeval letter-writers, the monks continue:

'Whereas our beloved brother in Christ, Robert of Fulham, professor of your Order (whom, owing to our special confidence in him above other men of great fame, we have long admitted among us in friendly wise as our lecturer), has for long past borne the labours of master in our schools; and whereas his teaching smells sweetly in the city of Canterbury, and has, by sprinkling the Holy Scripture in their hearts, made many brethren of our congregation, his diligent hearers, so fruitful that we consider them fit to undertake the office of lecturer in our schools: We have decided to substitute one of our brethren and fellow-monks in the place of the said Friar Robert, to undertake this duty. And lest, by reason of the aforesaid decision, any sinister opinion may arise concerning the said Friar Robert, We make known to you by these presents the certain cause of this change. Considering therefore the laudable character and imitable morals of the aforesaid Friar Robert, whose conversation we have found conformable to all honesty and his manner of lecturing agreeable, we recommend him specially to each and all of you as deserving of your good-will, heartily praying you to receive him favourably at our earnest request. And because it is pious to bear witness to truth, we have caused these our letters patent to be made. Given in our Chapter on the 18th of November, A.D. 1314.'

Some of the bearings of this letter on the subject before us are obvious and need not be pointed out. But it contains one important piece of evidence which does not lie quite on the surface. We have here the proof, if any proof be needed, that the Franciscan lecturers were employed in spreading, not elementary, but higher education. Otherwise we should be forced to the conclusion, that there was not a monk able to teach the 'three Rs' in a great Benedictine monastery, at Canterbury, in the beginning of the fourteenth century. This alternative has only to be stated for its absurdity to become apparent. The monks were well able to instruct their novices and choir boys; but they found themselves out of their depth when they began to turn their attention to the 'New Learning' of the thirteenth century, with all the profound questions which are included under the phrase, 'the scholastic philosophy.' In intellectual matters, the monks were a long way behind the friars. They were slow to see the importance of the Universities. The Dominicans had a house at Oxford in 1221; the Franciscans in 1225; the first Benedictine house was not founded till 1283.

It must be confessed, however, that there is a missing link in the chain which connects the Christchurch lectureship with the 'University Extension.' There is no evidence that either Wydeheye or Fulham was ever at a University. Suppose that neither of them studied at Oxford or Cambridge or Paris; still they must have studied in some convent of their Order under a teacher who had been trained at one of the Universities. What better proof could be given of the success of the mediaeval 'University Extension' and of the thoroughness of the instruction which it imparted? Here are two friars, not University men but merely 'Extension Students,' who are judged capable of lecturing, and whose pupils become lecturers after them.

(2) Under the term 'secular clergy,' are included all those clergy who did not live under a common rule, such as rectors and vicars of churches, chantry priests, and a large class of persons in minor orders, who eked out a precarious subsistence by singing psalms for the good of men's souls. Did any of these men attend the lectures of the Mendicants in the various towns of England? The only evidence to be hoped for on this question consists in incidental references in contemporary records and chronicles. To take an instance: Adam Marsh, a famous Franciscan of the thirteenth century, writing about his friend, Friar W. de Maddele, who was lecturing at some convent, says: 'he is pleasant (or persuasive) in lecturing, acute in arguing, and in his writings and words useful and acceptable both to friars and seculars.' If he had said that 'his *lectures* were acceptable both to friars and seculars,' this passage would have been important testimony on the matter before us. As it is, it cannot be considered as' of much value, and I do not recall any other instance. But this is the kind of casual allusions on which the case must rest; and points like these are easily passed over, unless one is expressly looking out for them [1].

At present we must be content with probabilities; and I will now bring forward some facts and considerations, which prove that the probabilities are in favour of an affirmative answer to the question under discussion. (1) Dominican lecturers were expressly enjoined to admit seculars to their lectures if commanded to do so by their priors [2]. (2) Considerable numbers of the secular clergy were eager for the education which the Universities afforded. Rectors frequently obtained licenses to leave their parishes in order to study at Oxford or Cambridge for a year or more; their period of residence was often too short to admit of their taking a degree. (3) In the thirteenth century the seculars considered the friars the most capable teachers of philosophy and theology. Roger Bacon, writing in 1271, says: 'The secular clergy for the last forty years have not composed a single treatise on theology, nor do they think that they can ever know anything, unless for ten years or more they attend the lectures of the boys of the two (Mendicant) Orders.' (4) Seculars attended the lectures of the friars in the Mendicant Convents at the Universities. This may be gathered from Roger Bacon's words just quoted, and from the complaint of the Oxford Dominicans in 1312, that, owing to a quarrel with the University, 'scholars (or 'clerks') are not per-

mitted to come to the schools of the friars.' It seems to be a reasonable inference from these facts, that the secular clergy, in non-University towns also, sometimes desired to attend the lectures of the friars, and were allowed to do so.

There are many other points of interest in connexion with the 'University Extension' in the Middle Ages; but enough has been said for our present purpose. This paper does not of course profess to be exhaustive even of the materials already to hand: its object is merely to draw attention to a curious and almost untrodden path in the maze of mediaeval history.

SOUTH KENSINGTON AND UNIVERSITY EXTENSION.

FROM time to time we have taken occasion in these columns to insist on the importance of cordial co-operation between South Kensington and University Extension work. Nothing in the nature of the University Extension system prevents such an alliance, which would be of great benefit to the educational interests of the country. The following letter will be read with interest by those who have watched the working of the two systems:—

Department of Science and Art,
London, S.W., April 30, 1894.

Reading University Extension College: School of Science and Art.

SIR,—I am directed to transmit, for your information, the following extract from the report of the Inspector of this department:—

'This school is doing a unique work.

'The literary and historical work is blended in a most satisfactory manner with the technical and scientific. The organization seems to be quite perfect. The blending of the University Extension and departmental systems has succeeded, and there are apparently not many difficulties in working the two systems together.

'An agricultural department has recently been added under the supervision of Mr. Gilchrist (formerly of Bangor), and Mr Ffoulkes, B.Sc. Edin. (Agriculture).

'The Physical Laboratory has been very conveniently planned, and the students are in course of making some of the apparatus required.

'The Morphological Laboratory is fully equipped for about ten students.

'The teaching in Electricity and Chemistry is of a thoroughly practical and efficient character.'

The Department is glad to learn that such satisfactory progress has been made in the development of the College.

I am, Sir,
Your obedient servant,
G. F. DUNCOMBE.

F. H. Wright, Esq.,
University Extension College,
Reading.

WHO ARE THE COBBLERS?

MR. JOHN MORLEY is reported to have said on May 4 that 'during the last fifty or sixty years successive generations of Radical cobblers have in political foresight and political insight beaten easily the University of Oxford.'

During the years referred to by Mr. Morley, the following are some of the Oxford graduates who have taken a leading part in the public or literary life of this country:—Sir Robert Peel, the Earl of Shaftesbury, Mr. Gladstone, Lord Salisbury, Dr. Arnold, Dr. Pusey, Archbishop Tait, Bishop Wilberforce, Dean Stanley, Dean Church, Cardinal Newman, Cardinal Manning, Mr. Matthew Arnold, Mr. Ruskin, Professor Freeman. Mr. J. R. Green, Professor T. H. Green, Mr. Arnold Toynbee, Bishop Stubbs, Lord Rosebery, and Mr. John Morley himself.

What are the names of the cobblers?

---

[1] Cf. Tanner, *Bibliotheca*, p. 509; an account of a Dominican and a Franciscan holding a theological disputation in the Cathedral Schools of York in 1355.
[2] *Archiv fur Litteratur- und Kirchengeschichte des Mittelalters*, i. 220, note.

SUMMER MEETING NOTES.

The inaugural address of the practical course on Hygiene will be delivered on August 7 by Dr. John Billings of Washington, U. S. A. Dr. Billings, who is Hon. D.C.L. of the University of Oxford, is one of the greatest living authorities on Hygiene. Dr. Billings has chosen for his subject 'Hygiene in University Education,' and his address will have special reference to defects in the scientific foundations of practical sanitation. The chair will be taken by Sir Henry Acland, the Regius Professor of Medicine.

•.•

Among the excursions during the Second Part will be visits to Edge Hill and, by kind invitation of Sir Edmund and Lady Verney, to Claydon House, where are preserved the portraits and documents of the seventeenth century familiar to the readers of the *Memoirs of the Verney Family.* Lady Verney, who was the editor of part of the memoirs, will read a paper during the meeting on the historical associations of Claydon House.

•.•

The Dean and Chapter of Christ Church have kindly given permission to members of the Cathedral choir to sing illustrations to Dr. Mee's lecture on the music of the seventeenth century, on August 2. Mr. Basil Harwood, Mus. Bac., Organist of Christ Church, will also play pianoforte illustrations at Dr. Mee's lecture.

•.•

Mr. Hudson Shaw's lectures at the Summer Meeting will be on Strafford, Pym and Hampden, and Falkland. These three lectures will all be delivered in the First Part.

•.•

Two lectures on Cromwell will be delivered in the First Part by Mr. A. L. Smith, Fellow and Tutor of Balliol College, and at the beginning of the Second Part the course on the foreign history of the seventeenth century will be happily supplemented by two lectures on France after Colbert, by Mr. Arthur Hassall, Student and Tutor of Christ Church. It is gratifying that so many resident members of the University are taking part in the instruction to be given at this year's Summer Meeting.

•.•

The subjects of the lectures to be given by Mr. Walter Pater have been changed at his request. Mr. Pater will lecture on Pascal and Rubens on July 28 and 30, at 4 p.m.

•.•

Some additions have been made to the course of lectures on the literature of the seventeenth century. Two lectures will be given on Dryden by Mr. Churton Collins, and two lectures on Wither, Crawshaw, Vaughan, Cowley, Denham, and Waller, by Mr. Warwick Bond. Much pleasure will be also felt at the announcement that Dr. Bailey has sufficiently recovered from his accident to deliver a lecture on George Herbert. Mr. Boas will give two lectures on Herrick and Sir Thomas Browne in the First Part, and six lectures on Milton in the Second Part of the Meeting.

•.•

A lecture on the progress of geographical discovery under the Stuarts will be given by Mr. Lyde, whose lecture at the Meeting in 1892 will be remembered by many students.

•.•

To the scientific section of the Meeting several additions have been made. Mr. Carus-Wilson will give two lectures, one of which will be upon Ice, the second on Volcanoes and Earthquakes ; and the Principal of the Exeter University Extension College (Mr. A. W. Clayden) will deliver two lectures on Clouds and Storms.

•.•

The Principal of the Reading University Extension College (Mr. Mackinder) will lecture on the Influence of Holland in the Seventeenth Century.

Professor Poulton, F.R.S., will, lecture at the Conversazione on

•.•

Dr. Wade, before beginning his practical ᒪᘛ Hygiene, will give two lectures upon the growth and development of modern Preventive Methods. The first will be devoted to Edward Jenner and Vaccination ; the second to Edwin Chadwick and his sanitary reforms.

•.•

Besides Dr. Devine's lectures (as announced in our last issue) the Economic class will have two lectures on Value from Mr. Arthur Berry of Cambridge, and will attend the six lectures to be given by Mr. Hewins on the Economic History of the Seventeenth Century. In addition to this, the class will study the Wage System, under the care of Mr. J. A. Hobson, from August 16–24. Mr. Hobson has drawn up the following scheme of work :—

The Wage System.

(1) The Structure of the modern Business.
(2) Modes of measuring the Shares of Labour.
(3) The Minimum Wage.
(4) The Economy of High Wages and Short Hours.
(5) Theory of Competition and Combination in Labour and Capital.
(6) Relations between Trades in their bearing on the Wages System.

•

The subject of Captain Abney's illustrated lecture on August 6 will be Sunlight and Moonlight.

•.•

We are glad to announce that Sir F. Pollock, Bart., Corpus Professor of Jurisprudence in the University of Oxford, will give a lecture on Hobbes, as part of the course on the Seventeenth Century.

•.•

The subjects of Mr. Arthur Sidgwick's three lectures will be —
(1) Primitive Language.
(2) Primitive Thought.
(3) Primitive Remains.
The lectures will form the introduction to Mr. Churton Collins' course on Homer.

•.•

Mr. W. M. Acworth will lecture on Thursday, August 16, at 5.30 p.m., on 'The Mechanism of Distribution.'

•.•

Lectures on Vandyck and Velasquez will be delivered on August 9 and 10 by Mr. C. W. Furse, the distinguished painter, whose work in this year's Academy has been the subject of much admiring comment.

•.•

Mr. Marriott will give three lectures on Ireland in the Seventeenth Century on the evenings of August 17, 18 and 20. This course will form a welcome addition to the chief sequence of lectures.

•.•

An addition has been made to the theological courses. The Rev. A. C. Headlam, Fellow of All Soul's College, will lecture from August 9 to 15 on 'The Church of the Apostolic Fathers.'

•.•

Miss Fanny Davies's pianoforte recital on the afternoon of Tuesday, July 31, will be given, by kind permission of the Governing Body, in the Hall of Christ Church.

•.•

Mr. A. L. Smith, Fellow and Tutor of Balliol College, has kindly given £5 to the Summer Meeting Scholarship Fund.

•.•

The time-table of the Summer Meeting has been published, and can be obtained on application from the University Extension Office, Oxford. The full programme and time-table are sent to any address, price 7d. post free. The time-table alone costs 2d.

PREPARATIVE READING FOR THE SUMMER MEETING.

MR. D. G. RITCHIE has drawn up the following suggestions to guide the reading of students in preparation for his lectures on Descartes, Spinoza and Locke :—

Suggested Reading.

*Descartes, *Discourse on Method,* transl. [by Prof. J. Veitch]. (Blackwood, 2s.).

[I do not know whether this separate edition of the *Method* can still be got. It can be got in combination with a translation of *The Meditation,* &c. 6s. 6d.] In the French it will be found in Descartes, *Œuvres choisies.* (Garnier, Paris, 3 fr.)

Mahaffy, *Descartes* in *Phil. Classics.* (Blackwood, 3s. 6d.)

Huxley, Lect. on Descartes in *Collected Essays,* vol. i.

E. Caird, *Cartesianism* in *Encycl. Brit.,* in his *Essays in Literature and Philosophy,* vol. ii. (Maclehose, Glasgow.)

Spinoza, *Chief Works,* transl. by Elwes. Two vols., each 5s. Bohn's Library. The 'Ethics' are in vol. ii.

Martineau, *A Study of Spinoza.* (Macmillan, 6s.)

Pollock, *Spinoza's Life and Philosophy.* (Kegan, Paul & Co., 16s.)

John Caird, *Spinoza* in *Philosophical Classics.* (3s. 6d.) ['Life' not given.]

Matthew Arnold, Essay in *Essays in Criticism.* (Macmillan, 9s.)

Lewes, *Biographical Hist. of Philosophy.* 'Spinoza.'

*Locke, *Conduct of the Understanding,* ed. Fowler. (Clar. Press, 2s.)

*Locke, *Civil Government.* [Bk. ii. along with first Letter on Toleration.] (Cassell's National Library, 3d.)

†Fowler, *Locke.* [Engl. Men of Letters.] (Macmillan, 1s.)

Fraser, *Locke* (*Philosophical Classics*). (3s. 6d.)

Fox Bourne, *Life.* 2 vols. [o. p. priced at 7s. 6d. in catalogues: is *the fullest life.*]

* All students purposing to attend the lectures are advised, if possible, to read these three books beforehand. Those quite unacquainted with philosophical books can hardly be recommended to attempt Spinoza, but if they have access to any of the books named, may read his 'Life,' and get some notion of his thought.

† Fowler's *Locke* will be found useful, as it gives a good deal of information about the relation of Locke to English politics.

GREEK CLASSES AT THE SUMMER MEETING.

IT is proposed to hold two classes for the study of the Greek language for one and a half hours daily from August 8 to August 24 (both days inclusive), at such times in the day as shall be decided upon by the vote of the students present at the first meeting of each class.

The elementary class is intended for those who have no previous knowledge of the language. Its aim will be to lay a solid foundation for further study by imparting—

(1) An accurate knowledge of the ordinary forms of nouns, adjectives, pronouns, and verbs.

(2) Facility in the translation of very simple English sentences into Greek.

The Text-Books used will be—

(a) Abbott and Mansfield's *Greek Accidence* (Percival & Co. 2s. 6d.).

(b) Underhill's *Easy Exercises in Greek Accidence* (Macmillan & Co., 2s.).

The more advanced class is intended only for such students as have already a sound and accurate knowledge of as much grammar, at the very least, as will be studied in the elementary class. It is proposed to read the whole of Book XI of Homer's *Odyssey,* and to devote some time to the grammar and syntax of the text.

The Text-Books used will be—

(a) Abbott and Mansfield's *Greek Grammar* (Edition of 1893), including syntax and Appendix on Homeric forms (Percival & Co., 3s. 6d.).

(b) Merry's *Odyssey,* Books VII—XII (Clarendon Press, 3s.).

N.B. It is essential to the success of the classes that all students should provide themselves with the Text-Books.

HENRY G. GIBSON, M.A.

PUPIL TEACHERS AND UNIVERSITY EXTENSION.

MANY Committees, though anxious to make their University Extension lectures directly advantageous to pupil teachers, have been unable to arrange a course of twenty-four lectures and classes in one session. Not only financial but educational considerations were against so long a course. With all their other work, pupil teachers cannot keep up with the reading required from those who would fully profit by weekly lectures of this type on historical, literary or economic subjects. And yet, if the lectures were at fortnightly intervals, the course of twenty-four would run into the summer—to the fatal injury of large attendance. But we are glad to learn that the Education Department interprets the clause in the Code (Schedule V. note 8, p. 88) as meaning that, if the certificate is awarded during the year preceding the Queen's Scholarship Examination, the twenty-four lectures and classes may have been spread over more than one year. Thus, if a Committee takes twelve lectures between next October and the following March, and twelve more lectures (in continuation of the former twelve) between October 1895 and March 1896, certificates gained by pupil teachers in the final examination held on the double series of lectures will be of value to them in the Queen's Scholarship Examination in the following December (1896). An incidental advantage of this arrangement is that pupil teachers will not be overpressed by the lectures in the year immediately preceding their Queen's Scholarship Examination. At the same time the fact that they are able to pass an examination on a course of study extending over a period of eighteen months will prove incontestably the educational advantage derived by them from their attendance at the University Extension lectures.

THE SCHOOL OF ENGLISH LITERATURE AT OXFORD.

ON May 1 the University of Oxford considered the preamble of the statute intended to carry out the resolution in favour of the establishment of a School of English Language and Literature, which was carried last December. The statute provides that every candidate shall be examined in (1) the history of the English language; (2) the history of English literature ; (3) the text and matter of certain authors, such authors to be studied in connexion with the history and thought of the time. Candidates for the highest honours will have to offer, in addition, one or more special subjects connected with the English language and literature.

Mr. Grose introduced the statute and Professor Pelham supported its adoption. The speakers against it were Professor Case and the Warden of All Souls. The latter remarked that the new school of English Literature was desired by University Extension lecturers and women. It is true that the experience of University Extension workers long ago convinced them of the desirability of giving academic recognition to the study of English Literature, and one of our lecturers, Mr. Churton Collins, distinguished himself by faithful advocacy of the scheme at a time when it was much less popular than at present. But it would appear that others in Oxford besides women and University Extension lecturers are in favour of the new School as the preamble of the statute was passed by the significant majority of 120 votes to 46.

THE PLACE OF UNIVERSITY EXTENSION.

A Review of Professor Simon N. Patten's Article in 'University Extension.' (Feb. 1894.)

UNIVERSITY Extension, as they say in America, 'has come to stay,' both there and here : and it is quite in accordance with the fitness of things that in the great American Republic, where system and order are prized so much more highly than in our somewhat unsystematic Old World, the first reasoned attempt should be made to state philosophically what the new movement proposes to do, and what part it claims for itself in the educational system of a nation. This Professor Patten has done, and done well ; we could only wish that he had not attempted to be so philosophic in his terminology—to the great prejudice of his style, and to the loss (we fear) of many readers : e. g. what is gained by such a sentence as the following ?— 'The utilitarian calculus of pleasures and pains had been displaced in these cases by psychologic motives, demanding a conformity between his conduct and the customs and ideals formed through the concrete relationship between himself and the local environment.' The writer has in the previous page explained admirably what he means ; the difference between the intensity of the political life of former times and that of the present day has been often dwelt on but has rarely been better put. Why then does he go on to cumber his argument with philosophic phrases, dragged out of their proper 'environment' ? (We apologize for using this much-overworked word, but Professor Patten's style is unfortunately infectious.)

Now, having had our grumble at the stiff reading which Professor Patten has so needlessly set us, and which we resent the more, because he can write, when he pleases, in a style which excites our envy, as much as his pseudo-philosophic one stirs our spleen, we would thank him for his definite statement of the principles of University Extension, and for the light which he throws on the methods which we all of us have been trying to put in practice ; and we would humbly essay to summarize his excellent pamphlet on what appear to be its most important points. We would add at once that we know we shall fail to do it justice, and that all who really care to think about University Extension, and the part which it is to play in the future, had better read Professor Patten for themselves.

He begins by pointing out the uncertain character of the 'theory of education' in its present state. It is to be feared that he will shock the educationalists ; but common-sense people will thank him for boldly venturing to call it 'an aggregation of the most miscellaneous character, a combination of platitudes, adages, maxims and traditions of uncertain value, mixed with crude generalizations, based upon the institutions of a given epoch or the tendencies of a given age.' Then after proceeding to show the changes in the educational machinery (in the widest sense) which mark our own day, and the need of revision of educational institutions to meet new conditions, he works out admirably one of the main differences between ancient and modern education ; the former was largely that of adults ; it is only in modern times, with the development of printing and the Revival of Learning, that the idea has grown up that education is a thing for children, and must be completed before a child reaches maturity : it may be a paradox, but it is one full of meaning, when Professor Patten says 'the reformers of to-day should be willing to let nature keep the boy as long as possible, and strive to educate the man.'

He then proceeds to the main point of his argument, the division of knowledge into three kinds, *memorised* which deals merely with isolated facts ; *reasoned*, which is 'serial' and based on purely intellectual processes ; and *visualised*, i. e. knowledge of the type which the average man acquires, the result of a process not based only on pure reason, but which enables him to form 'ideas more or less concrete in form,' and 'so definitely related to one another that they can appear simultaneously in consciousness.' The first kind of knowledge may be neglected ; the second is that of the scientific inquirer ;

but it is the third which forms 'race knowledge,' a knowledge which 'has the same interest to the individual who receives it as it has to the person who imparts it,' which is 'assimilated and becomes a motive for action.' 'Reasoned knowledge' is the knowledge of the scholar : it is 'race knowledge' on which 'depends the level of citizenship,' and which maintains the institutions and customs of the race, through which social progress is possible. 'It is like a panorama which combines a bit of real scenery with a painted background' : it 'becomes as real to the citizen as the mine or shop from which he earns his living.'

This kind of knowledge is largely neglected in modern education, which gives a boy the elements of knowledge, but neglects political instincts and national character ; yet it is these which are specially needed in our modern life. A good citizen must be more than a good producer : we, however, ignore the fact that the elements which make a man a good citizen have been the result of long training, not in books, but in the school of life. In old days actual experience taught the necessity of citizenship ; the state was a very real thing, and the 'obstacles to national liberty' were 'vivid and objective' ; 'there was little need of conscious political education.' But now that 'legislative halls are connected with corruption and bribery, not with deeds of patriotism ... and the constitution is only an uninteresting book,' 'organized and persistent efforts should be made to revive and perpetuate the traditions and ideals of the race.'

So then the University has to do with two kinds of knowledge, the reasoned knowledge of the scholar, and the race knowledge of the citizen ; it once gave the latter to the neglect of the former ; now that the former is taking its proper place, a new machinery is needed to secure the latter, and that machinery is furnished by the University Extension lecture. To it facts as facts are not of importance ; 'they cannot become part of the race knowledge without a transformation into some higher form. They are only the oil lost in the flame which lights the world.' But in order to effect this, the lecturer must proceed steadily from the known to the unknown, from the basis of interest in his hearers' minds to the new interest which he wishes to arouse in them. It will be seen that Professor Patten lays small stress on the side of University Extension work which seeks to create scholars ; he looks upon the special class work as largely accidental. In this we thoroughly agree with him ; it is true that if the work be sound, it will everywhere help the few who have in them the power and the wish to study a subject completely ; but these will always be few, partly because the number of those who wish to become scholars in the highest sense is limited, and because the nation has no need for more than a limited production of scholars. If it is the fault of the English University system that it produces too few, it must not be forgotten that, as the German Emperor has recently pointed out, the German system produces too many.

It would be interesting to dwell on the contrasts between English and American ideas which Professor Patten's paper reveals : e. g. it certainly is not true here that 'the term scholar now means only a specialist ' ; nor that 'the Church is not a national institution giving force and character to national life.' We hope too that, both in England and in America, Professor Patten is overstating his case when he says that recent 'changes have cut out the disciplinary character of home life.' But we must end with an apology to Professor Patten if we have misrepresented his points in endeavouring to state them with more brevity and simplicity. Perhaps he may think we have made them too commonplace ; but whether this be so or not, he can rest assured that they seem to us really valuable and timely in their utterance.

J. WELLS.

LECTURERS' RESERVE FUND.

SUBSCRIPTIONS RECEIVED SINCE MARCH 30, 1894.

	£	s.	d.
Anon.	5	15	0
Miss M. E. Holland	0	10	0

THE CORNWALL COUNTY COUNCIL AND UNIVERSITY TEACHING.

A SERIES of resolutions, which may have an important bearing on the educational policy of the County Councils, were adopted by the County Council of Cornwall on May 1. Excellent and fruitful as was the work of the lecturers who, in the early days of the technical instruction movement, visited many of the villages and small towns of the country on behalf of the County Councils, we have felt for long that their efforts were to be regarded as a preparative and introductory, rather than as a permanent, part of the educational system of the counties. Nothing could have been more stimulating to the country districts than the presence of highly-trained scientific teachers from the Universities. By this means trial was made of the intellectual aptitudes and desires of the country populations. The work of these lecturers, the reports which they based upon it, the advice which they tendered, the educational interests which they diffused broadcast, will ultimately be regarded as one of the most important initial elements in the movement for the popularizing of scientific and technical instruction. But the chief part of the work of these pioneers is done as soon as an educational map of the county has been constructed, when the dark places and light have all been set down in the educational records of the Technical Instruction Committee of the County Council. Moreover it is clear that peripatetic teaching at a distance from laboratories is not the most suitable method of imparting instruction in many scientific subjects. For hygiene, for astronomy, possibly for certain aspects of botany, for physiography, it is excellent. For physics, for chemistry, it is unsuitable. It is natural therefore that the work of the University Extension lecturers should now be concentrated by the County Councils in centres where laboratories exist, or as part of the organization of well-equipped agricultural or technical colleges. To this rule there are and may continue to be certain natural exceptions. Each county differs in need, and those which contain a large number of small towns are more adapted for the continuance of peripatetic teaching in science than are districts of which the greater part of the population is scattered in villages.

But there remains, within the limits of the technical instruction work of the County Councils, much ground which can be well covered by the travelling teacher and, under present circumstances, covered better by him than by any one else. We refer especially to such subjects as commercial and industrial history, the economics of industry and finance, certain forms of instruction in art, and lectures on colonial affairs, with especial regard to their bearing on the commercial interests of this country. It is important that stimulating and accurate instruction in these subjects should be brought within the reach of the great number of persons who would be advantaged by it, and we can see no other method by which this need can be better met than by a system of itinerant teachers.

Itinerant teaching however, if it is to be successful, involves efficient local organization. It is no use finding a good lecturer and then sending him out without preparation into towns or villages where no local organizers have taken the trouble to interest the people in the forthcoming course, to procure its proper advertisement, or to take the lead in the work of the class which should always follow the lecture. The success of University Extension has depended in large measure on the devoted service of many local committees. It is not enough, as many of the County Councils have already found to their cost, to dump down lecturers, however excellent, without having made sure of local organization to begin with.

But the problem is how to secure such local organization in places where it does not already exist. The fact is that under our present system, University Extension teaching is only established in those places where there happen to live a number of persons, who are deeply interested in its success. The project of having University Extension lectures is talked over and canvassed in a dozen places for one in which it is actually established. In short, there is a natural selection of those places where local conditions favourable to the success of peripatetic teaching already exist. A County Council, however, works from precisely the other direction. It takes a map of the county, and decides that teaching should be established in this place or in that. The problem then is to find persons in these chosen places who will undertake the arduous and often thankless duties of local organization. The odds therefore against the success of peripatetic teaching in towns where local organization has not already been prepared, are heavy as against the prospects of the same kind of teaching in towns where a self-formed local committee has for some time previously been at work.

So, whenever a County Council is anxious to adopt the system of peripatetic teaching (and for certain sides of their work there is nothing half so efficacious), it should make a point of using as far as possible the machinery of the University Extension Committees, wherever they may happen to exist in the district. It is to the credit of the Cornwall County Council that it has had the good sense to avail itself of the machinery of this kind which lies ready to its hand. On the recommendation of the Technical Instruction Committee, the County Council has decided to secure the services of an Oxford lecturer for the whole of next winter. In view of the intimate relations which connect Cornwall with our colonies, and especially with South Africa, to which country a steady stream of emigration constantly flows from the Cornish mining villages, the County Council has decided to choose courses of lectures on Australia, on South Africa and the colonies, as the subject of their new undertaking. For this work they have chosen Mr. W. B. Worsfold. After taking his degree from University College, Oxford, Mr. Worsfold went out in an educational capacity to South Africa, and afterwards to Australia, where he acquired first-hand knowledge of the chief problems of colonial life. His lectures in Cornwall will deal with the commercial, industrial, and social aspects of the countries under review. And it may be safely said that they will conduce to the patriotic interest and the industrial advantage of those who hear them.

But the County Council has naturally stipulated that the lectures should be made available for workmen. The problem is how to cheapen the lectures without embarrassing the financial aspect of the undertaking. This difficulty has been met by adopting the expedient of the Gilchrist trustees. It is stipulated that at each lecture a certain number of seats shall be available at a penny each.

The County Council will employ the aid of the existing University Extension Committees in Cornwall. Such of the latter as may desire to avail themselves of Mr. Worsfold's services, will be permitted to do so on the wise condition of their having a full course of twelve fortnightly lectures, extending throughout the whole winter session. And while the lecturer's fee will be paid by the County Council, each local committee will be called upon to defray the local expenses of room rent and advertisement, the cost of the lantern illustrations with which each lecture is to be accompanied, and its quota of the lecturer's railway expenses.

This scheme promises to combine economy, efficiency and adaptiveness. It secures due control to the County Council, while retaining the initiative, the enterprise, the responsibility of the local committees.

Miss Beatrice Vivian of Camborne, the honorary secretary of the South Western University Extension Association, has very kindly consented to act as the representative of the Cornish centres, and all communications with the County Council will be made through her. The movement is fortunate in having the aid of so experienced and judicious an adviser.

Mr. Worsfold has visited Cornwall during the last month, and has made the acquaintance of the local committees at the various centres. It is reported that up to the present eight centres have asked for the full course of twelve lectures, but it is thought that some other towns will apply. Every centre has chosen the course dealing with South Africa, a natural choice considering the particularly close connexion between South Africa and Cornwall. This unanimity of choice will also help the lecturer to make his courses more effective by enabling him to concentrate his efforts upon the one subject. Mr. Worsfold has forwarded to the secretaries of the various Students' Associations a preliminary list of books and subjects for study. These indispensable societies will therefore be able to commence their meetings without delay. We shall watch the working of the experiment with great interest ; and predict that, if successful, it will be imitated in other parts of England.

UNIVERSITY EXTENSION IN AUSTRALIA.

MR. ARNOLD TUBBS, an Oxford man who has distinguished himself as secretary of the University Extension movement in Melbourne, has been obliged to resign his office in consequence of having been appointed to an important position at Auckland University College, New Zealand. Those who have watched the progress of University Extension in Australia know how much of it has been due to the energy and wise courage of Mr. Tubbs. The new secretary is Professor Spencer, and we hope that under his care the advance of the Melbourne University Extension will continue unchecked. Professor Spencer has many friends in England, where he has recently been spending a year of leisure.

.[.].

Important news comes from New South Wales. The Sydney University Extension Board has decided to pay its secretary a salary in order to set him free for the work of organizing the local centres and delivering lectures, especially in the country districts. There is no doubt that this step will greatly enhance the efficiency of the Sydney organization. University Extension is too complex a matter for its administration to be conducted in the spare moments of a busy man. One chief interest of the system is that it gives opportunity for every degree and variety of paid and unpaid work, but if the movement is to be successful, the details of its business must be conducted with the punctuality, regularity and despatch, which an office and a regular staff alone have time and strength to compass.

.[.].

It appears that the Government has given State aid to University Extension in Sydney, and the question of State grants crops up in several pages of the March number of the *Melbourne University Extension Journal,* one of the most interesting of the magazines devoted to University Extension.

SUMMER COURSES FOR THE STUDY OF MODERN LANGUAGES.

WE are glad to see that steps have been taken to resume, during next summer, the summer courses at Jena, which were so successful in 1893. The course at Jena will last from August 1-23, and will comprise both elementary and advanced instruction. The members of the University at Jena have offered a hearty welcome to the English students, and the latter will have the opportunity of attending the *Ferien-Kurse,* a sort of summer meeting attended by schoolmasters, chiefly those studying science. For those who desire to learn French, there is to be a summer meeting at Caen, from August 6-26, and, if a sufficient number of entries are to hand by June 15, an extra course will be held at Caen from July 9-28, with special reference to the need of teachers in primary schools. For the Caen meeting, entries should be sent to R. Lancelot, Esq., Abbotsholme, Rocester, Staffs. For the German course at Jena, entries should be sent to J. J. Findlay, Esq., Rugby. These summer courses for modern language study owe very much to Mr. Findlay's enthusiasm, and we are glad that he is sufficiently recovered from his long illness to feel justified in taking renewed part in their organization.

RESEARCH DEGREES AT OXFORD.

Description of the Debate.

SEVEN resolutions of the first importance were proposed in Congregation on Tuesday, May 8. They had for their object the constitution of new degrees upon terms which have never before been recognized in this University. A blasphemous enemy might say that the result of the debate was characteristic of the academic mind. For the six resolutions that involved the most serious real change were passed (only one division being taken), while the one which dealt merely with the names of the new degrees was rejected after a somewhat acrimonious debate by the narrow majority of three votes.

The first resolution embodied the principle of the new degrees. It affirms that 'it is expedient to establish new degrees, to be granted after a course of special study or research to members of the University who have passed the examinations qualifying for the Degree of Bachelor of Arts, and to persons not being graduates of Oxford who have given satisfactory proof of general education and of fitness to enter on a course of special study.' The Dean of Christ Church—who was understood to have acted as Chairman of the Committee appointed by Council to prepare the scheme—was entrusted with the task of introducing the resolutions. In proposing the first on the list, the Dean explained the reasons which had led to the formation of the scheme. The most important part of his speech, and that which was listened to with the greatest interest, was that in which he dwelt upon the desirability of attracting learned Americans to Oxford, and impressing upon them an English rather than a German character. The resolution was passed without a division. The question of names called forth a series of criticisms. Professor A. Thomson objected on the ground that the ordinary scientific curriculum leading to the B.A. degree would tend to be thrown into the shade by the new degree. He suggested as an alternative to the name Master of Science, the monstrous title of Research Fellow of the University of Oxford—a term unknown to any historical English University. Professor Ray Lankester professed himself content with the title proposed, and made light of the gloomy anticipations of Professor Thomson. Mr. Rashdall of Hertford pleaded for the titles Bachelor of Science and Bachelor of Letters. This resolution was thrown out. Of the others, that which concerned the permission to graduates in Science and Letters to supplicate for the M.A. degree, and that which embodied the conditions of their residence in Oxford provoked some discussion. A division was taken upon the former, and it was passed by a majority of thirty-three. Widely different opinions were expressed as to the importance of residence—Mr. Snow of St. John's being anxious to give up this condition altogether—but the resolution passed without a division. It must not be hastily supposed that the matter is now at an end. As a result of the passing of the resolutions a motion was introduced, constituting a Select Committee of thirteen to draw up a statute to regulate these now nameless degrees. The statute, which the thirteen produce, will have, of course, to pass through Congregation and Convocation. Either body may deal murderously with it. *Absit omen.*

T. B. S.

.[.].

The following is the official statement of the resolutions and of the reception they met with :—

(1)

That it is expedient to establish new degrees, to be granted after a course of special study or research to members of the University who have passed the examinations qualifying for the degree of Bachelor of Arts, and to persons not being graduates of Oxford who have given satisfactory proof of general education and of fitness to enter on a course of special study.

[*Carried : nemine contradicente.*]

(2)

That these degrees should be entitled Master of Science and Master of Letters.

[*Rejected on a division: placets 55, non-placets 58.*]

(3)

That those who have received either of these degrees may supplicate for the M.A. degree on paying the usual fees, provided that they have completed the required number of Terms from their Matriculation.

That those candidates who have studied for at least two years in a University or Local College approved by Convocation, shall enjoy the same privilege with respect to standing as that conferred on students of Affiliated Colleges by Statt. Tit. II. Sect. VI. cl. 6 (*c*) (p. 7, ed. 1893).

[*Carried on a division: placets 73, non-placets 40.*]

(4)

That no candidate should be permitted to enter on any of the proposed courses of study under the age of twenty-one.

[*Carried: nemine contradicente.*]

(5)

That no candidate should be permitted to supplicate for either degree unless he has resided in the University for three years: Provided that residence for two years in a University or College approved by Convocation or in an Affiliated College should be reckoned as equivalent to one year's residence in Oxford.

[*Carried: nemine contradicente.*]

(6)

That a Delegacy should be appointed to decide upon applications for admission to the proposed courses of study, to arrange for the supervision of the candidate's work, and to grant certificates authorizing candidates to supplicate for the proposed degree. That such certificates should only be granted when the Delegacy is satisfied that a high standard of merit has been attained.

[*Carried: nemine contradicente.*]

(7)

That the Delegacy should be empowered to appoint Committees of graduates to report on each candidate's capacity for the course of study on which he proposes to enter, and to superintend his work if he is admitted thereto.

[*Carried: nemine contradicente.*]

The following Motions were then proposed:—

(1)

That a Select Committee be appointed to prepare a Statute for carrying into effect the said Resolutions.

[*Carried: nemine contradicente*]

(2)

That the number of the Committee be twelve, besides the Vice-Chancellor.

[*Carried: nemine contradicente.*]

KING'S COLLEGE AND THE TREASURY GRANT.

One View.

IT is a great pity that educational progress in England should be hindered by religious prejudice; but such is the case. Now that the Church has given up her old rights and privileges, and recognizes all as on a footing of equality, she has herself to struggle against the so-called friends of liberty, who construe it as meaning liberty to teach their own views and nothing else. This attitude is becoming more marked every year; the latest instance is the notice which has been given to King's College that it is to be deprived of its share in the Parliamentary grant of £15,000 to the local colleges, the giving of which was one of the many educational advances made by the late government. It is not contended that this is taken away because King's College is inefficient, nor that any penny of this public money is spent on religious teaching: it is to be lost simply because King's College is an institution where instruction in the doctrines and duties of Christianity, as 'taught by the Church of England' is to 'be for ever combined with other branches of useful education.' It is time that the great principles were recognized, that public money should be given for efficient secular teaching, equally wherever it is found, and that the presence or absence of religious instruction in any institution should have nothing to do with the matter of public grants. It is idle to appeal to the reasonableness of fanatics who find themselves in a temporary majority, but it may be suggested to them that the Church is too strong a body to be lightly provoked, and that if the present policy is continued, the Church of England may find herself forced into adopting a similar attitude to that which has been forced on the Church of France, to the great injury at once of educational and of religious progress in that country.

J. W.

.·.

Another View.

In 1889 Parliament voted, for an experimental period of five years, an annual subsidy of £15,000 in aid of the work of certain Colleges in Great Britain 'giving education of a University standard in Arts and Science.' Among the recipients was King's College (London), its quota being £1700 a year. Now, ever since the great University Commissions, it has been a common-place of public policy that in our national Universities religious tests shall not be permitted, save in one limited department of academic work. At King's College, however, the professors are required on appointment to give assurance of their membership of the Church of England. This requirement was (we may presume) overlooked when the Treasury Grant was first divided in 1889. But, on the grant coming up for review in the present year, the Government very rightly drew attention to the anomaly. One of two things is true. Either King's College, as an institution of university rank, must abandon religious tests, or, if it justifies its peculiar rules on the ground of being a denominational and non-university institution, then it has no claim to a share in this particular subsidy. If the supporters of King's College prefer the latter alternative, they only find themselves in the position which they occupied five years ago before the grant was made. If on the contrary their rules imposing religious tests are amended, the Government is prepared to renew the grant. There is no cruelty in this; nothing to deserve the shrill scolding which recently came from lips that should have known better; nothing which to the impartial critic recalls the conduct of Julian the Apostate. If the Council of King's College think it a matter of principle to allow no Dissenter to teach mineralogy or surveying, that is their own affair. And if it costs them £1700 a year to maintain such a principle, it does not lie in their mouth to complain. At any rate it is not the business of Parliament to subsidise such an arrangement, any more than it is its business to bolster up a belief that only Baptists should teach botany. In fact, were Parliament to accede to either demand, it would be giving its sanction to the revival of religious tests in secular studies. Who will deny that since the abolition of tests at Oxford and Cambridge religious work and feeling in the Universities have grown in strength and depth? We should be unwise therefore to blame the Government for refusing to revive the system of religious tests which was found by bitter experience, so far from safeguarding religion in the Universities, 'to habituate the mind to giving careless assent to truths which it has never considered, and to lead to sophistry in the interpretation of solemn obligations.'

X.

COMMENTS OF BY-STANDERS.

DURING the last few months, a string of comments on University Extension and other academic movements have appeared in various journals from the pens of Mr. Goldwin Smith, of Mr. Thomas Arnold, and of Mr. Selby-Bigge, the latter of whom has recently left Oxford to take up work in the Charity Commission.

The article of Mr. Goldwin Smith has naturally attracted much attention, as it appeared under the title of 'Oxford Revisited,' and in some measure consists of a comparison between the Oxford of to-day as recently revisited by him and that of the Oxford of forty years ago in which he was so brilliant a figure. Mr. Arnold, who bears a name honoured in Oxford, writes frankly in the capacity of *laudator temporis acti*. Mr. Selby-Bigge on the other hand, fresh from Oxford, may be regarded as speaking from a more intimate experience of the present conditions of University life.

Professor Goldwin Smith in the course of his article remarks that in Oxford 'a new feature is University Extension ; that is, a system of local lecturing and examination under the auspices of the University. By some it seems to be regarded as no less important than novel ; at least, I heard it described as one of the three great waves of beneficent change which had passed over the world, the other two being, if I recollect right, the Reformation and the Revolution. Some fear seems to be felt that the University may slide into the position of a popular lecturing bureau, and that in the end something may be done which would compromise the integrity of degrees. It may be said without any reference to University Extension or to any educational movement in particular, and it is hoped without incurring the charge of illiberality or obscurantism, that people will have presently to consider the economical, as well as the intellectual, effects of pressing on everybody what is called high education. The good founder of the Cornell University once confided to a friend his hope that the day would come when there would be 5,000 students in his institution. His friend replied, that if the day did come, the institution, instead of being, as it was, a blessing, would be in danger of being a curse to the State, since there would not be a market for anything like such a number of graduates, and the residue would be without suitable work, unhappy, discontented, and probably dangerous to the commonwealth. It is feared, by those who have been given opportunities of observation, that our high schools in Canada are estranging the farmers' sons and daughters from the farm and sending them to seek higher and more ambitious callings in the city where the market for clerks is already glutted. It is vain to imagine that people having received what they think a high education will go back and dignify with it what they deem a low employment. Even of youths educated at agricultural colleges many, it is said, do not return to the farm. The caution is the more necessary because, from the general ferment of opinion on the subject of national education, the activity of legislation, and the expenditure of public money, a race of educational projectors is pretty sure to arise.'

Referring to the above article in a letter addressed to the *Spectator* of February 17, Mr. T. K. Arnold wrote as follows :—

The idealism which Oxford's very stones seemed once to breathe, is gone. She has taken to 'University Extension,' which means the beating out of a small quantity of learning, much too small to begin with, into a thin film which will cover a multitude of persons of both sexes scattered about England, and make sufficient show to justify the conferring of the required number of distinctions, classes, prizes, degrees, and so forth.

It is hard to say which is the most absurd—the excessive praise which Mr. Goldwin Smith's friend poured on University Extension or the censure passed upon it by Mr. Arnold.

Finally in the *Contemporary Review* for May, Mr. L. A. Selby-Bigge comments on Mr. Goldwin Smith's article from the point of view of one who, till recently, was resident in Oxford as a fellow and tutor of University College. Mr. Selby-Bigge's reference to University Extension is as follows :—

Mr. Goldwin Smith's attitude towards University Extension is neither sympathetic nor distinguished. The great pretensions of the 'popular lecturing bureau,' the danger of overstocking the market with educated wares—are not these and many others among the amenities of the *National Observer*? It is not my business to take up the cudgels for a movement which has shown itself so eminently fitted to take care of itself, but I should wish to note how thoroughly—some would say how terribly—practical a movement it is. It is practical alike in inception and in execution. Here is something which we possess, and are willing to impart ; here are those who want that something, and have wanted it for a long time. What could be more practical than to bring the two parties together? The permanent value of this new combination as an organ in the educational system of the country may not be so great as its enthusiasts claim ; that it has some value, all but the most stubborn are compelled to admit. Its aims and results may be criticized, and its importance minimized, but its methods are admirably effective and claim the respect which is due to success. The Extension lecturer has been often sneered at as an incurably second-class man who doesn't know enough for a fellowship, and can't play cricket well enough to be schoolmaster. But every one who has heard him knows that he can lecture. . . .

But the Extension lecturer can write as well as lecture. A good syllabus of a subject is worth a great deal in itself, and, if the Extension manuals are written by men of such acknowledged eminence as Professor Minto, they are probably worth writing. An elementary book on a difficult subject is a very difficult thing to write. The most distinguished form of deep thinking is plain speaking, and at that rate there has been little deep thinking done among philosophers since some time in the eighteenth century.

UNIVERSITY EXTENSION COLLEGE, READING.

THE following official announcement appeared in the *Oxford University Gazette* for May 16 :—

CHRIST CHURCH.

Mr. HALFORD JOHN MACKINDER, M.A., of Christ Church, has been with the consent of the Visitor elected to a Studentship, held on condition that he acts as Principal of, and directs the educational work at or in connexion with, the University Extension College, Reading.

It is understood that this election is made under the provision of a new Statute recently granted to Christ Church by Her Majesty's Privy Council, and that the Lord Chancellor has, on being consulted in accordance with the terms of the Statute, signified his approval of the action of the Governing Body.

.·.

IN a Convocation of the University of Oxford, held on May 22, the following Decree was carried *nemine contradicente*, ' that the Delegates for the Extension of Teaching beyond the limits of the University be authorized to appoint representatives to co-operate with the Reading University Extension College in the organization of instruction and examination in Agriculture.'

Under the powers given by this Decree, it is possible that steps may be taken to provide systematic instruction in Agriculture at Reading.

.·.

THE *Reading Observer* of April 28 contains an account of a successful lecture delivered to the Reading Literary and Scientific Society by Mr. G. J. Burch, lecturer at the University Extension College in that town. The subject was the Language of Birds ; Mr. Wallis presided, and after the lecture a hearty vote of thanks was passed to the lecturer.

REPORTS FROM THE CENTRES.

BURY.—The secretaries regret that there was not a larger audience for the very able and most interesting course of twelve lectures given by Mr. Mallett on the French Revolution during last winter. There was an average attendance of fifty, many of whom were students; ten of these were qualified for the examination, eight undertook it, four passed with distinction. In his report the examiner said, 'A small but very good competition. The work of the first three was exceptionally good and so level that I do not think it would be fair to distinguish between them.' The delegates therefore generously gave three prizes to this centre. The lecturer's report also, from the students' point of view, was most gratifying; he spoke in the highest terms of the work done for him.—E. ROTHWELL, *Hon. Sec.*

CLEVEDON.—This centre has much enjoyed Dr. Fison's six lectures on 'The Life of a Planet.' He combines a clear, accurate statement of facts with a bright, pleasant style, while the lantern slides add to the attraction of the course. It is to be regretted that Clevedon audiences diminish rather than increase. The average attendance was about seventy, half of whom remained to the class. Dr. Fison's plan of explaining then by black-board diagrams, &c., the right answer to his questions dealt with in the students' papers on the previous fortnight's subjects was most helpful, and he spared no pains in his careful annotations written upon each paper. The whole of the students qualified entered for examination. This centre is venturing on a twelve-lecture course for the first time, six before, six after Christmas, and hopes to welcome Mr. Marriott.—J.WOODWARD, *Hon. Local Sec.*

SWINDON.—On Wednesday, April 4, a most successful course of six lectures at this centre was brought to a close. The subject chosen was the Puritan Revolution, the lecturer being the Rev. W. Hudson Shaw. The large hall of the Mechanics' Institute has been well filled on each occasion, the average attendance being 480, thus proving the selection of the subject by the Council to be a judicious one. A students' class in connexion with the course was formed, at which the average attendance was upwards of thirty, fifteen students qualifying themselves for examination. The lecturer expressed his entire satisfaction with the work done for him by his students, remarking that he had never been in a centre where the students displayed a better grasp of the subject, and a greater clearness in writing than at Swindon, the papers being exceptionally good. A hope was expressed that the Council of the Institute would endeavour to secure the services of Mr. Shaw as lecturer for the next session.—THOMAS JONES, *Hon. Sec. Students' Association.*

TAVISTOCK.—A new and most interesting course of six lectures on Shakespeare's England (Part III, Social Life) was delivered at Tavistock by Mr. K. D. Cotes, between February 26 and April 2. The titles of the lectures were Stratford-on-Avon, Kenilworth, London, The Stage, Magic, and Justice. It would be difficult to say which subjects evoked the most interest, the attendance (averaging fifty-six) being remarkably even throughout. Probably Kenilworth, with its picturesque account of the visit of Queen Elizabeth, and The Stage, a comprehensive survey of the Drama from the earliest times, would be generally considered the most popular. A Students' Association was most successfully started by Mr. Cotes after the first lecture. Periodical meetings for reading and discussion will be held in view of a continuance of the lectures next winter, and it is earnestly hoped that other West of England centres will combine with Tavistock in making application for them at an early date to secure convenient grouping. It may be mentioned that the Duke of Bedford kindly gave £5 to the recent course at Tavistock, with a promise of the continuance of the subscription. If owners of property in other small centres could be induced to follow this example, the financial difficulties of such places would be materially lessened. Emphasis must also be laid on the fact that, in asking for such help, it is quite unnecessary to endeavour to prove that working people will be directly benefitted. Country neighbourhoods contain a large proportion of educated people of small means anxious to enjoy the advantages of higher instruction, but unable to bear the whole cost of it. Ample machinery having been created by Parliament to provide public funds for the instruction of 'the people,' it is only fair that some portion of private benevolence should be devoted to the furtherance of mental cultivation among 'the other people,' whose margin available for self-improvement has been diminished in many cases by the fall of incomes, and in all cases by their contribution to the State education from which they derive no personal benefit.—GRACE JOHNSTONE, *Hon. Local Secretary.*

TEDDINGTON.—This may be looked on as practically a new .... is satisfactory to record that the revival of the ..... as given so much pleasure that the committee

are encouraged to hope that there will not be much difficulty in raising funds for an Autumn course, and also that in the near future the lectures may be a permanent institution. Of course till this can be done there will always be anxiety and uncertainty about each new course. The course just ended was most happily inaugurated on February 12 by a lecture from Mr. Sadler on 'Oxford; its History and Great Men.' The Rev. W. Hudson Shaw was our lecturer, and he considered the paper-work of the students (about twenty in number) very creditable, especially as 'Venice' was not the easiest subject to write upon. It is hoped that next session it will be possible to form a Students' Association.—MARY RYAN, *Hon. Sec.*

TUNBRIDGE WELLS.—It has been our privilege this Spring term to have Mr. Hudson Shaw as our afternoon lecturer. His course on 'Venice and Florence' was the most successful we have ever had, and aroused much enthusiasm among his audience, enthusiasm for Mr. Shaw in particular, and also for University Extension in general. The average audience was 160; there were about forty essay-writers, and thirty-one candidates for the examination. For the evening lectures, provided by the Borough Technical Education Committee, we had an excellent course on the Commercial Geography of the British Empire by Dr. Mill, making the third course he has given in Tunbridge Wells. We are sending three students with local scholarships to the Summer Meeting this year, two from the evening and one from the afternoon lectures.

VENTNOR.—An exceedingly interesting course of evening lectures by Dr. Fison upon 'Astronomy' was completed in March; the attendance throughout was very good, and increased interest was attached to each lecture. The subject was very ably treated by Dr. Fison, and the course resulted in an awakened interest in astronomy, and a large amount of home study. The number of papers was not so large, but the value of the lectures and the knowledge imparted could not be measured by this means at this centre. A very successful conversazione was held during the course, and was found to be of great assistance to students. Dr. Williamson then mentioned that good lectures such as they had had the advantage of attending was an invaluable way of imparting knowledge, but such knowledge could be deepened and made more usable in every day life if students could be induced to meet together and converse on the subject of their study. Then conversation was much helped by having before them objects which would provide suitable topics for it. The objects shewn in the room all tended in this direction, and a very beautiful help and factor in the study of astronomy, the spectroscope, would be illustrated, and form a centre of interest and investigation. The afternoon course on 'Tennyson' was delivered by Mr. Boas after Christmas. The lecturer was introduced by Dr. Whitehead, who has taken so great an interest in the centre. The course was received with great interest, but the attendance was not so large as that at the evening course. Nevertheless good work was done, and the efforts of Mr. Boas very greatly appreciated. The session, embracing two courses of lectures, was successful in carrying out a larger programme than is usual with a centre of this size, and in sustaining an interest in a higher education.—A. ARCHIBALD, *Hon. Sec.*

WEST BRIGHTON.—The first evening course of Extension lectures held at this centre concluded on April 5. The subject of the course was 'The Making of the English Empire: Trade, Adventure, and Discovery,' illustrated by lime-light, the lecturer being Mr. Kenelm Cotes, M.A. The average attendance of the audience was 115, the number qualifying for the examination being nine. The committee regret that there were not a larger number of writers, but they recognize that the audience consisted of a very busy class, to accommodate whom the lectures could not be held at an earlier hour than 8.30, and that for those the difficulty of finding leisure for regular work must have been great. That this class should have been reached by the lectures they consider encouraging. From the commencement of the course a Students' Association was formed, at which there has throughout been a regular attendance of from thirteen to sixteen. This Association hopes to continue its meetings throughout the summer in continuance of this course and in preparation for the next. Thanks are felt to be due to Mr. Cotes for the kindly interest he has taken in the students and the help and encouragement he has extended to them. The committee has offered prizes to all those attaining distinction in the examination.—Mr. Horsburgh's course of twelve lectures on 'The Renaissance in Italy and England,' which has been delivered at fortnightly intervals all through the winter, has been most interesting and very successful, though the average attendance has not been quite so large as at former courses on literature, which seems to be a more popular subject here. A large Students' Association has been formed in connexion with the course, and has been very successful in arousing interest amongst the students.—M. F. BASDEN, *Hon. Sec.*

WHITEHAVEN.—Referring to the former notices of the course of lectures on Physiography by Mr. C. Carus-Wilson, which appears in the *Gazette* for December, 1893, it is most satisfactory to be able to state that the interest evinced in the subject by the attendance at the first three lectures was fully maintained during the concluding part of the course in a manner that was highly gratifying to the joint committees of the two societies, and must have been most pleasing to the lecturer. It is, however, to be regretted that the number of students who qualified for examination was not much greater, but all those who did qualify passed in a very creditable manner. The course on the 'French Revolution,' by Mr. C. E. Mallet, which began on Feb. 6, 1894, two weeks later than originally arranged, a postponement which was most kindly acceded to by Mr. Mallet at the special request of the committee, has just been concluded. These lectures have been in themselves perhaps more appreciated than those on Physiography, although, except on the occasion of the last lecture. they have not had the advantage of lantern illustrations. This is a feature which seems to have a great attraction for many; the pictorial representation appealing more powerfully to the eye than the verbal description, however lucid and eloquent, does to the ear. The attendance has ranged from 250 to 320, and in nearly every instance more than half of the audience remained to the class. In regard to the paper work of the class, it commenced well but afterwards diminished very considerably, and only a small number of the students qualified for examination. This is a circumstance much to be deplored, considering that only two-thirds of the questions have to be attempted in order to qualify. It is just possible that if certificates of a minor degree were granted in connexion with the courses of six lectures, an additional stimulus might be given to this part of the work, for in reality the examination is a test of the permanent benefit derived from the University Extension lectures, and this I take to be the effect which all the various centres have in view.—R. RUSSELL, *Hon. Local Sec.*

LETTERS TO THE EDITOR.

[*We do not hold ourselves responsible for the opinions expressed by our correspondents.*]

Should 'Prizes' be given to Extension Students?

DEAR SIR,—A discussion took place at the Bournemouth Conference in April as to the advisability of giving prizes after courses of University Extension lectures. Of the limited number of lecturers and delegates present a large majority evidently favoured the retention of prizes, and we heard incidentally that most of the Oxford lecturers were of the same opinion. But it would be interesting and I think useful to have the views of others upon a subject respecting which there is certainly much to be said on both sides. Among the arguments used 'against' prizes were the two following:—(1) They encourage the evil results of competition, viz. pleasure to the winner at the expense of others, and envy and discouragement to the backward student. (2) Passing examinations is often a question of 'knack'; the position of prize-winner is therefore no effective guarantee of the student's knowledge. (Are not these two arguments slightly contradictory of each other?) Speakers 'for' prizes confined themselves almost entirely to asserting that these arguments were not borne out by facts; and here it would be well to learn the experience of students, and of those who are in close contact with them; of local secretaries, secretaries to Students' Associations, students who *are*, and students who *are not*, prize-winners. But absence of abuse is not a strong argument for use, and we should like to have better reasons for valuing our prizes than the knowledge that our possession of them does not arouse jealousy, or discourage students with fewer advantages or less luck than ourselves. One point which occurs to me is the sense of a personal link with the University which the Delegates' prize brings, and which inspires one to perseverance in study. Letters in your columns from such authorities as I have mentioned above, giving positive reasons for the retention of prizes in the Oxford University Extension scheme, will be welcomed by

A PRIZE-WINNER.

The Tone of Patronage.

SIR,—Much that I read in your columns strikes me as being full of promise for the future of English education. I catch the note of sympathy, of the desire for unity of effort. of contempt for the petty jealousies which are apt to estrange one branch of the teaching profession from another. May I, however, without being misunderstood, lodge a protest against the tone of patronage which here and there your correspondents adopt especially when speaking of those who are engaged in the work of primary schools? The tone no doubt is unconscious, but the harm which it does is real. It affronts those who are independent, and can be tolerable only to those who are weak, among the very men with whom your correspondents are anxious to co-operate.

BYSTANDER.

.·.

The Employment of Junior Lecturers.

DEAR SIR,—At the Bournemouth Conference Mr. Wells expressed a wish that centres would apply more frequently than they do at present for the 'comparatively young and untried lecturers.' One of his reasons was that they are able to spend more time with their students in morning classes and other forms of tutorial work than can be done by gentlemen whose lecture-circuits are full.

I send you a very brief outline of the history of an experiment somewhat of this nature which has just been tried at Wells. The natural history societies of the neighbouring towns of Glastonbury, Shepton Mallet and Wells proposed to invite Mr. Badger to spend the Easter vacation in the district, giving in each town a course of instruction in practical geology by means of lectures and excursions. Eventually two of the three societies were unable to carry out their wishes, but Mr. Badger very kindly consented to come for the sake of Wells only. A small grant from the District Technical Education Committee enabled the organizers to charge only 2s. 6d. for the course and to throw it open to all comers. These lectures took place (necessarily) in the daytime, when a large attendance could not be expected; an average of 37 was, however, steadily maintained. We had five lectures, each followed immediately by a walk or drive to places of geological interest in the neighbourhood, where the instruction was continued. The walks were arranged so as admirably to illustrate the lectures, and with their endless opportunities for question and answer they brought teacher and taught into that close contact which is so advantageous to the latter. The lecturer has practically been at our disposal during the whole time, and by walks *ad interim*, by small evening classes held in the reference library, and by private instruction when desired, he has devoted himself to the interests of his students.

They fully appreciate this, but he would not wish to be thanked in the *Gazette*, and my object in writing is simply to show the advantages which may be gained by employing a lecturer who has a little time to spend in his centre.

Yours faithfully,

Wells, April 26. M. A. G. LIVETT, *Local Sec.*

.·.

An [? Im]pertinent Query.

SIR,—Is the Yorkshire University Extension Association any use? Why should it go on meeting to arrange lectures? Is the Lancashire and Cheshire Association any better?

Yours truly,

NORTH COUNTRY.

Summer Meetings are becoming the fashion. One will be held in London this month for the study of Library organization.

PROFESSOR HUXLEY'S DEFENCE OF THE POPULAR LECTURE.

IF any man has made effective use of the popular lecture it is Professor Huxley. He has shewn it to be an instrument capable of changing public opinion, and by its means he has secured for certain academic schemes the driving force of popular enthusiasm. It is, for example, to his work as a lecturer, more than to any other single cause, that the movement for scientific education may trace much of its popularity and practical success.

On the work of a lecturer, therefore, Professor Huxley speaks as an expert, and that he still retains his old opinion as to the value of the lecture as an instrument in educational propaganda, is proved by the following characteristic paragraphs which appear in the preface to the new edition of his *Discourses, Biological and Geological*, just published by Messrs. Macmillan.

I have not been one of those fortunate persons who are able to regard a popular lecture as a mere *hors d'œuvre*, unworthy of being ranked among the serious efforts of a philosopher; and who keep their fame as scientific hierophants unsullied by attempts—at least of the successful sort—to be understanded of the people.

On the contrary, I found that the task of putting the truths learned in the field, the laboratory and the museum, into language which, without bating a jot of scientific accuracy, shall be generally intelligible, taxed such scientific and literary faculty as I possess to the uttermost. Indeed, my experience has furnished me with no better corrective of the tendency to scholastic pedantry which besets all those who are absorbed in pursuits remote from the common ways of men, and become habituated to think and speak in the technical dialect of their own little world, as if there were no other.

If the popular lecture thus, as I believe, finds one moiety of its justification in the self-discipline of the lecturer, it surely finds the other half in its effect on the auditory. For though various sadly comical experiences of the results of my own efforts have led me to entertain a very moderate estimate of the purely intellectual value of lectures; though I venture to doubt if more than one in ten of an average audience carries away an accurate notion of what the speaker has been driving at; yet is that not equally true of the oratory of the hustings, of the House of Commons, and even of the pulpit?

Yet the children of this world are wise in their generation, and both the politician and the priest are justified by results. The living voice has an influence over human action altogether independent of the intellectual worth of that which it utters.

. . . .

That sagacious person John Wesley is reported to have replied to some one who questioned the propriety of his adaptation of sacred words to extremely secular airs, that he did not see why the devil should be left in possession of all the best tunes. And I do not see why science should not turn to account the peculiarities of human nature thus exploited by other agencies: all the more because science, by the nature of its being, cannot desire to stir the passions, or profit by the weaknesses, of human nature. The most zealous of popular lecturers can aim at nothing more than the awakening of a sympathy for abstract truth in those who do not really follow his arguments; and of a desire to know more and better in the few who do.

At the same time it must be admitted that the popularization of science, whether by lecture or essay, has its drawbacks. Success in this department has its perils for those who succeed. The 'people who fail' take their revenge, as we have recently had occasion to observe, by ignoring all the rest of a man's work, and glibly labelling him a mere popularizer. If the falsehood were not too glaring, they would say the same of Faraday and Helmholtz and Kelvin.

LORD ROSEBERY ON THE POSITION OF THE TEACHER.

A CONVERSAZIONE organized by the head teachers of the London School Board was held on April 27, at which both Lord Rosebery and Mr. Acland were present. In response to the obvious desire of those present, Lord Rosebery delivered a short impromptu speech, which we reprint :—

'I will,' he said, ' break my compact if you like. I have found by experience that it is a very dangerous thing to say anything either in my capacity as Lord President or as any other person. I particularly wish not to say anything on this occasion, because I do not wish that any doubt should arise as to the absolute supremacy of the Vice-President of the Council in matters of education. You know very well that, at any rate when the Vice-President of the Council is a Cabinet Minister, the Lord President has merely nominal functions with regard to education. I am anxious that that should be known, for he has dragged me at the tail of his triumphal chariot; and I am quite willing to appear in the same way that the monarchs were dragged at the tails of the Roman chariots. Well, he has conquered you all, I believe, and I am quite willing to appear in this capacity; but it is with an interest apart from any relation to the Privy Council, that I may say it gives me great pleasure to be here. After all, this is a gathering not of unique interest, but of very singular interest. You are here to-night for a re-union, which, I believe, is rare and exceptional—to gather together, in an evening partly of pleasure and partly of improvement, some of your experience of the past year. Well, what is it that we politicians rely upon? Whether a man be a Tory Minister or a Liberal Minister in this country, he relies on one thing, and that is the better education of the people who control the Government. You especially are the captains and the guides who are making for the England of the future that population which is to make our destinies. Whether it makes Ministers or not is a matter of inferior importance. What it has to do is to make the destinies of this country, and, therefore, the more the Ministers can meet the teachers of the public schools of this country the better it may be for the teacher, but it is certainly the better for the Minister. I thank you for giving me this opportunity of meeting you face to face, if only for a minute or two.'

This is, we believe, the first occasion on which the Lord President of the Council has spoken on educational matters.

THE EXTENSION OF UNIVERSITY INFLUENCE.

IT is customary for the Proctors at the conclusion of their term of office to summarize the events of the academic year in a Latin speech. In the *Oxford Magazine* for May 9 is printed the address of Messrs. Hassall and Hardie, which contains the following paragraph referring to one of the most important events which took place during their year of authority :—

' Initio termini Michaelis ingens huc multitudo confluxit, invitante Vice-Cancellario. Susciperetne ipsa Res Publica curam secundariae, quae vocatur, educationis, sicut iam suscepit primariae? Hoc ambigebatur : contiones eiusmodi fuerunt unde qui adfuit τερψάμενος, ut Homeri verbis utar, ῥεῖται καὶ πλείονα εἰδὼς: et per Sireneas has voces fortasse evenit ut in eam rem nunc Quaestio Regia sit constituta. Hoc vero tempore rursus frequentiam hospitum videmus, haberi contiones : multa disceptari, multa sine dubio in melius provehi, multos multis, quibus antea omnino ignoti fuerint, fieri amicos : gratulamurque Academiae quod iam tandem aliquo pacto toti Angliae disciplinarum ludorumque litterariorum velut fautrix quaedam et adiutrix extiterit.'

OXFORD UNIVERSITY

EXTENSION GAZETTE.

VOL. IV. No. 46.]   JULY, 1894.   [ONE PENNY.

N.B.—Local Organizers of Oxford University Extension Lectures are invited to send to the Secretary, Extension Office, Examinaticn Schools, Oxford, copies of any journals containing notices of, or references to, Extension work.

OXFORD UNIVERSITY EXTENSION.

Award of Scholarships and Prizes.

SCHOLARSHIPS to enable University Extension Students to attend the Oxford Summer Meeting have been awarded as follows. The award was based on an essay competition confined to students who had passed the examination on a course of Oxford University Extension lectures during the preceding year. The alternative subjects for the essays were drawn from History, Literature, Economics and Natural Science. There were fifty-eight candidates.

Scholarships of £10.

In History:—

ALBERT BRITLAND (Matlock).
J. R. FARMERY (Louth).
EDWIN OLDHAM (Hyde).

In Literature:—

BENJAMIN F. BROOKE (Harrogate).
ANNIE L. C. HELE (Carlisle).
JOSEPH OWEN (Oldham).

In Economics:—

WILLIAM E. OWEN (Oldham).

In Natural Science:—

RICHARD HIGGS (Chislehurst).

Scholarships of £5.

In History:—

EVELINE M. DOWSETT (Reading).
JOSEPH EMES (Pucklechurch).
ELMINA MORGAN (Abergavenny).
THOMAS OWEN (Ancoats, Manchester).
JOHN A. SIMPSON (Todmorden).
JANE E. VANT (Ripon).

In Literature:—

LAURA E. GREEN (Huddersfield).
KATHARINE G. HARTLEY (Prestwich).
EUNICE M. HOLDEN (Todmorden).

In Economics:—

OWEN BALMFORTH (Huddersfield).
ROBERT HALSTEAD (Hebden Bridge).

In Natural Science:—

HENRY B. ROBINSON (Croydon).

Prizes of £1.

In History:—HANNAH BUTTON (Oldham), RICHARD J. CHIRGWIN (New Swindon), CHARLES DOWNES (Abergavenny), KERSHAW HADFIELD(Oldham), EMMA JAGGER (Oldham), CHARLES OWEN (Oldham), MARY THORNEWILL (Bakewell).

In Literature:—LAURA VEALE (Harrogate).

In Economics:—FRED. COOK (Gloucestsr), JOE DYSON (Huddersfield).

In Natural Science:—LUCY A. PARKINSON (Grange), GEORGE H. PICKLES (Hebden Bridge).

Report of the Awarders.

THE standard of the competition was higher than last year, and the number of candidates much larger. The work done is of a satisfactory character.

History.—' The essays sent in are on the whole decidedly good. A certain number, evidently written by young candidates, were hardly up to the mark, but even these showed considerable promise. Some of the writers had a tendency towards irrelevancy which detracted from the merits of their papers. A good many of those who chose the Norman Conquest spent too much time in writing about the Anglo-Saxons, while very few of those who wrote on the Stuart subject really understood James I's foreign policy or knew anything whatever about that of James II. A chapter or two in Gardiner's *History of England* would explain to them the drift of James I's policy, while a few chapters in Ranke's *History of England* would give them adequate information on the position of James II. The essays however were, generally speaking, very well done, being much superior to those of last year, showing great care, thought and accuracy. I consider the result of the competition to have been most satisfactory.'

Literature.—' In literature the essays were fully up to the usual standard, and there was a larger competition than there has yet been. There was a great deal of careful work, and here and there the answers showed original thought. The two besetting dangers of essays on literary subjects are *fine writing* and *vague generalizing without examples*: from these faults the work was on the whole creditably free. But it would improve the clearness of most of the essays if the writers carefully arranged the heads of their subject in proper order before beginning. This would prevent repetitions, and would tend to keep digression within the due limits.'

Economics.—' The essays sent in show a great advance on those of last year, and of any preceding year. The subjects were evidently popular, and brought out a good deal of well applied practical knowledge, as well as results of reading. As a rule, the manner of writing was good, but here and there it tended to become diffuse. There was also a want of arrangement in some essays, which might be remedied by an abstract drawn up before the essay is written. On the whole the industry shown was very praiseworthy, and the reasoning clear and concise.

Natural Science.—The essays on practical Science

1

teaching were both good. Two of those on the Weather were of considerable merit, and an essay on the Nitrogen of the Farm was thoughtful and well arranged.'

> Signed.　ARTHUR HASSALL.
> 　　　　　ARTHUR SIDGWICK.
> 　　　　　LANCELOT R. PHELPS.　} *Awarders.*
> 　　　　　W. W. FISHER.

June 25, 1894.

• The Awarders have transmitted the results of the Dixon-Galpin and Dorset County Council Competition to the Technical Instruction Committee of the Dorset County Council.

NOTES AND COMMENTS.

The late Bishop of Bath and Wells. One by one the pioneers of University Extension are dropping off. Last month we had to record the death of Professor Henry Morley. He has now been followed by the Bishop of Bath and Wells. So long ago as in 1855, Lord Arthur Hervey addressed a letter to his own University of Cambridge, strongly recommending the appointment of a staff of travelling professors, whose duty it would be to give courses of lectures at Mechanics' Institutes. In this way he hoped that the University might help forward the education of adult students who could not afford the advantages of academic life. The scheme was before its time. Financial difficulties alone would have been enough to prevent its realization. But a less obvious, though none the less fatal, obstacle lay in the unreadiness of the members of Mechanics' Institutes to undertake regular courses of instruction by University men. The Elementary Education Act had to work for a generation before a sufficiently large number of people were intellectually prepared for Lord Arthur's scheme. But the fact that he practically proposed what we now call University Extension (though without many of the more valuable provisions which were afterwards added by Mr. James Stuart) shows that Lord Arthur Hervey had the insight of a statesman. In later years he rejoiced to see the attainment of his earlier hopes. As Bishop of Bath and Wells, he was never tired of helping forward the University Extension movement. Chairman of the local committee, he always desired that its meetings should be held at the Palace in order that he might himself preside, and in many other ways he showed his practical interest in the work.

The new Junior Local Examination. On June 12 the University of Oxford decided to hold in 1895 a new Local Examination for candidates under fourteen years of age. This vote, which was carried by eighty-three to twenty, marks the present trend of academic policy. It was stated that the educational work of the County Councils has led to a demand for some authoritative test of juvenile merit at an age for which the existing forms of local examination were not designed. The question was whether this test should be supplied by the University or by some other body. It was finally decided that the University should carry forward its present policy of rendering all the aid in its power towards the improvement of secondary education in England, Professor Dicey making an eloquent speech in favour of this view. Serious objection, however, was taken to the proposal to institute this examination by decree instead of by the more lengthy process of statute. But the fact that, if the present opportunity was to be seized, there was not time to go through the stages of a statute, reconciled the University to the quicker, though unusual, procedure by decree. An undertaking was, however, given that next term there would be submitted a statute laying down general rules for the conduct of the new examination in future years. It would have been injudicious for the University to appear to shrink from what appears to be a matter of public duty. The more the State and local authorities concern themselves with public instruction, the greater is the need for the complementary service of great institutions like the Universities. The independent, though concerted, action of the Universities and of public authorities will tend to secure general efficiency without sacrificing order or freedom.

.•.

The Premier and two ex-Premiers are at the present time members of a single College in Oxford. Such a combination is probably without precedent. Lord Rosebery, Lord Salisbury and Mr. Gladstone were all educated at Christ Church, and are now Honorary Students of the House.

.•.

The Summer Meeting of 1895. The plan of holding the large Summer Meeting at Oxford and Cambridge in alternate years has been unexpectedly disturbed. A new system of drainage is being introduced into Cambridge, and some of the principal streets are likely to be opened up in August 1895. The Oxford Delegacy have therefore, after conference with the Cambridge Syndicate, decided to hold the large Summer Meeting in Oxford next year. The Summer Meeting of 1896 will be at Cambridge and, it is hoped, alternately from that time onwards in the two University towns. In continuation of the general sequence, the chief course of historical and literary lectures will next year be upon the eighteenth century.

.•.

Mrs. T. H. Green of Oxford has kindly given £10 to the funds of the Oxford University Extension.

.•.

The Cambridge Syndicate have decided to arrange two courses of instruction in Chemistry at Cambridge, from August 7 to August 28. The courses which it was proposed to hold in other subjects have been abandoned, as the number of entries was insufficient.

.•.

Abandonment of the Scheme of the Catholic Summer School at Oxford. A number of Catholics connected with Newman House in Kennington Park Road, S.E., arranged a number of courses of lectures to be delivered in Oxford from July 14 to July 26 for the benefit of Catholic teachers and others. Among the lecturers on literature were Messrs. Kegan Paul, Lionel Johnson, and Dr. Parry. There were also to have been courses of lectures in social science by Messrs. Costello, Devas and others. Among the historical lecturers were to have been Dr. Casartelli, Father Goldie, S.J., Mr. C. J. Gatty, &c., some of the subjects being Saint Anselm, Sir Thomas More, and the History of Oxford. We hear however that the scheme for holding the Summer School has been abandoned in deference to the wishes of an influential member of the Catholic Hierarchy in England. As the arrangements were far advanced towards completion, the abandonment of the scheme will cause much disappointment to those who were taking an active part in promoting its success. The Honorary Secretaries of the scheme were Messrs. Everard Feilding and Mr. Sidney Parry.

.•.

We are glad to see that Mr. H. T. Gerrans, Fellow and Tutor of Worcester College, and Secretary to the Oxford Local Examination Delegacy, has been appointed one of the Assistant Commissioners to the Royal Commission on Secondary Education.

.•.

The Rev. C. G. Lang, Fellow of Magdalen College, till recently one of the Staff-lecturers of the Oxford University Extension, will be the new Vicar of St. Mary's, the University Church in Oxford. It was as Vicar of St. Mary's that John Henry Newman preached many of his most famous sermons. The gift of the living is in the hands of Oriel College. One of Mr. Lang's first sermons as Vicar of St. Mary's will be that which he has promised to preach to the University Extension students during the Summer Meeting.

Two of the examiners of the Oxford University Extension have recently received deserved honour—the Rev. F. J. Smith by election as Fellow of the Royal Society, and Dr. Sydney Hickson by appointment to the Beyer Professorship of Zoology at Owens College, Manchester.

.˙.

Mr. J. H. Fowler of Manchester has been appointed Sixth Form Master at Clifton College, and is therefore obliged to resign the honorary secretaryship of the Lancashire and Cheshire Association for the Extension of University Teaching. Mr. Fowler has held this position, which is by no means a sinecure, for some years, during which time he has managed the affairs of the Association with tact and prudence. His work has done much to strengthen the position of the University Extension movement in the North of England.

.˙.

A noteworthy feature of this year's class lists at Cambridge has been the success of students who have begun their educational career in public elementary schools. Miss Baldwin, the daughter of the clerk of the Barnsley School Board, has gained new distinction by obtaining the only First Class won in the second part of the Natural Science Tripos this year. The first stages of her education were conducted by her father, when master of the High Green British School, midway between Barnsley and Sheffield.

.˙.

The Victoria University is considering a scheme for the award of Diplomas in the theory and practice of education.

.˙.

We are pleased to see from the *Bury Times* of June 13 that an effort is being made to place the University Extension lectures at Bury on a firmer basis. For many years two ladies, Mrs. Rothwell and Miss Kitchener, have worked hard for the scheme at Bury, and have not only given up much time to the work but have also borne the greater part of the financial responsibility. A large committee has now been formed consisting of seven ladies and seventeen gentlemen, as well the chairmen of the Athenaeum, the Y.M.C.A., the Technical Instruction Committee of the Corporation, the Co-operative Society's Educational Committee, and the High School for Girls. This is an excellently representative body, and we are glad to see that both the Rector and the Mayor of Bury were present and spoke at the meeting held to inaugurate the new departure. Mention was made at the meeting of the desirability of so framing the programme of lectures as to meet the needs of teachers in elementary schools. Hopes were also expressed that some of the operatives would attend the lectures.

.˙.

Visitors to Oxford will welcome the appearance of a new edition of Alden's Sixpenny *Guide*. We have formerly commended this handy little volume, and are now able to do so even more warmly, as the careful editor has corrected his description of Oxford in view of recent additions to our buildings, and the further light which has been thrown on the antiquity of part of the Cathedral.

.˙.

University Extension in Belgium. The *Revue Universitaire* (Brussels) for June 15 contains the annual report of the University Extension movement in Belgium. Twenty-five courses have been delivered during the year, comprising in all 183 lectures, at thirteen towns. The total attendance has been between 3,900 and 4,000. Six courses were given on history, five on sociology, two on law, five on physiology and hygiene, four on zoology, two on palaeontology, and one on agricultural chemistry. The audiences were mostly composed of 'fonctionnaires, instituteurs, employés et personnes appartenant à la petite bourgeoisie qui avaient déjà reçu une instruction relative-

ment supérieure.' Some graduates also attended. Workmen came in some numbers at Brussels and Charleroi. In other places they were apathetic. The audiences have apparently been too shy to ask questions, though invited to do so by the lecturers, nor have they done weekly exercises. The Central Committee advise the formation of 'classes' on the English model and propose to institute short examinations. Most of the courses have consisted of six lectures, given at weekly intervals. The attendance has been regular. During the year the University of Brussels approves of the movement, but declines to give it official sanction. The direction of the Belgian University Extension remains therefore in the hands of a private society, which now numbers 246 members.

.˙.

We understand that Miss Gould, who has just obtained a first class in the Honour School of Natural Science at Oxford, was originally an Oxford University Extension student, who did such good work in connexion with one of Mr. Poulton's courses in Devonshire, that he encouraged her to enter for the Scholarship competition at Somerville Hall. Miss Gould's success has now been crowned by the highest honours in one of the Final Schools.

.˙.

In *University Extension* for June Mr. John Russell Hayes, of Swarthmore College, has an appreciative article about the Oxford Summer Meeting.

.˙.

An honorary Inspector of University Extension. An important piece of news comes from Albany. The University of the State of New York has commissioned Mr. J. E. Whitney to serve as honorary inspector of Extension teaching in Western New York. Mr. Whitney, who has had practical experience in the organization of Extension work, will have his head-quarters at Rochester. His duty will be 'to inspect the methods and practical workings of Extension agencies referred to him by the University and, so far as practicable, to stimulate the formation of new centres, circles, clubs and libraries, and to assist in their organization and supervision.'

IMPRESSIONS OF THE UNIVERSITY EXTENSION CONGRESS.

IT has been a great occasion and a memorable success—not a mere beating of tom-toms but a deliberative gathering, from which the whole movement will gain encouragement, cohesion of interest, greater precision of purpose. Many expected far less than this to come out of a mixed and rather ornamental gathering. Some even feared that things might be said which would injure the prospects of University Extension work and emphasize differences without composing them. Both were happily wrong. It is true that in a certain sense the assembly was decorative rather than workmanlike. Some who seemed to be pillars were found to be nothing of the kind. One or two people who count themselves experts showed themselves ill-informed. But the mass of the meeting knew its own mind and meant to go forward. True, it was a demonstration rather than a debate. When you deduct the time spent on necessary futilities, six hours leave small margin for serious discussion. But, nevertheless, real work was done. The Congress unanimously ratified the three reports which were proposed for its acceptance, and did so, not with its eyes shut and in ignorance of the real bearing of what was thus approved, but of set purpose and in formal endorsement of what had previously been matters of sectional opinion rather than of collective policy.

In fact, the Congress has made peace and has cemented alliance between the various groups in the movement. This is a great achievement, the effects of which will be felt long after the Congress is forgotten. Of course, the mere fact of holding such a gathering at all, the joint

2

presidency of the Chancellors of the three Universities of Oxford, Cambridge and London (a combination without precedent in academic work), the attendance of delegates from every part of England, the evidence of the international character of the work,—all these things have impressed, and rightly impressed, public opinion. The movement takes its place among the recognized forces in modern education. It has come of age. It has strengthened its position. All this is good and at the present time specially desirable and appropriate. But the Congress was not merely a parade. It marks a consolidation of policy. What were thought at one time to be rival schemes have proved to be complementary parts of one whole. The long-course and the short-course systems are not alternative policies but both necessary parts of one policy. As a witty member of the Congress remarked, parodying the couplet from Bombastes Furioso,

> 'In short, so long as we your favours claim,
> Short course or long to us is all the same.'

That is to say, each system must be judged from the practical standpoint of educational efficiency. In one district, long-continued courses are possible and desirable : in another district, they are not. But in any well organized centre, both long and short courses will be found necessary, for both meet different needs which are permanently present among the students of a large institution.

Agreement, again, has been reached in respect of the method of University Extension teaching. The lecture *plus* class *plus* weekly exercise is not adapted to many subjects of which it is desirable that University Extension centres should take account. The old method, for example, is not applicable to instruction in languages and in mathematics. And therefore the Congress agreed that class teaching should have an accredited place in the University Extension system.

And so on all through the list of once vexed questions. The propriety of acting in concert with local authorities, the need for public subsidies for the higher education of adults who cannot go to a University, the claim of University Extension students for recognition in the degree-course of the new University of London—on all these points the Congress had no difficulty in speaking its mind. And public acknowledgment was handsomely made of the educational, as well as administrative, value of large Summer Meetings, and of the worthiness of such institutions as the University Extension Colleges at Reading and Exeter to be imitated in other places.

It is, therefore, with hearty gratitude that we express our sense of the obligation under which the whole University Extension movement lies to the Council of the London Society for its action in summoning the Congress. And thanks are especially due to Dr. Roberts and Dr. Lawrence, on whom fell the chief part of the burden of organization. They accomplished a difficult and often delicate task with tact, geniality and forethought.

What will be the practical outcome of the Congress ?

It is often said that Conferences end only in words. Of the University Extension Congress this criticism would be entirely untrue. Apart from the good feeling to which it has given rise (and on good feeling between coadjutors educational progress chiefly depends), the Congress leaves behind it a definite result in the carefully prepared reports which the assembly unanimously adopted. It is true that the different authorities are not pledged to everything which those reports contain—but, coming from a unanimous and representative gathering, the proposals will carry great weight with any person who carefully examines them. It is safe to predict that, during the next few years, the University Extension movement will advance on the lines broadly laid down in these reports.

No University Extension worker, therefore, should fail to study them in conjunction with the full report of the discussions which is to be published on July 16 by the London University Extension Society (Charterhouse, E.C., 1s. post free). A perusal of this volume will do more than anything else to convince the reader of the great work which still lies before the University Extension system, and of the practicability of the plans which have been

framed to secure its educational efficiency and thoroughness.

But the first thing to do in an administrative direction is to consider the propriety of forming a Joint Consultative Committee, representative of the four branches of the movement in England and of the two University Extension Colleges already in existence. We do not want any elaborate organization but simply an arrangement by which about ten or a dozen people, appointed by Oxford, Cambridge, London and Victoria, and the Colleges at Reading and Exeter, may meet in London or at some other central place three or four times a year in order to talk over matters affecting the common interests of the work. We need to federate, not to unify, the Extension movement in England. What the Railway Association does for the Railway Companies, what the School Board Association does for the School Boards, what the County Council Association does for the County Councils, such a Joint Committee might easily do for University Extension. Moot and delicate questions, like intrusion into areas in the immediate neighbourhood of Universities or University Colleges, the correlation of the standard of examinations, the nomenclature of certificates, and the interchange of Summer Meetings would all be profitably talked over in such a Committee as we have described. The Committee need have no executive authority. Its business would be to express opinions, leaving it to the several authorities concerned to act upon them.

And in negotiations with Parliament, with Government Departments, with local authorities, such a Committee would be useful and influential. The weight of the University Extension movement would be greatly increased if it had the means of readily expressing a collective opinion. We want something which will focus our influence, without depriving our work of its spontaneity and initiative.

Moreover, such a Committee might act in concert with representatives of the movement abroad. There is now an international side of our work which the presence of Colonial, American and foreign delegates at the Congress opportunely emphasized.

Finally, it is clear that we must have superintendent lecturers in charge of the various districts in which our work is carried on. Such directors would work with the local committee, promote combination, increase the number of centres, bring a long experience to bear on the local difficulties which will always tend to appear and to repeat themselves, and afford a means of training the younger lecturers to whom we look to carry on the work in the future. Mr. James Stuart and his friends saw the need for such superintendents at the beginning of the work. The need still exists. But in order to meet it, we want funds. And future appeals for funds will be strengthened by what passed at the Congress. The most pressing difficulty which now confronts our work is this need for funds. And the funds, which need not exceed a few thousands a year, must be administered by the central authorities in trust for the whole movement. Reading and Exeter, indeed, require subsidies paid direct into their accounts. But for the benefit of the ordinary run of centres, the most economical and effective means of employing subsidies will be through the central authorities.

As soon, however, as we get superintendent lecturers, the question of areas will become acute. An Oxford and a Cambridge superintendent cannot usefully work in the same district. How are we then to adjust the claims of the four central authorities? This is a pressing matter which must be discussed in common. A solution is by no means impossible, but we must have a joint committee to arrive at it.

In these columns, no detailed report of the proceedings of the Congress is necessary. That has appeared already to some extent in the daily papers. A full report—and nothing less can do justice to the importance of the gathering—is promised hereafter. What has been said here aims at summing up the general drift of the discussions and at pointing the way to the future action which those discussions have shown to be possible and expedient.

SUMMER MEETING NOTES.

We regret to announce that the heavy work which has fallen on Mr. Bryce in consequence of his appointment as President of the Board of Trade will prevent him from delivering the Inaugural Address at the Summer Meeting.

.·.

During the First Part of the Summer Meeting special services will be held in the Chapel of Mansfield College ; the Principal, Dr. Fairbairn, will be the preacher on July 29, and the Rev. Professor Francis Brown on August 5. During the first three days of the intervening week, Mr. J. V. Bartlet, M.A., tutor and lecturer at Mansfield College, will lecture on Seventeenth Century Religion in the light of its antecedents; and the Rev. Dr. Brown, Professor of Hebrew in Union Theological Seminary, New York, on the historical writing of the Old Testament on Thursday, Friday, and Saturday following. The lectures will be given at 9 a.m. at Mansfield College.

.·.

No public conference on University Extension will be held during the Summer Meeting, but conferences of a private nature will be held at times to be fixed later. Among subjects which will be discussed will be the arrangement of Students' Associations, and the best means of conducting them with success.

.·.

Mr. Balfour's class in Anthropology will be limited to twelve students. Applications for admission to the class are now being received. On Monday, July 30, the class will assemble in the Pitt Rivers Museum at 2.30, but the hour of meeting on other days may be put later in the afternoon. This point however will be settled by Mr. Balfour during the first meeting of the class.

.·.

Dr. Odling, F.R.S., Professor of Chemistry in the University of Oxford, will give two lectures on Chemistry in the First Part of the Summer Meeting. He has also kindly consented to exhibit part of his famous collection of Rembrandt etchings. Mr. C. W. Furse will give a lecture on Rembrandt in addition to the lectures previously announced on Velasquez and Vandyck.

.·.

Dr. Devine recommends students who will attend his lectures at the Summer Meeting to read Walker's *Political Economy*, Marshall's *Economics of Industry*, Gide's *Political Economics*, or any other standard text-book as general preparation. For the first lecture he specially recommends Mr. E. Cannan's book on *Production and Distribution of* 1848.

.·.

Class in Economics.　A class will study, under the guidance of Messrs. M. E. Sadler and Edward Grubb, M.A. (author of *The Economics of Luxury*) the historical development of the theory of Socialism. The class will meet daily from 12—1.45 from August 18—24 (excluding August 19). There will be a series of lectures on the subject, and those members of the class who write essays will receive individual tuition. The class will be limited to twenty. The subjects of the lectures will be—

1. French Revolutionary Socialism, including St. Simon.
2. Fourier and Owen.
3. Ferdinand Lassalle and the relation of the theory of socialism to the economics of Ricardo.
4. Karl Marx and Capital.
5. (i) Socialists of the chair. (ii) The logical antithesis of Collectivism and Anarchism.
6. Socialist thought in England. The collectivist tendency of central and local administration.

.·.

Mr. Headlam recommends students who propose to attend his theological lectures the following books for preparatory reading :—Bishop Lightfoot, *The Apostolic Fathers* and *The Apostolic Fathers* translated in the Golden Treasury Series.

.·.

The Rev. Charles Gore has, we regret to say, been again ordered abroad for his health, and will consequently be unable to deliver the lectures on the Elements of Theology, which were announced in the early editions of the Summer Meeting programme. The Rev. R. L. Ottley has, however, kindly consented to give six lectures on the Manifestation and Work of the Lord. Mr. Ottley, the late Principal of Cuddesdon and Fellow of Magdalen College, has succeeded Mr. Gore as Principal of the Pusey House in Oxford.

.·.

Further lectures have been arranged on three seventeenth century divines. The Rev. R. L. Ottley will lecture on Bishop Andrewes, the Rev. L. Pullan, Fellow of St. John's College, on Bossuet, and the Rev. H. C. Beeching on Jeremy Taylor.

.·.

We are glad to announce that the Rev. Dr. Lawrence, of Downing College, Cambridge, and Staff-lecturer to the Cambridge Syndicate for local lectures, has consented to deliver a lecture on Grotius, as part of the course on the Seventeenth Century.

.·.

An advertisement issued with this number of the *Gazette* will draw attention to a new departure in the programme of the Summer Meeting. For the first time a dramatic performance will be included. With eminent appropriateness to the historical period selected for the main work of the Meeting, Robert Browning's 'Strafford' has been chosen for performance. Two representations of this play will, therefore, be given in the New Theatre (in George Street) on Saturday, Aug. 4—a matinee at 2 o'clock and an evening performance at 8 o'clock. Summer Meeting students will be able, on presentation of their tickets, to obtain reserved seats in the stalls and dress circle at half price. The stage management has been most kindly undertaken by Mr. Alan Mackinnon, M.A., of Trinity, *facilè princeps* among amateur managers and with few equals among professionals. The characters will be played almost entirely by members, past or present, of the O.U.D.S., with the valuable assistance of Mrs. Charles Sim as Lady Carlisle. Among the members of the cast as at present arranged are : Mr. Lawrence Irving, Mr. A. Mackinnon, Mr. Arthur Ellis, Mr. R. A. Johnson, Mr. P. Comyns Carr, Mr. C. Croker King, Mr. Kidston, and Mr. F. U. Mugliston. For the parts of the 'Speaking Supers' we look for assistance to Summer Meeting students. Gentlemen who are prepared to help in this capacity are requested to send their names to Mr. J. A. R. Marriott, New College, under whose general management the piece will be produced. The rehearsals for the principals will take place mostly in London, but Summer Meeting volunteers will only be required to attend rehearsals on Aug. 1, 2, and 3 in Oxford.

.·.

Many students will hear with pleasure that Miss Edwards is forming a party of lady teachers to attend the course of lectures on Education at the Oxford Summer Meeting. Her intimate knowledge of education will enable her to render great service to those who are studying the subject of the course. She is hoping to find rooms for the party at 44 High Street, and the expense per head for board and lodging will not exceed 25s. a week. It may possibly be as low as 21s. Those who wish to join Miss Edwards' party should communicate with her direct, and as soon as possible, at 25 York Street Chambers, Bryanston Square, London, W.

.·.

Twelve or thirteen lady students can be accommodated at Wordsworth Hostel during the first fortnight of the Summer Meeting, at a charge of 25s. a week for board and lodging. Application should be made as soon as possible to Mrs. Arnold Toynbee, 10 Norham Gardens, Oxford.

RESIDENCE AS A FACTOR IN UNIVERSITY LIFE.

THERE is no doubt that public opinion is setting very fast in favour of regarding residence as an essential part of the best kind of University training. Thirty years ago, in the heyday of other influences, academic reformers spoke contemptuously of residence as a thing which should be curtailed in the case of one class of students after another and perhaps eventually abandoned.

All the time, however, there were many who believed that Cardinal Newman was right in insisting that, if you had to make the choice, it would be wiser to go to a University where there was residence without teaching than to one where there was examination without residence. And gradually the mass of opinion has swung slowly round to Cardinal Newman's view. Victoria University, founded as the result of the same impulse which had formerly given London University to the nation, has deliberately adopted residence as an essential part of its qualification for a degree, and, as if to make this change in policy more significant, it has taken place as the result of experience acquired during the new university's short career. In London itself a strong agitation for a residential university has produced first the scheme for the Gresham University, then a Royal Commission to investigate the subject, and finally a recognition from that high authority that the existing London University should so far remodel its constitution as to provide a special set of examinations for those who have resided for the purpose of receiving instruction.

And now in Edinburgh the same movement has shown itself. The energy of Professor Patrick Geddes, who is now well known in Great Britain and France as a vigorous thinker on academic questions, has brought about the erection on the Castle Hill of a new building, which will really form a college in the University of Edinburgh. For many years he has superintended on the Mound in Edinburgh a house called the University Hall, which has provided residential life for a few students of the University. But now his scheme has taken a more ambitious, and we hope a more definitely permanent, form. And on Friday, April 13, there took place the formal opening of the new buildings on the Castle Rock, which are to provide opportunities of residence for a larger number of students. The decoration of the Hall is said to be as artistic and its arrangements as ingenious as the friends of Professor Geddes would naturally expect it to be. We can do no more in these columns than extend a hearty welcome to the newest comer among University colleges and to wish it a long and prosperous future. In time to come the fame of Patrick Geddes may be to Edinburgh what that of Walter of Merton is to Oxford.

CO-OPERATORS AND THE UNIVERSITIES.

THE report of the Central Co-operative Board, presented to the Sunderland Congress in May, contains the following paragraphs under the heading 'University Education':—

The Hughes and Neale Scholarships.—(a) The third Hughes scholar, Mr. Alfred Hickling, who was successful in the examination held in October 1892, has not yet entered upon his University career, but it is expected that he will take up his residence at Oxford at the commencement of the next term. This further delay has taken place on the advice of the Provost of Oriel, who considered that, on account of his youth, Mr. Hickling would gain by the postponement. It will not, however, affect in any way the election of the next Hughes Scholar, in regard to which the examination will be held in October 1896. As the second examination for the Neale Scholarship will take place in October next, there appears every probability that we shall have two co-operative scholars commencing their studies at the same time.

(b) We have endeavoured to obtain information as to what has become of the students who have completed their University career, partly with the object of ascertaining how far these scholarships were instrumental in fitting the sons of co-operators for the higher walks of life, and part to help us in forming an opinion as to whether students so educated were likely to become good and useful co-operators Of the two scholars who have passed through the University by the aid of the co-operative scholarships, we find that one—Mr. James Stuart Ramsay—is now sub-editor of a Glasgow newspaper, and expresses his willingness to render what service he can to the movement.

While writing this paragraph, tidings were received of the sudden decease of the Rev. Theodore Parker Broadbent, B.A., the first Hughes Scholar, who died at the early age of twenty-six, after a few hours' illness. Coming at a time when we were just making inquiry as to his position in life, and in regard to his prospects for a bright and useful future, his sudden removal from our midst strikes us as inexpressibly sad. From the account which appeared in the *News* of April 21, it will be seen that Mr. Broadbent had made good use of the opportunities afforded by the co-operative scholarships at Oxford, and that his life was full of promise for future usefulness.

University Summer Meeting.—Owing to local circumstances there was no Summer Meeting held at Oxford in 1893, we therefore took advantage of the gathering which had been arranged to be held at Cambridge to continue our connexion with these Summer Meetings. The Educational Committee, as in former years, arranged to make grants to enable the six best students in our co-operative classes to attend at Cambridge last July or August. The successful students were as follows:—Messrs. R. Rose (Hyde), E. E. Hancock (Plymouth), E. Williams (Winsford), R. H. Townsend (Dewsbury), J. Grant (Sunderland), and J. E. Kilburn (Dewsbury).

The students, of this and former years, unite in bearing testimony to the value of these University gatherings, bringing together as they do students and thinkers from all parts of the United Kingdom, thus giving the opportunity for exchange of ideas and stimulating a desire for higher education.

Preparative Reading for Lectures on the Historical Development of the Theory of Socialism.

1. *Contemporary Socialism.* By John Rae. Second edition. (Sonnenschein, 1891, 10s. 6d.)

2. *Le Socialisme Contemporain.* Par Émile de Laveleye. (Paris, Felix Alcan, 1885, 3 fr. 50.)
   [*There is an English translation of this by Orpen.*]

3. *Socialism New and Old.* By William Graham. International Scientific Series. (Kegan, Paul & Co., 5s.)

4. *Les Origines du Socialisme Contemporain.* Par Paul Janet. (Paris, Germer Baillière, 1883, 2 fr. 50.)

5. *St. Simon et le St. Simonisme.* Par Paul Janet. (Paris, Germer Baillière, 1878, 2 fr. 50.)

6. *Capital.* By Karl Marx. Any edition. (An Eng. trans. by Moore and Aveling is published by Sonnenschein. 2 vols.)

7. *The Quintessence of Socialism.* Schäffle. (Sonnenschein, 2s. 6d.)

8. *The Co-operative Movement.* By Beatrice Potter (Mrs. Sidney Webb). (Sonnenschein, 5s.)

9. *Principles of State Interference.* By D. G. Ritchie. (Sonnenschein, 2s. 6d.)

10. *The London Programme.* By Sidney Webb. (Sonnenschein, 2s. 6d.)

11. *The Fabian Essays.* Edited by Bernard Shaw. (Walter Scott, 1s.)

12. *A Plea for Liberty.* Edited by Thomas Mackay. (John Murray, 1s.)

13. *The Labour Movement.* By L. T. Hobhouse. (Fisher, Unwin & Co., 3s. 6d.)

[*Nos. 1, 2 or 3 would serve as a general introduction to the course.*]

ON THE TRAINING OF TEACHERS.

[A Paper read by Mr. A. Sidgwick, M.A. (Fellow and Tutor of Corpus Christi College and Reader in Greek in the University of Oxford), before the Easter Conference of the N. U. T. at Oxford, on Tuesday, March 27, 1894.]

MR. PRESIDENT, LADIES AND GENTLEMEN,—I wish to state clearly from the outset that I decline to consider it an open question, whether all school teachers ought to be professionally trained and certified. In every other art or craft, professional training and apprenticeship is a practical or legal necessity. But in the profession, which is undeniably one of the greatest difficulty and of the first national importance, the public, over a large part of the field, has no sort of guarantee of the efficiency of the instruments it employs; and whether the teachers have natural aptitude or no, their professional skill has either to be acquired at the expense of the pupil, or never acquired at all. No serious person can deny that this state of things is *prima facie* a flagrant absurdity. And when we assert the necessity of training we are not blind to the limits that must be placed on what is to be expected from it. That training alone is not enough: that it will not by itself be able to convert a born incompetent into a good teacher: that some of the most valuable qualities of the teacher are neither taught nor teachable—these are truths which we do not only admit, but insist on; though we may suspect that it is not the untrained teacher who makes the best use of them. I will go further, and assert that training, like other forms of knowledge, may be used in too mechanical a way, and may be too highly valued by its possessor; though I do not assent to the inferences sometimes drawn from these statements. For the teacher innocent of training is at least equally liable to the same dangers. It is quite possible to be ignorant of method, and yet conceited; and it certainly is not necessary to be trained in order to be mechanical. But when all these tendencies and limitations are fully recognized it is obvious, from considerations of common sense and experience alike, that *ceteris paribus* the trained man is better than the untrained. As Dr. Fitch said before the Select Committee, 'a poor teacher is made better, a bad teacher can be made tolerably useful, and even the best is improved.' That puts the case in a nutshell; and I do not see what answer there is or can be to it.

I suppose I may assume a general agreement that training, to whatever grade of teaching it is to be applied, will consist of two elements—first, a general education, including, but not confined to, the subjects which the students will have to teach; and, secondly, specific education, both practical and theoretic, in what the Germans call by the rather terrible name of Paedagogics, but for which I shall prefer to use the easier term Method. It will, perhaps, be simplest and most convenient to take the different branches into which English education naturally falls, and briefly consider them in relation to this definition.

And though it may seem to lie outside our subject, and even outside the region of practical politics altogether, I, nevertheless, should like to begin with a word or two about the Universities. I am aware that nobody has ever ventured to suggest that University teachers should be trained before they commence work; and, more particularly, that when the question of establishing a national register of teachers was, three years ago, brought practically before Parliament by Sir Richard Temple and Mr. Arthur Acland, both these authorities expressly excluded the Universities from the purview of their respective Bills, and in the report of the Select Committee none but school teachers were considered. But though the question has not been raised in public, it is a fair one to raise; and it has certainly been discussed in private. There is in many quarters a suspicion of the Universities—less, I am thankful to say, than there was some time ago, and steadily diminishing—but it still undoubtedly exists. There is a feeling, none the less injurious because it is vague, that the Universities, though they are powerful by reason of their wealth, prestige, and influence in high quarters, yet are all the while no better than they should be. In view of such feelings, it is all the more important that no reasonable

criticism should be shirked, and that any special claim should be justified. Such a critic might be supposed to speak as follows:— 'Of the two elements of training, general culture and method, we do not, of course, deny that the University teachers possess the first; if they have it not, nobody has it. But they are professional teachers too, and yet they have no apprenticeship or professional training of any sort. They have difficult subjects and difficult pupils to teach; youths fresh from the class-lists are set to instruct those scarcely younger, in some cases no younger, than themselves; and there are stories from the lecture-room current which imply that the natural results follow. If we are going to insist on training, why should we not begin at the top!'

Now without attributing any weight to the stories which belong, as usual, some to Mythology rather than to History, and some to the past rather than to the present—I may say at once that in my view the principle of training applies here too, and that University teachers, like others, would be the better for systematic attention to method. But, quite apart from the insuperable difficulty of imposing any appropriate system of training, there are one or two points, tolerably obvious but often overlooked, which put a wholly different colour on the situation. It is plain, for instance, that the older and more advanced the student is the more important is the teacher's *matter*, and the less important his *manner*. With the youngest and most ignorant children Method is almost everything; and, though it never becomes indifferent, its relative value visibly decreases as you go up. Again, originality, always most precious in a teacher, in the early stages works best in detail, within the limits of a general system; in the higher studies, it works best unrestricted. Further, it should never be forgotten that University teachers belong to two distinct classes, corresponding to the two main functions of a University, namely, what I may call the Producers and the Distributors of knowledge. Of course all teachers have to distribute, and many do something to produce; but it would not be difficult to classify roughly the University staff under these two heads, according to their predominant activity. And though the producing class may, and do, differ very much in natural power of exposition, still their value and influence depend mainly on personal gifts and acquirements, and act in a way to which the very idea of training seems inapplicable. With those who are mainly distributors, on the other hand, the case is different; and here the question may be more relevantly raised. But here, too, there is much to remember which is often forgotten, and which makes a difference. First, the students being men, and not boys, all that part of method relating to discipline is not wanted. Again, the free interchange of teaching between the colleges gives the student a large choice, so that the best teachers are the most sought; and thus the law of gravitation, if I may so call it, reduces the evil, due to a deficiency of method, to a minimum. Further, much of the most important teaching is given *tête-à-tête*, or informally to very small classes; where again personal qualities are all-important, and method would have very little to say. Above all, the Commission of fifteen years ago introduced changes familiar enough to us, but perhaps not fully appreciated outside, which bear directly on this point. The teacher is no longer an Ordinary Fellow of a College, appointed after his degree for his attainments, but an Official Fellow, selected frequently from outside by his special fitness for the work. And the Colleges, which have the most cogent reasons for choosing well, have recently shown a remarkable tendency to appoint on their official staff men who have served apprenticeship, and can show a good record as teachers. I have counted no less than sixteen of the present Oxford teachers, including some of the most efficient, who have been so appointed in my time, and whose qualifications were both acquired and tested in the public schools or elsewhere. If these men have not exactly passed in Paedagogics, at any rate they cannot be called untrained.

Passing from the Universities to the higher secondary schools we are met at once with a paradox. Many very competent judges both at home and abroad are agreed that the English public school more nearly realizes the ideal of a sound, efficient, well-balanced system of education than any other extant institution. Without adopting self-complacent superlatives, there is no doubt that the English boy is well-cared for in body and mind, on the whole, in these schools, and that in after life—to my mind the greatest test—he is very loyal to his school, and anxious that his sons should have the same advantages. Of course these schools command every resource; they have money, prestige, tradition, and the best attention of the leisured, powerful and vocal classes; and they can attract the best material both of boys and men. I do not deny—I have the best grounds for assurance—that their boast is not baseless. On the other hand, every one of the teachers is absolutely devoid of professional training. Does not this throw doubt, it may be asked, on the assumption that the training of teachers, even if not equally indispensable for all grades and ages, is nevertheless universally desirable and profitable? The proof of the pudding is in the eating; and if the results are so good without training, is not training superfluous? This question not only *may* be asked, but *is* asked; and if you were to take the staffs of the best twenty public schools, who are confessedly the pick of the Universities, and put the question to them, a large majority of these eminent and select persons would confidently answer ' yes.' I need not say I cordially dissent. The true point is, in my view, not whether these schools succeed, but whether they might not succeed better; whether, in short, there is not *waste*. The first of living headmasters is certainly Dr. Percival; and on this point let me quote him. In answer to the question put to him on the Select Committee by Mr. Acland, how the lack of systematic preparation affected the young teacher, he said :—' Take an ordinary teacher, in nine cases out of ten the young man goes down from the University and plunges into work without any definite preparation of any kind; so that he starts with his own recollection of school life as his sole equipment, and with nothing more in the way of paedagogic theory and training; and my experience almost invariably was that at first there was *a great deal of waste*. There are all the preliminary difficulties with regard to discipline, and even the best masters often failed in this at first, simply because they did not know how to set about it—*they had never been taught*.' Such evidence as this, from a man who has made a striking success at two great schools, cannot be gainsaid. And the waste of which Dr. Percival speaks covers a vast deal more than the question of form-discipline, important as that is. It affects the whole attitude of mind of the young teacher towards his profession. If he begun with any adequate professional training, he would approach his work with some sort of modesty and knowledge, instead of ignorance and confidence. And his experience would be useful to him from the first. It would mean a gradually more assured progress along the right road, from which he had never strayed, instead of meaning, as it too often does now, that he reaches the right road ultimately, in a somewhat battered condition, after a series of futile excursions down blind alleys.

But, important as are the higher public schools, from many reasons, and wide as is the attention which they command, we must never forget that they form an insignificant fraction even of the inadequate supply of secondary schools which we possess. The College of Preceptors, which (pending the researches of the new Commission) has the best and fullest information about our secondary schools, calculates that there are about 780,000 children receiving intermediate education in about 11,000 schools, and that of these the public and proprietary schools number not more than 1,000, the remaining 10,000 being in private hands. In all these, the number of teachers who hold any sort of professional diploma is lamentably small; and of those who do by far the most important section are the trained and certificated primary masters who have transferred their energies to secondary teaching. The Endowed Schools have no doubt immensely improved since the days of the old Commission, and even among the Private Schools there have been strides of progress. The most intelligent private teachers have, for close on fifty years, been active, not only in cultivating their own corner of the field, but in uniting for the promotion of reforms to improve the rest. In the demand for training, in particular, they have been long to the front, thereby contrasting creditably with the supineness of the more highly favoured public schools. And I must note

in passing, that it is one of the most reassuring results of the improved education of women to find how promptly they have perceived the importance of training, and almost as a body have thrown their weight into the demand for it. Nevertheless there is no doubt that far the worst consequences of our *laissez faire* in secondary education are still, as ever, to be found among the lower ranks of these ten thousand private schools. I know myself of places where they have no real teaching or teaching-power, no system, no ideal, and of course no inspection, training, guarantee, or test of any kind; where it is hardly too much to say, that the whole energies of the place are devoted to gulling and exploiting the parents. Dr. Wormell, of the City Middle Class Schools, who receives about 30 per cent. of his boys from private teachers, says that though some of them have been very well taught, a good many have been very badly taught indeed, and the mischief done to them by unqualified teachers is nearly irreparable. The same authority speaks plainly of the private school masters ' purchasing bogus degrees,' and records the case of one such gentleman who printed a variety of letters after his name, amongst them being the well-known letters A.M. When he was pressed to explain these, he said they stood for *Art Master*, a degree awarded by himself for teaching drawing in his own school!

We have here a very miscellaneous set of evils which doubtless cannot be met by one remedy. Between the bona fide man who wastes power and time for want of training, and the absolutely unqualified and fraudulent humbug, there are plainly many intermediate degrees of unfitness.

The first step to take is certainly registration. This would be promptly fatal to the worst mischiefs, and would, undoubtedly, promote, though it would not of itself necessitate, more general training. At first we might probably have to accept degrees, and even experience, as qualification; and this, in the higher schools, would leave things pretty much as they are. But we ought never (in my view) to be permanently content with anything short of universal compulsory training. As long as it is left optional, even if it became vastly commoner, some of the best would escape; the training colleges would still complain, as they all do now, that they do not get the best material. The cleverest beginners can get places at once; and it tends to be the weaker vessels and the failures who are driven to eke out inferior qualifications with a training certificate. Even so the principle is justified, for they are vastly improved by training and enabled to compete with their natural betters. But this is obviously not what we want; the best oars must be trained as well as the feebler folk, or we shall be pulling at half power.

In spite, then, of the opinion of teachers of all ranks, of every conference, meeting, congress, and association; in spite of the experience of every foreign nation, to which I have no space to refer; in spite of strenuous isolated efforts in practice, among which none have been more striking or successful than those of the women; the English secondary teachers, from top to bottom, still suffer from one vital defect, the entire want of systematized professional preparation. Of the two sides of training which we have assumed—knowledge and method—the knowledge is more or less adequately present; the method is, with the rarest exceptions, absent.

And in the primary training, I would ask, in conclusion, is not the case reversed? The specific professional training has been adequately realized, that is the strong point; but is not the weak point a comparative deficiency of the other side, the general education? It will, of course, be understood that I speak with the greatest caution and diffidence—my whole direct experience lies in the higher and intermediate branches; but I wish to ask for information, and to put the case as it appears to me. May it not then be said, without much exaggeration, that culture and method being necessary for all school teachers, our system has resulted in giving to secondary teachers some culture but no method: and to the primary teachers adequate method, but defective culture?

I have myself talked to very intelligent men who had been through the training college and afterwards entered at the University, and who were deeply convinced of the narrowing effects of the system. Mr. H. Ll. Smith, who studied the question in Scotland, reports that all the authorities whom he consulted seemed convinced of the narrowing influence of a mere training college course, especially in the case of a residential college. And the same report adds, that the system of training which is combined with a University course is admitted by all to be far superior to a course at the normal school. There is evidence from abroad which points in the same direction. In Germany the training course is six years, in both general education and method; and there is a strong movement now to devote the whole of the first four years to general culture, and leave the professional part to the last two. In France, where the professional training seems distinctly inferior to ours, the general education, especially on the literary side, is allowed to be wider and better. Mr. Ward, a training college teacher, and a distinguished Oxford man, writes as follows: 'While here our students at most read a play of Shakespeare, some essays of Bacon, and a novel of Sir Walter Scott, in France almost all the classical writers are read.' And again, on language: 'Free from the necessity of preparing carefully a single book, which takes up almost the whole of the English student's energies, the Frenchman can study his languages in a more varied and interesting way.' And is there not some connexion between this defect and the following description by a master who has much experience in teaching ex-primary and secondary children together? 'A boy from an elementary school, who has passed the sixth or seventh standard, is generally very accurate in all the work he does; he objects, however, to enter into oral arguments; he prefers to answer all questions in monosyllables, and his general knowledge outside the subjects taught in the school is often rather limited : *one has to devote six months to open out his mind.*' These are the words of Dr. Wormell, in his evidence before the Select Committee on Registration. The suggestion is that if the teachers' training were wider, the pupils would be better off. Perhaps too much is expected, and we ought never to expect too much. Something is, no doubt, traceable to our apprenticeship system. I should like to hear the candid opinion of the conference on the pupil teacher question. The latter surely are overworked. I heard a very able Extension lecturer the other day, who had taught many hard-working people, say that the pupil teachers he taught were 'utterly jaded and played out.' The Inspectors complain of bad reading, unintelligent reciting, meagre and narrow text-books, mechanical arithmetic, and general lack of life. The masters complain of want of time to teach the students properly; and no doubt the complaint is often just. The training colleges complain that the first year is largely spent on elementary work that ought to have been done before. Without attempting to appraise or sift these various recriminations, one may feel that there is a defect somewhere. And the recent drift, both of changes and opinions, seems to point in the direction indicated. The demand for the accommodation of the syllabus to the London University course; the granting of the third year; the establishment of Day Training Colleges; the association of teachers to promote connexion with Universities; all these seem to have a common aim. I am aware that there is still, as I said above, much suspicion of Universities among the teachers; and Dr. Rigg in his address this year at the inaugural meeting of the Wesleyan Colleges, goes so far as to dissuade students from University residence altogether. He says it would be 'a radical mistake,' and the student would be 'running a great risk of unfitting himself' for the work of an elementary teacher. I can only say, I should be very sorry to believe that these fears were well grounded. I should be rather inclined, on the contrary, to look forward to a large extension of the Day Training College system, in which the secondary teachers might find a place side by side with the primary. This is not a mere amateur suggestion, for I see that such high and independent authorities as Dr. Fitch, Professor Laurie, and Dr. Wormell unite in recommending it. But in any case, whatever steps be taken to remedy it, the defect itself demands attention from all of us. I cordially agree that on this point, as on all others that affect national education, the voice of the teachers should be heard. And when I say teachers, I mean, first and foremost, the teachers mainly concerned; but also, not less certainly, the teachers in other branches, for we are all one profession, and we want light on our difficulties from every quarter. And I cannot better sum up the whole issue than in the excellent words of the Department Instructions of two years ago—words intended for the primary teachers, but applicable to all of us : 'The future usefulness of the teacher depends, not only on what he knows and can do, but on what he *is*—on his tastes, his aims in life, on his general mental cultivation, and on the spirit in which he does his work. Although such qualifications cannot be formulated in a schedule, or made the subject of examination, they are nevertheless indispensable as conditions of all true improvement in national education.'

INTERNATIONAL ASSOCIATION OF UNIVERSITY MEN.

A COMMITTEE, of which Mr. Hodgson Pratt is the President and Professor Richet of Paris the Vice-President, are trying to form what is called an 'Alliance Universitaire Internationale,' of which the following statement has just been published :—

Il vient de se constituer un Comité, dont l'intention est de créer des liens de plus en plus étroits entre tous ceux qui appartiennent, comme maîtres ou comme élèves, à l'enseignement supérieur.

N'est-il pas désirable qu'il s'établisse, entre les membres des diverses Universités, professeurs ou élèves, une union fondée sur des relations plus fréquentes et par conséquent plus cordiales ?

Bien des obstacles s'opposent encore à ce résultat. D'abord la différence entre les programmes d'enseignement et les conditions de scolarité dans les divers pays; ensuite les difficultés de voyage et de séjour à l'étranger, surtout pour les étudiants; enfin la rareté relative des occasions de rencontre, et l'absence presque absolue de ces rapports réguliers qui sont la condition de l'estime et de l'attachement mutuels.

La vie internationale ne sera possible entre les Universités que lorsque ces bornes, qui les séparent encore, auront complètement disparu. En conséquence, notre Comité propose à tous ceux qui auront à cœur la réalisation de notre but, de poursuivre l'exécution du programme suivant :

1°. Atténuer les divergences des conditions de scolarité, soit en cherchant à obtenir l'équivalence des grades dans les cas où elle est possible, soit en faisant admettre qu'un étudiant puisse se prévaloir, devant une Université, sinon des diplômes remportés à l'étranger, du moins des semestres d'études qu'il y aurait régulièrement passés; au cas bien entendu où, par la rigueur des examens, l'étendue des programmes et le mérite des professeurs, des garanties suffisantes pourraient être obtenues;

2°. Faciliter, dans chaque pays, les études réciproques, soit en obtenant que les programmes, conférences, travaux publics, y fassent une plus large part aux institutions comparées, soit en développant le système des bourses de voyage, qui ont donné jusqu'à ce jour de si bons résultats, soit enfin en favorisant l'organisation de Comités de patronage des étudiants étrangers;

3°. Faciliter les occasions de rapprochement entre les maîtres et les élèves des pays différents, par la multiplication et la périodicité des fêtes universitaires;

4°. Attirer l'attention des Universités sur les moyens de faire pénétrer plus de justice dans les relations internationales.

La réalisation des divers points de ce programme nécessite la formation d'une *Alliance universitaire internationale*, constituée par une série de Comités siégeant dans les principaux centres universitaires. Cette alliance sera définitivement constituée au Congrès qui sera convoqué dans le courant de l'année 1894 par les soins du Comité provisoire.

Among the members of the committee are the following :— Professors Nicholas Abricossoff (Moscow), Joachim Carvallo (Madrid), Osterrith (Heidelberg), Th. Ribot (Paris), and Armand Sabatier (Montpellier); Dr. Jacques Dumas, 109 Boulevard Saint-Michel, Paris, is the Secretary.

LETTERS TO THE EDITOR.

[We do not hold ourselves responsible for the opinions expressed by our correspondents.]

'The Tone of Patronage.'

DEAR SIR,—' Bystander's' letter on this theme, in the June *Gazette*, was ultimately prompted, no doubt, by the diction of an earnest and informed writer in the *Gazette* for May. Yet I do not find in that writer so much the tone of patronage as the 'note' of infelicitous expression. I could almost acquit him of any desire to patronize, but then, 'evil is wrought by want of thought as well as want of heart.' One regrets that words—apart from intentions, mere words—should have the power to wound and estrange; but so it is, and as I write I feel the responsibility that rests on those who use the pen. It is not enough to be well-meaning, not enough to convey one's intent in plain language; almost as important, in these days, is the art of putting things. Indeed, I should think (of course I speak with diffidence), that one's mode of expression is almost the accurate measure of one's degree of culture. Culture (again I write with diffidence) I take to be a relative matter so far as assimilative knowledge is concerned. In respect of 'light' there may be the culture of a Jowett, of a Faraday, and of a Jefferies or a Thoreau. But in respect of 'sweetness' there is only one type of culture, surely, and the highest degree of it is seen when manner and expression are most void of offence. One might almost say, perhaps, that sweetness is more than light,—nay even that light is absent where there is absence of sweetness. Now, in the article in question the light is a little obscured because of defects in the vehicle.

There are things that must be said, of course,—strong things and unpleasant things—because they are true things. But it is never quite impossible to say them gently. Then there is nomenclature; it is always open to select between name and name, or to periphrase. It was, therefore, not absolutely imperatve on the writer in question to use just the words he did in some parts of his article. To write, for instance, that 'in the elementary teacher there is material, although unpromising, of which an Extension student may be made,' and to inquire 'How, then, are we to get hold of the elementary teacher?' was to use not the most happy forms of expression. For one thing, the people referred to do not like to be dubbed 'elementary' teachers. Five years ago, at the risk of vagueness in the title of their Union, they formally disavowed the name. They say that the adjective 'elementary,' partly incorrect when applied to their schools, is wholly so when understood to apply to their trained and practised professional capacities. That may seem to others a small thing, and in itself, perchance, a sign of defective culture; but, rightly or wrongly, the teachers in question object to one name and prefer another, and 'sweetness' would suggest that their preference, since it involves no falsity or confusion, should be respected. Again, one cannot aptly say that the primary teachers are 'unpromising' as Extension students *in posse*; and the mere words 'made' and 'get hold of' suggest to the wincing mind them a kind of bustling evangelism and missionary patronage which I am sure the writer of the article did not intend. It may be hyper-sensitive and foolish to wince at such expressions; but there the wincing is, and 'sweetness' would suggest no touch on the tender spot.

But there are other writers and speakers to whom and to whose methods the delicate protest of ' Bystander' more fairly applies. One sometimes hears or sees things said or written about the certificated teachers as a class, which can only arise from want of knowledge of the modern facts or from the presence of prejudice. Sometimes, too, spokesmen or writers for the primary teachers criticize other people, as a class, in a parallel style. But these misconceptions and prejudices are now, I rejoice to believe it, waning and passing away. More and more as we know and regard one another as individuals and not as mere items in an alien class, our misunderstandings will vanish and our prejudices thaw. Years ago, when speaking at a gathering of secondary and primary teachers, to whom the clerical Chairman had propounded the idea that the clergy and secondary teachers might properly meet the 'elementary' teachers for pedagogic counsel, though of

course they could not do so socially, I ventured to retort (I fear, with some lack of sweetness) that the 'elementary' teachers were not proud, and would not seriously object to meet the clergy and the secondary teachers in a social way! And to-day, I believe that, as we meet one another oftener, and more and more on one plane, we shall experience less and less of the facile pride of patronage on the one part or of the awkward pride of humility on the other. So in the meantime let me enter this plea for careful modes of expression and considered choice of terms. One may afford to fight an open enemy, or to disregard the 'superior person' whose tone of patronage displays the very absence of culture or training which he presumes to lament in others; but one cannot afford to let mere words keep at arm's length those who wish to stand shoulder to shoulder, as do so many of us now.

J. H. YOXALL.

.·.

Schools of Citizenship in Denmark.

SIR,—I was glad to see the extracts from the Gilchrist Report on Schools of Citizenship in Scandinavia in your issue for March; and as I believe that the methods, aims and history of these will amply repay study on the part of the friends of University Extension in England, I hope you will allow me to indicate some other sources of information. There was no history of the movement, however brief, until Prof. D. M. Lewis, by his inquiries on the subject, induced Herr Schröder to draw up a short historical account, which will be found translated in the *Journal of Education* for May and June, 1890 (pp. 245-247, 303-305). In a short paper entitled 'To Esbjerg' (*Journal of Education*, April 1893), I have tried to show how easy it is to visit the schools themselves: this I shall be glad to forward to any one interested, on receipt of a stamped directed wrapper. But the schools are not at work in August, September and October. The men are at work from the beginning of November to the end of April; and the women in May, June and July. As the principal of one of these schools, Herr A. Poulsen, Ryslinge, Denmark, hopes to take part in the Extension course at Oxford in August, I have no doubt he would be glad to answer any inquiries. There are two magazines, *Danskeren* and *Höjskolebladet*, the one a monthly and the other a weekly, which are conducted by those engaged in the movement. The contents of the former are to be found catalogued each month in the *Review of Reviews*.

J. S. THORNTON.

Forest Place Villas, Leytonstone.

.·.

University Extension Scholarships and Prizes.

SIR,—'A Prize-winner' complains in your June number that the speakers at the recent Bournemouth Conference, who were in favour of prize-giving, confined themselves almost entirely to asserting that the principal arguments produced *against* prizes were not borne out by facts; and wishes to be given some positive reason in favour of their retention in the Oxford University Extension scheme.

I do not feel certain whether the prizes given by the Delegates are given on the best possible system, but I do think that some form of prize giving is desirable and if well arranged is beneficial. Many of the arguments for and against prizes apply almost equally to certificates and the whole examination system. But the most notable distinction between the certificates and prizes of inconsiderable money value lies in the rivalry and emulation excited by the latter: and in this, I believe, lies their chief value. Rivalry is undoubtedly a spur to endeavour. To those not far advanced in any study there must always be some drudgery in steady work even on a congenial subject; and the subject chosen by a centre cannot be the special favourite of *all* the students. It is well therefore to accept any harmless means of adding zest and interest to the work, and prize-competitions, under suitable conditions, seem one of the simplest ways of providing this help. At a centre where the students have caught anything of the real spirit of University Extension, nearly all will have (especially if they be members of a Students' Association) some opportunities of giving help to other students. And if these others be their rivals, they will find in such opportunities the needful condition for the most thorough enjoyment of the contest, everything done to help a rival adding to the delight of it. There will be an exhilarating sense that every advantage which others can be made to possess increases the credit of surpassing them, whilst all dread of defeat will be lost, for defeat will not be failure.

If the rivalry at any University Extension centre is ungenerous and leads to jealousy and ill-feeling, I cannot but think that something is radically wrong there, and the sooner that centre (or its Students' Association) is re-organized the better. I should be sorry indeed to see any trace of such a thing amongst our students, and if it tended to increase I should feel that we were making a bad failure somehow. I incline, however, to think that these unworthy feelings are feared or suspected more often than they really exist. Well-meaning people are often so much afraid that things may go wrong that they guard against imaginary dangers until they effectually preclude themselves from ever learning how many more people will do the right thing if it is taken simply for granted that they will than if they see that is not expected of them. In any case I do not think that the prizes could be the *cause* of so unfortunate a state of things. The competition for them might make it more apparent; but if it exists, this would be desirable: it is easier to fight a known and acknowledged enemy than a concealed one.

I have myself never won a prize at an examination, but have won a local prize for the poper-work done for the lecturer.

I am, Sir,
Yours faithfully,
A Students' Association Secretary.

THE PHILADELPHIA SUMMER MEETING.

THE course of lectures and classes on Economics which will be given during July at Philadelphia Summer Meeting form a very remarkable series, whether we have regard to the subjects of instruction, or to the distinction of the teachers. President Andrews will give a course of lectures on Money, and an address upon the Monetary Conference of 1892, at which he was one of the American delegates.

Professor Clark will give two lectures on the Distribution of Wealth; Professor Giddings five lectures on the Scientific Subdivision of Political Economy; Professor Seligman will deal with Political Finance; Professor Jenks with the relations of Economics and Politics; and Professor Patten with the Ricardian System of Economics, and the Theory of Dynamic Economics. Many English students of Economics would be thankful for the opportunity of attending such a course. As these Summer Meetings get better known, it is probable that we shall see a larger inter-change of students between America and England.

Another interesting feature of the American Summer Meeting is the course of lectures on Education in which special attention will be given to Herbartian Pedagogy. There will also be courses on Psychology, and on other subjects interesting to teachers.

Of the so-called 'Historical Pilgrimage' we have already spoken. The plans for it seem to have been well made. The travellers will leave Philadelphia on July 30, and after following as closely as possible Washington's revolutionary movements will return to Philadelphia on August 8. Among other places they will visit Hartford, Boston, Cambridge, Concord, Salem, Plymouth and New York. The charge, including railway fares and accommodation at hotels is fixed at £10. 8s. for 10 days.

BOOK EXCHANGE COLUMN.

Books to be lent by Bedford centre :—

On Modern European History :
  Life of Stein. (Seeley.) 3 vols.
  History of Napoleon. (Lanfrey.) 5 vols.
And a few books on French Revolution.
Also— Skottowe's *History of English Parliament.*
  Ashley's *Economic History.* Pt. II.

REPORTS FROM THE CENTRES.

ILKLEY.—On Tuesday, May 22, a small sale of work was held in order to raise a sum of money for this centre. The committee found at the close of last autumn's session that there was a deficiency of £10 11s. This was not a large sum to grapple with, and might easily have been cleared off; but the committee thought it was much wiser to raise a larger sum, and have a balance in the bank with which to begin next autumn's work. With this aim a sale of work and evening entertainment was organized, and resulted in a gain of £64 0s. 9d. After paying the debt the treasurer deposited in the bank a balance of £53 9s. 9d., and it is hoped that the work of next autumn will be carried on with renewed spirit in consequence. Mr. Mallet has promised to give a course of twelve lectures on 'England in the Eighteenth Century,' and the Students' Association will meet for the first time on June 21 in preparation for the course. This centre has a very good library of books needed for a course on Shakespeare, and would be glad to lend them to any other centre on the same terms as the Oxford Summer libraries are lent, or to exchange them for books needed for Mr. Mallet's lectures.

CAMBORNE (*Students' Association*).—Papers have been read at our Students' Association in a spring session, to continue the study of 'English Social Life,' Part I, the subject of the last course of lectures. The meetings were all thoroughly enjoyable, the papers being both interesting and instructive. That on Early Cornwall was reported at length by local papers, and has been widely read in this county. The other papers were also noticed in the columns of the press. The Students' Association is now enjoying a period of rest, in order to be better able to begin this month to study for the course of lectures arranged for next session; the subject—South Africa—being one which is very interesting to Cambornians. It is hoped that this preparatory session will be a fitting introduction to the first course of lectures delivered under the auspices of the Cornwall County Council.—CHARLES ROWE, *Hon. Sec. Students' Association.*

BEDFORD.—At this centre the summer term has been marked by the decided success of five lectures on Dante and the Divina Commedia, given by the kindness of the Rev. Alban Wright, between May 4 and June 1. The audience included many University Extension students, and the majority of those present stayed for the class, after each lecture, in order to study the original text under the lecturer's able guidance. Weekly classes are to be continued, as far as possible, during the remainder of this term, in order to help those who are anxious to pursue the study of this great subject. The funds of our Students' Association have also been increased by a gift of £5, as a result of the proceeds of this course. In answer to a letter issued by the local committee, many promises of annual subscriptions to our University Extension society have been received, but still further exertion is required to secure a sure basis for future work.

(*Students' Association*).—The Bedford Students' Association went a pilgrimage to St. Alban's on Saturday, June 9, with the object of seeing the Abbey of St. Alban and the ruins of Verulamium. Starting by the 2.25 p.m. train from Bedford, the students, on arriving at St. Alban's, went first to the house of the Rev. Mr. Glossop, who had kindly proffered his services to show them round the Abbey, a self-imposed task which he performed, much to the gratification of the students, giving valuable information, both as to the original parts of the Abbey and those which have been restored by the munificence of Lord Grimthorpe and Mr. Hucks Gibbs. After spending a very enjoyable time in the Abbey, and seeing the present buildings of the Grammar School, which is the oldest in England, the students assembled for tea, after which, though thinned in numbers by the departure of some who were obliged to return early to Bedford, the remaining few went to see the old church of St. Michael's, which stands in the centre of the site of Verulamium and is built on Roman foundations, and also contains the monument of Sir Francis Bacon, Lord Verulam and Viscount St. Alban's. The students returned to Bedford about 9.30 after a very enjoyable afternoon, for which they were chiefly indebted to the arrangements planned by the secretary of the Association, and a member of the Committee.

INFORMATION TO CONTRIBUTORS.

All communications should be addressed to the Editor, OXFORD UNIVERSITY EXTENSION GAZETTE, *University Press, Oxford.*

All matter intended for insertion in the August issue should reach him not later than July 20.

Contributions should be written on one side of the paper only, and must be accompanied by the name of the writer (not necessarily for publication).

N.B.—*All orders should carefully specify the full title,* OXFORD UNIVERSITY EXTENSION GAZETTE.

OXFORD UNIVERSITY

EXTENSION GAZETTE.

VOL. IV. NO. 47.]   AUGUST, 1894.   [ONE PENNY.

N.B.—Local Organizers of Oxford University Extension Lectures are invited to send to the Secretary, Extension Office, Examination Schools, Oxford, copies of any journals containing notices of, or references to, Extension work.

YOUNG MEN AND UNIVERSITY EXTENSION LECTURES.

How is it that young men attend Extension lectures in (comparatively speaking) such small numbers? This is a question I have been asked many times by those who having spared neither time nor trouble in making known and advertising the courses of lectures to be held, have been perplexed and disappointed at finding young men and boys in a decided minority among the audience. 'If the young men who have everything to gain by it, care so little for higher education,' they ask, 'what can we expect from older people whose careers have long ago been mapped out, and who are too often weighed down by the burdens and responsibilities of life? To begin with, I think people expect rather too much from the young working man. By the time he is twenty he is expected to have no other object before him than that of improving his mind, or taking up some serious work. Do we ever think of the lives those young fellows lead, do we realize that just when our own brothers are having the best of times at Eton or Harrow and the Universities, with compulsory games, and holidays often and long, the working boy is going through a monotonous round, day by day, and week by week, broken only by a Saturday half holiday (if he is not working overtime) with four bank holidays in the year? He is but a boy, with all a boy's animal spirits and tastes, and can we wonder very much if after a day's work, he feels more inclined to read or amuse himself, than to do anything else? 'I'm down in the pit all day; I don't want to go at night and hear mining lectures,' was the rather natural remark of a young collier, on seeing the bills of some County Council lectures pasted up, and if we put ourselves more in the place of young men who feel like this, we shall more readily recognize the fact, that we shall need special efforts to influence them with regard to the use they should make of their leisure hours. In my opinion too the athletic craze is responsible for many spoilt and wasted lives among our young working men. Professionalism, the ruination of all true sport, has a firm hold on Association football; its spirit is creeping into the Rugby game, while neither running nor cycling are free from it. The recreation then becomes a business, leisure time has a money value, training and football matches become the object of life, work and everything else go to the wall, and only too often the character goes too, for want of a nobler ideal just at the age when a man throws his whole heart into whatever he takes up.

But there are many young men who face life and its problems seriously, who amid the greatest difficulties and drawbacks, struggle after those things which 'make for righteousness,' and long for that sympathy and guidance which will help them to turn high ideals into noble and useful lives. How can we bring such as these into sympathy with the aims of University Extension?

We can do much by helping the individual. Wherever a number of young men are working there the Extension lecture secretary ought to go, and have a few words separately with each. In that way we find out the most convenient night and time, the kind of instruction wanted and the many little details, often so trivial and yet so necessary. We can also hear and answer the excuses and objections, and clear away the idea that attending Extension lectures would mean hours of hard work with frequent and compulsory examinations looming in the distance.

Then too we should be more in touch with the many young men's mutual improvement societies which exist in connexion with most dissenting chapels. Here we have a splendid neucleus, and I have always found the promoters and the members keen and enthusiastic in the cause of education. It is a good plan to give serial tickets at a reduced rate to such clubs, increasing the reduction on every ten tickets taken, and should the club own a reading room to allow one or two of the books from the travelling library to be placed there every week.

But above all we must make those young fellows who do join us into missionaries, and let them feel the responsibility resting on them of spreading the work. They have great influence, whether as members of a Trades Council or society, as officers in a benefit club, or simply as private individuals in the works. A recommendation from a Trades Union Secretary to its members to have wider ideas than simply fighting for a higher wage, a few earnest words from a member as to what education can do towards putting the position of a working man on its highest level, a credential from Jack to Bill that 'the lectures are just splendid, and he puts things quite different to what I ever thought'—all this goes further than the most enticing bill or programme. Why not have a guild of young men in every centre, who believe that by educating their thoughts, training their judgements and developing their intelligence on the highest lines, they are consecrating their lives in the true sense to the service of humanity here, and to His service also in the hereafter whose throne crowns the hill of knowledge? Such a guild might not produce a single genius, but it would give us a number of young men taking up the responsibilites of their position, educated and trained for the work that lies before them. For surely the position of the young working man *is* a very responsible one, and full of grand possibilities. Does not the future of England largely depend on his right judgement, his good sense, his justice and his foresight, and is he not helping to form public opinion, that sponsor of all legislation? We may hold different views as to the right and wrong of the great problems which are forcing themselves on us for solution, but at least we can have no doubt as to our duty towards the young in the matter of education, so let us look to it that we do not fail for want of a little sympathy, a good deal of patience and perseverance, and above all that real interest in the work which alone can influence or inspire.

V. B. H.

LECTURERS' RESERVE FUND.

UNIVERSITY EXTENSION COLLEGE, READING.

A PARTY from this college visited the Rothamsted experimental station on Monday, July 2, on the invitation of Sir John Lawes and Sir Henry Gilbert. The party was conducted over the station by Sir Henry Gilbert, who courteously explained as fully as time would permit the nature of the work which has been carried out since the foundation of the station in 1843. The experiments with different manures on the permanent meadow, which have now been carried out for thirty-eight years, were inspected. As the hay on the plots had not been mown, the party saw for themselves the results from different manures which are now of classic interest. The experiments on barley, in the Hoos field, which have been carried on since 1852, the experiments on leguminous crops and clover, on rich garden soil and on ordinary soil, and the experiments on mangel wurzel, potatoes and rotation of crops were also visited in turn. Finally, the renowned broad balk field, on which plots of wheat have been grown continuously, without manure and with different descriptions of manure, for fifty-one years, was inspected. The crops on some of the plots are remarkably good, and the results on the unmanured plots fully bear out Sir Henry's statement to the party—that the total exhaustion of soil like that at Rothamsted for wheat growing is practically impossible, if the land is kept free from weeds. The party was accompanied by Mr. Mackinder (the Principal), Mr. Gilchrist (the Director of the Agricultural Department) and Mr. Foulkes (one of the lecturers of the College). Among others present were—Mr. Henry Simmons (Bearwood), Mr. Henman (Caversham), Mr. Beaven (Wiltshire), Mr. Fidler (Reading), and Mr. Webb (Beenham). Before leaving Rothamsted Mr. Mackinder thanked, in suitable terms, Sir John Lawes and Sir Henry and Lady Gilbert for their great kindness and hospitality.—*Reading Observer.*

LONG AND SHORT COURSES.

THE discussion at the University Extension Congress brought into prominence the parts which long and short courses respectively play in the general scheme of our work. That a miscellaneous assortment of short courses will never satisfy real students is admitted by every one. The more advanced the student, the more does he feel the need of order, system, continuity in his method of study. On the other hand, no one now denies the fact that short courses have justified their existence, that they have rendered excellent service in preparing the way for more systematic teaching, that they are useful pioneers.

But are they more than this? At this point the discussion remains open. Are short courses a merely temporary provision,—something for which the need has already passed away in most centres, and will soon pass away in all—or are they likely to remain as a permanent feature of the University Extension system? To these questions we suspect that very different answers would be given by different people. In order, however, to test opinion on the subject, we have addressed to several University Extension workers of great experience, the following query:—

'Should short courses of six lectures be given up as a customary and regular part of the organization of University Extension teaching?'

To this question we have received the following replies:—

I. From Miss BEATRICE VIVIAN.

(*Hon. Sec. of the Camborne centre and of the South Western Association for the Extension of University Teaching.*)

No. Such was my reply some years ago on the occasion of a circular issued by the Oxford University Extension Delegacy with a view to obtaining the general opinion of local organizers on this important point. Further experience of the work has confirmed my old views on the subject.

The chief objections to the short courses have been based on two presumptions; first, the superficial character of the work done; second, the fact that because six lectures are cheaper than twelve, and require less trouble to organize, Local Committees will continue to take them in preference to the longer courses, and that therefore the short course will tend to retard the adoption of the long ones, and generally lower the standard of University Extension teaching.

With regard to the first. A short course is not necessarily more superficial than a long one. In most cases it simply covers half the ground, and if, as is often the case, the six lectures are delivered at fortnightly intervals, in a centre where there is a vigorous Students' Association, the work done by both lecturer and students is quite as thorough and valuable as far as it goes, as that done in connexion with long courses.

The standard required of the candidates for examination is the same for both, and I believe it will be found that the proportion of students obtaining distinction in examinations on short courses is quite as large as that in the examinations on the longer courses. In the group of centres with which I have been connected for some years no long courses have yet been delivered (with one exception), but that proportion just spoken of has always been very good, and further, the proportion of the students to the general audience has always been a high one.

With regard to the second. Here I can only speak from individual experience of the Cornish centres, but I am quite sure that, chiefly owing to financial reasons, it would have been hitherto impossible to organize courses of twelve lectures for the group of centres, unless some aid had been given from outside, as has now been done by the County Council. Nevertheless the tendency has always been to try and lengthen the courses, extending them to eight lectures whenever it could be done. From 1887 to 1893 short courses have been given every autumn in Cornwall, beginning with four centres, and increasing to eight, but after the first year at never less than five centres. This continuous record of work seemed sufficient justification to the County Council for a grant of £250, with the help of which a twelve-lecture course will be given at fortnightly intervals at nine centres in Cornwall in the autumn and winter of 1894-5. Had there been no short courses offered by the Delegacy, there is no doubt whatever that University Extension would have been quite unknown in West Cornwall.

So much for the comparison between the long and the short courses, which resolves itself into this—that half a loaf is much better than no bread, and that there is no special virtue in any given number of lectures which is lost immediately we drop below that figure.

But it is, perhaps, more important to notice that each system of long and short courses stands on its own merits, fulfils its own functions, and ought to be judged separately, not brought together for mere purposes of comparison. These differences of function have been so clearly and widely recognized that the discussion on the matter at the late Congress was perhaps unnecessary; but, at any rate, I venture to think that the general impressions and opinions held by a large number of University Extension organizers were there given a definite form and shape by the experts who took part in that discussion, and that there should no longer exist any confusion or misapprehension regarding the two systems, and also—may I say—there need be no further necessity for the apologetic manner in which University Extension organizers have hitherto felt bound to acknowledge the responsibility for short courses.

In the smaller country places, where it has been found so difficult, or impossible, to force the growth of the long courses, there is infinitely greater need of the introduction of fresh, new intellectual life than in the larger towns with their varied assortment of clubs, institutes, polytechnic colleges and the like, but there can rarely be found in the former an audience capable of supporting a long course, from the intellectual as well as the financial point of view, and this is where the great difference in the functions of the two systems can be best appreciated.

It not infrequently occurs that in some such country place one or two enthusiasts are moved to organize Extension lectures, the usual preliminaries are gone through, and a course of twelve lectures embarked on. All goes well for a time, but at the close the guarantors or subscribers have to be asked to pay the full amount for which they have put down their names, often then leaving an adverse balance, and except half a dozen students who have successfully taken the examination, no one is prepared to help to work up another course. For this reason, that all the money at the disposal of the organizers, as well as the public interest, which is quite as necessary as money for the success of the enterprise, has been already used up in providing twelve lectures in a town where the larger part of the audience was only fitted to receive a short course.

In the present state, not only of University Extension, but of the intellectual life and interest of most of the places outside the large towns, there is to be found an audience, perpetually recruited and enlarged from schools and other sources, fitted for short courses and able to profit by them to a really enormous extent, when the work of the Students' Association, the Summer Reading Circle, and the other parts of the machinery of organization is taken into account, but which cannot support the burden of a long course, and may not be able to do so for many a day to come.

No doubt these short courses are preparing the way for the further development of University Extension to which we are all looking forward, when the idea of the union of educational sequence and popular lectures, as exemplified in the Report presented by Committee I at the recent Congress, shall have moulded public opinion (i. e. that of the Local Committee) to view rightly the high importance of the subject.

In the meantime I maintain that if the short courses are abandoned, one of the most useful branches of the work will be cut off, and the University Extension movement itself will be deprived of one of its most valuable sources of vitality, thereby losing much of its influence on the people for whose benefit it was originally designed.

Camborne, Cornwall, *July*, 1894.

.·.

II. From MISS CATHERINE PUNCH.
(Hon. Sec. of the Bournemouth Centre.)

As a local secretary who would be exceedingly sorry to see the six-lecture course entirely abandoned, I will endeavour to show the reason for the faith that is in me by pointing out that the two arguments commonly brought forward for and against short courses, though strong and cogent, and easily to be understood by the multitude, do not cover the whole ground.

The main argument then in favour of the short course seems to be that it best suits the pockets of young, and weak, and small centres. There are many centres, probably some that are now flourishing ones, that would never have started at all if their local committees had been obliged in the first place to find or to guarantee funds for a twelve-lecture course; but I think it is more than possible that local committees are too easily content with the short course, and when they have made a successful start and enthusiasm is high, they let slip the opportunity of putting things on a better footing. But the want of money is not the only thing that makes the short course sometimes desirable. Want of the desire for higher education, entire lack of enthusiasm for the further education of adults, utter absence of any comprehension of what is meant by the University Extension scheme, are foes as formidable as poverty. The inhabitants of many a provincial town or village may be induced by the bait of something new and something interesting to start on a course of six lectures, the end of which does not seem indefinitely far off, when they would be staggered and daunted by the prospect of six months' lecturing. At the end of one or two short courses, in nine cases out of ten, sufficient people will have been inoculated with the Extension spirit to make the carrying out of the work a certainty.

Another way in which short courses are invaluable, is in promoting evening lectures in large towns where afternoon courses of twelve lectures have attained to a great degree of success. By means of the short course local committees in such places can feel their way without much danger of financial collapse towards the spread of the movement amongst an audience of a totally different class to that gathered together in the afternoon.

To turn now to the stock argument against the short course and in favour of the long one, viz. that the latter is much more highly educational, in that it allows of greater thoroughness of treatment on the part both of teacher and of taught. The truth of this argument is so self-evident, that there is no need to discuss it. The point that I wish to bring forward is, that it is possible to attain to something of the same end by the wise use of short courses, with less risk of tiring an audience that may not be too enthusiastic, and of utterly alienating the all-important ' fringe,' on which alas !˝financial success so often depends.

In defence of a long succession of short courses on utterly disconnected subjects I have little or nothing to say, nor do I not think that ordinary audiences imperiously demand this wild license of variety. Variety, change, they certainly do demand, and the local committee in a panic of fear that the centre will collapse under the weight of the much dreaded deficit, yield far more than they need, and rush wildly from six lectures on the Saxon Heptarchy, to six on Astronomy, followed by six on Victorian Poets, and six on Physiography ! The bulk of the ordinary audience will be satisfied with something much less exciting than this. A change from History to Literature, or vice versa, especially if accompanied by a change of lecturer, will be found as a rule to satisfy most people, and unless things are in a very bad way at the centre the few malcontents can safely be disregarded. To arrange such a change so as not to destroy the value of an educational sequence, requires only the exercise of a little wisdom and tact on the part of the local committee. They must be careful in the first place to choose a popular subject, and one that will admit of development in this way. Suppose for instance that a start is made with six fortnightly historical lectures on the Commonwealth, giving a general view of the subject, these might be succeeded by a course, by a different lecturer on the literature of the same period ; this again by a biographical course on some of the chief political and military leaders, and if the interest of the audience did not show signs of flagging, a final course might be given sketching the state of affairs on the Continent. Such an arrangement would provide sufficient variety of subject and style for those who appreciate the Extension lectures, but who do not wish to accompany them by earnest study, and the real students would be enabled to devote two years to something like thorough work in a comparatively short period.

Something more than at present might also be done, I think, to check the evil of short courses by the central authority, and something by the lecturers. I should suggest that a rule be made of never granting more than two, or at the most three, six-lecture courses to succeed each other, unless on connected subjects. Two or three courses it might be necessary to grant to allow a centre time and opportunity to decide as to what course of study would be most popular; but after a fair chance of selection had been given, the centre should be compelled to settle down to something like sequence, though by means if desired of short courses.

The lecturers, I think, might help us much by not covering so much ground in their courses (this I would humbly suggest applies to the long as well as the short courses). They do not yet seem to realize how difficult it is for many of their students to give much time to steady reading, and how impossible for them adequately to study the history or literature of 100 years or more in the fortnightly intervals of a course of lectures, or even in the few extra hours which some of the more ardent of them devote to a Summer Reading Circle.

It will doubtless be observed that on short courses of science lectures I have said absolutely nothing. In their favour there is, I think, nothing to say. Single popular science lectures, or even a course of six unconnected ones, such as are given under the Gilchrist Trust, serve an excellent purpose, but six lectures on one science subject are more than enough to awaken interest, and not enough for the acquirement of thorough and useful knowledge.

III. From a LOCAL SECRETARY.

The question as thus put to him came upon the present writer with a shock of surprise. He was aware certainly of the evidence of a controversy on the relative merits of long and short courses, but he did not imagine that the most ardent advocates of the former had gone so far as to propose the abolition of the latter.

But even as he took up a wrathful pen, a shrewd suspicion dawned upon him, that perhaps the form of the question was a clever ruse on the part of the Editor to enlist the sympathies of the short course advocates, and convert what would otherwise be a calm and judicial balancing of pros and cons into an over-whelming testimony in favour of short courses.

Such at all events was the effect of the question on him at first, and even now that he has somewhat recovered from his natural indignation, it would take very little to make him carry the war into the enemy's territory, and advocate the giving up, if giving up there must be, not of the shorter but of the longer courses.

In these days, and in the pages of an Oxford journal one may be allowed to find reasons for anything and everything, and to be paradoxical, if one cannot be brilliant.

For example, we might maintain that a lecturer, who cannot say what he has to say on a subject in six lectures, will not say it in twelve. Or thus, lengthiness is always tedious ; a course of twelve lectures is a lengthy course ; therefore it will be tedious. If we are to be academic and *a priori* in our reasoning, let us at least be so on both sides. We shall soon see that long courses are a dangerous and pernicious innovation. But for the sake of one good long course, which he did once hear, the present writer will restrain himself.

Let us however appeal to experience. Surely it is just to the short-course system, which rightly or wrongly (on *a priori* grounds) Oxford has allowed to prevail so widely, that she owes her many centres and her eminent and deserved popularity.

Surely it is too soon as yet to burn the ships which have brought us safely so far. We have still much exploring and pioneering to do ; we may have to pause awhile and wait ; we may have (*absit omen*) to fall back on our base of operations ; let us at least retain the means of communication.

It is the fault of most popular movements, that once started they tend to overshoot their mark. And academic leaders, when they put themselves at our head, catch this infection most easily, because of their previous immunity from anything of the kind. Extremes meet and they generally take the disease very badly. They seem indeed to think that the momentum, which it has taken them so long to accumulate, will *ipso facto* be sufficient to overcome all at once the *vis inertiae* of the popular mind. They forget too that we need time and patience—a fruit, which it has taken centuries to cultivate in academic gardens, and will at least require some decades before it springs up freely by the public road-sides.

To gain the ear of the public, to arouse its interest and curiosity, to show that knowledge is pleasant, healthy, elevating, is one thing, to train the popular mind in the ways of wisdom and sound learning is quite another.

The broad approaches to the gates of learning fill easily with eager pilgrims. But once pass the narrow doors and commence to mount the steep and stony path that lies beyond, how small the company and scant the enthusiasm ! To be interested in the results of knowledge is one thing, to learn truly is another. To reproduce in essays the generalizations of a clever lecturer is easy, interesting, and of its kind very good ; but to master and coordinate facts, to struggle with difficulties, to work patiently on while waiting for light, to wrestle with figures, dates, formulae and documents, this, though better, is incalculably harder. Few are they that from disinterested motives, and without compulsion, attain to it. And those that do have a bad habit of disregarding and dispensing with guides.

There are undoubtedly a few centres, where it is quite worth while to make an effort in this direction, to put the class-teacher in the place of the lecturer, and to adopt and encourage the longer and more systematic courses. But some sort of external

assistance or endorsement must be secured, and this all the more, if the shorter courses are at the same time discontinued. The student element alone cannot bear the financial burden of the shorter and much less of the longer course, and it will be by the student alone that the latter is mainly supported.

The writer is not blind to the faults of the short-course system, its sketchiness, its meagreness of fact and detail, its purely deductive method, its failure to bring the student into any real contact with the *material* of history or literature or science.

But these defects are certainly not to be remedied by doubling or trebling the number of lectures. What cannot be done in six cannot be done in twelve or twenty lectures. And a good deal of the force, freshness and variety of the lecture system is lost, as soon as the course has passed beyond a certain point. For either the lecturer simply attempts to cover more ground, or he goes over the same ground with fuller and more detailed treatment. In the former case the method remains the same, in the latter he tends to lose the lightness of touch and breadth of treatment which are essential in lecturing to a general audience.

No doubt what he desires is greater thoroughness. But this can hardly be secured on the fortnightly or weekly lecture system. If he attempts it, he becomes a class-teacher rather than a lecturer, and admirable as he may be in this function, he ceases to attract a popular audience, and it is the popular audience which as a matter of fact pays the piper.

Are there any instances, say even in Oxford, Cambridge or London, in which without endowment or external assistance long courses are successfully maintained ?

Let us look the matter in the face. Until University Extension is externally supported, we cannot afford to sacrifice the popular audience.

In the centre which the writer represents—a centre which is deeply indebted to the authorities for the admirable lecturers whom they have sent down—only one course for some years past has been financially unsuccessful, and it was a course of twelve lectures. The lecturer was popular, the lectures admirable, the number of students greater than ever before, but after the fifth or sixth lecture the audience rapidly diminished. Even the faithful few attended rather for the sake of the essays than because they felt that the lecturer had anything new to tell them. They felt in fact that by that time he had said nearly all he had to say that was new or stimulating. He had by that time taught them so far as he could how to study their subject.

In the writer's experience the course of six lectures seems by an almost providential arrangement to mark a natural limit, beyond which even a good lecturer cannot go without becoming diffuse or reiterative, or common-place, or dealing with his subject in too thorough and serious a manner for a general audience.

The true remedy for the defects of the short-course system lies in the provision of more and better class teaching. At present, so far as the writer's experience goes, this is largely a misnomer. There is no real class. The good lecturer is not always a good class teacher. The lecture has left him not merely exhausted, but in a frame of mind and feeling not conducive to patient and minute class-teaching. The audience too is in much the same condition. And it is no wonder that ' the class' degenerates into a few questions and answers, often irrelevant or superfluous, sometimes silly, often asked only for the sake of saying something.

What is really wanted is some systematic coherent work, to which lecturer and students can turn with relief, and the burden of which can be mainly borne by the latter. Study of a text-book will not do. University Extension students have enough and too much as it is of text books, big and little. The writer ventures to suggest that the concurrent study of some short and easy text or firsthand authority in history, or specimen piece in literature, should always form the basis of all class-work. It need not always relate to the particular lecture just given, but that would often be an advantage from the change and relief thus afforded.

Such texts are now for the most part easily and cheaply procurable. And how great the gain. The one thing the earnest

Extension student needs above all others is some corrective in the second and third hand nature of the mental food supplied to him. He is set to read big books on history and literature, and he bolts their philosophy and criticism wholesale. He acquires a false and voracious appetite for tendencies, views, paradoxes, essays. He reads Dowden before he knows his Shakespeare, and Freeman and Green before he knows anything about his own town or the existing institutions of his own country. He discusses theories of the formation of mountain-chains, when he cannot tell a piece of limestone from a piece of grit. He generalizes broadly in Biology who has never looked through a microscope. The more he reads, the further he is apt to get from the true materials of knowledge.

The difficulties are of course considerable. The lecturer comes by one train and goes by another. What more can he do? And first and foremost he is and must remain a lecturer. That qualification is too rare to be sunk in any other duty. But the lecturer might be helped in the class-work. Let recognition be given to some local helper or class-leader. Men with ample qualifications are often available, but are naturally shy in offering their services. Let it be an instruction to committees that they should secure the help of some decent scholar, let him work under the direction of the lecturer, and let the examiner test not merely the students' knowledge of what has been said in the lectures, but of the supplementary work that has been so done.

To sum up, the writer fears that longer courses, if made universal, will deter many centres on account of the increased liabilities they involve. They will increase the difficulties of the local secretary and committee, who are even at present sufficiently hard put to it to meet the wishes of those supporters who want history and will not come to literature or science, or who want say science and will not come to literature or history lectures. Single courses will certainly mean smaller audiences and less popularity. The lecturer will tend to become more and more a superior class-teacher, and his class-room will only be frequented by the few who have reasons for desiring to learn.

The present writer feels rather strongly on the subject. He has undergone many long courses of lectures in years gone by, but owes the two main intellectual impulses, which have been lasting and permanent, to two short courses, one an earlier course of six lectures intended only for a few students and delivered when he was at college, the other an Oxford Extension course also of six lectures. He would not exchange the influence these have had upon him for that of all the other lectures he ever heard.

Except in centres like Reading or Exeter or perhaps a few others, the ideal lecture course at present for student and general audience alike—the system that combines the greatest number of advantages with the fewest disadvantages is undoubtedly the course of six fortnightly lectures.

.·.

IV. From Miss COLMAN.

(Hon. Sec. of Peterborough centre.)

'Should short courses (i.e. of six lectures) be given up as a part of the customary organization of University Extension teaching?'—If by short courses is understood six lectures delivered fortnightly, one course only being given during the winter, their cessation would mean the extinction of many small or weak centres. In these the money difficulty is an insuperable barrier to a long course. Further, the most active and earnest workers and students have their hands so full of other undertakings that they cannot spend more time for Extension work (which cannot run of itself) and better results are obtained by concentrating their energies for the limited time on each. For instance, the Gilchrist lectures in our centre after Christmas make it wise for us only to have a short course in the autumn. The value of a short course depends mainly upon whether the lectures are delivered fortnightly or weekly. The general public may possibly prefer the latter, but to the student there is a great advantage in being able to study quietly the subject for the essays and to read more between the lectures. If there is a Students' Association, to the student who takes part and enters into the discussions, the personal gain may be almost equal to listening to a lecture. Possibly gentle pressure might be put on the centres which arrange *two* short courses during the winter to experiment with a continuous or linked one.

The scheme of allowing six-lecture courses, but withholding the examination seems rather hard on those students who have spent the same period in study as those who have had twelve weekly lectures, and for whom the same standard is set, as rightly or wrongly many find that they do better and more definite work with the stimulus of being tested by an examination before them.

UNIVERSITY EXTENSION AND WORKING MEN.

THE following is taken from an article recently communicated by Mr. E. L. S. Horsburgh to *University Extension,* the publication of the American Society for the Extension of University Teaching.

Even in America I find the old question is still a prominent one—How are we to reach the manual labourers? and this question, which everywhere I have found a burning one, is an indication that, as we do, you desire to reach the masses, and that, as we find, you have not yet reached them, and that you believe, as we believe, that they need to be reached.

The aim which we may justly have is to break through these barriers of caste and class which so much impede progress, and to show that it is not any class but the whole community which benefits by the improvement of even an individual member of it.

Great nations have been built up and for the most part this has been done without the co-operation in government of the masses composing these nations. The rod of empire has been wielded by the few, and is now passing into the hands of the many, and with it there passes a great heritage built up by the fostering care of our forefathers. We may ask, without offence, that those who are to receive this heritage shall know how to appreciate it—that the democracy 'shall have a greatness of character commensurate with the responsibilities of democratic control.'

Great questions are coming up for settlement every day. They are grave and perplexing, capable of being regarded from many sides and many points of view, and the decision of these questions is largely in the hands of the masses. They should know how to regard them with judgement and impartiality, and education will teach them this. The University teacher in History and Economics is constantly approaching such great questions which have agitated past ages; he is subjecting them to analysis, turning upon them the daylight of fact and reason, stripping them of the heat and passion which in the past may have surrounded them. He is not merely treating his subject; he is giving an object lesson of how subjects should be treated. The very spirit in which a lecturer examines a question should have an enormous educational influence upon his audience. They will unconsciously be drawn to apply his methods in dealing with the past in forming their own judgements on the problems of the present. A lecture may teach men how to act and the spirit in which they should judge, even though every fact it contains be forgotten. A robust and sturdy sense of citizenship, a sense of proprietorship in the whole fabric of the State—this is what we want to secure to every one, and we want to secure it as much in the interest of the individual as of the State.

There exists, moreover, another reason, a narrow but very forcible reason, why we must make every effort to reach the manual labourers. It is that in America and in England men have given their pecuniary support of the University Extension movement, because they believe it to be a great agency for the amelioration of the masses. If they find the masses are not touched by it, the money of many and the services of some will be withdrawn, and we want to retain within our ranks all the service and support we can.

The most essential reason, however, why we need thus to extend our efforts is that the labouring class have need of us. Can they be reached? is a question asked very often and despairingly. There is no doubt of it, and they themselves, by their own energy and through their own sense of need, are building a bridge between us and them. I can speak only of my own country, but in the character of their trusted leaders, 'in the patience of sympathy, of the suffering poor, in the simplicity and fortitude of the lives of the better workman, in the order and independence of good fellowship which mark the meetings of co-operative societies, benefit clubs and trade unions, in that degree of self-control which has been manifest even in the height of recent strikes, we see in the workmen of to-day indications of a character which will welcome and run to meet any advances we may make, a character which is unlikely to confuse interest with patronage. I have tried to show the area that exists for the further extension of our efforts towards the manual labourers, and also the fact that the manual labourer is prepared to receive and second our efforts. It remains to show how we may best reach and influence him. Three important factors in the life of the labourer have always to be uppermost in our minds: his independence, his want of leisure, and his want of previous training.

Every one hates patronage, none more so than the working-man. It is of the first importance, therefore, to lead the labourers to act for themselves, not to convey the impression that they are being acted for. The organization of the working-man's centre should be as much as possible in the hands of the working-men. They should form the majority of the local committee, one of their own number should be chairman and secretary, their own local leaders should be the men to explain, to encourage, and to incite. In the trades' councils, the co-operative stores and in the unions, plenty of leaders exist who recognize to the full the importance of the educational improvement of their class. It may be taken as an axiom that success in this direction is proportionate to the share in the management allotted to the workmen themselves.

In the second place, the working-man comes to a lecture at the close of a day of hard manual toil. He is weary and needs something in the nature of recreation as much or more than a further stimulus to effort. He is asked to write weekly papers, but it is sometimes forgotten that in his home he lives, perhaps, in a single room, surrounded by a large family in a hot, teeming and noisy district. Little opportunity is given him here for mental abstraction. The cares, anxieties and interests of his daily life are pressing close upon him. He may be full of the subject he is considering, full of the new spirit which a stimulating lecture excites, but he is untrained in the art of formulating and arranging his ideas: the mere manual art of writing may be pain and toil to him; he is often ill supplied with books. Here are the words of an English workman on this subject :—' The educational advantages which have fallen to the lot of artisans in early life, particularly if they be now over thirty years old, have hardly qualified them for the ready appropriation of what University Extension has to give. People who have spent the first twenty years of their lives under the direct influence of elaborate educational systems, will find some difficulty in fully realizing all the mental strain that heavy and prolonged reading, and composition in presentable English, as well as hard and systematic thinking, puts upon a mind but little trained in work of this kind.'

I am convinced that those who are working for the provision of better homes for the poor, shorter hours of labour, for securing more leisure for the artisan, are fellow-workers with us and to some extent must come before us. They are preparing the soil on which the good seed of education may fall and fructify, instead of withering away upon the stony ground of social disparity and distress.

The lecturer to working-men should, therefore, possess qualities which compel attendance and attention. Above all he must be sympathetic, for it is sympathy that wins men. He must be careful in the choice of subject, must know what to omit as well as what to include, and must always have in his mind the general conditions—as I have indicated them—which surround the lives

of the labourers. He may enlist the services of the eye, as well as the ear by well-chosen and well-executed illustrations shown in the lantern; but he must, if he uses this method, be content with nothing but the best, for the working man is quick to appreciate good illustrations and quicker to express his scorn of what is sensational and artistically bad.

There is a ready means of compelling attention in the locality where the audience live. There is scarcely a spot of ground that has not its own peculiar associations, history and inspiration. A new world of interest and delight is opened to the man who is brought to realize the fairy story of the stones, the trees, the plants, the rocks, which are at his doors. A new patriotism is inspired in the man who, living in some historic town or country, realizes the part which his own place has filled in the making of the nations, and where these direct object lessons are wanted there are always the heavens above him. The stars on which he has gazed so often that he is oblivious of their existence, may be made to disclose their glories to his gaze. The history of a single star may put new meaning for him into the universe, into the world in which he lives and the part he has to play in it.

It is obvious that the labourer cannot afford high fees. A dollar to a man with only five hundred of them or less every year means infinitely more to him than twenty to people with two thousand every year. Herein lies the need for the endowment of our work, whereby our forces may be brought to bear with regularity and precision, unimpeded by pecuniary fears and anxieties, instead of being fitfully applied as casual liberality may permit.

I have already said a word as to the qualities necessary in a lecturer to artisans and working-men. He must have magnetic influence, he must be sympathetic, he must never forget his local allusions, his treatment of his subject must be a pattern to his audience as to how subjects should be treated—judicial, impartial, clear. A question remains regarding him. Should he be a reader of his lecture or an extempore speaker?

A lecturer must have the gift of inspiration, and he will possess it in the fullest measure if he derive his inspiration directly from the audience he is addressing. Electric sparks of sympathy and feeling-feeling must flash between him and each member of his audience. He must gauge their capacity, their degree of comprehension of his meaning, their difficulties which arise as he speaks, the degree of interest with which they are receiving his teaching—he must judge, in short, of the present value of his efforts from the mental and physical attitude of his hearers *as they surround him.* He must be quick to mark the shades and shadows which pass in currents over every assembly of men and women, and the only way in which he can do all this is *by looking at them.* He must see the man who is asleep in the far corner and wake him up by vocal persuasiveness to interest and attention. He must *see* that such and such a point has not told, and must be prepared to put it in a different way; to present it from another point of view. He must be ready to change his own mental attitude, his style, his elocution, his whole method, until he finds he has at length hit the mark right between wind and water. Can he do this if he is reading from a manuscript? Some very gifted readers can; but, as a rule, the lecturer to working-men should speak extempore. I need not say that he must know his subject to his very finger tips. Extempore lecturing does not require less preparation than the written lecture, but more, for it is only when a man is fairly saturated with his subject that he can present it forcibly, scientifically and efficiently, even in its broad outline. Probably in lecturing to artisans it is broad outline and correct perspective at which the lecturer is chiefly aiming. He can only hope to hit the mark in proportion as his own detailed knowledge is exhaustive. A broad general view, to be of any value, must be based in the lecturer's mind upon exhaustive examination of details. In lecturing, then, to artisans, only the best you have got to give is likely to be of any real use. I will not attempt to determine dogmatically whether a lecturer should read or speak. He must fulfil the condition I have laid down, and if he feel he cannot fulfil them by reading—then he must speak extempore.

And lastly, the local organization must be efficient. I have already said it should be in the hands of the workmen themselves, but the lines on which they should work may be suggested by one fully versed in all the details of arrangement. A lecturer may be an angel from heaven and his lecture may harmonize in every way with his celestial qualifications, and yet without efficient management and organization the effort among the artisans will be a failure. Great as will be the results to them of extending University teaching to the workers, there will be another great result visible in the work of the Universities themselves. Some of the Universities do not know it, but it is true, that University Extension is doing as much for them as for the people outside their walls. They are, by its agency, being brought into touch with the masses, as they have never been before. Their own intra-mural methods are feeling the generous rebound of the work done outside their walls. They are emerging from their fossilized, their chrysalis condition, and putting on new harmonies of form and colour which are making them a thing of beauty, and enduring value to thousands who have regarded them hitherto as exclusive centres for the cultivation of so-called 'superior persons,' and reciprocally by the agency of University Extension, there may be brought before the eyes and minds of the masses the inestimable services which research, directed from the professor's chair, has conferred upon mankind at large.

But far more than this, there is the benefit which the community, as a whole, will derive from the Extension of sound learning widely among the masses who compose it. The elevated ideals, the manly sense of citizenship, the impartial view, the modification of passion, prejudice, and superstition, the brightness and sense of new life which will be infused into lives spent for the most part in privation and toil, the resolution of purpose, the joy of living and the glories of the universe, and of the world in which we live—all these things we have to hope for—all these things we may confidently expect by the Extension of our labours among our brothers and our sisters who compose the masses of mankind.

THE NATIONAL HOME READING UNION AT SALISBURY.

THE idea of the 'Summer Meeting' has become thoroughly at home in England; it has passed into the charmed circle of the Universities, and it has been adopted by younger and less exclusive bodies. Of these the N. H. R. U. is one of the youngest, for it has only just completed its fifth year with a meeting at Salisbury. Its supporters seem to think that the advantages of variety outbalance the charm of coming to the old Universities year after year: this matter we must leave to our own students to fight out, but certainly this year the gathering at Salisbury was delightful. Thanks to the surroundings of the sweetest cathedral city in England, to the energy of the local organizers, and to the lovely weather, all went off with a vigour of enjoyment and a keen sense of united energies, which reminded one continually of Oxford as it now is in August.

The main subject of the reading of the Union during the last year has been English History and Literature, down to the time of Edward III, and on this bore many of the lectures delivered at the meeting: Mr. York Powell, as was fitting, spoke on Saxon and Scandinavian England; Prof. Baldwin Brown of Edinburgh treated Early Architecture; Mr. Tanner of St. John's, Cambridge, lectured on Norman and Angevin England, with special reference to the history of Salisbury. In addition to this, there were evening lectures, given by the Dean on Browning, by Prof. Jebb on Dr. Johnson, and by Mr. Wells of Wadham College, Oxford, on the history of Oxford; while Sir Robert Ball cracked many jokes on 'Recent Discoveries as to the Sun,' though it was hard, after one and a half hours' listening, to say what the *recent* discoveries were.

A special feature of the meeting were the excursions. Every one of course knows that Stonehenge is within reach of Salisbury; but hardly less interesting were the Vandycks and the gardens at Wilton, the picture galleries at Longford, the church at Bemerton, and the old English folk-moot at Downton, and the other daily expeditions: many of these harmonized well with the studies of the meeting.

About 250 tickets were issued for the gathering as a whole, while as many more were sold for parts of it. Such gatherings are pleasant to all who take part in them, and they certainly, with all their popular elements, aid some of those who wish to do real work for themselves; but perhaps their most important function is their share in the rediscovery of England. English people need to find out the treasures of beauty and of historic interest which lie all around them: the best training for doing this at home is to do it thoroughly under good guidance in a few such favoured spots as Salisbury.

LETTERS TO THE EDITOR.

[*We do not hold ourselves responsible for the opinions expressed by our correspondents.*]

Short Courses.

DEAR SIR,—In reading the reports of the discussion on short courses of lectures at the London Congress, I find it is stated that two short courses of six lectures can be accepted as a full course, if carried on in sequence. But it is not stated that this advantage is refused to centres that are unable to arrange for the short courses to be held within six months of each other.

The present arrangement cannot but be felt as extremely hard by students at small centres. Work as long and as steadily as they may, the Certificate is still beyond their reach.

Perhaps therefore the following suggestion may be worth considering, viz. that Certificates should be granted to students who have passed the examinations on two short courses of lectures, held in sequence, in two successive years, and supplemented by summer work. Such summer work to consist of at least three essays on the subject of the lectures, and to be submitted to the lecturer or any other examiner appointed by the Delegacy.

This privilege, if granted, would act as an incentive to small centres to arrange courses in sequence, and the knowledge gained by the students would, I venture to think, be more thorough than that of the students of a single long course.

Yours truly,

AN ACCUMULATOR OF 'PASS LISTS.'

.'.

Prize-Giving.

DEAR SIR,—In compliance with the request of 'A Prize Winner' in your June issue, the Wells Students' Association was summoned to discuss this question at its annual meeting yesterday, and I am requested to tell you briefly what took place. The subject was introduced by my giving an account of the debate at the Bournemouth Conference, and summarizing the letters that have since appeared in your columns and in the *Bournemouth S. A. Gazette*. Canon Buckle considered that examinations and prizes were at one time needful to stir and stimulate to study, but that this was no longer the case; and for his part he should like to see such a body as the Students' Association setting an example of delight in knowledge and in the exercise of their mental faculties, without examinations, certificates, or prizes. The students generally did not rise quite to this height, and the opinion that prizes give a healthy zest and interest to the work was expressed by more than one speaker. The envy, jealousy, and self-glorification feared by some of the Bournemouth debaters will not, I hope, be created by being talked of; the whole Association agreed that they do not exist here, and that they might be dismissed from consideration. The idea of working for the prize only was also new to them; they thought that possibly 'knack' helped in passing examinations, but that this was but one of the many occasions in life where fortune does not always appear to favour merit, and was not a sufficient reason for altering the present system. The head-mistress of the High School thought (with the writer in your June number) that the Delegates' prize formed a tie to the University which it would be a great pity to sever, but she advised that the same student should be debarred from receiving it continually; also she deprecated the idea of any portion of the local funds being used for a second prize. Two members of the Committee (one the head master of the Grammar School) considered that prizes in the form of scholarships to the Summer Meeting were a most valuable help to promising students. Before the discussion came to a close I explained that the second prize does not come out of the local funds, but has hitherto been kindly offered by individual members of the committee. I also said that desirable as scholarships are, they cost £5 or £10 instead of the 5s. or 10s. which a book costs, a fact which renders their adoption difficult in many centres, certainly in this. The feeling which pervaded the meeting was evidently that of the Students' Association secretary, whose letter appeared in your columns last month. Mrs. Slater, who presided, summed up by saying that she agreed with what the students present appeared to her to think; namely, that prizes are not and ought not to be *necessary* to University Extension students, but that they are harmless and frequently useful adjuncts to their studies. A show of hands was unanimous in favour of the retention of prizes.

As far as my own opinion is worth anything, it is this. Where the majority of students have plenty of leisure for self-improvement, it is possible that the idea of competition may enter somewhat too largely into their work, and destroy its healthful pleasure, and perhaps lower its aims; and there I almost think it might be well to forego even examinations, to induce that delight in knowledge for its own sake which ought to inspire us all. But in many centres the students are busy men and women, with little money or time for books; there, every prize that is won is a well-deserved record of perseverance in overcoming difficulties for the sake of knowledge, is a source of great pleasure to the owner *and to his or her rivals*, and should not be denied on any consideration.

Yours faithfully,

MARY A. G. LIVETT (*Local Secretary*).

Wells, Somerset, *July* 19.

.ᐧ.

DEAR SIR,—I should be glad to know whether the Delegates wish to encourage students from all centres to compete for their scholarships and prizes, or whether they wish to limit as much as possible the number of competitors. Their regulations seem admirably adapted for the latter purpose, but might, I think, be so framed as to take similar effect in reducing the work of the examiners without making unfair distinctions between centre and centre. At our centre, both this year and last, students have been unable to qualify for this competition unless they had gained their certificates of distinction the *previous* year (I had done this, so have no personal ground of complaint). Our examinations took place on April 13, 1893, and April 14, 1894: this year our secretary received the examiner's report on June 11, last year a few days later—in both cases more than a week *after* the latest date at which the essays could be sent in. In previous years we received the examiner's verdict within five weeks after the examination; and this was the case also this year with neighbouring centres which had taken a different lecturer and subject.

I am, Sir,

Yours faithfully,

June 18, 1894.   G. C.

REPORTS FROM THE CENTRES.

GLOUCESTER.—Six scholarships to enable students to attend Part I of the Summer Meeting have been raised in Gloucester, four being given by the local committee, and two by private individuals. The competition was divided into two classes: (*a*) for artisans only; (*b*) for students earning not more than £100 a year. The subjects for the essays were arranged by the Rev. W. H. Hudson Shaw, who also kindly acted as judge. The following were the successful candidates:—F. Cooke, G. H. Draper, P. Deggan, W. Manning, J. Mansel, and W. H. Sayer.

NOTES FROM A NORTHERN CENTRE.

By Mr. JOHN V. BARROW.

IT has often been suggested that one of the most admirable features of the system of University Extension is the spirit of good fellowship which it develops among its students, brightening the isolation of individual study into the eagerness of collective energy, quickening healthy and friendly competition, strengthening good resolutions and legitimate ambitions, and uniting them by bonds of mutual help and common sympathy, into a band of earnest travellers in the realm of knowledge. What the well regulated centre does for the individual, the Summer Meeting does for the students of many centres, and the *Gazette* in turn, for the whole area of University Extension work. The main purpose of the *Gazette* is undoubtedly to give in broad outline the general progress of the work, but I think there can be no two opinions that one of its most valuable and interesting items is to be found in the news from the centres, giving personal experiences, detailing individual effort, and dropping by the way seeds of suggestion and helpfulness, from which may spring up a harvest of increased success in other centres adopting such methods, and the same plan of operation.

The columns of the *Gazette* being open for such records, no apology is needed for writing of a centre which, although not directly connected with Oxford, is nevertheless in hearty sympathy with all that concerns this great educational movement. Backworth has long been associated with University Extension, and has maintained an almost unbroken attachment to it since its pioneers first set up their banner in Northumberland. Out of the many mining centres established in the country in the early days of the movement Backworth alone can claim anything like a continuous connexion, and point to a record of many years. Only in very few instances has the generosity of the County Council in contributing thirty pounds to every course of University Extension lectures held under the Technical Education scheme, served to revive the interest in this system of higher education, and one course has usually been the extent of the effort. For the third time Backworth has decided on this means of assistance to secure a course of University Extension lectures. Indeed, but for the funds available through the County Council it would have been exceedingly difficult to have kept up the connexion so long existing between this centre and the University of Cambridge. Before the days of County Council grants, the money for the lectures was raised by purely local effort, and the strenuous perseverance of an active Students' Association. Bazaars, exhibitions, concerts, lectures, and a variety of other agencies were pressed into service, and enabled the centre to hold its head above the threatening waters of financial difficulty. When it is remembered that Backworth is a mining village, and that all the above named agencies get the worse for wear, it will not be difficult to see that it was with very bodeful thoughts that the students looked to the future. The grant obtainable from the County Council, however, has enabled us to pass the Rubicon, and although limited in the choice of subjects, we are content to accept the lists of the Technical Education committee as a means of keeping in touch with this beneficent movement. The spring course of lectures was delivered by Mr. H. S. Mundahl, B.A., LL.B., the subject being Political Economy, a subject of pressing and important interest to an industrial community. The previous course of lectures on Geology had not been very successful, and it was felt that special means must be taken to secure the prosperity of the Economic course. Having regard to the character of the district, one shilling is charged for the entire course, and twopence for single lectures. As the time approached for the lectures to begin, a special meeting of the members of the Students' Association was called, and every member present undertook to sell tickets. The lecturer was asked to forward a rough copy of his syllabus, and a committee was appointed to issue a leaflet setting forth in language free from technicalities the subject-matter of each lecture. Posters adorned the walls of the place, and handbills were distributed at every house. With these preparations and a list of the text-books before us, we felt ready for a beginning. The first lecture was very well attended, one of the miner's agents presiding, and ardently advocating the study of Economics and the benefits of University Extension. The lecturer impressed all who heard him, and maintained that impression throughout the course. The number of tickets sold was eighty, the average attendance at lecture being fifty, and at class thirty-four. Thirteen students sent in weekly papers, eight presenting themselves for examination, all of whom passed, three gaining the honour of distinction, one of the latter being the youngest candidate in the group, and a hitherto untried student in University Extension.

This may not be considered great success, but in a centre such as this it is not without its encouragements. Of course the inevitable difficulty creeps in, and the higher education is pronounced to be 'too high for those for whom it is designed.' It is certainly true that where education has been superficial or become rusted, it is very difficult to begin where University Extension begins, and it is worth the consideration of those in authority how best to meet this difficulty. Evening continuation schools will do something, but the level is often found too high even there. Where a good Students' Association exists, this seems the most fitting channel through which to approach the question. If the more advanced students would take in hand those less advanced than themselves, helping them over difficulties, training them in the use of books, and habits of study, by personal contact and influence, much might be done to overcome what is all too evident in the majority of centres. In the meantime this ought not to be a deterrent to the progress of the work, for it is to be remembered that genuine success is not always measured by numbers; and while heads undoubtedly count, no district can have these educational influences present without being the better for it.

I have referred to the work of the Students' Associations, and a brief description of that at Backworth may be of some interest. The owners of the colliery allow the use of a room and gas free of cost, and a local lady undertook to furnish, and annually pays for its cleaning. It is here that all the business of the centre is transacted, the whole of the members forming a committee, and generally interesting themselves in the work. The association is active throughout the year, having a 'Classical Novel Reading Union,' meeting once a month, a 'Literary Conversation Class,' meeting once in the same period, and just now an 'Experiment Class,' meeting once a week, preparatory to Dr. Kimmins' course on Chemistry in the autumn. The Association is something more than

an adjunct to the centre. It is the intellectual home of the student, combining equality of right with equality of opportunity. A recent addition to the Students' Association is worthy of note, having had its origin at Oxford. A little over a year ago one of the students was requested by a few men at the mine to undertake their tuition in elementary education. No other means being available he consented, and for six months held a class, for two nights in the week. During its progress, an Oxford lady, Miss E. Clare Huntington, became interested in the work, and suggested that a few books for general reading might be useful. The offer was made with such generous kindness that it was felt that a refusal would be ungracious, and it was accepted. It was anticipated that only a few books would be given; but principally through Miss Huntington's efforts and the generosity of many friends, the number multiplied until it was felt that it would be selfish to keep them within the narrow circle of the class. A proposal was therefore made to the Students' Association that they should be located there, for joint use and a wider sphere of service. The arrangement having been made, the Association can now boast of a library of over three hundred volumes, comprising some of the best works of the best authors in poetry, fiction, history, travels, science, essays, &c.

The library is a great boon, members borrowing once a month, and having brought within their reach those great legacies of literature which adorn our time.

In these brief notes some idea may be gained of the work of the Backworth centre, and if, by precept or example, we help on the good work in other places, then in that knowledge we are amply rewarded.

BOOK EXCHANGE AND LOAN COLUMN.

THE Bakewell University Students' Association have the following books to lend :—

Terms as follows :—

Twenty-five volumes on —

'The Stuarts and the Puritan Revolution': £1 for a year.

A small library on—

'The Age of Elizabeth': 1s. a volume for a year.

A small library on—

'England in the Eighteenth Century': 1s. a volume for a year. These books could also be exchanged for a library on 'English Novelists.'

Address :—Miss KATHLEEN MARTIN,
Edensor, Bakewell.

ARRANGEMENTS FOR 1894-5.

Autumn, 1894.

Centre.	No. of Lectures in Course.	Subject of Course.	Lecturer.	Course begins.	Course ends.
ALTRINCHAM (evening) ...	6	Making of England, Part I. ...	Rev. W. H. SHAW, M.A.	F. Oct. 5	Dec. 14
ASHTON (afternoon)	6	Florence	,, ,, ...	T. Oct. 9	Dec. 18
ASHTON (evening)	6	Making of England, Part II.	,, ,, ...	T. Oct. 9	Dec. 18
BIRMINGHAM, SEVERN STREET (evening)	6	Making of England, Part II. ...	,, ,, ...	T. Oct. 2	Dec. 11
BOLTON (afternoon)	6	Social Reformers	,, ,, ...	Th. Sept. 27	Dec. 6
BOLTON (evening)	6	Making of England, Part II.	,, ,, ...	Th. Sept. 27	Dec. 6
CHELTENHAM (afternoon) ...	6	Florence	,, ,, ...	Th. Oct. 4	Dec. 13
CHELTENHAM (evening) ...	6	Making of England, Part I. .	,, ,, ...	W. Oct. 3	Dec. 12
CHESTER (afternoon) ...	6	Making of England, Part II. ...	,, ,, ...	F. Sept. 28	Dec. 7
CIRENCESTER (afternoon) ...	6	Age of Elizabeth	,, ,, ...	M. Oct. 1	Dec. 10
GLOUCESTER (evening) ...	6	Making of England, Part I.	,, ,, ...	M. Oct. 1	Dec. 10
KENDAL (afternoon)	6	Puritan Revolution ...	,, ,, ...	M. Sept. 24	Dec. 3
MALVERN (afternoon)	6	Age of Elizabeth	,, ,, ...	W. Oct. 3	Dec. 12
MANCHESTER, CHEETHAM (evening)	6	Age of Elizabeth	,, ,, ...	F. Sept. 28	Dec. 7
OLDHAM (evening)	6	Making of England, Part II.	,, ,, ...	W. Sept. 26	Dec. 5
PRESTWICH (evening	6	Making of England, Part II.	,, · ,, ...	M. Sept. 24	Dec. 3
READING, UNIVERSITY EXTENSION COLLEGE (evening)	6	Not fixed	,, ,, ...	Th. Sept. 4	Dec. 13

Centre.	No. of Lectures in Course.	Subject of Course.	Lecturer.	Course begins.	Course ends.
STROUD (afternoon)	6	Not fixed	Rev. W. H. SHAW, M.A.	T. Oct. 2	Dec. 11
WIGAN (afternoon)	6	Florence	„ „ ...	W. Sept. 26	Dec. 5
BAKEWELL (evening)	6	English Novelists...	J. A. R. MARRIOTT, M.A.	Th. Sept. 27	Dec. 6
BIRMINGHAM, EDGBASTON (afternoon)	12	Age of Louis XIV and French Revolution	„ „ ...	T. Oct. 9	Dec. 18
BOURNEMOUTH (afternoon) ...	12	Europe since Waterloo	„ „ ...	W. Oct. 3	Dec. 12
CLEVEDON (afternoon)	12	Shakespeare's Historical Plays ...	„ „ ...	Th. Oct. 4	Dec. 13
LEAMINGTON (evening)	6	English in India	„ „ ...	F. Sept. 28	Dec. 7
LYMINGTON (afternoon)	6	English in India	„ „ ...	T. Oct. 2	Dec. 11
MATLOCK (afternoon)	6	The Stuarts & Puritan Revolution	„ „ ...	Th. Sept. 27	Dec. 6
*SOUTHBOURNE	12	Not fixed	„ „ ...	Not fixed.	Not fixed
STAFFORD (afternoon)	6	Shakespeare's Historical Plays ...	„ „ ...	W. Sept. 26	Dec. 5
WELLS (evening)	6	England in the 18th Century ...	„ „ ...	Th. Oct. 4	Dec. 13
WEYMOUTH (evening)	6	Not fixed	„ „ ...	W. Oct. 3	Dec. 12
READING, U. E. COLL. (aft.)	12	English Literature	J. CHURTON COLLINS, M.A	S. Sept. 29	Dec. 8
READING, U. E. COLL. (even.)	12	English Literature	„ „ ...	S. Sept. 29	Dec. 8
HARROGATE (evening)	12	Prose Writers	C. E. MALLET, B.A.	F. Sept. 28	Dec. 14
ILKLEY (afternoon)	12	England in the 18th Century ...	„ „ ...	Th. Sept. 27	Dec. 13
OTLEY (evening)	6	The Stuarts	„ „ ...	Th. Oct. 4	Dec. 13
RIPON (afternoon)	6	French Revolution	„ „ ...	T. Sept. 25	Dec. 4
RIPON (evening)	6	The Stuarts	„ „ ...	T. Sept. 25	Dec. 4
TAMWORTH (evening)... ...	10	England in the 18th Century ...	„ „ ...	T. Oct. 2	Dec. 11
TUNBRIDGE WELLS (afternoon)	10	Tudors and Stuarts	„ „ ...	M. Oct. 8	Dec. 10
WARRINGTON (evening) ...	6	Tudors	„ „ ...	W. Sept. 26	Not fixed.
BRADFORD (evening)	6	Shakespeare	F. S. BOAS, M.A.	Th. Oct. 4	Dec. 13
BURNLEY (evening)	12	Spencer & other Elizabethan Poets	„ „ ...	Th. Oct. 11	Dec. 20
CANTERBURY (afternoon) ...	12	Victorian Poets	„ „ ...	W. Oct. 10	Dec. 19
HODDESDON (afternoon) ...	12	Shakespeare	„ „ ...	T. Oct. 2	Dec. 18
RAMSGATE (afternoon) ...	12	Literature of Cavaliers & Puritans	„ „ ...	S. Oct. 6	Dec. 15
RUGBY (evening)	6	Browning	„ „ ...	W. Oct. 3	Dec. 12
SALE (evening)	6	Representative Men, Stuarts ...	„ „ ...	F. Oct. 12	Not fixed
WESTERHAM (afternoon) ...	6	Victorian Poets	„ „ ...	S. Oct. 13	Dec. 22
EASTBOURNE (afternoon) ...	6	Not fixed	Rev. J. G. BAILEY, M.A., LL.D.	Th. Oct. 11	Dec. 20
NEWBURY (afternoon)... ...	6	Shelley, Keats, Coleridge, and Wordsworth	„ „ ...	Th. Oct. 4	Dec. 13
ROCHESTER (evening)	6	Shakespeare	„ „ ...	T. Oct. 2	Dec. 11
WEST BRIGHTON (afternoon)...	12	Tennyson	„ „ ...	F. Oct. 12	Dec. 21
BEDFORD (evening)	12	The Colonies and India ...	H. MORSE STEPHENS, M.A.	M. Oct. 8	Dec. 17
BURY (evening)	6	Epochs from English History ...	E. L. S. HORSBURGH, M.A.	T. Oct. 2	Dec. 11
FOLKESTONE (morning) ...	6	Age of Elizabeth (Social & Lit.)	„ „ ...	M. Oct. 1	Dec. 10
HEBDEN BRIDGE (evening) ...	6	French Revolution	„ „ ...	S. Oct. 20	Dec. 29
HUDDERSFIELD (evening) ...	6	Epochs from English History ...	„ „ ...	W. Oct. 10	Dec. 19
OXFORD (evening)	12	The Making of England... ...	„ „ ...	F. Oct. 5	Dec. 14
REIGATE (afternoon)	12	The Early Tudors...	„ „ ...	M. Oct. 1	Dec. 10
THORNTON (evening)	6	Epochs from English History ...	„ „ ...	M. Oct. 8	Dec. 17
SOUTHAMPTON (evening) ...	6 or 12	Not fixed	„ „ ...	F. Sept. 28	Dec. 7
SWINDON (evening)	6	Epochs from English History ...	„ „ ...	W. Oct. 3	Dec. 12
*WAKEFIELD (evening) ...	6	Not fixed	„ „ ...	T. Oct. 9	Dec. 18
WINDSOR (afternoon)	6	Architecture	F. BOND, M.A.	Th. Oct. 4	Dec. 13
HENLOW (evening)	12	The English Citizen	W. M. CHILDS, B.A.	W. Oct. 10	Dec. 19
CIRENCESTER (evening) ...	6	Trade, Adventure, and Discovery	K. D. COTES, M.A. ...	M. Oct. 1	Dec. 10
KNOWLE (afternoon)	6	Shakespeare's England	„ „ ...	M. Sept. 24	Dec. 3
PETERBOROUGH (evening) ...	6	Trade, Adventure, and Discovery	„ „ ...	F. Sept. 28	Dec. 7
SWANSEA (evening)	6	Trade, Adventure, and Discovery	„ „ ...	F. Oct. 5	Dec. 14
TUNBRIDGE WELLS (evening)...	8	Commerce, Colonization & Empire	„ „ ...	T. Oct. 9	Nov. 27
WINSLOW (evening)	6	Relation of History to Painting ...	„ „ ...	Th.	Not fixed.
BANBURY (evening)	6	Economic Aspects of Social Questions	W. A. S. HEWINS, M.A.	Th. Oct. 4	Dec. 6
GRIMSBY (evening)	6	Not fixed	„ „ ..	T. Oct. 2	Dec. 11
HYDE (evening)	6	English Social Life	„ „ ...	M. Oct. 1	Dec. 10
WEST BRIGHTON (evening) ...	12	Three Centuries of Working Class History	„ „ ...	Th. Oct. 18	Dec. 13
ACCRINGTON (evening) ...	6	Structure of Modern Industry ...	J. A. HOBSON, M.A. ...	M. Oct. 1	Dec. 10
BRIDPORT (evening)	12	Industrial Revolution	„ „ ...	T. Oct. 9	Dec. 18
COVENTRY (evening)	6	Sharing of Wealth	„ „ ...	Th. Sept. 27	Dec. 6
TEAN (afternoon)	6	English Novelists	„ „ ...	S. Sept. 29	Dec. 8
BARNSLEY (evening)	6	Ruskin	J. E. PHYTHIAN	T. Oct. 9	Dec. 18
CARLISLE (afternoon)	12	Architecture	„ „ ...	T. Oct. 16	Dec. 11
GRANGE (evening)	6	Architecture	„ „ ...	M. Oct. 1	Dec. 10
KESWICK (evening)	6	Shakespeare	„ „ ...	M. Oct. 8	Dec. 17
MOSTON (evening)	8	Venice and Florentine Art ...	„ „ ...	F. Oct. 19	Dec. 7
RHYL (evening)	6	Architecture	„ „ ...	W. Oct. 10	Dec. 19
ROMSEY (afternoon)	6	Mediaeval Architecture	Rev. G. H, WEST, D.D.	W. Oct. 3	Dec. 12
BODMIN (evening)	12	South Africa	W. B. WORSFOLD, M.A.	F. Oct. 12	Dec. 21
CAMBORNE (evening)	12	South Africa	„ „ ...	F. Oct. 5	Dec. 14
FALMOUTH (evening)	12	South Africa	„ „ ...	Th. Oct. 4	Dec. 13
HELSTON (evening)	12	South Africa	„ „ ...	T. Oct. 9	Dec. 18
LAUNCESTON (evening) ...	12	South Africa	„ „ ...	W. Oct. 3	Dec. 12
PENZANCE (evening)	12	South Africa	„ „ ...	M. Oct. 8	Dec. 17
REDRUTH (evening)	12	South Africa	„ „ ...	Th. Oct. 11	Dec. 20
ST. AUSTELL (evening) ...	12	South Africa	„ „ ...	T. Oct. 2	Dec. 11
TRURO (evening)	12	South Africa	„ „ ...	M. Oct. 1	Dec. 10
HUNGERFORD (afternoon) ...	12	Physiography	G. J. BURCH, M.A. ...	T. Oct. 2	Dec. 18
CARLISLE (evening)	6	Outlines of Geology	C. CARUS-WILSON, F.G.S.	Th. Oct. 11	Dec. 20
LOUTH (evening)	6	Outlines of Geology	„ „ ...	M. Oct. 1	Dec. 10

* Arrangements not yet completed.

Centre.	No. of Lectures in Course.	Subject of Course.	Lecturer.	Course begins.	Course ends.
ST. HELENS (evening)	6	Crust of the Earth	C.CARUS-WILSON,F.G.S.	M. Oct. 8	Dec. 17
SETTLE (evening)	6	Physiography	,, ,,	T. Oct. 9	Dec. 18
*BATH (afternoon)	12	Not fixed	A. H. Fison, D.Sc.	Th. Sept. 27	Dec. 6
BATH (evening)	12	Life of a Planet	,, ,,	Th. Sept. 27	Dec. 6
BOURNEMOUTH (evening)	12	Forces of Nature	,, ,,	F. Sept. 28	Dec. 7
NEWPORT (evening)	12	Not fixed	,, ,,	Th. Oct. 4	Dec. 13
RYDE (afternoon)	12	Life of a Planet	,, ,,	Th. Oct. 4	Dec. 13
VENTNOR (evening)	12	Physical Astronomy	,, ,,	F. Oct. 5	Dec. 14

Spring, 1895.

Centre.	No. of Lectures in Course.	Subject of Course.	Lecturer.	Course begins.	Course ends.
†BIRMINGHAM, EDGBASTON (afternoon)	12	Age of Louis XIV and French Revolution	J.A.R.MARRIOTT,M.A.	T. Jan. 15	Mar. 26
†BOURNEMOUTH (afternoon)	12	Europe since Waterloo	,, ,,	W. Jan. 23	Apr. 3
BRADFORD (evening)	6	Colonies	,, ,,	Th. Jan. 17	Mar. 28
†BRIDPORT (evening)	12	Industrial Revolution	,, ,,	T. Jan. 22	Apr. 2
†CLEVEDON (afternoon)	12	Shakespeare's Historical Plays	,, ,,	F. Jan. 25	Apr. 5
†OXFORD (evening)	11	The Making of England	,, ,,	F. Jan. 18	Mar. 29
SALE (evening)	6	England in the 18th Century	,, ,,	W. Jan. 16	Mar. 27
*†SOUTHBOURNE	12	Not fixed	,, ,,	Not fixed	Not fixed
†READING, U. E. COLL. (aft.)	12	English Literature	J.CHURTONCOLLINS,M.A	S. Jan. 26	Apr. 6
†READING, U. E. COLL. (even.)	12	English Literature	,, ,,	S. Jan. 26	Apr. 6
†TAMWORTH (evening)	10	England in the 18th Century	C. E. MALLET, B.A.	T. Jan. 15	Feb. 26
†BURNLEY (evening)	12	Spenser & other Elizabethan Poets	F. S. BOAS, M.A.	Th. Jan. 17	Mar. 28
*†CANTERBURY (afternoon)	12	Victorian Poets	,, ,,	Th. Jan. 24	Apr. 4
†RAMSGATE (afternoon)	12	Literature of Cavaliers and Puritans	,, ,,	S. Jan. 26	Apr. 6
†WEST BRIGHTON (afternoon)	12	Tennyson	Rev. J. G. BAILEY, M.A., LL.D.	F. Jan. 18	Mar. 29
†BEDFORD (evening)	12	The Colonies and India	H.MORSESTEPHENS,M.A	M. Jan. 28	Apr. 8
*ABERGAVENNY (afternoon)	6	English History in Shakespeare	E. L. S. HORSBURGH,M.A	Not fixed	Not fixed
BRECON (afternoon)	6	Not fixed	,, ,,	Th. Jan. 24	Apr. 4
BRECON (evening)	6	Not fixed	,, ,,	Th. Jan. 24	Apr. 4
CHELTENHAM (afternoon)	6	Not fixed	,, ,,	W. Jan. 30	Apr. 10
CHELTENHAM (evening)	6	Not fixed	,, ,,	W. Jan. 30	Apr. 10
EVESHAM (evening)	6	Revolution and Age of Anne	,, ,,	W. Jan. 23	Apr. 3
GLOUCESTER (evening)	6	English History in Shakespeare	,, ,,	M. Jan. 28	Apr. 8
HEREFORD (evening)	6	Wyclif to Sir Thomas More	,, ,,	M. Jan. 21	Apr. 1
*LEOMINSTER (evening)	6	Not fixed	,, ,,	T. Jan. 22	Apr. 2
READING, U. E. COLL. (even.)	6	Not fixed	,, ,,	Th. Jan. 17	Mar. 28
*REIGATE (afternoon)	12	The Age of Elizabeth (political)	,, ,,	Th. Jan. 17	Mar. 28
ROSS (afternoon)	6	Literature of the 18th Century	,, ,,	T. Jan. 22	Apr. 2
*†SOUTHAMPTON (evening)	12	Not fixed	,, ,,	F. Jan. 18	May 29
STROUD (afternoon)	6	Not fixed	,, ,,	T. Jan. 29	Apr. 9
*STROUD (evening)	6	Not fixed	,, ,,	T. Jan. 29	Apr. 9
SWANSEA (evening)	6	Not fixed	,, ,,	F. Jan. 25	Apr. 5
*†WINDSOR & ETON (afternoon)	12	Architecture	F. BOND, M.A.	Th. Jan. 24	Apr. 4
†HENLOW (evening)	12	The English Citizen	W. M. CHILDS, B.A.	W. Jan. 16	Mar. 27
†WEST BRIGHTON (evening)	12	Three Centuries of Working-class History	W. A. S. HEWINS, M.A.	Th. Jan. 24	Apr. 18
GRIMSBY (evening)	6	Not fixed	J. A. HOBSON, M.A.	T. Jan. 22	Apr. 2
MIDHURST (afternoon)	6	English Novelists	,, ,,	W. Jan. 16	Mar. 27
†CARLISLE (afternoon)	12	Architecture	J. E. PHYTHIAN	T. Jan. 15	Apr. 9
CHESTER (afternoon)	6	Architecture	,, ,,	T. Jan. 22	Apr. 2
†BODMIN (evening)	12	South Africa	W. B. WORSFOLD M.A.	F. Jan. 25	Apr. 5
†CAMBORNE (evening)	12	South Africa	,, ,,	F. Jan. 18	Mar. 29
†FALMOUTH (evening)	12	South Africa	,, ,,	Th. Jan. 17	Mar. 28
†HELSTON (evening)	12	South Africa	,, ,,	T. Jan. 22	Apr. 2
†LAUNCESTON (evening)	12	South Africa	,, ,,	W. Jan. 16	Mar. 27
†PENZANCE (evening)	12	South Africa	,, ,,	M. Jan. 21	Apr. 1
†REDRUTH (evening)	12	South Africa	,, ,,	Th. Jan. 24	Apr. 4
†ST. AUSTELL (evening)	12	South Africa	,, ,,	T. Jan. 15	Mar. 26
†TRURO (evening)	12	South Africa	,, ,,	M. Jan. 14	Mar. 25
BANBURY (evening)	6	Crust of the Earth	C.CARUS-WILSON,F.G.S.	Th. Jan. 17	Mar. 28
*†BATH (afternoon)	12	Not fixed	A. H. FISON, D.Sc.	Th. Jan. 17	Mar. 28
†BATH (evening)	12	Recent Discoveries with the Telescope and Spectroscope	,, ,,	Th. Jan. 17	Mar. 28
†BOURNEMOUTH (evening)	12	Forces of Nature	,, ,,	F. Jan. 18	Mar. 29
†NEWPORT (evening)	12	Not fixed	,, ,,	Th. Jan. 24	Apr. 4
†RYDE (afternoon)	12	Recent Discoveries with the Telescope and Spectroscope	,, ,,	Th. Jan. 24	Apr. 4
†VENTNOR (evening)	12	Physical Astronomy	,, ,,	F. Jan. 25	Apr. 5

* Arrangements not yet completed. † Continued from Autumn Session.

Note.—Application for Courses and all information as to fees, &c., can be obtained from The Secretary, University Extension Office, Examination Schools, Oxford.

INFORMATION TO CONTRIBUTORS.

All communications should be addressed to the Editor, OXFORD UNIVERSITY EXTENSION GAZETTE, University Press, Oxford.

All matter intended for insertion in the September issue should reach him not later than August 20.

Contributions should be written on one side of the paper only, and must be accompanied by the name of the writer (not necessarily for publication).

N.B.—*All orders should carefully specify the full title,* OXFORD UNIVERSITY EXTENSION GAZETTE.

OXFORD UNIVERSITY

EXTENSION GAZETTE.

VOL. IV. NO. 48.] SEPTEMBER, 1894. [ONE PENNY.

N.B.—Local Organizers of Oxford University Extension Lectures are invited to send to the Secretary, Extension Office, Examination Schools, Oxford, copies of any journals containing notices of, or references to, Extension work.

NOTES AND COMMENTS.

The death of Mr. Walter Pater is a heavy blow to English letters and to Oxford life. The University can ill afford to lose a figure already so distinguished and destined to larger fame. To us, in particular, who had been looking forward to his promised lectures at the Summer Meeting, the news came with appalling suddenness. Almost the very day on which we had hoped to hear him brought the tidings of his death. He set a high example of exquisite patience in workmanship, of fine freshness of perception, of fastidious delicacy of thought. The 'elaborate and life-long education of receptive powers' was his message to the fellow-learners of his time. And, at the moment of his death, the memory travels back to the noble words in which he spoke of the last hours of Marius, the Epicurean. 'At this moment, his unclouded receptivity of soul, grown so steadily through all those years, from experience to experience, was at its height; the house was ready for the possible guest; the tablet of the mind white and smooth, for whatsoever divine fingers might choose to write there.'

.·.

Mr. Whibley's amusing article on 'The Farce of University Extension' will be answered, we believe, in another place. Here then it is enough to say that, if University Extension were what he imagines it to be, it would fully deserve his censure. We believe Mr. Whibley to be possessed by a sincere conviction that our work is an educational fraud. The odd thing is that he has taken no pains whatever to bring his suspicions to the test of facts. Had he done so, he would have had the satisfaction of finding that his fears are entirely without foundation. Instead of that, he now stands in the foolish position of having misled the public as well as himself. For our own part, however, we are obliged to him for his trouble. Intemperate and ill-founded criticism swiftly recoils on those who utter it.

.·.

Mr. Arthur Acland's speech on the Education Estimates the other day was a noteworthy utterance. It foreshadowed intelligent changes in the award of science grants by South Kensington, and it emphasized the view that the function of the State in public education is to supply ' test, stimulus, advice, dignity,' not to crush private initiative or to centralize administration.

.·.

Scholarships for the Summer Meeting, 1895. The students attending the Summer Meeting held in Oxford last month very kindly subscribed the sum of £45, which they placed in the hands of the Secretary with a request that he would devote it to the furtherance of the work. This gift, which was accompanied by many valued expressions of good will, has been made the nucleus of a fund to enable poor students to attend the Summer Meeting of 1895.

In the Vienna *Neue Freie Presse* for Aug. 10 there is a long account of the Oxford Summer Meeting from the pen of Dr. E. Nader, who gives a vivid description of the lectures and debates during the first few days of the Meeting.

.·.

The promising members of Mr. Gibson's Greek class have all consented to continue their study of the languages Some of them will join the London classes, while Mr. Gibson has kindly consented to direct the work of those who live at a distance, by means of correspondence.

.·.

We are glad to learn from the Report recently published by the local committee at Brighton that two Greek classes, one for elementary and the other for more advanced students, have been started in the town under the guidance of the Rev. E. Luce. There are nine students in the one and seven in the other. It is probable that there will be an increase in the numbers next session. During the past year the Committee applied to the Town Council for an increased grant to meet the expenses of the lectures, and in reply the Council expressed their wish to take over the work of University Extension as part of their scheme of technical education in the borough, and asked whether the Committee would agree to this transfer. The Committee have approved the scheme, and recommend that the Council should be requested to relieve the managers of the University Extension scheme of the branch of their work consisting of lectures in science and technical subjects, and with that object they suggest that the Council should institute courses of lectures on scientific and technical subjects in connexion with their Technical Institution. In the event of the Council agreeing to undertake this work, the University Extension committee would confine their own work to courses in history and literature for which subjects no grants from public money are as yet available. It is interesting to notice that the deficit for which the Committee is responsible amounts to £19 15s. 10d., of which as much as £18 5s. has been incurred in respect of science courses.

.·.

The essay which was placed first in the competition for the Bournemouth Students' Association Scholarship (tenable at the Summer Meeting), is printed in the new issue of the *Bournemouth Students' Association Gazette*. There is also a summary of the work which will be undertaken at the Bournemouth centre during the coming session. The attendance at the afternoon lectures has steadily risen since the spring of 1889, but the paper work has fallen off. This defect we hope that the Students' Association will be able to remove. The *Gazette* also contains an appreciative account of Part I of the Oxford Summer Meeting. We congratulate Miss Punch on the sustained interest of the journal which she conducts. The Bournemouth centre has made encouraging progress and may do great things for the movement in that part of England.

1

<table>
<tr><td>The Day
Training
College.</td><td></td></tr>
</table>

One of the most important duties of the University at the present time is to strengthen its connexion with the system of public education. Much depends upon the prosperity of the Day Training Colleges which have been established in recent years at the Universities and at some of the University Colleges. Dr. Pope, whose work as Censor of the Non-Collegiate Delegacy is well known both in Oxford and the country, has felt obliged owing to the pressure of other duties to resign his office of Secretary of the University Day Training College here. We are glad to see that Mr. G. N. Richardson, of Oriel and Pembroke Colleges, has been nominated for appointment in his place. A better choice could not have been made.

. . .

There is a judicious and thoughtful article in the current number of the *Church Quarterly Review* on the position of the Non-Collegiate Students in Oxford. The writer justly dwells on the historic importance of this element in academic life and points out the facilities for economical residence in the University which are now offered by the Non-Collegiate Delegacy.

. . .

Mr. J. A. Hobson contributes an interesting article on 'Popular Instruction in Economics' to the August number of *University Extension* (Philadelphia). He believes that economic teaching may be made as popular as it would admittedly be useful in the centres. The great interest shown in the Economic courses at the recent Summer Meeting supports his view.

. . .

Philadelphia Summer Meeting. One of the most satisfactory features in this year's work for University Extension has been the success of the Summer Meetings. We are glad to learn that the second Summer Meeting at Philadelphia has in every way rewarded the patient thought and labour of its promoters. Three hundred and fifty students attended the Meeting. Of these, 135 took the courses in the department of Music. The remainder were about equally divided between the courses in (1) Literature, Science and Art, (2) Mathematics, (3) Pedagogy, (4) History and Civics, and (5) Economics and Sociology. The last-mentioned course deserves specially honourable mention. Its staff of lecturers comprised many of the best-known economists in America, and the course of instruction was exactly what an advanced student of economics would most desire. We heartily congratulate the American University Extension Society, and Dr. James and Dr. Devine in particular, on the success of one of the most important experiments in economic teaching which has yet been made. To return to the statistics of the Meeting as a whole, we learn that the courses lasted four weeks, that more than sixty lecturers were engaged, and that the aggregate of lectures was 504.

. . .

The *University Extension Bulletin* for August gives an excellent report of the Philadelphia Summer Meeting.

. . .

In the current issue of the *University Extension World* there is an encouraging account of the first Summer Quarter (or, as we should call it in England, Long Vacation Term) at the University of Chicago. Alone, among the Universities of the world, Chicago is trying to make the work of its academic year continuous—the Long Vacation being abandoned. Last year the World's Fair interrupted the scheme, but this Summer the experiment has been tried in earnest. Seventy members of the Faculty remained in residence, offering between them 150 courses of instruction. The number of students who availed themselves of these facilities was 540. Of these, 200 were regular students of the University continuing their work instead of taking the usual vacation. The remainder were new students, the University Extension centres supplying a large contingent. A large number of

the new students were teachers in other Universities or in schools, the faculties of forty-one Universities or Colleges being represented. Forty graduates came from the Southern States. The *University Extension World* reports that the experiment has been an 'assured success' and points out that the 'Summer Quarter' is in effect the Summer Meeting of the University of Chicago.

. . .

University Extension in Australia. A very good number of the *Melbourne University Extension Journal* reaches us from the Antipodes. The movement in Australia has naturally suffered from the prevailing depression, but the Melbourne University Extension Board has not relaxed its efforts for a moment, and is now rewarded by satisfactory signs of revival. Taking the circumstances into account, it is a remarkable thing that University Extension has held its ground in Victoria all through the bad times. In New South Wales, the University of Sydney has thrown itself into the work with energy and deserved success, the energetic Secretary, Mr. Arthur W. Jose, reporting the arrangement of a considerable number of courses. We learn also that University Extension is prospering in Queensland, and that the University of Tasmania is also making experiments on Extension lines.

. . .

In the current number of the *Student* (R. Ward & Co., Newcastle on Tyne), there is a brightly written interview with Mr. James Stuart, M.P., from the pen of Mr. Keatley Moore.

. . .

The *University Extension World* (Chicago) appears in a new and improved form. The current issue is abundantly illustrated with portraits of professors of the University of Chicago. Four numbers will in future appear in each year—the months of publication being January, April, July, and October. Mr. Francis W. Shepardson is the editor of the magazine. The Director of the Chicago University Extension is Professor Nathaniel Butler, whose bright speeches at the London Congress will be long remembered. In his capable hands, we foresee a prosperous future for the important branch of University Extension now under his care.

. . .

Extension Day was celebrated at Melbourne on December 16. This festival is happily devised for the purpose of giving opportunities of reunion to University Extension students and their teachers. The University buildings and grounds were thrown open to the visitors, all of whom were members of town and country Extension centres. Lectures were given at frequent intervals during the morning and afternoon. In the evening a conversazione was held, at one point of which the chairman of the University Extension Board gave a report of the year's work, speaking hopefully of the future of the movement. The delegates from distant centres were hospitably entertained by professors of the University and others, and the opportunity was wisely seized of holding a conference of local secretaries and representatives, at which many matters of organization were frankly discussed.

. . .

We understand that Professor H. B. Adams of Johns Hopkins University is writing a monograph on University Extension in America for the series which Commissioner W. T. Harris issues from the Education Department at Washington.

. . .

We have received a parcel of excellent syllabuses from the Brussels University Extension. They are well arranged and carefully edited. Among them are syllabuses on Economics, Sociology, Belgian History, Palaeontology, Physiology and Hygiene. Each pamphlet contains a full analysis of the lectures, and a bibliography with suggestions for study.

THE SIXTH SUMMER MEETING.

AFTER the bustle of August, Oxford is empty again. And now we can take stock of the Summer Meeting and mark the signs of progress or change. The process is a pleasant one, for, beyond doubt, no previous Meeting has been so educationally successful as that which has just drawn to its close. So far from having lost its freshness or vitality, the gathering is fuller than ever of promise for the future.

First, there has been a marked growth of systematic work. The classes in Part II have become one of the most successful features of the Meeting. Many of them were twice as large as previous experience had allowed us to expect, and in all of them, the industry, regularity and enthusiasm of the students deserved the highest praise.

Next, we have welcomed a larger number of students from distant countries than ever before. Thirteen American and foreign Universities were represented in the roll of students. Friends from America were with us in considerable numbers and more than twenty students came from Scandinavia. In the old days, Oxford was an international University, and there are many signs that our more recent isolation is passing away. Among the lecturers were many distinguished members of the Faculties of other Universities, and specially welcome were Professor Rein of Jena, Dr. Buckham of the University of Vermont, Dr. Devine from Philadelphia, Dr. Billings from Washington and Herr Povlsen from Denmark. Their lectures were greatly valued by all who heard them. We were also fortunate in having with us Mr. Arthur Berry and Dr. Lawrence from Cambridge, and Captain Abney from South Kensington, whose presence marked the unity of purpose which inspires the educational work of the English Universities and of the Education Department. And among the visitors who did not lecture special mention should be made of Mr. Frederick Miles, Dr. Edmund James, and Mr. H. W. Rolfe, representatives of the American University Extension Society and all of them old and valued friends.

The staff of lecturers comprised almost all the senior lecturers of the Oxford University Extension and many more of the resident Oxford teachers than has been the case in former years. No less than twenty-seven tutors or lecturers of Colleges took part in the instruction. This will strengthen the connexion between the resident teachers of the University and the Extension work. It is not possible in these columns to give a detailed summary of the lectures or even to repeat the lecturers' names. It must suffice to say that, by general consent, the lecturers surpassed themselves. But special mention must be made of the fact that the course on the Seventeenth Century was inaugurated by one of the most honoured of living historians, the greatest living authority on the period under review, Dr. Samuel Rawson Gardiner.

Apart from the lectures on theological subjects, which were much appreciated, the chief courses of study were as follows : (1) The history, literature, art and philosophy of the Seventeenth Century ; (2) a series of non-partisan lectures on the Life and Duties of the Citizen ; (3) Greek Language and Literature ; (4) Economics ; (5) Chemistry ; (6) Hygiene ; (7) Geology ; and (8) The Theory and Art of Teaching. Special reports of some of these courses will appear in this, or the next, number of the *Gazette*; with regard to the others, it is satisfactory to note the keen interest aroused by the lectures of Mr. Graham Wallas and others on civic subjects, and the continued success of the sequence of historical lectures which began in 1891 and will be continued next year. Nowhere else, we believe, can a student hear a chosen period discussed from every point of view by a number of experts, each taking some aspect of its political or economic history, some master of its science, art or philosophy, or some leader of its religious thought. The seventeenth century raises many fundamental points of still-living controversy. And yet, though no problem was evaded, the students were impressed by a sense of underlying unity of purpose rather than confused by perplexing contradictions. The interest of the lectures was much increased by a successful performance of Browning's *Strafford*, which we owed to the kindness of past and present members of the O.U.D.S., aided by Mr. Mackinnon

of Trinity and Mr. J. A. R. Marriott. And not less helpful in giving vividness to the teaching were the visits to the Colleges, Mr. Wells' excellent lectures on the history of Oxford, and the excursions to places in the neighbourhood of Oxford associated with the events of the seventeenth century. Among the latter, the students will cherish grateful memories of Lady Verney's lecture and of the hospitality of Claydon House.

The one drawback was that our numbers in Part I were one hundred short of the maximum for which arrangements had been made. This was partly due to the fact that the Meeting began a few days before most of the teachers in secondary schools were liberated from their duties. School holidays began late this year and the Meeting was, it seems, fixed too early for teachers, from whose ranks the majority of the students come. This error will, we believe, be avoided in future years. Again, the British Association, which met this year in Oxford from Aug. 8–15, doubtless drew off a few who would otherwise have come to the Extension lectures. And, in the third place, many were deterred from applying for tickets because an impression had got abroad that all the tickets were sold. This misunderstanding was spread broadcast by a paragraph in the newspapers, and it is known that a large number of students gave up all thoughts of attending the Meeting in consequence of it.

Finally the success of the gathering was largely due to the *esprit de corps* which animated it, to the willing and courteous aid of the Committee of Reference, to the kindness of the University and College authorities, and to the hospitality and consideration which we received on every hand. Nor was the Meeting spoiled by the weather which, for August, was execrable.

The Hampshire County Council and the University Extension College, Reading.

THE following recommendation of its Technical Instruction Committee was adopted by the Hampshire County Council on August 13 last. The Council of the Reading University Extension College now includes the chairmen of one County Council and of the Technical Instruction Committee of two other County Councils.

' The Prospectus of the Agricultural Department of the College having been fully inquired into, it is proposed to make a grant of £75 to the Council of the College in respect of the session 1894-5, it being intended that this grant should be renewable annually, and should be paid out of the sums set aside for systematic day teaching under the Secondary Schools and scholarship scheme.

The Council of the College are prepared on their part in return for this grant to provide for the representation of the Hampshire County Council upon their body; to conduct experimental plots in the county in accordance with the system now adopted in several counties, in consideration of the reimbursement of actual out-of-pocket expenses only, and without charge for the services of the Instructor; and to admit all pupils from the administrative county who may attend the instruction in their Agricultural Department at a fee reduced by 25 per cent. from the ordinary College fee.

The objects to be kept in view in establishing the experimental plots will be (1) the conduct of scientific experiments bearing upon practical agricultural problems affecting the districts of the county where the plots would be established; (2) the dissemination by means of leaflets published at the expense of the Technical Education Committee of the data so obtained among the agriculturists of the district; and (3) the explanation by means of lectures, if thought advisable, of the scientific methods of investigating practical agricultural problems which are adopted in conducting such experimental plots. The localities for conducting the experiments and the nature of the experiments to be conducted will be settled by the Technical Education Committee and the College conjointly. The assistance of the above named members of the Royal Counties Agricultural Association has also been invited in making the arrangements.

2

It is proposed that steps should be taken to start these plots after the August meeting of the County Council.

Your Committee further propose that the Reading College shall be an institution for higher technical teaching at which Higher or Senior Scholarships shall be tenable, the probable date of the first award of such scholarships being September, 1895.

Your Committee are satisfied that the course of agricultural instruction, which includes farm work under the supervision of practical agriculturists, has been drawn up on sound lines, and is suitable for lads and young men who intend to become farmers.

At the same time it is satisfactory to observe that the organization of courses will permit a scholar to take a general scientific course during his first year at the College, entering afterwards the specialized agricultural course if he finds his bent to be in that direction.

It is recommended that the necessary representation of the County Council upon the Governing Body of the Reading College be provided for by the nomination of Mr. J. Bonham-Carter as the representative of the County Council.'

LECTURES IN AID OF EXTENSION CENTRES.

MR. J. WELLS, M.A., Fellow and Tutor of Wadham College, authorizes us to say that he is willing to lecture on Oxford at any centres in the South of England on Dec. 17, 18, 19 and 20, in aid of the funds of the local University Extension committees. The lecture will be fully illustrated by lantern slides. No charge will be made for the lecture or for the lecturer's travelling expenses, but the local committees must provide a lantern and make the necessary local arrangements. Communications should be addressed direct to Mr. Wells at Wadham College, Oxford.

Those who had the good fortune to hear Mr. Wells' lectures on the history of Oxford at the Summer Meeting will appreciate the kindness of the offer which he permits us to announce.

REPORTS FROM THE CENTRES.

BAKEWELL.—The General Annual Meeting of the 'Students' Association took place on Saturday, August 25. The committee provided afternoon tea for the students in the Town Hall before the meeting. About forty members of the Association were present. The prize and pass lists were presented to the successful candidates by Mr. H. Brooke-Taylor, who also presided at the meeting. All the students who passed the examination last year obtained 'Distinction.' The statement of account, showing a small balance in hand, was passed and arrangements were made for the work of the autumn session. We look forward to a successful term of work on the 'English Novelists' under the guidance of Mr. Marriott. The first students' meeting will be held on Thursday, Sept. 20.

OXFORD.—The special arrangements which have been made at this centre for pupil teachers are announced in the following circular:—'Extra marks are given in the Queen's Scholarship examination to pupil teachers who present certificates awarded during their fourth year, after examination on a course of twenty-four lectures, of which they have attended not less than twenty, and the subject of which has been approved by the Education Department. In order to meet the needs of pupil teachers who will sit for their Queen's Scholarship examination in December, 1896, the Oxford local committee have arranged for two courses of twelve lectures on the Making of England, with special reference to the history of Oxford, the first of which will be delivered in the winter of 1894-95, and the second in the winter of 1895-96. An examination on the subject-matter of the twenty-four lectures will be held at the end of the second course, and certificates gained in it will be recognized by the Department as entitling the holders to extra marks in the Queen's Scholarship examination held in December, 1896. Special arrangements will be made for the pupil teachers who wish to take their Queen's Scholarship examination in December, 1895.' The lecturers for the coming winter will be Mr. Horsburgh and Mr. Marriott.

THE GREEK CLASSES.

THE Advanced Class was a very small one (consisting only of three members), but worked with very keen interest. The text was Homer's *Odyssey*, Bk. i. lines 1-230. Special attention was given to the grammar, and almost every word was parsed.

The Elementary Class consisted of twenty members, who displayed an immense amount of enthusiasm. This was seen particularly in—

(*a*) The regularity of the attendances.

(*b*) The amount of time (not less than two hours *per diem*) devoted to the preparation for each meeting.

(*c*) The attendance of considerable numbers of the members at extra classes held at awkward times.

(*d*) The patience and sustained attention of the members during constant repetition and revision.

The ground covered by this class embraced the nouns, adjectives, pronouns and active voice of the regular verb in Abbott and Mansfield's *Greek Grammar*, together with thirty pages of Underhill's *Easy Exercises in Greek Accidence*. Both classes will be examined by Mr. Wells, Fellow and Tutor of Wadham, the Advanced *viva voce*, and the latter on paper. The result of this Examination (for which fourteen members have entered) may, I think, be expected with confidence, and I am very pleased to learn that it is the intention of most of the students to make the foundation laid at this Meeting a basis for further study.

HENRY G. GIBSON, M.A.

.•.

ONE of the most successful undertakings of the Extension course this summer has been the instruction in Greek of two classes, one for beginners, the other for advanced students. The difficulties of such a task are numberless. At a gathering like this at Oxford, the instructor finds himself confronted unavoidably by an ungraded class. His pupils are unequal in age, natural ability, previous mental discipline, knowledge of other languages, present power and willingness to apply themselves, and—as practical a difference as any among the beginners—varied degrees of ignorance of the language supposed to be studied for the first time. Only genius in teaching can harmonize these antagonistic elements, and make the class profitable to all.

The beginner's class—and that is without doubt the test class for a teacher—this year, in fifteen one-hour-and-a-half lessons, covering two weeks and a half, fairly mastered the declensions of Greek nouns, pronouns, and adjectives, the conjugation of λύω, gained a small vocabulary, and prepared illustrative exercises; in fact gave substantial promise of a not remote enjoyment of Greek literature. Such an accomplishment was made possible by the willingness of the class to recite, an advantageous spirit not always found in mixed classes. Evidence not only of the satisfactory work of the pupils, but also of the ability and excellent method of the instructor, was made in the two examinations taken by the elementary class, one after nine meetings, the other after thirteen meetings. The results of the latter were as follows :

Report of the Examiner.

I. The advanced class were examined by me *viva voce* in about 230 lines of Homer's *Odyssey*, Bk. i. There were three candidates : of these one did very well, one well, and the third only fairly : she had worked well, but her knowledge of constructions, &c., was very imperfect. The parsing of all three was good, that of Miss Lake very good.

II. In the elementary class the work offered was Greek Grammar up to (and including) the active voice of λύω, and fifty pages of Underhill's exercises. In other words the grammar was rather more than half what a candidate would offer for Responsions. I therefore made this examination my standard, both in setting the questions and in marking.

The result was at once surprising and satisfactory: 6 of the 11 candidates obtained more than 75 per cent., and 5 of these were over 85 per cent. The work was exceedingly sensible and accurate.

The five other candidates ranged from 45 to 23 per cent. Their papers showed signs of work, and were what I should rather have anticipated from the whole of a class, the majority of whom began Greek a fortnight ago. I am very glad to find my most sanguine expectations surpassed in the case of the majority. Mr. Gibson and his class are to be congratulated on a fortnight's excellent work.

J. WELLS, M.A.

Fellow and Tutor of Wadham College.

Perhaps the most insidious foe of all against which the instructor had to contend was discouragement. With the pace of the class set by the hard-working and capable half-dozen, the other twelve or fourteen found it difficult to keep up, and were ready to take refuge in despair, that impediment to all progress. But by judicious individual exercises in writing, extra time given to backward pupils, and untiring devotion to his work, Mr. Gibson resisted successfully this human weakness, and prevented the evaporation of original enthusiasm.

A. P. LOWELL.

[*Reports of Classes in Hygiene (Dr. Wade), Chemistry (Mr. Marsh), Geology (Prof. Green and Mr. Badger), Economics (Mr. Hobson), Education (Mr. Montgomery), and of the Greek Class are unavoidably held over till the October Number.*]

THE EDUCATION CLASS.

THE Education Class was a new experiment this year—but one which had about it many signs of success. The numbers attending the lectures fluctuated only very slightly. The largest attendance consisted of sixty-one women and fourteen men. The leading idea of the course was to show the relations of psychological theories to practical methods of teaching and how these methods may be realized in actual school-work. Twelve lectures were given, descriptive of the general character and results of psychological inquiry, and step by step the applications of the theories to practice were explained and exemplified by sketches of actual lessons. Immediately following upon each group of illustrative lessons came subjects on which the students were required themselves to sketch outlines of somewhat similar lessons; and these outlines were corrected by the lecturer and their *general* features criticized before the whole class—details of criticism being reserved for a personal interview between the lecturer and each student who had sent in a sketch. Altogether forty students sketched lessons of various kinds—nearly all doing so on every occasion. Thirty-seven of these were women, of whom thirty-two were teachers; and three were men, of whom one was a teacher already, and the others intended to become so very shortly. It may be mentioned that experience showed that great advantage was to be gained by two, or even three, students uniting to sketch a single lesson. Not only was the number of sketches to read and correct—no slight task—considerably lessened, but the sketches themselves were as a rule very much improved in quality.

The period over which the course extended (Aug. 8 to 23 inclusive) was too short for any very decided opinion to be expressed on the results produced; but the class as a whole showed unmistakeable interest in the work, and the sketches of lessons gave clear evidence of an advance in the appreciation of the value of psychology to the teacher, and of an improved insight into the true nature of teaching. Had the students found it possible to restrict themselves somewhat more to the course on Education, and to read concurrently with the lectures some text-book of psychology, such as Professor Sully's *Handbook for Teachers*, there can be no doubt that the results would have been still better. But even without this full concentration of interest the results were decidedly encouraging; and it is not rash to hope that in very many cases the work begun at Oxford this summer may hereafter be carried further by the students themselves, and so the desire to found teaching on a more scientific basis may become more general and be better understood.

The course was rendered much more interesting and much more valuable by the addition of other lectures besides those already mentioned. First amongst these

must be mentioned a set of six lectures on Hygiene for schools by Dr. Wade, in which the value of physiology to the teacher was very strikingly shown. Dr. Rein, the well-known professor of Pedagogy of the University of Jena, gave three lectures on the Development of German Pedagogy and Theoretical Pedagogics divided into the theory of the purpose and the theory of the means of Education—these two last being naturally from the Herbartan standpoint. Unfortunately for many these lectures were given in German; but those who could understand the language could not have failed to notice the remarkable skill and lucidity with which the subjects were treated. Mr. A. D. Hall gave a most useful exposition of the optical lantern, and the mode of using it in schools. The Rev. Dr. Buckham, President of the University of Vermont, gave a very suggestive address on Education in America—especially suitable to the present moment when we are considering the organization of Secondary Education; and Herr Alfred Povlsen described the High Schools of Denmark. Altogether students could hardly complain of any lack of variety in the course set before them.

H. COURTHOPE BOWEN.

LETTERS TO THE EDITOR.

[*We do not hold ourselves responsible for the opinions expressed by our correspondents.*]

The Education Class.

DEAR SIR,—As a teacher of many years' standing—one who, alas! has had to train herself in the midst of, and partly by means of, her work—I may perhaps venture to offer an opinion upon the course in education provided for Extension students at this Summer Meeting.

The Theory of Education is a subject in which I conclude we had most of us at any rate dabbled; but, unless we had gone through a regular course of instruction in Pedagogics, I suspect we had but small acquaintance with the systematic application of that theory to our every-day teaching. Far be it from me to assert that such a course of instruction has been given in little more than a fortnight, even by such a lecturer as Mr. Courthope Bowen. We shall make an enormous mistake, if we go away from Oxford pluming ourselves on having attended the classes, and thinking we have nothing further to do. We shall certainly need to take both time and pains to digest what we have learnt; for the very amount and weight of the information received, will have hindered its orderly assimilation. Then if we are wise, we shall carry on the good work which Mr. Bowen has taken such infinite pains to begin. Some of us may be able to do this under regular training; but doubtless there are many who, like myself, must be content with what they can snatch in the intervals of hard work, and to such in particular I consider this course an inestimable boon.

My own experience is: (1) that the lectures in the Theory of Education have recalled, modified and greatly enlarged my previous knowledge of Psychology; (2) that the practical lectures have done more than anything I ever learnt before, to help me in applying the principles of that science to the details of my work, and that in such a clear way as to be of real definite value; (3) the drawing up of lesson notes has shown me very plainly little unmethodical and inaccurate ways which I hope to mend; and lastly the lectures in general have made me determine to embrace every opportunity that may present itself for continuing my study of the science of Education, which, I take it, was the lecturer's chief aim. Further, the course has had the advantage of bringing me into contact with some of my fellow-workers in a way which has been both pleasurable and profitable.

Mr. Bowen will forgive my objecting that the methods be so ably advocates, involve a greater amount of leisure for preparation than has ever fallen to *my* lot as a teacher. I fully acknowledge the beauty of the path down which he would fain lead us; but, I fear me, I must be content to follow humbly a long way behind!

I might add, that in private schools and in families, teaching has many limitations. True, the march of educational reform is to improve away all these; but meanwhile will the pioneers of the movement make allowances for the shortcomings of the rank and file, often sadly hampered by the conditions of their work ?

If I may do so without impertinence, I should wish to pay my small tribute of gratitude to all connected with this new departure in University Extension teaching. The courtesy and self-devotion of the lecturers needs no comment of mine; but I should like to express my particular appreciation of the privilege of listening to Dr. Rein, and the intense pleasure it was to me, to be lifted for the moment above the clouds that too often envelop a teacher's daily life, into the pure atmosphere of a lofty educational ideal.

Yours faithfully,
ANNA M. LAKE.

Oxford, *Aug.* 18, 1894.

.'.

The Crush for Tickets.

DEAR SIR,—Before the first flush of the Summer Meeting enthusiasm has begun to fade, I should like to say a few words on a matter which very likely is not even known to some of the students, but which nevertheless concerns us all. I refer to the peculiar scenes enacted every morning during the First Part of the Meeting in the Reception Room when cards, admitting to the afternoon College visits, were given out.

Notwithstanding the convenient central position of the rooms in the High, the narrow dark stairs leading to them gave an almost unconscious impulse to try and get up as quickly as possible. There is always something stimulating to the British mind in a struggle to get the first place. Is there not the actual pleasure of the elbowing, the rush and push, and the prospective pleasure of the glorious moment when you have victoriously secured your morsel of pasteboard or what not—one instant in advance of your neighbour?

So astounding was the eagerness to get admission you might have supposed the Colleges were at vanishing point ; this opportunity missed, never would they be seen again ! The struggle to get up first and prevent your neighbour from gaining on you was so intense, that the most patient and persevering of Secretaries and her assistants were not allowed to come up the stairs and get to their desk for fear they should prove to be rivals in the race ! Not till much explanation and remonstrance had been employed were they even suffered to pass, though not till their arrival could the place be opened, and the ardently coveted tickets be given out ! I will pass over the state of confusion in the room, till forcible steps were taken to prevent the breaking of chairs and tables and the hurling themselves of Students against the Secretaries' desk while trampling on one another.

Now if our Summer Meeting have a moral side, the lesson taught is surely that blessings should be shared, privileges made common ; if we are drawn into a fellowship of work, a community of intellectual interest, why should there not be a fellowship in recreation and amusement also? The one occasion on which students could show individually their sense of the spirit in which the Summer Meetings have been planned and carried out for them by others, is employed in ousting one another in a rush and scramble to get each for him or herself a 'something' of which he seeks to deprive another !

The irony is complete when we add that the possessor does not even always value or make use of the dear-bought prize, for the tickets have been found flung aside, if another more amusing prospect presented itself at the last moment ! I feel confident that no students would for an instant have acted in this way had they stopped to think. Those dark stairs must momentarily have obliterated all consciousness of the duties and obligation they owed to the Secretaries and to one another. Now that we have returned to the cool light of day and reason, you will perhaps allow me this opportunity of drawing attention to what did happen, and expressing the hope that such scenes will never be enacted again (even by students hurrying on to their 9 a.m. theological lectures) at another Summer Meeting in Oxford.

I am, Sir,

Faithfully yours,

P. W. BRIDGES.

Proposed Ribbon for Extension Students.

DEAR SIR,—I shall be obliged if you will kindly make it known that it has been decided to start a ribbon, suitable for hat bands, &c., to be worn by Extension students. It will combine in equal proportions the colours of Oxford and Cambridge, dark and light blue, being divided by a narrow red stripe. The ribbon will not be ready for a fortnight. The price we hope will not exceed 1s. 3d. per yard.

Those who would like to see patterns before ordering may send stamped and addressed envelopes to—

Miss WESTALL,
c/o The Editor,
University Extension Gazette,
Clarendon Press, Oxford.

Yours truly,

Aug. 20, 1894.   E. A. W.

*Correspondence held over :—*E. B.W. ('Training of Teachers '); E. Wilson ('A Teacher's Thoughts about the Education Class '); Hermine Ritzhaupt ('Suggestion for next Summer Meeting ').

THE DANISH POPULAR HIGH SCHOOL.

By ALFRED POVLSEN.

(Director President of the Association of the Popular High Schools and Agricultural Colleges in Denmark).

THE Delegates of the University Extension have honoured me with permission to attend the Summer Meeting here in Oxford, and have invited me to deliver a lecture on the educational system in Denmark.

I am most happy to respond to this invitation, but first I must beg you to excuse my bad English, and hope you will bear with my shortcomings in that respect. With the aid of my papers and the patience of my auditors, I hope it will be possible for me to give a correct conception of the intellectual work with which I am to deal in this lecture. I must limit the task to a description of those principles and forms of popular education which in this century have had the greatest influence on our whole school-work, and have been most characteristically expressed in the so-called Popular High Schools.

The subject I am going to treat of is indeed a familiar one to me, as I have been connected with it for fifteen years. I also think that it would be particularly interesting for the present meeting to hear about work done in another country with the same object in view as the University Extension.

The term Popular High School must not confuse or mislead us. In Denmark the name High School is used in a far more extensive manner than in England. The highest educational establishment in Denmark is always called University, and never mentioned under any other name. Popular High Schools have of late been transplanted from Denmark to Norway, Sweden and Finland but they were first established in Denmark, and in this country they have also been most widely extended and have exercised most influence.

Now these schools have existed for fifty years, and next month teachers from all High Schools of the North will assemble in Denmark at a great meeting to celebrate the jubilee of the Danish High Schools. This festival will take place on September 8. On that day, 111 years ago, the man was born who founded Popular High Schools, the poet, the historian, the religious leader, Bishop Grundt-vig, unquestionably the only man to whose native genius we owe reform in Denmark. Though he has been already dead for more than twenty years, his thoughts and systems are as enthusiastically discussed as they were during the first half of the century, when he himself was the leader. Since then they have made progress, and firmly established themselves in every corner of the land, where they have borne ample testimony to the influence of his noble mind. If I were to compare him with any Englishman, it must be Carlyle. Like him, he is in the first place a deeply religious mind, but without laying any stress on dogma. Possessing the same poetical power, he chiefly used it as a historical philosopher. Like Carlyle, he does not dive into history for its own sake, never losing himself in details. Broadly speaking he does not treat history as a science, but seeks in it the unity and grandeur of life — God and man. Carlyle's grand prose-poems on hero-worship have their counterpart in the mythological and historical works of Grundtvig, and it is the same lyrical string that sounds in his numerous hymns and songs. These works of his are pearls, only found by him who sounds the depths of human hearts. · His hymns are now heard in all our churches of all denominations, and his songs are sung in all our schools and homes, regardless of political and social differences. If great genius for one thing is known by its power of uniting and binding together, then Grundtvig undoubtedly is our greatest man. He is, in a word, the national hero of ours.

Again, like Carlyle, he is a sworn enemy of all sorts of formalism, and is also strongly opposed to any set form of fashion in church, literature and politics. As for the rest, his views cannot be classed in ordinary categories, and he can absolutely not be ranked among ordinary partisans, for everywhere he stands on his own ground. Thus also in relation to schools and popular education.

In the first instance he was only incited by human sympathy to work for his fellow-men. This feeling especially shows itself in his love for the uncultivated, unartificial man. Like Carlyle, he venerates the common sense of the peasant and the horny hand of the labourer. The upper classes, the crown of society, must never forget its root and origin, and its dependence upon the lower strata for support. Yet his love for the lower classes is not this sickly, dim sentiment, which aims at revolutionizing existing order or disturbing existing relations of work, property and knowledge.

He sees no debasement in being a peasant or a working man, nor any grandeur in being rich in goods or knowledge. Misfortune lies only in poverty, when accompanied by ignorance, immorality and impiety. And the most invaluable treasure of man is, as he says in one of his best school songs, to know God and yourself. In this sentence his whole educational system is expressed. Make every man a servant of God and a master of his task. In these few words are contained the double object of school-work, namely universal and professional education. Universal education need not be scientific. Scientific education is professional, and can never become the possession of the multitude. Children, perhaps also grown-up people, can be trained to pick up the crumbs that fall from the table of science, but intelligence derived in that way will only be fractional, will only become a demi-civilization, a boyish science, as Grundtvig liked to call it, and has just as little to do with real science as with real education. From the Jews he learned that all education must be historical, from the Greeks that it must be poetical ; and the life of the Roman people taught him to shun that amassing of knowledge which has nothing at all to do with the development of conscience and heart.

He strongly opposes the old school system that to his mind is built up upon Roman principles and against the error that knowledge, without developing the inner man, should be able to ennoble the mind or cause a greater happiness. He wants to save the people from the errors which the upper classes labour under, and from the danger that results from bringing the working man too soon into contact with scientific research and book-learning, that is to say, before he has realized his own position and capacities. This must shield him from vain dreams, discontent and distaste for the humble position in which he is placed, and from dislike to manual work.

- Education ought never to be rendered in such a manner that it breeds despondency and contempt for work, but so that it ennobles a man's work and heightens his ability to perform it well. Therefore education must not only be scientific or taken from books, but the balance must be kept between knowledge of the world and knowledge of oneself. Of course every educational work, also the popular one, must make the freest use of science and literature, but these should only be a means to an end. If knowledge is to bear good fruit for the common people, it must first and foremost be educational and nourish the mind, strengthen its morals and its feelings of responsibility. This is the

only way to obtain thorough education, which is to be obtained as well by the peasant as the scholar.

The second aim of the individual ought to be to become an able man in his business and to further the claims of society. To this end instruction in certain subjects, and the communication of certain elementary rudiments of learning, are necessary in order to gain mastery over one's work and obtain influence in one's social position.

The reflections I have just put forth, indicating at once the aim and the impediments of popular education, may be said to express the views of Grundtvig and the men of the school who have assembled around him. They are certainly not new to the members of the University Extension. They naturally present themselves to every one who takes an interest in this matter.

To me it will be of the highest interest to examine the different ways in which this country has set about improving the minds of the people, by what means it has reached the greatest development, and how it has avoided mistakes. I shall now for my part try to illustrate how we in Denmark have exerted ourselves in the same cause and attempt to put forth more plainly how the work is carried on in accordance with the views I have now set forth.

The first impulse to this work was evidently brought about by the general craving for liberty in the middle of this century, and the national feeling of self-respect awakened by the encroachment of Germany.

Grundtvig loved the people, but at first he was no friend of democracy, which to his mind awoke too great expectations about the future and promised much more that it could fulfil. Time has proved he was in the right. But he also saw that the same law exists in popular movements as in natural forces—they must not be opposed but guided. He felt that the time had arrived for action in order that the people should receive education, before getting and making use of their liberty, for the freer the institutions of the people are, the better its education must be. Then he conceived his plan of a Popular High School on a grander scale, and brought it before the king. Denmark was then an absolute monarchy. The king approved the plan, the building-ground was laid out, the capital invested, everything was in order ; but then the king died, and with him the plan was buried. But only to arise in a new form. It has later been thought fortunate that it was not carried out upon the original plan ; it was not that way the thing was to be started.

Grundtvig's thoughts had inspired and brought up a whole staff of young teachers, who also were enthusiastic admirers of his religious and historical views. They now went out among the people to pave the way for the new school, and instead of the one large High School, there arose in the course of time by the assistance and exertion of the population itself minor schools all over the different parts of the country. There are now more than fifty such, and they are all founded by private means and owned by private men (almost without exception the principal himself) or by some local societies. They are all schools for grown-up people. Grundtvig held to the opinion, which experience has shown to be the right one, that it is at the age of from 18 to 25 that the intellectual faculties are most accessible to intellectual influence. Before that age the mind is not sufficiently developed and meditation cannot be awakened ; later on in a more advanced age most minds will be occupied by the practical duties of life. But the age of strong emotional feelings and arduous longings, the 'sturm und drang' period, natural to youth, is the best time for sowing the seed of knowledge and for exercising the personal influence of the teacher. For on the latter all depends.

You will not at all be able to conceive how these schools are arranged by examining their time-tables, the different subjects, &c. ; in this respect a foreigner would find one very much like another, but a native would easily distinguish between them. The head in each establishment makes all the difference. All intellectual influence must be personal. This is the fundamental principle of these schools. Everything depends upon *how* knowledge, education is given, or rather *who* it is that gives it. The first condition for working in this school is therefore that the teacher, besides possessing the pedagogical faculties and means, must himself feel the fervour and zealous warmth for his vocation and possess the power and influence, without which he will not be able to captivate the attention of his hearers or win their confidence. 'Che non arde, non incende,' says the Italian. If the eyes and ears of the pupils are to be opened, their abilities awakened and their will strengthened, then all this must first exist in the personality of the master, and from him it will impart itself to the pupil.

Therefore oral instruction is principally employed, while books only play a very subordinate part in the main work of the school. The mark to be aimed at is not to learn this or that, much or little, but to be made prepared for the teaching of life. If this preparation is made, if the young man has been roused to learn from books and men, he will certainly be able to help himself to that wisdom in life, which he mostly is in need of, and if this intellectual awakening does not take place in the mind of the youth it will be perfectly useless to equip him with a larger or smaller stock of book-learning or accomplishment, for they are in truth not his, and he will never learn to use them rightly.

As I have said before, history is the principal subject. It is also to the study of history that the pupils pay most attention. I venture to say, that it is for the sake of history that the pupils attend the school, and if *it* were withdrawn, the school would soon lose its character. It is very difficult for me to explain how history is taught, as it entirely depends upon the different teachers who treat the subject, but the chief object is to portray the characteristic qualities of historical personages and the predominant character of different ages and peoples, in order to throw a light on all great or small incidents that happen in our own time and life. This is the main point. Here we find mentioned the relation of man and woman, parents and children, master and servant, religious, social and political questions, which all agitate our own times. It is, if you like, a sort of unsystematical, practical life—philosophy, which in this way—the historical—we seek to convey to our pupils.

The prominent faculty of Carlyle, possessed also by Grundtvig, and designated by him as the historical-poetical faculty, must not be wanting in a teacher of history, who wishes to educate the people. He must be able to produce from out of the historical facts and details a vivid picture, for only by those means can he directly bring nourishment to the heterogeneous parts of the human soul.

The school does not teach religion as far as dogmatical instruction goes, neither are the pupils influenced in any certain religious direction; neither are separate lessons on this subject given. But historical teaching is all through religious; that is to say, the hand of God is shown all through the evolution of ages, and in this way the religious feeling is constantly kept awake and exercised. All political agitation is avoided in the school, but it awakens and sharpens judgement by explaining political principles and portraying historical strifes and struggles of society, partly by treating of the constitution of the state and its principal laws. Instruction is of course also given in elementary subjects: Danish, writing, arithmetic, drawing and surveying; moreover in physics, geography, botany and zoology. Clearly expressed lectures are delivered upon the human body and its functions, and we especially try to instil into the pupils rational ideas of those natural forces, which are of so great importance in the life and work of man.

Some schools, especially the Swedish ones, lay great stress upon the instruction in natural science, and make a point of testing the work by means of examinations. In all schools young girls are taught needle-work; in some few instruction is given in slöjd, and every day the pupils have their gymnastic exercises after the system of Ling, which has been universally used. It is especially well adapted to engage the interest of all young people, and helps to keep them healthy and in good spirits. Each large school is provided with a spacious gymnasium, where numbers of young girls suitably dressed assemble to have their lesson.

The work of the school does not terminate with any

examination, neither does it give any admission whatever to any higher academy, to any situation or other worldly advantages. It has always been understood that any appointed public examination would destroy the free and fertilizing communication and appropriation of knowledge, which is the basis of the power and authority of the school. There must not be any advantage gained by frequenting such a school but that which can neither be weighed or measured, or on which a pecuniary estimate can be placed ; no other profit must be derived from the instruction than *the* increase of inner worth, which all good learning gives[1].

The schools are all situated in the country, and nearly all the young men and women who attend them belong to the peasantry. Instruction is ordinarily given separately to the two sexes. The winter school, which lasts five months, is for the male, and the summer school, which lasts three months, for the female pupils. As attendance at school is voluntary, the number of pupils varies at the different schools. At *Ryslinge High School,* of which I am the principal, there were last winter 100 men pupils, and in the summer 110 female pupils.

Here I must mention a thing of the greatest importance. All the pupils board at the school, and thus live during their whole school-life together with the teachers and their families and their own comrades. The masters and their families are present at one or more of the daily meals ; the pupils have also free access to the home of the superintendent and the teachers. I have always found the pupils show great tact in availing themselves of this privilege.

It will easily be understood what an elevating influence this sort of education may exercise over the young. Not only do they learn to respect discipline and order, but their whole behaviour improves partly by dint of instruction, and partly by being brought into constant contact with the teachers and their homes. We all learn to know each other personally and form by degrees a union, so to say a great family or household, share together the labour and the enjoyment of the day, can speak openly and freely with each other, and become at last so familiar that the day of parting always is a sad one, especially for the young girls.

I myself was once a pupil at a High School, and I can testify that through my whole school-life I never heard an oath or indecent language, or ill-natured quarrelling. We were eighty young men living together for five months. This behaviour is not the fruit of prohibition or of strict discipline, but only of the tone that pervades the whole establishment. In social respects this mode of living, among other advantages, has the one that it contributes to equalize classes and abolish social prejudices. Here we find the son of the rich farmer sitting side by side by the common labourer, both receiving the same instruction and, what is more, being brought to know each other. I have often seen the good effects thereof in many parts of the country regarding the relation of farmer and labourer, master and servant.

Regarding the short school-time, five or three months, I must here observe that we are strongly opposed to having the time extended, partly because that would exclude numerous pupils of limited means, and partly because we do not like to take them from or make them unsuited for bodily exertion. If they remained longer at the school, they would doubtless acquire a distaste for their work and a liking for study.

Now it is a fact that almost all the pupils return to their former work. But in many cases the pupil will repeat his visit to the same school, or when some years have passed by to another school. Especially it is not uncommon that pupils, who have a great desire for learning, frequent the so-called Extended Popular High School of Askov, situated near the German frontier. This school has

[1] Here I may quote appropriately the words of Th. Hughes in *Tom Brown's School Days.* When asked, 'Why do you send your son to school,' he answers: 'If only he can become an honest, useful, truth-loving Englishman and a gentleman and a Christian—that is all I wish for!' The man who has said this thoroughly understands the aim and object of our Danish High School.

a better supply of school-materials, has more teachers and better means of instruction than the others. There also are courses extending over two winters for pupils who have formerly attended a Popular High School. Of course here much more stress is laid upon the acquisition of knowledge and professional education.

The proper professional education is however obtained at the so-called Agricultural and Technical Schools or Colleges. They are closely related to the High Schools. The persons who superintend them are on a friendly footing with the High Schools, and their whole plan is laid out upon the same principles ; they work hand in hand with them, receiving not only the majority, but as they say themselves, their best pupils from the High Schools. But it would take too much time to enter further into details concerning these schools.

Another offspring of the High Schools is the lecturing societies, which now by the hundred are established over the whole country. As a rule every lecturing club has its own meeting-house, and the lectures are commonly delivered by the principals and teachers of the High Schools. Every autumn the people from far and wide, country-people and town-people assemble at the several High Schools at a large meeting that lasts several days.

As far as I can see the High Schools have taken up part of the work which in this country is done by University Extension. But they take no part in the gratuitous instruction given to artisans and workmen in the towns. It is the students of Copenhagen who have here set the example and taken up a work, which undoubtedly has much more in common with the English undertaking. The High School has now existed for fifty years, but it is during the last thirty years, after the unfortunate German war, that it has grown in importance and increased in dimensions. The schools are now frequented by about 6,000 pupils. A considerable number of the young country-folk are thus brought under the influence of the schools, as the number of the entire rural population is only about 1,400,000.

The schools having been in existence for more than a generation, it may rightly be asked what fruits they have borne during that time. Before concluding, I am going to say a few words on this point.

In the first place I must mention the influence which the schools have had on the economical well-being of the country. From the year 1870 to 1880 agriculture, which is the principal industry of our country, underwent a serious crisis. The old-fashioned modes of culture did not suffice any longer. The exportation of corn was the main industry of farmers ; but the price of corn fell, and agriculture was on the brink of ruin. Then it was that a perfect revolution was brought about in a few years. From the production of corn and meat, the country now turned to dairy-work, especially the manufacturing of butter. This was the first reform. The second one came in the year 1880.

It was very soon understood that if we were to obtain good prices for our butter here in England, production of a better and more homogeneous quality and in greater quantities would be necessary. Then arose as by magic the large co-operative dairies, which get their milk from larger districts, ordinarily from a whole parish. By this mode of proceeding it was rendered possible for our butter to gain its good reputation in the English market. The quickness and precision with which this change was carried out, is due partly to the leading agriculturists of our country and partly to the High Schools. By their help a set of young, energetic men were brought up to understand the importance of the new ideas ; and to secure the success of the new principle of co-operative manufacture, some of them, after a very short course of instruction, were able to undertake the responsible work as managers of the larger and smaller co-operative dairies.

You all know the Danish butter, Ladies and gentlemen, and have perhaps already often partaken of it. Well, if this be so, you also have come in a sort of contact with the schools I am speaking of, for the greater part of the men and women who manufacture this butter are pupils of the High Schools.

I might, if time allowed it, quote many sayings of men, who in different branches of industry have made themselves prominent. They all agree in this, that the young people who have frequented the High Schools are much more to be relied upon, more industrious than their comrades who never have had the opportunity of attending them. To be brief, I shall content myself with stating a remark recently made at the Congress of Antwerp by Mr. Peschke Köedt, one of our most influential merchants. He said : the Popular High School is one of the most prominent factors in the economical life of the country.

In the management of municipal affairs, partly also in politics, the influence of the High School education cannot easily be over-estimated. Without exaggerating, I venture to say that the majority of the public offices that are laid in the hands of the people, have been entrusted to men influenced by High School training.

But the greatest importance I ascribe to another effect, which cannot be proved by statistics ; namely, the influence on the religious and moral state of the population. One of the most eager antagonists of the school has said : ' It must be admitted that depravity vanishes where the High School exists. In those social circles where the High School has obtained influence, neither drinking, gambling, or the like gross breaches of morals are to be met with. Now you must not think that puritanical severity reigns among our pupils. They are very fond of games, dancing and sport and all other recreations.'

Still the best result of this popular enlightenment and education is to my mind the awakening of the religious feeling of responsibility. The desire of serving God and living a life to His honour. Only where this fruit has ripened, the aim of the school is attained. And if the Danish Popular High School has been able to educate the common man and cultivate his abilities, it is because it has placed its standard so high. It has not aimed at or been satisfied by attaining certain material advantages, but has constantly kept its eye fixed on the ideal standard. Therefore, clearly, it has proved that it has taken up its mission in the right manner, and in spite of mistakes and errors, a result is attained which encourages us to continue in the same path.

I hope I have not wearied you or dwelt too long upon the results of our school, but I feel bound to speak as forcibly and impressively of this matter as I can. Perhaps it may be the only original gift our little country is able to contribute to the intellectual work of our neighbouring countries. We ourselves surely think we have found a precious pearl, a treasure of the greatest value, which we should proudly and gladly like to share with other nations.

Owing to my slight knowledge of English, I have been only able to give you a vague, unsatisfactory idea of the facts which I have tried to put before you. Should you ever want to know the Popular High Schools, you must visit them and see them at work. I cannot express this forcibly enough especially to those who still look in a sceptical way on this peculiar and novel educational work. Many antagonists have been won for the cause, when they had an opportunity of seeing and becoming personally acquainted with the schools.

I can offer you a hearty welcome, if you will visit us. And if I have succeeded in calling forth in any one who seeks the means of making the humble man partner in the best happiness in the world, the inclination to come into closer contact with our schoolwork, it would indeed be a satisfaction for me, and I should not have spoken in vain. Certainly Denmark is only a very small country, but thoughts can be fertile and deeds rich even there. The sky and the stars of heaven are also reflected in our sea. No doubt he who visits us will still find 'something rotten in the state of Denmark,' but I hope he will find something else besides. If, for instance, he seeks help for the solution of great social problems, it might not be impossible that something could be learned in our little country.

Here we have commenced to solve problems by beginning from within, and the Popular High School is not our smallest contribution to this work.

The strength, which of old sent the Vikings abroad over the seas, is not yet dead. Thoughts are called to life which can yet inspire and conquer.

ARRANGEMENTS FOR 1894-5.

Autumn, 1894.

Centre.	No. of Lectures in Course.	Subject of Course.	Lecturer.	Course begins.	Course ends.
UNIVERSITY EXTENSION COLLEGE, READING (evening)	12	Age of Elizabeth and Puritan Rebellion	Rev.W.H.SHAW,M.A. & E.L.S.HORSBURGH,M.A.	Th. Oct. 4	Dec. 13
,, (afternoon)	12	Tennyson and Browning ...	J.CHURTONCOLLINS,M.A	S. Sept. 29	Dec. 8
,, (evening) ...	12	Greek Drama	,, ,,	S. Sept. 29	Dec. 8
,, (evening) ...	12	The Study of Local History ...	W. M. CHILDS, B.A. ...	F. Sept. 28	Dec. 7
,, (evening) ...	12	La Littérature Française du XVIIe Siècle	M. J. MAURICE REY, B. es Sc.	W. Sept. 26	Dec. 5
,, (evening) ...	12	Geography of the British Isles ...	H. J. MACKINDER, M.A.	S. Oct. 6	Dec. 5
ALTRINCHAM (evening) ...	6	Making of England ...	Rev. W. H.SHAW,M.A.	F. Oct. 5	Dec. 14
ASHTON (afternoon) ...	6	Florence	,, ,, ...	T. Oct. 9	Dec. 18
ASHTON (evening)	6	Mediaeval England ...	,, ,, ...	T. Oct. 9	Dec. 18
BIRMINGHAM, SEVERN STREET (evening)	6	Mediaeval England ...	,, ,, ...	T. Oct. 2	Dec. 11
BOLTON (afternoon)	6	Social Reformers	,, ,, ...	Th. Sept. 27	Dec. 6
BOLTON (evening)	6	Mediaeval England ...	,, ,, ...	Th. Sept. 27	Dec. 6
CHELTENHAM (afternoon)	6	Florence	,, ,, ...	Th. Oct. 4	Dec. 13
CHELTENHAM (evening)	6	Making of England .	,, ,, ...	W. Oct. 3	Dec. 12
CHESTER (afternoon) ...	6	Mediaeval England ...	,, ,, ...	F. Sept. 28	Dec. 7
CIRENCESTER (afternoon)	6	Age of Elizabeth	,, ,, ...	M. Oct. 1	Dec. 10
GLOUCESTER (evening)	6	Making of England ...	,, ,, ...	M. Oct. 1	Dec. 10
KENDAL (afternoon)	6	Puritan Revolution ...	,, ,, ...	M. Sept. 24	Dec. 3
MALVERN (afternoon) ...	6	Age of Elizabeth	,, ,, ...	W. Oct. 3	Dec. 12
MANCHESTER, CHEETHAM (evening)	6	Age of Elizabeth	,, ,, ...	F. Sept. 28	Dec. 7
OLDHAM (evening)	6	Mediaeval England ...	,, ,, ...	W. Sept. 26	Dec. 5
PRESTWICH (evening	6	Mediaeval England ...	,, ,, ...	M. Sept. 24	Dec. 3
STROUD (afternoon)	6	Florence	,. ,, ...	T. Oct. 2	Dec. 11
WIGAN (evening)	6	Florence	,, ,, ...	W. Sept. 26	Dec. 5
BAKEWELL (evening)	6	English Novelists...	J. A. R. MARRIOTT, M.A	Th. Sept. 27	Dec. 6
BIRMINGHAM, EDGBASTON (afternoon)	12	Age of Louis XIV and French Revolution	,, ,. ...	T. Oct. 9	Dec. 18
BOURNEMOUTH (afternoon) ...	12	Europe since Waterloo ...	,, ,, ...	W. Oct. 3	Dec. 12
CLEVEDON (afternoon)	12	Shakespeare's Historical Plays ...	,, ,, ...	Th. Oct. 4	Dec 13
LEAMINGTON (evening)	6	English in India	,, ,, ...	F. Sept. 28	Dec. 7
LYMINGTON (afternoon) ...	6	English in India	,, ,, ...	T. Oct. 2	Dec. 11
MATLOCK (afternoon) ...	6	The Stuarts & Puritan Revolution	,, ,, ...	Th. Sept. 27	Dec. 6
SOUTHBOURNE	12	Not fixed	,, ,, ...	T. Oct. 2	Dec. 11
STAFFORD (afternoon) ...	6	Shakespeare's Historical Plays ...	,, ,, ...	W. Sept. 26	Dec. 5
WELLS (evening)	6	England in the 18th Century ...	,, ,, ...	Th. Oct. 4	Dec. 13
WEYMOUTH (evening)	6	Not fixed	,, ,, ...	W. Oct. 3	Dec. 12
HARROGATE (evening)	12	Prose Writers	C. E. MALLET, B.A. ...	F. Sept. 28	Dec. 14
ILKLEY (afternoon)	12	England in the 18th Century ...	,, ,, ...	Th. Sept. 27	Dec. 13
OTLEY (evening)	6	The Stuarts	,. ,, ...	Th. Oct. 4	Dec. 13
RIPON (afternoon)	6	French Revolution	,, ,, ...	T. Sept. 25	Dec. 4
RIPON (evening)	6	The Stuarts	,, ,, ...	T. Sept. 25	Dec. 4
TAMWORTH (evening) ..	10	England in the 18th Century ...	,, ,, ...	T. Oct. 2	Dec. 11
TUNBRIDGE WELLS (afternoon)	10	Tudors and Stuarts	,, ,, ...	M. Oct. 8	Dec. 10
WARRINGTON (evening) ...	6	Tudors	,, ,, ...	W. Sept. 26	Not fixed.
BRADFORD (evening) ...	6	Shakespeare	F. S. BOAS, M.A. ...	Th. Oct. 4	Dec. 13
BURNLEY (evening)	12	Spencer & other Elizabethan Poets	,, ,, ...	Th. Oct. 11	Dec. 20
CANTERBURY (afternoon)	12	Victorian Poets	,, ,, ...	W. Oct. 10	Dec. 19
HODDESDON (afternoon) ...	12	Shakespeare	,, ,, ...	T. Oct. 2	Dec. 18
RAMSGATE (afternoon) ...	12	Literature of Cavaliers & Puritans	,, ,, ...	S. Oct. 6	Dec. 15
RUGBY (evening)	6	Browning	,, ,, ...	W. Oct. 3	Dec. 12
SALE (evening)	6	Representative Men, Stuarts ...	,, ,, ...	F. Oct. 12	Not fixed
WESTERHAM (afternoon) ...	6	Victorian Poets	,, ,, ...	S. Oct. 13	Dec. 22
BRIGHTON (St. Michael's Hall) (morning)	6	The Merchant of Venice	Rev. J. G. BAILEY, M.A., LL.D.	F. Oct. 12	Dec. 21
EASTBOURNE (afternoon) ...	6	Shakespeare	,, ,, ...	Th. Oct. 11	Dec. 20
MAIDSTONE (afternoon) ...	6	Shelley, Keats, Coleridge, and Wordsworth	,, ., ...	W. Oct. 10	Dec. 19
NEWBURY (afternoon)... ...	6	Shelley, Keats, Coleridge, and Wordsworth	,, ,, ...	Th. Oct. 4	Dec. 13
ROCHESTER (evening)	6	Shakespeare	,, ,, ...	T. Oct. 2	Dec. 11
WEST BRIGHTON (afternoon)	12	Tennyson	,, ,, ...	F. Oct. 12	Dec. 21
BEDFORD (evening) ...	12	The Colonies and India ...	H.MORSESTEPHENS,M.A	M. Oct. 8	Dec. 17
BURY (evening)	6	Epochs from English History ...	E.L.S. HORSBURGH,M.A	T. Oct. 2	Dec. 11
FOLKESTONE (morning) ...	6	Age of Elizabeth (Social & Lit.)	,, ,, ...	M. Oct. 1	Dec. 10
HEBDEN BRIDGE (evening) ...	6	French Revolution	,, ,, ...	S. Oct. 20	Dec. 29
HUDDERSFIELD (evening)	6	Epochs from English History ...	,, ,, ...	W. Oct. 10	Dec. 19
OXFORD (evening)	12	The Making of England... ...	,, ,, ...	F. Oct. 5	Dec. 14
REIGATE (afternoon) ...	12	The Early Tudors...	,, ,, ...	M. Oct. 1	Dec. 10
THORNTON (evening) ...	6	Epochs from English History ...	,. ,, ...	M. Oct. 8	Dec. 17
SOUTHAMPTON (evening) ...	6 or 12	Not fixed	,, ,, ...	F. Sept. 28	Dec. 7
SWINDON (evening)	6	Epochs from English History ...	,, ,, ...	W. Oct. 3	Dec. 12
WAKEFIELD (evening) ...	6	Epochs from English History ...	,, ,, ...	T. Oct. 9	Dec. 18

Centre.	No. of Lectures in Course.	Subject of Course.	Lecturer.	Course begins.	Course ends.
*WINDSOR (afternoon)...	6	Architecture	F. BOND, M.A.	Th. Oct. 4	Dec. 13
HENLOW (evening)	12	The English Citizen	W. M. CHILDS, B.A.	W. Oct. 10	Dec. 19
CIRENCESTER (evening)	6	Trade, Adventure, and Discovery	K. D. COTES, M.A.	M. Oct. 1	Dec. 10
KNOWLE (afternoon)	6	Shakespeare's England	"	M. Sept. 24	Dec. 3
LLANELLY (evening)	6	Not fixed	" "	W. Oct. 3	Dec. 12
PETERBOROUGH (evening)	6	Trade, Adventure, and Discovery	" "	F. Sept. 28	Dec. 7
STROUD (evening)	6	Shakespeare's England	" "	Th. Oct. 4	Dec. 13
SWANSEA (evening)	6	Trade, Adventure, and Discovery	" "	F. Oct. 5	Dec. 14
TUNBRIDGE WELLS (evening)...	8	Commerce, Colonization & Empire	" "	T. Oct. 9	Nov. 27
WINSLOW (evening)	6	Relation of History to Painting ...	" "	Th. Sept. 27	Dec. 6
BANBURY (evening)	6	Economic Aspects of Social Questions	W. A S. HEWINS, M.A.	Th. Oct. 4	Dec. 6
GRIMSBY (evening)	6	Not fixed	" "	T. Oct. 2	Dec. 11
HYDE (evening)	6	English Social Life	" "	M. Oct. 1	Dec. 10
KIDDERMINSTER (afternoon)...	6	Economic Aspects of Social Questions	" "	W. Oct. 3	Dec 12
KIDDERMINSTER (evening)	6	Economic Aspects of Social Questions	" "	W. Oct. 3	Dec. 12
PUCKLECHURCH	6	Not fixed	" "	F. Oct. 12	Dec. 21
WEST BRIGHTON (evening)	12	Three Centuries of Working Class History	" "	Th. Oct. 18	Dec. 13
ACCRINGTON (evening)	6	Structure of Modern Industry	J. A. HOBSON, M.A.	M. Oct. 1	Dec. 10
BRIDPORT (evening)	12	Industrial Revolution	" "	T. Oct. 9	Dec. 18
COVENTRY (evening)	6	Sharing of Wealth	" "	Th. Sept. 27	Dec. 6
TEAN (afternoon)	6	English Novelists ...	" "	S. Sept. 29	Dec. 8
BARNSLEY (evening)	6	Ruskin	J. E. PHYTHIAN	T. Oct. 9	Dec. 18
CARLISLE (afternoon)	12	Architecture	" "	T. Oct. 16	Dec. 11
GRANGE (evening)	6	Architecture	" "	M. Oct. 1	Dec. 10
KESWICK (evening)	6	Shakespeare	" "	M. Oct. 8	Dec. 17
MOSTON (evening)	8	Venice and Venetian Art	" "	F. Oct. 19	Dec. 7
RHYL (evening)	6	Architecture	" "	W. Oct. 10	Dec. 19
ROMSEY (afternoon)	6	Mediaeval Architecture ...	Rev. G. H. WEST, D.D.	W. Oct. 3	Dec. 12
BODMIN (evening)	12	South Africa	W. B. WORSFOLD, M.A.	F. Oct. 12	Dec. 21
CAMBORNE (evening)	12	South Africa	" "	F. Oct. 5	Dec. 14
FALMOUTH (evening)	12	South Africa	" "	Th. Oct. 4	Dec. 13
HELSTON (evening)	12	South Africa	" "	T. Oct. 9	Dec. 18
LAUNCESTON (evening)	12	South Africa	" "	W. Oct. 3	Dec. 12
PENZANCE (evening)	12	South Africa	" "	M. Oct. 8	Dec. 17
REDRUTH (evening)	12	South Africa	" "	Th. Oct. 11	Dec. 20
ST. AUSTELL (evening)	12	South Africa	" "	T. Oct. 2	Dec. 11
TRURO (evening)	12	South Africa	" "	M. Oct. 1	Dec. 10
HUNGERFORD (afternoon)	12	Physiography	G. J. BURCH, M.A.	F. Oct. 5	Dec. 21
CARLISLE (evening)	6	Outlines of Geology	C. CARUS-WILSON, F.G.S.	Th. Oct. 11	Dec. 20
LOUTH (evening)	6	Outlines of Geology	" "	M. Oct. 1	Dec. 10
ST. HELENS (evening)...	6	Crust of the Earth	" "	M. Oct. 8	Dec. 17
SETTLE (evening)	6	Physiography	" "	T. Oct. 9	Dec. 18
BATH (afternoon)	12	Life of a Planet	A. H. FISON, D.Sc.	Th. Sept. 27	Dec. 6
BATH (evening)	12	Life of a Planet	" "	Th. Sept. 27	Dec. 6
BOURNEMOUTH (evening)	12	Forces of Nature ...	" "	F. Sept. 28	Dec. 7
NEWPORT (evening)	12	Physical Astronomy	" "	Th. Oct. 4	Dec. 13
RYDE (afternoon)	12	Life of a Planet	" "	Th. Oct. 4	Dec 13
VENTNOR (evening)	12	Physical Astronomy	" "	F. Oct. 5	Dec. 14
LITTLE BERKHAMPSTEAD	6	Astronomy	R. A. GREGORY, M.A.	Th. Oct. 4	Dec 13
Lancashire County Council					
5 Courses of	12	Hygiene	C.H.WADE,M.A.,D.P.H.	Oct.	Dec.
Somerset County Council					
5 Courses of	12	Management of Farm Stock	H. SESSIONS	Oct.	Dec.
5 Courses of	12	Agricultural Chemistry	H. E. NIBLETT, B A.	Oct.	Dec.

Spring, 1895.

Centre.	No. of Lectures in Course.	Subject of Course.	Lecturer.	Course begins.	Course ends.
†UNIVERSITY EXTENSION COLLEGE, READING (evening)	12	Age of Elizabeth and Puritan Rebellion	Rev.W.H.SHAW,M.A. & E.L.S.HORSBURGH,M.A.	Th. Jan. 17	Mar. 28
" (afternoon)	12	Tennyson and Browning ...	J.CHURTONCOLLINS,M.A	S. Jan. 26	Apr. 6
" (evening) ...	12	Greek Drama	" "	S. Jan. 26	Apr 6
" (evening) ...	12	The Study of Local History	W. M. CHILDS, B.A.	F. Jan 25	Apr. 5
" (evening) ...	12	La Littérature Française du XVII° Siècle	M. J. MAURICE REY, B. es Sc.	W. Jan. 23	Apr. 3
" (evening) ...	12	Geography of the British Isles	H. J. MACKINDER, M.A.	S. Jan. 19	Mar. 30
†BIRMINGHAM, EDGBASTON (afternoon)	12	Age of Louis XIV and French Revolution	J.A.R.MARRIOTT, M.A.	T. Jan. 15	Mar. 26
†BOURNEMOUTH (afternoon) ...	12	Europe since Waterloo ...	" "	W Jan. 23	Apr. 3
BRADFORD (evening) ...	6	Colonies	" "	Th. Jan. 17	Mar. 28
†BRIDPORT (evening) ...	12	Industrial Revolution	" "	T. Jan. 22	Apr. 2
†CLEVEDON (afternoon)	12	Shakespeare's Historical Plays ...	" "	F. Jan. 25	Apr. 5
†OXFORD (evening)	12	The Making of England ...	" "	F. Jan. 18	Mar. 29
SALE (evening) ...	6	England in the 18th Century	" "	W. Jan. 16	Mar. 27
*†SOUTHBOURNE	12	Not fixed	" "	Not fixed	Not fixed
†TAMWORTH (evening)	10	England in the 18th Century	C. E. MALLET, B.A.	T. Jan. 15	Feb. 26
FOLKESTONE	10	Not fixed	" "	M.Jan. 21 or 28	Mar. 25 or Apr. 1
†BURNLEY (evening)	12	Spenser & other Elizabethan Poets	F. S. BOAS, M.A.	Th. Jan. 17	Mar. 28

* Arrangements not yet completed.   † Continued from Autumn Session.

Centre.	No. of Lectures in Course.	Subject of Course.	Lecturer.	Course begins.	Course ends.
†CANTERBURY (afternoon)	12	Victorian Poets	F. S. BOAS, M.A.	W. Jan. 23	Apr. 3
†RAMSGATE (afternoon)	12	Literature of Cavaliers and Puritans	,, ,,	S. Jan. 26	Apr. 6
†WEST BRIGHTON (afternoon)	12	Tennyson	Rev. J. G. BAILEY, M.A., LL.D.	F. Jan. 18	Mar. 29
†BEDFORD (evening)	12	The Colonies and India	H. MORSE STEPHENS, M.A.	M. Jan. 28	Apr. 8
*ABERGAVENNY (afternoon)	6	English History in Shakespeare	E. L. S. HORSBURGH, M.A	S. Jan. 26	Apr. 6
BRECON (afternoon)	*6	Not fixed	,, ,,	Th. Jan. 24	Apr. 4
BRECON (evening)	6	Not fixed	,, ,,	Th. Jan. 24	Apr. 4
CHELTENHAM (afternoon)	6	Not fixed	,, ,,	W. Jan. 30	Apr. 10
CHELTENHAM (evening)	6	Not fixed	,, ,,	W. Jan. 30	Apr. 10
EVESHAM (evening)	6	Revolution and Age of Anne	,, ,,	W. Jan. 23	Apr. 3
GLOUCESTER (evening)	6	English History in Shakespeare	,, ,,	M. Jan. 28	Apr. 8
HEREFORD (evening)	6	Wyclif to Sir Thomas More	,, ,,	M. Jan. 21	Apr. 1
*LEOMINSTER (evening)	6	Industrial and Economic Questions since 1789	,, ,,	T. Jan. 22	Apr. 2
REIGATE (afternoon)	12	The Age of Elizabeth (political)	,, ,,	Th. Jan. 24	Mar. 28
ROSS (afternoon)	6	Literature of the 18th Century	,, ,,	T. Jan. 22	Apr. 2
*†SOUTHAMPTON (evening)	12	Not fixed	,, ,,	F. Jan. 18	May 29
STROUD (afternoon)	6	The Renaissance	,, ,,	T. Jan. 29	Apr. 9
STROUD (evening)	6	Age of Elizabeth	,, ,,	T. Jan. 29	Apr. 9
SWANSEA (evening)	6	Not fixed	,, ,,	F. Jan. 25	Apr. 5
*†WINDSOR & ETON (afternoon)	12	Architecture	F. BOND, M.A.	Th. Jan. 24	Apr. 4
†HENLOW (evening)	12	The English Citizen	W. M. CHILDS, B.A.	W. Jan. 16	Apr. 27
TAVISTOCK	6	Not fixed	K D. COTES, M.A.	W. Jan. 30	Apr. 10
WIRKSWORTH	6	Trade, Adventure, and Discovery	,, ,,	Th. Jan. 24	Apr. 4
†WEST BRIGHTON (evening)	12	Three Centuries of Working-class History	W. A. S. HEWINS, M.A.	Th. Jan. 24	Apr. 18
GRIMSBY (evening)	6	Not fixed	J. A. HOBSON, M.A.	T. Jan. 22	Apr. 2
MIDHURST (afternoon)	6	English Novelists	,, ,,	W. Jan. 16	Mar. 27
†CARLISLE (afternoon)	12	Architecture	J. E. PHYTHIAN	T. Jan. 15	Apr. 9
CHESTER (afternoon)	6	Architecture	,, ,,	T. Jan. 22	Apr. 2
KERSAL	8	Architecture	,, ,,	M. Jan. 28	Mar. 18
†BODMIN (evening)	12	South Africa	W. B. WORSFOLD M.A.	F. Jan. 25	Apr. 5
†CAMBORNE (evening)	12	South Africa	,, ,,	F. Jan. 18	Mar. 29
†FALMOUTH (evening)	12	South Africa	,, ,,	Th. Jan. 17	Mar. 28
†HELSTON (evening)	12	South Africa	,, ,,	T. Jan. 22	Apr. 2
†LAUNCESTON (evening)	12	South Africa	,, ,,	W. Jan. 16	Mar. 27
†PENZANCE (evening)	12	South Africa	,, ,,	M. Jan. 21	Apr 1
†REDRUTH (evening)	12	South Africa	,, ,,	T. Jan. 15	Mar. 26
†ST. AUSTELL (evening)	12	South Africa	,, ,,	M. Jan. 14	Mar. 25
†TRURO (evening)	12	South Africa	,, ,,	M. Jan. 14	Mar. 25
BRIGHTON (St. Michael's Hall)	6	Regions, Races, and Resources	H. R. MILL, D.Sc.	Not fixed.	Not fixed
BANBURY (evening)	6	Crust of the Earth	C CARUS-WILSON, F.G.S.	Th. Jan. 17	Mar. 28
†BATH (afternoon)	12	Recent Discoveries with the Telescope and Spectroscope	A. H. FISON, D.Sc.	Th. Jan. 17	Mar. 28
†BATH (evening)	12	Recent Discoveries with the Telescope and Spectroscope	,, ,,	Th. Jan. 17	Mar. 28
†BOURNEMOUTH (evening)	12	Forces of Nature	,, ,,	F. Jan. 18	Mar. 29
†NEWPORT (evening)	12	Physical Astronomy	,, ,,	Th. Jan. 24	Apr. 4
†RYDE (afternoon)	12	Recent Discoveries with the Telescope and Spectroscope	,, ,,	Th. Jan. 24	Apr. 4
†VENTNOR (evening)	12	Physical Astronomy	,, ,,	F. Jan. 25	Apr. 5
Somerset County Council :					
5 Courses of	12	Management of Farm Stock	H. SESSIONS	Jan.	Apr.
5 Courses of	12	Hygiene	C. H. WADE, M.A., D.P.H.	Jan.	Apr.

Summer, 1895.

| BRIGHTON (St. Michael's Hall) | 6 or 8 | England in the 18th Century | J. A. R. MARRIOTT, M.A. | Not fixed. | Not fixed |

* Arrangements not yet completed.   † Continued from Autumn Session.

Note.—Application for Courses and all information as to fees, &c., can be obtained from The Secretary, University Extension Office, Examination Schools, Oxford.

INFORMATION TO CONTRIBUTORS.

All communications should be addressed to the Editor, OXFORD UNIVERSITY EXTENSION GAZETTE, *University Press, Oxford.*

All matter intended for insertion in the October issue should reach him not later than September 20.

Contributions should be written on one side of the paper only, and must be accompanied by the name of the writer (not necessarily for publication).

N.B.—*All orders should carefully specify the full title,* OXFORD UNIVERSITY EXTENSION GAZETTE.

OXFORD UNIVERSITY

EXTENSION GAZETTE.

VOL. V. No. 49.]   OCTOBER, 1894.   [ONE PENNY.

N.B.—Local Organizers of Oxford University Extension Lectures are invited to send to the Secretary, University Extension Office, Examination Schools, Oxford, copies of any journals containing notices of, or references to, Extension work.

AWARD OF
SESSIONAL CERTIFICATES, 1893-4.

THE following students have received Sessional Certificates, having passed an examination on a course of not less than twenty-four lectures and classes during the past lecture year:—

Reading University Extension College.

(*a*) Botany:—EDYTH M. CLOSE (*distinction*), ALFRED GEORGE ARTHURS, JULIA EASTWOOD CHESSON, SARAH STOBO HASTINGS, ALICE BERTHA KENTISH, RICHARD GEORGE KNIGHT, WALTER ROBERTS, HERBERT JAMES SHARPE, GEORGE SHORTER, GEORGE ROBERT STEVENS.

(*b*) Elementary Chemistry accompanied by Practical Classes:—ALFRED GEORGE ARTHURS (*with distinction in practical work*), A. B. STEDMAN (*with distinction in practical work*), GEORGE ROBERT STEVENS (*with distinction in practical work*), WALTER ROBERTS.

(*c*) Electricity:—FRANK HENRY WISE.

Newbury, in conjunction with Reading University Extension College.

(*a*) Botany:—WILLIAM MARGETTS BASSETT.

(*b*) Chemistry of Common Metals:—EDWARD CAIN (*distinction*), GRACE D. FLINT (*distinction*), ROBERT WING (*distinction*), WILLIAM MARGETTS BASSETT, CECIL ALEXANDER ELLIOTT, EMILY JANE HABGOOD, JESSE MATHEWS, ALBERT ARTHUR ORVISS.

Oxford.

The English Citizen:—EMILY ELLIOTT (*distinction*), ANNIE C. FOWLER (*distinction*), L. GEORGIANA GREEN (*distinction*), R. C. KNIGHT, D. G. LANGE, W. J. OWENS, M. R. PETERS.

NOTES AND COMMENTS.

About the middle of September Dr. Creighton, Bishop of Peterborough, delivered a most interesting lecture on English Life during the reign of Elizabeth, introductory to the Autumn course of lectures which are to be given by Mr. Cotes. Dr. Creighton, after referring to the value of University Extension lectures as giving facts from which more general ideas may be gathered rather than as presenting ready-made notions, dealt with the social, commercial and maritime life of England under Elizabeth. He insisted upon the fact that the real interests of the country were then national rather than religious, and were indeed largely commercial. The consciousness of national existence produced Shakespeare, the unconsciousness of it led to religious persecution as a means of securing political unity. The Bishop later dealt with many phases of sixteenth-century life in England. At the conclusion a hearty vote of thanks was accorded to the lecturer.

.·.

Technical Instruction in Wiltshire does not seem to have been successful, at least in the rural parts of the county. At a recent meeting of one of the district committees, the following resolution was unanimously carried—'That this meeting desires to place on record its opinion that it is hopeless to secure adequate attendance at, and satisfactory results from, classes held under the present system, in the purely agricultural districts, and recommends that assistance should be given through the existing technical education committees to the Continuation Schools, with a view to preparing the way for technical instruction ; and hopes that, if it be necessary, the Education Department will secure such alteration in the law as will enable the money to be so applied.' The opinion was freely expressed that the students in country districts were not sufficiently well grounded in the principles of elementary education to be able to understand and profit by technical instruction.

.·.

That the same difficulty is felt in the Northern and manufacturing parts of the country is shown in the second annual report lately published by The Director of Technical Education at St. Helens, who states that 'as long as the standard for full time exemption remains at Standard V, so long will there be a distinct want of preparation on the part of the majority of the students who attend the evening classes '

.·.

Great interest was excited at Grindelwald on August 23 by a lecture on Ice delivered by Mr. Cecil Carus-Wilson high up among the mountains, close to a glacier which he made the text of his discourse.   A Geological Lecture among the Glaciers.

.·.

Mr. Morse Stephens, Staff Lecturer of the Oxford University Extension Delegacy, has accepted the appointment of Acting-Professor of Modern History at Cornell University, New York. We congratulate Mr. Morse Stephens and Cornell, but regret the loss to England of so distinguished an historian.

.·.

In the flood of literature which has recently appeared upon the life and duties of the citizen, a word of special praise should be given to the Introductory Remarks upon the subject which are published by Dr. Robert Spence Watson. Dr. Watson does not go into much detail, but his lectures would form an admirable introduction to a course of instruction on civic duty. They are full of sound truths plainly and vigorously said.

1

A New Constitutional History of England. Mr. D. J. Medley, who, before the pressure of work in Oxford made him unable to lecture outside the University, was one of the Oxford University Extension lecturers, has written a book which will be of great value to all students interested in Constitutional History. In an *English Constitutional History*, published by Mr. Blackwell, of Oxford, he has attempted to give in succinct form the results of recent researches in English Constitutional history which have hitherto been practically inaccessible to the ordinary reader. The author has succeeded in stating clearly and briefly the views held by various authorities; and the system of arrangement adopted — according to subject and not merely chronological — is of the greatest service. Mr. Medley has succeeded in writing a book which will be of the greatest use to all who are interested in the history of English Institutions.

∴

Mr. H. H. Cousins, M.A., one of the Oxford University Extension lecturers, has been making some experiments on the prevention and cure of hop mould on behalf of the County Council of Kent. At the August meeting of the Council he was able to suggest remedies which, if a practical success, would mean a saving of £100 a year on fifty acres of crops.

∴

Messrs. Macmillan have published in a half-crown volume, under the title of *Aspects of Modern Study*, the addresses which have been delivered at the annual meetings of the London University Extension Society since 1886. This handy little book contains the speeches of Lord Playfair, Mr. Goschen, Mr. John Morley, Sir James Paget, Professor Max Müller, the Duke of Argyle, Canon Browne, the Bishop of Durham, and Professor Jebb.

∴

The Rev. H. C. Beeching left behind him after his lecture in the South Writing Room of the Schools, the first volume of Bp. Heber's edition of Jeremy Taylor; if any student packed it up by mistake, it should be returned to Yattendon Rectory, Newbury.

GREEK CLASSES AT BRIGHTON.

MANY readers of the *Extension Gazette* will be aware that, early in 1893, a serious effort was made to formulate a scheme by which the study of Greek literature and philosophy could be associated with the study of the original language in a manner accessible to the general public. With this end in view, Greek classes had already been successfully formed in London, and in order to show that the scheme would meet a real want elsewhere, I was asked to start a voluntary elementary class in Brighton. This I did in June 1893, and in spite of short notice, fifteen members attended. Six classes were held, considerable progress was made, and great interest shown. A short examination on paper followed, and the results were very satisfactory. Enough was accomplished to prove that a demand for instruction in Greek existed, and that it could be met in the way proposed.

The present scheme was finally drawn up by a Joint Board of the Universities of Oxford, Cambridge and London, and the regulations (under which the classes in Brighton are now conducted) were issued by the Oxford Delegacy in April, 1894. In Brighton notices were circulated by the Local Extension Committee announcing the proposed formation of classes for the teaching of Greek; and although many residents are absent from Brighton during the Summer term, sixteen names were received—nine for the Elementary class and seven for the Intermediate. A start was made early in May, and twelve weekly classes of one-and-a-half hours each were held. The ground covered by the Elementary class embraced selected parts of Goodwin's *Greek Grammar for Schools*, a few chapters of Xenophon's *Anabasis*, Book i, and a weekly selected exercise from the early part of Sidgwick's *First Greek Writer*. In the Intermediate

class Thucyd. vii, 1–30 (omitting 11–15) and the whole of Homer, *Odyssey* vi, were read. Considerable attention was devoted to the simpler constructions in Thucydides, and to Homeric forms and scansion. Weekly exercises from Sidgwick were also written.

As teacher of the classes I have pleasure in saying that the sustained interest and attention of the students was most satisfactory. It is hoped that there will be a considerable increase in numbers this session, and that the work will go on steadily till the members are able to claim the Sessional Certificate.

The Elementary class will be held on Tuesdays, Oct. 9 and following, and the Intermediate on Wednesdays, Oct. 10 and following. Intending members should communicate at once with the Hon. Secs., Miss Knall and Miss Basden. In the Elementary class Xenophon's *Anabasis*, Bk. i, will be continued; in the Intermediate, Thucydides, Bk. vii, and the *Ajax* of Sophocles will be read.

It is pleasant to hear in this connexion that the Greek classes held at Oxford during the Summer Meeting by Mr. Gibson have been so successful. If, as we may hope, they become a yearly feature of the Oxford Meeting, they will no doubt do much to increase the number of students in the classes at the various centres.

EDMUND LUCE.

THE EDUCATION CLASS.

MR. COURTHOPE BOWEN in his lectures on the Theory of Education, addressed to the Oxford University Extension Students at Oxford, has opened the eyes of a number of teachers to many facts which should prove useful to them in their work. The titles to his lectures, 'Elementary Psychology for Teachers,' and 'Psychology applied to Class Teaching' did not sound very inviting; and moreover the question 'What has psychology got to do with teaching?' found frequent expression. It did not occur to many of the teachers that the Kindergarten system is entirely based on psychology; but one has only to have the fact made clear, to see at once the immense advantage it will be for teachers to understand something of the principles on which they work, instead of working by rule of thumb as most of them do at present. But it is not to the Kindergarten alone that the principles of psychology apply, and one of the foremost aims of Mr. Bowen's lectures has been to show how these principles apply to and ought to be the foundation-stone of teaching in more advanced schools. It is not our present intention to dilate on Elementary Psychology, but a few of the lessons brought home to his hearers by Mr. Bowen may be of interest to those of your readers who were not fortunate enough to be present.

In the first place the lecturer insists on the fact that the 'mind' is one; that each of the so-called 'faculties' is but a separate manifestation of the mind and that none of these faculties can act entirely without the others. Each therefore may and should be made to aid the others; thus observation should be made to assist imagination, imagination to assist reasoning and so on. At the same time he impressed upon his audience that there was a natural order for the development of these faculties, and that it was absurd to try to get children to understand an abstract conception before they are taught to observe and classify. For instance in giving a lesson on lines, the very last thing he would have us teach a child concerning them is that they have neither breadth nor thickness. Silence often conveys more than speech, and so it should do here. In all cases a scientific definition should be built up before the class, or better still by the class, by means of induction from numerous concrete examples: a definition should not be set to the class to learn by heart before the scholars understand it, and the facts (which they can understand) subsequently deduced from it: this, the usual method, is putting the cart before the horse.

Many of us are familiar with the pregnant words of Plato, συνοπτικὸς γὰρ ὁ διαλεκτικός, but most of us are content to say that children do not aim at being philosophers. Mr. Bowen however insists that even the smallest children should, in proportion to their powers, be taught to look on all knowledge as a whole, to take a synoptic view of the different branches, to see the interrelation of the various subjects they are taught. Not only is it important to aim from the beginning at this result for the sake of the result, but how much easier and more interesting is it for the children—and I may add for the teacher—what an incentive is it to them to learn dull subjects, when they perceive that their knowledge in one department will help them to understand another department.

Another fact—perhaps obvious though so often neglected —which the lecturer dwelt upon was the absolute necessity for keeping the attention of the class fixed and its interest always alive, and the advantage for this purpose of something which the scholars can touch or have a hand in constructing, such as models in clay, or drawings on the black-board—a sadly under-exercised article—made in class by teacher and scholars. Thus for instance in a lesson in geography, an ordinary printed map is quite inadequate to give a clear mental picture of the district dealt with : a model or a map growing under the hands and before the eyes of the pupils will hold the attention of the class and fix the lesson on their minds much more lastingly. Again in discussing a campaign of Caesar, to what great use modelling clay may be turned. Even more particularly in the case of 'object lessons' how ridiculous it is to think of giving an object lesson when the object under discussion, in addition to numerous other similar objects to compare and contrast with it, is not actually present in the room.

Another point which we have here only space simply to mention is the necessity for definiteness and clearness of mental images, and for the teacher to leave out features in a picture, which the child cannot be expected to understand. Want of accuracy is to be expected in small children, but in older pupils it is often the fault of the teacher rather than of the learner. Again, Mr. Bowen inveighs against the so-called thoroughness of many schools, a word which is made to cover a multitude of sins. The only thoroughness he would admit into any system of teaching is the gradual normal and uniform development of a child's *whole* nature.

Mr. Bowen, of course, believes in the *via media* between the old system of making children learn for themselves out of books, while the teacher merely makes sure of accurate verbal knowledge by 'hearing the lesson,' and the opposite extreme where the teacher does everything for the pupil. The true aim of teaching is to make the children observe, think and act for themselves while the teacher constantly guides and directs their mental activities into the right channels. The teacher should scarcely for a moment leave the class to itself: it needs constant superintendence and personal teaching and guidance to keep boys and girls interested. This system naturally requires a much wider and more accurate knowledge of any subject than is contained in the school text-books, with which teachers are too often contented. It also requires an endless fund of good nature and patience, qualities on which it is impossible to lay too much stress.

These are some of the salient points of Mr. Bowen's lectures. His large experience of teaching, in all kinds of schools, gives him a breadth of view and a sympathy with teacher and taught which are frequently conspicuous by their absence in lectures on 'theory.' His corrections of lessons sketched by his audience have been a most useful supplement to his lectures.

I am sure many teachers who have attended these lectures will be grateful to the Delegates of the University Extension, if they can provide a course of lectures by Mr. Courthorpe Bowen for next Summer Meeting, amplifying his instruction in the methods of teaching two or more particular subjects, though we are all aware he is the last person in the world to wish to stereotype any one form of teaching a subject.

Personally I may say that some course of lectures on the latest scientific methods of teaching by a man of very large and varied experience seems to me an invaluable, if not absolutely necessary, supplement to a University course, for any one who intends to make teaching his profession.

C. J. MONTGOMERY.

THE CLASS IN GEOLOGY.

THE Class in Geology was composed of fifteen members, there being ten ladies and five gentlemen. From Aug. 8 to 16 inclusive, Mr. A. B. Badger was responsible for the instruction given, subsequently Professor Green took charge of the work.

The aim of the first part of one course was to enable the students to learn as far as possible from their own observations the characters of the commoner minerals, rocks, and rock structures : with that object an explanatory lecture of about an hour was given each morning, and then followed practical work in the laboratory or in the field (excursions being made to places of geological interest in the neighbourhood), which extended over an ther four hours.

A good deal of ground was covered in the short time at our disposal, so that the knowledge gained could only be superficial, but at least it was obtained from actual contact with things geological and not from mere descriptions in books.

Most of the members of the class were punctual in their attendance, and were very diligent and enthusiastic in their studies.

A. B. BADGER, *Lecturer.*

.˙.

A large portion of the second week of the course was spent in the field, and the students were instructed in the use of maps and the methods of geological mapping. They took great interest in the work, and several of them seem to have fully grasped the structure of the district explored and the way of representing it on a map. In order to vary the work excursions were also made to spots of geological interest. When outdoor work could not be carried on on account of bad weather, the time was spent in demonstrations in the Museum and short lectures.

I feel sure that several members of the class derived real profit from their work, and went away better geologists than they came.

A. H. GREEN, *Lecturer.*

Aug. 24, 1894.

.˙.

Those who visited the Summer Meeting with the primary intention of applying themselves to the study of the fascinating science of Geology, were introduced to the subject by Professor Green, who in three preliminary lectures gave an interesting account of the history and progress of the science, together with a lucid exposition of the cardinal principles which must govern the methods of geological research. Settling down in the Second Part to the more serious pursuit of class work, the students underwent a course of instruction at the hands of Mr. Badger, whose able and perspicuous teaching in the lecture-room, supported by his conscientious and patient efforts in the laboratory, gave equal satisfaction with the enjoyment derived from the field-work, also under his guidance. He seems to have grasped the fact that students who come to Oxford for the working part of the Summer Meeting, look for that practical kind of tuition which it is impossible for most of them to obtain at home and from books ; for this was just what he took the greatest pains to provide, both in the laboratory and in the field. He taught them, by the aid of specimens, to recognize from personal experience in the laboratory the chief kinds of minerals and some of the fossils ; and in the field he imparted that information which cannot fail to heighten our appreciation of landscape beauty, together with an increasingly intelligent comprehension of the causes which have brought about the present conformation of our earth. It was almost with a half-regret, however, that one had to give way to a conviction of the fallacious nature of the delightful simplicity with which the diagrams contained in the text-books are liable to impress one. Then for the last week Professor Green resumed the task and conducted us over hill and dale, pointing out the signs by which the geologist is enabled to trace the outcrops of the various strata in a district, and to delineate on the map what he has observed in the field. The advantageous combination of scientific study

2

with health-promoting exercise in the invigorating air of the hill-tops, the gratification afforded by beautiful scenery, together with the helpful and genial presence of the Professor, more than counterbalanced the slight and temporary difficulties which occasionally beset the zealous student in the form of drenching rains, scrambles through thorny hedges, and unexpected plunges into muddy bogs —not to mention the onslaughts of ferocious dogs jealous of intruders, or the anger of scarcely less ferocious farmers careful of the 'young swedes.' From a student's point of view the class may be pronounced an unqualified success.

J. R. F.

THE CLASS FOR PRACTICAL CHEMISTRY.

AFTER introductory lectures by Professor Odling in the First Part of the Summer Meeting, the practical class began on Aug. 8, and continued daily, the hours being from 9 to 1. The proportion of beginners was less than in 1892. Some students, especially those from Surrey, having had the advantage of working at practical chemistry in their county, and some having previously attended a Summer Meeting in Oxford. For the beginners the same elementary course was adopted which on previous occasions had been found to work satisfactorily and to form a useful introduction to more systematic courses. The student began with operations with the thermometer and the balance. The phenomena of neutralization, crystallization, oxidation, and reduction were studied, in selected cases quantitatively. This course also included the preparation of gases and the general blowpipe reactions. The more advanced students took the qualitative analysis of mixtures, one worked on volumetric analysis, and one on the preparation of organic compounds in the pure state. Great interest was shown in the work and admirable progress was made, many becoming quite adept in the art of analysis. The result, I think, shows that, though the time is short, much may be done in it and the student may be put in the way of continuing chemical work by himself. This few could do without some assistance at the start. The County Councils are undoubtedly doing good work in finding facilities for their students to continue their practical work at home, so that when they return here they have not forgotten what they learnt before, but are able to begin more advanced work or work of a special or technical nature. I have no doubt that in this way after a few years we shall have students capable of attacking new problems in chemical science and of applying their skill, or of instructing others in the working and improvement of technical processes.

J. E. MARSH.

REPORT ON HYGIENE CLASSES.

DURING the Meeting of 1894, in addition to three introductory addresses, the last of which was given by Dr. J. S. Billings, of Washington, U.S.A., two courses of lectures were delivered on Hygiene, one to a limited class consisting mainly of teachers in elementary schools, and the second to a larger body of students attending the special classes on the Science and Art of Education. In connexion with the former course a series of practical demonstrations of the principles of sanitary science was rendered possible by the readiness with which the municipal and other authorities of Oxford afforded facilities to the Extension classes for visiting and inspecting the various works and institutions under their control. In this way the pumping-station and filter-beds of the city water supply, the drainage system at New Botley, the sewage farm at Littlemore, the city Workhouse and its Infirmary, the Radcliffe Infirmary, the Juxon Street and St. Barnabas schools, &c., were in turn visited, and opportunity taken to illustrate by their means the chief points dwelt on in the more didactic lectures. It is interesting to state here that the students showed a keen appreciation of the valuable nature of this supplement to the class teaching, the whole body of them availing themselves of

the leave given to join in the excursions, and showing by the intelligent nature of their frequent inquiries, that the demonstrations were of service in fixing their knowledge of details. Throughout the course, too, the regular attendance and undivided attention of the class were very gratifying evidence of the interest with which the study was pursued : and in the light of this evidence it may be worth consideration whether on another occasion, if the same subject is included in the Summer Meeting programme, it would not be desirable to afford a larger share of time to its study, and to include physiology as part of the course. Such a plan would tend to make the work done more permanently valuable in all probability, and it might be secured either by making the course of Hygiene sufficiently lengthy to admit of each lecture being subdivided to include the necessary consideration of physiological details, or by the two subjects being independently, even if concurrently, dealt with.

The shorter course of lectures on school Hygiene was attended by a considerable number of students, and these showed themselves to be deeply interested in the subject. It is proposed to supplement the course by a period of home-reading extending over three months, under direction of the lecturer; and a considerable proportion of the class have expressed the wish to take advantage of this means of adding to the work thus commenced at the Summer Meeting.

CHARLES H. WADE, *Lecturer.*

[*∗* The record of attendance at the Hygiene class shows that, out of 24 students, 22 attended every lecture and demonstration : the other two students each missed one lecture.—ED.]

ECONOMICS.

THE course upon the Wage System was designed as an introduction to the closer study of the many large questions suggested by that title. In the course of eight lectures an outline treatment of the structure of the modern Business was followed by the setting of the problems involved in the modern Labour Movement in England, the question of 'the Living Wage,' the policy of High Wages, the Eight Hours Day, and some general account of the economic relations between Capital and Labour in competitive industry. An examination of the several steps towards industrial peace, such as the Sliding Scale, Boards of Conciliation and Arbitration, &c., ensued, and the course ended with a setting of special problems connected with Woman's Work and the Unemployed Question.

The large scope of the study precluded the minute treatment of any of these large matters, my object being to help to form a basis of thought and work in students who designed to give further time to the subjects.

The numerous and well-pointed questions raised in the class showed that a strong interest was taken alike in the principles and in the practical issues involved. The magnitude of some questions and the minuteness of others were sometimes a cause of embarrassment. 'How far is Evolution traceable in modern industry?' and 'What practical reforms are desirable in the diet of the working classes?' may be taken as samples of the upper and lower limit of the questions to which I was subjected either *viva voce* or in writing. But as a rule the questions were short, well stated, and strictly pertinent The paper work was slight in quantity and showed more intelligence than reading. So far as relates to reading which bore directly on the course, it was of course impossible to expect much. I hope however that students will be induced to read carefully at their leisure at least the more important among the books named in the syllabus. Some three or four among the writers of paper-work showed some practical acquaintance with industrial facts, and with economic science, and a considerable number of members of the class were able to contribute some real thought to the discussion. Measured by regularity of attendance and sustained interest the work may be regarded as entirely satisfactory.

JOHN A. HOBSON, *Lecturer.*

GREEK FOR SUMMER MEETING STUDENTS.

THE critic who follows the Summer Meetings and regularly makes his moan has not deserted us this year. He is now specially disgusted with a certain housemaid who attended Extension lectures on Greek tragedy, and as a Greek scholar himself, is anxious that his beloved subject may be treated with due respect. For that reason he may welcome definite information on the teaching of Greek during the month of Extension work at Oxford this August.

A class of some twenty members assembled ; there may have been housemaids among them – one cannot tell, but in any case about half the number were entirely ignorant of the language, and had only a very slight acquaintance with the Greek characters. It was not a promising outlook for Mr. Gibson, who undertook the work, in spite of the article in the *Nineteenth Century.* He did not even worry about the possible housemaid student. He treated all his pupils with the greatest courtesy and patience, teaching them their letters in the first of the twelve lessons, enduring their repeated mistakes, which it is to be feared were a great trial to him. In twelve days the class managed the declensions of nouns and adjectives with most of the irregularities, the pronouns, half a dozen regular verbs in the active voice only, and fifty pages of easy translation. When the backward members found it impossible to follow, he gave them half an hour of supplementary help, and in a day or two he gave an hour of his time in his own rooms before breakfast to any one who liked to come to him.

This work went on for a week. The class had caught Mr. Gibson's enthusiasm, though surely never did enthusiasm wear so quiet an expression ; but it was there nevertheless. It was there so strongly that even Mr. Gibson's half-timid suggestion of an examination at the end of the fortnight was not received with any signs of disapproval by the class. The critics have at least done one service to the Summer Meeting students. When they so persistently call their studies only froth on the surface, they make the students angry enough to welcome any such test of their work, if only to put the critics in the wrong.

With a patient, never-tiring master, and an examination in prospect, the students worked with a will. Proposed excursions, even to Claydon, with its kind hostess Lady Verney, lost their attraction ; and the bad weather which spoiled one excursion was hailed with satisfaction, because it solved the difficulty of choice between a geological excursion and the Greek afternoon class. Greek dominated all for that fortnight. Three hours a day with the master, and as much time as one could give to the grammar by one's self, with Mr. Churton Collins' lectures on Homer, and Mr. A. Sidgwick's on Primitive Greek Thought, Language, and Remains, for recreation.

The critic can, of course, look down on the sum total of the fortnight's work with contempt, and will doubtless make merry over the meagre requirements of the examination paper, and the mistakes in the answers ; but, if Mr. Gibson is satisfied, as there is every reason to believe he is, it does not much matter what the critic says. About twelve took the paper in the hope that the result, whether brilliant or not, will show that they really meant work, and that they have made a start.

What they will do in the future remains to be proved ; whether, as so many men who learnt Greek at school and have forgotten it, they too will give it up ; whether, if they live in some out-of-the-way village, they can go on by themselves. or whether they will be able to continue their work with Mr. Gibson, or any of his colleagues, in the ensuing term.

For the present, the students who attended the Greek class owe their best thanks to Mr. Gibson for his enthusiasm in his work, his generous devotion of his time to them, and his courteous never-failing patience with them as beginners.

A MEMBER OF THE GREEK CLASS.

LETTERS TO THE EDITOR.

[We do not hold ourselves responsible for the opinions expressed by our correspondents.]

Training of Teachers.

SIR,—As a senior mistress of some years' standing in a large private school, and as one who has not had the advantage of studying at a training college, I should like to say a few words on the training of teachers in connexion with the courses of lectures on Education recently given to University Extension students by Mr. Courthope Bowen.

A few years ago, I felt the necessity of being trained as a teacher, and studied some works on the subject, soon after which I had the privilege of attending in one of the North German ' Hohere Töchterschulen,' the training class for teachers, and soon saw in the efficiency of the teachers, the advantage of such a system, and the absolute necessity of proper training for all those who wish to pursue the highest vocation of life—the mental, moral, and physical training of the young,—so that each child may be enabled to live usefully and happily, to the benefit of himself and those around him.

This necessity has been still more strongly brought before me when I have studied the work of the mistresses under me, and seen that, with the exception of one or two ' God-gifted ones,' (as Dr. Rein put it) their experience was obtained by a series of mistakes, which, as Mr. C. Bowen so forcibly told us, is a far too costly method both for teacher and taught.

Hence it was with the greatest delight I saw in the Programme of the Oxford Summer Meeting, that one of the special courses was to be on the Science and Art of Education, and that Mr. Courthope Bowen, whose life-work it has been to champion the cause of the young on this point, and to urge amid constant opposition the necessity of training, was to give two courses of lectures on this subject. I feel that this has been the most important section of the Programme, and has given teachers especially an opportunity of hearing one who has helped to raise in England the work of teaching the young into a science, and shown that *true* success can only be obtained by understanding the nature and development of the child, and that the only means of doing this, is by a proper and systematic study of the laws which govern that nature and development.

I shall be glad when the time comes, which I believe is not far distant, when it will be required of all who wish to educate the young to undergo a proper training themselves, and I feel that our heartiest thanks are due to Mr. C. Bowen for so kindly giving us so much valuable help and assistance, and for raising the ideal of a teacher's life work. I only hope that a similar course will be given at each Summer Meeting of Extension students, so that the advantages of this teaching may, in some small degree, supply the want of proper training in the Science and Art of Education.

I am,

Yours truly,

E. B. W.

∴

A Teacher's Thoughts about the Education Class.

SIR,—There are a few things which are not easy to set down in writing—among these are the advantages I have derived from the excellent course of lectures which have been delivered to the University Extension students at this Summer Meeting. Their advantages do not admit of being catalogued, real and substantial though they are

Speaking as one who has been for some years a teacher, I have found that many of the practical suggestions made by Mr. Bowen have been those I have learnt from painful experience; experience which, had I attended such lectures earlier, both teacher and pupils might have been spared.

Experiment is all very well in pioneer work, but when the principles we have had so clearly set before us have been ascertained it is sheer waste of time for many years to be spent in reaching the starting-point from which steady development in the right direction is possible. But these lectures have done more than this for me, they have opened a wide field of interest which I have been certain must exist in the training of undeveloped minds, but have never clearly perceived. Now there seems no end to the scientific enjoyment to be derived from giving the simplest lessons.

I have hitherto been content to give lessons on special subjects and have not been sufficiently careful to see that other teachers were interweaving their lessons with my own, the unity of every branch of education was hardly a working factor in my system. This could not continue to be the case after the emphasis which Mr. Bowen has laid upon the necessity for this unity throughout the course.

Again, before attending these lectures I had no clear idea of the connexion between the Kindergarten and ordinary school work. When the children reached a certain age, they dropped K. G. methods and took up others as quite a separate department. I now regard it as the starting-place for the child's education in a continuous line without any such gap. The practical lessons have been an efficient test of our comprehension of the principles placed before us; their value has been greatly enhanced by the unwearied attention Mr. Bowen has so kindly given to the individual members of his class.

Dr. Wade's lectures have been clear and emphatic; no one present can fail to have been impressed with the extreme importance of hygienic considerations. It is something new indeed to have a high authority for stating what one has often felt, that the training of girls requires even more care and attention than that of boys. The strong statements made to us will be so much reinforcement in the battle almost always to be fought, in country districts at least, for the adequate physical training of girls. Personally I leave Oxford to continue the studies which have been opened to us and to work on the system which has been put before us.

I am sure I am only speaking for the whole class when I say we shall always remember the lectures with gratitude and pleasure. They will make our work as teachers more interesting and more profitable.

E. WILSON.

.·.

A Suggestion for the next Summer Meeting.

DEAR SIR,—Let me first of all express my grateful sense of the benefit which the University Extension lectures confer on all those who have the privilege of attending them.

You kindly told me I might describe to you the plan adopted at Geneva, which has been found very helpful to German teachers in their study of the French language and literature. During the course which I attended two years ago, Monsieur Bouvier, one of the professors of the University of Geneva, who originated the scheme, gave lectures on the French writers of the Romantic School—Chateaubriand, Victor Hugo. &c.—which were followed by lessons on passages he had selected from these authors as characteristic of their language, style and thought. He also gave lessons in translation, and was good enough to correct some of our papers.

Another University professor gave lessons on French grammar, pronunciation and elocution. There were about ninety students. The fee for the whole course, which also gave free admission to the University Library, was 20 frcs.

I feel sure that if a somewhat similar course in English could be arranged for the Oxford Summer Extension lectures, many German teachers would gladly avail themselves of it.

I am, dear Sir,

Yours faithfully,

HERMINE RITZHAUPT.

Sofienstrasse 14, Karlsruhe i/Baden,
Aug. 19, 1894.

The Technical and University Extension College at Exeter.

DEAR SIR,—It is possible that some of your readers who are deciding on winter quarters, may be interested to hear of the educational advantages offered this winter at the new Technical and University Extension College at Exeter. In addition to the usual Science and Art classes in connexion with South Kensington (including a class in wood-carving) we have commercial classes in Shorthand, Book-keeping, French and German, and two Latin classes, all in the evening, and at very low fees. But we are introducing in addition a considerable amount of afternoon class work; advanced French (this class will be conducted wholly *in French*) and German; more elementary classes in these languages, Greek, and Anglo-Saxon. The fee for each class is two guineas a term for one and a half hours' lesson, on in Anglo-Saxon, for two hours. There are also classes for practical work in Chemistry and Physics, with the use of a good Laboratory and apparatus—fees 30s. a term. Then there will be three courses of lectures going on, two by Mr. Boyd Carpenter on 'The Revival of Learning' and 'The Colonial Empire'; and one on 'Problems of Life and Health' by Mr. Parkyn. The climate of Exeter, though not all that could be desired, is appreciably milder than the North or Midlands; the Cathedral is not only beautiful, but has a very good choir; and the history of Exeter is second to no city in England for interest. We have no Hostel at present connected with the College, but I should be most happy to give any assistance in my power to families or individual students desiring to find quarters; and living is not expensive in Devonshire. I shall be delighted to answer any questions about our work, and thank you for allowing me an opportunity of making it known through the *Gazette.*

I am, dear Sir,

Yours very faithfully,

JESSIE DOUGLAS MONTGOMERY,

Hon. Sec. U. E. Department.

.·.

The Danish Popular High Schools.

SIR,—The Editor of the *Daily Chronicle* in his first leader on September 8 evidently felt much attracted by many of Herr Povlsen's statements in your issue for September. But he must also have felt somewhat incredulous, for by the use of no less than twenty-one sets of inverted commas he has left Herr Povlsen severely responsible for the truth of the statements in question. I propose to supplement our Danish friend's lecture by some remarks, which shall also be incredible until inquired into, on points he had not time to touch upon.

(1) What does it cost to attend these schools? 'The expenses,' says a writer in the *Times* of Sept. 15, are reduced to a *minimum*—about £15 for six months' instruction, board and lodging, including all extras. And the poorer half of the students, on the recommendation of clergymen or other authority, receive State bursaries that defray half the cost.'

(2) I can imagine the authors of our 'Technical Instruction Act 1889' somewhat slow to believe that State money can be spent on private schools. But, to quote again from the article in the *Times,* 'In the *Stateman's Year Book* for 1894 it is stated that the Danish government expends nearly £17,000 a year on these schools. Three-fifths of this sum goes in bursaries. The rest is expended as follows:—£17 a year is paid to the principal of each school along with a capitation grant of half a guinea for each student in attendance; and a further grant is made that covers one-third of the cost of salaries, books, and apparatus. The State imposes no cast-iron code; it conducts no examination as a condition of these grants; there is no authority, whether local or central, that has the right of nominating members on any committee of management in proportion to the sum contributed. The only condition is that there shall be at least ten pupils, that the school shall have been in existence at least a year, and that it shall receive once a year a government inspector, who shall satisfy himself in a general way that the school is doing good work, and shall make a report accordingly.'

(3) But what I most wish to say is that the schools, as Herr Povlsen says, must be *seen* to be understood; and I should like to indicate how easy it is for Englishmen to pay a visit to Denmark. The old students at these schools, now of course very numerous, seek opportunities at various yearly gatherings of maintaining and renewing their acquaintance with their old comrades. They have also founded in the chief towns of Denmark twenty seven High School Homes or modest hotels where they can meet their friends when travelling, and be entertained at a cost that does not task their resources. There are three of these homes in Copenhagen, the chief of which in Helgolandsgade no. 14, about five minutes from the central station, is presided over by Mr. Harald Holm, who speaks excellent English, and is besides one of the liberal leaders in the lower house of parliament. At all these homes (of which a full list is given at page 46 of *Holiday Resorts*, which may be had from the Teachers' Guild, 74 Gower Street, W.C., price 1*s.*) the cost for board and lodging does not exceed half-a-crown a day, or £3 a month; and Englishmen are just as welcome there as Danes. I have stayed at five of these homes; and four of them I found so good that I should not hesitate to take wife or daughter to them.

J. S. T.

UNIVERSITY EXTENSION TEACHING IN A SECONDARY SCHOOL.

THE following report by Mr. Marriott on the sequence of courses which have recently been given at St. Michael's Hall, Brighton, will be read with interest.

'I desire to draw the special attention of the Delegates to the course of lectures recently delivered at St. Michael's Hall, Brighton. It was a course absolutely unique I believe in the history of University Extension. It began in May 1893, and went on continuously (interrupted only by the ordinary school vacations) for fourteen months. During that period I delivered at St. Michael's Hall twenty-eight lectures on the History of England from 1485—1714. It was a course more nearly resembling the ordinary teaching of an Oxford lecture-room than anything I have experienced before, and except the actual locale there was nothing to differentiate the teaching I was giving in Oxford on one day and in Brighton the next.'

REPORTS FROM THE CENTRES.

CAMBORNE.—The following report of Extension work in Cornwall appeared in the *Cornish Post* for Sept. 20, 1894:— 'The County Council of Cornwall has this year created a new precedent in the annals of County Councils, by engaging an Oxford Extension lecturer to reside in the county for six months of the year, and lecture during that period at twelve of the chief towns in Cornwall, on South Africa. The course will begin on October 5, and will be illustrated throughout by oxy-hydrogen light. Many of the slides are from particular sources, such as photographs, sections, &c., lent by the De Meers Mining Co., and all have been specially selected and prepared for the course which consists of the following lectures:—Description of South Africa and Early History; the Kaffir Wars; Subjugation of Native Races; Sir Bartle Frere, and Establishment of British Supremacy; The Dutch Republics; Natal and the Kaffir Problem: Native Territories; Agricultural and Pastoral Resources; The Diamond Mines (Kimberley); Gold Mining and other mine rals; Conflict of Nationalities and Races; South African Literature; and Cecil Rhodes, and the Mashonaland Development.'

VENTNOR.—According to the Report published in the *Isle of Wight Mercury*, the fifth year of University Extension in this centre has been on the whole an encouraging one. The evening course has proved that when all classes unite (which is only possible in an evening course) success is insured. Dr. Fison's lectures excited great interest, were well supported, and have more than paid their way. A successful conversazione was of great assistance in cementing the good understanding between lecturer and audience, and in strengthening the influence of the Extension movement. The Association is to be congratulated on having, in common with the other Island centres, secured Dr. Fison's services for the coming season. With regard to the educational results of the two courses, much satisfaction is expressed in the lecturers' reports, and in those of the examiners.

THE LIMITS OF 'TECHNICAL INSTRUCTION.'

THE duty of deciding what subjects fall within the definition of technical instruction, and are therefore lawful objects for County Council aid, is intrusted by the Technical Instruction Acts to the Science and Art Department at South Kensington. No question arises as to the subjects which are enumerated in the 'Science and Art Directory' as those towards instruction in which aid is granted. But some local authorities have naturally desired freedom to aid teaching in a multitude of other subjects as well. And in interpreting the limits of technical instruction, the Science and Art Department has had large influence in determining the educational scope of County Council aid. It is satisfactory therefore that the Department has taken a broad view of the question, and has sanctioned, among others, the following subjects as suitable for the different districts from which the several applications have come :—

Commercial History.
Commercial Geography.
Political Economy.
Instrumental and Orchestral Music.
Etching.
Engraving.
Photography.
Ambulance Work.
Science and Art of Teaching.
Design in application to pottery, furniture, needlework, silversmiths' and goldsmiths' work, textiles, bookbinding, printing, lace, metal work, carving in wood and stone, glass, plaster work, enamelling, and house decoration.
Entomology.

BOOKS ON OUR TABLE.

English Records: a Companion to the History of England, by H. E. MALDEN. London: Methuen & Co. Pp. viii, 239. Price 3*s.* 6*d.*
The idea which inspired this little volume deserves all praise. The author has attempted to introduce historical students to original authorities, and above all to a knowledge of the Statute Book. To a considerable extent he has been successful; but he has failed to write a really useful book, as owing to necessary limits of space, he has been able only to give the vaguest outline of the text and documents with which he deals.

The Economics of Commerce. By H. de B. GIBBINS, M.A., formerly University (Cobden) Prizeman in Political Economy, Oxford. London, Methuen & Co. (Commercial Series). Crown 8vo, pp. 94. Price 1*s.* 6*d.*
This little volume is in every way suited as a useful text-book to study in connexion with economic courses, and might be read with advantage by every young citizen. It is concise and clear in arrangement, and the definitions of Political Economy are given in simple language so as to be readily understood. There are interesting chapters on 'Bimetallism,' 'Money,' and 'Banking.' One cannot at the same time help noting a few slight typographical errors.

Sophocles: Electra. Text and Notes. Edited by J. THOMPSON, M.A. Camb. and B. J. HAYES, M.A. Lond. and Camb. London, Univ. Corr. Coll. Press. Extra fcap. 8vo, pp. 109. Price 3*s.* 6*d.*

Xenophon: Hellenica, Book IV. Text and Notes. Edited by A. WAUGH YOUNG, M.A. Lond. London, Univ. Corr. Coll. Press. Pp. xvi, 101. Price 3*s.* 6*d.*

London Matriculation Directory. No. XVI, June 1894. With Solutions. London, Univ. Corr. Coll. Press. Price 1*s.*

BOOK EXCHANGE COLUMN.

THE Ilkley centre has a valuable stock of books on Shakespeare and his Predecessors in the English Drama. The committee are willing to lend the books to any other centre requiring them, at the rate of 1*s.* a volume, or 10*s.* for twelve volumes, the borrowers paying the carriage. A list of the books will be sent on application to the Hon. Sec.—EMILY DALE, 27 Parish Ghyll, Ilkley, Yorkshire.

ARRANGEMENTS FOR 1894-5.

Autumn, 1894.

Centre.	No. of Lectures in Course.	Subject of Course.	Lecturer.	Course begins.	Course ends.
UNIVERSITY EXTENSION COL- LEGE, READING (evening)	12	Age of Elizabeth and } Puritan Rebellion }	Rev.W.H.SHAW,M.A. & E.L.S.HORSBURGH,M.A.	Th. Oct. 4	Dec. 13
,, (afternoon)	12	Tennyson and Browning	J.CHURTONCOLLINS,M.A	S. Sept. 29	Dec. 8
,, (evening) ...	12	Greek Drama	,, ,, ,,	S. Sept. 29	Dec. 8
,, (evening) ...	12	The Study of Local History	W. M. CHILDS, B.A. ...	F. Sept. 28	Dec. 7
,, (evening) ...	12	La Littérature Française du XVIIe Siècle	M. J. MAURICE REY, B. es Sc.	W. Sept. 26	Dec. 5
,, (evening) ...	12	Geography of the British Isles ...	H. J. MACKINDER,M.A.	S. Oct. 6	Dec. 5
ALTRINCHAM (evening)	6	Making of England	Rev. W.H.SHAW,M.A.	F. Oct. 5	Dec. 14
ASHTON (afternoon)	6	Florence	,, ,, ...	T. Oct. 9	Dec. 18
ASHTON (evening)	6	Mediaeval England	,, ,, ...	T. Oct. 9	Dec. 18
BIRMINGHAM, SEVERN STREET (evening)	6	Mediaeval England ...	,, ,,	T. Oct. 2	Dec. 11
BOLTON (afternoon)	6	Social Reformers	,, ,, ...	Th. Sept. 27	Dec. 6
BOLTON (evening)	6	Mediaeval England ...	,, ,, ...	Th. Sept. 27	Dec. 6
CHELTENHAM (afternoon)	6	Florence	,, ,, ...	Th. Oct. 4	Dec 13
CHELTENHAM (evening)	6	Making of England	,, ,, ...	W. Oct. 3	Dec. 12
CHESTER (afternoon) ...	6	Mediaeval England ...	,, ,, ...	F. Sept. 28	Dec. 7
CIRENCESTER (afternoon) ...	6	Age of Elizabeth	,, ,, ...	M. Oct. 1	Dec. 10
GLOUCESTER (evening) ...	6	Making of England ...	,, ,, ...	M. Oct. 1	Dec. 10
KENDAL (afternoon) ...	6	Puritan Revolution ...	,, ,, ...	M. Sept. 24	Dec. 3
MALVERN (afternoon) ...	6	Age of Elizabeth	,, ,, ...	W. Oct. 3	Dec. 12
MANCHESTER, CHEETHAM (evening)	6	Age of Elizabeth ...	,, ,, ...	F. Sept. 28	Dec. 7
OLDHAM (evening)	6	Mediaeval England	,, ,, ...	W. Sept. 26	Dec. 5
PRESTWICH (evening) ...	6	Mediaeval England	,, ,, ...	M. Sept. 24	Dec. 3
STROUD (afternoon) ...	6	Florence	,, ,, ...	T. Oct. 2	Dec. 11
WIGAN (afternoon) ...	6	Florence	,, ,, ...	W. Sept. 26	Dec. 5
BAKEWELL (evening)	6	English Novelists... ...	J. A. R. MARRIOTT, M.A.	Th. Sept. 27	Dec. 6
BIRMINGHAM, EDGBASTON (afternoon)	12	Age of Louis XIV and French Revolution	,, ,,	T. Oct. 9	Dec. 18
BOURNEMOUTH (afternoon) ...	12	Europe since Waterloo ...	,, ,,	W. Oct. 3	Dec. 12
CLEVEDON (afternoon) ...	12	Shakespeare's Historical Plays ...	,, ,,	Th. Oct. 4	Dec. 13
LEAMINGTON (evening)	6	English in India	,, ,,	F. Sept. 28	Dec. 7
LYMINGTON (afternoon)	6	English in India	,, ,,	T. Oct. 2	Dec. 11
MATLOCK (afternoon) ...	6	The Stuarts & Puritan Revolution	,, ,,	Th. Sept. 27	Dec. 6
REPTON (morning)	6	English Novelists... ...	,, ,,	F. Sept. 28	Dec. 7
SOUTHBOURNE (evening) ...	12	The Age of Napoleon ...	,, ,,	T. Oct. 2	Dec. 11
STAFFORD (afternoon) ...	6	Shakespeare's Historical Plays ...	,, ,,	W. Sept. 26	Dec. 5
STRATFORD-ON-AVON (evening)	6	Cavaliers and Roundheads	,, ,,	T. Oct. 9	Dec. 18
WELLS (evening)	6	England in the 18th Century	,, ,,	Th. Oct. 4	Dec. 13
WEYMOUTH (evening) ...	6	Shakespeare's Historical Plays ...	,, ,,	W. Oct. 3	Dec. 12
WORSLEY (evening) ...	6	English in India	,, ,,	W. Oct. 10	Dec. 19
HARROGATE (evening) ...	12	Prose Writers	C. E. MALLET, B.A. ...	F. Sept. 28	Dec. 14
ILKLEY (afternoon)	12	England in the 18th Century	,, ,,	Th Sept. 27	Dec. 13
OTLEY (evening)	6	The Stuarts	,, ,,	Th. Oct. 4	Dec. 13
PRESTON (afternoon) ...	6	Prose Writers	,, ,,	W. Oct. 10	Dec. 19
RIPON (afternoon) ...	6	French Revolution ...	,, ,,	T. Sept. 25	Dec. 4
RIPON (evening)	6	The Stuarts	,, ,,	T. Sept. 25	Dec. 4
TAMWORTH (evening) ...	10	England in the 18th Century	,, ,,	T. Oct. 2	Dec. 11
TUNBRIDGE WELLS (afternoon)	10	Tudors and Stuarts ...	,, ,,	M. Oct. 8	Dec. 10
WARRINGTON (evening) ..	6	Tudors	,, ,,	W. Sept. 26	Not fixed.
BRADFORD (evening) ...	6	Shakespeare ...	F. S. BOAS, M.A. ...	Th. Oct. 4	Dec. 13
BURNLEY (evening) ...	12	Spencer & other Elizabethan Poets	,, ,,	Th. Oct. 11	Dec. 20
CANTERBURY (afternoon) ...	12	Victorian Poets	,, ,,	W. Oct. 10	Dec. 19
HODDESDON (afternoon) ...	11	Shakespeare	,, ,,	T. Oct. 2	Dec. 18
RAMSGATE (afternoon) ...	12	Literature of Cavaliers & Puritans	,, ,,	S. Oct. 6	Dec. 15
RUGBY (evening)	6	Browning	,, ,,	W. Oct. 3	Dec. 12
SALE (evening)	6	Representative Men, Stuarts	,, ,,	F. Oct. 12	Dec. 14
WESTERHAM (afternoon) ...	6	Victorian Poets	,, ,,	S. Oct. 13	Dec. 22
BRIGHTON (St. Michael's Hall) (morning)	6	The Merchant of Venice ...	Rev. J.G. BAILEY, M.A., LL.D	F. Oct. 12	Dec. 21
EASTBOURNE (afternoon) ...	6	Shakespeare	,, ,,	Th. Oct. 11	Dec. 20
MAIDSTONE (afternoon) ...	6	Shelley, Keats, Coleridge, and Wordsworth	,, ,,	W. Oct. 10	Dec. 19
NEWBURY (afternoon)...	6	Shelley, Keats, Coleridge, and Wordsworth	,, ,,	Th. Oct. 4	Dec. 13
ROCHESTER (evening)	6	Shakespeare	,, ,,	T. Oct. 2	Dec. 11
WEST BRIGHTON (afternoon) ...	12	Tennyson	,, ,,	F. Oct. 12	Dec. 21
BURY (evening)	6	Epochs from English History	E.L.S. HORSBURGH,M.A	T. Oct. 2	Dec. 11
FOLKESTONE (morning)	6	Age of Elizabeth (Social & Lit.)	,, ,,	M. Oct. 1	Dec. 10
HEBDEN BRIDGE (evening) ...	6	French Revolution ...	,, ,,	S. Oct. 20	Dec. 29
HUDDERSFIELD (evening) ...	6	Epochs from English History	,, ,,	W. Oct. 10	Dec. 19
OXFORD (evening) ...	12	The Making of England...	,, ,,	F. Oct. 5	Dec. 14
REIGATE (afternoon) ...	12	The Early Tudors... ...	,, ,,	M. Oct. 1	Dec. 10
THORNTON (evening) ...	6	Epochs from English History ...	,, ,,	M. Oct. 8	Dec. 17

Centre.	No. of Lectures in Course.	Subject of Course.	Lecturer.	Course begins.	Course ends.
SOUTHAMPTON (evening) ...	12	The Reign of Elizabeth	E. L. S. HORSBURGH, B.A.	F. Sept. 28	Dec. 7
SWINDON (evening) ...	6	Epochs from English History ...	„ „	W. Oct. 3	Dec. 11
WAKEFIELD (evening) ...	6	Epochs from English History ...	„ „	T. Oct. 9	Dec. 18
HENLOW (evening) ...	12	The English Citizen	W. M. CHILDS, B.A. ...	W. Oct. 17	Dec. 19
CIRENCESTER (evening) ...	6	Trade, Adventure, and Discovery	K. D. COTES, M.A. ...	M. Oct. 1	Dec. 10
KNOWLE (afternoon) ...	6	Shakespeare's England	„ „ ...	M. Sept. 24	Dec. 3
LLANELLY (evening) ...	6	Trade, Adventure, and Discovery	„ „ ...	W. Oct. 3	Dec. 12
PETERBOROUGH (evening) ...	6	Trade, Adventure, and Discovery	„ „ ...	F. Sept. 28	Dec. 7
STROUD (evening) ...	6	Shakespeare's England	„ „ ...	Th. Oct. 4	Dec. 13
SWANSEA (afternoon) ...	6	Shakespeare's England	„ „ ...	F. Oct. 5	Dec. 14
SWANSEA (evening) ...	6	Trade, Adventure, and Discovery	„ „ ...	F. Oct. 5	Dec. 14
TUNBRIDGE WELLS (evening)...	8	Commerce, Colonization & Empire	„ „ ...	T. Oct. 9	Nov. 27
WINSLOW (evening) ...	6	Relation of History to Painting ...	„ „ ...	Th. Sept. 27	Dec. 6
BANBURY (evening)	6	Economic Aspects of Social Questions	W. A. S. HEWINS, M.A.	Th. Oct. 4	Dec. 6
GRIMSBY (evening)	6	Economic Aspects of Social Questions	„ „ ..	T. Oct. 16	Dec. 18
HYDE (evening)	6	English Social Life	„ „ ...	M. Oct. 1	Dec. 10
KIDDERMINSTER (afternoon)...	6	Economic Aspects of Social Questions	„ „ ...	W. Oct. 3	Dec. 12
KIDDERMINSTER (evening) ...	6	Economic Aspects of Social Questions	„ „ ...	W. Oct. 3	Dec. 12
PUCKLECHURCH (evening) ...	6	Not fixed	„ „ ...	F. Oct. 12	Dec. 21
WEST BRIGHTON (evening) ...	12	Three Centuries of Working Class History	„ „ ...	Th. Oct. 18	Dec. 13
ACCRINGTON (evening) ...	6	Structure of Modern Industry ...	J. A. HOBSON, M.A. ...	M. Oct. 1	Dec. 10
BRIDPORT (evening)	12	Industrial Revolution	„ „ ...	T. Oct. 9	Dec. 18
COVENTRY (evening)	6	Sharing of Wealth	„ „ ...	Th. Sept. 27	Dec. 6
TEAN (afternoon)	6	English Novelists	„ „ ...	S. Sept. 29	Dec. 8
BARNSLEY (evening) ...	6	Ruskin	J. E. PHYTHIAN	T. Oct. 9	Dec. 18
CARLISLE (afternoon) ...	12	Architecture	„ „ ...	T. Oct. 16	Dec. 11
GRANGE (evening)	6	Architecture	„ „ ...	M. Oct. 1	Dec. 10
KESWICK (evening)	6	Shakespeare	„ „ ...	M. Oct. 8	Dec. 17
MOSTON (evening)	8	Venice and Venetian Art ...	„ „ ...	F. Oct. 19	Dec. 7
RHYL (evening)	6	Architecture	„ „ ...	W. Oct. 10	Dec. 19
ROMSEY (afternoon)	6	Mediaeval Architecture	Rev. G. H. WEST, D.D.	W. Oct. 3	Dec. 12
HALIFAX (evening)	6	Dante	Rev. P. H. WICKSTEED, M.A.	F. Oct. 12	Nov. 30
BODMIN (evening)	12	South Africa	W. B. WORSFOLD, M.A.	F. Oct. 12	Dec. 21
CAMBORNE (evening)	12	South Africa	„ „ ...	F. Oct. 5	Dec. 14
FALMOUTH (evening)	12	South Africa	„ „ ...	Th. Oct. 4	Dec. 13
HELSTON (evening)	12	South Africa	„ „ ...	T. Oct. 9	Dec. 18
LAUNCESTON (evening) ...	12	South Africa	„ „ ...	W. Oct. 3	Dec. 12
PENZANCE (evening)	12	South Africa	„ „ ...	M. Oct. 8	Dec. 17
REDRUTH (evening)	12	South Africa	„ „ ...	Th. Oct. 11	Dec. 20
ST. AUSTELL (evening) ...	12	South Africa	„ „ ...	T. Oct. 2	Dec. 11
TRURO (evening)	12	South Africa	„ „ ...	M. Oct. 1	Dec. 10
HUNGERFORD (afternoon) ...	6	Physiography	G. J. BURCH, M.A. ...	F. Oct. 5	Dec. 21
CARLISLE (evening)	6	Outlines of Geology	C. CARUS-WILSON, F.G.S.	Th. Oct. 11	Dec. 20
LOUTH (evening)	6	Outlines of Geology	„ „ ...	M. Oct. 1	Dec. 10
ST. HELENS (evening)... ...	6	Crust of the Earth	„ „ ...	M. Oct. 8	Dec. 17
SETTLE (evening)	6	Physiography	„ „ ...	T. Oct. 9	Dec. 18
BATH (afternoon)	12	Life of a Planet	A. H. FISON, D.Sc. ...	Th. Sept. 27	Dec. 6
BATH (evening)	12	Life of a Planet	„ „ ...	Th. Sept. 27	Dec. 6
BOURNEMOUTH (evening) ...	12	Forces of Nature	„ „ ...	F. Sept. 28	Dec. 7
NEWPORT (evening)	12	Physical Astronomy	„ „ ...	Th. Oct. 4	Dec. 13
RYDE (afternoon)	12	Life of a Planet	„ „ ...	Th. Oct. 4	Dec. 13
VENTNOR (evening)	12	Physical Astronomy	„ „ ...	F. Oct. 5	Dec. 14
LITTLE BERKHAMPSTEAD (afternoon)	6	Astronomy	R. A. GREGORY, M.A.	Th. Oct. 4	Dec. 13
Somerset County Council					
4 Courses of	12	Management of Farm Stock ...	H. SESSIONS	Oct.	Dec.
5 Courses of	12	Agricultural Chemistry ...	H. E. NIBLETT, B.A....	Oct.	Dec.
Greek Classes					
BRIGHTON (Elementary)...	10	Xen. *Anab.* I	REV. E. LUCE, M.A. ...	T. Oct. 9	Dec. 11
„ (Intermediate)	10	Thucyd. VII and Soph. *Ajax* ...	„ „	W. Oct. 10	Dec. 12

Spring Term, 1895.

†UNIVERSITY EXTENSION COLLEGE, READING (evening)		Age of Elizabeth and Puritan Rebellion }	Rev. W. H. SHAW, M.A. & E. L. S. HORSBURGH, M.A.	Th. Jan. 17	Mar. 28
„ (afternoon)		Tennyson and Browning ...	J. CHURTON COLLINS, M.A.	S. Jan. 26	Apr. 6
„ (evening) ...		Greek Drama	„ „ ...	S. Jan. 26	Apr. 6
„ (evening) ...		The Study of Local History ...	W. M. CHILDS, B.A. ...	F. Jan. 25	Apr. 5
„ (evening) ...		La Littérature Française du XVII° Siècle	M. J. MAURICE REY, B. es Sc.	W. Jan. 23	Apr. 3
„ (evening) ...		Geography of the British Isles ...	H. J. MACKINDER, M.A.	S. Jan. 19	Mar. 30
†BIRMINGHAM, EDGBASTON (afternoon)		Age of Louis XIV and French Revolution	J. A. R. MARRIOTT, M.A.	T. Jan. 15	Mar. 26
†BOURNEMOUTH (afternoon) ...		Europe since Waterloo ...	„ „ ...	W. Jan. 23	Apr. 3
BRADFORD (evening)	6	Colonies	„ „ ...	Th. Jan. 17	Mar. 28
†BRIDPORT (evening) ...		Industrial Revolution ...	„ „ ...	T. Jan. 22	Apr. 2
†CLEVEDON (afternoon) ...		Shakespeare's Historical Plays ...	„ „ ...	F. Jan. 25	Apr. 5

† Continued from Autumn Session.

Centre.	No. of Lectures in Course.	Subject of Course.	Lecturer.	Course begins.	Course ends.
DORCHESTER (evening) ...	6	Colonies	J.A.R. MARRIOTT, M.A.	W. Jan. 23	Apr. 3
†OXFORD (evening) ...		The Making of England ...	,, ,, ...	F. Jan. 18	Mar. 29
SALE (evening)	6	England in the 18th Century ...	,, ,, ...	W. Jan. 16	Mar. 27
†SOUTHBOURNE (afternoon) ...		Europe since Waterloo ...	,, ,, ...	Th. Jan. 24	Apr. 4
†TAMWORTH (evening)		England in the 18th Century ...	C. E. MALLET, B.A. ...	T. Jan. 15	Feb. 26
FOLKESTONE (evening)	10	Europe since Waterloo ...	,, ,,	M.Jan. 21 or 28	Mar. 25 or Apr. 1
†BURNLEY (evening) ...		Spenser & other Elizabethan Poets	F. S. BOAS, M.A. ...	Th. Jan. 17	Mar. 28
†CANTERBURY (afternoon) ...		Victorian Poets	,, ,, ...	W. Jan. 23	Apr. 3
†RAMSGATE (afternoon)		Literature of Cavaliers and Puritans		S. Jan. 26	Apr. 6
†WEST BRIGHTON (afternoon)		Tennyson	Rev. J. G. BAILEY, M.A., LL.D.	F. Jan. 18	Mar. 29
ABERGAVENNY (afternoon) ...	6	Shakespeare	E. L. S. HORSBURGH, B.A.	S. Jan. 26	Apr. 6
BRECON (afternoon) ...	6	Not fixed	,, ,, ...	Th. Jan. 24	Apr. 4
BRECON (evening) ...	6	Not fixed	,, ,, ...	Th. Jan. 24	Apr. 4
CHELTENHAM (afternoon) ...	6	Not fixed	,, ,, ...	W. Jan. 30	Apr. 10
CHELTENHAM (evening)	6	Not fixed	,, ,, ...	W. Jan. 30	Apr. 10
EVESHAM (evening) ...	6	Revolution and Age of Anne ...	,, ,, ...	W. Jan. 23	Apr. 3
GLOUCESTER (evening)	6	English History in Shakespeare...	,, ,, ...	M. Jan. 28	Apr. 8
HEREFORD evening) ...	6	Wyclif to Sir Thomas More ...	,, ,, ...	M. Jan. 21	Apr. 1
LEOMINSTER (evening)	6	Industrial and Economic Questions since 1789	,, ,, ...	T. Jan. 22	Apr. 2
†REIGATE (afternoon)...		The Reign of Elizabeth ...	,, ,, ...	Th. Jan. 17	Mar. 28
ROSS (afternoon) ...	6	Literature of the 18th Century ...	,, ,, ...	T. Jan. 22	Apr. 2
†SOUTHAMPTON (evening)		The Age of Elizabeth ...	,, ,, ...	F. Jan. 18	May 29
STROUD (afternoon) ...	6	The Renaissance	,, ,, ...	T. Jan. 29	Apr. 9
STROUD (evening) ...	6	The Reign of Elizabeth ...	,, ,, ...	T. Jan. 29	Apr. 9
SWANSEA (evening) ...	6	Not fixed	,, ,, ...	F. Jan. 25	Apr. 5
†HENLOW (evening) ...		The English Citizen ...	W. M. CHILDS, B.A. ...	W. Jan. 16	Mar. 27
GLOSSOP (evening) ...	6	Trade, Adventure, and Discovery	K. D. COTES, M.A. ...	W. Jan. 23	Apr. 3
*WARRINGTON (evening)	6	Trade, Adventure, and Discovery	,, ,, ...	F. Jan. 25	Apr. 5
WIRKSWORTH (evening)	6	Trade, Adventure, and Discovery	,, ,, ...	Th. Jan. 24	Apr. 4
*TAVISTOCK (afternoon)	6	Puritan Revolution	W. G. DE BURGH, B.A.	M. Not fixed	Not fixed
†WEST BRIGHTON (evening) ...		Three Centuries of Working-class History	W. A. S. HEWINS, M.A.	Th. Jan. 24	Apr. 18
GRIMSBY (evening)	6	Not fixed	J. A. HOBSON, M.A. ...	T. Jan. 22	Apr. 2
MIDHURST (afternoon)	6	English Novelists	,, ,, ...	W. Jan. 16	Mar. 27
†CARLISLE (afternoon)		Architecture	J. E. PHYTHIAN ...	T. Jan. 15	Apr. 9
CHESTER (afternoon) ...	6	Architecture	,, ,, ...	T. Jan. 22	Apr. 2
HALIFAX (evening) ...	6	Florentine Art	,, ,, ...	Th. Not fixed	Not fixed
KERSAL (evening) ...	8	Architecture	,, ,, ...	M. Jan. 28	Mar. 18
†BODMIN (evening) ...		South Africa	W. B. WORSFOLD M.A.,	F. Jan. 25	Apr. 5
†CAMBORNE (evening)...		South Africa	,, ,, ...	F. Jan. 18	Mar. 29
†FALMOUTH (evening)...		South Africa	,, ,, ...	Th. Jan. 17	Mar. 28
†HELSTON (evening) ...		South Africa	,, ,, ...	T. Jan. 22	Apr. 2
†LAUNCESTON (evening)		South Africa	,, ,, ...	W. Jan. 16	Mar. 27
†PENZANCE (evening) ...		South Africa	,, ,, ...	M. Jan. 21	Apr. 1
†REDRUTH (evening) ...		South Africa	,, ,, ...	Th. Jan. 24	Apr. 4
†ST. AUSTELL (evening)		South Africa	,, ,, ...	T. Jan. 15	Mar. 26
†TRURO (evening)		South Africa	,, ,, ...	M. Jan. 14	Mar. 25
BRIGHTON (St. Michael's Hall)	6	Regions, Races, and Resources ...	H. R. MILL, D.Sc. ...	Not fixed.	Not fixed
BANBURY (evening)	6	Crust of the Earth	C.CARUS-WILSON,F.G.S.	Th. Jan. 17	Mar. 28
†BATH (afternoon)		Recent Discoveries with the Telescope and Spectroscope	A. H. FISON, D.Sc. ...	Th. Jan. 17	Mar. 28
†BATH (evening)		Recent Discoveries with the Telescope and Spectroscope	,, ,, ...	Th. Jan. 17	Mar. 28
†BOURNEMOUTH (evening) ...		Forces of Nature	,, ,, ...	F. Jan. 18	Mar. 29
†NEWPORT (evening) ...		Physical Astronomy	,, ,, ...	Th. Jan. 24	Apr. 4
†RYDE (afternoon)		Recent Discoveries with the Telescope and Spectroscope	,, ,, ...	Th. Jan. 24	Apr. 4
†VENTNOR (evening)		Physical Astronomy	,, ,, ...	F. Jan. 25	Apr. 5
Somerset County Council :					
5 Courses of	12	Management of Farm Stock ...	H. SESSIONS	Jan.	Apr.
5 Courses of	12	Hygiene	C.H.WADE,M.A.,D.P.H.	Jan.	Apr.

Summer Term, 1895.

BRIGHTON (St. Michael's Hall) | 6 or 8 | England in the 18th Century ... | J.A.R.MARRIOTT,M.A. | Not fixed. | Not fixed

† Continued from Autumn Term.   * Arrangements not yet completed.

Note.—Application for Courses and all information as to fees, &c., can be obtained from The Secretary, University Extension Office, Examination Schools, Oxford.

INFORMATION TO CONTRIBUTORS.

All communications should be addressed to the Editor, OXFORD UNIVERSITY EXTENSION GAZETTE, *University Press, Oxford.*

All matter intended for insertion in the December issue should reach him not later than November 20.

Contributions should be written on one side of the paper only, and must be accompanied by the name of the writer (not necessarily for publication).

N.B.—*All orders should carefully specify the full title,* OXFORD UNIVERSITY EXTENSION GAZETTE.

OXFORD UNIVERSITY

EXTENSION GAZETTE.

VOL. V. No. 51.]   DECEMBER, 1894.   [ONE PENNY.

N.B.—Local Organizers of Oxford University Extension Lectures are invited to send to the Secretary, University Extension Office, Examination Schools, Oxford, copies of any journals containing notices of, or references to, Extension work.

NOTES AND COMMENTS.

Mr. Acland, the Vice-President of the Council, in the course of an important address on educational matters to his constituents on Nov. 15, spoke warmly of the aims of University Extension, and offered to make a contribution towards the cost of a course of lectures if one could be arranged in Rotherham. This proposal of the Minister of Education is a high compliment to the work of the University Extension lecturers.

.·.

There is a great increase in the number of workmen attending University Extension lectures this session.

.·.

The audience attending Mr. Hudson Shaw's courses this Autumn number no less than 7,400. The wet fortnight at the end of October did not diminish this total by more than 50. At the end of this month Mr. Shaw sails for the United States, and will lecture during next term for the American Society for the Extension of University Teaching.

.·.

At an industrial centre in Yorkshire there is a larger attendance now that each member of the audience pays 2s. 6d. for a ticket, than there was when the lectures were free.

.·.

Instruction in Agriculture at Reading. Under the authority of the decree of May 22 last by which the University of Oxford empowered the Delegates to co-operate with the University Extension College, Reading, in organizing instruction and examination in Agriculture, a joint committee has been formed, consisting of five representatives of each of the two co-operating bodies. The following are the members of this committee :—Elected by the University Extension Delegacy : Rev. Dr. Magrath (Vice-Chancellor of the University of Oxford), Prof. E. B. Poulton, M.A., F.R.S., Mr. W. W. Fisher, M.A., F.C.S., Mr. P. E. Matheson, M.A. (Secretary of the Oxford and Cambridge Joint Examinations Board), and Mr. M. E. Sadler, M.A. Elected by the University Extension College, Reading : The Principal (Mr. H. J. Mackinder, M.A.), the Director of the Agricultural Department (Mr. D. A. Gilchrist, B.Sc.), Mr. W. H. Dunn, J.P. (Chairman of the Technical Education Committee of the Berks County Council), Mr. M. J. Sutton, J.P. (Member of the Councils of the Royal Agricultural Society and of the Bath and West of England Society), and the Right Hon. Viscount Valentia (Chairman of the Oxford County Council). At the first meeting of the Joint Board held at Oxford on Nov. 14 the Vice-Chancellor was elected chairman, and the College Secretary (Mr. F. H. Wright) secretary of the Board. The scheme is of a most practical and systematic character, and has attracted much favourable notice in agricultural and scientific circles.

On November 6 in a Convocation of the University of Oxford the following decree was carried unanimously :—

That the Delegates for the Extension of Teaching be authorized to issue Diplomas in Agriculture in connexion with the instruction and examination in Agriculture organized by the Delegacy in co-operation with the Reading University Extension College.

.·.

Mr. Graham Wallas' election adds a strong man to the London School Board at a time of great opportunity in English education. Our only regret is that his new duties will necessarily curtail the time that he can give to University Extension.

.·.

Among the lecturers announced in the programme of the Leeds Philosophical Society for the winter, are three who are closely identified with Extension work, Messrs. D. S. MacColl, C. Carus-Wilson and Oliver Elton.

.·.

The Delegates have received through Dr. Furnivall a gift of several copies of Parts 7-12 of the Browning Society's papers, and a set of the Chaucer Society's publications (97 volumes), which will form a valuable addition to their library.

.·.

Christmas Holidays. — The University Extension Office will be closed as usual between Christmas Eve and New Year's Day.

THE OXFORD SUMMER MEETING, 1895.

THE Meeting will begin on August 1 and end on August 26, these dates having been fixed in order to meet the convenience of teachers whose Summer Term does not end till late in July. The chief course of lectures will deal with the history, literature, art, and economics of the period from 1688 to 1789. More lectures on the literature of the period will be given in Part I (August 1-12) than was the case this year ; and a considerable part of the course in Part II will be thrown into the form of classes, in connexion with which students will have an opportunity of writing papers.

There will be a course on the Science of Education, which may extend over a large part of the Meeting, and will include lectures on educational history. Among the new features of the Meeting will be a course on Philosophy, in which reference will be made to the works of Berkeley, Hume, and Kant ; and an illustrated course on Architecture in relation to History, with special regard to the buildings in Oxford and its neighbourhood. Classes in Greek and in Economics will also be included in the programme.

In Natural Science, it is hoped to arrange courses of instruction in Chemistry, Geology, Botany, and Hygiene,

1

but further announcements will be made on this subject, which is still under consideration.

The excursions to places of historical interest, which proved popular last August, will be resumed, some being arranged to take place on August 12, on which day there will be no lectures. This day will form a break between the two parts of the Meeting. During the first part, a conference will be held on some subject relating to University Extension. The price of tickets will remain as before (30s. for the whole Meeting, £1 for either part alone), an extra charge being made for some of the classes. The programme, with list of lodgings, will be published at Easter, and a guide to preparative reading will be issued in due course.

THE OPPORTUNITY OF THE UNIVERSITIES.

By Miss J. D. MONTGOMERY.

AT the present moment there is a widespread feeling that we are on the eve of important changes in Secondary Education ; and while we are awaiting the Report of the Royal Commission, there are many points on which the public mind exercises itself; and surely not the least important is the question 'What part can and will the Universities play in any national scheme of Secondary Education?'

Fifty years ago such a question would have had no meaning at all; for the Universities then bore no direct relation whatever to the national life; only some 3,000 undergraduates were to be found at Oxford and Cambridge together; and although this small number of men may have had some indirect influence on the public life, as politicians, clergy, teachers, &c., they were but an inadequate conduit to convey the spirit of the Universities to the mass of the people. But now the case is widely different. Through the Local Examinations, and still more through the system known by the somewhat clumsy name of University Extension, or by the positively misleading name of Local Lectures (since the lecture is only a part of the machinery employed), the Universities have allowed themselves to be brought into touch with that larger portion of the nation which can never hope for the privileges of University residence.

Now is their opportunity for deepening, for extending, for systematizing their influence; will they see it? will they rise to it? or will they repudiate their debts to the nation at large, and content themselves with exercising only an indirect influence on it?

In the local committees for promoting University Extension and the Local Examinations, there are throughout the country organized bodies accustomed to look to the Universities for guidance ; the *principle* is recognized, the local bodies are ready, and the time has come for the Universities to make a voluntary step forward, and, as it were, offer to place their wide experience, their wealth of historic association, and some of their material resources at the service of the nation as a whole. Let it be noted, that hitherto every step taken in this direction has *not* been voluntary, but has been forced on them by the outside public. Sir Thomas Acland and his colleagues were the means of inducing the Universities to take in hand the Local Examinations; while the demand for systematic courses of lectures came from an association of ladies in Yorkshire, and from some Working Men's Co-operative Societies; and it was only listened to, thanks to the persistent and generous advocacy of Mr. James Stuart.

Where lies the present weakness of University Extension teaching? those of us who believe most in its possibilities are the first to recognize and deplore its want of system and continuity. But where is the remedy? We say boldly and frankly, it lies with the Universities.

We are deeply grateful for what they have done; we have shown our gratitude by untiring local effort. We have made, unassisted, great advances towards system ; we have borne the financial strain of 'Affiliation'; we have risked losing popular support by giving opportunities for gaining the Sessional Certificate ; we have strained every nerve to supplement the science courses by classes for practical work; we have started Greek classes in connexion with courses on Greek History and Art; we have almost everywhere organized Students' Associations for the encouragement of individual study.; we have made many efforts, and we feel we can do no more without fresh help and support. It is time for the Universities to recognize their responsibilities in the matter, and to make *their* sacrifices.

Two Institutions which have grown out of University Extension work seem to show the lines of possible development. At Reading and Exeter two permanent institutions have been established in organic connexion with the Universities. This has been rendered possible at Reading by the award of a Christ Church Studentship to the Principal of the College, thus enabling him to devote himself to the organization of higher education in Reading and the neighbourhood ; while at Exeter the Cambridge Syndicate 'recommended' a Principal to the local authorities, and guaranteed him lecturing work in the district to supplement the salary which the local funds could supply.

Great as is the help thus afforded, it is not wholly adequate ; the continued and regular absences of the Principal are detrimental to the work of his own College, especially if he himself undertakes a considerable share in the teaching. What we want is that some University Fellowships should be given to experienced 'Extension' workers, thus enabling them to devote their whole time to organizing the educational work of a district. Such an accredited agent of the Universities should prove a valuable assistance to the work of the Royal Commission on Secondary Education. That is chiefly concerned with *schools*; but the boys and girls who leave elementary, middle, and high schools at the age of twelve, sixteen, and eighteen respectively, are only provided with the *means* of education, not with education itself. To whatever body the Royal Commission commits the work of organizing Secondary Education, such an official should be of the greatest service. He should make it his business to become acquainted with all educational organizations, technical, commercial, secondary, or higher-grade, from the National Union of Teachers to the Head Masters' Association. He should have the tact to find out local needs, and the resource to suggest to the administering body means of supplying them. His advice would be the more readily listened to, because he would be independent of local prejudices, while understanding local conditions. His influence would be not only *personal*, for he would have the Universities behind him ; and his voice would be given to support those members of local bodies who wish to maintain a high standard, and not to pander to any desire for immediate and, above all, financially satisfactory results.

Will the Universities, as occasion offers, devote Fellowships to this work? There are Fellows not occupied in research, or original literary work, whose sole duty is lecturing to a mere handful of undergraduates ; such Fellows might be doing invaluable work for a whole district, while the University provides other means for its resident students to get 'all knowledge.'

'Statutes forbid!' Statutes are not like the laws of the Medes and Persians ; and even if no existing Fellowships can be spared for this work (which it would be hard to demonstrate), is England too poor to entrust a few hundreds a year to her Universities for the elevation and increased happiness of her adult citizens?

Let us frankly admit that new conditions have brought new needs. If the Universities feel that their means are inadequate to meet them, why should not individuals give them the means? If ten rich men would found ten Fellowships of £200 a year, the demand on each would not be unbearable, and the benefit to the country would be incalculable.

I believe that if the Universities realized their responsibility in the matter of general national education, and made it clear that they had not the means to meet it, the means would be forthcoming.

To speak quite plainly, we local workers feel that we want more sympathy and encouragement from the Universities; we want to be brought into closer personal relations with our benefactors; and a University Fellow resident among us would go far to supply the need.

Let us for a moment put aside all preconceived ideas as to what a University might, could, or should be, and consider what was the ideal proposed at its commencement. Ascertaining that, we shall at least know whether such a modification of existing conditions as we suggest would be evolution, revolution, or reversion to type.

Many tell us that the first and most important object of a University is to encourage 'research,' and that by undertaking any share in 'popular' teaching, the University misapplies its endowments and resources. Now if we go back to the original Statutes, we find uncommonly little about 'research.' In the Middle Ages 'research' and diffusion of knowledge were not differentiated. But this we do find everywhere:—while the Universities were for *all* who desired to learn, special care was taken for the poor.

Look at Walter de Merton's Statutes: his scholars were to be 'poor' boys, and to vacate their place on getting a benefice. Again, the first qualification for Bishop Stapledon's scholars was to be 'poverty': any who obtained a yearly income of sixty shillings were to forfeit their position. At Pembroke (Cambridge) every Fellow had to swear that he had not above forty shillings a year to spend. Read the objects set forth by Henry VIII in founding Trinity—'research' is not mentioned. Look again at the quaint phrases of the founder of Clare, who desires that knowledge may shine for '*all* who walk in the by-ways of ignorance.' Or see from what kind of homes the students of S. John's came, among whom we find the sons of a husbandman, groom, carrier, cook, miner, miller, drover, plumber, &c. Everywhere the obvious intention is the wide *diffusion* of knowledge among all who desire it.

And without for a moment disparaging the extreme value of 'research,' it may surely be contended that it is not the only, nor even the worthiest object of a University. If the explorer who discovers the source of the Nile renders a service to mankind, surely the engineer who supplies a big city with water, from sources already known but hitherto unutilized, is also a benefactor to the race.

And recalling Lessing's celebrated dictum, that 'It is better to seek for Truth than to find it,' may we not ask, 'Is there not sometimes a danger of the "research" worker using knowledge rather as a whetstone for his own intellect than as a mine from which to derive precious ore which may be shared with others?'

It is difficult to escape a suspicion that some of the objections put forward by those who deprecate any 'popularizing' of the Universities may have their roots in the tenacity with which we all cling to 'privilege.' 'If every one is educated, who will do *our work*?' was plaintively asked by a student at the Summer Meeting at Oxford. And a recent writer in the *Contemporary Review* does not hesitate to express some such views in language which has a real interest as the genuine survival of a spirit which we had thought to have died out in the last century, the spirit which shows how the exclusive possession of any privilege cramps and impedes the unhappy possessor who clutches it fast, and refuses to share it. The belief 'that knowledge is the heritage of all,' rests only on 'the slippery ground of sentiment'; 'why should our Universities exist if the unlettered are given their share in the privileges and patronage of learning?' 'Literature and Art must remain aristocratic and exclusive—the people never had and never can have the smallest interest in its privileges and penalties.' We had thought a Burns and a Giotto had done some service to Literature and Art. But better indeed to be without either, than to suffer such moral deterioration as could alone inspire such an absolute want of sympathy and perception.

Granting fully that the Universities should encourage 'research' to the utmost, it is surely not possible that all their members should have the talents required for such work; and when fresh knowledge has been acquired, is it to be the monopoly of one man, or to be shared only with a few kindred spirits? Is not knowledge, like mercy, 'twice blessed,' blessing 'him that gives, and him that takes'? We venture to think that while the 'research'

workers are exploring unknown regions, the Universities have also a noble work lying ready to their hand in giving wide publicity to knowledge already acquired.

By interesting themselves in the national education, the Universities have certainly reaped a material reward. If fifty years ago some wild fanatic had proposed a scheme for despoiling the Universities, it would indeed have raised a howl of fury from the 'privileged' classes; but the middle and working classes would have had little to say against such a plan. Now however, in manufacturing towns and mining villages, in watering-places and rural districts, 'our Universities' have a place in the affection of no inconsiderable portion of the nation.

And if the Universities reap some reward, the nation derives great benefit. There are, at any rate, three reasons which make the Universities specially valuable factors in organizing local education.

1. There is a real danger just now lest Technical Instruction should be supposed to cover the whole field, and lest Technical Instruction itself should be interpreted in its narrowest sense as being immediately concerned with commercial profits, which is undoubtedly not the intention of the Technical Instruction Act. The University spirit would tend to maintain the higher view, and to interpret it as instruction in the sciences underlying commercial processes.

2. The Universities are apart from party spirit. The bane of purely local administration of education is the extent to which it is dominated by politics. Long ago Sir Thomas Acland pointed out the favourable position of the Universities in this matter, inasmuch as their 'acknowledged position would be a strong security that no private crotchets or personal interests would be allowed to disturb the action of a great body of men for the mental cultivation of a free people'; and he further noted their power of combining 'much freedom with much exactness.'

3. The Universities have a power of stirring up and keeping alive some enthusiasm for education. It is possible to have a genuine enthusiasm for one of our old Universities; they touch our imagination, appeal to our historical sense, promote *esprit de corps*: it is *not* easy to be enthusiastic over a Government Department.

In conclusion, we earnestly trust that some influential members of the Universities will see the present opportunity, and induce the Governing Body to embrace it. Many noble spirits in all ages in the Universities have dreamt of 'a University co-extensive with the nation'; we almost hope that dream is now shared by the nation; for—

'The dreams that a nation dreams come true.'

WHAT THE WORKMAN NEEDS IN EDUCATION.

By a Member of the Independent Labour Party.

'*It is not for his toils that I lament for the poor; we must all toil, or steal (howsoever we name our stealing), which is worse; no faithful workman finds his task a pastime. But what I do mourn over is that the lamp of his soul should go out; that no ray of heavenly or even earthly knowledge should visit him; but only in the haggard darkness, like two spectres, fear and indignation bear him company.*'—CARLYLE.

OF late years 'the education of the workman' has become one of the most frequent subjects of discussion, and also one of active and extensive experiment. The old Mechanics' Institutions which existed in most centres, have blossomed into the more modern Technical School, and towns which hitherto had allowed the workman to shift for himself in matters educational, or not to shift at all, as the case may be, have suddenly expressed a desire to follow in the same direction and become possessed of an evening school; add to this the extension of the activity of the School Board in secondary and evening education, and a host of other agencies too numerous to name in a short article of this description, and one is obliged to recognize that there is a large amount of educational means at hand. But in spite of all the advantages and opportunities, I am afraid that the workman generally does not to any large extent benefit as he should do by the above institutions; not because the institutions themselves are wrongly directed or at fault, but because of the difficult circumstances and conditions that the workman has to fight against, and over which he has little or no control.

Now it is with these difficulties that I mainly wish to deal. But first let us see what are the actual needs of the workman. At present he is so narrow-minded and often wrong because he knows little of the history of his own country, and less of the history of other countries. He is bigoted and intolerant, because prejudice and personal or family connexions usually lead him to be indifferent to or leave him with fixed opinions on politics; and knowing nothing of the economic forces which affect and regulate his industrial conditions, he rarely changes his views on intelligent lines. His acquaintance with literature is meagre, unless indeed the dreadful trash read so extensively by the young men and women for its sensational excitement be considered literature. He has no admiration for art, because he fails to understand it; science is unknown to him, and languages he imagines to be altogether beyond his reach. Now observe, I do not mean that every workman is ignorant; far from it. I am myself indebted to the beneficial guidance of workmen whom I shall ever respect and revere. I have also known men who, because of their knowledge and education, have been respected and admired by the whole of their fellow-workmen in the factory. But these are exceptions, though on the whole the general tone of the workers is vastly improving, because they are beginning to realize that they will have to take their part in removing the industrial difficulties which surround them. Holding these views of the workman, I submit then, that in order to give him sound judgement, intellectual pleasure, and equip him to compete for the higher positions in the industrial world with his more favoured rival, the university man, it is necessary that he should know something of history, of political economy, of art, of science, of languages, and of course have a technical knowledge of the industry by which he earns his living. But there are insurmountable difficulties which prevent hundreds of workmen from undertaking the study of these branches of education. Under present industrial conditions there are thousands of young men and women working in our factories ten hours a day, until completely exhausted, who never have a moment's leisure to sit down and quietly take stock of their mental position; and how is it possible for a man wearied in physique to become a capable and efficient student? All the time that is left between sleep and work is spent in the pleasures that most immediately appeal to the overwrought body. The gin-palace and the low music-hall are the direct result of a system of overwork that destroys men's desire for, and therefore prohibits, mental leisure. This is the condition of things always found where the labour of eight or ten hours per day is physically exhausting, as in the factory, the workshop, and the mine; and where the labour is lighter, people have to work longer hours, as in the case of shop-assistants, railway-porters, &c. But apart from the question of the long hours and the exhausting nature of his work, the workman has few opportunities for that quiet and consistent study which is so necessary to enable him to become the thorough master of any subject he may take in hand. In nine cases out of ten his reading, writing, and everything else, must be done in the living-room, which also serves as kitchen; and here, amidst the noise of the children, the elder son of the family, or the young married man must pursue his study. Of course there are a considerable number of young men and women who live their lives independently, at any rate for a considerable period, of all family ties; but these can hardly be said to be more specially favoured, as in a large number of cases they have the same difficulties to meet. Apart from this, a working-man's home is, in many cases, neither roomy enough nor adaptable for one or more members of the family to sit at the table to read or write; the housewife

and mother must do her work, and the student is always in her way. This difficulty could, I think, be met for the present, if local authorities and the directors of evening schools would be at the small expense of erecting desks to write upon, as they now provide tables and stands to read at, in connexion with their reading-rooms and libraries. To many workmen who are hindered by none of these difficulties there is a mighty barrier in the way: it is, how to get the necessary cash to undertake even small instalments of education. Not only this, but the poor student always feels acutely any slight upon his poverty; and however unintentional it may be, he is often left to struggle coldly along by himself, with no help or kind word of encouragement or friendly association from his more favoured class-mate. It is not only a difficulty to the man who sets himself to study, but it is the great bugbear which deters others from beginning. During the past few years, for instance, Mr. Ruskin's works have been brought into prominence amongst the workers by various methods. I have myself often given addresses on his social and economic teachings, and the question asked has always been, How can we get hold of Mr. Ruskin's books? I have at all times advised the method adopted by a dozen of my comrades, of paying each sixpence a week and purchasing one book a week, reading it in turns, and casting lots which book each of us should possess as his own, when we had each read them all; but that is a method which they do not readily adopt. The Oxford Extension book-boxes might be made more useful in relieving this difficulty; for instance, the books, I think, should consist of what the lecturer advises students to read, which is not always the case at present, and more copies of each book in place of those now sent and never used [1]. This question of expense has been a real difficulty with me personally, and with many men whom I have tried to persuade to join the classes. For four years I had plenty of time and every other facility, but could not purchase the books and other requirements in various branches of study, because I was working short hours through bad trade, and as a consequence only earning part wages. Want of money is a difficulty with thousands, who live by weekly wages so scanty that nothing can be afforded for books or education. I know that the thrifty and successful man will say that the workers should spend less in beer and tobacco; but my answer is, that the men who often squander their money on those things are not the men who would otherwise spend it on education. I know that for many subjects undertaken by the Oxford Extension classes, books can be had from the public and school libraries; but there are many places where public libraries do not yet exist, and often enough the student applies for a book from the box or from the school library only to find that it is out, and the most important help—the very book he cannot afford to buy—is kept from him. In art, science, and language classes it is absolutely necessary in most cases that the books should be bought outright, and there are few young workmen of the manual labour class who can afford to do it. Then of course there are other expenses in many cases, such as tram and railway fares. Imagine, reader, if you are one who has never had to face these difficulties, a young man who, having finished his ten hours of hard physical labour, rushes from the mill-gates at six o'clock, to get his tea and change his dress in time for the lecture or class at the evening school. He is tired when he leaves the mill, has a mile to walk home, and another or more to walk to the school. Add to this the difficulties of study at home, and perhaps the cost of transit fare from some outside village; see him baffled in obtaining the text-book from the library; and can you wonder that the working classes do not take sufficient interest in Extension work? Those who have friends to guide them and relatives to help them may stick to their task until it becomes their pleasure and recreation, but the large mass seek the pleasures which are nearest and cheapest at hand, in which there is often more harm than good. There is one further difficulty which the new and young student often has to encounter—that is the difficulty of obtaining proper guidance and correct informa-

[1 Want of means alone prevents this from being done at once; in the meantime improvement is steadily being made.—ED.]

tion on the course of reading, the subject and the character of the examination he will have to undergo: as many neglect to go to an examination through the fear of being unable to make a good show of work. Older and more capable scholars can do much to assist the teacher to remove this, by a spirit of mutual helpfulness and kindly fellowship amongst the various classes of younger students. This, I think, will begin to take place as the workman realizes more generally that these advantages of higher education are for him, to improve in his leisure hours, be they few or many, whatever capacity and power nature has endowed him with; and every advance to cheapen and expand the facilities of obtaining a higher education will be a boon to the studious workman who desires by every means at his command to fit himself for the duties of true citizenship.

THE EXPERIMENT OF THE CORNWALL COUNTY COUNCIL.

IN the spring of the present year, as most of the readers of the *Gazette* are probably aware, the County Council of Cornwall determined to assist the University Extension movement in that county. The Extension lecture-system had been at work there for some years, without ever having received the smallest assistance from any public funds. Although the movement showed signs of strong vitality, and of much popularity in those centres which had kept an unbroken record for seven (in two cases eight) years, there were not wanting the usual tokens of the weakness caused by a constant struggle with pecuniary difficulties, with a total inability to keep pace with the larger ideas of the proper scope of University Extension work with which we have now become familiar, or with the demands of a body of students sufficiently large to make the local organizers see the value of the work with which they struggled, but yet not large enough to give the movement in Cornwall that appearance of importance and strength which it enjoys in more thickly populated districts.

Only one centre had ever been able to arrange a course of twelve lectures, and had never been able to repeat the experiment. Only four centres had ever taken even eight lectures; and never had more than seven centres been able to co-operate in securing the services of a lecturer. The Council resolved to appoint an Oxford University Extension lecturer to reside in the county for six months, the local centres being thus released from all costs but those of the University fees for library, syllabus, examination, &c., and the local expenses. The only conditions imposed were that each centre should take not less than twelve fortnightly lectures and classes, to be held in the evening when the artisan classes as well as others could attend, and that at each lecture a sufficient number of seats should be reserved at one penny each. Mr. W. B. Worsfold was selected as lecturer by the Council, and the centres were offered a choice of lectures on the English Colonies. There was a special appropriateness in this selection, Mr. Worsfold having recently spent five years in South Africa and Australasia, studying various colonial questions, and Cornwall being more interested in the Colonies as a field for emigration than any county in England.

Nine centres immediately applied to the Council for lectures under these conditions, and unanimously selected Mr. Worsfold's course on South Africa. Application was also received for six pioneer lectures to be given in the autumn term, on the one evening in the fortnight which would remain at Mr. Worsfold's disposal.

It will be seen that Mr. Worsfold's work in the district is thus roughly divisible into two parts, viz. University Extension lecturing proper, and pioneer lecturing, the latter being small in proportion to the former.

From the nine University Extension centres thus working together under the County Council the following figures have been received for the first three lectures, covering six weeks of Mr. Worsfold's work, from October 1 to November 6:—

	Attendance at			No. of persons writing papers.
	Lect. I.	Lect. II.	Lect. III.	
Truro	140	192	190	14
St. Austell	47	28	24	7
Launceston	75	52	34	4
Falmouth	88	98	70	6
Camborne	160	160	160	14
Penzance	140	110	76	6
Helston	65	30	50	7
Redruth	250	300	300	13
Bodmin	56	40	46	1
Total	1021	1010	950	72

It should here be noticed that in former years no centre has had more than 200 present at any one lecture, the highest average attendance being not more than 120.

The figures above given seem to justify a classification of the centres in three groups, thus:—(a) Strong (3 centres). (b) Weak (4 centres). (c) Intermediate, i.e. where the attendance might, and probably will, be improved (2 centres).

One at least of the centres in Class II shows signs of possible improvement, the interest in the lectures being considerable, the class of persons attending described as very satisfactory, and the paper-work excellent.

Of this branch of the work Mr. Worsfold says: 'The quality of the papers is extremely good. Among the papers received for the second set of questions were six marked A +.' (The system of marking being A, B, or C.)

The great increase in the work both in respect of (1) the number of centres and the number of lectures given at each centre, and (2) the number of persons attending the lectures, is of course very evident.

(1) The first is owing directly to the action of the Council in removing the payment of the lecturer's fees from the centres. Had this not been done, not more than five or six centres at the most would have been able to arrange a course of even six lectures this autumn, and not one could have taken a course of twelve lectures.

(2) The increase in the attendance may be attributed to the following, among other causes: the choice of subject, in this case unanimously popular; the general stimulus and incentive given by the action of the County Council in thus officially recognizing the value of the Oxford University Extension work already done in the district; the additional dignity and importance given to the work by the fact of nine centres working together; and the wise reservation of the penny seats, which has probably in several centres introduced an appreciable number of people, chiefly artisans, foundrymen, dock-labourers, &c., hitherto strangers to the movement. The special announcement of penny seats has in many cases seemed to act as a guarantee that the lectures were really intended for that class of persons, and to be taken as such by them. From personal observation in one centre I should say that the audience in the penny seats was one quite as regular in its attendance as the audience of ticket-holders for the course; but it is too early to say much about this yet. Possibly at most or all of the centres an increased attendance may be expected when the more practical lectures, on the Diamond and Gold Fields, &c., are reached after Christmas. It is perhaps hardly necessary to point out that in those cases where the attendance increases after the first lecture, or is even steadily maintained at the same point, a high tribute is paid to the excellence of the lectures themselves, and to the manner in which they are delivered. Good local organization may secure a large sale of tickets, but cannot possibly ensure the presence of the holders at the lectures on wet, stormy nights, such as we have lately had in extraordinary abundance. The weather has been so exceptionally bad since the first fortnight of the lectures, that a considerable falling off in the attendance was feared, but except in a few cases it seems to have had very little effect.

The six pioneer lectures are all being given in the Saltash district, with the following result as to numbers attending:—Saltash, 100; Torpoint, 60; Millbrook, 70. A second lecture will be given at each of these places during the remainder of the term.

The arrangements here have been made solely through the Saltash District Technical Instruction Committee, no University Extension lectures having been ever given here before. There has been no travelling library or syllabus used, and occasionally no lantern illustrations could be arranged.

Mr. Worsfold's experience here is especially valuable as it enables a comparison to be made with the other centres, in which the work of preparing the way had already been done by local committees and previous lecturers. He says: 'As regards the three pioneer lectures which I have delivered, my experience has shown me how very valuable the work of the Extension Committee is ; making all allowance for difference in population and in nature of population, the contrast between these audiences and the smallest Extension audience shows that the Extension organization introduces a new atmosphere into a place.'

This seems very plainly to show that the County Council has in this case been able to avail itself of a large amount—varying, of course, in different centres—of voluntary organization and labour, most valuable as a practical means of making the Technical Instruction Act really efficacious, in creating a demand for the higher teaching which the Council has been supplying in so many ways since 1890.

As far as we can judge at the present stage of the experiment, the County Council has had ample justification for its outlay in thus helping even the weakest of the centres now participating in the movement, because the previous work done by the Extension organizers has provided a basis for operations under the Council which could not have been obtained by other means without a very much larger outlay, extending over an indefinite period of time.

It may be doubted, also, with all due respect to other systems of teaching, and other means of providing teachers, whether any agency but that of the Oxford University Extension Delegacy could have supplied Cornwall with such a lecturer, on a subject so removed from the ordinary curriculum, and yet so important, so welcome, and so much appreciated by students of every rank.

One would be glad to be able to state with some degree of correctness the proportions in which the various classes attend the lectures, but at present this is a task of some difficulty. Judging from the number of penny seats taken, and the general remarks furnished by the local secretaries as to the nature of the audience, it may be inferred that in many centres the number of persons attending who, if not themselves engaged in manual labour, belong to the working classes, is much higher than has been the case on former occasions. In this respect the organizers owe a good deal to Mr. Worsfold, who has spared no pains to make the lectures known where the ordinary methods of advertising, &c., could not reach, by visiting docks, foundries, and similar places in the men's dinner-hour, and introducing the subject to them personally. In two centres free tickets have been given to children in the elementary schools, in the sixth and seventh standards. When there was not room for all the children in these standards, those who had made the highest attendances in the fortnight were invited. It may also be noted that the most earnest of the students who do the paper-work, and who do some of the best of that work, do not belong to the leisured classes, and could not possibly obtain any teaching of this class unless it were provided for them by public funds or private subscription. At three centres arrangements have been made by Mr. Worsfold for going through the papers with the students on the morning after the lecture, and the only limits to the further extension of this plan are those imposed by time and the railway company. Further applications for pioneer lectures after Christmas have already been received, and it is hoped that a short course will be given at a new working-class centre.

All those local committees in Cornwall who last year organized the courses given by Mr. K. D. Cotes must be now remembering with grateful feelings the help he gave in preparing the petition to the County Council which is now producing these results.

BEATRICE VIVIAN,
Hon. Sec. S. W. Association.

REPORTS FROM THE CENTRES.

ACCRINGTON.—University Extension teaching is of recent introduction in our neighbourhood. Our first course (last winter) was on the ' Problems of Poverty.' Our present course, on 'The Structure of Modern Industry,' was commenced on Oct. 1 under the presidency of the Mayor of Accrington, who spoke on the value of University Extension teaching generally, and the importance of all classes—employed and employers alike—possessing a sound knowledge of the principles under which our industries and commerce have been developed, and are at present conducted ; so that our commerce may extend and its benefits be more widely spread. We have been successful in securing Mr. John A. Hobson for both courses. His clear and impartial manner has aroused an interest in the study of Political Economy, which must be specially valuable in a centre like ours, composed of working men, with a fair sprinkling of trade unionists and others interested in similar institutions. The lecturer has had earnest and thoughtful auditors, but it is a matter for regret that the educational advantages have not been enjoyed by larger audiences. The average number attending lectures has been 65 ; classes, 40. The fact that a course of twelve lectures on ' The Principles of Health' has been proceeding simultaneously with ours may, to some extent, have caused a poor attendance. I am glad to say that our County Council has encouraged our efforts by granting pecuniary aid to the extent of half the cost of the lectures.— ISAAC MASON, *Hon. Sec.*

BEDFORD.—The interruption of our plans for work this term caused by Mr. Morse Stephens' acceptance of an appointment at Cornell University, U.S.A., was a severe trial to the resources of our centre. These, however, have not been found wanting for the Students' Association has been enabled, through the kind assistance of Mr. J. E. Morris, M.A. (Magdalen College, Oxford), to follow the lines of the first half of the syllabus prepared by Mr. Morse Stephens. There has been a fairly good attendance at the lectures on ' India and the Colonies,' showing that great interest is felt in the subject. Large audiences have been attracted by the Gilchrist lectures, given in the Corn Exchange, where seats can be found for fifteen hundred on these occasions. Our committee has decided to foster this enthusiasm for science by undertaking a short Astronomy course next spring. Our lecturer is to be Dr. Fison. We are fortunate in having the prospect of a lecture from Mr. J. Wells (Wadham College) on ' Oxford, and its part in English History,' to be given (with limelight views) on Dec. 17. The local committee fully appreciate this kind assistance to their funds, combined with valuable instruction in the history of Oxford.—E. BLAKE, *Hon. Sec.*

BIRMINGHAM, SEVERN STREET.—In no town has the adult school movement gained such a hold as in Birmingham. Adult schools are now established in every part of the city. They begin, in most cases, at half-past seven on Sunday morning, and are attended by several thousand working people. Many of these schools and classes send representatives to our organizing committee, which consists of three or four teachers and from thirty to forty scholars. The representatives acquaint their ' constituents ' with the arrangements for the lectures, and dispose of tickets in their respective schools. In this way a large audience is secured at a minimum of expense for advertising and printing. Our centre has received from time to time valuable help from the neighbouring and more wealthy organization at Edgbaston, to which it owes its existence in no small degree. This help, together with the encouragement received from the teachers in the various adult schools (whether belonging to the Society of Friends or to other denominations), has made the struggle for existence of the Severn Street centre less severe than at many other places. The present series of lectures on English History bids fair to surpass in interest and value any course we have yet had. The attendance at the opening lecture on October 2 was the largest we have ever known, amounting to 600 persons, a considerable number of whom had to be contented with standing room. There is an attendance of about fifty persons at the classes which are held before the lectures, and a large proportion of these students write papers for the lecturer. Owing to the kindness of friends, both here and at Oxford, the ' book difficulty' has been overcome. Few of our students are in a position to buy their own text-books, consequently the travelling library has proved entirely inadequate to supply the demand. Now, however, we can boast of a very complete little reference-library and reading-room in the centre of the city, where students can work and write papers under better conditions than obtain in most working-men's homes. Another new departure is the establishing of a students' class, which meets, under the guidance of Miss Smithson, on the Tuesday evenings not occupied by the lectures. This class is much valued by those working for Mr. Shaw.—W. H. STURGE, C. CARLESS, *Local Secretaries.*

BRIDPORT.—Mr. Hobson's course of lectures on 'The Indus-trial Revolution' has been fairly well attended, and the audience has manifested great interest in the subject and keen appreciation of Mr. Hobson's method of handling it. A large proportion has always remained for the class. Probably the slight decrease in numbers has been due to the many other classes which at present exist in the town.—K. C. BUSSELL, *Hon. Sec.*

BURY.—The newly-organized committee of this centre has every reason to congratulate itself on the success of Mr. Horsburgh's course of lectures on 'Some Epochs in the History of our Country.' The audience has been the largest known here, averaging 270, and the interest taken in the very able and brilliant lectures has not flagged. Mr. Horsburgh's rare and interesting collection of lantern slides adds greatly to the attraction of the course.— E. ROTHWELL, *Hon. Sec.*

CARLISLE.—A good beginning has been made here with the winter session. It was introduced by a visit from Mr. M. E. Sadler on October 5, who addressed the members of the general committee in the afternoon upon the relation of University Extension to the other educational agencies of the country. In the evening Mr. Sadler gave a popular lecture upon 'Oxford,' illustrated by lime-light views. The audience numbered 180. The proceeds, after payment of local expenses, all went towards the funds of the centre. Towards the cost of the session about £70 has been found by voluntary contributions. Mr. J. E. Phythian is giving a course of twelve fortnightly lectures on Tuesday afternoons at 3.30 p.m. on the History of Architecture. The number present at the first three lectures averaged 90. On the alternate Thursdays, when there is no lecture, the Archi-tectural Class of the Students' Association meets at the same time. Mr. Phythian kindly repeated freely his introductory lecture on the evening of his second visit. On Tuesday nights at 8 p.m., fortnightly, Mr. Carus-Wilson is lecturing on Geology, with an average attendance of about 70. The Committee has invited Mr. Carus-Wilson to give a second course of six lectures after Christmas, in continuation of that which he is now giving. The Students' Association Geological Class meets on the alternate Tuesday evenings. The lectures are given in the Lecture Theatre of Tullie House, which has been granted free of charge by the committee of that Institution. 'Tullie House' (which takes its name from an old house incorporated in it) consists of a large block of buildings recently opened in the city, to be the centre of its intellectual life. It contains a Library, Reading Room, Museum, School of Art, Lecture Theatre, Laboratory, and other rooms, and promises to do much for the objects which 'University Extension' is designed to promote.—A. R. HALL, *Hon. Sec.*

GLOUCESTER.—To say that Mr. Hudson Shaw is the lecturer, and 'The Making of England' the subject, naturally means that this centre is most flourishing. Our only difficulty is to get a good hall, large enough for our audience and moderate in price, as our present hall, which holds over 450, is literally packed. Two points are worthy of notice—viz., the energetic manner in which members of the Trades' Council disposed of artisan tickets, and the successful result of selling tickets at reduced rates to any one taking twelve or twenty-five, the reduction being increased according to the number taken. I shall hope later on to send an analysis of this plan. We have two Students' Associations, one in the afternoon and another in the evening for working men ; each has a membership of between 30 and 40, and the discussions are spirited and interesting. The following pro-gramme shows the work being done by the Evening Association— Mr. Shaw's lecture on the Coming of the English was supple-mented by a paper by Mr. S. Martland of the Folk Lore Society ; the other lectures on Augustine and the Conversion of England, the Norsemen and Alfred, the Normans, Henry II, John and the Great Charter, were respectively followed by papers on Cædmon and Bede by Miss Emily Hickey, editor of Browning's *Strafford ;* the early Church by the Rev. G. L. Bryans, the Doomsday Book as affecting Gloucestershire ; Becket, by the Rev. W. Owen of Cheltenham College. The last meeting of the Association will be for general discussion in preparation for the examination.

GRANGE-OVER-SANDS.—We are much pleased with our Autumn course of lectures on the History of Architecture, given by Mr. J. E. Phythian. Though a 'technical' subject, Mr. Phythian succeeds in filling it with human interest, and his many beautiful lime-light views help us to realize the gradual development of the different styles. In a village of this size we cannot expect a large audience, but our average attendance of seventy-five people is a proof that considerable interest is taken in the subject. Eleven students are writing papers for the lecturer, and the books in the travelling library are invaluable to them, and much appreciated by others who do not write. On November 12, Mr. Phythian kindly came early, and we had a pleasant excursion to Cartmel Church in the afternoon before the lecture. In spite of a depressingly dull November day, between thirty and forty

people met at Cartmel, and Mr. Phythian showed—with the help of Canon Cooper—how the beautiful old priory church told the history of its building in its arches, walls, and windows. Many points which Mr. Phythian noticed in the afternoon formed useful illustrations to the lecture on the rise of Gothic Architecture in the evening, and the little expedition has proved an interesting addition to the course.

HYDE.—Course of lectures by Mr. W. A. S. Hewins, M.A., subject 'English Social Life.' These lectures, which commenced in Hyde on October 1, deal with the industrial history of England from the Middle Ages up to the present day. They have been, up till now, well attended, the fourth lecture having just been given. The interest taken in the subject of the lectures has been shown in a marked degree by the numerous questions asked during the class after the lecture, and also in the gradually increasing number of papers written.—E. M. DOWSON, *Hon. Sec.*

ILKLEY.—We have now had the eighth of a course of twelve lectures from Mr. Mallet on 'England in the Eighteenth Century.' We have issued 199 tickets for the course, and we have an average attendance of about 170. All are very much interested, and many of them find the subject more attractive than they expected ; due in large measure to the clear and interesting way in which Mr. Mallet depicts the gradual rise of political parties, of the proper representation of the people in Parliament, and the gradual settlement of our government into a constitutional monarchy, along with his impartial and brilliant sketches of the many inter-esting characters who during that period so largely influenced the fortunes of our country. Our regret is, that in spite of the great interest felt, only nine students are writing papers, and it is feared Ilkley will present but a poor figure when the time comes for examination. Between sixty and seventy members remain for the class, and the books from the library are well used, but so few will write papers. This makes us feel very strongly that the examination is not a true test of the work actually done, though unfortunately it is the only proof the Delegacy can have of the success of University Extension work.—EMILY DALE, *Local Secretary.*

LITTLE BERKHAMSTED.—A course of six lectures on 'Astro-nomy' is being given here by Mr. R. A. Gregory, F.R.A.S. The greatest interest in the subject is shown by the audience, and the members of the class write papers regularly for the lecturer. The average attendance is very good, and shows an increase on former years. It is hoped that this course may be followed, in the spring, by another on 'The Astronomy of the Nineteenth Century.'—C. C. BARCLAY, *Local Secretary.*

MATLOCK.—Mr. Marriott's course on the Stuarts is progressing most satisfactory, the interest increasing with each lecture. The paper-work is of a very high standard of excellence, and has been frequently commended by Mr. Marriott, who says both the quantity and quality are far above the average for a centre the size of Matlock. The Students' Association meets at Cromford between the lectures, and is doing good work.—GEORGE H. BROWN, *Hon. Sec. Students' Association.*

OLDHAM.—On September 26 Mr. Shaw began his course of lectures here on 'Mediaeval England.' This is our eighth course of Extension lectures, all of which have been on history. From year to year the audiences have increased, and this year seems the most successful of all. In spite of the inclement weather which prevailed on several of the lecture-nights the 'Co-operative Hall '—capable of accommodating over a thousand people—has been comfortably filled ; and we know of many instances of people walking a few miles to be present. The lectures have been listened to with eager and intelligent attention. No point seemed to be missed. Whether the subject was the wars of Edward III, or the Vision of William Langland, the interest of the audience never flagged for a moment. One pleasing feature in the move-ment here is that our audiences are composed for the most part of real working men and women. There seems to be a difficulty in many towns in getting the working class to take their proper share in the movement. We are pleased to say that difficulty has not occurred here. Another thing which points to the success achieved here is that the same people attend year after year, so that we are attaining some of the objects aimed at by 'sequence of study.' In fact, University Extension has become quite an institution in the town. There is little need to advertise the lectures, they are always looked forward to long before they come.—A. SPENCER, *Hon. Sec.*

(*Students' Association.*)—It is too early yet to take stock of our position as compared with previous years, but so far as we *can* estimate we are in a better and more promising situation than ever before. We have had five meetings on alternate weeks with the lectures, with an attendance varying from twenty to thirty or more, for the most part bona-fide Extension students who are reading up and writing papers. The class is composed

. e. artisans, school-teachers, clerks,
ve free and informal discussion on
ch have arisen in the lecture or in
The meetings have been bright and
is centre it is no small element of
pleasant and attractive as possible
cial feeling among the students.
.... at all to disparage the usefulness of the
Examination, we should like to point out that in some respects
at least, it fails to entirely measure the work done in a centre
like our own. Being busy people some of the members cannot
find time every year to follow up the course of reading, &c.,
necessary, so that whilst we have received this session an addition
of some eight or nine new members our number for ' Exam '
may not be increased proportionately. Nevertheless, we have
to set off against this the fact that none of those who have ever
joined us have lost their interest in the work. They have not
fallen away from indifference, but have been prevented through
more pressing demands upon their scanty leisure. We have
therefore reason to believe that the class has done, and is doing,
an amount of good which it is not easy or perhaps possible to
express in statistics.—JOSEPH OWEN, *Hon. Sec.*

RAMSGATE.—The course of lectures which has just been begun
by Mr. F. S. Boas at this centre promises to be very interesting.
The subject is the ' Literature of the Cavaliers and Puritans,'
and includes Sir Thomas Browne, Milton, George Herbert, and
Bunyan, as well as Herrick and other Lyrists of the period.
The average attendance at present is 85. A fortnightly Students'
Meeting is held at Broadstairs in connexion with the course, at
which papers are read and discussed. Courses of lectures have
been given at this centre on Shakespeare and his Contemporaries,
and on Eighteenth and Nineteenth Century Literature, so that the
present course supplies the missing link in the chain of continuity.
The literature courses have been alternated with historical ones,
an arrangement which is found very satisfactory in meeting the
tastes of different students.—L. WHITING, *Hon. Sec.*

RIPON.—Two courses of lectures were begun at this centre on
Tuesday, September 25, by Mr Mallet, the subject in the afternoon being ' The French Revolution,' and that in the evening
' The Stuarts.' At the first lecture the chair was taken by the
most Hon. the Marquis of Ripon, K.G., who spoke at some
length on the very satisfactory reports given by the lecturer and
examiner on the work of the last session. We may add that one
of the students gained a £5 scholarship in the Essay Competition
conducted by the Delegates. The lectures given by Mr. Mallet
are highly appreciated, and the attendance is larger than on
former occasions. A fair number of papers are sent in, so it is
hoped that there will be a good muster for the examination, and
that the result may be as satisfactory as in former years, no
failure having ever been reported from this centre.—F. M. CROSS,
Hon. Sec.

ST. HELENS.—Under the auspices of the Technical Education
Committee of this county borough, the course of University
Extension lectures by Mr. Carus-Wilson on ' The Crust of the
Earth' was commenced on October 8 in the Town Hall. Three
lectures have been given, and they have been highly appreciated.
All those members of the audience who have spoken to me
with reference to this course of lectures have given unqualified
praise to the lecturer, his methods, and illustrations. The average
attendance has been about 300.—JEFF. J. BROOMHEAD, *Hon.
Sec.*

SOUTHAMPTON.—An interesting report presented to the local
Committee by one of the hon. secs. (Mr. Frank Perkins) thus
summarizes the results of last session's work here. During the
past year the Southampton centre has for the first time—(i) been
in a satisfactory financial position ; (ii) organized a twelve-lecture
course, with future courses in direct sequence ; (iii) had an
average attendance of 197; (iv) offered a scholarship for the
Summer Meeting ; (v) obtained four certificates in distinction ; (vi)
organized a Students' Association on a permanent basis ; (vii) received the co-operation of the School Board.

SWINDON.—On October 3 Mr. E. L. S. Horsburgh commenced here what has proved to be a very successful course of
lectures, entitled ' Epochs from the History of our Country,' at
the Mechanics' Institution, illustrated by lime-light views. The
lecturer had a large and appreciative audience, numbering
upwards of 500. The series was continued on Oct. 10 and 31.
The audiences attending these lectures have been thoroughly
representative. A large proportion are pupil teachers in public
elementary schools in the town, the School Board having recognized the importance of the work, and paid the fees of their
pupil teachers. A students' class, which is fairly well attended,
is held on alternate Wednesdays to the lectures.—THOMAS JONES,
Hon. Sec. Students' Association.

SUPERINTENDENT LECTURERS.

BY MISS G. CARTER.

IT would, I think, be difficult to study the reports of
the University Extension Congress held in London last
June, or of the Conference at Bournemouth last April,
without being impressed by the great and growing need
for more combination among lecture-centres. By better
organization, more satisfactory educational results might
be obtained at less cost both of money and labour ; but
the difficulties in the way of such organization are as
apparent as the need for it. These difficulties seem to me
to come under three heads. First, there is the reluctance
of local committees and their supporters to promote or
accept any arrangement which appears either to limit
their freedom of action, or to be more obviously to the
advantage of neighbouring centres than to their own.
Secondly, the difficulty of raising funds for the initial
experiments, which must involve a certain financial risk,
although they would, if successful, be also economical.
And thirdly, that not every capable lecturer is willing or
able to undertake organizing work, or to give his whole
time to one part of the country. But I believe that if the
difficulties of the kind that I have put first could be overcome, the others would not long present any serious
obstacle. Is it, then, possible to overcome these difficulties ?

I believe that it is possible : for must not far greater
difficulties of a similar nature have been overcome by
those who brought about the Extension of University
Teaching to the students at all these scattered centres ?
If a centre has caught anything of the real spirit of those
who, having themselves already a part in the intellectual
and social advantages of a University, seek as much as
possible to share those advantages with all who need
them, surely we may feel confident that such a centre
would be willing and ready to do its part in extending
those benefits yet more widely ? It needs only to be shown
clearly how its action could help forward this work without
diminishing its power of securing a full share of these
good things for those whose special interests it is bound
to consider first. It would, of course, be absolutely undesirable that local organizers should neglect local interests.
What, therefore, is needed is a sound system of district
organization which should commend itself to local committees, because, whilst adding nothing to the difficulties
of any one of them, it would smooth the way for many of
those which were struggling hardest against adverse circumstances ; would aid the development of new centres,
and the recovery of those which had succumbed ; and
would stimulate the progress of higher education throughout a district by making it clear that the strength and
success of any University Extension centre therein would
be a gain to every other centre.

Such an improvement in organization seems to be
possible through the appointment of resident Superintendent Lecturers to suitable districts.

When a measure of reform or progress appears wholly
desirable, it is natural for every one to wish for its early
adoption by those in whom one's own interest is strongest.
It would be gratifying to see one's own county or neighbourhood take a forward place in promoting such a
measure, as well as reap its fullest benefits. So, naturally,
the practical question which forces itself on my consideration is, Can we have a Superintendent Lecturer in the
Isle of Wight ?

The great advantages which we might gain thereby
come clearly before me : but at our present stage of
development there would not be sufficient *remunerative*
work for the lecturer to make it possible for the Island to
provide the necessary funds.

The solution that suggests itself to me is to seek the
alliance of the Hampshire centres. A Superintendent
Lecturer for Hampshire and the Isle of Wight together
would have plenty to occupy him ; and if the committees
of all the centres in the district would join cordially in the
scheme and use their influence to promote the formation
of new centres, I feel no doubt that the financial difficulties
could be met. But it would be necessary to secure

the co-operation of almost *all* these centres before such a scheme, in its entirety, could be set on foot; less than all the present number would leave to each centre the responsibility for a larger sum than is now expended on its lecturer. Therefore it would probably be best to begin with some plan less complete but less costly; and, learning experience alike of difficulties and of the best way to overcome them, to work on quietly and patiently till the time is ripe for the full development of the scheme. Probably such development would, when it came, be so different from the first ideal that it would be scarcely recognizable as the same. For the local organizers at every centre concerned, the lecturers, and the Oxford Delegacy, would each and all have had a share in shaping the measure. Thus it would possess the strength and vitality that belong only to a living growth; firmly rooted, it would have a power of expansion and adaptability to circumstances that could not be attained by the most perfect system if imposed by external authority.

If a few of the centres would resolve to make a beginning and unite in the effort to aid and complete the work done for them by Oxford, I feel sure that in a short time they could thus prepare the way for such a measure of organization as would permanently increase the influence and efficiency of University Extension work throughout the whole district. As the centres learned the possibility and the value of friendly co-operation, the Oxford Delegates would gain a new confidence in their stability and loyalty; and the knowledge of this would do much to strengthen that feeling of having a real relationship to their University which is so essential a part of the benefit conferred on lecture-centres by the extension to them of University teaching.

Ryde, November 19.

UNIVERSITY EXTENSION IN AUSTRALIA.

Past, Present, and Future.

By Mr. H. Arnold Tubbs.

I HAVE been requested by the Secretary to the Delegates to contribute to the *Gazette* some account of University Extension in Australia. In complying, I must crave a certain indulgence. With no actual experience of University Extension in England, I have been connected, in Australia, solely with the Victorian movement, and am imperfectly acquainted with the working of similar schemes in New South Wales and Queensland. Moreover, as I am no longer resident in Melbourne, and am without access to official records, I must draw upon memory more largely than I could have wished.

A short recapitulation will conduce to greater clearness. The movement to establish University Extension in Victoria took definite shape in August 1891: and the first suggestion was due to Mr. H. B. Higgins, of the University Council, who, as a member of the Extension Board has played throughout a most active and prominent part in furthering the interests of the scheme. The Board itself was strongly constituted: it had in Professor Jenks, now of Liverpool, the very ideal of a secretary: it was able from the first to offer a broad and comprehensive syllabus of subjects and the services of a staff of trained lecturers. During the first season, which extended over a period of four months only, eight centres were formed, ten courses—of six lectures each—were delivered, and 1,382 students enrolled. In 1892 the numbers rose to thirteen centres, nineteen courses, and 2,018 students. In 1893 came the commercial crisis, inevitable result of a perverse system of financial administration and the inflated prices to which it had given occasion. As bank after bank suspended payment, money became unprecedentedly scarce, and a general panic seized the community. Fortunately many of the effects of the crisis were confined to Melbourne and its immediate vicinity. Country towns like Bendigo, though they suffered inevitably through their dependence on Melbourne as the business heart of the colony, were prosperous in themselves. But for this

it must have gone hard with University Extension, in spite of the brave front which some of the town centres opposed to accumulated disasters. As it was, the season 1893 left us with seven centres, nine courses, 1,018 students. Of 1894 it is too early to speak: at present five centres are at work and have arranged for seven courses. Although the effects of the crisis of May 1893 must be felt even more severely during 1894, I do not doubt that some improvement in these figures will be shown before the end of the year.

A modified form of University Extension had been established in Sydney somewhat earlier. As is the case with other of our Australian Universities, though not with Melbourne, it was and is usual in Sydney to repeat in the evening to a different audience some of the lectures which have been given already in the course of the day. Enjoying a special grant of £500 a year from Government, Sydney University was enabled to give a wider scope and broader usefulness to these evening lectures, and to attract a larger circle of students, by allowing them to be delivered in some of the suburbs. But the movement wanted what I cannot but regard as the cardinal characteristic of University Extension,—local effort, local management, local responsibility, and local finance. Owing to the partial withdrawal of Government aid, the system in New South Wales was gradually modified, approximating more and more towards that in operation in Victoria, which again does not differ in any essential from the English system. This year inaugurates an important change of policy. Thanks to its stronger financial position, the Sydney Board has felt itself justified in creating a salaried secretaryship. The secretary thus appointed occupies at the same time the position of a staff-lecturer, with this difference, however, that a staff-lecturer merely accepts the invitation of a centre, while the Sydney secretary is bound to deliver, or hold himself ready to deliver, a certain number of lectures to country towns. At the same time, the services of the lecturer are granted at a rate less by one-half or two-thirds than that which the entirely self-supporting Melbourne system is compelled to exact. Differential charges too are made, favouring country towns and districts. Thus the work in the country in New South Wales differs somewhat from that carried on in Sydney and its suburbs, where local centres not differing essentially from those in Victoria enjoy a healthy life. Further details of the New South Wales scheme, with some criticisms upon it from a Victorian point of view, will be found in the *Melbourne Extension Journal*, especially in the numbers for September and December, 1893, March and June, 1894: to repeat them here would unduly increase the length of this article.

Two features of the work in New South Wales are important: they serve also to distinguish it from the system in vogue in Victoria. These are virtual state-aid and greater insistence upon long as against short courses. At first, the Sydney Board would hear of nothing but courses of ten or twelve lectures, latterly the strictness of the rule has been relaxed: and courses are now offered consisting of six, eight, ten, or twelve. Moreover, courses delivered in country towns by the travelling lecturer are, I understand, uniformly of the shorter length; but in this I speak merely from recollection of a talk I had in Sydney in the beginning of the year with Mr. Jose, an old Balliol man, and now as secretary the centre of the entire movement, and with Professors Scott and Wood, also both Oxford men, who have had most to do with the guidance of the movement.

In the autumn of 1892 Tasmania established a University at Hobart, adopting a system of tuition which embodies some of the methods of University Extension. Owing to the rivalry between North and South—Launceston and Hobart have always cherished a more or less good-humoured jealousy of one another—some concession had to be made to the Northerners to compensate for the choice of Hobart as the seat of the new University. An arrangement was accordingly made by which the lecturers of the University were required to deliver courses of lectures in Launceston (eight hours by rail from Hobart) in addition to those which were given within the University buildings. Extra-mural courses on University subjects, more popular in treatment, are also given in Hobart. The staff of the Tasmanian University is inevitably small in this its period of infancy : and the work thus thrown upon the shoulders of three lecturers is too heavy to allow of much development without an addition to their number. The University, too, is regarded by a strong party in the Tasmanian Parliament as no better than an experiment : it could, under the terms of agreement and of the Government grant, be dissolved at the end of three years from the date of its inauguration.

A development of a somewhat different character was brought about in Queensland last year. In spite of its relative importance, this colony has not hitherto possessed any organization for the dissemination of a higher culture, much less has it enjoyed the benefits of a university. On the other hand it is happy in the possession of some excellent schools which have always taken high rank. Its University requirements have been met by Melbourne and Sydney. To two graduates, one of Melbourne, the other of Sydney, is due the initiation of a new movement, which, organized as University Extension, and modelled closely on the Sydney system to which it is affiliated, aims at creating the educated demand, and the educated public from which ultimately will come a University of the North. In one important respect the Queensland system differs from that of Sydney : it has followed Melbourne in adopting the six-lecture course as against the longer series of nine or twelve. Again the Queensland scheme is not governed from any University : its Council certainly consists mainly of University men, but it has a large and popular Senate, and its subjugation to Sydney extends only to this, that the appointment of its lecturers is confirmed and its examinations are conducted by the Southern University. In all other respects it resembles more nearly a powerful local centre with several 'missions.' The work began last year with the appointment of two lecturers, both graduates of Melbourne, and one a lecturer on the Melbourne list. Three courses were delivered. Attendance was large and interest well sustained ; the results judged by examination returns were satisfactory. This year already shows an increase : and we understand that seven courses have been arranged. The Council and Senate are strongly constituted ; the movement has grown from popular demand. Success has been based in the more serious temper of a year of severest depression, not skimmed off the crest of a tide of prosperity ; and on every ground there is reason to believe that the movement inaugurated in Queensland has before it a prosperous future, and a speedy realization of the hopes of its promoters.

Finally, there is at present a possibility of the commencement of similar work in South Australia, where a sister organization, the Australasian Home Reading Union, has sent down an unusually vigorous root. Latterly there have been frequent suggestions for some form of amalgamation between the A. H. R. U. and the various University Extension Boards in the several colonies : and it is in connexion with such a proposal that the possibility of founding University Extension in South Australia has come to the front. Personally I am doubtful whether any direct advantage would follow from the proposed amalgamation. The A. H. R. U. deals with units ('circles') of from three to fifteen members. A normal University centre is not in healthy life unless it counts its 100 or 150. There is always sufficient difficulty in catering for the diversity of tastes among 150 members : organize this diversity, give it form and voice, by creating ten reading circles busied each with a different subject, and the result is liable to be endless word-making and energetic supineness. A degree of concerted action would be useful ; union would only disintegrate by the junction of unequal forces. Both have a good work to do ; both have their own way of doing it : to combine those ways is to make one of those roads, not seldom seen in the colonies, too wide to be kept in order, one-third in use, two-thirds a waste and an impediment.

To complete this portion of my subject I must add here that although New Zealand was represented at the 'Extension Congress,' yet of University Extension there is nothing in either the North or the South Island. At the same time tuition in the three University Colleges is so arranged as to meet the wants of a large audience : lectures are given in the evenings for those who cannot attend during the day, and special courses at special hours for the benefit of teachers. More might be done if the Board of Primary Education were better advised : but the regulations of the Board are purposely framed to deter the teachers under its control from aiming at a higher and broader culture.

(*To be continued in the next number.*)

QUALIFICATIONS OF TECHNICAL TEACHERS.

A THOUGHTFUL correspondent writes to the *County Council Times* to warn County Councils against engaging imperfectly trained teachers under the Technical Instruction Acts.

'With disastrous results,' he says, 'I have seen that a course of lectures on ambulance and hygiene, supplemented by skimming through a hospital ward for a few months, cannot qualify bright and intelligent ladies to teach the arts of health and nursing, and make the subject intelligible and practicable to the working classes and the lower middle classes. In cases within my own knowledge, such teachers, baffled by difficulties and inquiries not anticipated, have advised quack nostrums and risky remedies, that a nurse would have known to be harmful and dangerous.'

The great success of the lectures and classes on hygiene, delivered under the University Extension system by Dr. Wade and others, is largely due to the fact that the lecturers are medical men of high attainment and wide experience.

SCHOLARSHIPS FOR THE OXFORD SUMMER MEETING, 1895.

A FUND, to which subscriptions amounting to £60 have already been promised, has been opened for the provision of Scholarships to enable students from Oxford centres to attend the Summer Meeting, which will be held in Oxford from August 1 to August 26, 1895.

The Scholarships will be awarded after an Essay competition, and will be of two values—£10 and £5. Holders of the former must attend the whole Meeting ; those of the latter may, if they prefer, attend either the First or Second Part only. Part I lasts from Aug. 1 to Aug. 12 ; Part II from Aug. 12 to Aug. 26.

Conditions of Award.

The Scholarships will be awarded on or about July 1, 1895, for English Essays on subjects drawn from English Literature, English History, Natural Science, and Political Economy.

A. *Competition for Scholarships.*

The Scholarships will be awarded in three divisions :—

(*a*) Open to all Oxford University Extension Students *who need the assistance of the Scholarships* in order to study in Oxford, according to the intention of the donors.

(*b*) Open to all Elementary School Teachers (men or women), who are also Oxford University Extension Students.

(*c*) Open to all working men and women, who are also Oxford University Extension Students.

To qualify themselves for election to a Scholarship :—

(1) All competitors must be recommended by their Local Committee as suitable candidates.

(2) Competitors in *divisions* (*a*) and (*b*) must, in order to qualify, obtain *distinction* in an examination on a course of Oxford University Extension Lectures delivered between January 1894 and June 1895.

(3) Competitors in *division* (*c*) must pass an examination on a course of Oxford University Extension Lectures delivered between the same dates.

The Delegates, however, reserve to themselves the right of rejecting the name of any candidate ; and, unless compositions of sufficient merit are sent in, do not bind themselves to award Scholarships in any or all of the following four subjects.

B. *Competition for Prizes.*

A limited number of Prizes, of the value of £1, will be awarded in the same competition without any limitation as to the means of the competitors. Candidates for this branch of the competition must qualify as regards examinations, like the competitors in *divisions (a)* and *(b)*.

SUBJECTS.

(1) *History* 'one only to be selected'.

(i) The Growth of Nationality in the thirteenth century.

(ii) The causes of the Great Rebellion.

(iii) England's command of the Sea during the Revolutionary Wars (1793–1815).

(2) *Literature* (one only to be selected).

(i) How far is it possible to specify any general conditions which are necessary to the production of the best poetry?

(ii) Explain what is meant by Poetic Justice, and consider with full illustrations how far it should be observed in Drama or Fiction.

(iii) Estimate the importance in literary history of the works of Dryden, Pope, or Walter Scott.

(3) *Political Economy* (one only to be selected).

(i) Show the effect of different systems of land tenure on the production and distribution of wealth.

(ii) What remedies have been suggested for the existing depression, and how far are they likely to succeed?

(iii) What circumstances may be expected to determine the wages of labour in the future?

(4) *Science* (one only to be selected).

(i) Theories of Chemical Action.

(ii) Sewage disposal in towns and rural districts.

(iii) The Weeds of the Farm.

REGULATIONS.

1. Each candidate may write an essay *on one subject only*, but may select one from any of the above four groups.

2. All compositions must reach the Delegacy [addressed—The Secretary, University Extension Office, Examination Schools, Oxford] on or before Monday, June 3, 1895; must each bear the writer's full name and address, with a note saying whether the writer is competing for a Scholarship or a Prize, or both, and, if the former, in which division (*a*, *b*, or *c*, see above); must be written on foolscap paper, and on one side of the paper only; must state, at the top of the first page, the writer's occupation; and must be accompanied by a certificate of qualification from his or her Local Committee in the following form:—

' On behalf of the members of the Local Committee acting in concert with the Oxford University Delegates for the establishment of Lectures and Teaching at   , I certify that *A. B.* is in all respects a suitable person for election to a University Extension   , according to the regulations.

Signed on behalf of the Committee,

....

Secretary.'

3. Candidates are not debarred from the consultation of standard works, but quotations should be notified in the margin, and borrowed passages should be clearly distinguished from the rest.

4. No composition should exceed thirty foolscap pages, including a brief analysis which should be prefixed to the essay.

5. The names of the unsuccessful competitors will not be divulged by the Delegates, and all compositions may be obtained from them after the announcement of the result of the competition.

6. Successful candidates will be informed by the Delegacy of the result of the competition.

7. The students elected to the Scholarships will be required to visit Oxford during the Summer Meeting of University Extension Students, 1895.

8. Holders of Scholarships of £10 are required to reside in Oxford during the whole Meeting. If they are unable to do so, they must resign half their Scholarship, retaining, however, the position on the list of scholars to which the excellence of their essay entitled them.

9. The Programme of the Summer Meeting will be published at Easter, and copies (7*d.* each post free) can then be obtained on application to the Secretary, University Extension Office, Oxford.

Contributions to the Scholarship fund should be sent to the Secretary, University Extension Office, Oxford.

Copies of the above regulations can be obtained free of charge on application to the Secretary, University Extension Office, Oxford.

¹ *State whether Scholarship or Prize, or both.*

SCHOLARSHIP FUND FOR THE OXFORD SUMMER MEETING, 1895.

The Secretary's Scholarship (subscribed by students attending the Summer Meeting, 1894)	£45 0 0
Mr. F. Haverfield, Student and Tutor of Christ Church	5 0 0
Mr. M. E. Sadler	10 0 0

ARRANGEMENTS FOR SPRING, 1895.

Centre.	No. of Lectures in Course.	Subject of Course.	Lecturer.	Course begins.	Course ends.
†UNIVERSITY EXTENSION COLLEGE, READING (evening)	12	Age of Elizabeth and Puritan Rebellion	Rev.W.H.SHAW,M.A. & E.L.S.HORSBURGH,M.A.	Th. Jan. 17	Mar. 28
„ (afternoon)	12	Tennyson and Browning ...	J.CHURTONCOLLINS,M.A	S. Jan. 26	Apr. 6
„ (evening) ...	12	Greek Drama	„ „	S. Jan. 26	Apr. 6
„ (evening) ...	12	The Study of Local History ...	W. M. CHILDS, B.A. ...	F. Jan. 25	Apr. 5
„ (evening) ...	12	La Littérature Française du XVIIe Siècle	M. J. MAURICE REY, B. es Sc.	W. Jan. 23	Apr. 3
„ (evening) ...	12	Geography of the British Isles ...	H. J. MACKINDER, M.A.	S. Jan. 19	Mar. 30
†BIRMINGHAM, EDGBASTON (afternoon)	12	Age of Louis XIV and French Revolution	J.A.R.MARRIOTT, M.A.	T. Jan. 15	Mar. 26
BIRMINGHAM, Severn Street (evening)	6	English Colonies	„ „ ...	T. Jan. 15	Mar. 26
†BOURNEMOUTH (afternoon) ...	12	Europe since Waterloo	„ „ ...	W. Jan. 23	Apr. 3
BRADFORD (evening)	6	Colonies	„ „ ...	Th. Jan. 17	Mar. 28
†BRIDPORT (evening)	12	Industrial Revolution	„ „ ...	T. Jan. 22	Apr. 2
†CLEVEDON (afternoon) ...	12	Shakespeare's Historical Plays ...	„ „ ...	F. Jan. 25	Apr. 5
DORCHESTER (evening) ...	6	Colonies	„ „ ...	W. Jan. 23	Apr. 3
†OXFORD (evening)	12	The Making of England	„ „ ...	F. Jan. 18	Mar. 29
SALE (evening)	6	England in the 18th Century ...	„ „ ...	W. Jan. 16	Mar. 27
†SOUTHBOURNE (afternoon) ...	12	Europe since Waterloo	„ „ ...	Th. Jan. 24	Apr. 4
†TAMWORTH (evening) ...	10	England in the 18th Century ...	C. E. MALLET, B.A. ...	T. Jan. 15	Feb. 26
FOLKESTONE (evening) ...	10	England in the 18th Century ...	„ „ ...	M. Jan. 28	Apr. 1

† The figures in the second column include the lectures given in the Autumn Term, from which these courses are continued.

Centre.	No. of Lectures in Course.	Subject of Course.	Lecturer.	Course begins.	Course ends.
†Burnley (evening)	12	Spenser & other Elizabethan Poets	F. S. Boas, M.A. ...	Th. Jan. 17	Mar. 28
†Canterbury (afternoon) ...	12	Victorian Poets	,, ,,	W. Jan. 23	Apr. 3
†Ramsgate (afternoon) ...	12	Literature of Cavaliers and Puritans	,, ,,	S. Jan. 26	Apr. 6
Devizes (evening)	6	Tennyson	Rev. J. G. Bailey, M.A., LL.D.	Th. Jan. 24	Apr. 4
†West Brighton (afternoon)	12	Tennyson	,, ,,	F. Jan. 18	Mar. 29
Abergavenny (afternoon) ...	6	Shakespeare	E.L.S. Horsburgh, B.A.	S. Jan. 26	Apr. 6
Brecon (afternoon) ...	6	Literature of the 18th Century ...	,, ,, ...	Th. Jan. 24	Apr. 4
Brecon (evening)	6	Epochs from English History ...	,, ,,	Th. Jan. 24	Apr. 4
Cheltenham (afternoon) ...	6	Growth of Parliament ...	,, ,,	W. Jan. 30	Apr. 10
Cheltenham (evening) ...	6	Industrial and Economic Questions since 1789	,, ,,	W. Jan. 30	Apr. 10
Evesham (evening)	6	Revolution and Age of Anne ...	,, ,,	W. Jan. 23	Apr. 3
Gloucester (evening) ...	6	English History in Shakespeare...	,, ,,	M. Jan. 28	Apr. 8
Hereford evening)	6	Wyclif to Sir Thomas More ...	,, ,,	M. Jan. 21	Apr. 1
Leominster (evening) ...	6	Industrial and Economic Questions since 1789	,, ,,	T. Jan. 22	Apr. 2
Malvern (afternoon) ...	6	Puritan Revolution	,, ,,	W. Jan. 23	Apr. 3
†Reigate (afternoon)... ...	12	The Reign of Elizabeth ...	,, ,,	Th. Jan. 17	Mar. 28
Ross (afternoon)	6	Literature of the 18th Century ...	,, ,,	T. Jan. 22	Apr. 2
†Southampton (evening) ...	12	The Age of Elizabeth	,, ,,	F. Jan. 18	May 29
Stroud (afternoon) ...	6	The Renaissance	,, ,,	T. Jan. 29	Apr. 9
Stroud (evening)	6	The Reign of Elizabeth	,, ,,	T. Jan. 29	Apr. 9
Swansea (evening)	6	Not fixed	,, ,,	F. Jan. 25	Apr. 5
*Dover (afternoon) ...	6	Architecture	F. Bond, M.A.	M. Jan. 28	Apr. 8
*Tunbridge Wells (afternoon)	10	Architecture	,, ,,	Not fixed	Not fixed
†Henlow (evening)	12	The English Citizen	W. M. Childs, B.A....	W. Jan. 16	Mar. 27
Glossop (evening)	6	Trade, Adventure, and Discovery	K. D. Cotes, M.A. ...	W. Jan. 23	Apr. 3
Warrington (evening) ...	6	Trade, Invention, and Discovery	,, ,, ...	F. Jan. 25	Apr. 5
Wirksworth (evening) ...	6	Trade. Adventure. and Discovery	,, ,,	Th. Jan. 24	Apr. 4
*Tavistock (afternoon) ...	6	Puritan Revolution	W. G. de Burgh, B.A.	M. Jan. 28	Apr. 8
Frome (afternoon)	6	Wordsworth, Coleridge, and Scott	,, ,, ...	T. Jan. 29	Apr. 9
†West Brighton (evening) ...	12	Three Centuries of Working-class History	W. A. S. Hewins, M.A.	Th. Jan. 24	Apr. 18
Grimsby (evening)	6	Not fixed	J. A. Hobson, M.A. ...	T. Jan. 22	Apr. 2
Midhurst (evening) ...	6	English Novelists	,, ,,	W. Jan. 16	Mar. 27
†Carlisle (afternoon) ...	12	Architecture	J. E. Phythian ...	T. Jan. 15	Apr. 9
Chester (afternoon)	6	Architecture	,, ,,	T. Jan. 22	Apr. 2
Halifax (evening)	6	Florentine Art	,, ,,	Th. Not fixed	Not fixed
Kersal (evening)	8	Architecture	,, ,,	M. Jan. 28	Mar. 18
†Bodmin (evening)	12	South Africa	W. B. Worsfold, M.A.	F. Jan. 25	Apr. 5
†Camborne (evening) ...	12	South Africa	,, ,,	F. Jan. 18	Mar. 29
†Falmouth (evening) ...	12	South Africa	,, ,,	Th. Jan. 17	Mar. 28
†Helston (evening)	12	South Africa	,, ,,	T. Jan. 22	Apr. 2
†Launceston (evening) ...	12	South Africa	,, ,,	W. Jan. 16	Mar. 27
†Penzance (evening) ...	12	South Africa	,, ,,	M. Jan. 21	Apr. 1
†Redruth (evening)	12	South Africa	,, ,,	Th. Jan. 24	Apr. 4
†St. Austell (evening) ...	12	South Africa	,, ,,	T. Jan. 15	Apr. 9
†Truro (evening)	12	South Africa	,, ,,	M. Jan. 14	Mar. 25
Lewes (evening)	6	Physiography	G. J. Burch, M.A. ...	M. Jan. 21	Apr. 1
Brighton (St. Michael's Hall)	6	Regions, Races, and Resources ...	H. R. Mill, D.Sc. ...	Th. Jan. 31	Apr. 1
*Brighton (evening)	6	Regions, Races, and Resources ...	,, ,,	Th. Jan. 31	Apr. 1
Banbury (evening)	6	Crust of the Earth	C.Carus-Wilson,F.G.S.	Th. Jan. 17	Mar. 28
†Carlisle (evening)	12	Outlines of Geology	,, ,,	Th. Jan. 24	Apr. 4
†Bath (afternoon)	12	Recent Discoveries with the Telescope and Spectroscope	A. H. Fison, D.Sc. ...	Th. Jan. 17	Mar. 28
†Bath (evening)	12	Recent Discoveries with the Telescope and Spectroscope	,, ,, ...	Th. Jan. 17	Mar. 28
Bedford (evening)	6	Life of a Planet	,, ,,	T. Jan. 29	Apr. 9
†Bournemouth (evening) ...	12	Forces of Nature	,, ,, ...	F. Jan. 18	Mar. 29
†Newport (evening)	12	Physical Astronomy	,, ,,	Th. Jan. 24	Apr. 4
†Ryde (afternoon)	12	Recent Discoveries with the Telescope and Spectroscope	,, ,,	Th. Jan. 24	Apr. 4
†Ventnor (evening)	12	Physical Astronomy	,, ,,	F. Jan. 25	Apr. 5
Somerset County Council :					
5 Courses of	12	Management of Farm Stock ...	H. Sessions	Jan.	Apr.
5 Courses of	12	Hygiene	C.H.Wade,M.A.,D.P.H.	Jan.	Apr.

Summer Term, 1895.

Brighton (St. Michael's Hall) | 6 or 8 | England in the 18th Century ... | J.A.R.Marriott,M.A. | Not fixed | Not fixed

† The figures in the second column include the lectures given in the Autumn Term, from which these courses are continued.
* Arrangements not yet completed.

Note.—Application for Courses and all information as to fees, &c., can be obtained from The Secretary, University Extension Office, Examination Schools, Oxford.

INFORMATION TO CONTRIBUTORS.

All communications should be addressed to the Editor, Oxford University Extension Gazette, *University Press, Oxford. All matter intended for insertion in the January issue should reach him not later than December 20. Contributions should be written on* one *side of the paper only, and must be accompanied by the name of the writer (not necessarily for publication).*

N.B.—*All orders should carefully specify the full title,* Oxford University Extension Gazette.

OXFORD UNIVERSITY

 EXTENSION GAZETTE.

VOL. V.   NO. 52.]   JANUARY, 1895.   [ONE PENNY.

N.B.—Local Organizers of Oxford University Extension Lectures are invited to send to the Secretary, University Extension Office, Examination Schools, Oxford, copies of any journals containing notices of, or references to, Extension work.

NOTES AND COMMENTS.

The most important speech on educational matters delivered during the last month was Mr. Acland's address at Huddersfield on Dec. 20. It contained a striking statement that we shall not have got far in popular education until we have achieved on a large scale for adults of the working class something of the kind which is being done here and there by the University Extension courses. The chief obstacle to a national development of University Extension teaching is the lack of funds, causing the costliness of the lectures to which Mr. Acland referred. As soon as the State perceives its duty in regard to higher adult education, the difficulty of expense will be overcome. A few thousands a year to each University Extension authority would solve the problem.

.·.

Mr. F. York Powell's appointment as Regius Professor of Modern History will give great pleasure to University Extension students, large numbers of whom are indebted to him for guidance and encouragement in their work. As an examiner, as a lecturer at the Summer Meetings, and as a friend whose interest has never flagged, he has rendered most valuable service to University Extension. We heartily congratulate him on the honour which he has received.

.·.

Great changes have taken place in the University Extension offices during the past month. Mr. Arthur Berry, finding himself overburdened by the labours of the office superadded to his tutorial duties in College, has, to the regret of his wide circle of friends, given up his work as Secretary to the Cambridge Syndicate. Mr. Berry's years of office have coincided with a critical period in the history of University Extension. He saw the beginnings of the connexion between the work of the Universities and of the County Councils. He has been closely concerned with the more recent developments in connexion with the School Boards. And from first to last his colleagues in the movement have never failed to receive from him the benefits of prudent and temperate counsel. When the events of the last few years have fallen into perspective, it will probably be seen that the most remarkable change which has taken place in Extension work is the drawing together of the several Universities concerned in it. Estrangement has given way to unity of action; where divergence of policy still remains, we have amicably agreed to differ, realizing that in so large a field of work there is need for diversity of method and room for many kinds of experiment. To this happy change in the position of affairs—a change which has greatly strengthened the position of University Extension in the country—Mr. Berry has contributed much. During his secretaryship, the friendship between the four branches of the system has steadily grown stronger, and he leaves his post to the sincere regret of all engaged in University Extension, and more especially of those who have been thrown into intimate relationship with him during a time of momentous change in English education.

We are very glad to be able to welcome an old colleague as Mr. Berry's successor. Dr. Roberts has given up his work in the London office and becomes Secretary of the Cambridge Syndicate on Jan. 15. Of Dr. Roberts' labours for University Extension, this is not the time to speak—nor is it necessary to do so. He is a veteran in the cause, unfailing in energy and undaunted in educational purpose. We wish him health and prosperity in his new office.

.·.

Dr. Roberts is to be followed, as Secretary of the London Society, by a well-known and popular lecturer, Dr. Kimmins, who has recently been appointed on the educational staff of the Technical Education Board of the London County Council. Dr. Kimmins brings to his new duties a singularly wide and successful experience as a lecturer and organizer of University Extension work. His hearty and genial ways have gained him friends everywhere, and there is no question that under his charge the London Society will continue to advance in popularity and educational influence. The choice of a teacher so closely identified with the work of the County Council may point to plans of a more intimate connexion between University Extension teaching and the Technical Education Board.

.·.

After many years of service, by which he has earned the gratitude of all workers for University Extension, Mr. Goschen has resigned the presidency of the London Society. We are glad to see that Canon Browne has consented to undertake the duties attached to a new office—that of chairman of the Council. It would be well for the connexion between the London Society and the University of Oxford to be strengthened by the selection of some Oxonian as Mr. Goschen's successor. The name of Mr. Arthur Acland naturally suggests itself for the office.

.·.

The Rev. C. G. Lang, Fellow of Magdalen College and Vicar of St. Mary's, and Mr. C. Cannan, Fellow of Trinity College, have been appointed members of the University Extension Delegacy in the place of the Provost of Queen's College (now, as Vice-Chancellor, an ex-officio member of the Delegacy) and the President of Magdalen (resigned). Mr. Lang was for some years a Staff-Lecturer of the Oxford University Extension.

.·.

The University is to be asked next term to amend the Statute, under which the University Extension Delegacy works, by striking out the words which at present limit its undertakings to England and Wales. The immediate reason for the proposed enlargement of powers is that the Delegacy has been asked to provide lectures for English residents in Switzerland.

1

We have received the first number of the *Journal* of the University Extension College, Reading, a well-printed magazine, convenient in arrangement and size, which will record the varied interests and undertakings of the College. The appearance of the Journal is a sign of the rapid growth of the new institution.

.·.

Holiday Courses in the Theory and Practice of Teaching.

The detailed time-table of the course of instruction in the Theory and Practice of Teaching, which is to be given at Exeter between January 3 and 17, was published early last month, and is excellently arranged. Two courses, each consisting of twelve lectures, are to be given in the mornings; the one by Mr. H. Holman on Psychology in relation to Education, and the other by Dr. Wade on School Hygiene. In addition to these, Miss Hughes has undertaken to give three lectures on the Government of Children, and single lectures have been arranged in the evenings on various subjects connected with educational questions. These will begin with an inaugural address by the Master of Downing College, Cambridge, and will include lectures or addresses by Mr. Arthur Sidgwick, M. Paul Barbier, Miss Cooper, Mr. Sadler and others. The detailed time-table also contains a list of lodgings available for the students staying in Exeter, and it is stated that arrangements have been made to visit various buildings of historical interest in the city. Full information about the meeting can be obtained from the Hon. Secretary, Miss Montgomery, 10 Baring Crescent, Exeter.

.·.

In the *Bournemouth Students' Association Gazette* for December a correspondent makes the suggestion that the Delegates should be asked to grant Certificates in exchange for Pass-lists to students who have attended two courses of lectures delivered on connected subjects in two successive years, provided that the candidate shall have sent in supplementary summer work between the two courses. The object of this proposal is to encourage small centres to take courses in sequence two years running, and students' associations in such places to link together the two courses by intermediate work.

.·.

It is proposed to give in London next May performances in English of the Trilogy of Aeschylus—the *Agamemnon*, the *Choephori* and the *Eumenides*. Professor Stanford, who wrote the music for the production of the *Eumenides* at Cambridge, has promised to compose music for the other two plays. The arrangements are in the hands of an influential committee of which Professor Jebb, M.P., is President, and Mr. Owen Seaman (41 Great Russell Street, W.C.) Hon. Secretary. The proceeds of the performances will be handed over to the British School of Archaeology at Athens. Mr. Seaman's connexion with University Extension work will give many students at our centres a special interest in this excellent scheme.

.·.

Mr. Carus-Wilson has kindly offered to give a children's lecture on the making of the land in aid of the funds of the Women Lecturers' Association. The lecture will be delivered on January 5, and will be illustrated by lantern slides.

.·.

The Extension Department of the University of New York undertakes to help literary societies in drawing up courses of home study, and fourteen clubs have recently availed themselves of this arrangement. The course of study extends in each case over at least ten consecutive weeks.

.·.

The Columbian University (Washington D.C.) has affiliated itself in its Extension work to the American University Extension Society. The lecturers are either professors in the University, or specially approved by the University and by the American Society. Mr. W. C. Langdon, M.A., is the director of the scheme.

RESEARCH DEGREES AND GRADUATE STUDY AT OXFORD.

THE University of Oxford is now considering a plan for creating new degrees which will be accessible to persons who, having been students here or in other Universities or places of education, wish to pursue a course of special study or research. The subject is one of great importance and is exciting much interest. It is hoped that the number of those who, after graduating at other Universities, come to Oxford for further study will continue to grow, and that the new degrees may provide a fitting recognition of their labours. The text of the proposed statute is as follows:—

Of the Degrees of Bachelor of Letters and Bachelor of Science, and of the Times and Exercises Required for them.

§ 1. *Of the Degrees of Bachelor of Letters and Bachelor of Science.*

Any person who has been permitted by the authority and in the manner hereinafter provided to enter on a course of special study or research may supplicate for the Degree of Bachelor of Letters or Bachelor of Science, provided that he has satisfied the conditions prescribed by this Statute.

§ 2. *Of the Delegacy for the Supervision of Candidates for the Degrees of Bachelor of Letters and Bachelor of Science.*

1. For the purposes of this Statute there shall be a Delegacy consisting of the Vice-Chancellor, the Proctors, and twelve members of Convocation elected as follows: namely, four by the Hebdomadal Council, four by the Congregation of the University, and four by the Vice-Chancellor and Proctors. The first elections shall be made in February, 1895, and of the Delegates then elected the two junior Delegates in each section of four shall vacate office on the fifteenth day of February, 1898. Subject to the foregoing rule the Delegates shall be elected to serve for a period of six years. Vacancies occurring at any time before the expiration of the prescribed period shall be filled up only to the end of such period.

2. The Delegates may at any meeting by a majority of votes co-opt an additional member, provided that notice of the intention to propose such co-optation, and of the name of the person to be proposed, shall have been sent to all the Delegates at least fourteen days before the day of meeting, and that the number of co-opted members shall never be more than four. A person who is not a member of Convocation may be co-opted as a member of the Delegacy. Every co-opted member shall be elected for two years, and shall be re-eligible.

3. The Delegates shall make a Report of their proceedings every year to Convocation.

§ 3. *Of the Admission of Candidates for the Degrees of Bachelor of Letters and Bachelor of Science, and the Conditions of supplicating for these Degrees.*

1. Any person may give notice to the Secretary to the Boards of Faculties of his intention, subject to the approval of the Delegates, to enter on a course of special study or research as a Candidate for the Degree of Bachelor of Letters or of Science as the case may be: Provided that no such notice shall be given by any person under the age of twenty-one years. Every such notice shall state in general terms the subject and nature of the proposed course. The Secretary shall transmit every such notice received by him to the Delegates for their approval. Such approval shall not be granted unless the intending Candidate shall satisfy the Delegates (1) That he has passed the Examinations required for the Degree of Bachelor of Arts, or has given evidence of having received a good general education; (2) That he has given evidence of his fitness to enter on a course of special study or research; and (3) That the course of study or research on which he proposes to enter is such as may profitably be pursued within the University. If the notice given by an intending Candidate is approved by the Delegates, the Secretary shall enter

it in a book to be kept for the purpose; and the person giving notice shall be deemed to have been admitted as a Candidate for the Degree of Bachelor of Letters or of Science at the time when such notice was first received by the Secretary to the Boards of Faculties, or, if at the time when such notice was given he was not a member of the University, then from the time of his matriculation.

2. The Delegates shall have authority to direct and superintend the work of Candidates for the Degree of Bachelor of Letters or Bachelor of Science, and to make such general regulations and such arrangements in the case of individual Candidates as they shall think fit.

3. The Delegates may appoint Committees composed of graduate members of the University, or other competent persons, and may authorize any such Committee to report to them regarding the fitness of an intending Candidate for the course of study or research on which he proposes to enter, and to superintend the work of a Candidate and report thereon to the Delegates.

4. Any Candidate admitted as aforesaid may, after completing his proposed course of study or research, apply to the Delegates for a certificate authorizing him to supplicate for the Degree of Bachelor of Letters or Bachelor of Science. On receiving such application, the Delegates shall satisfy themselves as to the merit of the Candidate, and his proficiency in the subject of his course of special study or research, either by examination or by requiring from him such dissertation, report of work done, or other evidence as shall seem to them sufficient. Any Candidate who is directed to submit a dissertation or report of work done may be further examined in the subject of such dissertation or report. It shall be the duty of the Delegates to grant certificates to those Candidates only who have attained a high standard of merit; and to state in their annual Report the grounds on which the certificate has in each case been granted. ·

5. No Candidate shall be permitted to supplicate for the Degree of Bachelor of Letters or for the Degree of Bachelor of Science, unless he has kept at least twelve terms by residence within the University as a matriculated member thereof: Provided that any member of an Affiliated College who shall have completed a course of two years at such College shall be entitled for the purposes of this clause to reckon the term in which he is matriculated as the fifth term from his matriculation: Provided also that the Delegates shall be authorized with the approval of Convocation to extend the privilege hereby conferred on Affiliated Colleges to any other University or College.

(*Clauses 6 and 7 relate to certificates.*)

8. Bachelors of Letters and Science shall rank immediately after Bachelors of Civil Law and Medicine; and, among themselves, according to the date of admission to their respective degrees in Letters and Science.

(*A number of clauses follow relating to the admission of candidates, &c.*)

9. In Statt. Tit. VI. Sect. II. § 1, after clause 2 (p. 149, ed. 1894) the following clause shall be added:—

‘3. Any person who has been admitted to the Degree of Bachelor of Letters or Bachelor of Science may supplicate for the Degree of Master of Arts at the same time and under the same conditions as if he had been admitted to the Degree of Bachelor of Arts: Provided that on being admitted to the Degree of Master of Arts he shall not cease to be a Bachelor of Letters or of Science as the case may be.’

A number of amendments have been proposed to the above form of statute, and these will be discussed during the ensuing term. Some wish to reduce the necessary term of residence; some to entrust the oversight and administration of the scheme to the several Faculties, instead of to a new Delegacy; others to require that on the Delegacy there should sit a large proportion of Professors and other University teachers. Others, again, object to the titles proposed for the degrees, and would prefer to award the ordinary B.A. degree to approved students after a prescribed course of special research.

UNIVERSITY EXTENSION IN AUSTRALIA.

(*Continued from the December number.*)

WITH a rapid survey, inevitably meagre, I closed my account of the history of University Extension in Australasia. It remains to discuss the future of the movement in those colonies. Here there are several forces whose relative effect must be estimated. It shall not detract from the honour due to the founders and organizers of the movement in England if I say that, in proportion to its possible field, University Extension in the colonies presents a more difficult problem than did University Extension in England at its inauguration. There is so much that might be done, so little that is being done: the materials for a structure are there, but they are so scattered that the labour of getting them together is almost prohibitive. Higher education is an unworked field outside the walls of the several Universities; but these Universities, non-residential, with their low fees and democratic facilities, and their position in the great centres of population are available for, I do not say are used by, an immeasurably higher percentage of the citizen aggregate than those in England. In the country no special organizations for the teaching of a higher culture exist; beyond schools of mines and agriculture, whose title sufficiently indicates their scope, all is left to individual effort. Peripatetic lectures on farming, dairying and kindred subjects have been provided by Government at various times, with on the whole somewhat indifferent results. A demand for higher education exists, but, owing to the sparsity of population in country districts, the demand does not so readily formulate itself. The ignorant apathy of an agricultural class like that to be found at home in such counties as Hants, Berks, or Suffolk, does not exist in Australasia, where the average of intelligence and of education is much higher than in England. But the Australian as he matures too rapidly, is also less capable of persistent effort. Culture in the towns is as yet superficial: the blood of the restless spirits who made Australia in the fifties is still itching in the veins of their sons: virgin soil merely scratched will yield a sufficient sustenance, and whether field or brain be farmed intense culture is not as yet understood. Our Universities turn out practical men by the hundred—doctors, lawyers, schoolmasters; but a life devoted to study is scarcely known. On the other hand a legacy of restless activity which an earlier generation has bequeathed itself not merely in sport and athletics, but in the lighter forms of mental exercise. If a census were taken of amateur dramatic, musical, orchestral, sketching and debating clubs, their proportion to the population in any Australian town would somewhat astonish an Englishman. The Australian evening lacks repose. Music, sometimes good, generally of indifferent quality, recitation, dancing, cards—of these there is more than enough. The soberer arts of conversation and dialectic are little understood. It is a sign of general manners that dinner parties are rarely given, generally mismanaged, lack appreciation. Society allows no time for thought; Australia, like Nature, abhors a vacuum: to entertain means to keep your guest constantly on the move.

Again, the appetite for instruction is not unsupplied in the towns by existing agencies. As in the old days each new comer was exploited for whatever he could tell of the old world, so it is to-day: each professor, lecturer, parson, doctor, literateur, must pay his footing by essay, address, or lecture before some of the numerous clubs or institutes. Professors, more especially, have in Australia a very different position to that we associate with the name in England. They are expected to assume a certain recognized, though imperfectly conceived, social duty: and it is the failure to appreciate this which lies at the root of the not infrequent difficulties which have arisen between University teachers and the community in which they are placed. When the Australian buys a professor, he buys him out and out. Nothing hampers University Extension, especially among the working classes, so much as the wide-

2

spread system of single lectures on disconnected subjects. With artisan clubs the difficulty is almost insuperable. As for such lectures no payment is made, it becomes by no means easy to make the members of a club understand why, if they can obtain six disconnected lectures for the asking, it is to their interest to take a course of six lectures and pay for it.

But these disadvantages notwithstanding, there is abundant scope for University Extension, more especially in the country districts. The matter of organization is more difficult. In the towns there is little more to be done. Australian towns, with their wide circle of suburbs—the suburban radius of Melbourne is ten miles—lend themselves easily and naturally to the local centre system. With the country it is different. Here the great difficulty, a difficulty unknown in England, is the want of easy and rapid communication. Ballarat is one of our best centres in Victoria : to lecture there means that the lecturer must leave town by the 4.25 p.m. train, arriving at 7.30, lecture, hold his class, stay the night, catch the 6.25 a.m. express in the morning, and reach Melbourne again in time for a nine o'clock breakfast and his University duties at ten. The great majority of our lecturers in Australia it must be remembered are not men of leisure, still less men who, as in England, can give themselves entirely to Extension lecturing : they are men with their time fully occupied, who, out of a scanty leisure, must manufacture the means to spread University culture. But the smaller country towns are in a far worse position. Ballarat is seventy-five miles away, and has what we consider a good service of trains. To reach other towns a lecturer would have to sacrifice two full days—in most cases a condition absolutely prohibitive. Communities of 6,000 or 10,000 cannot be served ; still less the smaller towns ('townships' to use the Australian term). As for the districts where there is little or no urban life, these are wholly beyond reach. Thus the most important field is closed to us, because we have not, what has created University Extension in England, easy and rapid communication by rail.

An equally serious difficulty is the want of suitable books. Three months distant from our market, a course of lectures may be chosen and delivered before we can receive an adequate supply of text-books. Travelling libraries are absolutely essential, and hitherto the funds for their provision have been unattainable. The Melbourne Extension Board has not received a penny beyond fees paid by the centres ; which fees barely cover expense of payments to lecturers, and outlay on printing and general management. The secretaryship is honorary ; and surplus funds are fully employed in entertaining the students at the annual gathering on 'Extension Day' which closes the year's work.

It will be seen that the future of University Extension in Australia does not promise a wide usefulness unless these difficulties can be met. Given a small endowment, their solution would be easy ; without it, nothing can be done. It is imperative that the movement should receive aid, either from Government or from private generosity. Government has here an unmatched opportunity ; but in these days of retrenchment, when no vote has been more bitterly attacked than that for education, to ask for money is to court not a certain refusal only, but an angry rebuff, and an attention which would result in nothing but further reduction of grants for University purposes. Yet the expenditure would be infinitesimal. Much could be done if the Government would concede merely a free pass to lecturers travelling to and from country centres. The programme to which I look forward includes appointment of one or more peripatetic lecturers ; organization of country districts in groups of, say, five centres ; a minimum of twenty-five students at each centre ; courses of ten lectures lasting for thirty or forty weeks continuously and consecutive treatment of allied subjects ; utilization of the numberless state-schools for the holding of lectures ; payment by members of centres of a fee of 6d. per lecture. In this way the work would be nearly, if not quite, self-supporting : and with a small grant added for the maintenance of travelling libraries, it would be possible to organize a satisfactory system for the evangelization of country as well as town. Already, as I have mentioned,

Sydney University has made an important step in this direction, having turned its organizing secretary into a peripatetic lecturer with a fixed salary which enables him to give up his time entirely to the work. With Victorian prejudice I am loath that the self-supporting character of the work should be in any respect infringed ; yet some form of aid in money is essential. I would make this aid as little as is consistent with a true economy which does not sacrifice educational advantages to a narrow regard for pence. Short of such a system, I see no probability that the work in Victoria can be greatly extended beyond the limit already reached in 1892. In that year we had in work almost all possible centres, those excepted which in one way or another require a grant in aid.

There is a further difficulty to which I have indeed already alluded. Although the staff of lecturers on the list of the Melbourne Board contains the names of several who are not directly engaged in the teaching work of the University, yet the majority are so engaged. Moreover the centres have shown a very marked preference hitherto for members of the University staff. As a consequence it has been necessary more than once to refuse compliance with the wishes of a centre. The difficulty has been felt even more in New South Wales ; where, however, it has been partly obviated by appointing as lecturers competent persons residing in the district in which the centre is situated, a policy against which the Melbourne Board has for sufficient reasons set its face. Nor will it be found possible to increase to any degree the number of lecturers on the staff, except by very gradual steps, without appreciably lowering the standard. For Extension lecturing does not offer, and is not for many years likely to offer, in itself, a career and a livelihood. Such a position as is held by the more successful lecturers in England is beyond our horizon in Australia.

To sum up what I have said or implied as to the future of the movement in Australia. Given a revival of trade, I see no reason to doubt that Extension lectures will become a permanent institution in the chief towns. For country districts the problem is already being solved in New South Wales. It may be solved in a similar way in Victoria at any moment. Tasmania and Queensland will use University Extension to feed or create a University. A like movement may produce like results in due course in Western Australia. The several governments have here the opportunity of creating a system of higher education throughout the colonies, and so crowning the excellent work already done in primary education. But will they use the opportunity?

There are one or two questions arising out of our experience in Victoria, upon which a word may be not out of place. And first as to the duration of a course of lectures,—should six or more form the standard length? With entire dependence upon popular support it seems to me, judging from what has taken place in Victoria, that the only possible method at commencement is to adopt the six-lecture course. But I am not prepared to say that when the movement has made progress, courses of six lectures should be alone allowed. Our own system is flexible. A preliminary popular course of three lectures may be given (none as yet has been given) to introduce the system in a new centre ; but the centre is limited to one such course, and thereafter has the option of courses of six, nine, or twelve lectures. But the method which I think promises best is that which adopts a six-lecture course and extends it over a period of twelve weeks, lectures being fortnightly and supplemented, in addition to the ordinary class on lecture nights, by a class of regular students meeting fortnightly and following up the results of the lectures by more practical work. Such a class is supervised by the lecturer or by some competent deputy. In this way better work can be done than by a series of twelve lectures at weekly intervals. Moreover there is far better prospect of two connected courses of six, than of one course of twelve, upon the same subject. That is certainly our experience so far as the movement has yet developed itself. If the experience of the Sydney Board is somewhat contrary, that is to be set down, largely if not entirely, to the fact that the Board could afford to disregard popular support.

Secondly as to examinations. Perhaps the majority of our courses in Victoria have not been followed by examination : where examination has taken place, the number of candidates has been, with one exception, insignificant, and it is likely to remain so, unless a monetary value can be placed upon the Board's certificate. We have not pressed examination, the feeling of the Board has been rather against than for it. We can imagine the cry of heresy which will be raised against us in certain quarters, but in this case οὐ φροντὶς Ἱπποκλείδῃ. It is more than doubtful whether examination adds to the permanent value of the lectures : most of the evils of examination are present, few of its advantages. The student who is attracted by real love of his subject is only spoilt by examination : those who take an examination for the sake of display add no honour to the movement, and lose their knowledge faster than it was gained. Extension lectures are not a method of cram ; they are to solve the problem of the possibility of teaching the spirit of knowledge. We do not aim at increasing the sum of the known, but of the knowable ; at the widening and deepening of intellectual interests ; at a broader life, a fuller interest ; in a word, not at learning but at culture. The issue of the experiment in Victoria seems to show that examination is not essential to the success or utility of University Extension. But each case must be decided on its own merits ; and the fact that Victoria has minimized the importance of examination in no way prevents New South Wales or Queensland from utilizing examination to the fullest.

LETTER TO THE EDITOR.

[*We do not hold ourselves responsible for the opinions expressed by our correspondents.*]

Interchange of Books among Students.

DEAR SIR,—I have read with much interest the paper in the *Gazette* on 'What the Workman needs in Education' : and as a fellow student, you will perhaps kindly allow me to suggest a plan which may prove of some help to workmen. The great difficulty of buying books is one which all poor students can understand, and since 1887, when I first became a student, I have bought only a few, but they have been added to by kind friends, so that I now have a little stock of twenty-five volumes. besides Macaulay's and Motley's works. These I would willingly lend to any student for three months. They could be sent by parcels post at little cost ; and if you would allow any workman to insert in the *Extension Gazette* the name of the book wanted and his address, it would be easy to communicate. If other students, who have some books on History, Science, or Political Economy would do the same, the plan might prove of use to others, and the risk of loss would not I hope deter them, as I have already lent books to Students' Associations without the loss of any, and I think any workman who is anxious to learn would take care of the books entrusted to him.

I am, dear Sir, Yours truly,
A STUDENT.

[*** If our correspondent's suggestion meets with favour, we shall be glad to adopt it.—*Ed.*]

LECTURERS' RESERVE FUND.

SUBSCRIPTIONS AND DONATIONS RECEIVED UP TO DEC. 19 FOR THE YEAR 1894-95.

	£	s	d
Miss Mason (don.)	5	0	0
Miss E. B. Partridge	0	10	0
Miss S. S. Partridge	0	10	0
Miss Wilson	0	10	0
Miss Goldie	1	0	0
Mrs. Gibson Martin	0	10	0
Miss Purton	0	10	0
Mrs. Lelacheur	1	0	0
Miss A. Walton	1	0	0
Miss Cecil	0	5	0
Miss E. A. Slack	0	10	0
Miss M. B. Borlase	0	5	0
Miss A. Lund	0	5	0
Miss Beard	0	10	0
Miss M. E. Holland	0	10	0
Mrs. Le Lacheur Edwards	0	10	0
Mrs. R. Crompton Jones	0	10	0
The Misses Jones	1	0	0

REPORTS FROM THE CENTRES.

BEDFORD.—The close of our Autumn Session was marked by the distinct success of Mr. J. Wells' lecture on Oxford, given on Monday, Dec. 17, in the Modern School Hall. An audience of at least 150, showed keen appreciation both of the views of Oxford buildings, and of the history of its great men, vividly and impartially sketched by the lecturer. With regard to next Spring there is every reason to hope that Dr. Fison's course on 'The Life of a Planet,' will prove full of interest to the many, besides enabling the Students' Association to turn its attention to Astronomy, after three years' historical work. Mr. J. E. Morris kindly gave his last lecture on 'India from 1770 to 1856,' on Dec. 12, when a hearty vote of thanks was unanimously accorded to him for the great help given to our centre in its difficulties this term by his friendly assistance.—E. BLAKE, *Hon. Sec.*

BOLTON.—Mr. Hudson Shaw has just concluded the third course given at Bolton, and the second on 'The Making of England.' This subject is very popular here, as is also the lecturer, who treats his subject in a most vivid manner. The Technical School has been most inconveniently crowded. A large amount of paper-work has been done ; the examination takes place on Monday, January 28, when we hope to exceed the results of last year when twelve students passed, two of them going to the Summer Meeting at Oxford. We have also a very flourishing Students' Association under the able leadership of Mr. J. R. Barlow, who, with his sisters, spare no pains to make it a success, there being over seventy members. In addition to the travelling library sent from Oxford, our committee have kindly purchased a number of books for the use of the students, and judging from the number taken out, they are of immense value to the students.—JAMES MUNKS, *Hon. Librarian.*

BOURNEMOUTH. — A very successful Autumn Term was brought to a close on Friday, Dec. 21, by Mr. J. Wells' delightful illustrated lecture on Oxford University. The Local Committee had some fear that owing to bad weather, and the nearness of Christmas, the attendance at the lecture would not be large, but an audience of about 400 to 450 assembled in the Shaftesbury Hall when the evening arrived, and by their applause at the time, and their expressions of approval since, have testified to their appreciation of the lecture. Bournemouth, as well as the other centres at which the lecture has been so kindly given by Mr. Wells, owes him a debt of gratitude. The average attendance at both courses of lectures during the Autumn term has shown a decided, and in the case of the evening course, a very large increase. For the afternoon course the average has been 180, for the evening 380. The number remaining for the classes has been large, and the paper-work good. The paper-work however, especially for the evening lectures, is still deficient in quantity for such a large centre. The Students' Association has done well. Evening as well as afternoon meetings have been carried on, the papers read have been good, and the discussions brisk and lively.—CATHARINE PUNCH, *Hon. Sec.*

CHELTENHAM.—The great success of the afternoon lectures delivered last Spring, combined with the strong desire for an evening course, expressed by many who were occupied during the day, induced the Committee to try the experiment of two courses in the Autumn. The result has been most satisfactory. The attendance at both courses has been large—from 250 to 300 at every lecture—and it has been gratifying to notice the same faces time after time, proving that the lectures were able to compete successfully with the many counter attractions which this town offers. It need scarcely be added that with the Rev. W. Hudson Shaw as lecturer and 'The History of Florence' and 'The Making of England' for his subjects, the interest of the audience was well sustained. It is a matter of regret that the courses must be interrupted for the present, in consequence of Mr. Hudson Shaw's visit to America ; but the Committee have been fortunate in securing Mr. Horsburgh for the Spring Session. He will lecture in the afternoon on the 'Growth of Parliament,' and in the evening on 'Industrial and Economic Questions since 1789'—both subjects of peculiar interest at the present time. Owing to the kindness of the Governors of the Grammar School, the Committee have had the free use of their fine Assembly Hall, and have thus been saved considerable expense.—F. H. CRAWLEY, *Hon. Sec.*

HODDESDON AND BROXBOURNE.—The course of twelve lectures on Shakespeare by Mr. Boas has been most satisfactory. The attendance has been well maintained, and both intellectually and financially the lectures have proved a success. The number of students writing papers is less than last year, though the work is up to the usual standard. We have eight students going up for examination.—E. P. TAYLOR and M. E. BAIN, *joint Hon. Secs.*

LEAMINGTON.—Mr. Marriott's course upon the English in India concluded on Dec. 7 with a brief sketch of the leading events of the Indian Mutiny. Lime-light illustrations of prominent Indian statesmen and military commanders, furnished by the lecturer, and of the principal scenes of the Mutiny, lent and explained by Alderman Hinks, were exhibited. Mr. Marriott, in summing up, at the conclusion of his lecture, the position of the English in India, observed that by the strangest and most marvellous concatenation of events we found ourselves the possessors of a vast and thickly populated country, and we had accepted a vast responsibility which we could not shirk, even if we would. We could only pray that the English people as a whole would realize this responsibility, and would endeavour fearlessly to discharge a duty almost appalling in its magnitude; but at the same time unique and splendid in the opportunities it afforded for advancing the happiness, the good government, and the social peace of millions of the human race. The mayor, in moving a vote of thanks to the lecturer, struck the same key by adding that the audience would carry away that evening the consciousness of the responsibility, as well as of the glory, that our rule in India entailed upon us, and a desire to do the best we could for the people in India, before we began to think at all of ourselves. The course, which has been a marked success in every way, has had an average attendance of 143 persons. Nine students qualified for examination.—C. H. d'E. LEPPINGTON, *Local Secretary.*

MAIDSTONE.—For a new centre, the course of lectures held here on Shelley and Keats by Rev. J. G. Bailey, LL.D., has been very successful. The number who took tickets for the course was not large, but most of these entered with hearty appreciation into the subject of the lectures, and a large percentage wrote the weekly papers. It is hoped, however, that sufficient interest has been aroused to lead to the establishment of a permanent University centre. The course has been practically self-supporting. —E. STANGER, *Hon. Sec.*

OXFORD.—A two years' sequence of lectures on English History with special reference to the history of Oxford, arranged to meet the needs of pupil-teachers who are going in for their Queen's Scholarship examination in 1896, has been begun this autumn by a half-course of six lectures by Mr. Horsburgh on the Making of England from 1215 to 1485. The lectures have been most interesting, and though the audience has not been much over 100, a large proportion of that number are students, and about twenty-three papers have been sent every fortnight to the lecturer. Only ten pupil-teachers are attending the course, but this is perhaps as many as can be expected to take up an extra subject, when it is remembered that they are teaching all the week, both morning and afternoon, and have only the evenings in which to do all their preparation for examination. The special subject of Oxford has been treated of at the Students' Association meetings, held in the alternate weeks to the lectures. Mr. Sadler very kindly gave three lectures at Oxford, which were greatly appreciated by the students, and papers have been read by students on the same subject. The course will be continued next term by Mr. Marriott, who will give six lectures on the Renaissance and Reformation in England.—MARY S. BEARD, *Hon. Sec.*

REPTON.—A course of six lectures on ' English Novelists' by Mr. Marriott was begun on Friday, Sept. 28, and held in the Pears School on alternate Friday mornings up to Dec. 7. The average attendance has been sixty, which for a country centre is good. This is the first course of lectures under the auspices of the Oxford Extension scheme held in Repton, and it is hoped that another course will be arranged for next autumn. The number of papers done has only averaged five, but the library has been much used. On December 14 an examination on the subject of the course was held ; it was taken by six students.— M. CATTLEY, *Local Secretary.*

RIPON.—At the conclusion of the last of Mr. Mallet's lectures on the 'French Revolution,' which have been given in the afternoons during the present term, a hearty vote of thanks was given to the lecturer on the motion of the Dean of Ripon. In the evening Canon MacColl presided at the last of Mr. Mallet's lectures on the 'Stuarts,' and again a vote of thanks was accorded to the lecturer.

TUNBRIDGE WELLS.—The afternoon course here this last term on 'The Tudors and the Stuarts' has been very popular. The large and regular attendance we have had is good evidence that Mr. Mallet succeeded in making this period of English history thoroughly interesting to his audience, and the large number of students who qualified and entered for the Examination (33 —the highest number we have ever yet mustered) is very satisfactory. The audience was one of the best we have had, and its numbers increased as the course went on. About twenty-five stayed regularly to the class, and the time and trouble Mr. Cotes gave to this part of his work was much appreciated.— LAURA F. JONES, *Hon. Sec.*

WINSLOW.—The last of a course of six lectures on ' The

Relation of History to Painting' was delivered by Mr. Kenelm Cotes on December 6, to between seventy and eighty students. The numbers during the course have kept up well, and the interest has steadily increased. Any centre which can take twelve lectures would I am sure find that the second part of the same course, ' Five Cities' (whose art is explained by their history), adds much to the teaching value as well as to the interest of the course. —A. L. NEWCOMBE, *Hon. Sec.*

SCHOLARSHIPS FOR THE OXFORD SUMMER MEETING, 1895.

A FUND, to which subscriptions amounting to £60 have already been promised, has been opened for the provision of Scholarships to enable students from Oxford centres to attend the Summer Meeting, which will be held in Oxford from August 1 to August 26, 1895.

The Scholarships will be awarded after an Essay competition, and will be of two values—£10 and £5. Holders of the former must attend the whole Meeting; those of the latter may, if they prefer, attend either the First or Second Part only. Part I lasts from Aug. 1 to Aug. 12 ; Part II from Aug. 12 to Aug. 26.

Conditions of Award.

The Scholarships will be awarded on or about July 1, 1895, for English Essays on subjects drawn from English Literature, English History, Natural Science, and Political Economy.

A. *Competition for Scholarships.*

The Scholarships will be awarded in three divisions:—

(*a*) Open to all Oxford University Extension Students *who need the assistance of the Scholarships* in order to study in Oxford, according to the intention of the donors.

(*b*) Open to all Elementary School Teachers (men or women), who are also Oxford University Extension Students.

(*c*) Open to all working men and women, who are also Oxford University Extension Students.

To qualify themselves for election to a Scholarship :—

(1) All competitors must be recommended by their Local Committee as suitable candidates.

(2) Competitors in *divisions* (*a*) and (*b*) must, in order to qualify, obtain *distinction* in an examination on a course of Oxford University Extension Lectures delivered between January 1894 and June 1895.

(3) Competitors in *division* (*c*) must pass an examination on a course of Oxford University Extension Lectures delivered between the same dates.

The Delegates, however, reserve to themselves the right of rejecting the name of any candidate ; and, unless compositions of sufficient merit are sent in, do not bind themselves to award Scholarships in any or all of the following four subjects.

B. *Competition for Prizes.*

A limited number of Prizes, of the value of £1, will be awarded in the same competition without any limitation as to the means of the competitors. Candidates for this branch of the competition must qualify as regards examinations, like the competitors in *divisions* (*a*) and (*b*).

SUBJECTS.

(1) *History* (one only to be selected).

(i) The Growth of Nationality in the thirteenth century.

(ii) The causes of the Great Rebellion.

(iii) England's command of the Sea during the Revolutionary Wars (1793-1815).

(2) *Literature* (one only to be selected).

(i) How far is it possible to specify any general conditions which are necessary to the production of the best poetry ?

(ii) Explain what is meant by Poetic Justice, and consider with full illustrations how far it should be observed in Drama or Fiction.

(iii) Estimate the importance in literary history of the works of Dryden, Pope, or Walter Scott.

(3) *Political Economy* (one only to be selected).

(i) Show the effect of different systems of land tenure on the production and distribution of wealth.

(ii) What remedies have been suggested for the existing depression, and how far are they likely to succeed ?

(iii) What circumstances may be expected to determine the wages of labour in the future ?

(4) *Science* (one only to be selected).

(i) Theories of Chemical Action.
(ii) Sewage disposal in towns and rural districts.
(iii) The Weeds of the Farm.

REGULATIONS.

1. Each candidate may write an essay *on one subject only*, but may select one from any of the above four groups.

2. All compositions must reach the Delegacy [addressed—The Secretary, University Extension Office, Examination Schools, Oxford] on or before Monday, June 3, 1895; must each bear the writer's full name and address, with a note saying whether the writer is competing for a Scholarship or a Prize, or both, and, is the former, in which division (*a*, *b*, or *c*, see above); must be written on foolscap paper, and on one side of the paper only; must state, at the top of the first page, the writer's occupation ; and must be accompanied by a certificate of qualification from his or her Local Committee in the following form :—

' On behalf of the members of the Local Committee acting in concert with the Oxford University Delegates for the establishment of Lectures and Teaching at   ,
I certify that *A. B.* is in all respects a suitable person for election to a University Extension   [1],
according to the regulations.

   Signed on behalf of the Committee,

. ...

Secretary.'

[1] *State whether Scholarship or Prize, or both.*

3. Candidates are not debarred from the consultation of standard works, but quotations should be notified in the margin, and borrowed passages should be clearly distinguished from the rest.

4. No composition should exceed thirty foolscap pages, including a brief analysis which should be prefixed to the essay.

5. The names of the unsuccessful competitors will not be divulged by the Delegates, and all compositions may be obtained from them after the announcement of the result of the competition.

6. Successful candidates will be informed by the Delegacy of the result of the competition.

7. The students elected to the Scholarships will be required to visit Oxford during the Summer Meeting of University Extension Students, 1895.

8. Holders of Scholarships of £10 are required to reside in Oxford during the whole Meeting. If they are unable to do so, they must resign half their Scholarship, retaining, however, the position on the list of scholars to which the excellence of their essay entitled them.

9. The Programme of the Summer Meeting will be published at Easter, and copies (7*d*. each post free) can then be obtained on application to the Secretary, University Extension Office, Oxford.

Contributions to the Scholarship fund should be sent to the Secretary, University Extension Office, Oxford.

Copies of the above regulations can be obtained free of charge on application to the Secretary, University Extension Office, Oxford.

ARRANGEMENTS FOR SPRING, 1895.

All lectures are at fortnightly intervals except where otherwise stated.

Centre.	No. of Lectures in Course.	Subject of Course.	Lecturer.	Course or Half-Course begins.	Course ends.
†UNIVERSITY EXTENSION COLLEGE, READING (evening)	12	Age of Elizabeth and Puritan Rebellion	Rev.W.H SHAW,M.A. & E.L.S.HORSBURGH,M.A.	Th. Jan. 17	Mar. 28
,, (afternoon)	12	Tennyson and Browning	J.CHURTONCOLLINS,M.A	S. Jan. 26	Apr. 6
,, (evening) ...	12	Greek Drama	,, ,, ...	S. Jan. 26	Apr 6
,, (evening) ...	12	The Study of Local History ...	W. M. CHILDS, B.A. ...	F. Jan. 25	Apr. 5
,, (evening) ...	12	La Littérature Française du XVII* Siècle	M. J. MAURICE REY, B. es Sc.	W. Jan. 23	Apr. 3
,, (evening) ...	12	Geography of the British Isles ...	H. J. MACKINDER, M.A.	S. Jan. 19	Mar. 30
†BIRMINGHAM, EDGBASTON (afternoon)	12	Age of Louis XIV and French Revolution	J.A.R.MARRIOTT,M.A.	T. Jan. 15	Mar. 26
BIRMINGHAM, Severn Street (evening)	6	English Colonies	,, ,,	T. Jan. 15	Mar. 26
†BOURNEMOUTH (afternoon) ...	12	Europe since Waterloo	,, ,, ...	W. Jan. 23	Apr. 3
BRADFORD (evening)	6	Colonies	,, ,, ...	Th. Jan. 17	Mar. 28
†BRIDPORT (evening)	12	Industrial Revolution	,, ,, ...	T. Jan. 22	Apr. 2
†CLEVEDON (afternoon) ...	12	Shakespeare's Historical Plays ...	,, ,, ...	F. Jan. 25	Apr. 5
DORCHESTER (evening) ...	6	Colonies	,, ,, ...	W. Jan. 23	Apr. 3
OXFORD (evening)	6	The Renaissance and Reformation in England	,, ,, ...	F. Jan. 18	Mar. 29
SALE (evening)	6	England in the 18th Century ...	,, ,, ...	W. Jan. 16	Mar. 27
†SOUTHBOURNE (afternoon) ...	12	Europe since Waterloo	,, ,, ...	Th. Jan. 24	Apr. 4
WEYMOUTH (afternoon) ...	6	Age of Louis XIV ...	,, ,, ...	T. Jan. 22	Apr. 2
†TAMWORTH (evening) ...	10	England in the 18th Century ...	C. E. MALLET, B.A. ...	T. Jan. 15	Feb. 26
FOLKESTONE (evening, weekly)	10	England in the 18th Century ...	,, ,,	M. Jan. 28	Apr. 1
WHITEHAVEN (evening) ...	6	England in the 18th Century ...	,, ,,	W. Jan. 16	Mar. 27
†BURNLEY (evening)	12	Spenser & other Elizabethan Poets	F. S. BOAS, M.A. ...	Th. Jan. 24	Apr. 4
†CANTERBURY (afternoon) ...	12	Victorian Poets	,, ,,	Th. Jan. 17	Mar. 28
†RAMSGATE (afternoon) ...	12	Literature of Cavaliers and Puritans	,, ,,	S. Jan. 26	Apr. 6
DEVIZES (evening)	6	Tennyson	Rev. J.G. BAILEY, M.A., LL.D.	Th. Jan. 24	Apr. 4
†WEST BRIGHTON (afternoon)	12	Tennyson	,, ,,	F. Jan. 18	Mar. 29
ABERGAVENNY (afternoon) ...	6	Shakespeare	E.L.S.HORSBURGH,B.A.	S. Jan. 26	Apr. 6
BRECON (afternoon)	6	Literature of the 18th Century ...	,, ,, ...	Th. Jan. 24	Apr. 4
BRECON (evening)	6	Epochs from English History ...	,, ,, ...	Th. Jan. 24	Apr. 4
CHELTENHAM (afternoon) ...	6	Growth of Parliament	,, ,, ...	W. Jan. 30	Apr. 10
CHELTENHAM (evening) ...	6	Industrial and Economic Questions since 1789	,, ,, ...	W. Jan. 30	Apr. 10
EVESHAM (evening)	6	Revolution and Age of Anne ...	,, ,, ...	W. Jan. 23	Apr. 3

† The figures in the second column include the lectures given in the Autumn Term, from which these courses are continued.

Centre.	No. of Lectures in Course.	Subject of Course.	Lecturer.	Course or Half-Course begins.	Course ends.
GLOUCESTER (evening)	6	English History in Shakespeare...	E. L. S. HORSBURGH, B.A.	M. Jan. 28	Apr. 8
HEREFORD (evening) ...	6	Wyclif to Sir Thomas More	„ „	M. Jan. 21	Apr. 1
LEOMINSTER (evening)	6	Industrial and Economic Questions since 1789	„ „	T. Jan. 22	Apr. 2
MALVERN (afternoon)	6	Puritan Revolution ...	„ „	W. Jan. 23	Apr. 3
†REIGATE (afternoon)...	12	The Reign of Elizabeth	„ „	Th. Jan. 17	Mar. 28
ROSS (afternoon) ...	6	Literature of the 18th Century ..	„ „	T. Jan. 22	Apr. 2
†SOUTHAMPTON (evening)	12	The Age of Elizabeth ...	„ „	F. Jan. 18	May 29
STROUD (afternoon) ...	6	The Renaissance ...	„ „	T. Jan. 29	Apr. 9
STROUD (evening) ...	6	The Reign of Elizabeth ...	„ „	T. Jan. 29	Apr. 9
SWANSEA (evening) ...	6	Epochs from English History ...	„ „	F. Jan. 25	Apr. 5
DOVER (afternoon) ...	6	Architecture	F. BOND, M.A.	M. Jan. 28	Apr. 8
TUNBRIDGE WELLS (afternoon, weekly)	10	Architecture	„ „	F. Jan. 25	Mar. 29
FLEET (afternoon) ...	8	Chaucer to Shakespeare ...	R. WARWICK BOND, M.A.	Th. Jan. 24	Apr. 25
†HENLOW (evening) ...	12	The English Citizen ...	W. M. CHILDS, B.A....	W. Jan. 16	Mar. 27
GLOSSOP (evening) ...	6 .	Trade, Adventure, and Discovery	K. D. COTES, M.A. ...	W. Jan. 23	Apr. 3
WARRINGTON (evening)	6	Trade, Invention, and Discovery	„ „	F. Jan. 25	Apr. 5
WIRKSWORTH (evening)	6	Trade, Adventure, and Discovery	„ „	Th. Jan. 24	Apr. 4
TAVISTOCK (afternoon)	6	Puritan Revolution ...	W. G. DE BURGH, B.A.	M. Jan. 28	Apr. 8
FROME (afternoon) ...	6	Wordsworth, Coleridge, and Scott	„ „	T. Jan. 29	Apr. 9
†WEST BRIGHTON (evening)	12	Three Centuries of Working-class History	W. A. S. HEWINS, M.A.	Th. Jan. 24	Apr. 18
GRIMSBY (evening) ...	6	Problems of Poverty ...	J. A. HOBSON, M.A. ...	T. Jan. 22	Apr. 2
MIDHURST (afternoon)	6	English Novelists ...	„ „	W. Jan. 16	Mar. 27
TUNBRIDGE WELLS (evening)	6	Industrial Questions of the Day ...	„ „	W. Jan. 23	Apr. 3
†CARLISLE (afternoon)	12	Architecture	J. E. PHYTHIAN	T. Jan. 15	Apr. 9
CHESTER (afternoon) ...	6	Architecture	„ „	T. Jan. 22	Apr. 2
HALIFAX (evening) ...	6	Florentine Art	„ „	Th. Jan. 24	Mar. 28
KERSAL (evening, weekly)	8	Architecture	„ „	M. Jan. 28	Mar. 18
†BODMIN (evening) ...	12	South Africa ...	W. B. WORSFOLD, M.A.	F. Jan. 25	Apr. 5
†CAMBORNE (evening)...	12	South Africa ...	„ „	F. Jan. 18	Mar. 29
†FALMOUTH (evening)...	12	South Africa ...	„ „	Th. Jan. 17	Mar. 28
†HELSTON (evening) ...	12	South Africa ...	„ „	T. Jan. 22	Apr. 2
†LAUNCESTON (evening)	12	South Africa ...	„ „	W. Jan. 16	Mar. 27
†PENZANCE (evening) ...	12	South Africa ...	„ „	M. Jan. 21	Apr. 1
†REDRUTH (evening) ...	12	South Africa ...	„ „	Th. Jan. 24	Apr. 4
†ST. AUSTELL (evening)	12	South Africa ...	„ „	T. Jan. 15	Mar. 26
†TRURO (evening) ...	12	South Africa ...	„ „	M. Jan. 14	Mar. 25
LEWES (evening) ...	6	Physiography	G. J. BURCH, M.A. ...	M. Jan. 21	Apr. 1
BRIGHTON (St. Michael's Hall)	6	Regions, Races, and Resources ...	H. R. MILL, D.Sc.	Th. Jan. 31	Apr. 4
BRIGHTON (evening) ...	6	Regions, Races, and Resources ...	„ „	Th. Jan. 31	Apr. 4
†CARLISLE (evening) ...	12	Outlines of Geology ...	C. CARUS-WILSON, F.G.S.	Th. Jan. 24	Apr. 4
†ST. HELENS (evening)	12	Crust of the Earth	„ „	Th. Jan. 31	Apr. 3
†BATH (afternoon) ...	12	Recent Discoveries with the Telescope and Spectroscope	A. H. FISON, D.Sc. ...	Th. Jan. 31	Apr. 11
†BATH (evening) ...	12	Recent Discoveries with the Telescope and Spectroscope	„ „	Th. Jan. 31	Apr. 11
BEDFORD (evening) ...	6	Life of a Planet	„ „	T. Jan. 29	Apr. 9
†BOURNEMOUTH (evening)	12	Forces of Nature ...	„ „	F. Jan. 18	Mar. 29
LEAMINGTON (evening)	6	Life of a Planet	„ „	T. Feb. 5	Apr. 16
†NEWPORT (evening) ...	12	Physical Astronomy ...	„ „	Th. Jan. 24	Apr. 4
†RYDE (afternoon) ...	12	Recent Discoveries with the Telescope and Spectroscope	„ „	Th. Jan. 24	Apr. 4
†VENTNOR (evening) ...	12	Physical Astronomy ...	„ „	F. Jan. 25	Apr. 5
Greek Classes (afternoon, weekly) : BRIGHTON (Elementary)	10	Xen. *Anab.* I : Eurip. *Alc.* (scenes from)	REV. E. LUCE, M.A. ...	T. Jan. 29	Apr. 2
„ (Intermediate)	10	Thucyd. VII and Soph. *Ajax* ...	„ „	W. Jan. 30	Apr. 3
Somerset County Council : 5 Courses of ...	12	Management of Farm Stock ...	H. SESSIONS ...	Jan.	Apr.
5 Courses of ...	12	Hygiene	C. H. WADE, M.A., D.P.H.	Jan.	Apr.
Kent County Council : 2 Courses of	12	Chemistry	H. H. COUSINS, M.A.	Jan.	Apr.

Summer Term, 1895.

BRIGHTON (St. Michael's Hall) | 6 or 8 | England in the 18th Century ... | J. A. R. MARRIOTT, M.A. | Not fixed | Not fixed

† The figures in the second column include the lectures given in the Autumn Term, from which these courses are continued.

Note.—Application for Courses and all information as to fees, &c., can be obtained from The Secretary, University Extension Office, Examination Schools, Oxford.

INFORMATION TO CONTRIBUTORS.

All communications should be addressed to the Editor, OXFORD UNIVERSITY EXTENSION GAZETTE, *University Press, Oxford.*
All matter intended for insertion in the February issue should reach him not later than January 21.
Contributions should be written on one side of the paper only, and must be accompanied by the name of the writer (not necessarily for publication).
N.B.—*All orders should carefully specify the full title,* OXFORD UNIVERSITY EXTENSION GAZETTE.

OXFORD UNIVERSITY

EXTENSION GAZETTE.

VOL. V. NO. 53.]   FEBRUARY, 1895.   [ONE PENNY.

N.B.—Local Organizers of Oxford University Extension Lectures are invited to send to the Secretary, University Extension Office, Examination Schools, Oxford, copies of any journals containing notices of, or references to, Extension work.

NOTES AND COMMENTS.

New Member of the Delegacy. The Hebdomadal Council has appointed the Rev. L. R. Phelps, Fellow of Oriel College, as a member of the University Extension Delegacy in place of Mr. Chapman resigned. Mr. Phelps, who is widely known as one of the Editors of the *Economic Review*, has from the first taken an active interest in the Oxford University Extension and has for a long time been one of the Examiners of the Delegacy.

.·.

Dr. A. H. Fison has been appointed a Staff-Lecturer. The appointment will date from the end of the present session.

.·.

Applications for lectures from English residents in Switzerland and Cape Colony made it appear desirable to remove the statutory restrictions, which at present limit the action of the Oxford University Extension Delegacy to England and Wales. An amendment of the Statute was therefore promulgated in the Congregation of the University on Jan. 29. The proposal met with some opposition but was carried through the first stage by eleven votes to eight.

.·.

Oxford Colleges and Agricultural Depression. A paper read to the Statistical Society by a well-known Oxford University Extension lecturer, Mr. L. L. Price, on the Colleges of Oxford and Agricultural depression has deservedly received general notice. Mr. Price, it should be remembered, is both an economist of distinction and also, as Treasurer of Oriel, an expert in College finance. The fall in College revenues between 1883 and 1893 may be reckoned as being 'nearer 30 per cent. than 11.' The emoluments of the Heads of Colleges have fallen from £22,811 to £20,905 ; that of the Fellows from £83,820 to £74,749: and in some Colleges this represents a decline of more than 25 per cent. in the Fellows' incomes. The emoluments of Scholars, however, have increased from £44,776 to £48,378. Two Colleges were richer in 1883 than in 1893, seventeen were poorer, the net decline in receipts from external sources amounting to £26,877.

.·.

The Journal of Education and the older Universities. The *Journal of Education* is usually so just and sympathetic towards the efforts which are being made to draw closer the bonds of connexion between the Universities and the schools of the country, that a note in its January number strikes the reader as inconsistent and curiously ill-informed. 'The tendency of the recent developments at Oxford and Cambridge is to divert the younger generation of College tutors and fellows from their proper work and attract them to work for which they are not specially qualified. It is only human nature to neglect permanent work to which a fixed salary is attached, for occasional work which is paid for as an extra.' Those who know the Oxford of to-day will smile at the ineptitude of this attack. There never was a time when College tutors gave themselves more laboriously or with a more undivided attention to the care of their pupils. In fact, some people charge them with being so sedulous in the discharge of their duties as to impair the educational value of the undergraduate's training. And, in the second place, it is indisputable that one chief source of academic reform within the last thirty years has been the administrative connexion, formed by the Local Examination Delegacy between the University and the secondary schools.

.·.

The Vice-Chancellor of the University of Oxford was entertained last month at a complimentary dinner by past and present members of Queen's College, the society of which he has been for many years the distinguished Head. It will not, we hope, be thought improper if we take this opportunity of expressing to the Vice-Chancellor the gratitude of all University Extension students for the invaluable help which he has given to our work. Without his sympathy, counsel and encouragement, first as chairman of the original committee which had oversight of the Oxford University Extension in its early days, and during more recent years as Chairman of the Delegacy, much that has been done without friction or misunderstanding would have been regarded as impossible.

.·.

Sir Henry Acland's Resignation. The retirement of Sir Henry Acland removes a distinguished name from the roll of Oxford Professors. During his long tenure of office, Sir Henry has rendered the greatest services to the University. To him, more than to any other single man, was due the foundation of the Schools of Natural Science in the University. It is proposed to commemorate his life work by assisting the Sarah Acland Home for Nurses, an Oxford institution which was founded in memory of Sir Henry's wife. The Warden of All Souls is Treasurer of the fund.

.·.

Appeal for more Scholarships for the Summer Meeting. More Scholarships are wanted for the Oxford Summer Meeting of next August. At present the fund stands at £60. We ought to have £80 more. The fund is devoted to providing Scholarships of £10 and £5 to enable poor students to come to the Summer Meeting. The larger grant enables a student to attend the whole Meeting ; the smaller, for one or other part of it. Few gifts are more welcome or produce more lasting benefit to the recipients. The latter, it should be added, have to qualify themselves for election by attendance at a course of University Extension lectures and by success in the essay competition which follows the lecture-session.

.·.

The Lecturers' Reserve Fund was formed in order to provide against the misfortune which might otherwise befall a lecturer incapacitated from his duty by illness during a lecture season. The fund, upon which up to the present time no call has been necessary, now amounts to £964 15*s*. 6*d*., and our thanks are due to the many friends who by their goodwill and liberality have raised so large a sum. In the course of years we hope that the fund will largely increase, as it is our best guarantee against the anxiety and wearing care which are the worst enemies of efficient and happy work.

.·.

The reformed Curriculum of the organized Science Schools.
Public announcement was made on Jan. 28 of changes of almost revolutionary importance in the curriculum of the organized Science Schools under the Science and Art Department. Not only is the old system of 'payment by results' giving way year by year to the more educational method of distribution of grants according to the reports of visiting inspectors, who will observe the methods of teaching and the equipment of the school, but significant reforms are to be introduced into the balance of studies. Provision is to be made for literary instruction, as a curriculum of pure science has been found less profitable than one which pays regard to the humanities as well. Special courses are to be arranged for advanced students. And the educational needs of women students are to be remembered. Great credit will be given to Mr. Acland and to the South Kensington authorities for this timely and farsighted reform. There will in future be less difficulty in the way of an educational alliance between South Kensington workers and those primarily interested in the University Extension system. From the cordial co-operation of these two agencies, and their local representatives, much good may result to English education. And, as Captain Abney said at Oxford in August, the more the two agencies find it possible to work together and to sympathize with one another's aims and to supplement one another's deficiencies, the better will it be for educational progress in the country.

.·.

The Training of Teachers.
Sir George Kekewich delivered a noteworthy and suggestive address on Jan. 11 at the annual meeting of the Association of Principals and Lecturers in Training Colleges under Government inspection. He spoke strongly in favour of the introduction of elasticity and freedom into the curriculum of the Training Colleges. 'The teacher is thus more free to choose for the student, while at the same time the student is more free to adopt, the course most suited to his natural views, aptitude and capacity.' He also laid more stress on the cultivation of character, on the refinement of the mind and on the increase of interest in art, nature and social movements, than on mere drill and mechanical aptitudes. Teachers all over the country will welcome these statesmanlike words, which give expression to the University ideal of education.

.·.

The University of Wales.
Lord Aberdare has, we are glad to see, just been chosen as the first Chancellor of the University of Wales. This is a deserved honour to a pioneer of higher education in the Principality and to a family which for more than one generation has rendered great services to the same cause. Principal Viriamu Jones of Cardiff is to be the first Vice-Chancellor of the University. When the developments of the last few years fall into perspective, we shall see that we have been passing through a period of remarkable expansion of University influence. And as in the United Kingdom, the policy of one University has always affected the administrative aims of the rest, we may confidently foretell great results as likely to follow from this—the latest but not least welcome—addition to the roll of British Universities.

.·.

The many friends whom Mr. A. B. Badger has made at the University Extension centres and at the Summer Meetings will be glad to hear that he has been appointed Educational Adviser to the County Authority of Carnarvonshire. He enters on his new work at a critical time in Welsh education.

.·.

Professor Tout has become Chairman of the Victoria University Extension Committee and Mr. Hartog has been appointed Secretary in his place. We welcome this addition to the administrative strength of the University Extension system in the North of England.

.·.

It is announced that the University of Durham is seeking fresh powers in order to admit women to its degrees. When these powers are obtained, the majority of English Universities will be open to both sexes.

.·.

The University Extension College at Exeter.
An excellent programme has been published by the authorities of the Exeter University Extension College for the present term. There are classes in Latin, French, German, Italian, and English, in English History, in Geography, in Mathematics, Chemistry and Mechanics, and in Music. The public lectures comprise courses on Physiology by Mr. Parkyn, and on European History since the French Revolution by Mr. J. H. Rose. There is also a Normal Department for teachers. Why should not the latter be developed into a Day Training College? The staff of the College, on which both men and women teachers serve, includes the names of graduates of Cambridge, Oxford and Dublin.

.·.

The *U. E. Journal* and Miss Montgomery.
The leading article in the January number of the *University Extension Journal* criticizes the essay which was contributed to our December issue by Miss Montgomery on 'the opportunity of the Universities.' The criticism is admirably written, but much of it rests, in our judgement, on fallacious assumptions. The discussion, however, had better be continued in the columns where the criticism appeared. Here it must suffice to say that the *Journal* would have done well to make more adequate recognition of the great value of the services rendered by Miss Montgomery to the older Universities, and of her special knowledge of the opportunities offered to them by the present crisis in English education. We would, moreover, demur to the wisdom of congratulating ourselves at this stage on the part which the Universities have played in the guidance of public education. Let other people do that. It is for us rather to think of arrears than of achievements.

.·.

Annual Report of the Bournemouth Centre.
We have often had occasion to mention favourably the excellent work done by the Bournemouth centre, which is due in a large measure to the labours of the honorary secretary, Miss Punch, of the chairman of the local committee (Mr. Leveson Scarth), and of its treasurer (Mr. J. Thompson Ridley). The report for 1894 has lately been published and shows that the work of the year was satisfactory. Following the example of the University Extension Colleges at Reading and Exeter, the committee decided to strengthen themselves by asking various associations in the town to nominate a member to serve on the University Extension Committee. The People's Institute, Boscombe, the Bournemouth Science and Art and Technical School, the Young Women's Christian Association, the C.E.W.M. Union, the Carpenters' and Joiners' Amalgamated Society, the Teachers' Union, the Gardeners' Mutual Improvement Society, and the Scientific and Antiquarian Society have already nominated representatives. The report also mentions that the Committee arranged the first local conference of local organizers of University Extension, which was held in April, and proved most successful. The Bournemouth Visitors' Directory of Jan 19, contains an interesting notice of the successful annual conversazione of the Students' Association, and it is also stated in the same paper that, at the bazaar which is to be held in

Bournemouth in order to raise money for the local School of Science and Art, one of the stalls will be under the charge of the Students' Association. Such action is to be heartily commended, as it serves to increase the feeling of fellowship and unity which should exist between the various educational organizations in the same town.

.˙.

A Hint among the Chaff. The *Oxford Magazine* of January 23 contained a brilliant copy of verses chaffing, in amoebean strains, the University Extension movement and the endowment of research. It suggested that if the advocates of research and the advocates of University Extension joined forces (which there is nothing to prevent their doing, as the two movements are the complements, not the rivals, of one another), their united appeal for endowment would prove irresistible.

.˙.

The *Technical World*, which in its new form and under new auspices is coming to the front rank among educational papers, thinks that 'the University Extension movement is not destined to become a permanent factor in our educational system, but that nevertheless as a pioneer the movement has done and is doing thoroughly good work in arousing an interest in scientific problems among a class of people not reached by the ramifications of the Science and Art and Technical Classes.' We will not follow the *Technical World* into the region of prophecy—or would it be more correct to say 'of scientific prediction'?—but it will be observed that the author of this forecast of our future seems to be mainly thinking of the Extension lectures arranged in concert with County Councils. These, as we have always said, were of a preparative character. They were intended to pioneer the way for the more systematic instruction which must follow. And they have, by general admission, rendered fruitful service by mapping out the educational needs, and ascertaining the intellectual standard, of different districts. But, apart from County Council work, no method of imparting instruction by *lecture* can ever be regarded as more than a part of scientific education. Work in the laboratory, research, experiment, discovery—these are the chief elements of value in scientific training. On the side of literary and historical, and to some extent of economic, studies, the case is different. But even here the lecture, the mere giving of instruction, is only a subordinate part of true education. A student must make discoveries for himself. The things he discovers may have been known before. That, from the point of view of education, does not matter. The essential thing is that he should exert his own intellectual faculties by way of research, argument, construction of principles, coordination of ideas. Knowledge that is poured into the mind soon leaks away. The lecturer stimulates the student to work for himself. The power of University Extension is largely due to the fact that it insists on the primary need of the ethical element in instruction and in regarding the personality of the teacher as one of the chief instruments of education.

.˙.

In the report of the Brussels University Extension Congress, published by the *Indépendance Belge*, Mr. H. J. Mackinder is described as 'Professor of University Extension in the University of Oxford.' At least so the *Manchester Guardian* translates it. But the original report says 'Professeur de l'Extension Universitaire d'Oxford,' which is probably meant as a translation of 'Staff-Lecturer of the Oxford University Extension.'

.˙.

The central office of the Extension Universitaire of Brussels is at 8, Rue Zinner; and the general Secretary is Dr. Arthur Hirsch.

.˙.

The *Carlisle Journal* of Jan. 25 contains the following note which, if accurate, points to military exactitude on the part of the municipal officers in the discharge of their duties at Tullie House, an admirable institution which seems destined to play a great part in the intellectual life of Carlisle.

'A correspondent who signs himself "A Benighted Student" writes to protest against certain extraordinary regulations at Tullie House which are productive of great confusion and inconvenience at the close of every lecture which is given in the Lecture Theatre. He says:—"I am attending the singularly interesting and instructive course of lectures which are being delivered fortnightly by Mr. Cecil Carus-Wilson. These lectures are profusely illustrated by numerous limelight illustrations, and followed by questions·and a short discussion and an examination by the students of the many interesting and often unique specimens exhibited by the lecturer. Yet no sooner does the clock point to half-past nine than the engines are stopped, and the whole place is plunged into total darkness; the students are left to stumble out of the building as best they may, and the lecturer and those assisting him are left with the light of a sputtering match or a fortuitous tallow candle to collect and pack away the valuable specimens, books, lantern apparatus, slides, &c. I fail to see," adds our correspondent, "why a municipal institution which belongs to the citizens at large should be hampered by any such absurd regulations, which if not modified must very soon bring the place into disrepute."'

.˙.

The Warden of Toynbee Hall (Canon Barnett) issued in the early part of last month a circular invitation to a Conference which met in London on Jan. 28 to consider the best means of establishing University Settlements in other large towns in the United Kingdom, and the possibility of their federation. The meeting was successful and attended by a representative gathering from a large variety of towns. It was decided to take a step forward and seek to increase the number of settlements in the other great centres of population. Federation was approved, but the proposal to omit the word 'University' before 'Settlements,' though strongly urged by a speaker from Birmingham, was not pressed to a division.

.˙.

The thoughtful and impressive lecture on Arnold Toynbee recently given by Mr. Alfred Milner, C.B., at Toynbee Hall, is, we are glad to learn, in course of publication by Mr. Edward Arnold. Extracts appeared in the *Toynbee Record* for January.

.˙.

Those interested in what has been called 'Secondary Education for the Industrial Classes,' but would be more aptly spoken of as the Education of Citizens, will do well to look up the January number of the *Evening School Chronicle* which contains some excellent suggestions for the future development of this necessary, but hitherto much neglected, branch of national instruction.

.˙.

An excellent report on the methods of Economic Training in this and other countries has been issued by a British Association Committee including Professors Cunningham, Edgeworth, Gonner, Shield-Nicholson and Foxwell, and Messrs. H. Higgs and L. L. Price. The Committee regard the condition of economic studies at the Universities and Colleges of the United Kingdom as unsatisfactory. There is individual energy among the teachers, but too little organization of studies. Pedagogy excepted, economic science offers to the student the least inducement in the way of academic reward. Great improvements, however, have been rendered inevitable by the rising tide of economic interest in the country. The programme of the Independent Labour Party, the sale of *Merrie England* (a work which has had a wider circulation even than *Progress and Poverty*), the influence of the *Clarion*, are all signs of the times. And Professor Gonner's careful appendix on the condition of economic science in the United Kingdom does not fail to notice the rising popularity of economics as a subject for Extension courses. To take the Oxford branch alone, the attendance at the lectures of Mr. Hobson, Mr. Hewins and Mr. Graham Wallas has been significant and full of promise for the future.

2

University Extension in Ireland.

A start has been made at Belfast with a course of ten lectures on 'Present-day Questions—Economic and Social,' by Professor Graham, the author of a well-known and discriminating handbook on Socialism. We are glad that this subject has been chosen at the beginning of the Irish movement, glad too that it has been entrusted to such able hands. A German visitor, Herr Tönnies of Kiel, published last September in a Berlin journal an elaborate disquisition on our movement. In this, he argued, and quite rightly, that University Extension teaching would have to deal with the problems of civic and social life. But he was unaware that it had done so directly and indirectly from the very beginning. The sympathy of the movement, its insistence on the ideal of a healthy and reasonable life for all citizens, has been the real source of its strength.

.·.

The Lecture as an Educational Instrument.

In an able and suggestive letter, part of which might have been omitted with advantage, Professor Armstrong recently argued in the *Times* in favour of reform in the methods of scientific teaching, and with much that he said we are in hearty agreement. But, to heighten the force of his argument, he condemned the ordinary practice of lecturing, and, in so doing, overlooked the value of the stimulative force of the lecturer's personality. Taken alone, the lecture is inadequate as an educational instrument ; its real place in teaching is that of stimulus, preparative direction, comprehensive summary. In other words, it is *part* of a plan of teaching, not a method satisfactory by itself. It must be supplemented by the class, in which the student should set to attack difficulties for himself, to practise induction, to make discoveries, i. e. not to memorize the ready-made reasoning of other people, and to record his arguments and conclusions in writing. The last portion of the method is of great importance as cultivating the power of literary expression. It should also be followed by discussion with the teacher and with fellow-students in order that the gift of argument, of dialectic, of verbal resource may be trained and developed by means of struggle with those who are the student's equals, and also with one who is presumably his superior, in intellectual attainment.

.·.

It is announced in the *Athenaeum* that 'the *Contemporary Review* for February will contain the latest contribution of Water Pater to literature in the form of a study on Pascal, upon which he was engaged at the time of his death, and which he had not quite completed.' This essay was written in order to be read as a lecture at the last Oxford Summer Meeting as part of the course on the Seventeenth Century.

.·.

Among the most successful lectures given in London during the Christmas Vacation were the courses of two Oxford University Extension lecturers—Dr. H. R. Mill's on 'Holiday Geography' at the Geographical Society, and Mr. Mackinder's on the Geography of the Netherlands at the Royal Institution.

.·.

A book has just appeared in which many Summer Meeting Students will take an almost personal interest. We refer to Lady Verney's *Memoirs of the Verney Family* 1650-1660, which has been published during the last month by Messrs. Longman. The volume will recall two brilliant lectures and much gracious hospitality.

.·.

University Extension in Tasmania.

The University Extension system may be said to have secured for itself a good position in Tasmania. Last year courses were given at Hobart and Launceston with considerable success. This year, we learn from the *Melbourne University Extension Journal*, the courses have been renewed at the same centres, and the good attendance has been maintained. It is reported that 'the lectures have been useful, not only directly in the com-

munication of knowledge but also indirectly and perhaps with even greater benefit in arousing an interest in learning and inducing students to read for themselves on definite and exact lines.

.·.

It is feared that financial reasons may lead to the abandonment of the *Melbourne University Extension Journal.* We hope that strenuous efforts will be made to avert what would be a serious blow to the fortunes of University Extension in Australia. The Melbourne *Journal* has already secured for itself a place among the most ably conducted of the numerous magazines devoted to the interests of the University Extension movement. We should greatly regret its disappearance, as it has been from the first a very useful organ of educational opinion and a link between the work of the Australian and of the English Universities.

.·.

'A Yorkshire Secretary' writes as follows :—
'A neighbouring centre has asked us, even thus early, to join in a common invitation to a certain lecturer for next autumn ; and this leads me to make to you a suggestion which occurred to me last spring, and commended itself to several other secretaries. I think we are all spending each year an unnecessarily large sum on railway expenses —partly, no doubt, because of our distance from town and from Oxford, but in great measure, also, for lack of combination. What I venture to suggest is that the secretaries of the various Oxford centres in the West Riding and in the neighbouring Lancashire towns should meet, early in the year, at some central place, and arrange circuits for lecturers. At present we are organized according to Counties, but this is obviously inconvenient, especially in the case of large counties. To take this neighbourhood, Bradford or Leeds could join much more profitably with Bury or Manchester, than could Halifax or Hebden Bridge with Hull or Scarborough. I am only putting our own case, you see ; but I suspect that, in many other parts of the country, centres grouped round the main lines of railway might meet and combine with great advantage. Of course it would be necessary for each secretary to come to the meeting with a complete list of courses desired by his committee, and with full powers to act. And perhaps, before any such meeting, you would be able to issue a list of possible courses for the district, so that no secretary might arrive with a list full of impossible ones.'

.·.

School Boards and University Extension.

We are glad to see that the School Boards of Leeds and Bradford have both arranged University Extension courses for the present term. At Leeds Professor Jenks of Liverpool is giving lectures on the Life and Duties of the Citizen ; at Bradford Dr. E. S. Reynolds of Manchester takes as his subject 'The Principles of Health as applied to Home Life.' These we believe are the only School Boards which have so far undertaken the sole responsibility for courses of University Extension lectures, but the Boards in many other towns are giving valuable support towards the courses arranged by the Local Committees.

.·.

The first meetings of the newly established Committee of General Secretaries of the four English branches of the University Extension system will be held in Oxford on Feb. 23 and 24. We would suggest that it would be a wise step to add to the Committee representatives of the re-invigorated Durham University Extension scheme, and of the Reading and Exeter University Extension Colleges. To be effective the new Committee must be fully representative.

.·.

We hear from Professor Rein that the Jena Summer Meeting 1895 (University Extension) will begin on August 1 and on August 26 (Part I, Aug. 1-12 ; Part II, Aug. 13-26). The chief courses of lectures will deal with the Natural Sciences, physiology, psychology, school-hygiene, pedagogy, German language and German literature (Schiller and Goethe in Jena and Weimar). The programme will be published before Easter.

UNIVERSITY EXTENSION DELEGACY.

Resignation of the Secretary.

ON Jan. 5 the following official notification was issued from the Privy Council office :—

A new post has been created under the Education Department for the purpose of obtaining special information and issuing special reports, from time to time, in relation to educational work at home and abroad. The frequent demand for fuller information on many educational subjects and the great increase of purely administrative work both at the Education Department in Whitehall and at the Science and Art Department have made it desirable to have a separate officer in charge of a small additional branch for the above-named purpose, who will be designated ' Director of Special Inquiries and Reports.'

This appointment has been offered to and accepted by Mr. M. E. Sadler, Student of Christ Church, and Secretary of the University Extension Delegacy at Oxford.

At their first meeting of term, held on Jan. 25, the University Extension Delegates passed the following resolution *nem. con.* :—

' The Delegates, while congratulating the Education Department on obtaining the services of Mr. Sadler, wish to express in the strongest terms their regret that one who has had so large and distinguished a part in the movement represented by the Delegacy should be compelled to withdraw from it ; and their thanks to him for his unwearied attention to the business of the Delegacy and the eminent services which he has rendered to it.'

[It is understood that the Delegates are now considering the appointment of a successor to the present Secretary, who will retire at Lady Day next.]

.·.

Local Directors, or Superintendents, of University Extension Teaching.

AT the same meeting of the Delegates the following letter was read from a member of Delegacy, who does not wish his name to be known :—

OXFORD, *Jan.*, 1895.

DEAR MR. VICE-CHANCELLOR,—It seems to be generally agreed that many of the local committees, engaged in the extension of University teaching, are feeling the need of more advice in the organization of their courses and the development of their work.

The resolutions of the University Extension Congress, and several articles which have since appeared in the *University Extension Journal* and *Gazette*, recommend that experienced lecturers, or other persons familiar with the local conditions of the work, should be appointed as superintendents or directors of University Extension teaching in certain districts where railway communications make combined effort natural and easy.

It is felt that such directors should be nominated by the University authorities (preferably after private consultation with some of the more experienced organizers resident in the districts concerned), and should serve for a short term of years, as their influence would depend on their becoming familiar with local conditions and personally acquainted with the teachers and others closely concerned with education in the district. Their first duties would lie in the direction of forming lecture-circuits to be served by one lecturer at a time, in promoting sequence of studies, and in encouraging the establishment of classes for systematic work alongside of, or between, the lecture-courses.

I believe that at least two districts, almost entirely served by Oxford lecturers, are ready to welcome, and to gain great advantage from the visits of, such a director, who would strengthen the connexion and the good understanding which already exists between the Delegacy and the centres. These districts are (1) Hampshire with the Isle of Wight and (2) Gloucestershire, with parts of North Oxfordshire and of Worcestershire.

The initial difficulty is want of funds to start an experiment.

which, if once tried and successful, would doubtless be continued by help from public sources or private liberality.

In order that the experiment may have a trial, at a time which those chiefly concerned with the Delegacy's work regard as being one of special opportunity in the two districts I have named, I venture to ask the Delegacy to accept from me a sum of £600, which will I think suffice to provide the necessary remuneration for directors in two districts for a term of three years each. The appointment would not involve residence in the chosen district, and its duties would, I think, be amply discharged by visits to the district at fairly frequent intervals, by longer visits in the Christmas and Easter vacations, and by correspondence.

With your leave I should prefer to withhold my name and simply to subscribe myself

A MEMBER OF THE DELEGACY.

The Delegates resolved ' (1) to accept this generous gift and to give the heartiest thanks of the Delegacy to the anonymous donor, and (2) to refer the question of the disposal of the gift and the selection to a Committee of persons suitable for the purpose.'

THE BRUSSELS CONFERENCE.

THE Brussels Conference marks an epoch in the history of University Extension. The movement has now definitely spread to the Continent of Europe. Hitherto it has been confined to the English-speaking peoples ; it will gain strength and will find new developments by its introduction into Belgium. We are glad that the University Extension Delegacy was represented at Brussels by so fit a representative as Mr. Mackinder, whose speeches seem to have made a marked impression on the debate and who, according to the *Petit Bleu* which publishes an unrecognizable portrait of him, set forth ' avec beaucoup de clarté dans un français très pur, l'organisation de l'Extension Universitaire anglaise.' The Cambridge branch of the system was represented by another veteran lecturer, Mr. Parkyn.

The Brussels Congress on University Extension.

.·.

The Conference was one of critical importance to the movement in Belgium. The real point at issue was whether the Brussels University Extension Society should adopt the full method of the English system — lectures, followed by classes, accompanied by essay work and leading up to a final examination — or drift into a mere lecture-agency for the supply of more or less isolated addresses on different subjects. The battle was fought with spirit and pertinacity. But at last the English idea prevailed, and the Brussels committee and its secretary Mr. Hirsch will have the satisfaction of feeling that their work, instead of being doomed to early failure, has been systematized and strengthened by the Conference.

The Question at issue in the Belgian Movement.

.·.

This is an intensely interesting period in Belgian affairs. Public opinion is seething with excitement. The mind of the nation is open to new ideals of social organization and public duty. Now, if ever, is the opportunity for educated men, armed with an educational method of tried efficacy, to spread far and wide disinterested views of civic action and to diffuse a belief in the necessity of strengthening the higher education in a democratic state.

The Crisis in Belgium.

.·.

The University Extension movement does not exclude single lectures, but any number of single lectures do not make University Extension. Courses, however, guide the student and bear fruit in a number of other educational undertakings. We are glad to see that travelling libraries are to be established, for one of the main objects of the lecturers will always be to make their hearers read and think and reason for themselves. And

The aim of University Extension.

Mr. Mackinder did well to remind the Conference that University Extension does not address itself to any one class in the community. It is one of the pioneers of a national system of higher education for all citizens who are worthy to take advantage of such an opportunity. It makes no distinction between classes; it appeals to men and women, to rich and poor. It does not act as the rival of other organizations; it supplements their efforts or welcomes them as allies. And above all it insists on the strengthening and bettering of character as the chief end of education, and protests against the foolish notion that the mere multiplication of subjects improves a curriculum, or that a man can be made a better citizen by any increase in the volume of his attainments, unless at the same time his moral character is elevated by the method and subject-matter of his studies; unless his reasoning power is developed by intellectual and moral discipline; unless the course of his training gives him the gist of a liberal education, which was never better defined than in John Henry Newman's words as that which ' opens the mind, corrects it, refines it, enables it to know, and to digest, master, rule and use its knowledge; to give it power over its faculties; application, flexibility, method, critical exactness, sagacity, resource, address, and eloquent expression.'

CONGRÈS DE L'EXTENSION UNIVERSITAIRE.

LES membres des comités locaux de l'Extension Universitaire, les professeurs et généralement toutes les personnes s'intéressant au mouvement extensionniste belge se sont réunis en Congrès le dimanche 20 janvier 1895, à Bruxelles.

En attendant la publication du compte-rendu des travaux de cette assemblée, qui aura lieu dans la Revue Universitaire du 15 février, qu'il nous soit permis de constater le très grand succès qui a couronné les efforts des organisateurs.

Malgré l'abstention de l'Extension de l'Université Libre de Bruxelles et de l'Extension Universitaire de Gand — les questions à l'ordre du jour ne préoccupent point ces sociétés, semble-t-il,—le Congrès a réuni un nombre imposant d'adhérents, parmi lesquels on remarquait MM. les Professeurs Denis et Vandervelde, membres de la Chambre des Représentants, MM. les Professeurs Lameere, Boulenger, Leyder, de Brouckère, Wilmotte, etc., etc., MM. les sénateurs Janson et Bufquin des Essarts, M. Anseele, membre de la Chambre des Représentants, M. Vercamer, conseiller provincial, etc., etc.

La séance était présidée par M. le Professeur Houzeau de Lehaie, ancien membre de la Chambre des Représentants, président de la Société.

L'Extension Universitaire d'Oxford avait bien voulu se faire représenter par M. le professeur Mackinder, celle de Cambridge, par M. le professeur Parkyn. La Société ' Hooger Onderwijs voor het volk' avait délégué MM. De Saegher et De Raet, l'Extension Universitaire de Liége M. Blondieux. L'Extension Universitaire de Londres, dans une lettre fort aimable, avait exprimé le regret de l'impossibilité dans laquelle elle se trouvait de se faire représenter au Congrès. La haute compétence de MM. Mackinder et Parkyn—dont les discours prononcés avec beaucoup de clarté en un français très pur—n'a pas peu contribué à l'adoption par le Congrès de décisions des plus heureuses.

Le Congrès s'est occupé successivement de la Méthode, du Syllabus, de la Bibliothèque Circulante, des Comités Locaux, des Associations de Garantie des comités locaux, du Traitement des Professeurs et de la Statistique du mouvement extensionniste.

La méthode a soulevé la discussion la plus longue : le Congrès s'est d'abord prononcé en faveur du maintien du minimum de six leçons par cours. Il a décidé de laisser aux comités locaux le soin d'organiser les conférences de propagande, et a émis le vœu de voir appliquer, partout où il serait possible, la méthode anglaise en son intégralité, réservant cependant pour plus tard l'organisation systématique d'examens.

Une suggestion heureuse a été faite, quant à la méthode, par M. le Professeur Wilmotte : il a proposé l'institution de 'Cours Concentriques.' Le professeur commencerait d'abord par faire un cours de six leçons, sans classes ni travaux écrits, dans lequel il traiterait du sujet choisi d'une façon tout à fait générale. A la suite de ce cours, les auditeurs se livreraient à la lecture de tous les ouvrages indiqués. Puis, quelques mois plus tard, le professeur reviendrait, et appliquerait cette fois la méthode anglaise, avec les classes, les travaux écrits et l'examen, à un cours plus spécial, mais traitant de la même matière que celle qui faisait l'objet des premières leçons.

Le Congrès a décidé d'expérimenter ce système.

Les autres points à l'ordre du jour ont suscité également des discussions des plus intéressantes: en ce qui concerne le Syllabus, la Bibliothèque Circulante, les Comités Locaux et leurs associations de garantie, l'assemblée a adopté les mesures prises depuis longtemps en Angleterre.

Elle a voté une protestation énergique contre l'injustifiable décision du Conseil d'Administration de l'Université Libre interdisant aux professeurs de cette Université de collaborer à l'œuvre entreprise par l'Extension Universitaire.

D'ailleurs, malgré toutes les attaques auxquelles elle est en lutte, l'Extension Universitaire continue avec un plein succès son œuvre de diffusion scientifique. Elle a dès à présent organisé, pour l'année académique 1894-1895, les cours suivants : la plupart ont déjà commencé; les autres seront inaugurés incessamment. Tous comptent six leçons.

à Andenne, M. Wilmotte: Histoire de la langue française.

à Anvers, M. Vandervelde: L'Evolution Industrielle; M. Boulenger: La Nutrition Normale et Viciée; M. L. de Brouckère: Les Philosophes français au XVIIIème siècle.

à Arlon, M. Elisée Reclus : L'Amérique du Sud

à Bruxelles, M. Boulenger: La Nutrition Normale et Viciée; M. Kufferath: Historique et Esthétique Musicales.

à Charleroi, M. Elisée Reclus: L'Amérique du Sud; M. Vandervelde : L'Evolution Industrielle; M. Wilmotte : Les Patois Wallons.

à Courtrai, M. Vandervelde: L'Art Industriel.

à Ixelles, M. Picard : Evolution du Droit Civil français.

à Nieuport, M. Frank : Hoofdperioden in de geschiedenis des Vaderlands.

à Tournai, M. Elisée Reclus : La Philosophie des Mythes.

à Verviers, M. de Brouckère : Les Philosophes français au XVIIIème siècle; M. Mahaun : Les Syndicats Professionnels; M. Wilmotte : Les Patois Wallons.

Les comités locaux de Gand, de La Louvrère, de Namur et de Quevaucamps n'ont pas encore arrêté définitivement leur programme. De nouveaux comités locaux sont en voie de formation à Ypres, à Bruges, à Antoing, à Peruwelz, à Ougrée, à Morlanwelz, à Huy, à Saintes, à Herve et à Ath.

Tous ces cours, maintenant que la méthode anglaise a été définitivement adoptée, ne peuvent manquer de produire de féconds résultats. Leur succès sera dû pour beaucoup au sympathique appui que les Extensions Universitaires anglaises ne cessent de prêter à l'Extension Universitaire de Bruxelles. Qu'il me soit permis de les en remercier publiquement ici, au nom du comité central.

Dr. ARTHUR HIRSCH,
Secrétaire Général.

DIRECTORY OF SECRETARIES OF STUDENTS' ASSOCIATIONS.

IN order to render communication easier, we propose to publish in the next number of the *Gazette* a directory of the names and addresses of the Hon. Secs. of the Students' Associations at centres where Oxford lectures are given. For insertion in this list, names and addresses should reach the Editor by February 15. Local Secretaries and others concerned in the work are specially requested to send the necessary information in order that the directory may be complete.

TRAINING OF TEACHERS FOR SECONDARY SCHOOLS.

By PROFESSOR WILLIAM REIN *of the University of Jena.*

IN the last week of December 1894 the Pedagogical Seminary in the University of Jena celebrated its fiftieth anniversary. This institute, the first and the only one in the German Universities, can now review the work of fifty years. The experience gained during this long period may be summed up as follows :—

1. The best method of training teachers must comprise both the Theory and Practice of Education. As the young medical student learns the theory combined with the practice in the hospital, so must the young educator combine the theoretical studies with practice in a school.

2. The theory of education contains the following branches :—

(*a*) Ethics and Psychology--the fundamental sciences of Pedagogy.

(*b*) System of Pedagogy or the Enclyclopaedia of Pedagogy.

(*c*) General Didactic or General Method : the outlines of the theory of instruction.

(*d*) Special Didactic— or Special Method of instruction in every school subject.

3. In the University of Jena the theory of Pedagogy, including these four, is given by the Professor of Pedagogy. The student of Pedagogy must at first attend lectures on Ethics and Psycho ogy and the System of Pedagogy.

4. After this theoretical preparation the young man enters the Pedagogical Seminary. At this stage he hears in the University the special pedagogical principles : General Method and Special Method. At the same time he takes part in the exercises in the practice-school, at first as an auditor, then as a practising teacher.

5. The Professor of Pedagogy in the University is the Principal of the Pedagogical Seminary. With the Seminary is combined a practice-school, the field for the first exercises of the young students of education.

6. The Practice-School of the Pedagogical Seminary has two parts: (1) An Elementary School ; (2) A Secondary School, in which practice should be given in the lower classes at least. The work in the Elementary School is the fundamental work for every educator. Every educator must first teach in the Elementary School combined with the Pedagogical Seminary in order to develop the greatest skill in secondary education.

7. A Student's entrance into the Pedagogical Seminary in the University usually takes place in his twenty-second year, when he has completed his special studies, e. g. Philology, Theology, Natural Sciences, History or Literature.

8. In the Pedagogical Seminary in the University are included all the branches of the teaching profession. The Pedagogical Seminary in the University aims at giving the educational spirit for the work of education of the people in all classes.

9. The Pedagogical Seminary has three meetings every week during the Semester : (*a*) The Theoreticum. The members of the Seminary read the themes, referats and reports, dissertations, &c., which they have prepared independently. This work is criticized by the members and the Director. (*b*) The Practicum. One lesson per week is given by one of the students in the presence of the other members and the Director. (*c*) The Criticum or the Konferenz. In this meeting this lesson is criticized by the members and by the Director, who passes final judgement.

That is the chief aim : the Pedagogical Seminary in the University is not an Institution to prepare a young man for a special kind of schools or for special branches of school-instruction, but to equip him with the highest ideas of education, and to show him the best way of realizing these ideas. The power of education in the life of the people is very strong ; but the education must be founded and systematized on a definite plan. The Pedagogical Seminary gives the outlines of this plan. The Pedagogical Seminary of the Jena University has in the fifty years of its existence trained about 1000 educators, who have worked or are working as Professors in the University, as Prin-

cipals in Secondary, Normal, and Elementary Schools, as Teachers in High Schools for Girls, &c. The Pedagogical Seminary in the University is the alma mater of all. Attachment to it binds all its students together even when they are scattered in different countries. Thus, through its Pedagogical Seminary, the University permeates the life of the people. From this centre proceed the ideas of education and educational reforms. The Pedagogical Seminary sets before itself two problems : (1) The education of educators ; (2) The development of Pedagogy. The two problems are connected. The Pedagogical Seminary is the workshop for the development of Pedagogical Science, in which each student takes an active part in the investigations. Thus his interest is surely aroused, because he sees himself as a co-worker in this important field.

In this way the University can provide the best means for the development of Pedagogical Science, and also the best means for the education of teachers, who will bring the ideas of education to all classes of the people.

UNIVERSITY EXTENSION COLLEGE, READING.

A STEP of the first importance has been taken towards securing the permanent usefulness of the University Extension College. The Town Council of Reading, acting with wise liberality and foresight, have resolved to co-operate with the Council of the College in conveying to the Trustees representing the College the freehold land and buildings belonging to the Town Council which are now in use for College purposes.

The *Journal* of the College (an interesting second number of which has just been published) contains the following report of the negotiations. That the negotiations have proceeded so smoothly, that indeed at this early stage they have been possible at all, reflects credit alike on the Corporation and on the Council and Principal of the College.

The following report of the Committee of the Whole Town Council of Reading, was, on the motion of the Mayor, seconded by the Deputy Mayor, agreed to at a meeting of the Town Council, on January 3 :—

'On the 13th ult. the Committee of the Whole Council met a deputation, consisting of Mr. Herbert Sutton (Chairman), Mr. Mackinder (Principal), Mr. F. H. Wright (Secretary), Mr. W. H. Dunn, Mr. Alfred Palmer, Mr. Ravenscroft, the Rev. J. W. Spurling, and Mr. S. S. Stallwood, representing the Council of the University Extension College, who submitted proposals having reference to the College buildings. From these proposals it appeared that it had become necessary, with a view to further progress, to make more permanent provision for the continuance of the College. There were difficulties due to the present tenure of the buildings which must be removed before steps could be taken with this object. The buildings now occupied are the Art School, the Hospitium, and the Vicarage. The Art School stands apart from the remainder of the buildings, has a separate entrance, and is no longer large enough for its purpose. The other two buildings being held of separate owners cannot be treated as a single property for the purpose of enlargement. The College has to deal with many public bodies, and requires a secure basis if it is to compete successfully with institutions of a similar nature in other towns. It was suggested that in return for a surrender of the use of the present Art School, the Corporation should convey to the College the freehold of the Hospitium building and the land held therewith by the College under the Corporation. If this could be done the College Council was willing—(*a*) That the College should be incorporated for the purpose of holding property. (*b*) To raise a subscription for the purpose of purchasing the Vicarage, within the prescribed period, at the relatively small price fixed by Mr. Sutton. (*c*) To provide new Art Rooms in connexion with the main buildings. (*d*) To approach the Department of Science and Art with the view of transferring to the other College buildings the liability of about

£700 at present secured on the Art School. (e) To enter into covenants to be agreed upon, having reference to a possible extension of the Large Town Hall. The Town Council, on the other hand, would obtain possession, free from existing restrictions, of the present Art School, with power to use it for whatever purpose might seem good to them. The Chairman of the College Council and the Principal explained the object of the deputation in meeting the Committee, and Mr. Mackinder also explained in full detail the proposals of the College Council, and answered numerous questions on the subject. The deputation from the College having withdrawn, and the Committee having discussed the matter in all its bearings, it was resolved—That this Committee do recommend to the Council of the Borough that the Council do approve generally of the scheme set forth in the proposals of the Reading University Extension College, and do to the extent of the powers of the Corporation co-operate with the Council of the College in carrying out the scheme, subject to the reservation by the Council of the Borough of such portion of the property now held by the College under the Corporation as the Council of the Borough may deem to be necessary for the purpose of providing for the future extension of the New Town Hall, and by a subsequent resolution the settlement of details was referred to the Financial Committee in consultation with the Town Clerk.'

.·.

The courses of public lectures at the College this term include lectures on the Puritan Rebellion (Mr. Horsburgh), Local History (Mr. Childs), Greek Drama (Mr. Churton Collins), Tennyson and Browning (Mr. Churton Collins), French Literature of Seventeenth Century (Mons. J. Rey), Geography of the British Isles (the Principal, Mr. H. J. Mackinder), and Great Musical Composers (Mr. Tirbutt).

.·.

Gallia, the association for the study of French literature and language, continues its successful career under the enthusiastic leadership of Mons. Rey.

.·.

A College Athletic Club has been founded, with a strong Committee which includes Mr. Foulkes (Chairman), Mr. Childs and Mr. Aston (Vice-Chairman), Mr. Waugh (Treasurer), Mr. Donne (Secretary), Mr. Adams (Assistant-Secretary), Miss Pollard, Miss Downes, Mr. Barkas and others. The club should do much to further the popularity of the College and to establish its success.

.·.

We are glad to see that the College stands firm to its fundamental principle of granting equal recognition and equal privileges to men and women students. In the future, it will be regarded in this as in other things, as having been a pioneer in educational organization.

.·.

In the College Debating Society there has been a brisk and protracted discussion on the House of Lords. On a division, the Lords were saved by a narrow majority (23-18).

.·.

One of the most noteworthy and satisfactory signs of the progress of the work in Reading is the growth of a College spirit. The *esprit de corps* is showing itself on every side.

THE PHILADELPHIA SUMMER MEETING, 1895.

THE American University Extension Society is preparing an excellent programme for its Summer Meeting in Philadelphia next July. The Chairman of the Committee of Organization is Mr. F. B. Miles, and the Director of the Meeting Dr. E. T. Devine—both of whom were among the most welcome visitors to the last Oxford Summer Meeting. The *University Extension Bulletin* publishes an outline of the programme, from which we extract the following.

The third session of the Summer Meeting for University Extension students will be held in Philadelphia, July 1-26, 1895.

The University of Pennsylvania, as in previous years, has by a unanimous vote of the Board of Trustees granted the use of its buildings, libraries, laboratories and museums so far as they are needed for the purposes of the meeting. The Board of Directors of the society has entrusted the management of the meeting to the same committee that made so conspicuous a success of the last meeting. The Summer Meeting committee contemplates the organization of at least five departments to be designated as follows: (A) Literature and History; (B) Pedagogy; (C) Music; (D) Biology; (E) Civics and Politics. In department (A) it is proposed to introduce, with the next meeting, a cycle of study covering five or more years. The first year will be devoted to the history and literature of Greece. Some of the subjects on which courses will be given are: I—Pre-Grecian Civilizations; II—Physical Environment of the Greeks; III—Homeric Poems; IV—Ethical and Religious Ideals of the Greeks; V—Biographical Survey of Greek History; VI—Greek Drama: VII—Translations, with running comment, from Aeschylus, Euripides and Sophocles; VIII—Plato; IX—Greek Art; X—Greek Civilization in General; XI—Influence of Greece on Subsequent History of the Race; XII—Accessible English Translations of Greek Masterpieces. It is hoped that Professor John H. Wright, of Harvard; Professor B. Perrin, of Yale; Professor Benjamin I. Wheeler, of Cornell, and other Hellenic specialists of equal eminence will supplement the work of staff-lecturers William Cranston Lawton and Henry W. Rolfe in making this department of literature and history one of the most attractive and profitable which it is possible to offer to vacation students. Considerable progress has also been made in outlining the programme for the department of Civics and Politics. This department will be of interest not only to special students of political history and political science, but also to that large and increasing number of citizens, men and women, who are beginning to take a deeper interest in their citizenship. Courses will be offered on Constitutional Government in America; Political and Constitutional History; Federal Government; Political and Patriotic Literature; Needed Political Reforms; Problems of Municipal Government; Contemporary Statesmen, and a number of allied topics. The aid of some of the most eminent specialists in America and England will be secured. Students who confine their attention to this department will still find a variety of subjects of fresh and intense interest. It is probable that enough work will be offered in each of the two departments above outlined to fill about four hours daily for the four weeks. A full provisional programme will be issued about February 1. Applications should be sent to Edward T. Devine, Director, 111 South Fifteenth Street, Philadelphia.

THE HOLIDAY COURSE
FOR TEACHERS AT EXETER.

By AMY M. SHORTO, *Student of the Exeter Centre.*

THE year 1895, young as it is, has already seen the marked success of an experiment of great importance in the history of education. For the first time in any provincial centre a Holiday Course in the Theory and Practice of Teaching has been provided by the University Extension Department of the Exeter Technical and University Extension College, which, even in this its early youth, has proved itself capable of ministering to far more than merely local needs. The suggestion of this course is due to Miss Montgomery, to whom already Exeter owes so much, and who, aided by Mr. Clayden, the Principal of the College, devised every possible plan for the benefit, comfort and enjoyment of the visitors. The result of their efforts was that on the evening of January 3, about sixty-five teachers assembled from many parts of England to listen to the Inaugural Address delivered by the Master of Downing College, Cambridge, as a preliminary to a fortnight's work, which should prove more refreshing than a longer time spent in conventional holiday fashion.

Next morning began the regular work of the Meeting. Mr. Holman's course of twelve lectures on 'Psychology applied to Education' was followed with the deepest interest. It could not fail to be of value to those engaged in training and developing the minds of children, for it stimulated the study of individual character, and showed how psychological principles could be applied. Abundant opportunity was afforded for discussion, which proved neither the least profitable nor the least interesting part of the course, and, in response to a general desire, the lecturer gave a model lesson to a class of children from a Higher Grade Elementary School in the city. Mr. Holman's ideal teacher who 'possesses all the graces, and every grace in its most gracious form,' may never be found in real life, but at least his work during the Holiday Course should result in the more intelligent training of children than in the past. It is impossible to deal with these most useful lectures at any length, but all those who heard them, and many who did not, will welcome with pleasure the announcement that they may possibly be published.

The healthy development of the mind must go hand in hand with that of the body, and the Psychology lecture was appropriately followed every day by one on School Hygiene by Dr. Wade, well known to Summer Meeting students. This course was also most interesting and of the greatest possible importance, for since teachers are to a great extent responsible for the physical as well as the mental health of many hundreds of children, and can besides do so much as ' Missionaries of Hygiene,' it behoves them to lose no opportunity of increasing their own knowledge of the subject.

Six readings in French were given by M. Joël, and were a source of great profit and enjoyment to all who heard them. Each was delightful, whether the subject were Lamartine's *Jocelyn*, or Pailleron's *Le Monde où l'on s'ennuie*, and in no other way could the beauties of French poetry, or the wit of modern French comedy, so well have been revea'ed.

In the evenings lectures of a more general character were given, including ' The Teaching of Literature' by Mr. Sidgwick, ' History of the Universities' by Mr. Sadler, ' The Teaching of Modern Languages' by M. Paul Barbier, ' Esprit de Corps among Teachers' by Miss Cooper, and ' The practical use of the optical lantern in Schools' by the Principal. Besides these Miss Hughes gave three addresses on ' The Government of School-children,' which were extremely suggestive and valuable, besides being interesting to all concerned in the training of children either separately or in numbers ; by these lectures, as well as by her presence during the greater part of the Holiday Course, Miss Hughes has added not only to the pleasure of the Meeting, but also to the debt of gratitude which all interested in education owe her.

On the occasion of the first of these three lectures the Chai r was taken by the Vice-Chancellor of Cambridge, ' Visitor' of the College; Mr. Berry was also present and bore testimony to the great interest which was taken in the new experiment.

Exeter is rich in historical associations, and arrange- ments were made for visiting the Cathedral under the guidance of the Rev. Canon Edmonds, and of inspecting some of the precious manuscripts in possession of the Chapter, including the famous ' Exeter Book.' The Guildhall, too, was visited, and some ancient charters were shown by the Town Clerk, as well as the civic regalia, including the swords presented to the city by Edward IV and Henry VII, together with the Cap of Maintenance. In the Guildhall was held the final evening meeting, when those attending the course were received by the Mayor in full civic state, testifying to the honour Exeter wished to show to those in its midst, because of the greatness of their calling.

The votes of thanks passed on this occasion were no empty form, for everybody felt more gratitude than could be expressed towards the organizers of the course, the lecturers and those who by their kindness and hospitality had given opportunities for social enjoyment, especially the Bishop and Mrs. Bickersteth, the Principal and Mrs. Clayden, and Miss Montgomery.

Regrets were heard on every side that the fortnight which had been so full of delight, so productive of sympathy and friendly feeling, had passed away, leaving behind it, however, memories which will give strength and courage in the many trials which are inevitable in a teacher's life. Hope was expressed that the experiment would be repeated, and the teachers, who had been only learners for a time, went their way, filled with gratitude and admiration for those who had devised and carried out this novel plan.

The value of this new movement must be great, but cannot yet be fully estimated. Anything that encourages sympathy and *esprit de corps* among teachers cannot but be good, and a meeting such as this may go far to counteract the practical isolation in which many a teacher lives, and the tendency to become the ' prunes and prisms, sour-lemon' personage, who, according to Mr. Holman's parting warning, so often turns ' the milk of human kind- ness' sour.

REPORTS FROM THE CENTRES.

BAKEWELL.—By the kind consent of the Duke and Duchess of Devonshire, an entertainment was given in the Chatsworth Carriage House on January 1, and repeated on January 2. The proceeds were divided between the Edensor Library and the Bakewell University Extension Association. The Carriage House was fitted up as a Theatre, and Mr. Cecil Crofton kindly gave his services in producing a new One Act Play, *Mr. Dick's Heir*, written by himself and Harcourt Brooke. The characters were taken by Miss Emily Cross (of the Lyric Theatre), Mrs. Cory, Miss Elsie Cross, Mr. Cory, and Mr. Cecil Crofton (of the Garrick Theatre). The cast was admirable and the little play, which is full of bright repartee. was well received. The Play was preceded by a Conceit, in which several ladies and gentlemen kindly took part, and the exquisite violin playing of Miss Lilian Wright, A R.C.M., secured most justly repeated rounds of applause. The promoters of the entertainment were able to hand over £6 to the Bakewell U. E. Association, which will form a useful reserve fund. The Students' Association has decided to have, if possible, three lectures instead of monthly meetings this spring. Professor Raleigh and Mr. Kenelm Cotes have already most kindly promised to give single lectures in February and March.—K. MARTIN, *Hon. Sec.*

BRECON.—The *Brecknock Beacon* of Jan. 18 contains an account of a conversazione held in the Brecon Guildhall to inaugurate a course of University Extension lectures in that centre. The arrangements, which had been made by the ener- getic honorary secretary, Miss Garnons-Williams, assisted by a number of other ladies, were excellent, and the gathering was a great success. During the evening Mr. E. L. S. Horsburgh delivered an address on University Extension, in the course of which he said that ' University Extension claimed to be an agency in the intellectual and well-being of the people. What it designed was, first, to make better scholars ; secondly, to make them better citizens ; and, lastly, to make them better men and women. What they, who were engaged in the work, felt was that among the many great social questions confronting them at the present moment, there was not one so burning, not one which lay so much at the root of all evils, as the question of national education. They all constantly heard it said that this was the age of democracy, and he thought that was to a large extent true. It was an age when the power for the government of the country lay in the hands of the people as a whole, rather than in one class of the people. He, for one, was not in any way inclined to complain that the government was in the hands of the democracy—in the hands of the people at large— supposing they were instructed and understood the responsibilities which power entailed. What was to be dreaded, not only in this country, but in all other countries, what had proved so large a source of revolution and disorder, was power in the hands of men who were uninstructed and who did not recognize the responsibilities which power brought. When the democracy was intelligent, instructed, and understood something of the country it governed, of the glory of the past and the splendid future it had before it, then he could not help thinking that the nation at large would be benefited by the fact that the nation at large took an interest in the government of it. That then was one of the objects which they, who were engaged in the work of national education, put prominently before themselves. They desired to bring instruction with reference to the glories of the country to those who had the power in their hands to use it for good or evil. And that was not the only object which they had in view. They also desired to open up to the minds of the people the splendours of the universe and the joy of life. There was a joy in life which it was only by means of education that they could thoroughly and entirely appreciate. Nature herself, for example, was a great picture; many people spoke of her as an open book. But at the same time the language of Nature was a language which many of them did not understand or comprehend . . . It was not merely for the purpose of instructing the people at large that they endeavoured to bring the advantages of education among them; it was also for the purpose of elevating the minds of the people to recognize the greatness of the world in which they lived, and the place in life which they ought to occupy. Those were some of the ideals which they placed before themselves. His hearers might say that the views he had endeavoured to put forward were very ideal indeed, that they were dreams—dreams associated with youth, and enthusiasm, and inexperience. At the same time he trusted that the time was long distant when they should cease to have men amongst them who dreamed dreams and who had ideals which might possibly never be realized. If it came to dreams and ideals, they might do well to remember that they were all of "such stuff as dreams were made of, and that their little world was rounded by a sleep." Supposing they aimed high, if they did not hit the mark they were more likely to hit something, if they aimed high and placed noble and enthusiastic ideals before their minds.'

BRIGHTON (GREEK CLASSES).—October Term, 1894. The Elementary class consisted of ten members, all of whom were regular in their attendance, and enthusiastic in their work. The ground covered embraced selected parts of Goodwin's Greek Grammar for schools, a few chapters of Xenophon's *Anabasis*, Book I, about 200 lines of Sidgwick's Scenes from the *Alcestis* of Euripides, and a weekly written exercise from Sidgwick's *First Greek Writer*. There is good reason to hope that the numbers of this class may be considerably increased during the Spring Term. As only five students sent in their names for the Intermediate class, it was thought advisable to allow the class to lapse for the October Term. The class will however be started again, if seven names are sent in. No doubt, as time goes on, the Elementary class will supply students for the higher grade, and so lead up to the formation of an advanced class. I should like to add that the lectures on Greek History by Mr. A. J. Grant of Cambridge were well attended, and were much appreciated.— A. S. VERRALL. *Hon. Sec.*

DEVIZES.—An interesting meeting of students and other persons interested in University Extension work was held in the Town Hall in December, for the distribution of the prizes and certificates gained at the recent examination after Dr. Bailey's course of lectures on Shakespeare. The attendance was large, and the lecturer's address on University Extension work was full of interest. Dr. Bailey paid a deservedly high tribute to the late Secretary, Mrs. H. J. Sainsbury, who has taken such keen interest in the work in Devizes, and whose retirement is greatly to be regretted. The distribution of certificates and prizes was followed by a Conversazione.

EVESHAM.—On Jan. 8 a successful conversazione was held in the Farmers' and Merchants' Hall in order to inaugurate a course of University Extension lectures by Mr. Horsburgh. By invitation of the local committee, of which Mr. Gill Smith is hon. secretary, the central office was represented by Miss Beard. A varied programme was given to a large audience and the President of the Institute (Mr. Smith) delivered an address.—(*Corr.*)

LEOMINSTER—A public meeting, introductory to the course of lectures, was held here on Jan. 15. Mr. J. S. Arkwright (of Christ Church, Oxford) presided and delivered an able speech in support of the University Extension movement. He maintained that it was every one's duty to encourage the scheme, the aims of which would, he thought, be summed up by some future historian as follows—'That at a very critical time in the nation's history, when there was a great spread of education and a great growth of a desire for education, a scheme was started which did a great deal for that education in laying down fixed principles on which men of different creeds and different political parties could unite and discuss questions with solid principles set down for their discussion.' He thought it would be found that such an educational movement, coming as it did from a body that was divorced entirely from any political creed or any political party, would form a groundwork of unity, and certainly must do a great deal of good in settling the way in which great questions before the country should be discussed, and it was his hope that such schemes as that would tend to the solidity and peace of the Empire. Mr. Horsburgh then delivered an eloquent address upon the purpose and methods of University Extension teaching.

LITTLE BERKHAMPSTEAD.—The Autumn course of lectures on Astronomy delivered by Mr. R. A. Gregory at this centre has been most successful. The lectures have been clear and full of interest, and it is exceedingly regretted that, owing to the want of a sufficient number of guarantors, the lectures cannot be continued this Spring.

LLANELLY.—The course of lectures on 'Trade, Adventure and Discovery,' delivered at this centre by Mr. Kenelm D. Cotes, M.A., has been very successful—the average attendance having been

about 300. It is paying Mr. Cotes a high compliment to say that his style met the approval of this eminently Welsh audience, while the amount of information imparted and the sequence observed left nothing to be desired. The audience at the last lecture was the most enthusiastic of any. A vote of thanks to Mr. Cotes with a hope that his services would again be secured, was carried with acclamation.

OTLEY.—Mr. Mallet's second course of historical lectures on the Stuart period ended on December 13. This—the fourth series of University Extension lectures from Oxford—was equally if not more successful than any of the preceding ones, Mr. Mallet having further established himself in the favour of his audience by the sustained interest and high literary character of his lectures. His happy gift of condensing without confusing the rapidly succeeding incidents of that stormy period, his graphic sketches of the prominent actors, with his eloquent appreciation of the ideas or principles that moved them, were thoroughly enjoyed by an interested and enthusiastic audience. The travelling library was not in great request, the paper work meagre. Let us hope this part of the work in the future may be more commensurate with our appreciation of a gifted lecturer.—JANETTE DUNCAN, *Hon. Sec.*

OXFORD.—By kind invitation of Mr. and Mrs. Estlin Carpenter and Miss M. S. Beard (the hon. secs. of the local centre) a very pleasant evening was spent by the University Extension students at Manchester College on Jan. 11. There was a large company including the students of the centre, Sir William and Lady Markby, Principal and Mrs Drummond, Professor Poulton, F.R.S, Mr. Alfred Robinson of New College, Mr. and Mrs. F. H. Peters and Mr. and Mrs. Odgers. In the students' Common Room were arranged illustrated books lent by Miss Swann, and microscopes lent by Mr. Carpenter. Mr. G. J. Burch kindly exhibited a spectroscope. During the evening Mr. Arthur Sidgwick gave a delightful lecture on Ancient Athens, illustrated by slides. After this, Mr. Carpenter thanked the lecturer on behalf of the students, who also had the pleasure of hearing admirable addresses from their two last lecturers, Mr. Graham Wallas and Mr. E. L. S. Horsburgh. Much regret was felt at the absence of Mr. Marriott, whose lectures began in the following week. The conversazione gave the students an opportunity of welcoming Mr. Estlin Carpenter on his return from America where he has been fulfilling a term of office as special preacher at Harvard College.—(*Corr.*)

THE NEW UNIVERSITY FOR LONDON.

WITH the approach of the Parliamentary Session, the Gresham University question shows signs of life. On Jan. 22 the Prime Minister, with whom were Mr. Acland and Mr. Bryce, received two deputations in turn ; the one supporting, the other opposing, the scheme of the Royal Commission. The balance of argument, the evident sympathies of Ministers, and, as has since appeared, the weight of public opinion, are on the side of the Commissioners' scheme. It is not an ideal plan; in the practical working of it numerous difficulties will crop up ; it attempts to combine two different ideals and traditions of academic policy. But nevertheless it is probably the best scheme which could have been devised under the complicated circumstances of the case. It deserves a fair and sympathetic trial, and, if due forbearance is shown, it will probably prove a successful solution of the problem. Among other things, the scheme is fair to University Extension, though we hope that the London Society will not sacrifice the right of making educational experiments in order to obtain what, at such a price, would be the baleful privilege of academic recognition. At a subsequent meeting, also held on Jan. 22, Convocation of the University of London passed, by a considerable majority of votes, a resolution approving of the Commissioners' plan. The way, therefore, is now open for the appointment of a Statutory Commission to give effect to the scheme. To the old London University, English education owes a great debt of gratitude. The University of London vindicated the rights of the poor and isolated student ; it helped to free University education from the paralyzing influence of religious tests ; it reacted on the older Universities and stimulated them to the development of their own special excellence and tradition ; it has firmly maintained a high and unchallenged standard of intellectual attainment. But the changes in English ideals of education, of which the work and experience of the London University have partly been the cause, have made it necessary to review and recreate academic organization in the Metropolis. We now feel the need, in the centre of the Empire, of a great University which shall teach as well as examine, and which shall combine the complementary, but not mutually hostile, elements in University life—namely the provision of the highest instruction in a form available for all citizens, and the encouragement of profound learning and original research without which national life and public policy become narrow and sterile.

A MODEL PROGRAMME FOR A STUDENTS' ASSOCIATION.

AN admirable scheme of work has been drawn up by the Students' Association at Peterborough. Its object is to encourage the study of the city and its neighbourhood from the point of view of the geologist, the geographer and the historian. Though few places are so fortunate as to have the historic interest of Peterborough, it is obvious that the same idea would be found fruitful in other centres. Teachers especially would find it helpful to take part in such a course of organized study as that proposed by the Peterborough Association. As a model of other societies, we print the greater part of the programme in full.

The Early History of Peterborough.
Programme, 1895.

Jan. 18.—Physiographical description of Peterborough. Paper by Miss Colman. Questions for discussion :—(1) What reasons were likely to have induced people first to form a settlement here? (2) Where are the nearest fords up or down the river, and what relation do they bear to past and present roads? (3) Do the physical features of a district affect the character of the inhabitants?

Feb. 1.—The Geology of Peterborough. Paper by Mr. E. Wheeler. Discussion on the Gilchrist lecture on the 'Evolution of the British Isles,' as far as it affects this neighbourhood.

Feb. 15.—Roman occupation of Peterborough. Paper by Miss Eddison. Questions for discussion :—(1) Did the fact of the existence of suitable clay for pottery at Water Newton attract the Romans to the neighbourhood, or was it the situation on the river? (2) What was the exact extent of Durobrivae? (3) Where are the nearest remains of Roman Camps? Specimens of Roman remains will be on view.

March 1.—The Early Saxon Settlement. Paper by Mr. C. S. Colman. Questions for discussion :—(1) How recently were Peterborough Common lands enclosed, (*a*) ordinary for pasturage, (*b*) cultivated? (2) What was the Castor Common land that has just been enclosed by Act of Parliament? (3) What does the word Thorpe mean? How many Thorpes are there in this neighbourhood? (4) Is the Parish Council a reversion to former customs, or a new departure?

March 15.—Legendary Peterborough. Paper by Dr. Phillips. Questions for discussion :—(1) Were the Saints Chad, Kyneburga, Guthlac, Oswald, Pega, Wolstan, and Botolph, known anywhere but in the neighbourhood of Peterborough? (2) Is anything known of the hermit who lived beside the Holy Well at Thorpe? When did he live there? Did he use the subterranean passage?

March 29.—The Soke of Peterborough—its origin, extent, privileges and various forms of local government. Paper by Miss Argles Questions for discussion :—(1) When was the first Custos Rotolorum appointed? (2) What were his duties? (3) What are his present functions?

April 5.—The History of the Saxon Abbey. Paper by Miss E. Argles. Questions for discussion :—(1) Why was the name changed from Medehampstede to Peterborough? (2) What buildings in the neighbourhood formed part of the Abbey property? (3) What were (*a*) the limits of the Abbot's jurisdiction? (*b*) the extent of the Abbey lands?

May 3.—Annual Meeting; Election of Officers.

** *It will tend to promote the interest of the meetings if members will do their best to obtain all possible information on the subjects for discussion.*

LETTER TO THE EDITOR.

[We do not hold ourselves responsible for the opinions expressed by our correspondents.]

Secondary Education—What does it Mean?

DEAR SIR,—It is humiliating to have to confess utter ignorance on a subject about which 'everybody ought to know,' but I think you would be surprised at the large number of educated people who share my ignorance as to the real meaning of the term 'Secondary Education.' I have vainly sought enlightenment from, or have in turn been asked for it by, friends and acquaintances, comprising amongst others a prominent member of a Technical Education Committee, the Hon. Sec. of a University Extension centre, and the master of a first-rate private school, besides sundry University Extension students. Now it seems to me that either my friends are a singularly benighted set—and they do not belong to one neighbourhood—or else that there is such widespread ignorance on this matter, that it would be well to bring it to your knowledge, in order that you may find an opportunity of doing something to dispel it from the minds of your readers.

The prevalent idea seems to be that 'Secondary' means 'Second-rate.' When I receive this simple explanation, I suggest that Board-schools are called 'Primary,' which disturbs the theory that 'First' and 'Highest' are equivalent terms; and after that come nothing but vague suggestions. Will you please tell me whether Secondary Schools and Secondary Education fill up the whole interval between the Elementary Schools and the Universities? Does this qualification apply to *all* Private Schools? To such Public Schools as Eton and Harrow? To all Grammar Schools and High Schools? To the Technical Education given by County Councils? To the classes of the South Kensington Science and Art Schools? Even to University Extension lectures?

If you would kindly give a full answer to these questions, and define clearly the scope and limits of 'Secondary Education,' I feel sure that you would interest a good many besides

Yours faithfully,

'A STUDENTS' ASSOCIATION SECRETARY.'

[**** 'Secondary Education' includes all education between the University and the 'Standards' of an Elementary School.—*Editor.*]

The Southampton School Board and University Extension Lectures.

THE following circular has been issued by the Southampton School Board :—

The Board are desirous of giving all their teachers the opportunity of attending the lectures given under the auspices of the Oxford University Extension Delegacy, and they offer any teacher wishing to take advantage of this opportunity a free ticket of admission on the following conditions :—

(1) Any teacher accepting such ticket shall attend regularly and punctually.

(2) He shall, as far as possible, make a study of the subject of the lectures and write essays thereon.

(3) He shall endeavour to qualify himself to sit for the examination which is held at the end of each session.

The Board wish to leave the Head and Assistant Teachers the utmost freedom in their use of these lectures, but they think that they have a right to expect that all teachers accepting tickets shall endeavour to acquire some solid educational advantages from these lectures, and the Board is of opinion that if this result is to be attained, private study must supplement the public lecture.

Pupil Teachers may further their interests and better their position in the Scholarship Examination by diligent study under the University Extension scheme, and the Board desire that all their Pupil Teachers should attend these lectures and make the fullest possible use of them, that is to say, all Pupil Teachers will be expected to attend and to fulfil the three conditions stated above.

It may be, however, that in individual cases a narrower range of studies will be desirable for some Pupil Teachers; and if any Pupil Teachers experience any difficulty owing to the subjects of instruction being too numerous, they are expected to make a written application to the Education and Pupil Teachers' Instruction Committee, stating their difficulties and asking to be relieved from attending the University Extension lectures.

The Board desire to ask the assistance of the Head Teachers in making these lectures thoroughly useful to their Assistants and Pupil Teachers.

If only the Head Teacher in each department will act as a centre of enthusiasm for the studies of the teachers working with them, it is impossible to exaggerate the good which may result both to the teachers and to the work of education generally in our Elementary Schools.

Signed   { F. J. ASHMALL, *Chairman.*
               { J. CRUICKSHANK, *Clerk.*

The action of the Southampton School Board is highly to be commended from the point of view of those who desire to see the bonds between the Universities and the teachers drawn closer. In the conduct of negotiation between the Board and the Local University Extension Committee, one of the hon. local secs., Mr. F. Perkins, has rendered specially useful service.

A Plan for Directing Study before and after a Course of Lectures.

1. DIRECTIONS should be drawn up for a course of reading before and after the lectures, with suitable questions and subjects for essays.

2. These directions should be prepared in connexion with all future syllabuses of lectures. With regard to syllabuses already in print, it might be sufficient to prepare directions for study only for the lectures generally in demand.

3. The lecturer who writes the syllabus should generally be requested to prepare the directions and should receive a special fee, the amount to be determined by the Delegates, for so doing. In some cases it might be desirable to employ some person other than the lecturer.

4. Such directions to be obtainable by any student from the office, or through the Local Secretary.

5. The lecturer, or some substitute approved by the Delegates and the Local Committee, should visit the centre and deliver a preparatory lecture, on the invitation of the Local Committee.

For so doing he should receive a fee, to be hereafter determined, and second class railway expenses.

6. For the lecture-fee, the lecturer would also undertake to look over essays sent to him at certain intervals, and of a certain length. [If the number of essays were large, it might be desirable to arrange for additional remuneration. This however would be unlikely at first.]

7. The lecturer would pay a second and a third visit preparatory to the course on the same terms.

[Generally speaking, two visits would be quite sufficient: but I would recommend the preparation of a scale of charges for one, two, or three visits. The first visit would naturally take place when the Local Committee had decided on the course to be given, sufficient time having elapsed for making the lectures known, &c.; the second about half-way through the period of preparation, when the lecturer would have received a sufficient number of essays to enable him to detect the weak points of the students; the third, if it was thought desirable, some little time before the commencement of the course, when the lecturer could sum up the results so far obtained.]

8. The Local Committee should be encouraged to arrange if possible additional meetings of the students, and to obtain the services of some local person of sufficient ability to supervise the work of the students, acting in conjunction with the lecturer.

9. The lecturer should keep a register of all students undertaking this preparatory course of study, and the fact should (1) be specially mentioned on their certificates, or (2) have weight in awarding distinctions.

10. The subjects so dealt with should have special prominence in the Summer Meeting programme. A special but, at present, a subordinate department of the Summer Meeting might be devoted to such subjects.

11. A few Summer Meeting scholarships might be confined to students undertaking the preparatory course.

12. It is unnecessary to propose special arrangements for reading *subsequent* to the course of lectures. Centres adopting this plan would find it best to have one course of twelve lectures extending over the Autumn and Spring sessions, or two courses of six lectures on similar subjects. The *after-course* of reading would naturally be the preparatory course for the next lectures.

If some such plan as this could be adopted, the following results would follow:—

1. The work of the Students' Associations would be systematized, and would receive ample recognition from the Delegates.

2. There would be established a continuous course of study of twelve months on one subject,—viz., from Easter to Easter.

3. The number of students writing essays would be greatly increased. From my own experience, I should say that many students are deterred from writing essays merely by the fact that they know little or nothing of the subject before the course begins, and then they feel that it is too late to acquire the necessary knowledge.

4. Such a plan would pave the way for a three years' course, with classes continued throughout the year, vacations at Christmas, Easter and in the Summer excepted, and lectures in the winter months.

5. The plan could be *partially* adopted without putting any great financial strain on the centres,—at any rate, the stronger ones.

                         W. A. S. HEWINS.

UNIVERSITY EXTENSION IN CORNWALL.

THE following account of the University Extension work, now being done in Cornwall under the County Council, appeared in the *West Briton* for Jan. 3. We should like to take this opportunity of saying how much the cause of University Extension in Cornwall owes to the tact and indefatigable labours of Miss Beatrice Vivian of Camborne, the Hon. Sec. of the South-Western Association for the Extension of University teaching.

The first term's work of University Extension lecturing under the Cornwall County Council has just come to an end. Mr. W. B. Worsfold's lectures on South Africa have been delivered in ten towns or districts, from Launceston to Penzance, to audiences varying from 300 to 18, the lowest of any one attendance. These lectures do not by any means represent the sum total of the teaching achieved. Classes are attended; paper-work is done; books read and original authorities consulted at every one of these centres, with the exception of Saltash, where the lectures have been given solely as pioneer work in the Torpoint, Millbrook, and Saltash districts.

An immense amount of facts, bearing on all the most important relations between South Africa and the rest of the British Empire, is being amassed and digested by Mr. Worsfold's pupils. All reliable information on this subject is just now of the greatest possible interest and importance to most Englishmen, at a time when successful and peaceful expansion of the empire, under conditions favourable to all races and populations, constitutes our most hopeful prospect for the future. This is especially the case with Cornwall. It is not a pleasant fact, but it is a fact, nevertheless, that South African money alone keeps a very large proportion of the population in the most populous district of Cornwall from coming on the rates in this time of depression and cut wages.

The lectures on South Africa, up to this point, have dealt principally with the history and settlement of the conglomeration of states, colonies, Crown dependencies, and protectorates, familiarly comprehended in the term South Africa. In the spring, the resources of the country—agricultural, mineral, and otherwise—with other questions of material interest, will be dealt with. Just at present no part of the world offers such a hopeful prospect for all classes, in view of a speedy and successful development, as South Africa. It is evident that European action in that country must be far-reaching in its consequences, not only to the whole English race, but to humanity at large. There are problems essentially connected with the well-being of the country, on which great questions of commerce and trade, and of the maintenance of the empire, depend, with which not the best-informed or the wisest of statesmen is capable of dealing adequately without the support of his party and of his country.

This course of lectures, under the Cornwall County Council, has recently received a gratuitous advertisement in the columns of *Truth*. It has been stated in that journal, on the authority of correspondents whose statements are not substantiated by their names, that Mr. Worsfold 'has not only allowed his discourse to assume a pronounced political or partisan colour, but has even seasoned it, from time to time, with pointed allusions to Mr. Gladstone's part in South African politics.' In a later issue the editor says he has received a letter from Mr. W. C. Vivian, vice-chairman of the Camborne Radical Association, praising the lecturer highly, and stating that, although condemnation had been expressed by the lecturer in the past, 'it had been applied without evincing, so far as he (Mr. Vivian) could see, a partiality for either Conservative or Liberal Governments.' This, however, is not the whole of *Truth's* indictment, which does not stop at the lecturer, but 'goes for' the Cornwall County Council, on the ground that no conceivable advantages are to be derived from lectures on South Africa by a graduate of Oxford. 'The country has only been of importance during the last fifteen years.' (This would rather surprise our African friends.) 'It has played no part in the world's history; and all that is required to be known about it may be learned from the daily newspapers.' The Council is further recommended, if it persists in desiring lectures, to engage some intelligent colonist or traveller, 'such as my friend Mr. Selous,' who 'could give a lecture replete with information and——amusement!' It seems that any attempt to take the colonies seriously (except, perhaps, in the neighbourhood of the Stock and Share Market) is enough to arouse the antagonism of the Editor of *Truth*.

About the same time, the Right Hon. James Bryce, President of the Board of Trade, speaking at the distribution of prizes to the students under the scheme of commercial education of the London Chamber of Commerce (a body quick to recognize the value of lectures such as those now being aided by the Council), says—'He especially desired to impress on the students the *necessity* for studying recent history, particularly of foreign countries and of our own colonies.'

It is not very likely that the chairman and members of the Technical Instruction Committee, on whose recommendation the Council instituted these lectures, will be much moved by *Truth's obiter dicta*, as they probably had ample grounds for their judgement as to the value of lectures on South Africa, and the particular fitness and special knowledge of the lecturer before they engaged him. But, under any circumstances, the authoritative statements of the President of the Board of Trade convey some idea of the importance which ought to be attached to the serious study of this branch of commercial education. In the country places and remote districts of Cornwall there are numbers of young men growing up to take a part in the serious business of life, who have absolutely no opportunity of such study, unless it is offered them by some such action as that of the County Council, who are now taking the lead in providing such a useful branch of public instruction.

PRINCIPAL RENDALL ON UNIVERSITY EXTENSION.

SPEAKING at the Autumn Conference of the Lancashire and Cheshire University Extension Association, held at University College, Liverpool, last Autumn, Principal Rendall referred as follows to Mr. Whibley's exploits in the *Nineteenth Century*.

If one looked at University Extension through one's very bluest academic spectacles it was easy to see that it might be regarded as work that was not properly the function of the Universities. To the esoteric student of mathematics—to the Mahatma of mathematics—he had no doubt that arithmetic and Euclid and such pastimes would appear the most infantile trifling, and of course, if he might draw an illustration from the subject that was his own particular study, he would not think it a wise or wholesome recommendation to introduce students to Greek dramas or Greek works of literature entirely through the mediums of translations from the original. They must realize—and he thought all the advocates and supporters of the movement did realize—the difference between the ideal of University residence and the ideal of University Extension. The ideal of University residence he took to be this, that life for a time was consecrated entirely to study. That was the object and meaning of University residence, however it might be relieved and varied by other pursuits. The ideal of University Extension was something different. It was not to consecrate the whole of life to study, but to render study an element of life; in fact, to extend the idea of leisure and the idea of pleasure to comprehend the more serious intellectual pursuits which were a legitimate way of varying, relaxing, and recreating the leisured parts of busy lives. He thought it had been found in practice that for University Extension the severer disciplines of learning were naturally impossible, because very much of the technical basis or background of learning was absent, and that it worked best where the technical basis was ready to hand in our own native language, where thought required no artificial mechanism or technique to carry on its processes, and it was therefore in the realms of such subjects as history, literature, and philosophy, not subjects that required less thought, but where the means of thought were more ready to hand and existed in our own native language, that University Extension had most thriven. It had been singularly successful in giving companionship in study to those persons who would otherwise have been severed and isolated; it had given stimulus to study to those who otherwise would not have found the stimulus to study within themselves, and it had given more breadth to study through the agency employed—minds of academic culture and breadth. It had utilized, too, just those who, in youth and in the first vigour and freshness of interest in every subject, had been able more effectively than others to communicate freshness and variety to the studies which they had laid before the University Extension audiences. These were perhaps the principal and obvious aims of University Extension work, and such were to some extent the natural limits of its successes.

MR. CHARLES ACLAND ON TRAVELLING TEACHERS IN SECONDARY EDUCATION.

THE Chairman of the Technical Instruction Committee of the Devon County Council, speaking at the prize-giving of the prosperous Grammar School at Ashburton, said (we quote from the *Western Times*) that 'he had a dream before him, a vision which he scarcely dared hope to see fulfilled. It was the establishment of an organized system of well-trained travelling teachers going round among continuation schools to make periodical visits, and working cordially with the teachers in elementary schools.' . . . . Passing on to the organization and control of secondary education in rural districts, Mr. Acland said that was preeminently the function of the local authority and not of a central department of Government in London. Local knowledge and local interest, local initiative and local maintenance were all essential. Scholarships, exhibitions, bursaries (that was to say, payment of travelling expenses to and from schools) would be necessary, and there should also be organized centres of training, and circles of peripatetic work for teachers.

ORGANIZATION OF 'THE TEACHING INTEREST.'

JANUARY has been a month of educational activity. Never before have so many gatherings of interest to teachers been crowded into the same short period of time. One of the most significant gatherings was that of the Association of Headmasters, now 'incorporated' under Board of Trade rules. With much that was said at this gathering we are in sharp disagreement. Young University men who have been assistant masters well know that the assistants in secondary schools need the protection given by right of appeal against a headmaster's sometimes arbitrary decisions. There was also a note of jealous rivalry and misunderstanding in the critical comments on the new Oxford Local Junior Examination. The true significance of these criticisms, by the way, has been missed by a writer in the *Oxford Magazine.* A more promising feature of the conference was its resolve to reform the teaching of science in schools. Professor Armstrong will do good work for education if he pegs away at that matter. But after all the most remarkable thing about the Headmasters' Association is that the grade of Headmasters, which this association chiefly represents, should have been induced to organize themselves at all. Dr. Scott's power of persuasion, and the compressive force of circumstances, must indeed be great to have effected this combination. By the way, the only educational ' interest ' in England which is now at the disadvantage of being uncombined, unorganized and devoid of a standing committee to watch the bearing of parliamentary or local affairs upon its fortunes, is the University interest. Would it not be possible to have a joint committee to look after academic interests in parliament or elsewhere, and to report to the several Universities from term to term ? The existence of such a watching committee would not in any way affect the freedom of the individual Universities, which would lose their best hope for the future if they were deprived of the full opportunity for separate development on their own traditional lines.

ARRANGEMENTS FOR SPRING, 1895.

All lectures are at fortnightly intervals except where otherwise stated.

Centre.	No. of Lectures in Course.	Subject of Course.	Lecturer.	Course or Half-Course begins.	Course ends.
†UNIVERSITY EXTENSION COLLEGE, READING (evening)	12	Age of Elizabeth and Puritan Rebellion }	Rev. W.H. SHAW, M.A. & E.L.S. HORSBURGH, M.A.	Th. Jan. 17	Mar. 28
,, (afternoon)	12	Tennyson and Browning	J. CHURTON COLLINS, M.A	S. Jan. 26	Apr. 6
,, (evening) ...	12	Greek Drama	,, ,,	S. Jan. 26	Apr. 6
,, (evening) ...	12	The Study of Local History ...	W. M. CHILDS, B.A. ...	F. Jan. 25	Apr. 5
,, (evening) ...	12	La Littérature Française du XVII* Siècle	M. J. MAURICE REY, B. es Sc.	W. Jan. 23	Apr. 3
,, (evening) ...	12	Geography of the British Isles ...	H. J. MACKINDER, M.A.	S. Jan. 19	Mar. 30
†BIRMINGHAM, EDGBASTON (afternoon)	12	Age of Louis XIV and French Revolution	J.A.R.MARRIOTT, M.A.	T. Jan. 15	Mar. 26
BIRMINGHAM, Severn Street (evening)	6	English Colonies	,, ,,	T. Jan. 15	Mar. 26
†BOURNEMOUTH (afternoon) ...	12	Europe since Waterloo	,, ,, ...	W. Jan. 23	Apr. 3
BRADFORD (evening)	6	Colonies	,, ,, ...	Th. Jan. 17	Mar. 28
†BRIDPORT (evening)	12	Industrial Revolution	,, ,, ...	T. Jan. 22	Apr. 2
†CLEVEDON (afternoon) ..	12	Shakespeare's Historical Plays ...	,, ,, ...	F. Jan. 25	Apr. 5
DORCHESTER (evening)	6	Colonies	,, ,, ...	W. Jan. 23	Apr. 3
OXFORD (evening) ...	6	The Renaissance and Reformation in England	,, ,, ...	F. Jan. 18	Mar. 29
SALE (evening)	6	England in the 18th Century ...	,, ,, ...	W. Jan. 16	Mar. 27
†SOUTHBOURNE (afternoon) ...	12	Europe since Waterloo	,, ,, ...	Th. Jan. 24	Apr. 4
WEYMOUTH (afternoon) ...	6	Age of Louis XIV	,, ,,	T. Jan. 22	Apr. 2
†TAMWORTH (evening) ...	10	England in the 18th Century ...	C. E. MALLET, B.A. ...	T. Jan. 15	Feb. 26
FOLKESTONE (evening, weekly)	10	England in the 18th Century	,, ,,	M. Jan. 28	Apr. 1
WHITEHAVEN (evening)	6	England in the 18th Century ...	,, ,,	W. Jan. 16	Mar. 27
†BURNLEY (evening) ...	12	Spenser & other Elizabethan Poets	F. S. BOAS, M.A. ...	Th. Jan. 24	Apr. 4
†CANTERBURY (afternoon) ...	12	Victorian Poets	,, ,, ...	Th. Jan. 17	Mar. 28
†RAMSGATE (afternoon) ...	12	Literature of Cavaliers and Puritans	,, ,, ...	S. Jan. 26	Apr. 6
DEVIZES (evening) ...	6	Tennyson	Rev. J. G. BAILEY, M.A., LL.D.	Th. Jan. 24	Apr. 4
†WEST BRIGHTON (afternoon)	12	Tennyson	,, ,, ...	F. Jan. 18	Mar. 29
ABERGAVENNY (afternoon) ...	6	Shakespeare	E.L.S. HORSBURGH, B.A.	S. Jan. 26	Apr. 6
BRECON (afternoon) ...	6	Literature of the 18th Century ...	,, ,, ...	Th. Jan. 24	Apr. 4
BRECON (evening)	6	Epochs from English History ...	,, ,, ...	Th. Jan. 24	Apr. 4
CHELTENHAM (afternoon) ...	6	Growth of Parliament	,, ,, ...	W. Jan. 30	Apr. 10
CHELTENHAM (evening)	6	Industrial and Economic Questions since 1789	,, ,, ...	W. Jan. 30	Apr. 10
EVESHAM (evening) ...	6	Revolution and Age of Anne ...	,, ,, ...	W. Jan. 23	Apr. 3
GLOUCESTER (evening) ...	6	English History in Shakespeare...	,, ,, ...	M. Jan. 28	Apr. 8
HEREFORD (evening) ...	6	Wyclif to Sir Thomas More ...	,, ,, ...	M. Jan. 21	Apr. 1
LEOMINSTER (evening) ...	6	Industrial and Economic Questions since 1789	,, ,, ...	T. Jan. 22	Apr. 2
MALVERN (afternoon) ...	12	Puritan Revolution	,, ,, ...	W. Jan. 23	Apr. 3
†REIGATE (afternoon) ...	6	The Reign of Elizabeth	,, ,, ...	Th. Jan. 17	Mar. 28

† The figures in the second column include the lectures given in the Autumn Term, from which these courses are continued.

Centre.	No. of Lectures in Course.	Subject of Course.	Lecturer.	Course or Half-Course begins.	Course ends.
Ross (afternoon)	6	Literature of the 18th Century ..	E. L. S. Horsburgh, B.A.	T. Jan. 22	Apr. 2
†Southampton (evening) ...	12	The Age of Elizabeth	„ „ ...	F. Jan. 18	May 29
Stroud (afternoon)	6	The Renaissance	„ „ ...	T. Jan. 29	Apr. 9
Stroud (evening)	6	The Reign of Elizabeth	„ „ ...	T. Jan. 29	Apr. 9
Swansea (evening)	6	Epochs from English History ...	„ „ ...	F. Jan. 25	Apr. 5
Dover (afternoon)	6	Architecture	F. Bond, M.A.	M. Jan. 28	Apr. 8
Dover (evening)	6	Architecture	„ „ ...	M. Jan. 28	Apr. 8
Tunbridge Wells (afternoon, weekly)	10	Architecture	„ „	F. Jan. 25	Mar. 29
Fleet (afternoon)	8	Chaucer to Bacon...	R. Warwick Bond, M.A.	Th. Jan. 24	Apr. 25
†Henlow (evening)	12	The English Citizen	W. M. Childs, B.A. ...	W. Jan. 16	Mar. 27
Glossop (evening)	6	Trade, Adventure, and Discovery	K. D. Cotes, M.A. ...	W. Jan. 23	Apr. 3
Warrington (evening) ...	6	Trade, Invention, and Discovery	„ „ ...	F. Jan. 25	Apr. 5
Wirksworth (evening) ...	6	Trade, Adventure, and Discovery	„ „ ...	Th. Jan. 24	Apr. 4
Tavistock (afternoon) ...	6	Puritan Revolution	W. G. de Burgh, B.A.	M. Jan. 28	Apr. 8
Frome (afternoon)	6	Wordsworth, Coleridge, and Scott	„ „ ...	T. Jan. 29	Apr. 9
†West Brighton (evening) ...	12	Three Centuries of Working-class History	W. A. S. Hewins, M.A.	Th. Jan. 24	Apr. 18
Grimsby (evening)	6	Problems of Poverty	J. A. Hobson, M.A. ...	T. Jan. 22	Apr. 2
Midhurst (afternoon) ...	6	English Novelists	„ „ ...	W. Jan. 16	Mar. 27
Tunbridge Wells (evening)	6	Industrial Questions of the Day ...	„ „ ...	W. Jan. 23	Apr. 3
†Carlisle (afternoon) ...	12	Architecture	J. E. Phythian ...	T. Jan. 15	Apr. 9
Chester (afternoon)	6	Architecture	„ „ ...	T. Jan. 22	Apr. 2
Halifax (evening)	6	Florentine Art	„ „ ...	Th. Jan. 24	Mar. 28
Kersal (evening, weekly) ...	8	Architecture	„ „ ...	M. Jan. 28	Mar. 18
†Bodmin (evening)	12	South Africa	W. B. Worsfold, M.A	F. Jan. 25	Apr. 5
†Camborne (evening)... ...	12	South Africa	„ „ ...	F. Jan. 18	Mar. 29
†Falmouth (evening)... ...	12	South Africa	„ „ ...	Th. Jan. 17	Mar. 28
†Helston (evening)	12	South Africa	„ „ ...	T. Jan. 22	Apr. 2
†Launceston (evening) ...	12	South Africa	„ „ ...	W. Jan. 16	Mar. 27
†Penzance (evening)	12	South Africa	„ „ ...	M. Jan. 21	Apr. 1
†Redruth (evening)	12	South Africa	„ „ ...	Th. Jan. 24	Apr. 4
†St. Austell (evening) ...	12	South Africa	„ „ ...	T. Jan. 15	Mar. 26
†Truro (evening)	12	South Africa	„ „ ...	M. Jan. 14	Mar. 25
Lewes (evening)	6	Physiography	G. J. Burch, M.A. ...	M. Jan. 21	Apr. 1
Brighton (St. Michael's Hall) (afternoon)	6	Regions, Races, and Resources ...	H. R. Mill, D.Sc. ...	Th. Jan. 31	Apr. 4
Brighton (evening)	6	Regions, Races, and Resources ...	„ „ ...	Th. Jan. 31	Apr. 4
†Carlisle (evening)	12	Outlines of Geology	C. Carus-Wilson, F.G.S.	Th. Jan. 24	Apr. 4
†St. Helens (evening) ...	12	Crust of the Earth	„ „ ...	Th. Jan. 31	Apr. 3
†Bath (afternoon)	12	Recent Discoveries with the Telescope and Spectroscope	A. H. Fison, D.Sc. ...	Th. Jan. 31	Apr. 11
†Bath (evening)	12	Recent Discoveries with the Telescope and Spectroscope	„ „ ...	Th. Jan. 31	Apr. 11
Bedford (evening)	6	Life of a Planet	„ „ ...	T. Jan. 29	Apr. 9
†Bournemouth (evening) ...	6	Forces of Nature	„ „ ...	F. Jan. 18	Mar. 29
Leamington (evening) ...	12	Life of a Planet	„ „ ...	T. Feb. 5	Mar. 16
†Ryde (afternoon)	12	Recent Discoveries with the Telescope and Spectroscope	„ „ ...	Th. Jan. 24	Apr. 4
Sandown (afternoon)... ...	6	Recent Discoveries with the Telescope and Spectroscope	„ „ ...	F. Jan. 25	Apr. 5
†Ventnor (evening)	12	Physical Astronomy	„ „ ...	F. Jan. 25	Apr. 5
Greek Classes (afternoon, weekly) :					
Brighton (Elementary)	10	Xen. *Anab.* I: Eurip. *Alc.* (scenes from)	Rev. E. Luce, M.A. ...	T. Jan. 29	Apr. 2
„ (Intermediate)	10	Thucyd. VII and Soph. *Ajax* ...	„ „ ...	W. Jan. 30	Apr. 3
Somerset County Council :					
5 Courses of	12	{ Prevention of Disease among Animals Physiology of Domestic Animals }	H. Sessions	Jan.	Apr.
5 Courses of	12	Hygiene	C. H. Wade, M.A., D.P.H.	Jan.	Apr.
Kent County Council :					
2 Courses of	12	Chemistry	H. H. Cousins, M.A.	Jan.	Apr.

Summer Term, 1895.

Brighton (St. Michael's Hall) | 6 or 8 | England in the 18th Century ... | J. A. R. Marriott, M.A. | Not fixed | Not fixed

† The figures in the second column include the lectures given in the Autumn Term, from which these courses are continued.

Note.—Application for Courses and all information as to fees, &c., can be obtained from The Secretary, University Extension Office, Examination Schools, Oxford.

POPULAR EDUCATION IN THE FIFTIES.

'THE people in the early part of the century were only groping in the dark for the kind of higher education which they desired. The Mechanics' Institutes supplemented small and defective libraries by single and unconnected lectures. In fact, the associated members of these institutes scarcely knew what they wanted. Some joined the institutes for amusement, some for instruction. Both were proper objects of desire, but were difficult to amalgamate, so a strange mixture was made of both, often not very wisely, by the inexperienced managers of the new Mechanics' Institutes. One of the most prosperous of them asked me to give a single lecture on chemistry, in the year 1846, and sent me its programme for the preceding year. It was as follows:—

"Wit and humour, with comic songs—Women Treated in a Novel Manner—Legerdemain and Spirit-rapping—The Devil (with illustrations)—the Heavenly Bodies and the Stellar System – Palestine and the Holy Land.—Speeches by Eminent Friends of Education, interspersed with music, to be followed by a ball. Price to the whole 2s. 6d. Refreshments in an ante-room."

Compare your programme of sound work with this motley assemblage of professors, ventriloquists, conjurors and musicians, and you will see how much the scheme University Extension has moulded the demand for knowledge among the people, and turned it into channels which will refresh and irrigate the various districts through which it passes.'—*From Lord Playfair's Address on University Extension.*

LECTURERS' RESERVE FUND.

SUBSCRIPTIONS AND DONATIONS RECEIVED SINCE DEC. 19, 1894.

	£	s.	d.
Sir John Conroy	0	10	0
Miss Fletcher	0	10	0
Miss Tetley	0	10	0
Miss Lawford	0	10	0
Miss Williams	0	10	0
Miss Hills	1	0	0
Miss Prideaux	0	10	0
Miss Brassey	1	1	0
Miss Cowley	0	10	0
Miss Harlow	0	10	0
Miss Marion Harrison . .	0	10	0
Miss S. M. Scott . . .	0	10	6
Miss D. Harris . . .	0	10	0
Miss J. Harris . . .	0	10	0
Miss Woolston (7th subs.) . .	5	0	0
The Misses Nicholson . .	0	15	0
The Misses Coultate . .	0	10	0
Mr. and Mrs Sadler . .	1	0	0
Mr. and Mrs Sadler (don.) .	5	0	0
L. A. F.	1	0	0
Miss Edwards	1	1	0

INFORMATION TO CONTRIBUTORS.

All communications should be addressed to the Editor, OXFORD UNIVERSITY EXTENSION GAZETTE, *University Press, Oxford.*

All matter intended for insertion in the March issue should reach him not later than February 18.

Contributions should be written on one side of the paper only, and must be accompanied by the name of the writer (not necessarily for publication .

N.B.—*All orders should carefully specify the full title,* OXFORD UNIVERSITY EXTENSION GAZETTE.

OXFORD UNIVERSITY

EXTENSION GAZETTE.

| VOL. V. NO. 54.] | MARCH, 1895. | [ONE PENNY. |

N.B.—Local Organizers of Oxford University Extension Lectures are invited to send to the Secretary, University Extension Office, Examination Schools, Oxford, copies of any journals containing notices of, or references to, Extension work.

NOTES AND COMMENTS.

To Oxford the death of Mr. Alfred Robinson, Fellow and Bursar of New College, brings irreparable loss. And whatever there is in England that is influenced by Oxford or cares for her, will henceforth be the poorer and the weaker for the want of him. For he was a pillar of our state—*the* pillar indeed of parts of it. All his great powers he gladly gave to Oxford. Fame of the common kind he never sought or won. But he received what is better than fame—the grateful love of those who were daily helped by his example. He was a statesman and a leader, but yet his heart 'the lowliest duties on herself did lay.' Through his singleness of purpose and faithful service, many ancient things have passed from death to life. In his temper, zeal and caution were so finely blended as to become one virtue—wisdom. To us in Oxford he seemed to stand for what is the north-country character at its best,—for its steadfastness, its warm-hearted reserve, its rectitude, its simplicity of aim. He did much, felt deeply, said little. Dixit; Custodiam vias meas ut non delinquam in lingua mea. He had suffered secretly and in silence. For he chose to die at his post—the only sign of his decision a 'sudden brightness' which his friends noticed, but did not understand.

.·.

Mr. J. A. R. Marriott, M.A. of New College, has been elected Secretary of the Oxford University Extension Delegacy from Lady Day next. He will enter upon his new duties with the hearty good-will of his colleagues and of the many friends whom he has made at the Summer Meetings and in every part of England. Having been connected with the Oxford University Extension almost since its revival in 1885, Mr. Marriott is intimately acquainted with the working of the system and with the needs and difficulties of the local committee. As a member of the Delegacy since its establishment in 1892, he is familiar with the circumstances which have guided its policy, and he has also had experience of the management of the Summer Meeting. We cordially wish him good health and prosperity in his work.

.·.

Mr. G. N. Richardson, who has rendered valuable assistance in the University Extension office and at the Summer Meetings during recent years, did not offer himself for election as Secretary of the Delegacy.

.·.

The Delegates have during the past month appointed two Directors of University Extension teaching in selected districts. As Director of the work in Gloucestershire and part of Herefordshire, they have chosen Mr. J. Wells, M.A., Fellow and Tutor of Wadham College, while the oversight of University Extension teaching in Hampshire and the Isle of Wight has been entrusted to Mr. E. L. S. Horsburgh, B.A., Queen's College, Staff-Lecturer of the Oxford University Extension. The main duty of the Directors will be to co-operate with the local committees in improving and systematizing the organization of their work. We are glad to learn that the appointment of Mr. Wells and Mr. Horsburgh, both of whom have rendered distinguished services to University Extension, has

been received with much approval in the two districts, which—on account partly of their convenient neighbourhood to Oxford, partly of the energy and enterprise of some of their local organizers—have been chosen for this new and promising experiment. It is hoped that several other centres, lying just outside the above-mentioned districts, may also derive help from the Directors' work.

.·.

The Rev. P. H. Wicksteed has been appointed a Staff-Lecturer by the Delegacy. Mr. Wicksteed has for some time lectured in connexion with the London Society for University Extension, and, by special invitation, at some Oxford centres also. His courses on Dante and Economics are well known and have been much appreciated throughout England.

.·.

By the death of the Dowager Lady Stanley of Alderley, at the advanced age of 86, England loses a stately figure and University Extension, like many other educational movements, a staunch friend. Lady Stanley was a member of the Council of the London University Extension Society, and hospitably entertained many of the visitors to the Congress last June. But her chief work lay in the promotion of Queen's and Girton Colleges, and in the directorate of the Girls' Public Day School Company.

.·.

The election of Professor Rhys as Principal of Jesus College gives Oxford a great opportunity. Wales is stirred to its depths by an educational movement which has already established a public system of intermediate education and crowned the whole by a national University. In this movement Professor Rhys has borne a leading part. A scholar of European reputation, a man of affairs, and a teacher who has had experience in every grade of school, the new Principal will, we hope, bring Jesus College, and through Jesus College the University of Oxford, into direct and fruitful relation with the educational enthusiasm of Wales.

.·.

To commemorate the great services rendered by Mrs. Arthur Johnson to the Association for the Education of Women in Oxford, a fund has been started which will be used in helping women students to obtain University training here. Hitherto, it is stated, this need has been met by the London Education Loan Society, now no longer available. The experience, however, of this society will guide the Council of the Association in framing rules for the loan-fund, advances from which are to be repaid when the borrower obtains employment. Contributions to the fund may be sent to Mr. Arthur Sidgwick or to Mrs. Poole at the Clarendon Building, Oxford.

.·.

In the course of his Inaugural Address as Sibthorpian Professor of Rural Economy, delivered in the University Museum, Oxford, on Feb. 4, Mr. Warington remarked that 'the attempts which have been made to teach agriculture in Elementary Day Schools, or in evening classes under the

Professor Warington on University Extension Teaching in Agriculture.

Department of Science and Art, or in connexion with the County Councils, or again by University Extension lectures, cannot on the whole be pronounced a success.' He laid stress on the importance of Experiment Stations in agricultural science, on the desirability of giving farmers' sons some practical experience as workers on other farms of acknowledged excellence, on the necessity of obtaining 'teachers with a sufficient knowledge of practical agriculture to be really in touch with the farming community,' and on the unsuitability of the more expensive Colleges for the majority of our tenant-farmers. We may congratulate ourselves on the fact that these four points have all been borne in mind by those who have instituted the Agricultural Department of the University Extension College, Reading.

.·.

A new life of Archbishop Laud

Students who attended last year's Summer Meeting will give a hearty welcome to the Rev. W. H. Hutton's book on Archbishop Laud, which is the latest addition to the series of monographs on Leaders of Religion, edited by another Summer Meeting lecturer, the Rev. H. C. Beeching. Those who listened last year to Mr. Hutton's lectures on the Laudian movement will find much of the essence of the lectures in the book mentioned, and others who were not in Oxford last summer but who are interested in the struggle between Laud and the Puritans, will find a scholarly and interesting account of Laud's work in this study written with sympathetic reverence by a Fellow of the College of which the Archbishop was President. Further, Mr. Hutton has availed himself of all that the recent researchers into the history of the period have discovered ; so that his book presents the most complete account of Laud's life that has as yet been published. We heartily commend the book to all students of seventeenth century history. The price of it is three shillings and sixpence, and the publishers Messrs Methuen & Co.

.·.

The Award granted by the authorities of the Chicago Exhibition to the Oxford University Extension Delegacy is a curious document. It reads thus—'An excellent collection showing the equipment, facilities and high standing of this well-known University.'

.·.

Fortnightly Lectures as facilitating Sequence of Study.

The value of fortnightly lectures for centres which are not well off is very well exemplified in the report which the Bedford Local Committee have issued of the work accomplished under their auspices since the revival of the centre in January 1890. Between January 1890 and April 1891 three courses of twelve weekly lectures were given on Astronomy, Victorian Poets, and Geology respectively. Since then fortnightly lectures have been given, and, relieved from the financial strain of weekly lectures all through the session, the Committee have been able to arrange courses in sequence. Between October 1891 and April 1893 the subjects have been the French Revolution, the Napoleonic Era, and Europe since Waterloo, twenty-four lectures in all. A flourishing Students' Association has also been formed since 1891, to carry on the work in the alternate weeks to the lectures, and has added much to the strength of the centre. In 1893-94 a new sequence was begun by a course of twelve lectures on the English Citizen, Past and Present, by Mr. Graham Wallas. This was to have been followed in 1894-95 by twelve lectures on The Colonies and India by Mr. Morse Stephens, but his appointment to a Professorship at Cornell University prevented his delivering the course. The subject has, however, been studied all through the Summer and Autumn by the Students' Association, who have thus more than ever proved their great value to the centre.

.·.

A correspondent writes : 'Yours are not columns for dramatic criticism, but should nevertheless record the success of a comedy which is ascribed to one of the Oxford University Extension staff. Some days before *A Leader of Men* appeared on the stage of the Comedy Theatre, the new playwright was rumoured to be a Balliol man, a University Extension lecturer and the author of a book on the French Revolution. And, from a conversation between the door-keeper and neighbouring cabmen, which I could not help over-hearing on the night of my visit to the theatre, I am disposed to guess that the author's pseudonym, "Mr. Charles E. D. Ward," is rather more than half—say, two-thirds—of the truth. The writer is certainly to be congratulated on the welcome which has been given to his play.'

.·.

The Union of Cambridge Local Secretaries at Cambridge.

The honorary local secretaries of the Cambridge University Extension Committees have formed an association for conference and concerted action. This step, which will do much to unify the work of the centres, has been welcomed by the Cambridge Syndicate. The first meeting of the new association was held during February at Cambridge, and in spite of the cold, eighteen secretaries attended. On the second day of the meeting, a deputation of the members was invited to meet the Syndicate. They also enjoyed the hospitality of the Vice-Chancellor.

.·.

The Hants County Council and the University Extension College, Reading.

The Technical Education Committee of the Hampshire County Council have made arrangements for agricultural experimental stations, to be conducted by the Agricultural Department of the Reading University Extension College, at or near Petersfield, Havant, Fareham, Botley and Milford.

.·.

In view of the remarks of Herr Tonnies that University Extension must concern itself more largely with economic questions, it may be pointed out that the current list of the Council and officers of the British Economic Association comprises the names of one Delegate, two Staff-Lecturers, and one former Staff-Lecturer, of the Oxford University Extension.

.·.

A writer in the *Cornish Telegram* of Penzance thus refers to the absence of workmen from Mr. Worsfold's lectures at that centre. Happily in the industrial districts of the county, the attendance of workmen at Mr. Worsfold's course on South Africa is eminently satisfactory. Perhaps the workmen, and certainly the fishermen, of Penzance are not very much concerned with questions of emigration.

'Mr. W. B. WORSFOLD, the University Extension lecturer, must be sadly disappointed in the Cornish working men, if the attendance at the lectures at Penzance can be taken as a criterion of the interest taken in them in other centres of the country. It was expected that Cornish working men would rush to hear lectures by so well informed an authority on South Africa. The price per lecture was fixed at the modest sum of one penny, and it has been published broadcast that "these lectures are paid for by the County Council for the benefit of the working men." Yet the working men seem content with the knowledge of this wonderful country they may glean from some chance acquaintance who has "done" Africa in a superficial way, and are conspicuous by their total absence from these excellent lectures. Mr. Worsfold has dealt in the past half dozen lectures with the history of the dark continent, and on Monday gave a most engrossing and comprehensive account of the agricultural and pastoral resources of the country. If the history of South Africa has no charms for the working men, surely the more "dazzling" subjects of the diamond and gold and other mines should prove sufficiently fascinating to secure their attendance. These subjects will occupy the next two discourses, and will be characterized by that deep research and completeness which mark all Mr. Worsfold's lectures. It is worthy of note that several persons who have spent many years in exploring South Africa, among them Mr. H. F. Gros, than whom we suppose there are few people in Cornwall more fully acquainted with the country, regularly attend the lectures and learn much that is new and of absorbing interest to them. If such people can obtain benefit by sitting at the feet of Mr. Worsfold, can the working men, many of whom it may be assumed contemplate emigration, afford to lose these valuable opportunities of acquiring information from such an abundant and reliable fountain head?'

It is stated that the Right Hon. Cecil Rhodes, who was an undergraduate at Oriel and has more than once revisited Oxford since taking his degree, has it in mind to build at Cape Town a copy of Oriel College as the centre of the African University.

.·.

The last number of the well-edited organ of the American Society, *University Extension*, contains an interesting discussion of the educational aims of our movement. Dr. Roberts is the exponent of one view, the Editor of the magazine forcibly states the other in some notes at the end of the number. The former inclines to the intensive, the latter to the propagandist, policy. Except in their extreme forms (both of which seem to us to be false), the two policies are not really antagonistic to one another. One is needed in one district, the second in others. The two are needed in succession in the same district at different stages in the development of the work. And the most systematic form of Extension teaching is often none the worse for being occasionally brisked up by propaganda.

.·.

The University of Chicago, from which we have received an assortment of carefully-devised, though somewhat elaborate, 'blanks' and circulars, issues as an official paper an essay by Miss Montgomery of Exeter. in which she well describes the manifold responsibilities of the honorary local secretary of a University Extension centre.

.·.

Those who attended Dr. Devine's course on Economics at the last Summer Meeting will be glad to learn that the American Academy of Political and Social Science have published a paper from his pen entitled 'The Economic Function of Woman.' The price is 15 cents, and the London agents are P. S. King & Son, 12 King Street, Westminster.

.·.

State Aid for University Extension in Austria. In its estimate of expenditure for 1895, the Financial Committee of the Lower House of the Austrian Parliament has (we learn from Dr. Nader of Vienna) set aside the sum of 6000 florins to promote the work of University Extension, or 'Universitäts-Ausdehnung.' This success, our correspondent informs us, is due to the efforts of the 'Society for promoting the education of the people' (Volksbildungs-Verein). A chief object of the work of this society has been the foundation of free libraries. In 1892-3, 235 lectures were delivered under its auspices in thirteen districts. Courses of weekly lectures on German literature are a recent feature in the programme of the Vienna Society.

.·.

University Extension in Belgium is growing fast. Courses are now being delivered, or are in the way of arrangement, at Brussels, Charleroi, Vervier, Antwerp, Ixelles, Courtrai, Nieuport, Arlon and Namur. In all sixteen local committees are at work.

.·.

Among the distinguished members of the Belgian University Extension staff are Mm. Émile and Henri Vandervelde, one of whom has taken of late a prominent part in Belgian public affairs.

.·.

M. Élisée Reclus has become a University Extension lecturer and is giving courses on South America at Arlon and Charleroi.

.·.

Extension de l'Université Libre de Bruxelles. We have received from Dr. Vandervelde, Secretary of the Extension de l'Université Libre de Bruxelles, copies of the statutes of the Society and some syllabuses on historical, economic and scientific subjects. The list of lecturers comprises twenty-seven names. Most of the courses are scientific or technical. No statement of the centres actually established, or of courses

already delivered, has reached us. The third article of the statutes ordains that 'no one can be a member of the Extension of the Université Libre de Bruxelles who undertakes any duties in connexion with any other Faculty or foreign institution of University rank.' This seems to us an ill-judged ordinance, and rather calculated to injure than to benefit the society which has adopted it.

.·.

An interesting pamphlet has been written by MM. Arthur Hirsch and Michael Huisman, entitled *L'Extension Universitaire Belge ; ce qu'elle devrait être, ce qu'elle est.* We hope to refer to it further in a later number. The publisher is Henri Lamertin, Marché-au-Bois, Brussels.

.·.

Those who are interested in the Danish People's High Schools, which present perhaps the closest of all continental analogies to the work of our own University Extension in the industrial districts will be glad to hear that Herr H. Rosendal has published a full catalogue of these Schools, giving the names of the teachers and statistics of the number of scholars. The book is called *Danmarks Folkehojskoler og Landbrugskolar, 1844-1894'* (Odense, Trykt i Milo'ske Bogtrykkeri). The writings of Professor Morgan Lewis of Aberyswyth and of Mr. J. S. Thornton, and Herr Povlsen's lecture at the last Oxford Summer Meeting, have drawn considerable attention in England to the remarkable work of these Schools.

.·.

University Extension in North Wales. At the meeting of the Welsh Land Commission on February 6, evidence was given from the Welsh University Colleges in regard to their efforts for the furtherance of Agricultural Education in the Principality. Principal Reichel of Bangor spoke in favour of providing for agricultural students short vacation courses of instruction with laboratory practice. Mr. T. Winter, lecturer on agriculture and agricultural organizer of the University College of North Wales (Bangor), said that the demand for University Extension lectures showed that the interest of the farmers was steadily maintained.

.·.

Decentralization of Educational Control. A recent Parliamentary Paper shows that, up to March 31, 1894, the County and County Borough Councils in England and Wales (including London) had received, under the Local Taxation (Customs and Excise) Act 1890, £3,126,353. Of this amount, £1,508,958 had been already expended on technical or intermediate education, while an additional sum of £695,687 had been appropriated to the same purpose, but not yet actually spent. Partly in consequence of a movement in public opinion, partly through the operation of the Local Taxation Act of 1890, there is at present a strong tendency in England to decentralize educational control. Permanent educational work will more and more be drawn into some sort of relation to local authorities.

.·.

In *Nature* for Feb. 14 appeared a valuable article on 'the advance of Technical Education' by Mr. R. A. Gregory, a lecturer of the Oxford University Extension. The writer points out that the County Councils have rendered valuable service by calling public attention to the defects in our system of secondary education.

.·.

One of the agencies which has done most to guide and strengthen the educational policy of the County Councils is the 'Association of Directors and Organizing Secretaries for Technical and Secondary Education.' Three of the founders of this society—Mr. Arthur Acland, Mr. Llewellyn Smith and Mr. H. Macan—have been closely connected with University Extension work.

2

Mr. Macan, who is well known as the Organizing Secretary of the Surrey County Council, suggests in the *Technical World* of Feb. 16 that when the new Urban District Councils build offices they should attach to them suitable class-rooms for educational purposes. In one case in Surrey an urban Council is going to flank its administrative building by a free library and a secondary school. Mr. Macan also refers to a ' design of an ideal parish hall,' which has class-rooms and a library attached to it. Institutes of this kind would incidentally furnish accommodation for University Extension teaching.

.·.

A County Council and Economic Teaching. We regret to hear that an application made by the committee of the Malvern Church Institute to the County Council for a grant towards the expenses of a course of lectures on Political Economy by Mr. J. A. Hobson was rejected on the ground that the Council did not approve the subject. This decision has necessitated the abandonment of the proposed course. In view of the present movement of public opinion, and the desirability of teaching economics to workmen (who would have largely composed the audience at these lectures), the action of the County Council is much to be regretted.

.·.

To the *Glasgow Evening News* Professor R. M. Wenley is contributing a series of articles on University Extension. He points out that there are thousands of men and women who cannot possibly devote three or four years in their youth to residence at a University, and yet ought not, on this account, to be debarred from participating in the pleasures and discipline which systematized study brings. He sees in University Extension an attempt to supply this type of student with opportunities of following out a course of higher study while not ceasing to work for a livelihood, or to leave the scene of their daily labour.

THE NEW BISHOP OF HEREFORD.

FEW men have done so much for University Extension as Dr. Percival, Bishop-Designate of Hereford. It was largely due to his influence that the University of Oxford revived its Extension work on a new footing in 1885. At that time he was President of Trinity College, Oxford, and he served from the first on the Committee to which the Local Examinations Delegacy entrusted the charge of this branch of its multifarious undertakings. The earlier sittings of that Committee were held in his lodgings at Trinity. His efforts led to the establishment of many of our earlier centres, and the Endowment Fund, which enabled the Delegates to guarantee a stipend to Mr. Hudson Shaw for a short term of years, owed much of its success to his appeals. Later on, when he had become Headmaster of Rugby, he acted as chairman of the small committee which framed a scheme for home-reading circles, and thus prepared the way for the formation of the Home Reading Union. It was at a meeting of this Committee, held in the drawing-room of the School House at Rugby, that Dr. Paton of Nottingham and Mr. Charles Rowley of Manchester made the suggestions, based on the experience of Chautauqua, which led to the establishment of the Oxford Summer Meeting. Since that time Dr. Percival has frequently aided the University Extension movement by public addresses or by letters in the newspapers, while he has evinced his practical interest in the details of local organization by serving as chairman of the local committee at Rugby.

His support has from the first been given to University Extension in the large, as well as in the special, sense of the term. He has always discussed its plans in their wider bearings and in their relation to other parts of academic policy. In Sept. 1872, while still Headmaster of Clifton College, he addressed 'a letter to the Governing Bodies of the various Colleges in the University of Oxford,' in which, as a resident in a provincial city, he invited consideration of 'the possibility of establishing some closer connexion between the Universities and the great towns of the country.' This pamphlet, published in 1873 by Messrs. Macmillan under the title of *The connexion of the Universities and the great Towns*, is one of the earliest and most statesmanlike proposals for University Extension.

He urged that, if the Universities were to maintain a really national position amidst all the new conditions of commercial life, it was time to consider how their influence might penetrate into the great provincial cities. The foundation of local Colleges, as he saw, was certain to come; but, if such Colleges were established without direct connexion with the old seats of learning, they would tend to be too provincial in their character, too technical in their studies, and lacking in liberal culture. To avert this danger, Dr. Percival proposed that 'the Universities of Oxford and Cambridge should offer to plant in the chief provincial towns, under certain conditions, branches or faculties, consisting of various Professorships, which should be looked upon as integral parts of the parent University. Each of the wealthier colleges should convert two or more of its non-resident Fellowships into Professorships to be held in some great town such as Birmingham, Bristol, Leeds, Liverpool, &c., provided that the town were willing to comply with the conditions on which they were offered.' He further suggested that ' all students possessing certificates of having attended the required course of instruction under such Professors, and able to pass the ordinary University examinations, should be entitled to a University degree. The degree of B.A. would thus be thrown open to all such students on condition of passing the examinations required of residents, the higher degrees being reserved for those who had completed the usual term of residence within the walls of the University.

To the suggestion that the B.A. degree at Oxford and Cambridge should be thrown open to non-resident students, exception was justly taken at the time. To-day the feeling against such a scheme would be stronger than ever. And rightly so. An essential part of an Oxford or Cambridge education is that which can only be gained by residence at Oxford or Cambridge. The idea, however, that the Universities and the University Colleges of England should in a way be federated, was a bold and statesmanlike plan. But, when he proposed it, Dr. Percival was thirty years before his time. There are signs, however, that by the pressure of affairs, some sort of academic unity, though falling short of acknowledged federation, may be brought about.

But, whatever may be said about some of the details, the general purpose and spirit of Dr. Percival's plan will commend itself to every one who is in sympathy with University Extension work and practically acquainted with the educational needs of the country. There is no doubt that the pamphlet, from which we have quoted, has had a strong influence on the University Extension movement, and that much, which we are accomplishing with difficulty to-day, would have been still impossible had not the public mind been prepared more than twenty years ago by his far-sighted and generous appeals. Dr. Percival saw how much the great towns needed organized opportunities for higher education; how beneficial an influence may be exerted by a body of highly trained teachers in a commercial or industrial community; how much in their turn the national centres of learning and scholarship may gain from contact with the energy and practical sense of men of business and affairs. He foretold how large a part would be borne by the local Colleges and by University Extension teaching in the higher education of women. And experience has proved the truth of his contention that 'the mass of the people in the great towns would welcome with gratitude any prospect of a closer connexion with the old homes of learning,' and that one of the most pressing needs of our time is to spread 'among our commercial population all those higher influences for the sake of which Universities exist.'

THE AMERICAN UNIVERSITY EXTENSION SOCIETY.

FIFTY-TWO courses of lectures are being given this term under the direction of the American University Extension Society, the headquarters of which are in Phi'adelphia. Thirty-two of the centres, at which courses are now in progress, are in Pennsylvania, seven are in New Jersey, two in Delaware, one in Ohio, two in Massachussetts, two in Maryland and one in Virginia. The work of the Society, which occasionally extends to even more distant places, is thus naturally concerned with the Eastern States.

.·.

The courses consist for the most part of six lectures each, though in three cases a smaller number has been permitted. The favourite branch of study—so far as this term's figures go—is Literature, on which twenty-four courses have been arranged. Then follows History with fifteen. Natural Science accounts for four (one on Physiology, one on Botany and two on Astronomy); Economics (including Railway Management and the li'e and Duties of the Citizen) for five: and music for three. The remaining course is on Comparative Religion. We hope that a special report will be made on the musical courses as treating of a subject which has not yet taken its fitting place in University Extension work. The success of the musical section of the Philadelphia Summer Meeting encourages us to think that much will be learnt from the experience of the American Society in this matter. The course on Comparative Religion seems to be an entirely new experiment.

.·.

The *University Extension Bulletin*, the current number of which is the best wh'ch has yet reached us, announces that it and the other organ of the American Society, *University Extension*, will in future be merged in a new journal to be called the *Citizen*. This magazine will carry on the work of the two present papers but will also give space to the discussion of the general problems of civic education. In America, as in England, it is becoming clear that University Extension work, when once undertaken in a vigorous and comprehensive manner, raises questions which necessitate a review of a wide field of public education. If you regard Extension as a mere plaything, as nothing more than a temporary expression of academic benevolence, the work involves no larger questions of educational policy than would the operations of a lecture-agency. The task of finding, training and commissioning Extension lecturers and teachers is indeed a necessary part of the work of Universities if they are to maintain their proper place in the higher education of the modern state. But the business of arranging courses and negotiating with centres, though for their own credit and for the further efficiency of their work it must be as well and accurately done by the Universities as by any commercial agency, is only the preliminary part of their true function in this matter which is, by means of Extension teaching as an instrument, to ascertain the needs of the country in regard to higher instruction, to adapt academic methods to satisfy those needs, to inspire enthusiasm for great ideals in education, and to rally, encourage and support those who in each locality will embody those ideals in practical administration.

.·.

Mr. Hudson Shaw is at present lecturing for the American University Extension Society, and has indeed been enrolled as one of its staff-lecturers—a welcome sign of the unity which marks the work of the American and English branches of the system. He is now giving courses in Philadelphia, Camden, Germantown, Lancaster, Ogontz, Scranton, Wilmington, Brooklyn and Baltimore. The *Bulletin* thus refers to the success of his work :—

The presence in American University Extension centres of an Oxford or Cambridge lecturer is so frequent an occurrence as not to call for special comment, but the extraordinary success of the present mission of W. Hudson Shaw to this country cannot be passed over without remark. Mr. Shaw, in the week closing January 19, reached, we believe, the high-water mark of University Extension attendance in either country during a single week, the number reported being over 4 000. Nearly all of the centres in which he lectured in 18(3 are included in his present circuit, and it is widened to include towns as far distant as Baltimore, Brooklyn and Scranton. Mr. Shaw comes this year, not as a stranger, and not merely as an Oxford lecturer. His enthusiastic and affectionate welcome in every quarter, the tacit assumption that his visit is to be repeated next year, and the next, underlying the selection of courses in the various centres, his appointment as staff-lecturer by the society, and the unprecedented attendance to which attention has been called, are all so many indications that this foremost representative of the Extension platform in England, has been imperatively called upon to consider this country as much his field of labour as the other. Mr. Shaw loses no opportunity to point out that his lectures on the Making of England trace the early stages of our own history no less than that of the other branch of our race, which is called English.

But, delighted as they will be to hear of the enthusiasm which he has aroused, English centres cannot be expected to welcome the news that he may again be absent in America in the Spring Terms of 1896 and 1897.

.·.

The Philadelphia Summer Meeting promises to be as useful and successful a gathering this year as last. Special arrangements are being made for courses on Greek History, Music, Pedagogy, Biology, Political Science and Mathematics. The development of the Summer Meeting into courses of advanced instruction in a group of subjects is one of the distinctive marks of the successful work of the American Society.

.·.

The *Bulletin* contains three other articles of special interest—an account of the Reading University Extension College by its Secretary, Mr. Francis Wright; a summary of the educational advantages of writing the papers set by the lecturers, 'addressed to students by a student,' and by far the best (and the only candid) account which has yet been published of the University Extension movement in Scotland. The last is from the pen of Dr. R. M. Wenley, hon. sec. of the Glasgow University Extension Board.

UNIVERSITY EXTENSION COLLEGE, READING.

THE cordial relations that exist between the College and the neighbouring County Councils promise to become still more intimate. The College has lately entered into a contract with the Technical Instruction Committee of the Oxfordshire County Council to carry out all the instruction in Dairy-work in that county. Arrangements are being made for the classes to begin early in March.

.·.

One of the lecturers on the staff of the Delegacy, Mr. H. N. Dickson, is delivering a course of lectures at the College to agricultural students on Meteorology. This, it is said, is the first attempt that has been made in England to give scientific instruction concerning the weather to the class of persons who are most affected by it.

.·.

A meeting of the members of the French society called 'Gallia' was held in December last, and it was decided to offer three sets of prizes (Junior, Senior and Teachers), amounting to £25, for competition at an examination in practical French, open to all the schools in Reading.

THE DEBATE ON OXFORD RESEARCH DEGREES.

THE statute printed in the January number of the *Extension Gazette* has been the subject of considerable discussion in Oxford during the present term. The usual decorous and formal business of the Congregation of the University has given place to long and animated debates, and the Masters of Arts qualified to vote on the subject have received numerous papers urging them at length to vote for some or other of the sixty-three amendments to the statute that have been proposed. This activity in debate and in writing shows how fully Oxford feels the responsibility of creating this new degree, and affords assurance that not only the principle but the details of it will receive full and careful consideration.

Already on two occasions Congregation has sat for an unusual length of time to discuss the amendments to the statute which have been proposed, and at least one further meeting will be needed to dispose of the remainder; but sufficient progress has been made to show the opinion of the University on most of the points at issue.

The first series of amendments proposed that the new degree should confer the old name of Bachelor of Arts, and not the new one of Bachelor of Letters or Science. In support of this, it was urged that the new name is unnecessary, and the old one being better known would be more valued; but the sense of the University was clearly against any such 'tampering with the time-honoured degree,' and refused to be persuaded by the Provost of Oriel, who proposed the amendment. It was felt too that if the new studies and research formed an alternative course for the B.A. degree, the meaning and value of that degree would be still more confused than it is at present.

Having decided that the new degree should bear a new name, the Congregation was asked to consider how it should be granted. That the encouragement of research and of graduate study is the object the University has in view was accepted by all, but the question how that research is to be tested and approved before the degree is conferred showed some difference of opinion. Professor Holland raised the whole question by proposing to amend the statute by only granting the degree after public examination of the candidate, in addition to the approval of his essay or thesis by persons specially competent to judge its merits. The proposal—keenly discussed—won the favour of Congregation and was carried by the narrow majority of three, apparently on the ground that the University could not trust a board elected by itself to maintain the high standard of work to be required for the degree. It is to be feared that the prospect of examination will deter many and especially older students from coming to Oxford for the purpose of research; and this is particularly to be regretted as we should learn much from the presence of such students residing among us for two years or more.

The keenest discussion was aroused by the question as to what length of residence should be required from candidates for the new degree. Oxford has always strongly resisted any attempts to shorten the period of residence necessary for the degree of B.A., and the statute proposed to require that the student for the new degree should reside in Oxford for the same length of time. Amendments reducing the time to two years were introduced on the ground that, if residence for three years was required, many foreign and especially American students, who can obtain the degree of Ph.D. in one year in Germany, would not come to Oxford. It was urged that as the object of establishing the research degree is largely to attract students from other Universities, we should defeat our object by insisting on anything more than two years' residence. This view was strongly pressed by Mr. Wells and Prof. Poulton. It was pointed out that the coming of non-Oxford students would be a mutual benefit, as we should learn from them probably as much as they from us; further, that the healthy competition of intellect caused by their presence would be of infinite value to the University, and that, therefore, no unnecessary difficulty should be allowed to remain in their way. In spite of the eloquent defence of the three years' residence by the Dean of Christ Church, who spoke strongly of the influence exerted by Oxford life as being of greater value than knowledge, and of Mr. Raleigh, the feeling of Congregation decided by eighty-three votes to twenty-seven in favour of reducing the time of residence to two years, with the view of facilitating the international comity in education so much to be desired.

An interesting point was raised as to the position of the Professors towards the new degree and the research that it is hoped will follow its establishment. The opinion seemed to be general that their present position was anomalous, and that the statute would give them definite and suitable work in the University, especially so 'as the advancement of research is naturally the first work a professor has at heart.' Considerable amusement was created by the few words of a sentence, the latter part of which was inaudible. The speaker believed that much of the work connected with the new degree would be gladly undertaken by the professors, who, as he said, 'at present have absolutely no duties'—the members of Congregation did not allow the concluding words of the sentence to mar the sweeping condemnation of the professoriate—they were drowned by the applause of the professors themselves.

It is interesting to gather together the general impressions of the whole discussion. The University has seriously and honestly committed itself to the encouragement of research by creating the new degree of Bachelor of Letters or Science, with a clear recognition of the difficulties and dangers involved in doing so. Seldom has Congregation shown such sustained interest in any question brought before it, and seldom has any statute been so fully and minutely discussed. Whatever form the statute may finally take, it will go out to the world as the deliberate and carefully considered attempt of the University to solve a difficult problem and to meet a pressing need. It is a sign of healthy life and vigour that at one and the same time Oxford is providing additional facilities for research, and extending its influence over and guidance of elementary and secondary education throughout the country. This new form of University Extension will be heartily welcomed by all who desire to see the Universities the centre of all educational life, whether national or international.

G. N. R.

LECTURES TO CLERGY AT OXFORD, July 15-27, 1895.

[These lectures are open to all Clergy, whether graduates or non-graduates, who belong to the Church of England, or to Churches in Communion with the Church of England.]

THE following arrangements have been made by the Committee, and may be regarded as final, except in so far as additions or alterations may be found inevitable.

I. *Lectures.* The Lectures will, by permission of the Curators, be given in the Examination Schools, High Street, and will begin each morning at 9.45, 11, and 12.15, with an interval of a quarter of an hour between each lecture. There will be one other lecture each day, alternately in the afternoon at 5.30, and in the evening at 8.30. The opening meeting will be held on Monday, July 15, at 8.30, and the last lecture will be given on Saturday, July 27, at 9.30 a.m.

First Week: Morning Lectures.

Dr. Bright, 'Certain periods of Church History' (five lectures—probably); Rev. J. R. Illingworth, 'Christian Ethics' (five lectures); Rev. R. L. Ottley, 'The Messianic Hope, and Belief in a future life, in the Psalms and Prophets' (five lectures).

Second Week: Morning Lectures.

The Bishop of Colombo, 'Christianity and other Religions' (three lectures); The Dean of Christ Church, 'The Pastoral

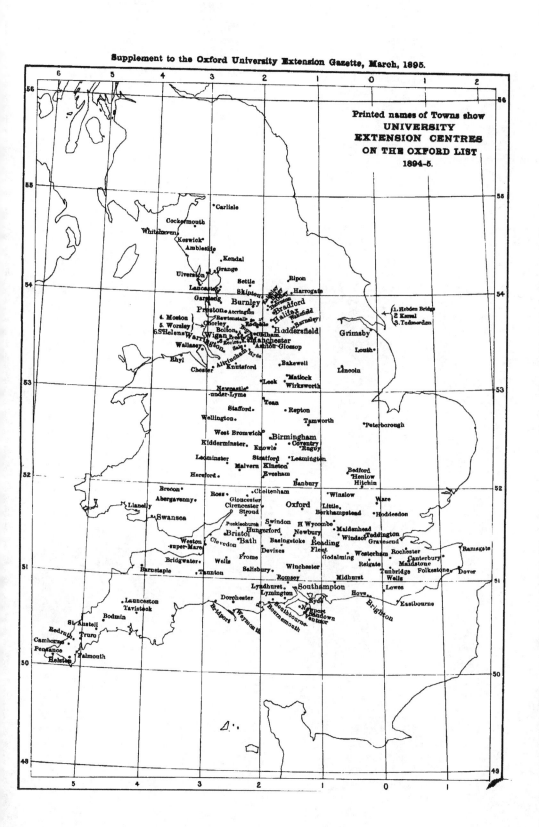

Printed names of Towns show
**UNIVERSITY
EXTENSION CENTRES
ON THE OXFORD LIST
1894-5.**

Epistles' (three lectures); Rev. C. Gore, 'The Atonement' (five lectures); Dr. Sanday, 'The Jewish Background of our Lord's Ministry' (two lectures); Dr. Wace, 'Christian Apologetics' (three lectures).

The following have promised to give one or more lectures, which will be in the afternoon or evening:— Dr. Moore, 'Dante as a Religious Teacher'; Rev. F. J. Chavasse, 'Preaching'; Rev. G. H. Gwilliam, 'The new Syriac Gospels'; Rev. H. C. Shuttleworth, 'Some defects of Clerical delivery and their remedies'; Rev. A. F. Winnington Ingram, 'Parochial Missions'; Rev. A. T. Lyttleton, 'Browning as a Religious Teacher'; Rev. E. Jacob.

The Bishop of London will preach in the morning of Sunday, July 21, and the Bishop of Winchester in the evening.

II. *Accommodation.* Those Clergy who attend may *either* (i) be lodged and boarded at an inclusive charge, without wine, of 5s. a day at Keble College, Wycliffe Hall, or St. Stephen's House. Those who wish for this should communicate with Mr. Bebb, who will reserve rooms in order of application; *or* (ii) apply to the authorities of their own college for the use of rooms, &c., there, *or* (iii) get, through the Secretary, the names and addresses of lodging-house keepers, with whom *all arrangements as to cost, &c., must be made direct, and not through the Secretary.*

III. *Fees.* The fee for attendance at the lectures is £1 for the whole time, or 15s. for either week. This fee should be sent, with the application for a ticket, to the Secretary,

Rev. Ll. J. M. BEBB,
Brasenose College, Oxford.

COUNTY COUNCILS AND UNIVERSITY EXTENSION.

THE following summary has been drawn up for the guidance of University Extension Committees. It is chiefly based on official papers, but in preparing the statement we have received assistance from the excellent *Record* published at quarterly intervals by the National Association for the promotion of Technical and Secondary Education.

I. The following County Councils, and County Borough Councils, have made grants in aid of University Extension teaching during the years 1894-5:—

(a) *County Councils.*

Berkshire.	London.
Cornwall.	Norfolk.
Dorset.	Oxfordshire.
Durham.	Somerset.
Gloucestershire.	Suffolk (West).
Hants.	*Surrey.
Herefordshire.	Warwickshire.
*Kent.	Yorkshire (East Riding).
Lancashire.	Yorkshire (West Riding).
Lincolnshire (Holland).	

* not renewed for 1895.

(b) *County Borough Councils.*

Brighton.	Reading.
Exeter.	Southampton.
Hastings.	West Ham.
Newcastle-on-Tyne.	York.

II. The definition of technical instruction is given in clause 8 of the Technical Instruction Act 1889. It is as follows:—

'The expression "technical instruction" shall mean instruction in the principles of science and art applicable to industries, and in the application of special branches of science and art to specific industries or employments. It shall not include the teaching of the practice of any trade, industry or employment, but, save as aforesaid, shall include instruction in the branches of science and art with respect to which grants are for the time being made by the Department of Science and Art, and any form of instruction (including modern languages and commercial and agricultural subjects) which may for the time being be sanctioned by that Department by a minute laid before Parliament and made on the representation of a local authority that such a form of instruction is required by the circumstances of its district.'

[The Local Taxation (Customs and Excise) Act 1890, clause I (2), enables 'the Council of any County or County Borough to contribute any sum received by the Council (under this act) for the purpose of technical education within the meaning of the Technical Instruction Act 1889.]

III. The following are the branches of Science with respect to which grants are at present made by the Department of Science and Art:—

Practical Plane and Solid Geometry.	Geology.
Machine Construction and Drawing.	Mineralogy.
Building Construction.	Human Physiology.
Naval Architecture.	General Biology.
Mathematics.	Zoology.
Theoretical Mechanics (Solids).	Botany.
Theoretical Mechanics (Fluids).	Principles of Mining.
Applied Mechanics.	Metallurgy.
Sound, Light and Heat (Elementary Stage).	Metallurgy (Practical). Navigation.
Sound (Advanced Stage and Honours).	Nautical Astronomy.
Light.	Steam.
Heat.	Physiography.
Magnetism and Electricity.	Principles of Agriculture.
Inorganic Chemistry.	Hygiene.
Inorganic Chemistry (Practical).	
Organic Chemistry.	
Organic Chemistry (Practical).	

IV. The following are *among* the branches of Art with respect to which grants are at present made by the Department of Science and Art:—

Principles of Ornament.	Historic Ornament.
Design.	Architectural Design.
Architecture.	

V. The following are *among* the subjects which have been sanctioned (as special subjects of technical instruction) on the representation of local authorities that they were required by the circumstances of the respective districts.

[N.B. Minutes of special sanction have been applied for by 43 local authorities, and the number of minutes issued under the Act is now 275. But a minute, issued for one local authority, does not *ipso facto* give sanction to the same subject in all districts.]

Principles of Banking and Financial Science.
Principles of Commerce.
Commercial History.
Economic Science.
Theory and Practice of Kindergarten.
Modern Languages:—
French, German, Spanish, Italian, Portuguese, Norwegian, Swedish, Danish, Russian, Irish.
Political Economy.

VI. Summary of the forms of aid given by County Councils and County Borough Councils to University Extension teaching in 1894 and 1895.

(a) *County Councils.*

Berkshire.—£200 to the University Extension College, Reading.

Cornwall.—£250 for payment of the lecturer's fee for courses of twelve lectures and classes on South Africa arranged at nine centres by local University Extension Committees.

Dorset.—£60 for Scholarships tenable at Oxford Summer Meeting.

Durham.—Aids University Extension lectures up to half the maximum cost.

Gloucershire.—Gives grants in aid of University Extension lectures.

Hants.—£75 to the University Extension College, Reading.

Herefordshire.—Gives aid to University Extension lectures.

Kent.—Employed Oxford University Extension lecturer in 1894. The lecturer having since been appointed to the Wye College (maintained by the County Councils of Kent and Surrey), the grant is not renewed for 1895.

Lancashire.—£500 set aside in 1894 and in 1895 for aid of University Extension teaching.

Lincolnshire (Holland).—Arranges University Extension lectures (£185 in 1891-2).

London.—£250 towards cost of five courses of ten lectures on Chemistry and other kindred subjects (repeated).

Norfolk.—Provides University Extension lectures.

Oxfordshire.—£75 to University Extension College, Reading.

Somerset.—Employed three Oxford University Extension lecturers in 1894-5. Subjects: Hygiene; Soils, Plants and Animals; Veterinary Science.

Suffolk (West).—Has arranged lectures.

Surrey—Same as Kent- see above.

Warwickshire.—Has provided Summer Meeting Scholarships.

Yorkshire East Riding).—£100 for University Extension lectures.

Yorkshire (West Riding).—Aids University Extension work.

(b) *County Borough Councils.*

Brighton.—£50 to the University Extension Committee.

Exeter.—Makes grants to the University Extension College, Exeter.

Hastings.—£40 15s. in aid of University Extension and other lectures.

Newcastle-on-Tyne.—University Extension lectures to be aided.

Reading.—£600 to the University Extension College, Reading.

Southampton.—Grants aid to University Extension lectures.

West Ham.—Estimated expenditure of £400 (1893-4) on University Extension courses.

York.— Grants aid to University Extension lectures.

** This list does not enumerate the towns in which local University Extension Committees in non-County Boroughs have received grants in aid, directly or indirectly, from the Technical Instruction Committee of the County Council. Among these are Accrington (Economics), Barnstaple (Design), Bodmin (English Colonies), Bridport (Economics), Camborne (English Colonies), Falmouth (English Colonies), Garstang (Astronomy), Grange (i. Geology; ii. Architecture), Helston (English Colonies), Launceston (English Colonies), Leominster (Economic History), Penzance (English Colonies), Pucklechurch (Geology), Redruth (Colonies), St. Austell (Colonies), St. Helen's (Geology), Thornton (Science), Truro (Colonies), Tunbridge Wells (Physiography, Hygiene, Commercial History and Economics), Warrington (Commercial History).

VII. Local Committees may find the following references useful :—

Technical Instruction Act 1889 (1d.), Eyre & Spottiswoode, East Harding Street, E.C.

Local Taxation (Customs and Excise) (1d.), Eyre & Spottiswoode, East Harding Street, E.C.

Forty-first Annual Report of the Department of Science and Art, 1894 (1s. 9d.), Eyre & Spottiswoode, East Harding Street.

National Association for promotion of Technical and Secondary Education, 14 Dean's Yard, London, S.W.

SCHOLARSHIP FUND FOR THE OXFORD SUMMER MEETING, 1895.

The Secretary's Scholarship (subscribed by students attending the Summer Meeting, 1894)	.	. £45	0	0
Mr. F. Haverfield, Student and Tutor of Christ Church	.	. 5	0	0
Mr. M. E. Sadler	.	. 10	0	0
Mr. J. Wells, Fellow and Tutor of Wadham	.	. 5	0	0

REPORTS FROM THE CENTRES.

ABERGAVENNY.—At the conclusion of the preliminary readings and before the commencement of Mr. Horsburgh's course of lectures on some of Shakespeare's plays, the ladies of the Students' Association gave a Dramatic Entertainment at the Town Hall. The scenes selected were *Merchant of Venice*, The Trial, Act iv, Scene 1, and *Macbeth*, Act i, Scene 3, Act iii, Sc. 5 and Act iv, Sc. 1, while a tableau of the fairy scene from the *Midsummer Night's Dream* was very prettily represented by children. The mise-en-scène in 'The Merchant' was very good. All the parts were excellently rendered with due dignity, and a clear enunciation which rendered every voice audible throughout the hall. The part of Shylock must be mentioned for the excellence of the make-up, and the histrionic power of the representation. The scenes from *Macbeth* showed the same careful and successful study on the part of the performers, with well-devised dresses and scenic effect. The tableau from ' The Dream,' accompanied by the singing of 'I know a bank,' was but too soon closed. The entertainment concluded with a little operetta entitled *The Spanish Gipsies*. The spectators evidently remembered the successful representation by the students on a former occasion of scenes from *The Princes*, and the hall was crowded in every part, consequently the financial result was highly satisfactory.—H. STFEL, *Hon. Sec.*

BAKEWELL.—The first of a series of three Miscellaneous lectures arranged for the Spring Term by the Students' Association Committee was held on Tuesday, Feb. 5. The lecture on 'Stratford-on-Avon as Shakespeare saw it' was most kindly given by Mr. Kenelm Cotes, who, as editor of the 'Social England Series,' had much to say that was interesting on English social life in Shakespeare's time. Mr. Cotes had also brought an excellent collection of lantern slides, which added greatly to the success of the lecture. In spite of a heavy fall of snow the audience numbered sixty, and a very hearty vote of thanks was passed to Mr. Cotes for his kindness in coming to give such valuable help to the Bakewell Students' Association.

BOLTON.—Considerable interest is taken in the work of the Students' Association here and meetings are held every fortnight. At each meeting a paper is read—usually by some member of the Association. But on Feb. 14, Mr. J. B. Gass, F.R.I.B.A.—a very active worker for University Extension in Bolton—gave to a numerous audience assembled in the Technical School an interesting lecture on Mediaeval Architecture as a supplement to the course recently delivered by Mr. Hudson Shaw.—JAMES MONKS, *Hon. Sec.*

BRIGHTON.—Dr. Mill's first lecture of the course on ' Regions, Races and Resources' was delivered to an audience which, owing to the inclement weather, was smaller than was expected. Prebendary J. J. Hannah presided. The report states that the lecture was full of instruction and interest.

DORCHESTER.—The *Dorset County Chronicle* of January 31 contains a full and detailed report of the first of Mr. Marriott's lectures on the ' Rise and Progress of the English Colonies.' The attendance was most encouraging and promises well for the success of the course. The Rev. J. M. Collard, who presided, briefly introduced the lecturer, and pointed out the usefulness of the Students' Association which has just been formed at this centre.

EVESHAM.—A course of six lectures on the Revolution and the Age of Anne is now being delivered at the Institute by Mr. E. L. S. Horsburgh. The lectures are delivered fortnightly. Mr. Horsburgh's lectures are much appreciated by the audiences, but unfortunately these are somewhat small, and the number of students is disappointing. Last winter Mr. J. A. R. Marriott delivered a course of lectures on ' Cavaliers and Roundheads,' and these were so successful that the Council of the Institute determined to make Extension lectures a fixed part of their programme. This year however the interest in the movement seems to be abated, notwithstanding the efforts of the committee and Mr. Gill Smith (the hard-working Hon. Secretary) to maintain it. Only one paper was written on the subjects submitted to the students after the first lecture, and this, as Mr. Horsburgh pointed out, is very discouraging. An Evesham correspondent suggests that the upper classes in the town should attend the lectures in larger numbers. Evesham contains about six thousand inhabitants, and it is a pity that the young people of the town do not avail themselves to a larger extent of this means of education. We hope to be able to report in our next issue that the state of things has improved.

HEREFORD.—We are glad to learn from the *Hereford Times* that the hon. sec., Miss Bull, was successful in bringing together for the first lecture of Mr. Horsburgh's course the largest attendance that has yet assembled for a University Extension lecture in Hereford. The course is a continuation of that given by Mr. Horsburgh in Hereford last year. Hereford is one of the oldest centres of the Oxford University Extension.

KINETON.—During the Autumn, an interesting course of lectures on 'The Making of the English Empire' was given to the neighbourhood of Kineton. The average attendance was very small, and the number of papers written for the lecturer was very small also; but, taking into consideration that the population of Kineton is only 1,000 and that we are said to be the smallest of all the centres, the local committee do not feel at all disheartened (especially as the Treasurer's accounts show a small balance on the right side), and they propose 'trying again' next Autumn. The course was much appreciated by all who attended, and a hearty vote of thanks was passed to Mr. Cotes at the last afternoon lecture. A Students' Association is now being formed on the lines suggested by the Peterborough Association for the purpose of studying local history in the neighbourhood of Kineton.—HELEN MALCOLM, *Hon. Sec.*

NEATH.—The *South Wales Daily News*, of February 16 last, contains the following account of a lecture delivered in this town with the object of arousing interest in University Extension work, and of establishing a lecture centre at Neath:—'Mr. Kenelm D. Cotes, M.A., University Extension lecturer, delivered a deeply-interesting lecture to a large audience at the Gwyn-hall on Thursday night, on "Stratford-on-Avon in Shakespeare's Time." The mayor of Neath (Councillor Hopkin Morgan) presided. At the close of the lecture it was resolved to establish a University Extension lecture centre at Neath for next autumn, and a committee was appointed.'

PENZANCE.—On January 15 a very successful and interesting Conversazione was given by the members of the Penzance Students' Association. Two gentlemen kindly read papers on African subjects. It may be remembered that the Cornish centres are having an exceedingly able course of lectures from Mr. Worsfold, on 'Africa south of the Zambesi.' Mr. Gros, who read the first paper, started an interesting theory that it is not the bite of the tsetse-fly that causes the death of animals, but something else, say malaria. He argued this from the fact that the tsetse-fly is not harmful to man. The tsetse-fly is found in malarious districts. Malaria is fatal to man—then why not to an animal whose head is nearer the ground, and that drinks water of whatever kind it finds however bad, and therefore ought certainly to be a victim before human beings, who walk erect and prepare their water by boiling, &c. Mr. Norman Garstin, the well-known artist, followed with some remarks on the very early days on the Diamond fields. He described the journey there and the style of living, his narrative being especially interesting, as he was in the same party with the now famous Cecil Rhodes (then a tall lad, rather delicate looking, of seventeen or eighteen) and his brothers. Captain Bates, who was in the Dark Continent this time last year, made some comments on both the foregoing speeches, and spoke in great praise of the climate of Africa. A vote of thanks from Miss Ross, a former President of the Students' Association, to the speakers, seconded by Miss M. B. Borlase, closed the proceedings.—F. M. MARCAUDE, *Hon. Sec.*

RAMSGATE.—The local papers say that the work of the present term has opened well, with a most interesting lecture by Mr. Boas on 'Paradise Lost,' which formed the seventh lecture of the course on the 'Literature of the Cavaliers and Puritans.'

TUNBRIDGE WELLS.—The exceptionally cold weather, with its counter-attraction of skating, has somewhat affected the audiences at both the afternoon and evening lectures this term. Still we have quite a satisfactory attendance at the afternoon course on Architecture, by Mr. Francis Bond, and the subject proves to be a popular one with the students. At the evening lectures, on 'Industrial Problems,' we have so far only had an average attendance of sixty. The working people are very fairly represented, and are evidently interested in the course; but it is disappointing that we cannot get a larger number of people of all classes to listen to teaching on these important social questions, the more so as Mr. Hobson is such an admirable lecturer.

WELLS (Somerset).—We have received from the Hon. Sec., Miss Livett, an interesting report of the work done at this centre during 1894. The following passages occur in the report:—'The Committee are glad to report that 1894 has been a very fairly successful year at this centre. A public meeting was held at the Palace on May 10, when, before a large audience, the Lord Bishop distributed the prizes gained by U. E. students at this centre in January, and Mr. Goodford gave an Address on U. E. work under the County Education Committee. This was one of the last meetings held in Wells by the late Bishop, Lord Arthur Hervey, President of your Committee. He had a strong belief in the possibilities of University Extension, constantly asserting that a systematic course of teaching by qualified University men must be of great benefit to persons unable to go to the University. By liberal donations, by regular attendance and counsel at committee meetings, and by hospitality to lecturers, he proved his readiness to act up to his belief, and to assist the movement here in every possible way.

In this connexion, as in so many others, he wi[ll be] remembered with gratitude. Our present Bishop [held] the office of President, and we look forward with h[....]..ess to his lively interest . . . The term was pleasantly brought to a close on December 18, by an illustrated lecture on the University of Oxford, most kindly given in aid of our funds, by Mr. J. Wells, Member of the Oxford U. E. Delegacy. It was unfortunate that prevalent illness and a very stormy evening prevented many of the students and their friends from hearing a most interesting lecture, which was much appreciated by an audience of about 120. The Committee here record their grateful thanks to Mr. Wells . . . A large number of the audience (obtaining tickets at 2s. 6d.) were teachers in schools, shop assistants, and artisans. This is in itself very satisfactory to the Committee, whose desire it is that all classes should profit by University Extension teaching, and we notice with special pleasure the regular attendance of several paper makers from Wookey Hole. But there is need to remind all our supporters that this class of subscriptions must greatly increase in number, and also be largely supplemented by subscriptions of 5s. and upwards, in order to maintain a sound financial condition, without which this form of Higher Education cannot be carried on. The necessary sum *per annum* would be produced by 350 half-crown tickets! an impossible number from our little city. The committee venture to hope that very many persons more or less wealthy will subscribe for their own benefit or for that of others; and to request that all those whom we may call our 'half-crown friends,' will appear in the lecture-room next autumn, *each accompanied by a new student.*'

WIRKSWORTH.—A course of lectures on 'The Making of England' (Trade, Adventure and Discovery) by Mr. Kenelm D. Cotes, M.A., was commenced at this centre on Jan. 24. After the lecture, which was illustrated by lantern slides, Mr. Cotes took the names of those desirous of joining the Students' Association, which has been formed and will meet alternate weeks with the lectures. As this is virtually a new centre (only one course of Extension lectures having been given here five years ago), the paper-work is not of a high standard, but the students are showing a keen interest in the subject, and there is every reason to believe that the work will improve.—N. GIBBS, *Hon. Sec.*

CO-OPERATORS AND UNIVERSITY EXTENSION.

THE Educational Committee of the Co-operative Union have been considering the best means by which Co-operative Societies may utilize their educational funds. From the *Co-operative News* of Feb. 16 we learn that the Committee, though submitting no definite programme, has made four suggestions. The first is that Co-operative Societies should combine in establishing permanent courses of University Extension lectures. On this point the experience of the Oldham Industrial, the Accrington, and the Hebden Bridge Manufacturing, Co-operative Societies will be found instructive. The second suggestion is that Societies should make grants to enable deserving co-operative students to attend the Summer Meetings at Oxford and Cambridge. The Co-operative Union has itself adopted the plan for several years, and announces further scholarships for competition during the present session. The third and fourth suggestions are the payment of the fees of children of members who desire to attend scientific and technical classes, and the engagement of the best lecturers on social and other subjects more or less allied to co-operative work.

LETTERS TO THE EDITOR.

[*We do not hold ourselves responsible for the opinions expressed by our correspondents.*]

Mr. Wells' Lectures.

AN 'Epsom Student' writes in terms of cordial appreciation of Mr. J. Wells' lecture on Oxford, which he kindly delivered last January at Epsom in aid of the funds of the local University Extension committee; and suggests that, as the invitation to Mr. Wells was made owing to a notice in the *Oxford University Extension Gazette*, all local secretaries should read the *Gazette*— a suggestion we heartily endorse. Mr. Wells' lecture resulted in a welcome addition to the funds of the Local Committee.

.·.

To Correspondents —R. HALSTEAD. Next month.

CHICAGO UNIVERSITY EXTENSION.

THE current number of the *University Extension World* (Chicago) contains a report of the work of the Autumn Quarter 1894 in the University Extension Division of the University of Chicago. Teaching has been carried on in five states—Illinois, Michigan, Indiana, Iowa, Missouri. With more lecturers available for distant service, the field of operations could have been widened. As it is, eighteen lecturers have been engaged, some giving part, some the whole, of their time. In all, sixty-four courses were delivered, nine being in Chicago itself. Sociology, including Economics, heads the list with twenty-nine courses. History presses it hard with twenty-one. English Language and Literature comes third with eleven. Two courses were on Art and one on Geology. The absence of other courses on Natural Science is singular and not explained.

Several lecture-circuits have been formed in neighbouring groups of towns—one comprising eight and three others five centres. Complaint, however, is made of three towns which, though 'to all intents and purposes united,' had three distinct lecturers, each of whom made a special trip of 180 miles to meet his engagements, although one lecturer might have served the three centres, giving three distinct courses.' The electoral campaign, it is stated, disturbed many centres and interrupted educational work.

In several places, the ordinary class (or 'lecture-review' as it is technically called in Chicago) was supplemented by a second meeting for special study. Where the lectures were given at fortnightly intervals, the 'students'-club' often met in the intervening weeks.

The report, which is from the pens of Messrs. F. W. Shepardson and R. N. Miller, is of an encouraging character, and is illustrated by a number of clearly-arranged summaries. The latter, however, so far as they concern the lecture-courses, wou'd be made more complete by the insertion of figures showing the attendance at the lectures.

Perhaps the most satisfactory feature in the report is the table showing the progress of the 'class-study department,' in which the Director of the Chicago University Extension (Professor Butler) takes a special interest. These classes, which are distinct from those held after or in connexion with the lecture-courses, numbered forty-nine, and were attended by 1,156 persons. The average number in each class was twenty-four. Biblical literature, Philosophy and English were the favourite subjects, but the list also comprises Geology, Botany, Zoology and Physiology; Greek, Latin, German and French; Scandinavian Literature; History, Political Economy, Political Science and Mathematics. Fifteen of these classes were held at schools. This valuable development of University Extension teaching will be watched with interest.

Professor R. G. Moulton delivered five courses. In the pages of the *University Extension World* cordial acknowledgment is made of the services rendered by women as local secretaries and of their zeal as students, but no woman's name appears in the list of those who have delivered lectures, though one is recorded as having given class instruction.

DIRECTORY OF SECRETARIES OF STUDENTS' ASSOCIATIONS.

Bakewell.— { Miss KATHLEEN MARTIN, Edensor, Bakewell.
{ Miss EDITH TAYLOR, King Street, Bakewell.

Bolton.— { FRED. WILKINSON, Esq., Technical School, Bolton.
{ JAMES MONKS, 22 Halliwell Street, Great Lever, Bolton.

Bournemouth.—Miss H. BOGUE, Wootton Hill, Bournemouth.

Dorchester.—Miss EMILY HILL, Southfield School, Dorchester.

Harrogate.—Miss VEALE, Roxburgh House, Harrogate.

Oxford.—Mr. E. W. B. MADGE, 49 Walton Street, Oxford.

Reading.—Miss CLARA E. STRACHAN, 6 Carnarvon Road, Reading.

Wells.—Miss T. E. CHURCH, Wells, Somerset.

Weymouth.—Mrs. SAUNDERS, Longhills, Rodwell, Weymouth.
[*Local Secretaries are desired to send addresses to complete this Directory.*]

SCHOLARSHIPS FOR THE OXFORD SUMMER MEETING, 1895.

A FUND, to which subscriptions amounting to £60 have already been promised, has been opened for the provision of Scholarships to enable students from Oxford centres to attend the Summer Meeting, which will be held in Oxford from August 1 to August 26, 1895.

The Scholarships will be awarded after an Essay competition, and will be of two values—£10 and £5. Holders of the former must attend the whole Meeting; those of the latter may, if they prefer, attend either the First or Second Part only. Part I lasts from Aug. 1 to Aug. 12; Part II from Aug. 12 to Aug. 26.

Conditions of Award.

The Scholarships will be awarded on or about July 1, 1895, for English Essays on subjects drawn from English Literature, English History, Natural Science, and Political Economy.

A. *Competition for Scholarships.*

The Scholarships will be awarded in three divisions:—

(*a*) Open to all Oxford University Extension Students *who need the assistance of the Scholarships* in order to study in Oxford, according to the intention of the donors.

(*b*) Open to all Elementary School Teachers (men or women), who are also Oxford University Extension Students.

(*c*) Open to all working men and women, who are also Oxford University Extension Students.

To qualify themselves for election to a Scholarship:—

(1) All competitors must be recommended by their Local Committee as suitable candidates.

(2) Competitors in *divisions* (*a*) and (*b*) must, in order to qualify, obtain *distinction* in an examination on a course of Oxford University Extension Lectures delivered between January 1894 and June 1895.

(3) Competitors in *division* (*c*) must pass an examination on a course of Oxford University Extension Lectures delivered between the same dates.

The Delegates, however, reserve to themselves the right of rejecting the name of any candidate; and, unless compositions of sufficient merit are sent in, do not bind themselves to award Scholarships in any or all of the following four subjects.

B. *Competition for Prizes.*

A limited number of Prizes, of the value of £1, will be awarded in the same competition without any limitation as to the means of the competitors. Candidates for this branch of the competition must qualify as regards examinations, like the competitors in *divisions* (*a*) and (*b*).

SUBJECTS.

(1) *History* (one only to be selected).

(i) The Growth of Nationality in the thirteenth century.

(ii) The causes of the Great Rebellion.

(iii) England's command of the Sea during the Revolutionary Wars (1793–1815).

(2) *Literature* (one only to be selected).

(i) How far is it possible to specify any general conditions which are necessary to the production of the best poetry?

(ii) Explain what is meant by Poetic Justice, and consider with full illustrations how far it should be observed in Drama or Fiction.

(iii) Estimate the importance in literary history of the works of Dryden, Pope, or Walter Scott.

(3) *Political Economy* (one only to be selected).

(i) Show the effect of different systems of land tenure on the production and distribution of wealth.

(ii) What remedies have been suggested for the existing depression, and how far are they likely to succeed?

(iii) What circumstances may be expected to determine the wages of labour in the future?

(4) *Science* (one only to be selected).

(i) Theories of Chemical Action.

(ii) Sewage disposal in towns and rural districts.

(iii) The Weeds of the Farm.

REGULATIONS.

1. Each candidate may write an essay *on one subject only*, but may select one from any of the above four groups.

2. All compositions must reach the Delegacy [addressed—The Secretary, University Extension Office, Examination Schools, Oxford] on or before Monday, June 3, 1895; must each bear the writer's full name and address, with a note saying whether the writer is competing for a Scholarship or a Prize, or both, and, if the former, in which division (*a, b,* or *c,* see above); must be written on foolscap paper, and on one side of the paper only; must state, at the top of the first page, the writer's occupation; and must be accompanied by a certificate of qualification from his or her Local Committee in the following form :—

'On behalf of the members of the Local Committee acting in concert with the Oxford University Delegates for the establishment of Lectures and Teaching at   , I certify that *A. B.* is in all respects a suitable person for election to a University Extension   [1], according to the regulations.

Signed on behalf of the Committee,

....
Secretary.[2]

3. Candidates are not debarred from the consultation of standard works, but quotations should be notified in the margin,

[1] *State whether Scholarship or Prize, or both.*

and borrowed passages should be clearly distinguished from the rest.

4. No composition should exceed thirty foolscap pages, including a brief analysis which should be prefixed to the essay.

5. The names of the unsuccessful competitors will not be divulged by the Delegates, and all compositions may be obtained from them after the announcement of the result of the competition.

6. Successful candidates will be informed by the Delegacy of the result of the competition.

7. The students elected to the Scholarships will be required to visit Oxford during the Summer Meeting of University Extension Students, 1895.

8. Holders of Scholarships of £10 are required to reside in Oxford during the whole Meeting. If they are unable to do so, they must resign half their Scholarship, retaining, however, the position on the list of scholars to which the excellence of their essay entitled them.

9. The Programme of the Summer Meeting will be published at Easter, and copies (7*d.* each post free) can then be obtained on application to the Secretary, University Extension Office, Oxford.

Contributions to the Scholarship fund should be sent to the Secretary, University Extension Office, Oxford.

Copies of the above regulations can be obtained free of charge on application to the Secretary, University Extension Office, Oxford.

ARRANGEMENTS FOR SPRING, 1895.

All lectures are at fortnightly intervals except where otherwise stated.

Centre.	No. of Lectures in Course.	Subject of Course.	Lecturer.	Course or Half-Course begins.	Course ends.
†UNIVERSITY EXTENSION COLLEGE, READING (evening)	12	Age of Elizabeth and Puritan Rebellion }	Rev.W.H.SHAW,M.A. & E.L.S.HORSBURGH,M.A.	Th. Jan. 17	Mar. 28
,, (afternoon)	12	Tennyson and Browning	J.CHURTONCOLLINS,M.A	S. Jan. 26	Apr. 6
,, (evening) ...	12	Greek Drama	,, ,,	S. Jan. 26	Apr 6
,, (evening) ...	12	The Study of Local History ...	W. M. CHILDS, B.A ...	F. Jan 25	Apr. 5
,, (evening) ...	12	La Littérature Française du XVII* Siècle	M. J. MAURICE REY, B. es Sc.	W. Jan. 23	Apr. 3
,, (evening) ...	12	Geography of the British Isles ...	H. J. MACKINDER, M.A.	S. Jan. 19	Mar. 30
†BIRMINGHAM, EDGBASTON (afternoon)	12	Age of Louis XIV and French Revolution	J.A.R.MARRIOTT, M.A.	T. Jan. 15	Mar. 26
BIRMINGHAM, Severn Street (evening)	6	English Colonies	,, ,, ...	T. Jan. 15	Mar. 26
†BOURNEMOUTH (afternoon) ...	12	Europe since Waterloo	,, ,, ...	W. Jan. 23	Apr. 3
BRADFORD (evening) ...	6	Colonies	,, ,, ...	Th. Jan. 17	Mar. 28
†BRIDPORT (evening)	12	Industrial Revolution	,, ,, ...	T. Jan. 22	Apr. 2
†CLEVEDON (afternoon) ...	12	Shakespeare's Historical Plays ...	,, ,, ...	F. Jan. 25	Apr. 5
DORCHESTER (evening) ...	6	Colonies	,, ,, ...	W. Jan. 23	Apr. 3
OXFORD (evening)	6	The Renaissance and Reformation in England	,, ,, ...	F. Jan. 18	Mar. 29
SALE (evening)	6	England in the 18th Century ...	,, ,, ...	W. Jan. 16	Mar. 27
†SOUTHBOURNE (afternoon) ...	12	Europe since Waterloo	,, ,, ...	Th. Jan. 24	Apr. 4
WEYMOUTH (evening) ...	6	Age of Louis XIV	,, ,, ...	T. Jan. 22	Apr. 2
†TAMWORTH (evening) ...	10	England in the 18th Century ...	C. E. MALLET, B.A. ...	T. Jan. 15	Feb. 26
FOLKESTONE (evening, weekly)	10	England in the 18th Century ...	,, ,,	M. Jan. 28	Apr. 1
WHITEHAVEN (evening)	6	England in the 18th Century ...	,, ,, ...	W. Jan. 16	Mar. 27
†BURNLEY (evening)	12	Spenser & other Elizabethan Poets	F. S. BOAS, M.A. ...	Th. Jan. 24	Apr. 4
†CANTERBURY (afternoon) ...	12	Victorian Poets	,, ,, ...	Th. Jan. 17	Mar. 28
†RAMSGATE (afternoon) ...	12	Literature of Cavaliers and Puritans	,, ,, ...	S. Jan. 26	Apr. 6
DEVIZES (evening)	6	Tennyson	Rev. J. G. BAILEY, M.A., LL.D.	Th. Feb. 7	Apr. 18
†WEST BRIGHTON (afternoon)	12	Tennyson	,, ,, ...	F. Jan. 18	Mar. 29
ABERGAVENNY (afternoon) ...	6	Shakespeare	E.L.S.HORSBURGH,B.A.	S. Jan. 26	Apr. 6
BRECON (afternoon)	6	Literature of the 18th Century ...	,, ,, ...	Th. Jan. 24	Apr. 4
BRECON (evening)	6	Epochs from English History ...	,, ,, ...	Th. Jan. 24	Apr. 4
CHELTENHAM (afternoon) ...	6	Growth of Parliament	,, ,, ...	W. Jan. 30	Apr. 10
CHELTENHAM (evening)	6	Industrial and Economic Questions since 1789	,, ,, ...	W. Jan. 30	Apr. 10
EVESHAM (evening)	6	Revolution and Age of Anne ...	,, ,, ...	W. Jan. 23	Apr. 3
GLOUCESTER (evening) ...	6	English History in Shakespeare...	,, ,, ...	M. Jan. 28	Apr. 8
HEREFORD (evening)	6	Wyclif to Sir Thomas More ...	,, ,, ...	M. Jan. 21	Apr. 1
LEOMINSTER (evening) ...	6	Industrial and Economic Questions since 1789	,, ,, ...	T. Jan. 22	Apr. 2
MALVERN (afternoon) ...	12	Puritan Revolution	,, ,, ...	W. Jan. 23	Apr. 3
†REIGATE (afternoon)... ...	6	The Reign of Elizabeth	,, ,, ...	Th. Jan. 17	Mar. 28

† The figures in the second column include the lectures given in the Autumn Term, from which these courses are continued.

Centre.	No. of Lectures in Course.	Subject of Course.	Lecturer.	Course or Half-Course begins.	Course ends.
Ross (afternoon)	6	Literature of the 18th Century ..	E. L. S. Horsburgh, B.A.	T. Jan. 22	Apr. 2
†Southampton (evening) ...	12	The Age of Elizabeth	„ „ ...	F. Jan. 18	May 29
Stroud (afternoon)	6	The Renaissance	„ „ ...	T. Jan. 29	Apr. 9
Stroud (evening)	6	The Reign of Elizabeth ...	„ „ ...	T. Jan. 29	Apr. 9
Swansea (evening)	6	Epochs from English History ...	„ „ ...	F. Jan. 25	Apr. 5
Dover (afternoon)	6	Architecture	F. Bond, M.A.	M. Jan. 28	Apr. 8
Dover (evening)	6	Architecture	„ „ ...	M. Jan. 28	Apr. 8
Tunbridge Wells (afternoon, weekly)	10	Architecture	„ „ ...	F. Jan. 25	Mar. 29
Fleet (afternoon)	8	Chaucer to Bacon	R. Warwick Bond, M.A.	Th. Jan. 24	Apr. 25
†Henlow (evening)	12	The English Citizen	W. M. Childs, B.A....	W. Jan. 16	Mar. 27
Glossop (evening)	6	Trade, Adventure, and Discovery	K. D. Cotes, M.A. ...	W. Jan. 23	Apr. 3
Warrington (evening) ...	6	Trade, Invention, and Discovery	„ „ ...	F. Jan. 25	Apr. 5
Wirksworth (evening) ...	6	Trade, Adventure, and Discovery	„ „ ...	Th. Jan. 24	Apr. 4
Tavistock (afternoon) ...	6	Puritan Revolution	W. G. de Burgh, B.A.	M. Jan. 28	Apr. 8
Frome (afternoon)	6	Wordsworth, Coleridge, and Scott	„ „ ...	T. Jan. 29	Apr. 9
†West Brighton (evening) ...	12	Three Centuries of Working-class History	W. A. S. Hewins, M.A.	Th. Jan. 24	Apr. 18
Grimsby (evening)	6	Problems of Poverty	J. A. Hobson, M.A. ...	T. Jan. 22	Apr. 2
Midhurst (afternoon) ...	6	English Novelists ... • ...	„ „ ...	W. Jan. 16	Mar. 27
Tunbridge Wells (evening) ...	6	Industrial Questions of the Day ...	„ „ ...	W. Jan. 23	Apr. 3
†Carlisle (afternoon) ...	12	Architecture	J. E. Phythian	T. Jan. 15	Apr. 9
Chester (afternoon)	6	Architecture	„ „ ...	T. Jan. 22	Apr. 2
Halifax (evening)	6	Florentine Art	„ „ ...	Th. Jan. 24	Mar. 28
Kersal (evening, weekly) ...	8	Architecture	„ „ ...	M. Jan. 28	Mar. 18
†Bodmin (evening)	12	South Africa	W. B. Worsfold, M.A.	F. Jan. 25	Apr. 5
†Camborne (evening)... ...	12	South Africa	„ „ ...	F. Jan. 18	Mar. 29
†Falmouth (evening) ...	12	South Africa	„ „ ...	Th. Jan. 17	Mar. 28
†Helston (evening)	12	South Africa	„ „ ...	T. Jan. 22	Apr. 2
†Launceston (evening) ...	12	South Africa	„ „ ...	W. Jan. 16	Mar. 27
†Penzance (evening)	12	South Africa	„ „ ...	M. Jan. 21	Apr. 1
†Redruth (evening)	12	South Africa	„ „ ...	Th. Jan. 24	Apr. 4
†St. Austell (evening) ...	12	South Africa	„ „ ...	T. Jan. 15	Mar. 26
†Truro (evening)	12	South Africa	„ „ ...	M. Jan. 14	Mar. 25
Lewes (evening)	6	Physiography	G. J. Burch, M.A. ...	M. Jan. 21	Apr. 1
Brighton (St. Michael's Hall) (afternoon)	6	Regions, Races, and Resources ...	H. R. Mill, D.Sc. ...	Th. Jan. 31	Apr. 4
Brighton (evening)	6	Regions, Races, and Resources ...	„ „ ...	Th. Jan. 31	Apr. 4
†Carlisle (evening)	12	Outlines of Geology	C. Carus-Wilson, F.G.S.	Th. Jan. 24	Apr. 4
†St. Helens (evening) ...	12	Crust of the Earth	„ „ ...	Th. Jan. 31	Apr. 3
†Bath (afternoon)	12	Recent Discoveries with the Telescope and Spectroscope	A. H. Fison, D.Sc. ...	Th. Jan. 31	Apr. 11
†Bath (evening)	12	Recent Discoveries with the Telescope and Spectroscope	„ „ ...	Th. Jan. 31	Apr. 11
Bedford (evening)	6	Life of a Planet	„ „ ...	T. Jan. 29	Apr. 9
†Bournemouth (evening) ...	6	Forces of Nature	„ „ ...	F. Jan. 18	Mar. 29
Leamington (evening) ...	12	Life of a Planet	„ „ ...	T. Feb. 5	Apr. 16
†Ryde (afternoon)	12	Recent Discoveries with the Telescope and Spectroscope	„ „ ...	Th. Jan. 24	Apr. 4
Sandown (afternoon)... ...	6	Recent Discoveries with the Telescope and Spectroscope	„ „ ...	F. Jan. 25	Apr. 5
†Ventnor (evening)	12	Physical Astronomy	„ „ ...	F. Jan. 25	Apr. 5
Greek Classes (afternoon, weekly) :					
Brighton (Elementary)	10	Xen. *Anab.* I: Eurip. *Alc.* (scenes from)	Rev. E. Luce, M.A. ...	T. Jan. 29	Apr. 2
„ (Intermediate)	10	Thucyd. VII and Soph. *Ajax* ...	„ „ ...	W. Jan. 30	Apr. 3
Somerset County Council :					
5 Courses of	12	{ Prevention of Disease among Animals { Physiology of Domestic Animals }	H. Sessions	Jan.	Apr.
5 Courses of	12	Hygiene	C. H. Wade, M.A., D.P.H.	Jan.	Apr.
Kent County Council :					
2 Courses of	12	Chemistry	H. H. Cousins, M.A.	Jan.	Apr.

Summer Term, 1895.

Brighton (St. Michael's Hall)	6 or 8	England in the 18th Century ...	J. A. R. Marriott, M.A.	Not fixed	Not fixed

† The figures in the second column include the lectures given in the Autumn Term, from which these courses are continued.

Note.—Application for Courses and all information as to fees, &c., can be obtained from The Secretary, University Extension Office, Examination Schools, Oxford.

INFORMATION TO CONTRIBUTORS.

All communications should be addressed to the Editor, Oxford University Extension Gazette, *University Press, Oxford.*

All matter intended for insertion in the April issue should reach him not later than March 20.

Contributions should be written on one side of the paper only, and must be accompanied by the name of the writer (not necessarily for publication).

N.B.—*All orders should carefully specify the full title,* Oxford University Extension Gazette.

OXFORD UNIVERSITY

EXTENSION GAZETTE.

VOL. V. NO. 55.]   APRIL, 1895.   [ONE PENNY.

N.B.—Local Organizers of Oxford University Extension Lectures are invited to send to the Secretary, University Extension Office, Examination Schools, Oxford, copies of any journals containing notices of, or references to, Extension work.

NOTES AND COMMENTS.

On March 5 last, Convocation of the University of Oxford passed *nem. con.* through its final stage the Statute which removes the present geographical limitation to the work of the University Extension Delegacy. The Delegates may now superintend courses beyond the limits of England and Wales. It is unlikely, however, that there will—at first at all events—be frequent occasion for the use of these extended powers; and, in organizing any course in a foreign country, the Delegates will naturally seek to act with the approval of the neighbouring University.

．·．

It is hoped that local committees will pardon some unavoidable delay in the arrangement of the lecturers' programmes for next session. Committees were asked to send in their invitations by an early date in order that they might be considered by Mr. Sadler before his resignation of the Secretaryship on March 25. Mr. Marrriott, however, is prevented by his lecture engagements from being regularly at the Office till towards the end of April. The result is that the programmes cannot be finally arranged till the beginning of May, but it is hoped that in the intervening period much may be done to arrange the lecturer's work in harmony with the convenience of the centres.

．·．

From several communications recently received it seems that the intimation in the 'Green File' with regard to Mr. Marriott's position on the list of lecturers is not clearly understood. In consequence of his appointment as Secretary to the Delegates, Mr. Marriott will unfortunately be compelled to withdraw from the list of 'active' lecturers. But it is hoped that he will still be able to accept a very limited number of invitations from centres where there exist special reasons for his presence.

．·．

There appears to be some uncertainty as to the position which in future Mr. Horsburgh will occupy as regards centres of University Extension teaching, within and without his appointed Directorial District. It is well, therefore, to make it clear that Mr. Horsburgh will still be able to accept invitations to lecture in any district. His appointment will not preclude him from accepting invitations from centres outside his immediate district; still less will it preclude him from accepting invitations within his district. A memorandum drawn up conjointly by Mr. Wells and Mr. Horsburgh will shortly be issued to all centres within their respective districts.

．·．

Outline programmes of the Oxford Summer Meeting, 1895, can now be obtained, post free, from the Secretary, University Extension Office, Oxford. The courses will be as follows : (1) The History, Literature, Art and Economics of the Eighteenth Century (to 1789); (2) Lectures on the Science and Art of Education; (3) the Philosophy of Plato, with some reference to the philosophical work of the Eighteenth Century; (4) the History of Architecture, with special reference to the buildings of Oxford and its neighbourhood; (5) Economics; (6) Chemistry; (7) Geology; (8) Botany; (9) Hygiene, with excursion; (10) the Greek Language.

Parties of University Extension students, making application before May 1, will be able to obtain the same reduced terms for tickets as were offered last year, viz. five tickets for Part I for £4 10s.   *Summer Meeting Tickets.*

．·．

University Extension, in its broader sense, finds ideal representation in the Proctors for the year 1895-6, as the Senior Proctor, Mr. P. E. Matheson, is Secretary of the Delegacy for the Inspection and Examination of Schools, and the Junior Proctor, Mr. H. T. Gerrans (junior to Mr. Matheson by about five minutes of academic existence), is Secretary of the Delegacy of Local Examinations.

．·．

Mr. Francis Gotch, who was at one time an Oxford University Extension lecturer, has been appointed Waynflete Professor of Physiology in the University of Oxford.

．·．

Mr. M. E. Sadler, late Secretary of the Oxford University Extension Delegacy, has been appointed by the University to be a perpetual member of the Delegacy.

．·．

The Delegates have decided that the courses of lectures delivered under their auspices shall in future be classified in two departments, namely those on which certificates are awarded, and those on which no certificates are given.

．·．

The recent appointment of Directors of University Extension teaching in two districts of England will facilitate the combination and co-operation of local centres, and go far to prevent the waste of energy and money which have so long resulted from the want of local supervision. At the same time it is not intended that the Directors shall in the least interfere with the freedom of the local committees to make arrangements with any University according to their educational needs. This perfect freedom of choice on the part of the centres has been formally approved by the Delegacy at various times, and at the last meeting a resolution was unanimously passed by the Delegates re-affirming, in regard to the newly-appointed Directors, the principle which has hitherto guided their policy. In this way it is hoped that the advantages of central supervision and local independence may be combined, and lead to the better organization of lecture circuits.   *The new Directorships and the freedom of the Centres.*

．·．

No development of University work in England has been more remarkable in the last few years than the expansion of the Oxford Local Examinations during the Secretaryship of Mr. H. T. Gerrans. It is well known that the system of Local Examination, adopted by the University of Oxford at the instance of Sir Thomas Acland and the present Bishop of London, was first tried by the

College of Preceptors, and the article, which we publish in this number from the pen of Mr. J. S. Thornton, will therefore prove of special interest to those who have studied the origins of the University Extension movement.

.˙.

Influenza has been rife among the lecturers on the Oxford staff. Mr. Mackinder, Dr. Bailey, Mr. Hobson, Mr. Burch, and Mr. Cotes have all been on the sick list. Mr. Hobson for a day or two was very seriously ill, but we are glad to say that he is now better.

.˙.

The number of Oxford University Extension courses delivered, since the revival of the work in 1885, is 1673.

.˙.

University Extension College, Reading. The Board of Agriculture have made to the College a grant of £500 for the present financial year. The grant made to the College for the preceding year was £150. This substantial increase in the grant will be regarded as a signal mark of the Board's approval of the provision which has been made at Reading for the teaching of agriculture.

.˙.

A correspondent sends us the following note :—'The Association for the Education of Women in Oxford has been this term discussing the question of Degrees. It is suggested that since all University Examinations are now open to women, they should also be admitted to the B.A. Degree. A meeting of women interested in the question was held on February 19; and next term there is to be a meeting of the whole Association, which consists of all those connected with Women's Education in Oxford, as well as of former students. At the preliminary meeting no formal vote was taken. The chief speakers were Miss Maitland (Principal of Somerville College), Mrs. A. Johnson (former Secretary of the Association), Miss Soulsby (Head-mistress of the Girls' High School), and Miss Rogers (present Secretary of the Association). The discussion showed spirit and interest; most of the speakers thought that the Degree would be ultimately inevitable; but some opposed it on the ground that, in accepting the Degree, women would give up much of their present freedom as regards residence and choice of study. It was urged on the other hand that the present confusion is a real disadvantage to Oxford students; there is great variety in their work— some take special Women's Examinations; some omit an Intermediate Examination; others omit a Final School, and so on. Even if this variety is advisable, there should be some way of distinguishing a student who has followed any complete University course, but who is practically often ranked lower than a B.A. of another University. The question will be more fully discussed at the General Meeting on May 4; as it is important to ascertain the opinions of all those concerned in the work of women's education.'

.˙.

The Rev. C. W. Boase, who died in his rooms in Exeter College on March 11, will be widely mourned. Few men have done more to awaken interest in the history of Oxford, and to vindicate the claims of poor scholars.

.˙.

The late Lord Aberdare was intimately and honourably connected with the Welsh educational movement, which has deeply influenced educational opinion in England. He served as chairman of the Departmental Committee on intermediate and higher education in Wales, the report of which, presented in 1881, was the basis of the Welsh Intermediate Education Act. The work of this Committee did much to stimulate the movement which led to the establishment of the University Colleges at Bangor and Cardiff. In the foundation of the new University of Wales Lord Aberdare also took a prominent part. His services, given without stint at a critical period in the history of Welsh education, will be remembered with gratitude. And in Oxford, where he was well known, his name will long be held in honour as one of the pioneers of the University movement which has played an important part in British education during the last quarter of a century.

.˙.

The late Mr. Alfred Robinson's work for University Extension. It is right that these columns should contain a brief record of the special services rendered to University Extension by the late Mr. Alfred Robinson, whose death we lamented in our last issue. One result of the work of the Schools Inquiry Commission was to create a feeling in favour of some organized test of the work of the great Secondary Schools in England. For a time it appeared as if the State would have to undertake this needful but difficult task. We owe it, however, to the statesmanship of Oxford and Cambridge that the two ancient Universities stepped into the gap and undertook a duty for which their experience and prestige preeminently fitted them. Of the Delegacy appointed at Oxford to carry out this purpose, Mr. Robinson was one of the original members, and at its first meeting, held on May 22, 1873, Mr. Robinson was elected to be its Secretary. Among the members of the Delegacy present at this historic meeting were Dean Liddell of Christ Church (then Vice-Chancellor and, consequently, chairman), Professor Jowett (Master of Balliol), Archdeacon Palmer and Mr. Kitchin (now Dean of Durham), Professor Henry Smith and Thorold Rogers and Mr. Thorley (now Warden of Wadham). In the same year the Oxford Delegacy co-operated with the corresponding Cambridge Syndicate in the formation of the Joint Board—which, as an examining and advisory agency, has ever since rendered most valuable service to the higher secondary education of the country. Its present Secretary, Mr. Matheson of New College, is Senior Proctor for the current year and a member of the University Extension Delegacy. In 1876 Balliol and New Colleges (Mr. Alfred Robinson being Bursar of the latter society) joined in making a grant of £300 a year towards the establishment and maintenance of University College, Bristol—a step which probably had some connexion with the efforts of Dr. Percival recorded in the March *Gazette*. In later years, Mr. Robinson was a member of the Local Examination Delegacy and was appointed a member of the Committee to which that Delegacy entrusted in 1885 the oversight of University Extension teaching. From that time to the month of his death, he took a constant interest in our work, helping it liberally by his influence and by his contributions to our funds, and acting as auditor of its accounts and, though he ceased to be a member of the new University Extension Delegacy shortly after its formation, never failing to give us assistance whenever we needed it. Our movement never had a truer friend.

.˙.

Victoria University Extension. Nineteen courses of Extension lectures are being delivered during the present session in connexion with the Victoria University. The length of these courses varies from six to twenty-four lectures, the average being slightly above nine. Among the courses are three on literature, three on history, one on economics, two on astronomy, three on chemistry, two on geology, and four on biology. Twelve lecturers are engaged in the work, one being a woman. The attendance, which is recorded in the case of fifteen courses, amounts to 1710, or an average of 114. In addition to the above courses, twenty-one pioneer lectures have been given at five centres. The following courses have also been delivered under arrangements with the County Councils of the North, East and West Ridings of Yorkshire—six on coal-mining, twenty on agricultural subjects, and three on sanitary science, as well as twenty-eight pioneer lectures on the latter subject. In this, the technical, department of the Victoria University Extension, eight lecturers have been employed and the total number of lectures delivered is 311. Thus the aggregate of lectures which have been given during this session under the auspices of the Victoria University is 532—a record which presages the increasing success in the future of this important branch of the University Extension movement.

.˙.

The National Union of Teachers are contemplating the establishment of a system of Local Examinations for elder scholars in primary schools. It is thought that the gradual abolition of the examinations hitherto conducted by the Government inspectors in elementary schools will cause a demand for some other test for the elder pupils, who may further be induced to remain at school, after the exemption standard is passed, if opportunity is afforded to them of obtaining in a non-competitive examination, proof of their intellectual attainments.

.˙.

Those who are interested in the proposal to place primary school-teachers on a civil service footing, which has been raised by the recent report of the Archbishops' Committee (and the scheme has its bearing on the interests of every branch of the teaching profession), will find in the *Schoolmaster* for March 23, a very able memorandum on the subject from the pen of Mr. Yoxall, General Secretary of the National Union of Teachers.

.˙.

The Wells Town Council and University Extension. The *Wells Journal* of March 7, in its report of the meeting of the Town Council, contains the following paragraph relating to University Extension :—

Miss Livett (Hon. Sec. of the University Extension Committee), in sending a copy of the report for 1894, and applying for a continuance of the grant of £5 5s., stated that this grant had enabled the committee to offer tickets for the English History lectures at half-price to assistant teachers in schools, shop-assistants, artisans, and boys and girls under eighteen years of age; and to give a certain number of persons of these classes free admission. She was glad to say that fifteen assistant teachers, nineteen shop-assistants and artisans, and about thirteen boys and girls availed themselves of these facilities. Alderman Harte proposed that the grant be continued. Alderman Slater seconded the proposal, and remarked that Miss Livett's report was very encouraging. The grant would be money well spent, as it would give assistance in the education of those who otherwise could not afford to attend the lectures. The motion was carried.

.˙.

Edinburgh Summer Meeting. The ninth session of the Edinburgh Summer Meeting is arranged to take place in August. In the section of Philosophy, Social Science and Anthropology the list of lecturers includes the names of Professor Geddes, Mr. William Sharp, M. Demolins, Editor of the *Science Sociale*, Dr. Wenley, Dr. Delius, and others. There will also be lectures on History, Literature and Language; while the Social and Natural Sciences will not be overlooked; Civics, Hygiene, Geography and Biology have each a fair share of attention. Amongst the many other features of interest, a series of Educational Conferences will, it is hoped, be especially useful to those who are engaged in educational work.

.˙.

The Brussels Conference on University Extension. In the *Revue Universitaire* for Feb. 15 (Brussels, H. Lamertin, 20 Rue du Marché-au-Bois), there is a full report of the Brussels Congress on University Extension. Mr. Mackinder's speeches, which were delivered in French, are printed in full. As it has been alleged in Belgium that the sole aim of the movement is to promote an educational propaganda among working men, he did well, in the course of one of his addresses, to remove this misconception by the following words, which were received with significant applause : 'L'Extension Universitaire s'adresse au peuple tout entier et non pas aux seuls ouvriers. Elle est utile à la petite bourgeoisie, aux dames, à tous ceux qui n'ont pu suivre les cours des universités.'

Some University Extension students may be glad to hear that a holiday course for the study of the French language will be held at Caen from April 15-27. There will be an elementary as well as an advanced course. The French language will itself be taken as the medium of instruction. In the elementary course there will be a daily lesson of one and a half hours, and each class in it will be limited to fifteen members, all of whom will be expected to take their part in question and answer. The fee for either course is 30s., or for both courses together 50s. The arrangements are in the hands of a Committee, which comprises the names of Miss Dodd of Owens College, Dr. Findlay of the Secondary Training College, Mr. R. A. Jones of Queen's College, Oxford, and Mr. J. W. Richards (the Grammar School, Stoke Newington, London, N.), to the last-named of whom correspondence about the Caen courses should be addressed. **Easter holiday course for Teachers at Caen.**

.˙.

There are 119 Universities in the world. Dr. Kukula in his list names 114, but he omits the Universities of London, of Paris, of the State of New York and of Wales and the New University of Brussels. Excluding the first three which, being of the Napoleonic type, have no resident students, the undergraduate population of the Universities of the world is estimated by this academic statistician as amounting to 157,513 persons. Berlin is the most populous University, Urbino the smallest. The first has 7,771 students, the latter only 74. In point of numbers Oxford comes tenth on the list; Cambridge, twelfth; Victoria, sixty-fourth, and Durham ninety-eighth. **The roll of Universities.**

.˙.

The first number of the *Citizen*, the new journal of the American University Extension Society, has reached us— and we give it a hearty welcome. The motto is as follows : 'University Extension is for the people. It aims, through instruction by University men, to make life more interesting and enjoyable; to awaken a sense of responsibility; and to encourage habits of sound thinking and right conduct.' The *Citizen* carries on the work of the *Bulletin* and of *University Extension*, both of which it replaces. While preserving the chief features of those journals, it spreads its net more widely than before. It is to be an educational paper rather than the organ of one educational organization.

.˙.

The first number redeems the promise of its editors by publishing articles on the establishment of free public libraries, on the improvement of the educational system of Pennsylvania, on the Massachusetts Library Commission, and on the 'New departure in English Education,' as well as University Extension news and announcements. It refers in cordial terms to the appointment of Professor York Powell and of Mr. Sadler, and to the movement for giving research degrees in the University of Oxford. We cannot do better than echo the greeting from Mr. Hudson Shaw (so close are the ties attaching the American to the English movement for University Extension) which appears in its columns :

'I send you greeting from all English friends of the University Extension movement, and hearty congratulations for the *Citizen*, name and thing both. It promises to do what many of us have long desired, to preach University Extension in its widest sense as a system of adult education for the whole people. More and more as the years go on, one sees that the ultimate aim of the movement, and its greatest opportunity, is to train good citizens, to extend high ideals from the few to the many, to aid England and America in the great task which has been entrusted to them jointly of forming what the world has never yet seen—a true, cultured, educated democracy. It should be our work, as Matthew Arnold urged, to make accessible to the whole body of our fellow-citizens "the best that can be known in the world, to come as near as we can to the firm, intelligible law of things, and thus to get a basis for a less confused action and a more complete perfection."

'The *Citizen*, therefore, I hope, will stand for social progress.

2

It will not limit itself, I understand, to the technical details of Extension work, but will appeal to all who desire for men and women of the English stock clearer thinking, sounder opinions, higher ethics, fuller and nobler life. To-day Europe and America are confronted by complex, vital social problems, and the Sphinx of Destiny demands that we solve her riddle or perish. Religion and education, these, I believe, and these alone, can save us from strife and anarchy.'

.˙.

Lady Verney has kindly presented to the University Extension Library a beautifully bound copy of the third volume of *Memoirs of the Verney Family.* The first two volumes of the *Memoirs* formed an earlier gift.

.˙.

Easter Holidays.—The University Extension Office will be closed from Thursday, April 11, to Tuesday April 16.

MR. HUDSON SHAW IN AMERICA.

MR. HUDSON SHAW, as I write, is just finishing the first half of his present visit, and is consequently, as all who know him might have predicted, in the midst of a most successful series of courses. An English cousin who was a welcome visitor in 1893, when putting on record his impressions of America, spoke banteringly of our habit of saying of such things as appeal to us strongly, 'that they have come to stay.' Perhaps it will not be a matter for rejoicing altogether in English University Extension centres that Americans are applying this complimentary expression to Mr. Shaw's lectures, and this not as a compliment merely, but as the expression of an earnest conviction that nothing less than a permanent engagement covering a series of years can be contemplated.

What, then, are the reasons for Mr. Shaw's extraordinary hold on his American audiences? Largely, no doubt, they are the same reasons that have accounted also for his repeated and permanent success in English centres. His unsparing labours in the preparation of his courses, the purity and directness of his speech, the absence of all straining for effect in his delivery, his intense earnestness, his passionate conviction that religion and education, and these only, can bring us social salvation—in many Oxford centres these noble qualities must be even more familiar than to us. But there is one additional reason for Mr. Shaw's popularity in America, which, by the thoughtless, might be ascribed to the success of a shrewd candidate for public favour in playing upon a well-known national foible, but which, in reality, has a significance much more creditable to both teacher and students. In two of the larger centres, he is lecturing upon the earlier periods of English history. This subject offers wide opportunity for teaching the great lesson of the essential unity of the English-speaking race. The lectures are upon the History of the English—the forefathers of those who dwell in Britain, in the colonies, and in the United States. There was a common origin, there are no doubt separate tasks, but there is also a common destiny for these English races in the civilization of the earth. He who can teach that lesson in a way that does no violence either to historical accuracy, or to national aspirations, deserves well of both England and America. Mr. Shaw accomplishes it not by indulging in cheap compliments, nor by insisting on truisms, nor by slandering other races. His method is that of the teacher, of the warm friend, yet also that of the preacher and leader of men. His faith in the possibility of a spiritual union of all those who trace their ancestry and their institutions to a common English origin is strong and abiding. Though never unduly obtruded, it appears in every lecture, in every discussion, and in every private talk. It is not put forward as a device to win applause, but it colours his entire work. He will not have his hearers praise the great Alfred and pronounce unfavourable verdict upon John merely as historical students, he will rather compel them, Anglo-Americans as they are, to rejoice with Englishmen in the virtues and in the deliverance from the vices of the men who have made their history. And to this teaching there is hearty response.

Mr. Shaw finds in every centre, whether his subject be the Making of England, the Age of Elizabeth, Florence, or Venice, an attentive hearing from large audiences. Though the numbers are in part estimated, as many as 4,000 people have probably attended his lectures within one week, and the aggregate attendance upon the two series of courses will be not far from 7,500. The course which has been most in demand during the present season is that on the History of the Republic of Venice—a fact which I am inclined to contribute chiefly to the great success of the lecture on the Venetian Painters at the University Extension Reunion on the eve of Mr. Shaw's departure in April, 1893, when possibly for the first time, Mr. Moulton and Mr. Shaw spoke from the same platform. Both the Florentine and the Venetian courses have been successful, but I venture to predict that when centres have another opportunity for choice, the English History courses will find favour in a larger number of centres than was the case for the present season.

Before the close of his present engagement Mr. Shaw will have an opportunity to become acquainted with a unique and admirable form of University Extension in the Brooklyn Institute, under the auspices of which he is to lecture on Venice, to visit the enterprising town of Scranton in the Pennsylvania coal regions, Lancaster, the seat of government of a prosperous agricultural county, inhabited chiefly by sturdy Pennsylvania Germans; Ogontz, a suburb of Philadelphia, and Orange, a residential suburb of New York City; besides continuing his longer courses in Philadelphia and Germantown, and opening a new course in North Philadelphia. During the period which has just ended, he has lectured in Wilmington, under the auspices of a Woman's Club, in West Philadelphia, in Camden, and in Baltimore, where a strong centre has been established as the result of the course. An afternoon course has also been given before the University Lecture Association.

I have attempted to tell you briefly of Mr. Shaw's work in this country, and the report may seem enthusiastic, but no other than an enthusiastic report would be accurate. If my task were to report this work as seen by the lecturer himself, it would probably be necessary for me to make slight deductions from the satisfaction with which it is to be regarded on two grounds—both important. As compared with the best English centres, there are few papers from students and there are no 'working-class' centres. It would take too much space to explain the reasons or to explain why these deductions are not so serious as an active local secretary in England might suppose. I can only assure you that the good counsel of Mr. Sadler in the Philadelphia Conference of December, 1891, and of Dr. Roberts in the Summer Meeting of 1893, has not been forgotten.

EDWARD T. DEVINE.

Office of the American Society for the Extension of University Teaching;
Philadelphia, *February,* 1895.

SPECIAL DIRECTION OF STUDENTS' WORK.

STUDENTS who wish to continue their work under the guidance of the lecturer, or to prepare themselves for a future course under the lecturer's direction, are invited to communicate with him upon the subject. Letters addressed to the 'University Extension Office, Examination Schools, Oxford,' will be forwarded. Many of the lecturers have consented to give such guidance by looking over essays, &c. As soon as the arrangements have been made between the lecturer and students, the latter should send to the University Extension Office a fee of one shilling and sixpence in respect of each essay which he proposes to submit for the lecturer's correction. No essay, or paper of answers, should exceed five foolscap pages; and the postage must always be fully prepaid.

ON THE BEGINNINGS OF THE LOCAL EXAMINATION MOVEMENT.

WHEN the two Universities in 1858 stepped outside the bounds within which their work had previously been confined, and commenced examining the work of secondary schools, the excitement and stir were such as almost to drive into the background some previous work of a similar kind, which has an interest and value of its own. As the whole apparatus of our secondary instruction is undergoing searching examination, with a view to its co-ordination and fuller development, it may be useful to bring these early efforts and experiments, promoted by different bodies and proceeding for the most part on parallel lines, into some sort of chronological relation. In so doing I shall not trench upon Sir Thomas Acland's very full account of the *Origin and Objects of the New Oxford Examinations* (London, 1858), but shall confine myself for the most part to matter lying outside his limits.

The charter granted by the Crown to the College of Preceptors on March 28, 1849 (which, by the by, does not specifically contemplate the examination of school pupils at all, but only of school teachers), had scarcely been in existence thirteen months, when a paper was sent out by the secretary, Mr. John Parker, to the members (then about one thousand in number), bearing the somewhat grandiose title: 'A Rough Sketch of a Scheme for rendering the College of Preceptors the University of the People by means of Examinations of the Schools of its Members and other measures which will be developed in due course.' This, and most of my other facts, I may say, are drawn from the pages of the *Educational Times*, which has had a continuous existence since 1847, and was from 1883 to 1893 edited by one of the Vice-Presidents of the College, Dr. Richard Wormell. On May 18, 1850, the scheme was referred to the Examination Committee, whose second and fullest report came before the council September 28. One recommendation, to which the examinations have owed much of their success, is that 'the examiners be men of experience as teachers of youth in schools but not actively engaged in conducting schools of their own.' Another recommendation, which, as the years have gone on, has been found difficult to carry out, is nevertheless interesting as anticipating the demand that the examination shall follow the teaching, as it does in the *Abiturienten* examinations on the continent. It is to this effect : ' that the examination be conducted chiefly by the principal of the school or his own assistant master (unless he desires the contrary), the College examiners adding such questions and exercises, and taking such steps as they consider requisite to assure a bona fide examination and to discountenance any attempt at cram.' At the first examination of pupils, held December 23 and 24, 1850, at Mr. Goodacre's school in Nottingham, three higher certificates and two lower ones were given, not to speak of twelve honourable mentions. It is interesting to note that the examiner was the Dean of the College, Dr. Richard Wilson, a Fellow of the same College at Cambridge as Mr. H. J. Roby, who was first Secretary to the Cambridge Syndicate. In the following summer schools were examined at St. Heliers, at Kelvedon, at Seacombe near Liverpool, and in Brighton. At Christmas, 1851, the first girls' school was examined, consisting of thirty-five pupils, who gained two higher certificates and five lower. Neither teacher nor pupils had their names publicly recorded ; that was an ordeal which was found more tolerable on subsequent occasions than it was at the beginning. At the following midsummer one town and four country schools obtained forty-four certificates ; and at Christmas a country school won five certificates. It was in this year that Dr. Jacob, formerly scholar and tutor of Worcester College, Oxford, who had been a member of the College of Preceptors from the first, but had not, so long as he was principal of the Collegiate School at Sheffield, been able to take any active part in its management, became headmaster of Christ's Hospital and was appointed third President of the College (1852–56). All its officers—those who had by great exertions started it, drawn up its charter, and fixed the lines of its activity

—had up to this time been private teachers. Dr. Jacob seems to have been the first of those public schoolmasters who earnestly espoused the cause of the College and contributed so largely to its success. He rendered still greater service, on the retirement of Dr. Wilson in 1859, by making himself responsible as Dean for the way in which the examinations were conducted during the next fourteen years. Public schoolmasters like Dr. Jacob were rare at the Preceptors in those early days ; but by degrees they became more numerous ; and in later years it has come about, by a tacit understanding rather than by any written law, that one half of the members of council are drawn from public schools.

In the summer of 1853 six country schools were examined from Chester in the north to Jersey in the Channel Isles. In the following December began the experiment of collecting pupils to a centre and examining them by identical papers, the boys winning twenty - five certificates and the girls five, of different grades. About this time, too, it is possible to see what the early examination papers were like, some of them being reprinted in the *Educational Times*: the reprint in separate book form commences only with the year 1857. The experiment of Christmas, 1853, was repeated on a much larger scale the following Midsummer. Pupils from ten scho ls in London and its environs were examined at the College rooms, winning 126 certificates ; whilst eleven other schools from New Brighton to Jersey had their examination at their own schools and won 114 certificates. And at Christmas 227 candidates won 82 certificates of varying grades. As the examinations have been continued every half year since 1854 without a break and with steadily increasing success, the College henceforth regarded the period of initial experiment as over, and is accustomed to give the year 1854 as the date of the establishment of local examinations in England. It was in this same year 1854, also, as Prof. J. S. Brewer informs us in the letter referred to below, that the Society of Arts first undertook to examine candidates. There was one candidate in 1854 and none in 1855. But in 1856, after some change of plan, there were 52 candidates, the Rev. F. Temple, now the Bishop of London, being one of the examiners ; and in the following year the examinations were held at Huddersfield as well as in London, and the candidates went up to 300. In this way Mr. Harry Chester and Sir H. Cole gained valuable experience for the South Kensington examinations in Art and Science which were commenced soon afterwards. For the further history of the Society's examinations, a report by Sir H. Trueman Wood may be consulted in the Society's *Journal* for August, 1879.

Meanwhile the Preceptors' Examinations went steadily forward. At the two examinations in 1855, 321 certificates were won ; in 1856, 493 ; in 1857, 749 ; and in 1858 (when the University Locals began) 1002. It is to be noted that at Christmas, 1856, some of the country schools were examined on a 'new plan,' that is, by ' proctors,' whose duty was not to set papers or examine, but to give out the questions they had brought in sealed packets and to forward the answers to be looked over by the examiners in chief. In this new way the examinations in town and country were made absolutely identical. It was essential this should be done, if the examinations were to be of a highly competitive nature like a Tripos at Cambridge. But as the aim has always been to restrain such excessive competition, and to obtain from the examinations as large an educational result as possible, it is to be regretted that the earlier type of examination, which made some approach to the *Abiturienten-examina* abroad, had after a while to be abandoned.

On December 17, 1856, an interesting Conference took place at the rooms of the Society of Arts between Dr. Booth and two of his friends on one side, and Dr. Wilson and two friends from the College of Preceptors on the other, with the result that the Society of Arts expressed their ' cordial appreciation of the valuable labours of the College,' and agreed to confine their examinations to those who had left school. Nearly five months later (May 1), Mr. Temple's two letters to Dr. Jeune, the Master of Pembroke College, which were printed next year at pp. 75-81 of Mr. T. D. (now Sir Thos.) Acland's *Account of the Origin and Objects of the New Oxford Examinations.* appeared in the columns of the *Daily News.* On May 5, Mr. J. S. Brewer writing from King's College in the Strand, Dr. Booth, and the President of the College of Preceptors in three long letters criticized Mr. Temple's plan. There were two other letters, but apparently no answer from Mr. Temple himself. Not less interesting was the criticism inside the College itself. In January, 1858, a paragraph in the half-yearly report, animadverting on the Oxford Locals, was ordered to be struck out, on the ground that 'it was not such a declaration with reference to an educational movement as ought to emanate from a body like theirs.' Two months before it had even been gravely proposed by a young member of Council that the Midsummer Examination of the College should 'be in future conducted by the Universities.' But the proposer after a long and grave debate was left in a minority of one, the Dean remarking that learned University men were not necessarily scholastic experts, and that there were some subjects taught in schools to which University men (in 1857) were not expected to pay particular attention. But there was a financial reason in addition why the pupils' examinations should not be given up. The College membership had declined during the Crimean War, and a debt of £300 (toward the payment of which the twenty members of Council had an hour or two before contributed £85) much hindered its work ; and the examinations, notwithstanding the low fee, were beginning to yield a small income.

But no one made a more accurate forecast of the future than one of the Vice-Presidents, the Rev. W. Taylor Jones, who had said in the preceding June that 'there was plenty of work for all parties to do ; and he thought if the scholastic body would rally round the College and act with it, they would find that the Universities would do them no real injury, but rather assist them in attaining that status in society which the schoolmasters ought to hold.' The prevalence of such moderate counsels amidst some of an opposite character had its reward. On May 1, 1858, just twelve months after the appearance of his two letters in the *Daily News,* Mr. Temple became a member of the College and of its Council, a position which he still retains ; and in 1869 Sir Thos. Acland presided at a distribution of College prizes at Willis's rooms and made an interesting speech. Paradoxical as it may appear, the competition of the Universities helped the College ultimately to a wider success. When once the two ancient Universities followed the College so closely in affirming the necessity of some outside test of school work, a new and powerful sanction was given to the movement, which had the effect, after some years, of vastly increasing, instead of diminishing, its own range of activity.

J. S. THORNTON.

A SUCCESSFUL STUDENTS' ASSOCIATION.

THE Students' Association at Bournemouth has arranged for the present term a series of seven fortnightly meetings for the discussion of historical subjects in connexion with the course of University Extension lectures. The following is the programme :—

Meeting I, January. 30.—' The Kingdom of Piedmont, and its part in the early struggles of Italy for freedom,' Mrs. Shipley. 'Mazzini's contribution to the Liberation of Italy,' Miss Fairbrother. 'Daniel Manin,' Miss Helen Bogue.

Meeting II, February 13.—' Can Cavour be fairly called the creator of Italian Unity?' Miss Punch. 'Was the French Alliance of 1859 a blunder?' Miss A. Drury.

Meeting III, February 27. 'Victor Emmanuel,' Miss C. Robertson. 'Garibaldi, his share in the work of Italian Unification,' Miss Fiennes. 'The Problem of Church and State in Italy.'

Meeting IV, March 13.—'A Criticism of the Constitution of 1815,' Miss A. Arnold. 'The Rise of Liberty in Germany,' Miss H. Bogue.

Meeting V, March 27.—'The work of the Frankfort Vor Parliament, Was it a failure?' Miss Punch. 'Bismarck—his contribution to the work of German Unification,' 'The Schleswig Holstein question.'

Meeting VI, April 10.—'The Foreign Policy of Canning,' Miss H. Bogue. 'The Foreign Policy of Palmerston.' 'The Foreign Policy of Lord Beaconsfield,' Miss Moyle Rogers.

Meeting VII, April 24.—Readings and recitations relating to the subjects of the historical lectures by members and friends.

At the annual conversazione of the Association, held on January 16, there was an historical exhibition illustrating Mr. Marriott's course. Among the objects of special interest were several relics of the French Revolution and the Napoleonic wars.

∴

A second series of students' meetings is also being held this term to carry on the work of Dr. Fison's scientific course.

∴

The members of the Students' Association have taken an active part in the establishment of a Public Free Library at Bournemouth. The desire for a Public Library, now fulfilled, was much stimulated by the liberality of Mr. Leveson Scarth, chairman of the Students' Association, who threw open for the use of the students a well-chosen library in his own house. In an interesting address on educational topics delivered by Mr. Scarth at the annual meeting of the Students' Association, he pointed out that the students' would be able to help the Free Library Committee by making suggestions for the expansion of the Library and for increasing its usefulness to the cause of higher education. In fact Bournemouth is preparing to make its Public Library a part of the organized educational machinery of the town. This is what Mr. Melvil Dewcy, the distinguished Director of the State Library at Albany, has strongly impressed upon the pupils in his Library School.

∴

A still more satisfactory feature of the work of the Bournemouth Students' Association is the vigorous interest which it takes in all forms of educational effort. The more a centre understands the real significance of University Extension, the more will it begin to realize the unity of education and the need for concerted action among educators. 'Bournemouth,' says the *Students' Association Gazette* for February—an excellent number, by the way—'feels more and more strongly the educational wave which is passing over the country and responds by pressing all educational schemes to the front in its local affairs.' As a result of this feeling, the 'Bournemouth Central Council of Education' was formed about twelve months ago. Its general object is 'to bring together representatives of the various educational bodies in the town, so that information may be collected about the agencies at present at work and ideas put forward for future developments.' The Mayor is President, and Mr. Leveson Scarth (representative of the Public Library Committee) is chairman of the Council. Among the members are representatives of the County Council, Science, Art and Technical Schools, the University Extension Committee, all grades of schools in the town, the National Union of Teachers, the various scientific associations in Bournemouth, and the Co-operative Society. The *Students' Association Gazette* summarizes the aims and programme of the Council as follows.

∴

The Council consists at present of about thirty-five members' each being especially connected with a particular school, association, or committee, and although, of course, many belong to two, three, or more such bodies, yet the Council may fairly be said to represent nearly, if not quite, 200 persons actively engaged in the cause of education in Bournemouth.

Such a Council of experts, meeting monthly for the interchange of ideas, ought in course of time to effect much by their influence, although they have no executive power, and do not claim any sort of right or wish to interfere with the detailed work of each local institution. Nevertheless, by the mere fact of their meeting to talk things over, thereby learning to know one another better, and gaining closer information of what others are doing, a vast amount of indirect good must accrue, of which all grades of education in the borough and neighbourhood—Primary, Secondary, Technical and Higher Education—will surely reap the benefit.

In order to give an indication as to the kind of subjects which might be profitably and pleasantly discussed, the subjoined list of suggestions has been drawn up. It is a list that may be indefinitely prolonged, but it will serve to show the wide field which is open to the Council. Education is broadening every day. It is the great question and problem of this generation, and no one local worker can pretend to know more than a fraction of what is going on around him amongst other workers in the same cause, unless by the aid of some such harmonizing and co-ordinating machinery as this Council of Education.

Suggested Subjects for Discussion at the Monthly Meetings.

The work of the two Schools of Science, Art, and Technical Instruction. The Connexion between the Municipality and Education. Recreative and Practical Evening Classes. The Art Department of the Public Library. The Status, Organization and Registration of the Teaching Profession. The Relation of Elementary Schools to Schools of Science and Art. The Scope of the Public Library as an Educational Force. Oxford University Extension. Associations of Students. High Schools for Girls. Educational Apparatus, Libraries, Methods. The Kindergarten System. Experience of Open Access System in the Public Library. School Hygiene. Suggestions for Improving the Public Library. The Historical Value of the Neighbourhood for Teaching Purposes. The Technical Education Committee of the County Council. American School System. Sloyd School Inspection. The Examination System. The Training of Teachers, &c., &c.

CLASS TEACHING AT THE CENTRES.

Meeting at Leamington.

ON Friday, March 1, a meeting was held at the Town Hall to receive from Mr. M. E. Sadler and Mr. J. A. R. Marriott some more detailed account of the scheme for forming teaching-classes at the local centres, in addition to the lecturer's classes. The chair was taken by the Rev. R. Arnold Edgell, Headmaster of Leamington College, and the audience, which numbered between forty and fifty, included representatives from the Banbury and Stratford-on-Avon University Extension Committees, the heads of several elementary and secondary schools, and members of the Corporation and the Technical Education Committee. In the earlier portion of his speech, Mr. Sadler touched incidentally upon the benefits conferred by the Extension movement. But, effective as the lectures were, they were after all rather a valuable stimulus than an attainment in themselves. Most of those who attended them had been conscious of a need for some means of pursuing the subject farther, and of systematizing the knowledge already acquired. It was in this matter that Students' Associations had come to their assistance, and in some centres the lectures had become but one element in a regular system of class teaching. The proposed scheme would be another means of supplying this need. There were many who were anxious to obtain that further and systematic guidance of a teacher which could be given in a class and not in a lecture. Again, the want of continuity in the subjects chosen from term to term, necessitated by the circumstances under which the arrangements for lectures were made, would be supplied by the scheme. Mr. Marriott dwelt very strongly on the growing need for some movement to be made in the direction of intension as well as extension. They wanted to consolidate and deepen the work already being carried on. The munificent gift of an anonymous donor had recently put it into the power of the Delegacy to appoint Directors, whose work it would be to systematize the arrangements made by local centres for lecturers, and also to organize the proposed classes. He thought the

classes might serve two very useful purposes. They might be supplementary to existing lectures, following their lines and developing their points; or they might deal with subjects not intrinsically suitable for lecture teaching. A suggestion was made by the local secretary, Mr. Leppington, that neighbouring towns might send students to classes meeting in Leamington, but it was doubted if this would be practicable in a number of cases, though Mr. Marriott pointed out that a saving of expense might be secured if adjacent towns joined in engaging the services of the same teacher. An animated discussion took place between the members of the Delegacy and the scholastic authorities present, as to the possibilities and limitations of the proposed class teaching, in the course of which Mr. Sadler cordially agreed with the chairman's suggestion that the study of philosophy would not only form a suitable subject for such treatment but would be likely to enlist much interest in times of great and momentous change like these, when a spirit of inquiry is abroad amongst us. Finally, a resolution was passed to the effect that it was desirable that an effort should be made to organize teaching-classes in Leamington, and that those present pledged themselves to use their best endeavours to support the movement; but that no arrangement should be finally made until enough pupils had been secured to defray expenses.

A. M. STUBBS, *Hon. Sec. Students' Association.*

HOLIDAY COURSE FOR YOUNG TEACHERS.

IT is proposed to arrange a Holiday Course for Young Teachers, to be held in Oxford from Monday, August 19, to Monday, August 26. The aim of the gathering will be to enable young teachers working in schools in the neighbourhood of Oxford to combine with a pleasant holiday opportunities of friendly intercourse and recreative instruction. The programme will be somewhat as follows :— The meeting will begin with a social evening on Monday evening, August 19. On each morning, except August 25, two classes will be held (probably at ten o'clock and at noon)—one on ' Great Men in English History,' the other on ' The Science of Every-Day Life.' The afternoons will be given up wholly to recreation—boating, lawn tennis, &c. In the evenings it is hoped that the students will be invited to attend the lectures of the University Extension Summer Meeting. Those who stay for the evening of August 26 will be invited to the University Extension Conversazione, which will take place on that night. A club-room will be provided for the students, and the social arrangements will be in the hands of a committee which includes the names of Mrs. T. H. Green; Mrs. Arnold Toynbee; Mrs. Gerrans (Hon. Secretary to the Oxford Branch of the Teachers' Guild); Miss Rogers (Hon. Secretary to the Association for the Education of Women in Oxford); Miss McNiel (Head Mistress Central British School for Girls); Miss Soulsby (Head Mistress of the Oxford High School for Girls); Miss Elliott (Head Mistress of Holy Trinity Infants' School); Miss Bruce, Somerville College; Miss Hayllar, Somerville College; Miss Beard (Assistant Secretary to the University Extension Delegacy); Mr. A. W. Cave (Headmaster of the Oxford High School for Boys); Mr. M. E. Sadler; Mr. J. A. R. Marriott (Secretary to the University Extension Delegacy); Mr. G. N. Richardson (Secretary to the Oxford University Day Training College); Mr. J. W. Horne (Headmaster of St. Barnabas' Boys' School); and Miss Hoskyns-Abrahall, Somerville College, *Hon. Secretary.*

It is believed that those who have friends in Oxford will prefer to make their own arrangements for board and lodging during the holiday course. Those who have no friends in Oxford are desired to communicate with the Hon. Sec., who will suggest lodgings which the Committee can recommend. The price of tickets, admitting to all the classes and lectures, will be 2s. 6d. each.

All communications should be addressed to—Miss HOSKYNS-ABRAHALL, Somerville College, Oxford.

PREPARATIVE READING FOR THE SUMMER MEETING, 1895.

List of Books.

A. ENGLISH HISTORY AND LITERATURE. 1689—1789.

(1) *Elementary Books.*

Gardiner, *Students' History of England*, Part III. (Longmans, 4s.) Or

Bright, *History of England*, 1689—1837. (Longmans, 7s. 6d.)

Stopford Brooke, *Primer of English Literature.* (Macmillan, 1s.)

** The short biographies of William III, Walpole and Pitt in the Twelve English Statesmen Series (Macmillan, 2s. 6d. each); of Bolingbroke and Fox in the Statesmen Series (Allen & Co., 2s. 6d. each); of Marlborough in the English Worthies Series (Longmans, 2s. 6d.); and of Burke in the English Men of Letters Series (Macmillan, 1s. 6d.) will be found useful.

(2) *Advanced Books.*

Macaulay, *History of England.* (Longmans, 5s.)

Lecky, *History of England in the Eighteenth Century.* 12 vols. (Longmans, each 6s.)

Seeley, *Expansion of England.* (Macmillan, 4s. 6d.)

Thwaites, *The Colonies* (Epochs of American History Series). (Longmans, 2s. 6d.)

Hart, *Formation of the Union.* (Longmans, 2s. 6d.)

Parkman, *Montcalm and Wolfe.* 2 vols. (Macm., 12s. 6d. each.)

Fiske, *The American Revolution.* 2 vols. (Macmillan, 18s.)

Toynbee, *The Industrial Revolution.* 10s. 6d.

Sir A. Lyall, *British Dominion in India.* (Murray, 12s. net.)

Seeley, *Clive* (' Rulers of India '). (Clarendon Press, 2s. 6d.)

Trotter, *Warren Hastings.* (Clarendon Press.)

Seton-Karr, *Cornwallis.* (Clarendon Press.)

(3) *Miscellaneous Books.*

Churton Collins, *Bolingbroke and Voltaire.* (Murray, 7s. 6d.)

Lecky, *Leaders of Public Opinion in Ireland* (out of print).

Boswell, *Life of Dr. Johnson.* (Nimmo, 5s.)

Southey, *Life of Wesley.* (Bell, 5s.)

Leslie Stephen, *History of English Thought in the Eighteenth Century.* 2 vols. (Smith Elder, 28s.)

(4) *Literature.*

Taine, *History of English Literature.* Vol. II. (Chatto & Windus, 7s. 6d.)

Bolingbroke, *Select Pieces.* (Ward & Lock, 3s. 6d.)

Dobson, *Selections from Steele.* (Clarendon Press, 5s.)

Dobson, *Eighteenth Century Essays.* (Kegan Paul, 1s. 6d.)

Arnold, *Selections from Papers in the Spectator.* (Clar. Press, 4s. 6d.)

Gibbon, *Autobiography.* (Ward & Lock, 3s. 6d.)

Pope, *Poetical Works.* (Macmillan, 3s. 6d.)

Goldsmith, *Poetical Works.* (Bell, 1s. 6d.)

Cowper, *Poetical Works.* (Macmillan, 3s. 6d.)

** The lives of eighteenth century writers in the English Men of Letters Series are most useful. The price of each volume is 1s. 6d.; the Publishers, Macmillan & Co.

B. FOREIGN HISTORY AND LITERATURE.

i. *Elementary.*

Jallifier and Vast, *Histoire de l'Europe*, 1610—1789. (Paris, Garnier Frères, 5s.)

Or Lodge, *Modern Europe* (7s. 6d.).

ii. *Advanced.*

Kitchin, *Hist. of France.* Vol. III. (Clarendon Press, 10s. 6d.)

Hassall, *Louis XIV and the Zenith of the French Monarchy.* (Putnam, 5s.)

Perkins, *France under the Regency.* (Macmillan, 8s. 6d.)

De Tocqueville, *France before the Revolution.* (Murray, 14s.)

John Morley, *Rousseau.* 2 vols. (Macmillan, 10s.)

John Morley, *Voltaire.* (Macmillan, 5s.)

John Morley, *Miscellanies.* Vol. II. (Macmillan, 5s.)

Longman, *Frederick the Great* (' Epochs of Modern History '). (Longmans, 2s. 6d.)

Carlyle, *Frederick the Great.* 10 vols. (Chapman, Hall & Co., 10s.)

Rousseau, *Le Contrat Social.* (3s.)

[N.B.—*A further list of books on other subjects will be published shortly.*]

LETTER TO THE EDITOR.

[*We do not hold ourselves responsible for the opinions expressed by our correspondents.*]

Books for Students.

DEAR SIR,—The suggestion of ' A Student' with regard to interchange of books among students, in the January *Gazette*, seems to me an admirable one for workmen, and the practical difficulties about its working are slight. The main difficulty will be how to get books for interchange, and I am venturing to add a suggestion to meet this. Workmen are generally unable or unwilling to lay a large lump sum down for what, in their condition of life, is a luxury. Many of them will make weekly outlays which would stagger them, if they were obliged at the beginning or the end of the year to put down the annual total of such outlays. Of course, if they could or would do this, they would get some advantages which they now miss; but when small incomes and growing tastes for luxuries are found together, economizing for future gratifications is a rather precarious operation unless there are some special expedients adopted for assisting the latter. The expedient I have to suggest for workmen with an ambition for a good library, and others who may be interested, is the formation of ' book clubs' for the purpose of buying the more expensive works of high-class authorities. These might be worked very much in the same way as ' watch clubs,' ' portrait clubs,' and other devices of the ' Philistine ' for making limited and precarious means accomplish otherwise unattainable ends. A number of students might club together and agree to contribute so much weekly (or periodically) toward a common fund. The periodical contributions should be within easy reach of the poorest member likely to join—say, sixpence or a shilling. At a stated period lots should be cast as to who shall have the benefit of spending the entire contributions for that period, minus any expenses incurred, on books, which may or may not be left to the member's own choice.

The amount available, and the time for paying out all the members, will of course depend on the number of people who join the club, and the terms of subscription. The scheme is capable of adoption by a good many agencies, by a temporary combination of readers either in a given locality or distributed over the country, by members of a permanent Students' Association, or by an amalgamation of associations. It might even be adopted by an ordinary bookseller, and worked on purely commercial lines. Where the clubs were large and worked by those buying books, special terms might be made either with publishers or local booksellers, if they were guaranteed the custom of the club for some stated period.

Some of the advantages incident to this suggestion have already been hinted at. Others might be mentioned. Where there are no Students' Associations the formation of local book clubs might lead to the formation of such societies, by bringing the educationally-minded, through the ' cash nexus,' into closer sympathy and social contact. Where there are Students' Associations it would help the poorer students out of their special disabilities. Perhaps I might be allowed to point out that the wealthier students might give assistance in this matter. They may not need such devices for purchasing books, but their co-operation would improve conditions for those who do, as well as have some possible social effects that are worth while working for. If Extension work gets on such a basis that a course of lectures to be given at any local centre may be known six or twelve months in advance, the formation of such clubs might put an intending student into possession of a library, which would equip him for his future work at the lectures, and might remain with him as a permanent memorial of inspiring studies. Many a workman would probably get into the habit of spending his surplus cash on his higher education, and be induced to make outlays on books which might never come within the reach of his unassisted resources.

It does not need any large gift of the imagination to see that this scheme would fit in with that indicated by ' A Student,' and it appears to me it would materially add to its effectiveness. On the other hand, the interchange of books would do away to some extent with one of the most serious objections to my suggestion, namely, that some of the members would get the benefits much sooner than others. This however need not deter any one, seeing that in other clubs worked on similar lines people who are working for material ends submit to the inevitable; and shall 'the children of this world be wiser in their generation than the children of light ?'

Apologizing for this lengthy epistle,

I am,

Yours truly,

Hebden Bridge.   R. HALSTEAD.

How about the Gambling Laws?—*Ed.*

REPORTS FROM THE CENTRES.

BAKEWELL.—The second of the series of Spring lectures arranged by the Students' Association was held on Friday, March 15, when Professor Raleigh most kindly came from Liverpool to address the students on 'The Mediaeval Novel'—a subject chosen on account of its connexion with the Autumn course on 'The Novelists.' Professor Raleigh was already known to many of the students by his excellent 'University Extension Manual,' *The English Novel,* and he received a very hearty welcome. The lecturer, by his own keen sympathy, gave warmth and colour to the intensely interesting age of the 'Fabliaux, Lais and Dits,' nor was he, in bringing to light the rich humour of these compositions, forgetful of the intense pathos so frequently underlying them. It was clearly evident throughout the lecture that Professor Raleigh was giving us the result of much original research, and we venture to take this opportunity of placing upon record our gratitude for the honour that he so generously conferred on the Students' Association of Bakewell.—KATHLEEN MARTIN, *Hon. Sec.*

BEDFORD.—The 'Life of a Planet' has proved a very attractive subject at our centre this Spring, and Dr. Fison's lectures are attended by audiences numbering, as a rule, nearly 300, of whom more than 100 are artisans, or other weekly wage earners. Our first experience of a 'short course' is so far encouraging, and the Local Committee has decided to ask for another six lectures on Astronomy, from Dr. Fison, next autumn, so that in the course of this year we shall have had twelve on the one subject. A fair number of papers has been sent in each fortnight, some of these being written by working gardeners and other artisans. The Students' Association holds meetings as usual, at which papers are read, and opportunities sometimes found for telescopic observation of the planets and stars. This is due to the kindness of Mr. Mellor, a new member of the Association, who has placed his telescope at the disposal of the students, when the weather is fit for observations of the sky. Compared with the experience of other centres this year, our success is the more marked, for (until perhaps the fourth lecture) the attendance showed no diminution, in spite of the trials of severe frost and consequent illness.—G. BLAKE, *Hon. Sec.*

CARLISLE.—Mr. Phythian has continued his course on the History of Architecture on Tuesday afternoons. The numbers of the audiences have been much decreased by the severe weather during the first two months of the year. The interest of the lectures has increased. Before his tenth lecture Mr. Phythian visited the Cathedral, Carlisle, with his class, and pointed out the illustrations of his subject which it furnished. Mr. Carus-Wilson on Thursday evenings is giving a second course of six lectures on Geology, illustrated with magic lantern views. The numbers have been well maintained, and there is a large proportion of men among the audience.—A. R. HALL, *Hon. Sec.*

DEVIZES.—In this centre, Dr. Bailey is giving a course of lectures on 'Tennyson,' which promises to be a great success. The audience, for a country town, is a large one: nearly 150 course tickets have been taken, and, at each lecture, our Town Hall has been well filled. This is the third Spring in which Dr. Bailey has come to Devizes, so that he is well known and is welcomed with great pleasure.—MARGARET HART, *Hon. Sec.*

EDGBASTON.—A successful course of twelve lectures is just being brought to a close at this centre. Mr. Marriott gave six lectures before Christmas on the Age of Louis XIV, and has since January followed these up by his interesting course on the French Revolution. The lectures have been thoroughly enjoyed by all those who have attended them. Much reading has been done, and the essay work has been satisfactory. The attendance has been very regular, though the audience has not been so large as could have been desired. This may be accounted for partly by the severe weather and partly by the numerous other lecture courses taking place in Birmingham. The Students' Association continues gradually to increase, and great interest is felt at the fortnightly meetings, in the discussion of questions arising out of the essays.—PHOEBE TIMMINS, *Hon. Sec.*

SWANSEA.—The *Cambrian* remarks that Mr. Horsburgh's lectures on Epochs of English History are characterized by clever treatment and impartial judgement.

WEST BRIGHTON.—Our *Evening* course of twelve lectures on 'Social Questions of To-day' by Mr. Hewins, M.A., commenced in October, and being given at fortnightly intervals are still continuing. The lectures have been of extreme interest, and the committee greatly regret that the subject of the course has not appealed to a larger audience, as the number attending is but small. In the hope of making the course better known, Mr. Hewins most kindly gave a free lecture after Christmas on 'Labour and Life in England,' but unfortunately it appears impossible to arouse any wide interest in economic questions at this centre. Those however who have attended have shown great interest in the course, as a consequence of which the Students' Association has increased in number, and the average of papers has been good both as to number and quality. The bad weather and general illness prevailing has still further thinned our numbers of late. In connexion with our *Afternoon* course on 'Tennyson' by Dr. Bailey, a performance of Tennyson Tableaux with Tennyson Songs and Descriptive Music was given by the students on Feb. 15. The poems selected for tableaux illustrations were : 'Ode to Memory,' 'The Dream of Fair Women,' 'Cophetua and the Beggar-Maid' (after Burne Jones' picture), and some of the 'Idylls of the King.' In spite of the very inclement weather the financial result of the performance was very satisfactory, and the appreciation of the representations expressed by the audience was highly gratifying.—M. F. BASDEN, *Hon. Sec.*

WEYMOUTH (*Students' Subsidiary Class*).—We are glad to learn from a correspondent that the desire for University teaching, which on some former occasions has been but feebly manifested in Weymouth, seems at last to be 'taking hold' there in earnest. The attendance on Mr. Marriott's present course on 'The Age of Louis XIV' is nearly double of that which was attracted by his late lectures on 'English History in Shakespeare,' and excellent accounts have been received of the paper-work sent in from the class. A further and satisfactory evidence of the interest created in the subject is afforded by the formation of a 'Students' Subsidiary Class,' which holds its meetings in the alternate weeks between Mr. Marriott's lectures, and at which essays commended by the lecturer are read and criticized, and questions bearing on the subject are proposed, to which other members of the class are invited to furnish answers. Apposite illustrations from the private reading of members of the class are also welcomed. Valuable help has also been secured from 'experts' connected mainly with the educational institutions of the town, one of whom kindly undertakes to attend each meeting of the class, and to take a leading part in its proceedings. An excellent beginning in this way was made at the first meeting the Rev. J. Miller, Head Master of Weymouth College, to whom Weymouth is indebted for much previous service in the cause of University Extension, and who on the present occasion offered some valuable suggestions as to the spirit in which the study should be pursued, the need of forming an independent judgement on what is heard or read, and on the value of a deeper study of history in its original and authentic contemporary records, of late made easily accessible to students. At the first and second meetings approved essays (three in number in each case) were read and discussed, and questions proposed, to be answered at the ensuing meetings. We subjoin the names of the 'experts' who have kindly given or promised their help as above : Rev. J. Miller, B.D., Head Master of Weymouth College ; Rev. A. E. Shaw, M.A., Lodmoor House, Assistant Master of Weymouth College ; Rev. S. Lambert, M.A., Curate-in-Charge of Westham ; Rev. A. A. Carré, M.A., Assistant Master, Weymouth College ; Miss L. Owen Snow, M.A., Lansdowne School, Rodwell, Weymouth ; R. F. Davis, Esq., M.A., Assistant Master, Weymouth College.— Rev. Canon TWEED, St. John's, Weymouth, President of the Class ; Mrs. SAUNDERS, Longbills, Rodwell, *Hon. Sec.*

DIRECTORY OF SECRETARIES OF STUDENTS' ASSOCIATIONS.

Bedford.—Miss KETT, Hamslade, Clapham Road, Bedford.

Edgbaston.—{ Miss SARGANT, 29 Clarendon Road, Edgbaston. Miss MURIEL HARRISON, Glenbolme, Richmond Hill Road, Edgbaston.

Leamington.—{ Miss A. M. STUBBS, Normanton House, Leamington.

Ryde.—Miss G. CARTER, East Upton, Ryde.

PROPOSED TESTIMONIAL TO MR. SADLER.

WE have been asked to print the following circular in the present number of the *Gazette*:—

It will be known to all those who are interested in the work of University Extension that Mr. Sadler has been appointed to the post of Director of Special Enquiries in the Education Department: a desire has been expressed in several quarters that his long connexion with the Oxford branch of the movement should be commemorated in some permanent way; many it is thought who have enjoyed his kindness, been guided by his counsel, and stirred by his enthusiasm, will welcome the opportunity of giving something to such an object.

In the present stage of the Extension work we believe that no purpose would be more sympathetic to Mr. Sadler than the foundation of a scholarship or scholarships, to be held by working men at the Summer Meeting: it is hoped that such a proposal will meet with general approval.

It is proposed to communicate to Mr. Sadler the names of all who give, but to add no further particulars; and we are quite sure that it would be his wish that no one should be asked personally, but that all subscriptions should be quite spontaneous.

A desire has been expressed in many quarters that some small part of the sum raised should be used for a personal gift to Mr. Sadler; it is proposed to carry out this suggestion.

A copy of this paper is being sent to each local secretary, and to the various papers connected in any way with education.

Subscriptions will be received by—Miss Basden, 21 The Drive, Brighton (*Local Secretary at Brighton*); Miss Brooke Hunt, Rikenel, Gloucester (*Local Secretary at Gloucester*,; Miss Colman, Bridge Street, Peterborough (*Local Secretary at Peterborough*); Rev. Arthur H. Fish, Arnold House School, Chester (*Local Secretary at Chester*); Miss Jones, 37 Broadwater Down, Tunbridge Wells (*Local Secretary at Tunbridge Wells*); Miss Montgomery, 10 Baring Crescent, Exeter (*Local Secretary at Exeter*); Miss Punch, Brackendene, Bournemouth (*Local Secretary at Bournemouth*); Mr. Charles Rowley, Ancoats, Manchester (*Local Secretary at Ancoats*); Mrs. Rothwell, Limefield, Bury, Lancashire (*Local Secretary at Bury*); Miss Sharp, Horton House, Rugby (*Local Secretary at Rugby*); Miss Snowden, The Grove, Ilkley; Miss Dale, 27 Parson Ghyll, Ilkley (*Local Secretaries at Ilkley*,; Miss Beatrice Vivian, Reskadinnick, Camborne (*Hon. Sec. South Western Association and Camborne Centre*); Mr. F. H. Wright (*Secretary of University Extension College, Reading*).

N.B.—*It is suggested that all subscriptions should be sent in by May 1.*

EXETER UNIVERSITY EXTENSION COLLEGE.

THE *Devon and Exeter Daily Gazette* recently contained an interesting account of an interview with Miss Montgomery, Secretary to the Exeter University Extension Committee. As such wide interest is felt in the aims and work of the College, we print the following extracts from the fuller report:—

'To begin at the beginning, as it were,' Miss Montgomery observed 'there were already two good technical schools existing in Devonshire—at Plymouth and Tiverton, I mean—and I am not sure there was not another at Devonport. But I thought we might do something on a more comprehensive scale, for I am not aware that there is an institution west of Bristol with anything like a complete curriculum for adults. We had a Science and Art School, to which it seemed to me technological and commercial subjects might be added. We had also a strong centre of University Extension lectures. Everywhere there was a growing desire to supplement that well-established system by direct tutorial work, and I felt if this could be done, and the whole placed under a first-rate Principal and be kept in organic connexion with the University, we should then have a technical school *plus* a University Extension College.'

'Was that the first introduction to Exeter of the University Extension movement?'

'Not exactly. I think there had been several single courses got up by a small number of people who felt an interest in the matter, among whom Mr. Dallas was one of the prime movers; but, if I recollect aright, Mr. Moulton was the person who first really put the thing on a permanent basis, and at the time he came to Exeter as a University Extension lecturer, Cambridge University had just passed its Affiliation statute, enabling students, according to the work they had done and the examinations they had passed at a local centre, to go up to the University as already "first-year" students, so that they could obtain a degree in two instead of three years. But I fear I am drifting rather away from my point. Mr. Moulton, who has been very popular wherever he has gone, stirred up a great deal of local interest in the movement, and he suggested we should affiliate ourselves to Cambridge. This suggestion was acted upon, so that while we can boast of our centre having been established regularly for eight years, we are in our seventh year of affiliation. I have myself been connected with the centre throughout that period of affiliation, and in that connexion I should like to mention with gratitude the able services rendered from the outset by my former co-secretary, Mr. Macan, who is now Organizing Secretary for Technical Education to the Surrey County Council.'

'The difficulty when I took up the matter,' Miss Montgomery continued, 'was not only a question of funds. People say, "I know my London." Well, I did flatter myself that I knew Exeter as well as any West of England woman. But I can assure you that I had no conception, previous to entering upon the preliminary work, of the number of isolated organized bodies that existed, each of which had to be communicated with and their interest secured before anything like a feasible scheme of co-operation could be launched with any hope of success. I found, also, that we had to contend against what I suppose is a characteristic of most provincial places—the existence of classes within classes, of people and bodies who were, or professed to be, ignorant that other people and other bodies existed. It was quite a novel experience for me; but, however, the thing was done, and Mr. Clayden has given you a very clear account of it since it became *un fait accompli*. In regard to the all-important financial question, you should understand that while the technical side, including the art school, has some endowment, we on the University Extension side have none. From time to time great efforts have been made to secure a separate form of endowment. About two years ago, when Lord Cranbrook was President of the Council, there was a deputation to his lordship, and I went up to represent Exeter. We were received very courteously; there was a great deal said that was flattering and hopeful; but no money was given, which, however, was no unusual result of an appeal to the Treasury. Last year our College, in conjunction with Reading U. E. College, applied for a share in the local college grant of £15,000 given annually.'

'From local or Imperial funds?'

'Oh, from Imperial funds; and we applied for a share in such local grant. But even that action has not as yet led to any definite result. However, there was a special Committee appointed to try and raise funds, and we may, I suppose, keep our hopes alive. But at present we are in this position of difficulty—our sole means of support consist of a small subscription list and fees, and the result of that is, we cannot start classes unless we can make them self-supporting. But there is always a degree of consolatory reflection in the knowledge that, from time immemorial, higher education in England has never been self-supporting. None of the public schools have been, nor any of the Universities. Higher education has had to be developed as far as could be by some form of endowment. We should, of course, be able to develop more rapidly if we had an endowment fund to trust to, and that is what I am extremely anxious to secure. This leads me to another point, which I think should be widely known and understood, namely, that if we get any endowment on the University Extension side it would be really a great help to the technical side. In this way: we should be able to give extra employment to the technical teachers in doing work such as may not be subsidized from the Technical Fund ; we should be able to enhance their individual incomes and retain the services of our best teachers. For instance, they have a most admirable teacher in the technical department teaching physiology, but the income they were able to offer would not have been enough alone, whereas we employ him likewise for two of our normal classes, which supplements the salary. Similarly, the services of Mr. Clayden could not have been secured without a union of resources, derived from the University guarantee and the Technical Instruction Committee.'

' What was your main underlying motive, Miss Montgomery, in entering upon this project ? '

' In proposing the conjunction of the two local Committees, I had in my mind this : To succeed in any scheme you must have something wherewith to kindle enthusiasm ; you must stir up a spirit to start with, that will also keep alive enthusiasm, and I don't think it is so easy to be enthusiastic over a Government Department. Really, I think connexion with the Universities is a means of keeping up a corporate spirit. A Government Department is, by its very constitution, too official to effect that. When you arouse a national movement, it goes throughout the length and breadth of the country, and this movement, in which we have played, I think I may claim, a not inconsiderable part, was national ; and being centered in the Universities, by means of Summer Meetings, smaller meetings locally, continual correspondence between the Secretaries, and the University's Travelling Library, a room open to all the students, where the books sent down could be consulted, my view was that a feeling was created of being part and parcel of a "floating" University. You see, there is a constant connexion between all the Secretaries. Every week I am receiving letters from all corners of England, asking questions about our work here, or making suggestions for the common good. I have had letters from four towns asking particulars of how our College was started, and especially how the co-operation between the Technical Instruction and the University Extension Committees was effected. Also, just the other day, I was invited to Gloucester to see the ex-Mayor personally with a similar object, and that gentleman hopes shortly to visit Exeter and see our work for himself. So we are really helping to start kindred institutions in other places. I would like to add my view that this always present idea of connexion with the University is advantageous to a far-away place such as Exeter, inasmuch as it tends to check and counteract the danger of our becoming too distinctly local. The stream of fresh life brought in, by new lecturers, the newest books, and information as to most recent discoveries, it seems to me, must necessarily help to counteract the tendency to fall into a purely local groove. In every town I have known there are many separatist influences at work, while our want is that of a common bond of interest. Unfortunately, though religious and political objects unite certain people, they separate them wholly from others. But as regards University Extension, I know literally of no other agency which has so successfully provided a platform wide enough for all parties and all classes. There is another way in which its teaching has a beneficial influence. If you take Technical Education alone, and confine yourself to it, you get a tendency to regard it only as a question of pounds, shillings, and pence ; it is here I find the usefulness of the University Extension side in keeping always before our minds the idea that our object is, after all, to make life higher and better and of fuller interest, rather than of the pecuniary betterment of the people.'

' There is an ideal, then ? '

' Oh yes. Of course, the Universities have not themselves always carried out their ideal. But that ideal is really "study for its own sake," and that we try to keep before us to a great extent. I think it would be worth while saying that we have been fairly successful, considering the state of things in the West of England, in reaching the artisans. Of course, there is nothing here like the keen desire for knowledge which prevails in the North. I imagine the climate makes people feel tired when their

day's work is over, and disinclined to turn out in the evening for the purpose of study. I have met several times at our "Summer Meetings" a Northumbrian miner who has taught himself Greek, and who is an enthusiast in University Extension work in his own locality. I like these Northern people. They are rough and out-spoken, perhaps not quite so good-mannered as our Devonshire folks, but when you know them, you cannot but appreciate their earnestness and intelligence. That by the way, however. What I was coming to is this, that on the whole we have been very successful with the working-men here. We had a large meeting two years ago, for which the then Mayor lent the Guildhall. It was certainly the largest gathering of working-men for an educational object ever held in Exeter. About 150 were present, all working-men. An organizing sub-committee was elected of seven artisans, who should assist the University Extension Committee in making the scheme known in the workshops and among the artisans of the city ; and then six of our Central Committee were appointed to serve with them. Before any course of lectures, or any "new departure," I call them together, give full information, and ask them for any suggestions they can make, and they undertake to distribute tickets in the workshops and among their own friends. By that means, and through the Co-operative Society, we have reached a large number of artisans. Last year sixty tickets were taken for our lectures by bona-fide working-men. We cannot get them as yet to do any large amount of private study in connexion with the lectures, partly owing to want of time, but also, I take it, more largely owing to defective previous education. Very few of the older ones have the power of putting their thoughts into writing. But I think that is coming. We have had instances of regular and steady paper-work being done by artisans ; for the rising generation I think our normal classes in English, History, and Geography will help, and we hope the good effect will increase with the increased attendance at the classes.'

' Considered broadly, what would you regard as the most useful characteristic of your method of working ? '

' I think the most useful function of all in the University Extension work is the stimulus it gives to private study. Of course, the great tendency is to think it means only lectures. I don't think any of us who care for the work regard the lectures as the principal part. I myself look upon them only as a starting-point, and I apprehend we are rather apt to allude too scornfully to those who merely attend the lectures. We sometimes call them, among ourselves, "the casuals !" and are apt to fall into the mistake of regarding them only as money-making machines. This is a little bit unjust, for often work is done by them which cannot be classified and tabulated ; in many instances people look upon themselves as too busy or too advanced in years to undertake paper-work, but their reading is helped and directed by the lectures. One of the most famous of the Extension lecturers, the Mr. Moulton I alluded to already, used always at the end of a course to try and get from his audience a record of the private reading they had done. I regret to say that for some time at least he has been permanently annexed by our American friends in connexion with their great enterprise, the Chicago University, mention of which reminds me that I have myself an invitation to go there next year and talk to them about this University Extension scheme in which I am so much interested.'

' How have these "Summer Meetings" been supported from this centre ? '

' Exeter, I am pleased to know, has generally sent the largest contingent to every Summer Meeting. Scholarships have been offered by the local committee, to which Sir Thomas Acland has been a very liberal contributor. Our scholarships have been held by pupil teachers, by an elementary school teacher, by a young artisan, and by a young watchmaker. Does the scholarship meet all the expenses of the trip ? No, it does not ; it has not been thought advisable that it should, our feeling being that students will appreciate the more something to which they have to contribute out of their own pockets. Last year we had seventeen from Exeter at Oxford. A point on which I feel rather strongly, personally, is, that we must in some manner elevate ourselves above passing and local, and look to permanent and national interests—a very difficult task, I admit. To that end we need to strengthen and utilize to the utmost the wholesome influence of our connexion with the Universities. I attach the highest importance to this. It is necessary to have a worthy ideal ever present to our minds. There is an inherent danger in popularization. You must never bring down your standard; you do not want to "teach down" to people, but rather to gradually raise your standard, and by so doing induce the people to ascend thereto. It is very necessary to provide technical education. But the needs of those capable of receiving a higher education should ever be remembered, and where it is possible to have a central institution catering for both classes, within easy reach of all, I conceive the whole community must be greatly benefited. It seems to me to be a bigger thing altogether to possess a college connected intimately with a great national institution, than to have merely a local college standing on its own footing.'

'Is not that much like a self-evident proposition? Would the advantage not seem to be obvious?'

'Not to every one. We all rather like managing our own affairs, you know! The larger my knowledge of local needs becomes, the more it is forced upon me that our chief want is local centralization. We require the feeling of support which emanates from a central body, combined with the enthusiasm that comes from local spontaneity.'

'Do you, Miss Montgomery, look forward to any specific benefit accruing to Exeter from this University Extension movement — I mean as one of the factors in our exceptionally advantageous position relative to education as a whole?'

'I do. I am sanguine enough to look upon the establishment of this College as a great and direct means of attracting people to Exeter. I think there must be numbers of people who have no special reason for settling in one place more than another, and who for the sake of the higher education facilities we can afford would definitely fix themselves here, if a knowledge of our position in that respect were widespread. I am just now in correspondence with a lady at Oxford, who has no special plans for the coming winter; she has been writing me for full particulars of our University Extension College, and is attracted by Exeter, if for no other reason, for the sake of our language classes. One other matter in this connexion. I look forward also to the time when we shall have a hostel in connexion with the College—a place where people from the outside could come for, perhaps, a five days' residence every week. Other places have established hostels of this kind, and I feel sure that it is fast becoming a necessity of the situation here. For example, though we are ordinarily considered admirably provided for in the way of railway travelling accommodation, still, the existing train service does not suit country students. There are no evening trains to and from many districts. Honiton and all that side is entirely cut off from us through lack of late trains. I do not know whether local pressure might not be brought to bear on the Railway Companies, but I can testify that I have had a good many letters complaining that country people were absolutely prohibited from coming to us by the utter absence of railway facilities.'

Reverting to the general subject-matter of our interview, Miss Montgomery, in course of further conversation, observed:—

'One student already has gone up from Exeter to Cambridge as an affiliated student, and a second hopes to do so this year. The circumstance that under affiliation the term of residence at the University can be reduced by one year, is a great consideration to many who cannot afford the full time as ordinary students. Representatives of affiliated centres are always regarded as in a different position at, for instance, the Summer Meetings and Conferences to those of non-affiliated centres. Indeed, it has been rather a theme of complaint that too much has been made of the affiliated element! It has just occurred to me that I omitted to mention, when treating of Mr. Moulton's work at our start, his suggestion of the foundation of a "Students' Association." This has been of very great use both in procuring new students, in promoting *esprit de corps,* and also in collecting a certain amount of money. A small fund has been collected during the last three years by the students, and specially entered in the

accounts. They are not a very rich body, and the total may not appear large—it reached about £13 in one year, from sums under five shillings—but that represents a good deal of work, besides a good deal of interest. Then, again, as our students became very numerous, and some of those who had got certificates, but were unable to continue work, did not want to break their bond of connexion, I proposed the formation of a University Extension Guild, the qualifications of membership being, first, a small subscription every year to cover the supply of one of the Extension magazines, as a means of keeping them in touch with the movement as a whole; and, second, the possession of at least one certificate. But the question of honorary members is under consideration. A prime function of this Guild is to promote social meetings and excursions to places of interest in the neighbourhood. We have had three social evenings and three or four excursions in connexion with courses of lectures on architecture. That Guild numbers now between fifty and sixty members. When we began originally we had only one course of lectures at a time; then we advanced to two; and now we have three courses each term, or six per year. During the last two years the cost of our Science lectures has been defrayed by a grant from the City Council of £100 a year. I think we may well say we have always received the greatest assistance and sympathy from the respective Mayors from the time we have been in existence, and from the city authorities generally. We pride ourselves, somewhat, upon having been the first centre in England to start a Committee on the basis in existence here, and a good many other places have since followed our example. The Mayor for the time being is president; then come certain vice-presidents; next various *ex-officio* members, really practical educational experts; then representatives of public bodies in the city, embracing the Council, the Chapter, the School Board, the Museum Committee, the Literary Society, the Co-operative Society, and the Association of Certified Teachers—we make it a condition that they shall become subscribers, so that the principle of "representation and taxation going together" is carried out; and lastly, we have the representatives of the subscribers, to whom an addition has just been made by the appointment of Mr. E. H. Brodie, one of H.M. Chief Inspectors of Schools, whose selection is calculated to inspire the teaching section of the community with confidence, and who has been exceedingly cordial to us in the past. Our pupil-teacher classes are conducted entirely in accordance with the Educational Department, and that is our sole connexion with it.'

'Before we close our talk, I want to emphasize one point as strongly as I can. I do not think any institution has been started on so comprehensive a plan as ours with such a small income. It is a venture of faith in the local patriotism of Devonshire. Reading, with about a similar number of students, enjoys a yearly turn-over of £6,000: we have only about £2,000. It is sometimes easier to get a big amount than a small one; and so I must say, if we are to be worthy of the county, at least £5,000 will be wanted, and that soon. Our classes have already outgrown our class-rooms; in eighteen months' time the guarantee from Cambridge will cease, and the money will have to be made up. I am loth to believe that when the North has found so many "pious founders" the West can produce none. Were only a few to come forward and promise substantial aid, I am fain to believe others would at once follow. Will you let my last words be these: Who will just give us, say, £1,000 as a start!'

INFORMATION TO CONTRIBUTORS.

All communications should be addressed to the Editor, OXFORD UNIVERSITY EXTENSION GAZETTE, *University Press, Oxford.*

All matter intended for insertion in the May issue should reach him not later than April 20.

Contributions should be written on one side of the paper only, and must be accompanied by the name of the writer (not necessarily for publication).

N.B.—*All orders should carefully specify the full title,* OXFORD UNIVERSITY EXTENSION GAZETTE.

OXFORD UNIVERSITY

EXTENSION GAZETTE.

VOL. V. NO. 56.]   MAY, 1895.   [ONE PENNY.

N.B.—Local Organizers of Oxford University Extension Lectures are invited to send to the Secretary, University Extension Office, Examination Schools, Oxford, copies of any journals containing notices of, or references to, Extension work.

NOTES AND COMMENTS.

The Delegates regret that, owing to the change in the Secretaryship, there has been some delay in the completion of the Summer Meeting arrangements, but the detailed Programme is now ready, and may be obtained (price 7*d.*) on application to the Secretary, University Extension Office, Examination Schools, Oxford. There are still a few gaps in the programme, but the Delegates are in communication with several distinguished specialists whose services they hope to secure. It is never very easy to induce hard-worked litterateurs or politicians to make definite lecturing engagements for August, and in the case of the latter, the uncertainty of the political outlook renders it especially difficult. All the greater, however, is the gratitude of the Delegates to those who have, frequently at great personal inconvenience, undertaken to be present.

.·.

The opposition offered to Mr. Sadler's appointment to the post of Director of Special Inquiries in the Education Department met with but little support in the House of Commons. The consideration of the Education Estimates afforded a last opportunity for again raising the question. Fitting and appropriate testimony to the excellent choice made by Mr. Acland was given by the senior member for the University of Oxford, Sir John Mowbray, and by Professor Jebb, who represents the sister University of Cambridge. Mr. Acland's reply, brief as it was, contained a clear and straightforward reason for his choice; he had selected for the post the person best qualified, in his opinion, to discharge the duties of the office. This view was shared by a large majority of the House, as was shown in the division that followed. Mr. Sadler therefore begins his new work with the pleasant assurance that he has with him the support of the House of Commons.

.·.

The question of seeking admission for women to the Oxford B.A. degree is rapidly approaching a critical stage. A meeting of the Association for the Education of Women is to be held in Oxford on Saturday, May 4, 'to consider a proposal to petition the Hebdomadal Council for the recognition by the University of resident women students who are duly qualified, whether by admission to the B.A. degree or by a diploma certifying that they have fulfilled all the conditions required from men for that degree.' We have been fortunate enough to secure a short statement of the case, for and against, from two of the doughtiest champions of the opposing parties: Miss Rogers, the recently appointed Hon. Secretary of the Association for the Education of Women in Oxford, and Mrs. Arthur Johnson, who resigned that office only a few months ago, and whose services to the cause of women's education are well known and widely appreciated. It should be added in fairness to both writers that in neither case was the article of the one seen by the other, though leave for their collocation was of course obtained.

.·.

We are glad to see that the movement in favour of holding Summer Meetings is becoming increasingly popular. In the thirteenth Report of the Technical Education Committee recently published, it is announced that the Governors may establish a Summer Meeting at the Wye College for students from Kent and Surrey in analogy to the University Extension Meetings held at Oxford and Cambridge.

.·.

The Bournemouth Educational Council have recently done a very graceful and at the same time a very wise thing in co-opting Mr. E. L. S. Horsburgh to a seat on their body. It is a compliment to Mr. Horsburgh, a compliment to the Oxford Delegacy, which he will informally represent, and above all, it affords a most happy augury of the relations which we trust will be established between the new superintendent directors and the existing educational agencies in their respective districts. We heartily congratulate both Mr. Horsburgh and the Bournemouth Council.

.·.

The Southern Counties Federation of University Extension centres, inaugurated **Southern** last year at Bournemouth, has accepted the **Counties** invitation of the College Council to meet this **Federation.** year at Reading. The Conference will take place on Tuesday and Wednesday, May 14 and 15, when a number of important questions will be discussed. Particulars can be obtained from the Secretary, Mr. F. H. Wright, University Extension College, Reading.

.·.

It is with very great regret that we learn that Miss Snowdon, who has been Honorary **Yorkshire** Secretary for the Oxford centres in the York- **Association** shire Association ever since its foundation, **Meeting.** in 1890, is leaving England next autumn for several months, and has felt obliged, therefore, to resign the Secretaryship. Extension work in the West Riding owes almost more to Miss Snowdon than to any other single person, and her ever-ready help and sympathy in difficulties will be keenly missed by the centres which have been under her care during the last five years. We hope that when she returns she will be able again to take part in the work for which she has already done so much. The Association have been fortunate in securing Miss Cooke of Ilkley as successor to Miss Snowdon. Miss Cooke has rendered great assistance to Miss Snowdon in her work, and she does not therefore come to it as in any sense a stranger. Her visits to the Yorkshire and Lancashire centres this spring on behalf of the Delegates have given her a special knowledge of the wants of the district.

.·.

We hope that the suggestion of amalgamation with the Lancashire and Cheshire Association which was made at the close of the meeting, but about which no formal resolution was passed, will not be lost sight of. Extension work must be organized according to railway systems rather than according to counties; and the West Riding and Lancashire are so closely connected by rail that it is impossible to consider them separately when planning lecturers' circuits. We venture to think that the opportunities for usefulness of both Associations would be

1

immensely increased by some plan for conjoint action. But even an amalgamated Yorkshire, Lancashire and Cheshire Association will not be able properly to carry out its work, if the centres within those counties do not perform their part, and one and all become members. There should now be no difficulty about this, as the fee for the Yorkshire Association has been reduced from 7s. 6d. to 2s. 6d. for the year, and we understand that the Lancashire and Cheshire Association has just made a similar reduction.

.˙.

Another important proposal was that brought forward by Mr. Wilson for the appointment of a superintendent and organizing lecturer for Yorkshire. The need for some local supervision of Extension work is being more and more recognized, and we are very glad that the question is being seriously considered. The Marquis of Ripon has, with his usual liberality to Extension work, already promised £25 for five years on condition that the rest of the necessary money be forthcoming ; and we hope Mr. Wilson may be very successful in his further appeal for funds.

.˙.

The athletic mania is not confined, it would appear, to the Old Country, nor even to those of her colonies which are still politically connected with herself. In some of the American Universities there are loud laments as to the decay in college oratory and in the writing of prize essays. 'It is of course,' says the *New York Evening Post,* 'unreasonable to expect students whose first duty is to athletics, to do high-grade literary work in the intervals of training.' An enterprising firm in Ohio has consequently stepped into the breach. Messrs. Colchester, Roberts & Co. are prepared to provide original orations,' ranging in price from three to fifteen dollars, according to 'style, length, nature of subject,' &c. Political speeches can be had for from ten to thirty dollars, and it will be good news to many of the over-worked lecturers on our staff to learn that 'lectures can be obtained ranging from ten to fifty dollars.' Sermons can be got cheaper, but intending purchasers are requested to note that no guarantee of originality accompanies 'low-priced sermons.'

.˙.

We have received from Mr. Murray a new volume of the series of University Extension Manuals, Professor Allan Menzies' *Comparative Religion.* We shall hope to notice it in detail at an early opportunity. Seven other volumes in the same admirable series are reported to be in progress ; among them Mr. Sadler's volume on *Problems of Political Economy,* Mr. Bury's *History of Astronomy,* Mr. Boas's *Shakespeare and his Predecessors in the English Drama,* and Mr. J. W. Mackail's *Latin Literature.*

SUMMER MEETING NOTES.

It has been decided to extend the time during which University Extension students can obtain Summer Meeting tickets on reduced terms from May 1 to June 1.

.˙.

It is a signal, but by no means solitary, instance of the persistent goodwill of the new Bishop of Hereford towards the University Extension movement that he has undertaken to preach at the Special Service in the University Church (St. Mary's) on Sunday morning, August 4. It was largely owing to Dr. Percival, as we pointed out in a recent number of this *Gazette,* that the University of Oxford revived its Extension work on a new footing in 1885. From first to last the movement has never had a truer or stauncher friend. The news, therefore, that he has consented, despite the multifarious claims of his new work upon his strength and time, to be present at the Summer Meeting of this year, will be warmly welcomed by all Extension students.

The special sermon at St. Mary's on Sunday, August 11, will be preached by the Rev. Charles Gore, M.A., the new Canon of Westminster. The conjunction of his name with that of the Bishop of Hereford is curiously coincidental, as it was Canon Gore who was appointed to preach at the new Bishop's Consecration on March 25. To many of our students, especially to those who attended the Summer Meeting of 1892, Canon Gore is personally a familiar figure. To almost all he is well known as the editor of *Lux Mundi,* and as the author of the most remarkable series of Bampton Lectures delivered since those of Dr. Liddon. As a preacher he has leapt, almost at a bound, into the very front rank of pulpit orators. Were proof of this needed, the thronged condition of the Abbey when Canon Gore has preached during these last two months would afford it. But by Summer Meeting students it will not be.

.˙.

With characteristic kindness Canon Gore has consented not only to preach at the special service, but also, on the evening of the same day, to address a meeting to make known the work and aims of the Christian Social Union. To the latter meeting all holders of Summer Meeting tickets will be invited.

.˙.

We have very great pleasure in announcing that Mr. Augustine Birrell, Q.C., M.P., has just accepted an invitation to deliver a lecture at the Summer Meeting. All who are acquainted (and who is not?) with Mr. Birrell's brilliant *obiter dicta* will look forward with the pleasantest anticipation to his promised lecture on Dr. Johnson.

.˙.

Mr. C. W. Furse, whose lectures on the Painters of the Seventeenth Century were among the most brilliant successes of last year's Meeting, has most kindly promised to give a further series of lectures, at the forthcoming Meeting, on Sir Joshua Reynolds, Gainsborough and Hogarth.

.˙.

We are glad to be able to announce that Sir Charles Aitchison, K.C.S.I., M.A., has just accepted the invitation of the Delegacy to deliver a lecture on the 'Rise of British Dominion in India.' Sir Charles Aitchison is, as our readers are aware, one of the most distinguished of Anglo-Indian officials, and he has recently contributed to Sir William Hunter's well-known series on the Rulers of India a most interesting volume on Lord Lawrence.

.˙.

Professor Richard Lodge, M.A., who for the past ten years has been one of the most active and prominent members of the Modern History Faculty in Oxford, and who was at one time a member of the University Extension staff, has consented to deliver two lectures at the Summer Meeting on Scotch History in the Eighteenth Century. There is a special appropriateness in the selection of subject, as Mr. Lodge has been recently appointed the first Professor of Modern History in the University of Glasgow.

.˙.

A special feature of the Meeting of this year, as of that of 1894, will be the lectures and classes on the Science and Art of Education. The inaugural lecture in this section will be given by Miss Dorothea Beale, Principal of the Ladies College, Cheltenham. Classes on special subjects will be conducted by Mr. Holman, H. M. Inspector of Schools, and formerly Master of Method at the University College, Aberystwyth ; by Mr. Hugh Gordon, B.A. (on the Teaching of Science), and by Mr. Cooke on the Teaching of Art. Miss Bishop, the well-known mistress of the Edgbaston Kinder-Garten, has given a provisional promise to deliver the lectures on the Fröbel method.

.˙.

The Committee of the Gloucester centre of University Extension Teaching have again wisely and generously determined to spend part of their balance in offering Scholarships for the Summer Meeting. Two Scholarships of £4 each are to be open for award to any artisan who has attended the lectures during the past session, and two others of the same value to any one who has attended the lectures, 'provided they are not in receipt of a salary exceeding £100 per annum.' Gloucester is well to the fore in this as in every other matter connected with the organization of University Extension work, and we cordially commend its example to other centres who end their session in the same fortunate condition with a 'balance in hand.'

.·.

It is hoped that Mr. Leslie Stephen and Professor Dicey will be able to accept the invitation of the Delegacy to lecture at the Summer Meeting.

.·.

Lectures on Music.
It was generally agreed by the students attending the last Summer Meeting that one of the most delightful lectures in the main sequence was that of Dr. Mee on 'Seventeenth Century Music.' The Delegates have been in communication with several distinguished musicians for similar lectures on the Music and Musicians of the Eighteenth Century, and it is hoped that Dr. Bridge of Westminster will be able to accept an invitation to deliver one or two of the lectures. It is somewhat remarkable that hitherto there has been little or no demand for lectures on music at the centres themselves. In Philadelphia great enthusiasm is being aroused by a course of lectures on the history and literature of Music now being delivered under the auspices of the American University Extension Society. There is reason to hope that the subject is one which will receive more attention from the Oxford centres in the future than it has in the recent past.

THE DISTRICT DIRECTORS OF UNIVERSITY EXTENSION TEACHING.

THE newly-appointed Directors, Mr. Wells and Mr. Horsburgh, have issued the following circular to all the centres in their respective districts. They have both been attending meetings during the past month.

Oxford University Extension.

Western and Southern Circuits.

The terms of the appointment of the directors of University Extension Teaching (which dates from March 25, 1895) are somewhat vague; the *Oxford University Extension Gazette* of March only says 'the main duty of the directors will be to co-operate with the local committees in improving and systematizing the organization of the work.'

It is therefore desirable to explain at once the ways by which it seems to us that these ends may be attained; no doubt the local experience of secretaries and the consciousness of local needs will suggest others: it is of the utmost importance that the duties of these new offices, which have been created, should be developed and defined with the assistance of our centres.

The objects to be aimed at are :—

(1) The organization—as far as is possible—of lecture circuits in adjoining centres, with a view to economy in travelling expenses and in the strength and time of lecturers.

(2) The development of strong centres (*a*) encouraging the development of students' associations; (*b*) where possible forming classes for special study under local teachers in connexion with the general lectures; (*c*) drawing closer the relations between University Extension work and other educational societies, e. g. mutual improvement classes, branches of the Y. M. C. A. &c. already existing in the locality; (*d*) if possible, bringing other educational agencies into connexion with University Extension work, with a view to prevent competition and to promote general efficiency. This might be done especially in the matter of training pupil teachers for the Queen's Scholarship examinations.

(3) The general assistance of centres from time to time by special lectures with a view to raising funds, and by attending

conversaziones, prize distributions, &c., when courses are beginning or ending.

(4) The formation of new centres in adjoining places within the districts, where at present University Extension has not taken root.

We propose the following means to attaining these ends :—

(1) It would be very desirable if, as far as possible, lectures for the ensuing year could be arranged in concert by the secretaries of centres conveniently placed for co-operation; this might be done at small local conferences in March or April each year, at which the directors would be present.

(2) We propose to hold ourselves free at certain times in each year for public lectures, meetings, &c. at the centres.

The times that seem most suitable are :— (*a*) The last ten days in September and the first ten days of October. (Mr. Horsburgh will be free throughout September, but not in October when his ordinary courses will have begun.) (*b*) If convenient to the centres, for a week either before or after Christmas. (*c*) For ten days or so in the weeks immediately following Easter.

(3) We should be glad to assist at public meetings with a view to forming new University Extension centres.

(4) When visiting the centres, we should be very glad to meet all persons engaged in educational work of any kind, whether directly connected with University Extension or not.

The principle of University Extension work hitherto has been its direct growth out of local needs nd from local energy: this has been its strength, and must be, if it is to continue to flourish. We look upon ourselves as appointed to assist and not to 'direct': but our aim will be everywhere to lay stress on the fact that University Extension is not merely a movement for the provision of intellectual amusement, or even for the cultivation of the individual student; both these aims it fulfils and ought to fulfil : but we believe we shall be only expressing the feelings of all local workers when we say that we regard University Extension as a means for the education of citizens in the widest sense, as a movement for the promotion of unity and fellowship in those higher interests, which make life not merely a round of routine duties and pleasures, but a privilege and a charge.

J. WELLS, *Wadham College, Oxford.*

E. L. S. HORSBURGH, 18 *Maddox Street, London, W.*

. It will be understood that the directors will be glad to hear *at any time* from local organizers as to questions that may arise, or as to difficulties in their work, and to assist in any way that may be possible.

CERTIFICATES ON CONNECTED SHORT COURSES.

MANY students have suffered from the fact that the towns in which they live can only afford to arrange one course of six lectures in a session; they have consequently been unable to obtain any recognition of their work from the University in connexion with which the lectures are arranged, beyond the publication of their names on the printed lists. As an increasing number of such centres have lately arranged their short courses in sequence of subject, the question of treating these two short courses as equal to one full course of twelve lectures has become important. After careful consideration the Delegacy have resolved to grant certificates on certain conditions to students who have attended two successive courses of six lectures each (the subjects of the courses being in sequence), and have undertaken some connecting work during the intervening Summer. As it is desirable that the certificate should imply, as it does at present, knowledge of the subject-matter of the whole course of twelve lectures, the Delegates have decided that the certificate shall only be awarded to students who, in addition to having passed the examination at the end of the first six lectures, shall, at the end of the second six, pass a final examination on the subject-matter of the whole of the twelve lectures. Moreover, students will be required in the period between the two courses, to undertake a course of study connected with the

2

subject of the lectures. Such a course of study must be sanctioned by the lecturer and the University authority, and must be conducted in a Students' Association, or in a class recognized by the University authority.

It is hoped that this scheme will afford additional stimulus to local committees—where short courses alone are possible—to arrange them in educational sequence, and that it will act as an incentive to Students' Associations to carry out a definite scheme of organized study in the intervals between the courses. At the same time the student who attends only one course will be able as at present to enter for the examination on that course, and the names of the successful candidates will continue to be published in the printed lists issued by the Delegates.

PREPARATIVE READING FOR THE SUMMER MEETING, 1895.

EDUCATION COURSES.

Ladd, *Primer of Psychology* (for beginners). (Longmans.)
Sully, *Outlines of Psychology*. (Longmans.)
Compayre, *Lectures on Teaching*. (Isbister.)
De Garmo, *Essentials of Method*. (Isbister.)
Lange, *Apperception*. (Isbister.)
De Garmo, *Herbart*. (Heinemann.)
Herbart, *The Science of Education*. (Sonnenschein.)

GENERAL GEOLOGY.

Page and Lapworth, *Introductory Text-book of Geology*. Twelfth Edition (*not an earlier* edition). (Blackwood, 3*s*. 6*d*.)
Or Sir A. Geikie, *Class Book of Geology*. (Macmillan, 4*s*. 6*d*.)

Advanced Works.

Sir A. Geikie, *A Text-book of Geology*. (Macmillan, 28*s*.)
A. H. Green, *Physical Geology*. (Longmans, 21*s*.)
Sir A. Ramsay, *The Physical Geography and Geology of Great Britain*. (Stanford.)

FOR THE GEOLOGY OF THE NEIGHBOURHOOD OF OXFORD.

The Geology of the Country round Banbury, Woodstock, Bicester, and Buckingham (Memoirs of the Geological Survey, Sheet 45). (Longmans, 2*s*.)
The Geology of Parts of Oxfordshire and Berkshire (Memoirs of the Geol. Survey, Sheet 13). (Longmans, 3*s*.)
Phillips, *The Geology of Oxford and the Valley of the Thames* (may be consulted, if accessible). (Clarendon Press, 21*s*.)

BOTANY.

Oliver, *Lessons in Elementary Botany*. (Macmillan, 4*s*. 6*d*.)
Lubbock, *British Wild Flowers in Relation to Insects*. (Macmillan, 4*s*. 6*d*.)
Grant Allen, *Colours of Flowers*. (Macmillan, 3*s*. 6*d*.)
Wallace, *Darwinism*. (Macmillan, 9*s*.)

HYGIENE.

Students proposing to attend the course of lectures on Hygiene are recommended to make perusal of the little manual on *The Laws of Health*, by Professor Corfield, and published (price 1*s*. 6*d*.) by Longmans & Co., London. The text-book best adapted to the course for all who can give the necessary time to its study is Dr. Whitelegge's *Hygiene and Public Health*, published (price 2*s*. 6*d*.) by Cassell & Co., London. In addition to either or both of these works, an elementary introduction to animal and human physiology, if it can be read, will afford valuable aid to the student of Hygiene; and perhaps the most suitable volume in this connexion is the recently issued and most excellent *Physiology for Beginners*, by Prof. M. Foster and Dr. Shore, and published by Macmillan & Co, London (price 2*s*. 6*d*.).

For supplementary reading, whenever time and opportunity permits, the following are specially recommended:—
Our Secret Friends and Foes, by Dr. Percy Frankland; *Treatise on Hygiene and Public Health*, edited by Dr. Stevenson and Murphy; the sections dealing with air, water, the dwelling, food and infection, in vols. i. and ii.
The Micro organisms of Water, Frankland; *The Chemistry of Cookery*, W. M. Williams; *Healthy Dwellings*, Galton; *Rural Hygiene*, Dr. V. Poore.

ANNUAL CONFERENCE OF THE YORKSHIRE ASSOCIATION.

THE annual conference of the Yorkshire Association for the Extension of University Teaching was held at York, on Saturday, April 6. Representatives were present from York, Scarborough, Hull, Pontefract, Barnsley, Harrogate, Ripon, Ilkley and Halifax, as well as from Oxford, Cambridge and Victoria. The statement of accounts, the receipt of which was the first business of the meeting, showed a balance on the general account of £6 1*s*. 6*d*., and on the Scholarship account of £5 8*s*. 0*d*. All the officers were re-elected for the ensuing year, with the exception of Miss Snowdon, the Hon. Secretary for the Oxford centres, who is obliged to resign her post and whose place will be taken by Miss Cooke of Ilkley. The Marquis of Ripon is again President, the Archbishop of York, the Bishop of Ripon and the Earl of Carlisle Vice-Presidents, Miss Thompson of Scarborough Hon. Treasurer, and Mr. Wilson of Hull general Hon. Secretary. Arrangements were made with the University representatives for lectures for next session. The subscription for the ensuing year was fixed at 2*s*. 6*d*. Mr. Wilson presented an interesting report of the work of the Yorkshire centres during the past year, from which it appeared that twenty-five centres had carried on University Extension work, ten of these connected with Oxford, six with Cambridge and nine with Victoria. He also reported that the Association had been able to send three scholars last year to the Oxford Summer Meeting, and the continuance of the Scholarship Fund was resolved upon. The report was adopted with thanks to the Secretary for preparing it.

Mr. Wilson then proposed, 'That this Association considers it advisable to endeavour with the least possible delay to arrange for the appointment of a superintendent and organizing lecturer for Yorkshire.' He remarked that the matter was mentioned at the annual meeting last year, and that the only difficulty appeared to be the question of finance. He saw no reason why that Association should not be able to raise sufficient funds to justify such an appointment as he proposed. His idea was that they should get the individual friends of the movement in the county to promise contributions for a term of five or six years. If they could get together £100 in this way, and could, in addition, guarantee the lecturer work in the county to the value of £250, they would be in a position to ask a superintendent to come down, say for three years, at £350 a year. A short time ago he communicated on the subject with Lord Ripon, their President, who replied that he should be glad to see the first step in such a scheme taken in Yorkshire, and to contribute £25 a year for five years providing the rest of the necessary funds could be raised.

After some discussion, the proposal was seconded by Miss Thompson and carried; and the Secretary was requested to endeavour to raise the necessary funds. It was decided to hold the conference next year at Leeds, and the meeting closed with an informal discussion of the desirability of endeavouring to bring about some sort of amalgamation with the Lancashire and Cheshire Association, with a view to the better arrangement of the lecturers' work in the three counties. No resolution was passed, but it was understood that the Hon. Secretary of the Oxford centres would communicate with the Hon. Secretary of the Lancashire and Cheshire Association on the subject.

SCHOLARSHIP FUND FOR THE OXFORD SUMMER MEETING, 1895.

	£	s.	d.
The Secretary's Scholarship (subscribed by students attending the Summer Meeting, 1894)	45	0	0
Mr. F. Haverfield, Student and Tutor of Christ Church	5	0	0
Mr. M. E. Sadler	10	0	0
Mr. J. Wells, Fellow and Tutor of Wadham	5	0	0
Messrs. Methuen & Co.	10	0	0

SHALL WOMEN HAVE THE B.A. DEGREE?

I.

By Miss A. M. A. H. ROGERS, *Hon. Sec. to the Association for the Education of Women in Oxford.*

WHEN Oxford confers the degree of B.A. upon a man it requires that three conditions shall have been fulfilled. He must have been for three years a member of the University, and therefore, by its constitution, a member of a College, a Hall, or of the body of Non-Collegiate students. He must have passed at least three University Examinations, in the first of which Latin, Greek and Mathematics are required. He must have resided in Oxford for three academical years.

There is in Oxford a body of students, registered under an Association and members of a College, a Hall, or the body of Home Students, but not matriculated. Some of these students are following exactly the same courses of study as members of the University. They intend to enter for the same examinations, at the same time, in the same room, and under the same conditions as to paper-work and viva-voce: they purpose to reside for three academical years, and the bodies to which they belong are prepared to present them for matriculation. These students, we are told, cannot graduate. They are, through the misfortune of their birth, women; and though Oxford examines women and encourages them to reside, it provides them no teaching, and gives the world no guarantee that they have received an Oxford education.

Through the favour of Colleges and individual teachers women are educated in Oxford, but they go out into professions at a considerable disadvantage. They can with truth say for themselves that they have studied in Oxford, have attended lectures, have been members of a Hall or other body, but Oxford, though it has educated them, is silent on this point. Like other Universities when it educates a man it gives him a degree, unlike most Universities, it does not allow the women it examines to graduate.

Oxford has however not refused the degree, for it has not been asked for it. The Council of the Association for the Education of Women, which has led the movement for women's University education in Oxford for fifteen years, while acknowledging the value of the concessions made to women who do not take the full course, is, by a large majority, in favour of making the request that qualified women (that is, those who fulfil all the requirements for the B.A.) should receive the degree. The B.A. itself is the only mark of recognition that the outside world will acknowledge, and anything short of it must be only a temporary expedient. While women, whose qualifications are the same as those of men, are not declared in the customary and recognized way to be duly qualified, they must necessarily be looked upon as their inferiors; and even the concessions and privileges granted by Oxford to women, though valuable in the early days of the movement and to individual students at all times, are of doubtful benefit to the status of Oxford students. Certainly Oxford, where more liberty is given to modify the course than at Cambridge, does not yet fill so large a place as Cambridge in the University life of women, and we are credibly informed that the uncertainty as to the exact meaning of its certificates does harm. It is therefore on the general ground that a woman, whose University course has been identical with a man's, should have the right to state it in the only way that will be fully recognized, that I hope to see women, as soon as they have fulfilled the necessary conditions, admitted to the B.A. degree of the University of Oxford, and thereby placed on a level with the women graduates of other Universities.

Much, though not all, of what I have said applies equally to Cambridge students, but their position is in many ways different, and I have preferred to leave their claims to be dealt with by a representative of their own University.

II.

By Mrs. A. H. JOHNSON, *Principal of the Home-Students, Hon. Sec. to Lady Margaret Hall, Formerly Hon. Sec. to the A. E. W.*

THE important question which is to be decided on May 4, at the General Meeting of the Association, has for the first time divided the friends of the Education of Women in Oxford into two camps. Seven years ago, when the same question of asking the University to grant the B.A. degree to women was discussed at Cambridge, our committee agreed that it would not be wise to raise the question in Oxford. They held—and this was the view which finally prevailed at Cambridge—that the granting of the degree would hinder rather than further the higher education of women, taking the expression in its widest and best sense; and that no evidence existed to show that the want of the mystic letters was in any way a drawback to our students, when applying for educational or other posts.

The dispute now is, therefore, not as between supporters and opponents of women's University education, but between those who equally believe in its value, who are equally pledged to further it, who equally desire to place it on a satisfactory and permanent footing.

That, at some future time, it might be well on all grounds that women students should have the B.A. both sides would probably allow; the question is, whether at this particular moment the University should be asked to grant it to those women students who shall have fulfilled exactly the same requirements as regards examination and statutable residence as the undergraduate. We propose to show that the reasons which induced the Association not to ask for the B.A. in 1888 still hold good, and that their decision has been justified by the result.

(1) It is asserted by the advocates for the change that women students are at a disadvantage, because they cannot take the B.A. degree, and are not even recognized by the University. It is quite true that the residence in Oxford of women students is not technically recognized, but this has not prevented their participating in all the educational advantages the University can give, while at the same time the authorities of the Association and Halls have enjoyed a freedom of action which has certainly been of value hitherto. Not only have all the Honour Examinations of the University been opened to women, but they have practically the same privileges as the men with regard to public libraries, laboratories, and lectures, and the high classes obtained in every Honour School are a proof that women are at no disadvantage. Nor is there any likelihood that these privileges will be withdrawn, unless, indeed, a demand for actual recognition at this present juncture should irritate the opponents of women's education—a contingency by no means impossible.

From the University point of view there is a good deal to be said for a longer trial of the experiment on its present basis. No doubt lately women students have been put on the same footing as men in Scotch and other Universities. But Oxford and Cambridge stand alone in their conditions of life and work, and it is not easy to base any argument with regard to them on experience elsewhere.

(2) Nor, though it is often stated, can it be proved that a lack of the B.A. degree has put our students and those of Cambridge at a disadvantage in competing for work with graduates of London, Victoria and other Universities. Positive proof on this point is difficult; but the present writer can only say that in fifteen years' experience as Secretary of Lady Margaret Hall, and ten years in experience as Secretary of the Association, she cannot recall one single case of a post lost for want of the degree, or even a complaint that there was no degree. It is true that in advertisements appears sometimes 'A graduate preferred '; but if an Oxford student can offer the required subjects, a certificate of residence from her Principal, and her University Certificate of Examination, she is not refused because she cannot call herself a B.A. Moreover the expression 'a degree,' or an equivalent to a degree, includes the Oxford student.

Further, of the 178 students who are permanently on the Register of the Association, 18 are, or have been, principals, vice-principals, or lecturers, 4 head-mistresses, 83 assistant-mistresses, not to mention those who have obtained private work, or posts other than teaching. Surely it is idle, in the face of these facts, to insist any more on the disadvantages under which our students have hitherto laboured.

But the chief objection to the change is that it would not conduce to the educational advantage of women students. In this respect the conditions remain nearly as they were in 1888, and indeed in one respect are less favourable. No doubt the introduction of a Final Honour School for men in the subject of English Language and Literature has added one more branch of study to the degree course. But in the subject of Modern Languages—a subject much required by those women who are preparing for the post of school-mistresses—there is still no Honour course which qualifies for a degree. So that, should the B.A. be granted, a student wishing to study this subject would have to forego the hope of a degree and sink to a lower position than her companions.

A still more serious objection remains. Until the other day, the friends of Women's University Education at Cambridge and Oxford have steadily refused to ask for the opening to women of the Pass Examinations. It was felt that there was nothing to be said for bringing young women up to the Universities to do Pass work. It is true that at Oxford there had always been a Pass Examination for women; but this had none of the attractions of a regular University Examination, and has chiefly been used, when thought advisable, as an intermediate examination.

During the last year, however, all the Oxford Pass Examinations have been opened to women, while Cambridge has kept to its resolve to have none but Honour students. Under these circumstances it is easy to foretell the result of now granting the B.A. Who can doubt that it would lead to a large increase of applicants for the Pass Schools?

The educational difficulty of forcing matriculated women students into the exact curriculum of the men remains the same as it was in '88. It must be remembered that there is no entrance to the B.A. except through Responsions, which means Latin and Greek books and Latin prose; and, after Responsions, either Classical Moderations or, if the alternatives to Moderations be taken instead, at any rate more Latin or Greek Testament.

It seems just as unreasonable now as it did in '88 to train girls in modern subjects at school or at home, and when they come to the University, presumably to carry on their work in a really complete manner, and to specialize in those subjects in which they have already shown aptitude or interest, to turn them suddenly into the classical road, and compel them to compete with boys who for years have been imbibing Latin and Greek.

There never was any difficulty in cramming girls up for Pass Examinations. But surely the whole theory of 'a lift to women's education throughout the country' by opening a University career to them demands that cram should cease, that we should root out the pernicious idea that any subject—languages least of all, perhaps—can be 'got up' in a few months, if it is to be worth anything either for teaching or for self-culture. Hitherto the mistake in women's education has been held to be that it has been shallow and scattered, and in no part serious enough. How is it to be 'lifted' by crowning at the University that course only which, in by far the largest number of cases, means the cramming up in a few months of subjects which it has taken boys years to learn—subjects too which will often be abandoned as soon as learnt?

It is no doubt difficult for those who are not acquainted with the details of the University Education of Women, during the fifteen years of its existence in Oxford, to realize the very great change which this apparently simple and graceful concession of the B.A. degree would cause. No ambitious student, no young woman, obliged to earn her own living, could dare to accept the lower place of a student who does not aim at a degree, a student who has not even had the honour of belonging to the University at all—for it is not proposed to matriculate any but those who are to take the B.A. course. At present all are alike, and the world accepts them on their achievements, and indeed

has been well satisfied with them; but if we mark out some for special preference, the others must be at a disadvantage.

What are the facts as regards Oxford women students hitherto? From the first it was open to them to take Latin and Greek exactly as the men do, though until 1884, not in the identical Examinations; for a time also women had a special final Honour School of Literae Humaniores, in which Philosophy and Ancient History were divided, and it was possible to obtain a First in Philosophy without a knowledge of Latin and Greek, the authors being read in translations. But for the last seven years women have been free to choose any of the Examinations open to men, and in any order deemed advisable. From the first they could have chosen the Latin and Greek course, exactly as a man might choose it, except that up to 1888 they would have taken their classical 'Greats' in two parts.

If the laws of supply and demand and the results of freedom of choice can be held to teach us anything, it ought to be instructive to see what were the subjects which earnest students and their thoroughly competent advisers thought the best for them both educationally and practically.

But what are the facts? In the fifteen years, 191 students have obtained classes in the Honour Schools. Of these sixty-two have taken Modern History, fifty-two of them having taken no intermediate examination answering to Moderations; two or three only Latin at any stage, and none Greek. Thirty-six have taken Modern Languages, four only with an intermediate examination, none with Greek at any stage, one or two only with Latin. Twenty-nine took English, two only with an intermediate, none with Latin or Greek. Fourteen took Science with the usual Science preliminaries, but were able to go straight to them from the ordinary Women's Pass Examination in Modern Languages and Mathematics, or an equivalent taken at school. Nine took Mathematics in the same way, and, with one exception, did not do more than Mathematical Moderations in their three years. Three took Philosophy under the old system, two of these without Greek, and one took Ancient History.

Leaving out the two who took Latin and Greek for their Philosophy and Ancient History, we get a total of 152 who have done the highest quality of University work—for forty-one obtained a First Class—and all have preferred other subjects to Classics. None found it advisable to get up Greek (one Science student took Greek, but not Latin, for her First Examination for Women) for their preliminary examination; few, to take any intermediate examination.

In Classical Moderations, we have had in the fifteen years thirty-two only, most of whom have taken three years at least to obtain their class, although the greater number had shown a decided bent towards classics before they came up, and had worked at one or other classical language. One took the final Honour School of Lit. Hum. after Honour Moderations, and four more are now working for it. To the thirty-two should be added five who took the Final School only: two of these had taken Moderations from Holloway; the others did not take Moderations at all. Thus, with the two mentioned above who took Philosophy and History under the old system, we get a total of thirty-nine choosing classics as against 154 choosing other subjects. Nor has the number of students taking classics, or offering Greek in a preliminary examination, grown of late years.

If, therefore, we force students into the men's curriculum—as practically we shall—a serious change in the course of their education at Oxford must ensue. One thing we fancied our experience had taught us; that it was a great disadvantage to students to be obliged to waste any of their time at the University over a Preliminary Entrance Examination, or even, in most cases, over a Pass Intermediate Examination. Now, unless it be proposed to force Latin and Greek, at any rate up to the standard of Responsions, upon Girls' Schools, our best students will most of them spend a year or more of their precious time at the University over the elements of Latin, Greek and other Pass subjects.

Two facts should also be remembered. Whereas the

large majority of undergraduates have money enough and to spare, and also are occupying at Oxford a few years between boyhood and manhood, by far the greater number of women students come up with barely enough money to carry them through their University career and, in a large number of cases, not enough to cover more than two years. Many of them, too, when they come up, are already fitted to earn their own living, and every month is precious to them. In order to get the B.A. as quickly as possible many of them must inevitably drop down to Pass work.

There is a great deal to be said for the received method of making a path across a field, namely, waiting to see where the grass is the most worn by footsteps. And in our experiment of University education for women, where we are dealing with persons who do not need driving, but earnestly desire to do thorough work, it might be wisest, before we make for the new and attractive way offered by University recognition and the B.A., to wait for a longer experience of the needs of our women students.

It may even be that in the future we must have the courage to confess that, while there is no educational subject which women cannot study with advantage, and while the highest subject for men is also the highest for women, the necessary circumstances of women's lives and temperament may render it more fitting, as it certainly is more easy, to allow them greater freedom in the choice of their University work. So that, as the late Professor Nettleship has said : 'A larger variety of subjects may be selected from the vast and increasing mass of knowledge for the purposes of serious mental training; that the study of Latin and Greek Classics may be as far as possible confined to those who are likely to profit by it, and thus the ideal of education may be reached, and no single mind be thrown away upon a study for which it is unfit.'

REPORTS FROM THE CENTRES.

CAMBORNE.—Our first course of lectures under the Cornwall County Council has now come to its conclusion. On March 29 Mr. W. B. Worsfold gave the last of his lectures on South Africa to the Camborne audience, which much regretted that the course had now come to an end. The course, which consisted of twelve lectures at fortnightly intervals, began in October last, and the attendance has averaged 100, with 55 per cent. of industrial attendance. This is our first long course, and our first experience of fortnightly lectures, and we all feel that we would never willingly return to a short course of weekly lectures. This must be regarded as quite the most successful course of lectures we have had, both in the character of the attendance, and the numbers, although, owing to various circumstances, a large portion of the audience was not able to keep up attendance after Christmas. In conjunction with the other Cornish centres we have petitioned our County Council for a repetition of the grant made last year, and we are hoping that we may be thus enabled to have a second course on some similar subject from Mr. Worsfold during the winter 1895-6.—BEATRICE VIVIAN, *Hon. Sec.*

BRIGHTON AND HOVE (Greek Classes).—The elementary class has during the Spring Term again numbered ten members, and has continued its work most satisfactorily. Alternate weekly exercises from Abbott's Arnold and Sidgwick's *First Greek Writer* have been sent in, and Chapters 1-3 of the *Anabasis*, and scenes from the first 250 lines of the *Alcestis* of Euripides, have been read. We are glad to report the revival of the intermediate class with seven members. The work here has included weekly exercises from the latter half of Sidgwick's *First Writer*, and from Sidgwick and Morice's *Greek Verse Composition*, with translation of Thucydides, Bk. i, Chapters 33-43, and of lines 1-692 of the *Ajax* of Sophocles (omitting choruses). This has been accomplished in spite of interruptions from influenza, which reduced the number of classes in each section from ten to eight. Special interest has been awakened in both classes in the construction of Greek Verse. Enthusiasm is, indeed, at all times, irresistible, and we are fortunate in having in Mr. Luce a lecturer whose own love of the subject commends its study even to beginners. There is promise of an increase in the elementary. class in the Summer Term, and it is hoped that the intermediate class will also muster sufficient numbers to justify its continuance.—A. S. VERRALL, *Hon. Sec.*

REIGATE.—Mr. Horsburgh has just finished a course of

lectures at this centre on 'The Tudor Monarchy.' We have been fortunate in having the same lecturer for the last five years, and each course has been in every way successful. It is satisfactory to find that interest in the lectures increases, as during the last course more students wrote papers for the lecturer, and also more entered for the examination. The first six lectures were especially well attended, the average being 112. After Christmas the long frost, and the great prevalence of influenza, somewhat reduced the attendance, which seemed a great pity as the lectures on the Elizabethan period were perhaps even more interesting than those on the earlier Tudors. As usual, at the end of the course, the vote of the students was taken as to the subject for next session, and the choice this time proved to be in favour of literature.—FRANCES T. BAKER, *Hon. Sec.*

RHYL.—We extract the following from the *North Wales Chronicle* of March 30 last :—' The annual meeting of the Rhyl University Extension Society was held at Colet House, Rhyl, Mr. W. J. P. Storey in the chair. Mr. Hugh Jones, M.A., presented the balance sheet, which showed a deficit of £1 2s. 2d. as the result of the course of lectures given on the 'History of Architecture,' by Mr. J. E. Phythian. The fund of the society amounted to £19 9s. 7d., and it was decided to draw £1 2s. 2d. to cover the deficit. The visit to Chester Cathedral, under Mr. Phythian's guidance, was arranged for Thursday, April 4, and it was decided to apply to the County Council for a grant towards the cost of continuing the lectures, and to await their reply before deciding whether another course should be arranged or not.'

TUNBRIDGE WELLS.—We have made a new departure this term, in connexion with the afternoon lectures on Architecture. We have taken advantage of Mr. Bond's generous offer to conduct his students to some of the places of architectural interest in the neighbourhood, and three excursions have been made—the first to Rotherfield Church, the second to the ruins of Bayham Abbey, and the third to Canterbury. They have been a decided success, especially the visit to Canterbury, for which a party of nearly forty was made up. Besides their educational value, the social advantages of these expeditions are not to be despised, and we feel much indebted to Mr. Bond for his kindness in undertaking them.—L. F. JONES, *Hon. Sec.*

[Reports received from the following centres are unavoidably held over :—Dover, Tavistock, Weymouth, Wirksworth.]

BOOKS ON OUR TABLE.

The Revolutionary and Napoleonic Era, 1789-1815 (Cambridge Historical Series). By J. H. ROSE. (Cambridge : the University Press.)

Like Mr. Morse Stephens, Mr. Rose has contributed an admirable volume on the Revolutionary and Napoleonic Era. He thoroughly appreciates the causes of the overthrow of Old Europe by France ; his account of the Revolution is excellent ; his description of Napoleon's career is masterly. It is impossible that a volume dealing with so complicated a period should be entirely free from errors ; it is equally impossible that Mr. Rose's conclusions should satisfy all historical students. He does not, perhaps, attach sufficient importance to the Peninsular War as one of the causes of the fall of Napoleon ; he is not at his best when describing the Emperor's preparations for invading England. But the volume is one of great merit ; it is carefully arranged ; it bears evidence of honest research ; it is in every respect attractive. We can congratulate Mr. Rose on his book, and Professor Prothero on the first volume of his series.

A. H.

Outlines of English Industrial History. By W. CUNNINGHAM, D.D., and ELLEN MⁱARTHUR. Cambridge University Press. 1895.

A concise presentment of the industrial history of England will be welcome everywhere, and Dr. Prothero is to be congratulated on the latest volume of the *Cambridge Historical Series.* The plan of the writers is to trace economic progress from the beginning of things down to the present day—and even beyond. This is done under a variety of heads. Thus we are shown, first of all, the making of industrial England, the national features of the country, the immigrants, their character and work. Country and town life are then illustrated by a sketch of the manor and a history of the mediaeval gilds. Lastly, we have the first beginnings of national as against local economic life set out in a valuable chapter. From this point the authors pass to a historical survey of the development of the various germs contained in the earlier state of things. The choice of heads is excellent, and, on the whole, the method is successful. True, there is something a little bewildering in the way in which the

reader is carried backwards and forwards over the same ground whilst tracing the history of the various sides of economic life. He feels at times as if he was living in a watertight compartment, or at any rate is compelled to close his eyes and ears to a good deal. But this is inevitable, and the gain in clearness compensates for a certain weakening of the power of realizing history as a whole. On particular points a good deal might be said; the work of Dr. Cunningham, even when shared by so excellent a colleague as Miss McArthur, is sure to contain debatable matter. Thus it is a little rash to indulge in forecasts as to the future, and these are certain to be criticized by every reader—it is the fate of prophets! Would it be possible in a second edition to add a few more references to works in which the student can follow up various branches of the subject?—
　　　　　　　　　　　　　　　　　　　　L. R. PHELPS.

London Matriculation Directory. No. XVII, January 1895. With Solutions to the Examination Papers. London, Univ. Corr. Coll. Press. Price 1s. net.

Intermediate Text-Book of English Literature. Vol. III (1660—1798). By W. H. LOW, M.A. Lond. London, Univ. Corr. Coll. Press. Pp. viii, 207. Price 3s. 6d.

Text-Book of Dynamics. By WILLIAM BRIGGS, M.A., LL.B. and G. H. BRYAN, M.A. London, Univ. Corr. Coll. Press. Pp. xiv. 192, Price 2s.

Text-Book of Statics. By WILLIAM BRIGGS, M.A., LL.B. and G. H. BRYAN, M.A. London, Univ. Corr. Coll. Press. Pp. viii, 220. Price 1s. 6d.

Steps to French. By A. M. M. STEDMAN, M.A., Wadham Coll., Oxon. London, Methuen & Co. Limp cloth, pp. 79. Price 8d.

European History: A.D. 1789—1815. By H. MORSE STEPHENS, M.A., Lecturer in Indian History at Cambridge. London, Rivington, Percival & Co. Crown 8vo, pp. xvi, 423. With maps.

SCHOLARSHIPS FOR THE OXFORD SUMMER MEETING, 1895.

A FUND, to which subscriptions amounting to £60 have already been promised, has been opened for the provision of Scholarships to enable students from Oxford centres to attend the Summer Meeting, which will be held in Oxford from August 1 to August 26, 1895.

The Scholarships will be awarded after an Essay competition, and will be of two values—£10 and £5. Holders of the former must attend the whole Meeting; those of the latter may, if they prefer, attend either the First or Second Part only. Part I lasts from Aug. 1 to Aug. 12; Part II from Aug. 12 to Aug. 26.

Conditions of Award.

The Scholarships will be awarded on or about July 1, 1895, for English Essays on subjects drawn from English Literature, English History, Natural Science, and Political Economy.

A. *Competition for Scholarships.*

The Scholarships will be awarded in three divisions:—

(a) Open to all Oxford University Extension Students *who need the assistance of the Scholarships* in order to study in Oxford, according to the intention of the donors.

(b) Open to all Elementary School Teachers (men or women), who are also Oxford University Extension Students.

(c) Open to all working men and women, who are also Oxford University Extension Students.

To qualify themselves for election to a Scholarship:—

(1) All competitors must be recommended by their Local Committee as suitable candidates.

(2) Competitors in *divisions* (a) and (b) must, in order to qualify, obtain *distinction* in an examination on a course of Oxford University Extension Lectures delivered between January 1894 and June 1895.

(3) Competitors in *division* (c) must pass an examination on a course of Oxford University Extension Lectures delivered between the same dates.

The Delegates, however, reserve to themselves the right of rejecting the name of any candidate; and, unless compositions of sufficient merit are sent in, do not bind themselves to award Scholarships in any or all of the following four subjects.

B. *Competition for Prizes.*

A limited number of Prizes, of the value of £1, will be awarded in the same competition without any limitation as to the means of the competitors. Candidates for this branch of the competition must qualify as regards examinations, like the competitors in *divisions* (a) and (b).

SUBJECTS.

(1) *History* (one only to be selected).

(i) The Growth of Nationality in the thirteenth century.
(ii) The causes of the Great Rebellion.
(iii) England's command of the Sea during the Revolutionary Wars (1793–1815).

(2) *Literature* (one only to be selected).

(i) How far is it possible to specify any general conditions which are necessary to the production of the best poetry?
(ii) Explain what is meant by Poetic Justice, and consider with full illustrations how far it should be observed in Drama or Fiction.
(iii) Estimate the importance in literary history of the works of Dryden, Pope, or Walter Scott.

(3) *Political Economy* (one only to be selected).

(i) Show the effect of different systems of land tenure on the production and distribution of wealth.
(ii) What remedies have been suggested for the existing depression, and how far are they likely to succeed?
(iii) What circumstances may be expected to determine the wages of labour in the future?

(4) *Science* (one only to be selected).

(i) Theories of Chemical Action.
(ii) Sewage disposal in towns and rural districts.
(iii) The Weeds of the Farm.

REGULATIONS.

1. Each candidate may write an essay *on one subject only*, but may select one from any of the above four groups.

2. All compositions must reach the Delegacy [addressed—The Secretary, University Extension Office, Examination Schools, Oxford] on or before Monday, June 3, 1895; must each bear the writer's full name and address, with a note saying whether the writer is competing for a Scholarship or a Prize, or both, and, if the former, in which division (a, b, or c, see above); must be written on foolscap paper, and on one side of the paper only; must state, at the top of the first page, the writer's occupation; and must be accompanied by a certificate of qualification from his or her Local Committee in the following form :—

> 'On behalf of the members of the Local Committee acting in concert with the Oxford University Delegates for the establishment of Lectures and Teaching at　　，
> I certify that *A. B.* is in all respects a suitable person for election to a University Extension　　　¹，
> according to the regulations.
>
> 　　Signed on behalf of the Committee,
>
> 　　　　　　　　　　　　　　　　Secretary.'

3. Candidates are not debarred from the consultation of standard works, but quotations should be notified in the margin, and borrowed passages should be clearly distinguished from the rest.

4. No composition should exceed thirty foolscap pages, including a brief analysis which should be prefixed to the essay.

5. The names of the unsuccessful competitors will not be divulged by the Delegates, and all compositions may be obtained from them after the announcement of the result of the competition.

6. Successful candidates will be informed by the Delegacy of the result of the competition.

7. The students elected to the Scholarships will be required to visit Oxford during the Summer Meeting of University Extension Students, 1895.

8. Holders of Scholarships of £10 are required to reside in Oxford during the whole Meeting. If they are unable to do so, they must resign half their Scholarship, retaining, however, the position on the list of scholars to which the excellence of their essay entitled them.

9. Copies (7d. each, post free) of the Programme of the Summer Meeting can be obtained on application to the Secretary, University Extension Office, Oxford.

Contributions o the Scholarship fund should be sent to the Secretary, University Extension Office, Oxford.

Copies of the above regulations can be obtained, free of charge, on application to the Secretary, University Extension Office, Oxford.

　　　¹ *State whether Scholarship or Prize, or both.*

OXFORD UNIVERSITY

EXTENSION GAZETTE.

Vol. V. No 57.]   JUNE, 1895.   [One Penny.

N.B.—Local Organizers of Oxford University Extension Lectures are invited to send to the Secretary, University Extension Office, Examination Schools, Oxford, copies of any journals containing notices of, or references to, Extension work.

NOTES AND COMMENTS.

The Vice-Chancellor and Proctors have appointed the Rev. W. Inge, D.D., Provost of Worcester College, to be a Delegate for the Extension of Teaching beyond the limits of the University in the place of Mr. Sadler, who has been constituted by decree of Congregation a Perpetual Delegate. The appointment is in every way a singularly happy and auspicious one. The Provost of Worcester is not only a good friend to the Extension of the University (in the older and wider sense of the term), but a man of great influence in the University itself. He is a member of the Hebdomadal Council—the most important body in the University; a Delegate of Appeals; a Delegate of University Police, and a member of the Delegacies for Local Examinations, and for the Training of Teachers. The Delegates for Extension teaching will warmly welcome his accession to their ranks.

.·.

It is with much regret that we announce Professor Poulton's resignation of his place on the Delegacy. He has been closely connected with University Extension work almost since the beginning of its revival under Mr. Sadler. His appointment as a lecturer dates from the auspicious Session 1886-1887, the same year which witnessed the appointment of Mr. Hudson Shaw, Mr. Marriott, Mr. Lang, Mr. Boas, Mr. Mallet, Mr. Churton Collins and Mr. Llewelyn Smith—truly a notable year in the history of University Extension. On the inauguration of the Delegacy in 1892, Professor Poulton was appropriately nominated to be a member of it, and in 1893 was appointed an honorary member of the Staff, a position which he shares with Mr. Arthur Acland and Mr. Llewelyn Smith, and reserved for those who ' have rendered specially distinguished service to the Extension work of the University.'

.·.

Mr. W. M. Childs, B.A., of Keble College, has been placed by the Delegates upon the list of regular lecturers. He has been for some time past a member of the permanent staff at the University Extension College, Reading, where he has done admirable work, more especially in connexion with the Students' Association and the affiliated clubs. He has also during the past winter delivered, under the sanction of the Delegacy, a successful course of twelve lectures on the ' Life and Duties of the Citizen.'

.·.

In the current number of *Englische Studien* (xxi, pp. 79-98. Leipzig, O. R. Reisland) there is an admirable account of the last Oxford Summer Meeting from the pen of Dr. E. Nader of Vienna. This is by far the best description of the gathering which has yet appeared in German and, so far as last year's Meeting is concerned, the fullest and most systematic which has been published in any language. We hope that the appearance of Dr. Nader's essay will increase the number of German teachers at the Meeting next August. Anything which promotes conference and intimacy between English and German teachers is a gain to our national system of education. At every important stage in our educational history during the last fifty years, it is possible to trace the influence of German theories and German experience. And now as before the two countries have much to learn from one another.

.·.

The authorities of the University Extension College, Reading, and particularly the indefatigable Secretary, Mr. F. H. Wright, are to be warmly congratulated on the success of the Conference organized by them on May 14 and 15. We print elsewhere a detailed account of the Conference. The utility of such Conferences is so obvious that it is highly satisfactory to learn that they are likely to become an annual institution in the district covered by the Southern Counties Federation. The Conference next year will probably be held either at Gloucester or Winchester. In either place it cannot fail to be of great service to the University Extension cause, if it attains the high standard of Bournemouth and Reading.

.·.

We publish elsewhere an account of the progress of the University Extension movement in Scotland contributed to the *Bulletin* by Mr. R. M. Wenley, M.A. Since the article has been in print we have received a copy of a pamphlet from the same pen, to which we would draw the attention of all who are interested in the movement. Within the space of some fifty pages Mr. Wenley has given an account of the movement in Scotland full of suggestiveness to the anxious organizer. Unfortunately Mr. Wenley—for very obvious reasons—is compelled to chronicle more of failure than of success. Hence the extreme value of his analysis of the conditions which have militated against the scheme in Scotland. The conditions in Scotland are quite other than those in England. None the less there are valuable hints to be gleaned from Mr. Wenley's pages.

.·.

The Governors of Cheltenham College have done a wise thing in electing as their Headmaster in succession to Dr. James, the Rev. R. de C. Laffan. A Wykehamist trained in the traditions of the Prince of Headmasters, Dr. Ridding; a distinguished alumnus of Merton : a teacher and administrator of tried capacity Mr. Laffan will prove, we doubt not, a successor worthy even of Dr. James. But while we congratulate Cheltenham, we cannot ignore the fact that the removal of Mr. Laffan involves a heavy loss to the cause of University Extension teaching in Stratford-on-Avon. As Headmaster of Edward VI's famous school, Mr. Laffan was in a position to give much help and encouragement to Extension work, and to inspire his fellow-townsmen with the confidence in its methods to which he himself had attained.

.·.

We warmly congratulate Miss Jane Harrison upon being, as far as we know, the first lady to receive an honorary degree from any British University. In well-deserved recognition of her work in Greek Art and Mythology, the University of Aberdeen has conferred

1

upon her the degree of LL.D. *honoris causa.* Many of our readers will be aware that Miss Harrison has long been a staff-lecturer to the Oxford University Extension Delegacy.

．·．

A further University honour has been gained by Miss Chisholm, of whom both Oxford and Cambridge may be justly proud. Miss Chisholm is the first woman student who has taken the degree of Ph.D. in the University of Göttingen.

．·．

We learn with much regret that Dr. Edmund J. James, the well-known President of the American Society for the Extension of University teaching, has felt himself compelled to resign the position he has held since 1891. Dr. James has addressed to the Board of Directors an interesting valedictory letter, in which he reviews the work done by the American Society between 1890 (the year of its inception) and 1894. The record is one of continuous and uninterrupted progress. In the year 1890 seven courses only were arranged ; in the year 1894 no less than 135, with an attendance of something like 20,000 students. Dr. James pays a handsome tribute to the help derived from English friends, notably from Messrs. Moulton and Shaw, and from his own colleagues —hardly less well known in Oxford than in Philadelphia— Mr. H. W. Rolfe and Dr. Devine.

．·．

The congratulations of all who are interested in the work of University Extension are due to Canon G. F. Browne, who has been appointed to succeed Dr. Billings as Bishop of East London. Canon Browne, who will henceforth be known as Bishop of Stepney, has a distinct advantage over his two predecessors in nomenclature. Why—apart from legal pedantry—the 'Bishop of the Slums' (as Dr. Walsham How loved to term himself) should be designated Bishop of Bedford—the home of superannuated respectability—has been one of those things which Lord Dundreary was ever ' wanting to know.' Most heartily, therefore, we congratulate Bishop Browne. He will carry into a new sphere of work not only the zeal and high capacity for affairs which distinguished his work at Cambridge and at St. Paul's, but the sincerest good wishes of all who are acquainted with his notable services to the cause of higher education.

．·．

We desire once again to draw the attention of local organizers to new regulations made by the Delegates with respect to Certificates on short courses, and announced in the May number of the *Gazette.* In order to encourage sequence of study in centres which are unable to arrange twelve-lecture courses the Delegates have decided to award Certificates after an Examination in the subject-matter of two courses, comprising not less than twelve lectures and classes in all provided that—
(i) The courses are delivered in successive sessions and in educational sequence.
(ii) The candidate has in the intervening period under-taken a course of connecting study approved by the lecturer and the Delegacy, and conducted in a Students' Association or in a class recognized by the Delegacy.

．·．

We are glad to learn that the new departure which is common to the Oxford Delegacy and the Cambridge Syndicate is warmly approved by those who are most intimately associated with University Extension work. For some time past it has been recognized as a real hardship that students, however excellent their individual work, who may chance to belong to a small or weak centre unable to afford more than a six-lecture course, should be debarred from adequate University recognition. Moreover, there has been no inducement or encourage-ment to the small centres themselves to arrange their lectures in educational sequence. We trust and believe that the new regulation will act as a powerful stimulus alike to the centre and to the individual student.

We have frequently laid stress in these columns on the necessity of education in Economics. Mr. Goschen has lately been enforcing the moral, though he somewhat underrates to our thinking, the extent to which the science is already studied. Speaking at the first annual dinner of the British Economic Association early in May, he emphasized strongly the necessity of including the study of Economics in any curriculum of higher education. Economic science, he said, was not given its proper place in this country, either by politicians or practical men of business. On the Continent students of law and philosophy were required to pass through a course of study of Political Economy, which was greatly discouraged in this country. The great difficulty was to get men to study Economics, and those who dwelt on the Olympian heights and calmly studied the science which after all was at the base of all society had not the satisfaction which other men experienced in finding their labours generally appreciated. He believed, however, that the study of Economics would grow in this country, and that many of the social difficulties with which we were now confronted in relation to capital and labour were largely to be attributed to the want of knowledge on matters regulated by the laws of Political Economy.

．·．

Mr. G. Claridge Druce, whom many students will grate-fully remember as having given a course of instruction in Botany at the Summer Meeting of 1892, has in preparation a book on the Flora of Berkshire. The book which will be not only a catalogue, but also a history of the plants of the county, will serve as a companion volume to Mr. Druce's well-known books on the Flora of Oxford-shire and Northamptonshire. It was largely in recognition of the value of these earlier works that the University conferred upon their author the honorary degree of Master of Arts.

．·．

In the current number of the *Toynbee Record* there is a very interesting article on 'The Casual Ward System.' It consists of the abstract of an inquiry at the White-chapel Union conducted, during the winter months, by Mr. H. W. Pyddoke. Over 500 cases came under his notice. Detailed statistics as to the causes and motives which brought men into the wards will be found in the article to which we refer. Perhaps the most interesting passage in it is the following : —

Canon Barnett thought that some of the younger lads who had never had any real chance in life might perhaps be got away from the ward and saved from the contamination of the older and more hardened hands. I was instructed therefore to make the following offer to the more promising lads and men under thirty years of age. If they would go into the Whitechapel Workhouse for a fortnight while their references were being verified, and if their past history was found to be satisfactory, we would do our best to find them work on a farm, or to afford them an opportunity for emigration. The Whitechapel branch of the Charity Organization Society was good enough to under-take to make the necessary investigations. Twenty accepted the offer, and promised to go into the workhouse. Of these twenty, fourteen never got to the workhouse at all ; one told me he remembered he would have to join the militia, and therefore he must take back his acceptance of our offer ; and of the five who really did go to the workhouse, only one stopped long enough for the Charity Organization Society to complete its inquiries into his character. In that case the man's character appeared to be good, and the act which brought him down from his former more prosperous circumstances was either not a fault at all, or a very small one. He has since found work again at his employment as a brass-finisher.

．·．

The following extract from the advertisement column of an April paper is an interesting example of the pro-minence of athletic interests in school life. In this case it would seem, however, that athletics do possess a definite and substantial value : ' Small boy, who could strengthen the cricket team in a Preparatory School, might receive a First Class Education on very advantageous terms.'

SUMMER MEETING NOTES.

The Delegates announce that there will be no Summer Meeting in Oxford in 1896.

.·.

The Delegates are glad to be able to announce that the Inaugural Lecture will be delivered by Professor Odling, M.A., F.R.S., Waynflete Professor of Chemistry in the University of Oxford.

.·.

The lec'ure on Garrick will be given by Sir Edward Russell, well known as a dramatic critic, as a Scotch M.P., and best of all perhaps as editor of the *Liverpool Da·ly Post*. The Delegates had hoped that Mr. Henry Irving would have been able to accept their invitation to deliver this lecture, but owing to the labour involved in prepara-tions for his American tour, he was eventually compelled to decline it.

.·.

The Right Hon. Sir John Mowbray, Bart., M.P., the senior Member for the University, has consented with characteristic kindness to curtail his holiday in order to preside at the Conference to be held on Monday, August 5. The Conference is to discuss the 'Relation of University Extension to Secondary Education.' Dr. Roberts, Secretary to the Cambridge Syndicate, and Mr. H. J. Mackinder, Principal of the University Extension College, Reading, have promised to attend and speak, and it is hoped that Dr. Kimmins, Secretary to the London Society, Professor Jebb, M.P. for the University of Cambridge, and other members of the Secondary Education Commission will take part in the discussion.

.·.

The Rev. W. Hudson Shaw will lecture in Part I on William III and the Revolution of 1688; in Part II he will lecture on the Wesleyan Revival of the Eighteenth Century and the Philanthropists (Wilberforce, &c.), and will also preach one of the special sermons.

.·.

The Rev. C. G. Lang, Fellow of Magdalen College, will preside at the Debate on Thursday, August 8. The subject of the Debate will be connected with Mr. Robert Blatchford's remarkable little book, *Merrie England.*

.·.

The subject of Mr. Mackinder's lecture at the Summer Meeting will be Captain Cook.

.·.

We have much pleasure in announcing that Professor Mahaffy of Trinity College, Dublin, has accepted the invitation of the Delegacy to give a lecture at the Summer Meeting.

.·.

The proceedings of the Summer Meeting will this year be opened by a Reception in the Examination Schools, which will take place on Thursday evening, August 1, at 8.30. It has been felt that those who attend the Meeting for the first time are frequently bewildered by the abundance of good things set before them in the official Programme. It has been decided, therefore, that a portion of the evening shall be devoted to an exposition of the leading lines of the Programme, and 'hints to beginners' as to the most profitable disposition of their time. These 'hints' will be conveyed to the students of History by Mr. Hudson Shaw, senior staff-lecturer in History; to students of Literature by Mr. F. S. Boas, staff-lecturer; and to students of Science by Mr. W. W. Fisher, Aldrichian Demonstrator in Chemistry, and one of the most inde-fatigable members of the Delegacy.

STATE-AID FOR LECTURI IN FRANCE.

THERE are many points of resemblance between the educational movements which are stirring France and England at the present time, but none more interesting, from the point of view of University Extension, than the recent decision of the Conseil supérieur of public instruc-tion to vote one hundred thousand francs in aid of lecture-courses for adult students. On both sides of the Channel people are beginning to see that the welfare of a demo-cratic state must largely depend on the education which we provide for the masses of the peop'e, and that a training which ends when the lad is thirteen or fourteen years of age, while it may lay an excellent foundation, is in itself inadequate to educate men for the complex duties and responsibility of citizenship. In France, as in England, it is admitted that night schools of the old kind are no longer required. The adults who need to be taught reading and writing are few in number. What we want are continuation schools for youths and courses of higher instruction for adults. When we get these in well-ordered variety, then, and not till then, will our system of public education be complete.

Two societies — the 'National Association for popular lectures' and the 'Republican Association for popular lectures' — have done an excellent work in preparing French opinion on this subject. Just as in England the University Extension movement has made people think of education as a whole, and in its bearings on citizenship and the public welfare, so in France have private or semi-private enterprises prepared the way for State recognition and support. For, without the latter in some form or other, the complete realization of our plans seems to be impossible.

So active and successful have been the two French societies which I have named, that the Higher Council of public instruction has recently decided that an additional vote of one hundred thousand francs should be given to convert the old night school curriculum into one bearing a close resemblance to the programme of some of our good University Extension centres. As, however, the Govern-ment did not see its way to insert this vote in the budget of the present year, a debate was raised on the subject in the Chamber of Deputies by M. Prudent-Dervilliers. The speaker, in an effective address, dwelt on the waste of public resources caused at present by the neglect of the State to encourage the agencies which continue education through youth and manhood. Much of the advantage of the system of primary education is lost by this neglect. Indeed, new and unforeseen dangers are encountered by the State which gives its children the instruments of learning, but fails to take the necessary steps to secure their best and most profitable use. 'We must do some-thing,' he urged, 'to develop the education of citizens : the State ought to come to the aid of the private societies, which have already addressed themselves to this important work.'

The Government instructed M. Buisson, the Director of primary education, to answer on their behalf. His remarkable speech, loudly applauded by the Centre and the Left of the Chamber, was practically a statement of the chief principles which underlie the educational aims of University Extension teaching. The address, which is printed in full in the *Revue de l'enseignement prima·re et primaire supérieure* (Paris, 15 Rue de Cluny) for March 17 last, might well be made accessible for our English workers. M. Buisson promised that the Government would not after this year ignore the vote which the Educational Council had come to in the matter, but pointed out that, to meet the needs of next session, other credits of 20,000 francs were available for the organiza-tion of such lecture-courses as the Council had approved. Of the educational value and necessity of these courses of instruction, M. Buisson spoke in terms of strong con-viction. He has evidently come to the conclusion that what we shou'd call a sequence of University Extension courses should be provided in towns all over France.

But the most significant and encouraging feature of the discussion was the applause which greeted M. Buisson's emphatic declaration that the State, instead of imposing a rigid curriculum and destroying freedom of initiative in this educational enterprise, should rather seek to give its aid, without harassing formalities, to those societies which have already thrown themselves into the work. 'We need,' he said, facilities for all, aid for all, no requirements of uniformity, no iron rule. We must help those who have shown that they can help themselves. We must encourage them to go forward freely and with courage on the lines which they have themselves preferred.' This is State-aid in its healthiest and less demoralizing form.

S.

LETTER TO THE EDITOR.

[*We do not hold ourselves responsible for the opinions expressed by our correspondents.*]

University Extension Ribbon.

DEAR SIR,—Will you kindly allow me to remind your numerous readers that the ribbon for hat-bands, waistbands, and neckties may be obtained on application to me.

On account of the difficulty of obtaining from the maker the required colours (light and dark blue, and red), a more expensive ribbon has been ordered. The charge therefore in future will be 2s. per yard. I feel confident however that the improvement in texture and tone will be found satisfactory.

Please address as before—Miss Westall, c/o the Editor, *Oxford University Extension Gazette*, Oxford.

A pattern will be sent, when desired, on receipt of stamped and addressed envelope.

Yours truly,
EDITH A. WESTALL.

Conference of the Southern Counties Federation at Reading.

THE success of the University Extension Conference which was held at Bournemouth last year (and the proceedings of which were described in the *Gazette* for May, 1894) was so great, that it was felt on all sides that it was desirable to hold one again this year: accordingly the Council of the Reading Extension College kindly undertook the duty of hosts, and at their invitation a large gathering was held at Reading on May 14 and 15. Among those present were Mr. Marriott (the Secretary), Miss Beard, Mr. Fisher, Mr. Mackinder, Professor Poulton, Mr. Richardson and Mr. Wells, from the central office, Mr. Burch, Mr. Childs, Mr. Churton Collins, Mr. de Burgh and Mr. Horsburgh from among the lecturers, and representatives from the following centres, Basingstoke, Bournemouth, Cheltenham, Gloucester, Henslow, Hereford, Newport I.W., Oxford, Ross, Ryde, Southampton, Stroud, Swindon, Wells (Somerset) and Winchester: Mr. Sadler, too, the late Secretary, was present during the greater part of the first day of the Conference.

The guests were received soon after noon by the Mayor in the Council Chamber, and over 100 were entertained by him at lunch in the New Town Hall. In responding to the toast of 'Success to the Oxford branch of University Extension,' Prof. Poulton referred especially to the services of the late Secretary, Mr. Sadler, who had not only created their work, but had laid its foundation so strong and sure, that even his retirement from the post of Secretary was not likely to injure its continued development.

The actual business of the Conference began at 2.30, when Mr. Herbert Sutton, the Chairman of the Council of the Reading Extension College presided: he spoke especially of the need for the development of all branches of University Extension; and he pointed out that while the success of the Reading College had been mainly on its scientific and technical side, yet there was good evidence that other departments of the work were flourishing too. Mr. Shaw had told him that he had never had larger audiences anywhere than at Reading, where 1,400 people had sometimes attended the lectures.

The first subject for discussion was the 'Relation of Municipalities to the work of University Extension.' Mr. Horsburgh spoke first on the subject of the relation

of University Extension to the elementary schools of a town: he dwelt on the necessity of unity in education, in which all concerned were engaged in one great work, that of developing the nation on its best and most important side. If teachers were to be induced to attend, they must have the lectures made cheap, and they must be brought to see that attendance at them was worth their while: the former result was attained at Southampton, where the School Board made a grant of the fees to all teachers who attended the course of twenty-four lectures. The result had been most marked; the number of papers had increased tenfold, and the Inspector had drawn special attention to the improvement in style and interest shown in the final examination. Mr. Horsburgh also pointed out that the University Extension certificates for twenty-four lectures had a definite value in marks assigned to it in the Queen's Scholarship Examination. Mr. Theodore White, who spoke on the relation of Secondary schools to education, urged that there was need for the Universities to supplement by teaching the work which they had been doing for more than a generation by their 'Locals' examinations: but if University Extension was to be widely adopted in schools, there must be a simpler type of lecture organized.

Miss Brooke Hunt (Secretary of Gloucester centre) then spoke on 'Working men's clubs and University Extension.' After a bright and amusing description of the various types of clubs, she pointed out how unreasonable it was to expect young working men to show a devotion to learning for learning's sake, which was neither expected from, nor found in, the young public-school, or even University, man of the same age. Personal contact was above all things necessary, if working men's clubs were to be brought into relation with University Extension.

In the discussion that followed Mr. Perkins of Southampton gave some further interesting details as to the educational experiment there, which had been tried by Mr. Horsburgh: he thought it was a mistake that compulsion had been introduced for those teachers who chose to attend: such compulsion was contrary to the spirit of University Extension.

There also spoke Canon Scannel, the Chairman of the Southampton School Board, Mr. Mackinder, Mr. Wells, Mr. Childs, and Mr. Councillor Nicholson: Mr. Mackinder lifted the discussion out of the region of details on to a higher level, while he pointed out that University Extension represented rather a principle than a method; it had many methods, but its principle was always the supplementing of the work of the general teacher, who had perforce to deal with many subjects, by that of the specialist, who had made one subject specially his own. He dwelt too on the need of actuality in all teaching: we nowadays went too much to books, and this was the case in science as well as in literature or history: it was necessary to appeal to a pupil's eyes as well as to his memory; he must be taught to see for himself. Mr. Wells briefly pointed out that the heads of Secondary schools could not only encourage University Extension directly by employing the services of its lecturers, but still more indirectly by encouraging their under teachers to attend the courses and making it easy for them to do so, and by endeavouring to maintain the interests which they themselves had aroused among their pupils at school, by inducing them to pursue the same subjects later in University Extension lectures.

The second part of the afternoon was devoted to the subject of 'Schemes for Local Organization.' Mr. Leveson Scarth of Bournemouth read a paper, in which he dwelt especially on the need for a good library in connexion with students' work, and described the unity which had been given to educational work at Bournemouth by a council which had on it representatives of all the educational bodies of the town. Mr. Horsburgh described how Mr. Scarth at Bournemouth had given practical effect to his own recommendations by putting his fine private library at the disposal of the Students' Association: unlike most book-collectors, Mr. Scarth carried out to the full the motto of his book-plate ' sibi et amicis.'

At the close of the afternoon a provisional invitation was given, by Miss Brooke Hunt and Mr. Seekings, to the Federation to visit Gloucester next year.

In the evening there was a most enjoyable conversazione given at the College by Mr. Herbert Sutton. The picturesque old buildings, representing all ages of English architecture from the fifteenth century to our own day, were admirably decorated; and the College garden was illuminated. The more serious visitors were invited to watch scientific experiments, especially the display in the physical laboratory of the spectrum of the new element argon, while music and songs were provided for those who wished to enjoy themselves more lightly.

At the second part of the Conference on Wednesday morning, Mr. Mackinder, the President of the College, presided: the subject was the Students' Association. Mr. Childs, one of the lecturers at Reading, read an admirable paper on the work of historical research, which might be done by a well-organized Students' Association. He pointed out the materials for local history which were lying still unused in the records of municipalities, in the piles of old newspapers, and elsewhere: students working in common could both attain valuable results for the more general historian, and familiarize themselves with the spirit of historical work in a way which could never be attained by the mere study of literary authorities, however excellent. Mr. Churton Collins spoke of the Students' Association as a means of preserving culture in the best sense: there was a danger everywhere, in University Extension as well as in other systems of education, of 'substituting for the liberal information of the adult citizen, cram work for mere examinees; the Students' Association should provide a rallying point for all who were interested in liberal study. There also spoke Mr. Cunningham, Mr. White, the Rev. J. M. Guilding, Miss Brooke Hunt and Mr. Wells: much stress was laid on the difficulty of maintaining a Students' Association permanently (that at Reading was just dissolving itself, although it was about to be reformed on a new basis), and on the need as far as possible of breaking down class distinctions in a common enthusiasm for the work. Mr. Mackinder, in summing up, expressed strongly the hope that the Reading Students' Association would enjoy a new and vigorous life on its wider basis of connexion with all departments of the Extension College. The old one was dying, but it had given the model to various special associations which were vigorously at work; the new one must unite itself with all these, and guide and form the general life of them all.

During the last hour of the meeting Mr. Marriott, the Secretary of the Oxford Delegacy, presided: the subject of discussion was the work of the new 'district superintendents'; he pointed out that it should be at once 'extensive and intensive,' in spreading University Extension in places and among classes where it was still unknown, and in developing thoroughness and continuity where University Extension was already at work. Mr. Wells and Mr. Horsburgh then described briefly the work they had already done in their respective districts, on the lines of the paper which they had issued (which was published in the *Extension Gazette* for May).

Before the meeting broke up, some discussion arose as to the meeting-place of the Southern Counties Federation for next year; Winchester and Southampton as well as Gloucester wished to have the pleasure of entertaining its members. It was finally decided that the question should be settled by the two district superintendents in conjunction with the local secretaries. In the afternoon very pleasant visits were organized to the Library and Museum, the Reading Abbey, St. Laurence's Church, and other objects of interest in the town.

To those who were not present, such a brief summary as the above can give but a faint impression of the sustained interest of the meeting: educational experiments were compared, the teaching to be derived from the successes (and also from the failures) of the past was clearly set forth, and the principles which underlie all University work were stated and emphasized. It is only those who are themselves at work, who know how useful such a meeting of workers and organizers is; and not less important, though less formal, are the opportunities for forming personal friendships among those who, under different circumstances and by different means, are pursuing one common end. That end is the spreading in every department of English educational life of the principles which the old Universities represent, of freedom of study combined with ordered subordination, of the pursuit of new truths and the application of the old ones to even new spheres. The entertainers of the Conference at Reading showed themselves apt pupils of Oxford in their open hospitality, and in the way in which they combined instruction and pleasure in a well-proportioned and organized whole.

THE ADMISSION OF WOMEN TO THE B.A. DEGREE.

A SPECIAL meeting of the members of the Association for the Education of Women in Oxford was held in the Examination Schools on May 4. The movement for the granting of the B.A. degree to women students—the subject considered at the meeting – is the outcome of a feeling that has been steadily growing in weight in Oxford during the last few years. Many persons in the University who have taken part in the higher education of women have felt for some time that, if the conditions of residence and examination laid down by the University for the degree of Bachelor of Arts are complied with by women students, it is only right to give them the same recognition as is given to men.

In expression of this feeling it was resolved by 115 votes to 26—'That it is desirable that women students who have complied with the statutable conditions as regards residence and examination should be admitted to the B.A. degree, and that a University Diploma, recording their residence and qualifications, should be granted to women students who have resided at least three years, have passed a preliminary and an intermediate Examination, and have obtained a class in any honour Examination recognized in the University.' It was also further decided to make immediate application to the University to confer the degree and the diploma upon women students duly qualified to receive one or the other. In consequence of this vote a petition to the Hebdomadal Council has been drawn up, which the resident Masters of Arts, composing the Congregation of the University, were requested to sign expressing their preference for the granting either of the degree or of a diploma after the fulfilment of the University conditions of residence and examination: 146 persons have signed the petition; of these 123 are in favour of the B.A. degree, and 23 prefer the diploma. The Council has received the petition and has appointed a committee to consider it.

The large number of signatures to the petition is significant of the strength of opinion in Oxford, but many difficulties will have to be overcome before the University will give such formal recognition as is asked for to women students.

THE UNIVERSITY EXTENSION MOVEMENT IN SCOTLAND.

THE following article by Dr. R. M. Wenley, Hon. Sec. of the Glasgow University Extension Board, appeared in a recent number of the *University Extension Bulletin* (Philadelphia). The history and comparative failure of University Extension work in Scotland have never before been so fully summarized and explained.

Although short courses of lectures to women were delivered by professors of the University of Glasgow, in the early seventies, the first real attempt at genuine University Extension in Scotland took shape, so far as I am aware, in the autumn of 1884. Five distinguished graduates of the University then delivered three courses in the Philosophical Institution. The same lecturers, along with a few others, continued their personal efforts in this direction for several years. Mr. William Smart, the well-known economist, was instrumental in originating this work. The movement to this point, was private and entirely unconnected with the University. In 1885, however, Queen

Margaret Guild, an association of former students of Queen Margaret College, Glasgow (now the Women's Department of the University of Glasgow), organized the scheme, and carried it on with considerable educational and financial success. Some half-dozen centres were formed, and about 500 students attended the various courses each session. For three years the Guild managed the movement in the west and south-west of Scotland.

Meanwhile the other Universities began to bestir themselves St. Andrews organized the scheme and put it into operation in the autumn of 1888; and, during the six months following, fifteen courses were given. In session 1889-90 the number fell to thirteen, but the students enrolled were 1346 strong. Then came a rapid decline, and, in 1892, Professor Geddes, of St. Andrews, tells me, the work of the association practically ceased, although since then an occasional course has been supplied, especially to Perth, where a University Education Society has been formed and still continues to manage local lectures. The Edinburgh University Association was founded at about the same time as that of St. Andrews. It made a fair start. But even so soon as April, 1891, the committee regretted to report that ' the number of courses delivered was not in advance of that stated in their second annual report.' The number of courses given during this year had been eight, but only two fell within the area of Scotland allotted to Edinburgh. In the six other cases Edinburgh lecturers were sent to St. Andrews or Glasgow. The number of students was about 500, of whom, however, only seventy-eight attended the Edinburgh centres proper. In the session of 1891-92 the number of courses had fallen to two, and shortly thereafter the Edinburgh Association announced its intention of suspending operations *sine die*. During these years the University of Aberdeen sent representatives to joint meetings of the various Extension associations, but so far as I know, Extension was never organized in the North, and I cannot find that any centres were ever successfully formed.

Returning once more to the West, we find that during three years Queen Margaret Guild carried on the work, but at length approached the University of Glasgow and offered to hand over its Extension scheme as a ' going concern ' to a board constituted by the University authorities. As a result, the Glasgow University Extension Board was constituted on February 1, 1888; it has continued to control, organize, and carry on Extension lectures ever since. In the session (the Scottish University session extends from October to April) 1888-89, 17 courses were delivered, with an attendance of 1400; in 1889-90, the courses were 17, and the attendance about 1100. Then came the sudden decline experienced elsewhere. In the session of 1890-91. the courses were 8, and the attendance 680; in 1891-92, the courses were 8, and the attendance 1065; in 1892-93, the courses were 9, and the attendance 1400; in 1893-94, the courses were 7, and the attendance 400; in 1894-95 10 courses have been arranged, and the attendance will probably run to 600. It should be added that, during the last three years, lecturers of the Glasgow Board have given from five to ten Extension courses—in addition to those mentioned above—at the Glasgow Athenaeum and other centres which are not under the direct control of the board. The annual average of courses may thus be taken at twelve, and of students at about 1000. When one considers that in Glasgow and its immediate neighbourhood more than one-third of the entire population of Scotland is concentrated—about 1,750,000, this success, great as it is compared with that of the other Scottish Universities, cannot be termed startling. What causes can be assigned for the comparative failure of the movement in Scotland? Limits of space forbid more than a summary statement.

The causes may be divided into two classes: (*A*) Those traceable to conditions of popular life in Scotland; (*B*) Those proceeding from the University organization itself.

(*A*)—1. The wide diffusion of popular education for generations has to a large extent prevented the growth of that need for Extension teaching which has been so strongly experienced in England. And the very fact that, until within the past two years, the Universities have been open to all comers without preliminary examination, and at very moderate fees, has operated forcibly in the same direction. 2. As a consequence, partly of the foregoing, and partly of ecclesiastical conditions, Scotland is covered by a network of local ' Literary ' and ' Philosophical ' and ' Dialectic ' societies, a main aim of which is to provide popular, but usually disconnected, lectures. The entertainment or attraction of lectures is supplied, but not the teaching. 3. The Combe Trust and the Gilchrist Trust, both possessing considerable endowments, have furnished regular courses very much of the Extension type—though only in the field of science—to the principal centres of population, and at fees which the unendowed Extension Board cannot accord. 4. The population, outside of some few considerable towns, is sparse and scattered, so that the formation of centres is difficult. (In passing I may say that seventy centres would be a large number for all Scotland.) In addition to this, the Scotchman's well-known virtue, or failing, of looking at both sides of the sixpence ere he parts with it, is a surprisingly formidable element. 5. When the County Councils found themselves in a financial position to arrange for technical education by local lectures, the Extension movement was not strong enough to step into the breach as it has done to some extent in England.

(*B*)—1. Unfortunately for Extension, the Scottish Universities have been in a state of transition for some years past. During the most critical stage for the movement, the initial one, University circles were broken into parties busied in the discussion of the *pros* and *cons* of reform, a discussion which had a tendency to become bitter and, therefore, absorbing. Deliberating thus on the machinery of their own organization University magnates had little time, and perhaps little inclination, to enter upon new paths. Moreover, one of the defects of our academic life, which it is anticipated the reforms, now carried out, may remove, was the lack of means whereby distinguished graduates might be retained as junior teachers at the University seat. The field for selection of lecturers was, thus, very limited, and I am convinced that this has had much to do with our rapidly accumulated difficulties. 2. The certificates issued by the various University Extension associations have hitherto had no academic value. They lead to nothing; and I fear that the Commission, now sitting, is most unlikely to legislate toward remedying this. 3. The organization of the movement has itself been insufficient, mainly owing to a lack of interest and belief in Extension on the part of the University officials. For this they are not to be harshly judged. The Universities have hitherto been undermanned, and a teacher with a class of 200 students, or more, has his hands so full of routine work that he can overtake it with difficulty, and is left with little time, and less energy, for extras. 4. The want of a central association, embracing the four Universities has been widely felt by the local organizers of the movement. Nevertheless, peculiar difficulties, which I shall not call jealousies, have rendered its formation almost impossible, and so the force of united, concentrated action has been lost.

It is possible that, after the stiff entrance examination now imposed at the Universities has done its work of exclusion for some years, the need of Extension teaching may become more clamant. At the present moment the only hopeful signs are the fairly satisfactory, but yet undeveloping, results of the Glasgow Board's effort, and the flourishing state of the Summer School at Edinburgh—now about to enter on its ninth year. This meeting owes its inception and success wholly to the unsparing efforts of Professor Geddes to whom, along with Professor Edward Caird, Extension in Scotland is indebted for its foundation and early, but unfulfilled, promise.

In closing, it may be noted that our Board and the Edinburgh Summer School have no endowments. The £60,000 recently bequeathed to Glasgow, and the £100,000 or more in process of collection by Aberdeen for ' University Extension purposes,' are to be applied to Extension in the utilitarian sense of stone and lime.

DIRECTORY OF STUDENTS' ASSOCIATIONS.
(*Secretaries.*)

Camborne.—CHARLES ROWE, 1 Foundry Row, Camborne.

Southampton.—{ H. M. COLEBROOK, Orwell, Portswood, Southampton.

REPORTS FROM THE CENTRES.

BEDFORD.—The interest aroused in Astronomy by Dr. Fison's lectures was well maintained through the course, which ended on April 9. Nine students entered for the Examination held the next day, and all passed, three gaining the mark of distinction. General satisfaction is expressed at the prospect of another course in continuation of the subject, to be given by Dr. Fison here next autumn. In the meantime the students, with the help of advice from the lecturer, hope to carry on regular work to some extent during May and June. At a preliminary meeting on May 17, a short lecture, illustrated by lantern slides, was kindly given by Mr. T. G. Elger, whose name is well known in the astronomical world as an authority on the physical features of the moon. The audience showed great interest in listening to the results of some recent observations made by American as well as English astronomers on the moon's surface. Our first attempt at summer work in connexion with Spring and Autumn lectures has thus had valuable encouragement at its outset.—E. BLAKE, *Hon. Secretary.*

DOVER.—We have had a very interesting course of lectures on Architecture by Mr F. Bond. The subject was fresh and in such competent hands has proved very fascinating. It has given a new interest to our old churches in the town and neighbourhood, while the students have also found in the modern churches many windows illustrating ancient forms. Mr. Bond has taught not only from his magnificent collection of photographs, but has taken his students abroad and given them instruction in the churches and other buildings with which this district abounds.

FROME.—An important public meeting was held at the Auction Mart on Thursday evening, May 2, in support of the University Extension movement in Frome. The Rev. the Hon. A. F. A. Hanbury-Tracy, Vicar of Frome, presided, and was supported by the Rev. Sydney Cooper, Rev. J. Walker, Mr. E. W. Bennett, the Secretary of the Local Committee, and other gentlemen. The principal speakers were Mr. J. A. R. Marriott, M.A., of New College and Worcester College, Oxford, Secretary to the Oxford Delegates, and W. J. de Burgh, B.A., who has recently delivered a course of Literature lectures at this centre. The Chairman introduced Mr. Marriott, who delivered an exceedingly powerful and interesting address. He sketched the history of the University Extension movement in England, explained the aims which its promoters had in view, and the methods they pursue. He laid great stress upon the importance of the annual Summer Meetings, and advised those who wished to get an idea of the movement as a whole to attend at least one of them. Finally he concluded a speech which was listened to with rapt attention by contending that ' most if not all the aims and anticipations of the pioneers of the Extension movement had been fulfilled ; that those aims were worthy of the Universities and not a mere " cheap smattering masquerade " ; and that they were useful in themselves and worthy of a permanent place in the economy of national education.' Mr. de Burgh spoke mainly of the great importance of Students' Associations, and the desirability of extending the movement to neighbouring towns, so as to form organized groups or lecture circuits. A considerable amount of discussion followed the delivery of the principal speeches, and on the motion of Mr. A. H. Coombs, seconded by Rev. J. Walker, it was decided to recommend the Committee to form a Students' Association in Frome. The outcome of the meeting was thus eminently practical. The meeting concluded with hearty votes of thanks to the speakers, and to Mr. and Mrs. E. W. Bennett, to whose energy the formation of the Frome centre has been due. It is a matter of general regret that Mr. and Mrs. Bennett are leaving the town ; but it is hoped that others will be found to carry on their excellent work.—*Somerset and Wilts Journal* (condensed).

ROSS.—Mr. Horsburgh's interesting course of six lectures on ' The Literature of the Eighteenth Century ' concluded on April 2. The lectures have been much appreciated, though the attendance, owing to the severe weather and prevalence of influenza, was small, averaging only fifty. The number of students regularly writing papers was about twelve. On April 24 Mr. Wells kindly gave his lecture on Oxford University, illustrated by limelight views, which was greatly appreciated and enjoyed by the audience. We owe Mr. Wells a debt of gratitude for the great assistance given to this centre in its difficulties this term, and feel we have already received great benefit from the appointment of the District Directors.—EDITH HUGHES, *Hon. Sec.*

TAVISTOCK.—A very clear and instructive course of lectures on ' The Puritan Revolution, with special reference to the Thought and Manners of the Time,' has been given during the Spring Term at Tavistock by Mr. W. G. de Burgh, B.A., Merton College, University Extension lecturer. Mr. de Burgh's experience as a lecturer at Toynbee Hall enables him to put the subject in a concise form with bold outlines extremely helpful to students of limited leisure, and also most pleasantly intelligible to a general audience. The interest was well sustained throughout the lectures and classes, and an opinion was generally expressed that the work begun last year by Mr. Kenelm D. Cotes, M.A., on 'Shakespeare's England' could not have been more satisfactorily carried on under the circumstances of his inability to prepare his projected course on the Puritan period. It is hoped that the historical sequence of the lectures at Tavistock will be maintained by a course on the later Stuart period next Spring.— GRACE JOHNSTONE, *Local Sec.*

WEYMOUTH.—The following regulations provisionally adopted for the ' Students' Subsidiary Class,' Weymouth, have been forwarded to us, in the hope that they might possibly supply a point of departure for other centres proposing to form the like. Comments or suggestions for their improvement will be welcome, if forwarded to the *Gazette.* *Order of proceedings for Subsidiary Class*—1. *Essays* written for and approved by the University lecturer, if marked by him ⅒ or upward, shall be read to the class. Writers to read their own essays : or, if objecting to do so, to leave them with the President not less than three days before the meeting. 2. *Discussion* to follow the reading. Remarks and criticism on the essays, or on matters suggested by the University lectures will be invited. It is hoped that ' experts ' specially invited will take a leading part in this. 3. *Questions* on special points or difficulties connected with the subject may be brought before the meeting. Members are requested to bring them *in writing*; and any member present will oblige by volunteering to furnish—(4) *Answers* to the same; either *in writing*, at the *next* meeting; or *vivâ voce* and at once, if preferred. 5. *Illustrative Extracts* from standard works, which any member may consider exceptionally helpful or valuable, may by permission be read to the meeting.

WIRKSWORTH.—This new centre has every reason to congratulate itself on the success of Mr. Cotes' course of lectures on ' Trade, Adventure and Discovery,' the last lecture of which was given on April 11. The average attendance has been eighty-five, a large proportion of whom have remained for the class.

[** *Report from Bakewell unavoidably held over.*]

BOOKS ON OUR TABLE.

History of Religion, a Sketch of Primitive Religious Beliefs and Practices, and of the Origin and Character of the Great Systems. By ALLAN MENZIES, D.D. London, John Murray, 1895.

The series of University Extension Manuals edited by Prof. Knight is greatly enriched by the volume now under notice. In little more than 400 pages Prof. Menzies has passed under review the principal facts concerning the development of religion from its earlier and ruder beliefs and usages into the great faiths which have aspired to embrace the world. A comparison with the nearest available book, Tiele's *Outlines of the History of Religion,* shows at once what a wealth of materials the labours of the last twenty years have placed in the scholar's hands. In his main view of the significant steps in the whole process, Prof. Menzies approaches his Dutch predecessor ; but his handbook is far richer in detail, and condenses with singular skill an amazing quantity of well-established results. The writer's style is rarely inspiring, but it is also rarely obscure ; and in the interest of the successive pictures which he unfolds, the student's attention should seldom flag. The most vigorous chapter perhaps is that on the religion of Israel, where the author steps firmly along the lines of independent study on the modern critical basis.

The key to the whole book is of course found in the general conception of evolution. The theory of a primitive revelation is so completely abandoned that it only deserves a passing mention. It is assumed at the outset that the growth of religion is to be explained on the same general principles as the advance of civilization. Regarding religion as ' the worship of higher powers,' Prof. Menzies traces the conception of these powers through the tribal and national stage to the higher spiritual forms in which racial limitations drop away, and religion is recognized as a relation between the soul and God. In the inevitable limitations of space much must be taken for granted, and statements must be made broadly without too much qualification. These early chapters, therefore, are in some respects less satisfactory. Thus the writer does not seem to us quite just to Prof. Max Müller's amended definition (p. 9) ; the dream theory of the origin of the soul is insufficiently explained (p. 30) ; the statements made about the chief deity of the North American tribes (p. 34) ' an animal, e.g. the hare or the musk-rat ; p. 28, ' heaven blowing, the sky with a wind in it ') need revision ; the Babylonian religion is surely treated too confidently (p. 90) as the ' mother ' of the Egyptian and the Chinese. In the description of the Chinese religion Prof. Menzies refers to the controversy about the proper term for ' God,' apropos of the conception of the living sky as the Supreme Ruler, or ' Shang Ti.' The Catholic missionaries wished to prove that 'Shang Ti' signified a being other than the sky, but the Chinese, says our author (p. 109), denied that they had ever made such a distinction, and declared that they could not understand it. In the catena of passages which Dr. Legge collected more than fifty years ago, there is more than one instance of the use by Chinese writers of the analogy of body and soul to explain the relation of the Supreme Ruler to the actual sky (*Notions, &c.,* pp. 52, 106). There is a worse confusion about a supposed Chinese Buddhist Amhita (p. 120).

Prof. Menzies is at his best in sketching the processes of growth and modification; he has a keen eye for what may be called the working of intellectual and moral causation. His estimates are warm and generous; he combines in an eminent degree both breadth of view and vividness of sympathy. Every reader will of course wish for something more, perhaps for something different, in departments which have awakened especial interest in him. One will wonder why the gracious figure of Apollo should be so lightly touched (p. 294) and Pindar should not even be named; another will think that the judgement on Mohammedanism does not take account either of the achievements of Arab culture or of the mystic schools of Sufism (p. 239); a third will protest against the phrase about the deification of the Buddha (p. 363). In the interest of future readers we would plead for an enlargement of the meagre lists of books at the end of each chapter, and the preparation of a really complete index—in the present index it is impossible to tell why some names are inserted, when so many more are omitted. The printing is on the whole singularly free from mistakes, but the persistent recurrence of such forms as *Maccabbean* (pp. 176, 208, 410), *Bhikku* (pp. 344, 361, 373, 375), *Pragapati* (p. 346), *Heidenthume* (pp. 215, 233, 239), calls for more care somewhere; and Mohammed was not born in 570 B.C. (p. 222). These are small blemishes in a work which marks a great advance in English thinking and knowledge on this subject. We are grateful to Prof. Knight and the publishers of his series for including the topic at all; and all students will owe deep acknowledgments to Dr. Menzies for a treatment so catholic, so thorough, and so clear.

J. ESTLIN CARPENTER.

SCHOLARSHIPS FOR THE OXFORD SUMMER MEETING, 1895.

A FUND, to which subscriptions amounting to £60 have already been promised, has been opened for the provision of Scholarships to enable students from Oxford centres to attend the Summer Meeting, which will be held in Oxford from August 1 to August 26, 1895.

The Scholarships will be awarded after an Essay competition, and will be of two values—£10 and £5. Holders of the former must attend the whole Meeting; those of the latter may, if they prefer, attend either the First or Second Part only. Part I lasts from Aug. 1 to Aug. 12; Part II from Aug. 12 to Aug. 26.

Conditions of Award.

The Scholarships will be awarded on or about July 1, 1895, for English Essays on subjects drawn from English Literature, English History, Natural Science, and Political Economy.

A. Competition for Scholarships.

The Scholarships will be awarded in three divisions:—

(a) Open to all Oxford University Extension Students *who need the assistance of the Scholarships* in order to study in Oxford, according to the intention of the donors.

(b) Open to all Elementary School Teachers (men or women), who are also Oxford University Extension Students.

(c) Open to all working men and women, who are also Oxford University Extension Students.

To qualify themselves for election to a Scholarship:—

(1) All competitors must be recommended by their Local Committee as suitable candidates.

(2) Competitors in *divisions (a)* and *(b)* must, in order to qualify, obtain *distinction* in an examination on a course of Oxford University Extension Lectures delivered between January 1894 and June 1895.

(3) Competitors in *division (c)* must pass an examination on a course of Oxford University Extension Lectures delivered between the same dates.

The Delegates, however, reserve to themselves the right of rejecting the name of any candidate; and, unless compositions of sufficient merit are sent in, do not bind themselves to award Scholarships in any or all of the following four subjects.

B. Competition for Prizes.

A limited number of Prizes, of the value of £1, will be awarded in the same competition without any limitation as to the means of the competitors. Candidates for this branch of the competition must qualify as regards examinations, like the competitors in *divisions (a)* and *(b)*.

SUBJECTS.

(1) *History* (one only to be selected).

(i) The Growth of Nationality in the thirteenth century.
(ii) The causes of the Great Rebellion.
(iii) England's command of the Sea during the Revolutionary Wars (1793-1815).

(2) *Literature* (one only to be selected).

(i) How far is it possible to specify any general conditions which are necessary to the production of the best poetry?
(ii) Explain what is meant by Poetic Justice, and consider with full illustrations how far it should be observed in Drama or Fiction.
(iii) Estimate the importance in literary history of the works of Dryden, Pope, or Walter Scott.

(3) *Political Economy* (one only to be selected).

(i) Show the effect of different systems of land tenure on the production and distribution of wealth.
(ii) What remedies have been suggested for the existing depression, and how far are they likely to succeed?
(iii) What circumstances may be expected to determine the wages of labour in the future?

(4) *Science* (one only to be selected).

(i) Theories of Chemical Action.
(ii) Sewage disposal in towns and rural districts.
(iii) The Weeds of the Farm.

REGULATIONS.

1. Each candidate may write an essay *on one subject only*, but may select one from any of the above four groups.

2. All compositions must reach the Delegacy [addressed—The Secretary, University Extension Office, Examination Schools, Oxford] on or before Monday, June 3, 1895; must each bear the writer's full name and address, with a note saying whether the writer is competing for a Scholarship or a Prize, or both, and, if the former, in which division (*a*, *b*, or *c*, see above); must be written on foolscap paper, and on one side of the paper only; must state, at the top of the first page, the writer's occupation; and must be accompanied by a certificate of qualification from his or her Local Committee in the following form:—

'On behalf of the members of the Local Committee acting in concert with the Oxford University Delegates for the establishment of Lectures and Teaching at   ,
I certify that *A. B.* is in all respects a suitable person for election to a University Extension   [1],
according to the regulations.

Signed on behalf of the Committee,

....
Secretary.'

3. Candidates are not debarred from the consultation of standard works, but quotations should be notified in the margin, and borrowed passages should be clearly distinguished from the rest.

4. No composition should exceed thirty foolscap pages, including a brief analysis which should be prefixed to the essay.

5. The names of the unsuccessful competitors will not be divulged by the Delegates, and all compositions may be obtained from them after the announcement of the result of the competition.

6. Successful candidates will be informed by the Delegacy of the result of the competition.

7. The students elected to the Scholarships will be required to visit Oxford during the Summer Meeting of University Extension Students, 1895.

8. Holders of Scholarships of £10 are required to reside in Oxford during the whole Meeting. If they are unable to do so, they must resign half their Scholarship, retaining, however, the position on the list of scholars to which the excellence of their essay entitled them.

9. Copies (7d. each, post free) of the Programme of the Summer Meeting can be obtained on application to the Secretary, University Extension Office, Oxford.

Contributions to the Scholarship fund should be sent to the Secretary, University Extension Office, Oxford.

Copies of the above regulations can be obtained, free of charge, on application to the Secretary, University Extension Office, Oxford.

[1] *State whether Scholarship or Prize, or both.*

OXFORD UNIVERSITY

EXTENSION GAZETTE.

VOL. V. NO. 58.]   JULY, 1895.   [ONE PENNY.

N.B.—Local Organizers of Oxford University Extension Lectures are invited to send to the Secretary, University Extension Office, Examination Schools, Oxford, copies of any journals containing notices of, or references to, Extension work.

OXFORD UNIVERSITY EXTENSION.

Award of Scholarships and Prizes. .

SCHOLARSHIPS to enable University Extension students to attend the Oxford Summer Meeting have been awarded as follows. The award was based on an essay competition confined to students who had passed the Examination on a course of Oxford University Extension lectures during the preceding year. The subjects for the essays were drawn from History, Literature, Economics, and Natural Science. There were thirty-one Candidates.

Class A (open to all Oxford University Extension students *who need the assistance of the Scholarships* in order to study in Oxford, according to the intention of the donors).

Scholarships of £10.

WILLIAM SYKES (Oldham), in History.
THEODORA NUNNS (Launceston), in Literature (honorary scholar).
JOSEPH OWEN (Oldham), in Political Economy (honorary scholar).

Scholarships of £5.

ALBERT BRITLAND (Matlock), in History.
CHARLES OWEN (Oldham), in History.
BEATRICE VIVIAN (Camborne), in Political Economy.
JOSEPH R. FARMERY (Louth), in Natural Science.

Class B (open to all Elementary School Teachers (men or women), who are also Oxford University Extension students).

Scholarship of £10.

BENJAMIN F. BROOKE (Harrogate), in Literature.

Class C (open to all working men and women, who are also Oxford University Extension students).

Scholarship of £10.

THOMAS H. TREGIDGA (Rawtenstall), in Political Economy.

Scholarship of £5.

G. HENRY DRAPER (Gloucester), in History.
GEORGE H. PICKLES (Hebden Bridge), in Natural Science.

Prizes of £1.

In History:— SAMUEL V. BRACHER (Gloucester), HANNAH BUTTON (Oldham), FRED. COOK (Gloucester), LOUISE J. HENSHALL (Altrincham), CONSTANCE D. SAUNDERS (Hoddesdon), JANE E. VANT (Ripon).

In Literature:—ETHEL HEYWOOD (Kersal), THEODORA NUNNS (Launceston), LAURA E. VEALE (Harrogate).

In Political Economy:—JOSEPH OWEN (Oldham).

Reports of the Examiners.

History:—' I have examined the essays of sixteen competitors for Scholarships and Prizes, and I am glad to be able to state that the compositions were carefully prepared, and were marked by accuracy and thoroughness. A tendency to drift into historical narrative detracted from the merits of several of the essays, and on a future occasion this tendency should be checked. The essays, however, almost without exception, represented conscientious study no less than keen historical interest, and reflect very great credit upon the diligence of the writers.'—ARTHUR HASSALL, *Examiner in History.*

Literature:—' I have pleasure in reporting that the work done in the English Literature Essays was very satisfactory. Of the six essays sent in four had real merit, and showed much thoughtfulness and considerable study. The two best were up to the very highest standard attained in previous years, the one which I put first being to my mind the best I have yet seen in competitions of this kind, and one which may fairly be called an essay of *remarkable* merit. In the two next, the chief defects were a want of clearness in grasping the exact limits of the subject, or in the arrangement of the points argued in the essay. But in these also there was evidence of care and thought, and of profitable study. The remaining two were much weaker in grasp and power of expression, and wanted more reading and thought. On the whole, the result was decidedly good.'— A. SIDGWICK, *Examiner in Literature.*

Political Economy:—' The total number of essays sent in is five, but small as the number is, they contain some very good work. I am especially struck with the improvements on those of last year. In the two best essays not only is the matter thoroughly sound, the fruit of good observation and well-directed reading, but the arrangement and style both call for praise. One other candidate sent in a strong well-reasoned essay, which contains much in a small compass. The other two essays are promising, the style perhaps a little exuberant, and the matter not always quite to the point, but at the same time they show a great width of knowledge, and which is even more valuable, a real interest in the subject. I hope that every year these scholarships may be the means of calling out a similar amount of good work, and in an even larger number of writers.'— LANCELOT R. PHELPS, *Examiner in Political Economy.*

Natural Science:—' If the essays are not quite as good as some of the successful compositions last year, they are generally meritorious, and the three on the subject of the treatment and disposal of sewage are very equal in character. In the main they are well arranged and show appreciation of the nature and difficulties of the problem to be dealt with, and contain a fairly complete summary of the chief methods in actual use more or less successfully in different localities. Only one candidate chose the subject of chemical action : his essay had many good points but was rather incomplete, especially in respect of modern developments of chemical theory.'—W. W. FISHER, *Examiner in Natural Science.*

[Holders of Scholarships are invited by the Delegates to meet at Manchester College on Friday, August 2, from 4 to 5 p.m.]

1

NOTES AND COMMENTS.

The publication of this *Gazette* will cease with the September issue of this year. The publication of the *University Extension Journal*, the organ of the Cambridge Syndicate and the London Society, has ceased already. With the commencement of the session 1895-1896, there will appear a new publication the *University Extension Journal*. It will be issued under the official sanction of the Oxford, Cambridge, London, and Victoria University Extension Authorities, and will be conducted by a joint Editorial Committee nominated by these four bodies. It will appear (in its first year) nine times, viz., from October to May, on the first day of the month, and about the middle of July. The price of each number will be 3*d.*; post free 3½*d.* The annual subscription will be 2*s.* 3*d.*; post free 2*s.* 6*d.* Secretaries of University Extension centres will be entitled to order packets of not less than a dozen at trade rates, particulars of which may be obtained from the publishers, Messrs. Archibald Constable & Co., 14 Parliament Street, Westminster, to whom orders may be sent.

.·.

Mr. Arthur Hassall, M.A., Student and Tutor of Ch.Ch. has been nominated by the Delegates to represent them upon the recently formed Extension Board of the Durham University. Mr. Hassall was one of the earliest of Oxford Extension lecturers, he is still an examiner, and has been one of the most zealous members of the Delegacy since its formation in 1892.

.·.

Mr. Gilbert C. Bourne, M.A., Fellow of New College and Demonstrator at the University Museum, has been appointed by the Vice-Chancellor and Proctors to fill the place on the Delegacy vacated by Professor Poulton. Mr. Bourne was one of the local secretaries for the Oxford meeting of the British Association in 1894, and the conspicuous success of the meeting was very largely due to the untiring energy and high administrative capacity which he displayed. That he will serve the Delegacy with equal zeal no one who knows him can doubt. The new Delegate will be seen and heard at the Summer Meeting where he has promised to deliver three lectures on 'Evolution with special reference to Biology.'

.·.

We tender our warm congratulations to Mr. W. A. S. Hewins, M.A., Lecturer of Pembroke College. Mr. Hewins, who has for some years past been one of our most active lecturers in Economics has been recently appointed to be the first Director of the London School of Economics and Political Science. No appointment could be more appropriate and we heartily wish success alike to Mr. Hewins and to the new enterprise.

.·.

During the past month the University movement in England and Wales has been marked by two events of considerable importance. The University of Durham has received its supplemental charter and now enjoys the right of conferring all its degrees on women, with the exception of those in Divinity. The charter also empowers the University to hold convocations in Newcastle and elsewhere, a provision which will give its academic constitution something of a federal character. And the University of Wales, of which the Prince of Wales has consented to be the first Chancellor, has held its first matriculation examination. About eighty candidates presented themselves, coming in fair proportions from the three constituent Colleges at Bangor, Cardiff and Aberystwith. Of these three Colleges, only one—Bangor, has as yet determined to subordinate its whole curriculum to the requirements of the new University of Wales. The other two will at present continue their work of preparation for the examinations of the University of London. This however will probably be only a transitional arrangement. Thus the foundation of new Universities necessarily curtails the constituency to which the University of London has hitherto rendered important service. And, as this process develops, the University of London will find itself free to give special regard to the educational interests of students resident in London and receiving instruction at the London Colleges. The success, therefore, of the University of Wales will be a factor in the movement for the establishment of a new Teaching University for London.

.·.

The annual public meeting organized by the Extension Committee of the Victoria University was announced to be held in the Chemistry Theatre of the Owens College, Manchester, on Saturday, June 29. The Vice-Chancellor (Principal Ward, of Owens College) promised to preside, and the Address was to be given by the Lord Bishop of Manchester. This meeting organized on the lines of those which are annually held under the auspices of the London Society is only one of many evidences of the enterprise and energy of Mr. P. J. Hartog, the new secretary of the Victoria University Extension Committee.

.·.

At a meeting of the Convocation of the University held on June 25, a decree was passed unanimously authorizing the Delegates of the University Press to contribute a grant of Clarendon Press books in sheets up to the value of £50 to the Library of the University Extension College at Reading.

.·.

A well-attended Conference was held at Toynbee Hall on May 18 to consider whether the educational work of co-operative societies might not with advantage be drawn into closer alliance with the various branches of University Extension work,—lectures, settlements and the rest. Mr. E. O. Greening took the chair, and Mr. Aves laid his plans before the meeting in a careful speech. Neighbouring co-operative societies, he contended, should combine to secure the services of a University lecturer and might well arrange a series of connected courses on the industrial history of England. The usual kind of discussion followed and the Conference committed itself to a resolution. Of course it has all been said before—said over and over again—but Mr. Aves is right to peg away at his point even at the risk of seeming prosy and importunate. The fact is that, with a few honourable and brilliant exceptions, co-operators have done less for the new ideals of civic education than at one time seemed likely to be the case. It has not been the fault of those in the co-operative movement who really care for education. They have never flagged in their enthusiasm or flinched from their high ideals. It has been the ordinary members who have been apathetic. And in the meantime the more quick-witted workmen have been tasting heady draughts of revolutionary speculation. But there are signs of change, and we must peg away.

.·.

Mr. C. E. Mallet, having taken over at Mr. Marriott's request, the Secretaryship of this Association, wishes to state that it is proposed to hold a conference of lecturers at Oxford during the Summer Meeting, the time of which will be announced later. He would therefore be glad if any lecturer who has any subject to bring forward for discussion at the Conference, would kindly communicate with him beforehand at 132 Cromwell Road, London, S. W.   *Oxford University Extension Lecturers' Association.*

.·.

Much discussion has arisen from time to time as to the desirability of throwing open University Extension lectures free to the public, especially in industrial centres. At the Conference of School Board Clerks held at Leeds in June, Mr. Wyatt, the clerk of the Manchester School Board, stated that he thought 'free evening schools were a frightful mistake . . . In cases where School Boards had freed their evening schools and had reported at the beginning of a session the attendance of thousands of eager students, he noticed that they were very reticent about the attendance at these schools when the session closed . . . Students should be led to see that the education they would receive was worth money.' Some local organizers of University Extension would be disposed to agree with Mr. Wyatt. On the other hand, the experience of the Oldham Industrial Co-operative Society, which has recorded year by year an increased attendance at its free University Extension lectures, may be cited on the other side. Possibly the explanation is that, as the courses at Oldham are paid for by the Co-operative Society, each individual co-operator feels that he has contributed towards the lectures. When the Barnsley British Co-operative Society had Extension lectures, it threw them open to the public. The result was a larger attendance. But so many of those present did not belong to the Co-operative Society, that a section of the members took umbrage and refused to continue the lectures.

.·.

We have received the Spring number of the *Cheltenham Ladies College Magazine.* It is, as usual, full of interest, primarily of course to those who are or have been associated with the famous institution whose prosperity and progress it records, but hardly less to all who are interested in higher education. The present number contains the annual report of the Lady Principal to the Council for the year 1893-1894. It presents a remarkable record of varied and many-sided activities. Everybody knows the high place to which the College has attained in respect of the higher studies, and the Principal therefore lays especial and most judicious stress on the progress of the Musical, Art, and Physical Education Departments. All educationalists will welcome the news of the steady increase in the Training Department for teachers. The success of this experiment at Cheltenham, on which Miss Peale is to be warmly congratulated, will lend additional interest to the address which she has most kindly consented to deliver at the Summer Meeting.

SUMMER MEETING NOTES.

Worcester College has most kindly placed thirty-five sets of rooms at the disposal of Summer Meeting students (men). Rooms will be allotted in order of application. As the privilege of a brief residence within College walls is very highly prized, early application should be made to the Secretary, University Extension Office, Oxford. The cost of board and lodging will not exceed 30s. a week. We need not remind those of our readers who have been present at previous Summer Meetings that Worcester College, with its extensive and beautiful gardens, is among the most attractive of Oxford Colleges. The kindness of the Governing Body in placing it at our disposal will be very warmly appreciated.

.·.

Visitors to the Summer Meeting will be welcomed at the Reception on Thursday, August 1, by the Provost of Worcester, Pro-Vice-Chancellor, on behalf of the Delegacy.

•·.

The Right Hon. Sir W. Hart Dyke, M.P., formerly Minister of Education, has most kindly undertaken to preside at the Conference on August 3, in place of Sir John Mowbray ; the latter is, we regret to say, compelled to seek a holiday after his arduous parliamentary labours. Professor Jebb, M.P. for the University of Cambridge, has also promised, if possible, to attend and speak.

.·.

We are glad to be able to announce that Professor York-Powell, the recently appointed successor to Professor Froude will lecture on Defoe.

.·.

Special prominence will be given in this Meeting as in the last, to the study of Economics. In addition to Sir Robert Edgcumbe's lectures, Mr. Graham Wallas will

give three lectures on the ' English Town in the Eighteenth Century' ; Mr. L. L. Price will lecture on Adam Smith ; and Mr. Hobson will conduct six lecture-classes in Economical Theory. Mr. Hobson's lectures will take the work of Adam Smith as their basis, and will trace the development of his theories in the work of later economists.

.·.

The Rev. T. W. Fowle, M.A., Rector of Islip, the well-known author of *The Poor Law*, in Macmillan's ' English Citizen ' Series, has kindly consented to deliver lectures in the First Part of the Meeting, on ' English Pauperism in the Eighteenth Century,' and to supplement them during the Second, by classes for the study of problems connected with the Poor Law. Students of Economics will thus have an opportunity of studying this important but intricate subject under the guidance of one who is acknowledged to be the leading English authority on the question.

.·.

The Delegates are glad to announce that the Rev. W. Bayard Hale has accepted an invitation to lecture on the ' Making of the American Constitution.' Mr. Hale is one of the most distinguished and popular lecturers on the staff of the American Society for the Extension of University Teaching, and will be welcomed to Oxford as a worthy successor to Dr. Devine and Mr. Rolfe. It is hoped that he will also be induced to preach one of the special sermons during the Second Part. The other special sermons as we have already announced, will be preached by the Lord Bishop of Hereford, Canon Gore, the Rev. W. Hudson Shaw, and the Rev. J. E. Odgers.

.·.

A large number of lecturers will this year be heard for the first time at the Summer Meeting. Among those who are well known in other spheres we may mention the names of Professor J. P. Mahaffy, the well-known and genial Professor of Ancient History in Trinity College, Dublin ; Sir Edward Russell of Liverpool ; Professor Reichel, formerly Fellow of All Souls College, and now Principal of the University College of North Wales at Bangor ; Professor Lodge, formerly Fellow of B.N.C., and now Professor of History in the University of Glasgow ; Dr. Kimmins, the Secretary to the London Society for the Extension of University Teaching, and Sir Robert Pearce-Edgcumbe.

.·.

Principal Reichel's lecture on the ' Influence of Sea Power in the Eighteenth Century,' will be given on the first evening of the Second Part, and Sir Robert Pearce-Edgcumbe's lectures on ' The History and Principles of the Currency ' on the two succeeding evenings. These lectures are expected to be devoted largely to an exposition of the Bimetallic theory.

.·.

The lectures on the Music and Musicians of the Eighteenth Century will be given by Mr. F. Cunningham Woods, M.A., Mus. Bac., Exeter College, on August 5 at 8.30, and August 6 at 3 o'clock. The first lecture will deal with the instrumental, the second with the vocal music of the period. There will be full musical illustrations, in which Miss Bué, Miss Taphouse, and Mr. Sunman (of Christ Church Cathedral choir) have kindly consented to take part. To render these illustrations more complete, Mr. Taphouse, of Magdalen Street, Oxford, has most generously placed at the lecturer's disposal his unique collection of musical instruments. Mr. Cunningham Wood will be known by reputation at least to many of our readers. Organist of Exeter College, and Honorary Conductor of the Oxford Philharmonic and Choral Society, he is by no means the least distinguished of a group of young musicians whom Sir John Stainer, by his conspicuous personal tact and strong but unobtrusive enthusiasm is gathering round him in Oxford.

2

At the meeting to be held in New College Hall on August 11, to consider the aims and objects of the Christian Social Union, the chair will be taken by the Rev. F. J. Chavasse, Principal of Wycliffe Hall, Oxford. The two chief speakers will be the Rev. Canon Gore and the Rev. C. G. Lang, Vicar of St. Mary's.

.·.

The lecture on Swift will be delivered, in the regrettable absence of Mr. Leslie Stephen, by Mr. F. S. Boas. Mr. Boas will also deliver during the Second Part of the Meeting, a series of lectures on the Poets and Novelists of the Eighteenth Century.

.·.

A course of theological lectures will be delivered by the Rev. C. G. Lang, M.A., Fellow and Dean of Divinity, Magdalen College, the recently appointed Vicar of St. Mary's. Mr. Lang's subject will be ' The Theology of St. Paul, especially in relation to English religion in the Eighteenth Century.' Lectures will also be delivered daily between August 2 and 10 at Manchester College.

.·.

By kind permission of the Union Society, a debate will take place in their famous Debating Hall, on Thursday, August 8. The subject will be connected with *Merrie England.*

.·.

Mr. Arthur Sidgwick's lectures will be on Addison and Pope.

.·.

An opportunity will be given to local secretaries and others to hear several new lecturers at the Summer Meeting, among them Mr. Garstang, Fellow of Lincoln College, who will lecture on 'Division of Labour in Animal Communities'; Mr. Hilaire Belloc, who will lecture on 'France before the Revolution'; Mr. F. E. Smith of Wadham College, who will lecture on ' John Wilkes,' and Mr. de Selincourt, of University College, on 'Letter-writing in the Eighteenth Century.' Mr. Belloc and Mr. F. E. Smith are among the most recent Ex-Presidents of the Union, where the reputation they made is exceptionally high.

.·.

Mr. Horsburgh will lecture during the First Part of the Summer Meeting on Sir Robert Walpole, and during the Second Part upon the Eastern Question in the Eighteenth Century, and on Reformers before the European Revolution. The lectures on the History of the Eighteenth Century will be given by Mr. A. L. Smith, M.A., Fellow and Tutor of Balliol College; Mr. E. Armstrong, M.A., Fellow and Tutor of Queen's College, and Mr. Arthur Hassall, M.A., Student and Tutor of Christ Church.

.·.

A pianoforte recital will be given by Miss Carrie Townshend, a gifted young pianist, whose performances in London have recently attracted much favourable attention.

.·.

Mrs. F. S. Boas has kindly undertaken, as before, the management of the Ladies' Cricket Match and the Lawn Tennis arrangements. It is proposed to arrange a match between the students and the Long Vacation Tennis Club on Thursday, August 8, and a Ladies' Cricket Match *v.* the Ladies of Oxford on Friday, Aug. 9. Ladies who are willing to play in the Cricket match, and ladies and gentlemen willing to play in the Tennis match are requested kindly to send their names and Oxford addresses to Mrs. F. S. Boas, Fairlie, Bickley, Kent, before Aug. 6.

.·.

The Delegates have decided that Monday, August 12, the last day of the First Part of the Meeting, shall be devoted entirely to excursions. The conversazione will take place in the evening, but there will be no lectures during the day. By kind permission of the Duke of

Marlborough, an excursion will be made to the Park, Gardens, and Palace of Blenheim, which is of course rich in eighteenth century associations. A visit will also be made to the ancient town of Woodstock, where the Town Clerk has most kindly consented to exhibit some of the interesting municipal records of the Borough. Mr. Ballard is himself no mean antiquarian, and under his expert guidance this visit should prove of singular interest. Nuneham House, thanks to the kindness of Mr. Aubrey Harcourt, will also be visited during the Meeting, and other excursions are in course of arrangement.

.·.

In the June number of the *L'Enseignement Chrétien,* there is an exceedingly interesting article from the pen of L'Abbé Félix Klein on the forthcoming Summer Meetings at Oxford and Edinburgh, to which he strongly recommends a visit :—

Édimbourg et Oxford ! Pourquoi ces villes plutôt que d'autres ? Un peu parce que je les connais mieux, y ayant séjourné plus longuement, mais aussi parce qu'elles me semblent posséder en fait d'agréments, de pittoresque et d'utilité, des avantages qu'on ne trouverait à un si haut degré dans aucune autre cité du Royaume-Uni. Telle n'est pas cependant la véritable raison de ce choix.

Cette raison, la voici : Édimbourg et Oxford possèdent, pendant le mois d'août, un *Summer Meeting.*

Un *Summer Meeting,* c'est tout un ensemble de cours, de conférences, d'excursions agréables ou instructives, de réunions diverses, qui ont lieu en été sons la direction plus ou moins officielle de certaines Universités ou grâce à l'initiative d'un comité de professeurs. Les personnes qui participent au *Summer Meeting* entrent par là même dans un certain groupement qui, sans leur imposer d'obligation pénible, leur procure comme spontanément toutes sortes de relations, de moyens de s'instruire et d'agréables distractions. Au lieu de se trouver seules en pays étranger, elles font partie d'une société extrêmement variée et très accueillante. Les professeurs comme les disciples sont généralement des gens à l'esprit tolérant et ouvert, très intéressants dans leur variété d'esprit, d'origine et de langage.

.·.

The visits to the Colleges will be arranged somewhat more systematically than in former years. They will be made under the direction of Mr. J. Wells, M.A., Fellow of Wadham College. Mr. Wells proposes to conduct a series of visits to the Colleges in chronological sequence with a view to illustrating the most important epochs in the development of the University.

.·.

The visits will be arranged as follows :—
(1) The Cathedral and St. Mary's Church with the beginnings of the University system.
(2) Merton College, the commencement of the College system.
(3) New College, the triumph of the College system.
(4) All Souls and Magdalen Colleges—the end of mediaeval Oxford.
(5) Corpus Christi College and Christ Church—the Colleges of the new learning.
(6) St. John's and Wadham Colleges with the struggles of the seventeenth century.
It will be obvious that the whole history of the Colleges mentioned is not connected with the periods they have been chosen to represent. Mr. Wells hopes to touch on other points of interest connected with them, but less formally than in an ordinary College visit; nor will his parties be in the first instance architectural. His main object is to study the history of each period in the most important building or buildings which represent it in Oxford.

The parties will of necessity be limited to 100, but if it be wished, Mr. Wells will gladly conduct the series of visits again in Part II of the Meeting. So far as is possible each visit will be strictly limited to an hour.

THE NEW 'JOURNAL.'

WE make elsewhere an official announcement which will be received, as it is made, with mingled feelings. When the time comes we shall say good-bye to the *Extension Gazette* with genuine regret. We hope some at least of our readers will share that feeling. None the less heartily shall we welcome the appearance of the new *University Extension Journal.* In outward form it will closely resemble the existing *Gazette*, a fact which may we trust help to reconcile some of our friends to a change, which there may be some disposition to resent. The Delegacy have not arrived at a decision in this matter without the most anxious deliberation, and constant consultation with the representatives of Cambridge, Victoria University, and the London Society for the Extension of University Teaching. The new *Journal* will appear under the official sanction of these four authorities, and will be conducted by a joint Editorial Committee appointed by them.

The step thus taken possesses a significance out of all proportion to its immediate importance, and may not impossibly lead to far-reaching developments in the future. It must be regarded as the first fruits of closer association between the various authorities engaged in the work of University Extension. Of that association the great London Congress of 1894 was at once the visible symbol and the outcome. Shortly after the Congress, and as a direct result of it, the leading University Extension authorities in England decided upon the formation of a representative joint Committee. This Committee has met frequently during the last few months, and it is thence that the idea of a joint Journal has issued. It is felt, and very strongly, that the fundamental unity of aim and principle which underlies the work of all the bodies responsible for the Extension of University Teaching, will best find adequate expression in a single Journal under their joint control, but representative of the movement as a whole ; and thus added emphasis will be given to an unquestionable fact. University Extension has taken its place among the great educational forces of our day ; it is prepared to claim its share in the national economy of education ; it has from the first advocated a single principle ; it will henceforth speak with one official voice. That diversity of views, as to administrative detail, will find expression in the new Journal we do not doubt. Were it otherwise we should despair of the state. But on all 'fundamentals' there is complete unanimity between the various authorities, and it is primarily for the dissemination and enforcement of these that the new Journal is established. We heartily wish Godspeed to the combined enterprise.

THE CONFERENCE ON ADULT EDUCATION AT HAVRE.

THE programme of this Conference, to which the recent discussion in the French Chamber has given considerable importance, is now published. Of the four subjects which will be considered at the Conference, the first three have a close connexion with University Extension work. They are as follows :—

(1) *Courses of adult instruction.* Their organization, programme of studies, methods and experience. Special courses for girls.

(2) *Popular lectures* in industrial and rural centres : methods of organization : subjects of lectures and choice of lecturers.

(3) *Illustration of lectures* : lantern slides ; their use and classification : the provision of circulating collections of slides.

The Conference will be held at Havre on Aug. 30 and 31 and Sept. 1. Each society can send two (or, in special cases, five) delegates. The names of delegates should be sent before August 10 to the Secretary, M. Édouard Petit at the Musée Pédagogique, Paris. Written communications should be sent before August 1 to M. G. Serrurier, Société havraise d'enseignement par l'aspect, Havre.

Universities in Democratic States.

M. Poincaré's Speech at Lille.

THE probable fate of Universities in a democratic state used to be a favourite subject of foreboding. Happily the danger of the situation was realized in time both by statesmen responsible for the interests of higher education and by the Universities themselves. The result is that in France and America, as in England, the Universities so far from being crippled by popular jealousies are being encouraged by public opinion to take a more influential part than ever in the guidance of educational policy. And nowhere is this changed attitude towards the Universities more apparent than in France where the antagonism to their influence, tacit or veiled in this country, had gone to open extremes. Successive Ministers of Public Instruction have gradually adopted a policy which will admittedly end in the restoration of the Universities to their former state of self-governing corporations. The results of the revolutionary and Napoleonic reform of the French Universities, the now baneful effects of the centralization which made each provincial Faculty dependent on the central office in Paris, cannot indeed be easily removed. Vested interests and ingrained habit make immediate reform impossible. But, as the French Minister of Education, M. Poincaré, said at the Fête Universitaire at Lille on June 2, the day cannot be long distant when the law, which has already given autonomy to the reunited Faculties, will confer upon some of them the full name and powers of a University. M. Poincaré was emphatic in his description of the services which Universities may render to the modern State. It is not, he said, merely as schools of professional training for doctors and lawyers that the State needs the Universities, it is because they are the workshops of thought, the centres of research and disinterested study. And alongside of their intellectual functions are their social duties which daily grow in importance. Universities, he urged, must not be inaccessible places, withdrawn and remote from practical interests and everyday life. Their work and influence are needed in the great centres of industrial and commercial activity. Nor is it they only who confer benefits -- they also receive stimulus and advantage from the stir, the practical experience, the munificence of the great cities. The need is reciprocal ; the Universities gain from the industrial life around them, the industry of the district is the better for the higher standard of attainment which the Universities diffuse and maintain. In fact the University of Lille stands to the busy district in which it is situate as the Victoria University stands to Lancashire. Finally, M. Poincaré insisted that the prosperity and activity of the Universities was essential to the welfare of a democratic State. It is admitted that primary education is a necessity : but primary education can only be fertilized by the influence of higher education which trains its teachers, revives their energies, is the source of further advance. C'est à l'enseignement supérieur de régler, pour ainsi dire, le diapason de l'instruction populaire, c'est à lui d'en marquer le rhythme et d'en as. urer l'harmonie. Que la démocratie se réjouisse donc de voir naître et prospérer les Universités françaises. C'est elles qui, en partie, décideront de son avenir ; c'est à elles peut-être, qu'elle devra le meilleur de ses destinées.

S.

SCHOOL BOARDS AND UNIVERSITY EXTENSION.

AT the Conference of School Board Clerks (one of the most important educational gatherings of the year) several references were made to University Extension work. Mr. Adams of Tottenham said that they had had a course of Extension lectures on 'The Life and Duties of the Citizen' with most satisfactory results. 'The lecturer clothed the subject with the breadth, intelligence and interest which it deserved.' Mr. Packer gave an account of the Extension lectures on Central and Local Government arranged last session by the Leeds School Board. 'The lecturers were able men, thoroughly conversant with their subject and spared no pains to make the lectures interesting.'

The attendance however was not well maintained, though twenty-three students passed the examination on Central Government and seventeen students that on Local Government. 'One of the students who passed in both courses with distinction is a day school teacher, who is willing to take up the subject as a special teacher in evening schools: thus a linking agency may be established for sound instruction from the University to the Elementary School.' But at Manchester, Mr. Broadfield said, they had 'endeavoured to introduce their pupil-teachers to University Extension lectures, and had found the young people unprepared to take full advantage of the instruction.' The position seems to be that University Extension teaching is finding a place in the programmes of the evening schools under the direction of the School Boards (the action of the Southampton School Board is a case in point), but that in many places the pupil-teachers and others attending the lectures are insufficiently prepared by previous education to make full use of the Extension courses. This is a difficulty, however, which is likely to diminish year by year.

The London School of Economics and Political Science.

IN spite of the growing importance of social and economic subjects, we have as yet done little in this country to further systematically the study of them. France has the École Libre des Sciences Politiques in Paris; the United States Columbia College, New York; and other countries similar institutions. We are glad, therefore, to see that in October next the London School of Economics and Political Science will provide organized courses of instruction in these subjects, and will offer facilities for original investigation and research.

Funds for this new school have been placed at the disposal of the trustees, and Mr. W. A. S. Hewins, well known as an Oxford University Extension lecturer, and as an able student of Economics, will undertake the direction of the work. That this sphere of work will be a wide one is proved by the fact that among its proposed aims are the holding of public lectures and classes on Economics (including both theory and history), and of special classes arranged in a three years' course of study; the promotion of original research by means of scholarships and in other ways; the formation of a library for the use of the students; and the organization of an 'information department' for the assistance of British and foreign students.

Courses of lectures and classes have been already arranged in many subjects. These will be given by various well-known lecturers, among others, by the Director (Mr. Hewins), Prof. Cunningham, Mr. Acworth, Mr. H. J. Mackinder, Prof. Munro, Prof. Foxwell, Mr. Graham Wallas.

It will be seen that the new School is to be a teaching body, and not an examining board. No definite preparation for special examinations will be undertaken, but there can be little doubt that the lectures and classes already arranged will be found helpful to students reading for many examinations such as those for the Civil Service, and those of the London Chamber of Commerce, and the Society of Arts.

It need only be added that the School has the cordial co-operation and support not only of leading economists and students of political science, but also of the Society of Arts and the London Chamber of Commerce, in whose rooms many of the lectures will be given. The advantages of the School will be open to all who are able to profit by them, whether men or women; and by arranging evening courses of instruction and by granting scholarships to deserving students it is hoped that all classes of persons may be able, should they wish, to avail themselves of the opportunities of scientific training now offered to them.

The progress of this new educational experiment will be watched with interest. We have long hoped for the establishment of some similar institution, and we look forward to the rapid growth in influence and activity of the London School. Of its usefulness we feel assured; of its success we feel equally confident.

REPORTS FROM THE CENTRES.

BAKEWELL.—On Thursday April 25, the concluding lecture of the short series arranged this Spring in connexion with the Students' Association was given by Professor Gotch. We are specially indebted to Professor Gotch for his great kindness in coming to Bakewell at a time when his recent appointment to be Waynflete Professor of Physiology in the University of Oxford had involved him in so many pressing engagements. The lecture was on 'Hypnotism,' and may be roughly divided into two parts. The scientific explanation of the physiological changes that take place in the various stages of the hypnotic trance, resulting in a serious derangement of the nervous system, and the moral effect upon a subject who voluntarily submits to the paralysis of his will, whereby he surrenders to another the strongest power in his nature. It is impossible to describe Professor Gotch's marvellous clearness of exposition, his avoidance of technicalities, and the intense interest that he threw into his whole subject, and we are sure that no one who heard the lecture could fail to realize not only the danger of Hypnotism generally, but also the responsibility given to every man in his possession of will-power. There was an attendance of eighty-one at the lecture, and the vote of thanks to Professor Gotch was passed with most enthusiastic applause.

CORNISH CENTRES.—The examiner on the course of lectures on South Africa, recently delivered throughout Cornwall by Mr. W. B. Worsfold, M.A., reports as follows:—'I have had papers sent me from six centres, Truro, Falmouth, Camborne, Redruth, Launceston, and Penzance. I am glad to report a high level of excellence in almost all the papers submitted to me. I am surprised at the amount of knowledge and of intelligent criticism in some of the best papers, e. g. those of Janette Clift and Olive Tresidder in the Falmouth centre; that of Laura Smith in the Truro centre; that of Charles Rowe in the Camborne centre; that of Harry Rich in the Redruth centre; and that of Maria B. Borlase in the Penzance centre. Especially the political history and political geography of the country seem to have been most ably taught by the lecturer. The result of the examination seems to prove what a really useful as well as fascinating study South Africa is. From my own experience Cornishmen and Cornishwomen are frequently in the habit of emigrating to South Africa, the land of mines and mining. It must be now useful to them to know by tuition something beforehand of the country to which they may drift. If report is true, there must be a great exodus shortly of Cornishmen to 'fresh fields and pastures new.' No country would suit them better than South Africa. These lectures must be very helpful to them if they are contemplating such an exodus. From a wider point of view:—No colony or dependency can offer a more attractive and, in the highest sense, educative study than South Africa. I doubt whether India is a better subject. In South Africa there are many practical problems, e. g., in the sphere of native administration, that touch the individual Colonist and challenge his judgement—in India these questions are left to departments and possess no educative value for any class of laymen. The race questions in South Africa are ever growing with an ever-widening field. It is well for all, whether at home or in our Colonies, to know something about them. Unless we do, our Parliamentary proceedings must be often without a meaning, and our national determinations a puzzle. As far as Colonial History is concerned, a criticism, e.g., of the late Sir Bartle Frere's administration must be useful. Without being partisans, we may, nevertheless, gather much from the knowledge we may gain of the inner workings of our system of government. It is the duty of our citizenship to grasp Colonial questions—and an ever-growing duty. From many points of view South Africa strikes me as an extremely fertile subject, and the Cornish centres must be congratulated upon the way their candidates have studied and written upon it.—WILLIAM GRESWELL, M.A., F.R.G.S.'

BOOK EXCHANGE AND LOAN COLUMN.

THE Bakewell Students' Association has for hire the following Libraries:—

Course: 'England in the Eighteenth Century.' 12 volumes for 10s. for a year.

Course: 'English Novelists.'
Fielding's Works, 12 vols.
Jane Austen's Works (5 vols.).
History of the English Novel. (Univ. Extension Manual.)
18 vols. for 15s. for a year; or Miss Austen's Works separately for 5s.

Detailed lists sent on application. Address:—Miss KATHLEEN MARTIN, Edensor, Bakewell.

BOOKS ON OUR TABLE.

The Marquess Wellesley. ('Rulers of India' Series.) By Rev. W. H. HUTTON, M.A., Fellow and Tutor of St. John's College, Oxford.

The two most commanding figures among the English 'Rulers of India' are undoubtedly those of Warren Hastings and the Marquess Wellesley. But there is this difference between them— that whereas the career of the former was entirely Indian and would therefore rightly need the hand of a specialist, Wellesley was nothing if he was not more than Indian. It seems to us, therefore, that Sir W. Hunter was well advised when he entrusted to a layman perhaps the most important and the most likely to be widely read in the whole of his fascinating series. And Mr. Hutton has not betrayed the trust reposed in him, but has given us a book in every way worthy of the subject. For, while on the one side his treatment of it is concise, judicial, proportioned, on the other side there is the measured enthusiasm which we look for in a biographer, and the literary instinct which

makes it plain that the writer is not only a compiler of accurate facts, but a most skilful interpreter of them. Mr. Hutton has very cleverly avoided any pitfalls of Indian technicalities. We have neither noticed nor heard of any complaints on that score. His professional feelings, if we may so call them, have evidently been aroused and interested by the problems of Wellesley's private life. What he has given us makes us wish that he could have dealt with them at greater length and would have been at pains to reconcile the Governor-General's ostentatious reverence for religious ordinances with the unsatisfactory nature, to put it no stronger, of his domestic relations, though Mr. Hutton hints not obscurely his opinion that these had much to do with Wellesley's failure to reach the very first rank of statesmen. We are, however, not disposed to complain. Mr. Hutton has made us feel Wellesley's greatness as an imperial administrator, and incidentally he has been at pains also to portray the weaknesses of the man. The result is an admirable piece of work, interesting alike to the general reader and the student.

ARRANGEMENTS FOR 1895-6.

Autumn, 1895.

All lectures are at fortnightly intervals except where otherwise stated.

Certificates are awarded on courses of 12 Lectures only.

Centre.	No. of Lectures in Course.	Subject of Course.	Lecturer.	Course begins.	Course (or Half-Course) ends.
UNIVERSITY EXTENSION COLLEGE, READING (evening, weekly)	12	Citizen Education...	A. L. SMITH, M.A. ...	Th. Oct. 3	Dec. 19
ALTRINCHAM (evening) ...	6	Mediaeval England	Rev. W. H. SHAW, M.A.	F. Oct. 11	Dec. 20
ASHTON-UNDER-LYNE (aftern.)	6	Puritan Revolution	" " ...	T. Oct. 8	Dec. 17
BIRMINGHAM, SEVERN STREET (evening)	6	The Reformation to the Revolution	" " ...	T. Sept. 24	Dec. 10
BOLTON (evening)	6	The Reformation to the Revolution	" " ...	Th. Oct. 10	Dec. 19
†BURY (evening) ...	12	History of Florence and Florentine Art	Rev. W. H. SHAW, M.A. & J. E. PHYTHIAN ...	F. Oct. 4	Dec. 13
CHELTENHAM (afternoon)	6	History of Venice...	Rev. W. H. SHAW, M.A.	Th. Oct. 3	Dec. 12
CHELTENHAM (evening) ...	6	Mediaeval England	" "	W. Oct. 2	Dec. 11
CIRENCESTER (afternoon) ...	6	History of Florence	" "	M. Sept. 30	Dec. 9
GLOUCESTER (evening) ...	6	Mediaeval England	" "	M. Sept. 30	Dec. 9
HEBDEN BRIDGE (evening) ...	6	Making of England	" "	S. Oct. 12	Dec. 21
KESWICK (evening)	6	Making of England	" "	M. Oct. 7	Dec. 16
MALVERN (afternoon)	6	History of Florence	" "	W. Oct. 2	Dec. 11
OLDHAM (evening)	6	The Reformation to the Revolution	" "	W. Oct. 9	Dec. 18
†OXFORD (evening)	12	Age of Elizabeth	Rev. W. H. SHAW, M.A. & E. L. S. HORSBURGH, B.A.	Th. Oct. 3	Dec. 12
SALE (evening)	6	English Social Reformers ...	Rev. W. H. SHAW, M.A.	T. Oct. 8	Dec. 17
†STROUD (afternoon)	12	Puritan Revolution and the Later Stuarts	Rev. W. H. SHAW, M.A. & E. L. S. HORSBURGH, B.A.	T. Oct. 1	Dec. 10
WIGAN (afternoon)	6	History of Venice...	Rev. W. H. SHAW, M.A.	W. Sept. 25	Dec. 4
†*DORCHESTER (evening) ...	12	Industrial Revolution	J. A. R. MARRIOTT, M.A.	Not fixed	Not fixed
STRATFORD ON-AVON (evening)	6	Age of Louis XIV	" " ...	M. Sept. 30	Dec. 9
*WEYMOUTH (afternoon) ...	6	Not fixed	" "	Not fixed	Not fixed
BARNSLEY (evening)	6	Shakespeare	F. S. BOAS, M.A.	T. Oct. 8	Dec. 17
ROCHDALE (afternoon) ...	6	Browning	" " ...	W. Oct. 9	Dec. 18
SETTLE (evening)	6	Shakespeare	" " ...	W. Oct. 2	Dec. 11
WAKEFIELD (evening) ...	6	Not fixed	" "	T. Oct. 1	Dec. 10
BRADFORD (evening)	6	Eighteenth Century	C. E. MALLET, B.A. ...	Th. Oct. 3	Dec. 12
NEATH (afternoon) ...	6	English Colonies	" " ...	F. Oct. 11	Dec. 20
NEATH (evening)	6	The Stuarts	" " ...	F. Oct. 11	Dec. 20
OTLEY (evening)	6	Not fixed	" " ...	F. Oct. 4	Dec. 13
SWANSEA (afternoon)	6	English Novelists	" " ...	Th. Oct. 10	Dec. 19
†WEST BRIGHTON (afternoon)	12	Age of Elizabeth	" " ...	M. Oct. 7	Dec. 16
EASTBOURNE (afternoon) ...	6	Shakespeare	Rev. J. G. BAILEY, M.A., LL.D.	W. Oct. 2	Dec. 11
TUNBRIDGE WELLS (afternoon, weekly)	10	Shelley, Keats, Coleridge, and Wordsworth	" " ...	T. Oct. 8	Dec. 10
†WEST BRIGHTON (evening) ...	12	Shakespeare	" " ...	Th. Oct. 17	Dec. 12
†BOURNEMOUTH (afternoon) ...	12	18th & 19th Century Literature ...	E. L. S. HORSBURGH, B.A.	S. Oct. 5	Dec. 14
BOURNEMOUTH (evening)	6	Puritan Revolution	" " ...	F. Oct. 4	Dec. 13
CANTERBURY (afternoon) ...	6	Age of Elizabeth	" " ...	T. Oct. 1	Dec. 10
CHESTER (evening)	6	Not fixed	" " ...	W. Oct. 9	Dec. 18

† The figures in the second column include lectures to be delivered in the Spring Term, when these courses will be continued.

* Arrangements not yet completed.

Centre.	No. of Lectures in Course.	Subject of Course.	Lecturer.	Course begins.	Course (or Half-Course) ends.
†FOLKESTONE (afternoon) ...	12	Shakespeare	E. L. S. HORSBURGH, B.A.	M. Sept. 30	Dec. 9
HYDE (evening)	6	French Revolution	„ „ ...	M. Oct. 7	Dec. 16
LYMINGTON (afternoon) ...	6	Age of Elizabeth	„ „ ...	F. Oct. 4	Dec. 13
†RAMSGATE (afternoon) ...	12	Napoleonic Era	„ „ ...	S. Sept. 28	Dec. 7
†REIGATE (afternoon)... ...	12	Shakespeare	„ „ ...	F. Oct. 11	Dec. 20
ROCHESTER (evening) ...	6	Studies from the 18th and 19th Centuries	„ „ ...	T. Oct. 1	Dec. 10
†RYDE (afternoon)	12	Not fixed	„ „ ...	Th. Oct. 3	Dec. 12
†SANDOWN & SHANKLIN (aft.)	12	Not fixed	„ „ ...	W. Oct. 2	Dec. 11
THORNTON (evening) ...	6	Industrial and Economic Questions since 1789	„ „ ...	T. Oct. 8	Dec. 17
†VENTNOR (evening)	12	The Stuart Monarchy	„ „ ...	Th. Oct. 3	Dec. 12
HALIFAX (evening, weekly) ...	12	Wordsworth	Rev. P. H. WICKSTEED, M.A.	Th. Sept. 26	Dec. 19
HARROGATE (evening, weekly)	12	Dante	M.A.	F. Sept. 27	Dec. 20
ILKLEY (afternoon, weekly) ...	12	Dante	„ „ ...	F. Sept. 27	Dec. 20
RIPON (afternoon, weekly) ...	12	Dante	„ „ ...	W. Sept. 25	Dec. 18
BATH (afternoon)	6	The Work of the Air ...	H. R. MILL, D.Sc.	Th. Oct. 10	Dec. 19
BATH (evening)	6	The Work of the Air ...	„ „ ...	Th. Oct. 10	Dec. 19
BEDFORD (evening)	6	Astronomy	A. H. FISON, D.Sc. ...	F. Sept. 27	Dec. 6
CARLISLE (afternoon)	6	Astronomy...	„ „ ...	F. Oct. 4	Dec. 13
COCKERMOUTH (evening) ...	6	Astronomy...	„ „ ...	W. Oct. 2	Dec. 11
EDGBASTON (afternoon) ...	6	Astronomy...	„ „ ...	Th. Oct. 10	Dec. 19
GRANGE (evening)	6	Not fixed	„ „ ...	Th. Oct. 3	Dec. 12
HODDESDON (afternoon, weekly)	12	Astronomy...	„ „ ...	T. Oct. 1	Dec. 17
KENDAL (evening)	6	Sound and Light (probably) ...	„ „ ...	F. Oct. 4	Dec. 13
†STROUD (evening)	12	Forces of Nature	„ „ ...	W. Oct. 9	Dec. 18
WINSLOW (evening)	6	Architecture	F. BOND, M.A. ...	T. Oct. 8	Dec. 17
WELLS (evening)	6	Shakespeare	R. W. BOND, M.A. ...	Th. Sept. 26	Oct 5
WESTON-SUPER-MARE (even.)	6	Shakespeare	„ „ ...	W. Sept. 25	Oct. 4
PETERBOROUGH (evening) ...	6	The English Citizen	W. M. CHILDS, B.A ...	T. Oct. 1	Dec. 10
*ASHTON-UNDER-LYNE (even.)	6	The Reformation to the Revolution	W. G. DE BURGH, B.A.	T. Not fixed	Not fixed.
BANBURY (evening)	6	Astronomy...	R. A. GREGORY, M.A. ...	Th. Sept. 26	Dec. 5
CIRENCESTER (evening) ...	6	Industrial Problems of To-day ...	J. A. HOBSON, M.A. ...	M. Oct. 7	Dec. 16
NEWCASTLE-UNDER-LYME (evening)	6	Problems of Poverty	„ „ ...	W. Sept. 25	Dec. 4
TEAN (afternoon)	6	Modern Thinkers upon Life ...	„ „ ...	Th. Sept. 26	De.. 5
KIDDERMINSTER (afternoon)...	6	Architecture	J. E. PHYTHIAN ...	W. Oct. 2	Dec. 11
BAKEWELL (evening)	6	South Africa	W. B. WORSFOLD, M.A. ...	T. Oct. 1	Dec. 10
MATLOCK (afternoon)	6	English Poetry & Fiction since 1851	„ „ ...	W. Oct. 2	Dec. 11

Spring, 1896.

Centre.	No. of Lectures in Course.	Subject of Course.	Lecturer.	Course begins.	Course (or Half-Course) ends.
UNIVERSITY EXTENSION COLLEGE, READING (afternoon, weekly)	12	Literature	Not fixed	Not fixed	Not fixed.
„ (evening) ...	6	Astronomy...	A. H. FISON, D.Sc. ...	Th. Jan. 16	Mar. 26
BATH (afternoon) ...	6	Not fixed	J. A. R. MARRIOTT, M.A.	Th. Jan. 23	Apr. 2
BATH (evening)	6	Not fixed	„ „ ...	Th. Jan. 23	Apr. 2
†DORCHESTER (evening) ...	12	Industrial Revolution ...	„ „ ...	Th. Jan. 16	Mar. 26
SWINDON (evening)	6	Not fixed	„ „ ...	W. Jan. 15	Mar. 25
†WEST BRIGHTON (afternoon)	12	Age of Elizabeth	C. E. MALLET, B.A...	M. Jan. 20	Mar. 30
†WEST BRIGHTON (evening) ...	12	Shakespeare	Rev. J. G. BAILEY, M.A., LL.D.	Th. Jan. 30	Apr. 23
†BOURNEMOUTH (afternoon)...	12	18th & 19th Century Literature ...	E. L. S. HORSBURGH, B.A.	S. Feb. 1	Apr. 11
*BRECON (evening) ...		Not fixed	„ „ ...	T. Jan. 21	Mar. 31
CHELTENHAM (afternoon) ...	6	Not fixed	„ „ ...	Th. Jan. 23	Apr. 2
CHELTENHAM (evening) ...	6	Not fixed	„ „ ...	W. Jan. 22	Apr. 1
*DOVER (evening)		Not fixed	„ „ ...	M. Jan. 27	Apr. 6
†FOLKESTONE (afternoon) ...	12	Shakespeare	„ „ ...	M. Jan. 27	Apr. 6
†OXFORD (evening)	12	Age of Elizabeth	„ „ ...	F. Jan. 31	Apr. 10
†RAMSGATE (afternoon) ...	12	Napoleonic Era	„ „ ...	S. Jan 25	Apr. 4
†REIGATE (afternoon)... ...	12	Shakespeare	„ „ ...	F. Jan. 24	Apr. 3
†RYDE (afternoon)	12	Not fixed	„ „ ...	Th. Jan. 30	Apr. 9
†SANDOWN & SHANKLIN (aft.)	12	Not fixed	„ „ ...	W. Jan. 29	Apr. 8
†STROUD (afternoon)	12	Later Stuarts	„ „ ...	W. Jan. 22	Apr. 1
†VENTNOR (evening)	12	Not fixed	„ „ ...	Th. Jan. 30	Apr. 9
LEAMINGTON (evening) ...	6	Astronomy...	A. H. FISON, D.Sc. ...	F. Jan. 17	Mar. 27
†STROUD (evening)	12	Forces of Nature	„ „ ...	W. Jan. 15	Mar. 25
WIRKSWORTH (evening) ...	6	Commerce, Colonization & Empire	K. D. COTES, M.A. ...	Th. Jan. 30	Apr. 9
ABERGAVENNY (afternoon) ...	6	Not fixed	W. G. DE BURGH, B.A.	S. Jan. 18	Mar. 28
HEREFORD (evening)	6	English Exploration & Discovery	„ „ ...	M. Jan. 20	Mar. 30
LEAMINGTON (evening) ...	6	English Exploration & Discovery	„ „ ...	T. Jan. 21	Mar. 31
GLOUCESTER (afternoon) ...	6	Literature	J. A. HOBSON, M.A. ...	Not fixed	Not fixed.
GLOUCESTER (evening) ...	6	Problems of Poverty	„ „ ...	Not fixed	Not fixed.
†BURY (evening)	12	Florentine Art	J. E. PHYTHIAN ...	Not fixed	Not fixed.

† The figures in the second column include the lectures given in the Autumn Term, from which these courses are continued.

* Arrangements not yet completed.

Note.—Application for Courses and all information as to fees, &c., can be obtained from The Secretary, University Extension Office, Examination Schools, Oxford.

OXFORD UNIVERSITY

EXTENSION GAZETTE.

VOL. V. NO. 59.]   AUGUST, 1895.   [ONE PENNY.

N.B.—Local Organizers of Oxford University Extension Lectures are invited to send to the Secretary, University Extension Office, Examination Schools, Oxford, copies of any journals containing notices of, or references to, Extension work.

NOTES AND COMMENTS.

Reports on the Summer Meeting will appear in the September number of the *Gazette*.

．˙．

The new *University Extension Journal* will be sent gratuitously, as is the case with the existing *Gazette*, to Local Secretaries.

．˙．

By far the most important event connected with University Extension work during the past month was the opening of a new wing of the Albert Memorial Museum and Free Library, which is to become the home of the Technical and University Extension College at Exeter. The Duke of Devonshire in declaring the building open, delivered a speech full of sympathy with the aims and work of University Extension, which had now, he said, passed out of the experimental stage and become recognized as one of the educational agencies in the country. We hope next month to print a full report of the speech.

．˙．

The Duke of Devonshire has found an answer to a question which has long been a sore puzzle to many people ; he has discovered the true function of the Chancellor of a University. This high officer, though the nominal head of the University, has little to do with its internal affairs ; but his duty is rather to serve as a connecting link between the outer world and the University, to bring its ideas and thoughts into contact with those of persons outside its limits. Certainly the Duke has formed a high ideal of the duties of his office, and his speech at Exeter shows that the Chancellor of the University of Cambridge will not be behindhand in fulfilling those duties.

．˙．

Our critics, happily, are still with us. They have even invaded the Summer Meeting itself. Few will resent Professor Mahaffy's genial but shallow witticisms at our expense. But in the *Morning Post* for August 6 there appears an attack upon the whole system, which appears to reproduce Mr. Mahaffy's sophistries without the compensating wit. The attack is as ungenerous as it is untrue. The ideal of University Extension is *not* to help to 'push' men up 'into more exalted rungs on the intellectual and social ladder,' but to extend to the many all those intellectual delights which have been, but will never again be, the exclusive monopoly of the few.

．˙．

In the recent award of Honours issued by the Examiners in the Final School of Modern History, there appears in the Second Class the name of 'Miss E. M. Dowsett, University Extension College, Reading.' The announcement in these terms will be read with interest by many, and with something like amazement by all. It is by far the most distinguished honour as yet obtained by a genuine University Extension student, and is an achievement of which the youthful institution at Reading may be justly proud. We offer our hearty congratulations alike to Miss Dowsett and to Mr. Mackinder.

．˙．

The last number of the *University Extension Journal* contains the official announcement of Mr. A. W. Clayden's appointment by the Cambridge Syndicate as resident superintendent lecturer for Devon and district. Mr. Clayden's position as Principal of the Exeter University Extension and Technical College will give him an excellent position and opportunity for directing and superintending the educational work of the centres in his district. The editorial comment on the appointment we can hardly pass by without notice. It is true that 'the experiment of superintendent lecturers is as yet young and untried,' but it does not necessarily follow that the fact of Mr. Clayden residing in the district, which he is to administer, will probably 'enable him both more quickly to master the details of his work, and with more intimate sympathy to organize his centres, than is practicable in the case of a Director who can only visit his district at certain periods of the year.'

．˙．

The question of resident or non-resident Directors has been much discussed, and is still an open one. Is it better that they should be in close and personal contact with the central administrative authority, or that such close connexion be sacrificed to residence in their district? An answer can only be given after both experiments have been tried ; and at present it is somewhat premature to claim such preponderating advantages for either of two untried systems over non-resident Directors.

．˙．

In the same editorial notes a slight inaccuracy occurs. It is stated that Mr. Clayden's appointment differs from those that have been made by the Oxford Delegacy in that he is to be permanently resident in the district which he is to administer. One of the Directors appointed by the Delegates has already taken a permanent residence in his district ; the other, though non-resident, is within easy reach of it. The Delegacy is in fact trying the two experiments side by side, and only experience can decide which is the better.

．˙．

'Summer Meetings' increase apace. In addition to the Edinburgh Meeting, which will be held as usual during this month, gatherings of considerable educational importance will take place at Caen, Jena, Geneva, &c.

．˙．

A congress of societies engaged in the work of public education is to be held at Havre on August 30 and 31 and September 1. The object of the meeting is to discuss, from the practical point of view, the best means of organizing courses of instruction, by class or lecture, for adult students. All societies for the furtherance of public education are invited to send representatives. In view of the recent discussion in the French Chamber, the Congress will be discussing matters of pressing public importance. It would be a good thing if some of our best University Extension centres could be represented at the Congress. Reading, Exeter, Oldham, Bournemouth—to name only a few out of the many names which suggest themselves—have each a record of practical experience, which would be a valuable contribution to the discussions of the Congress. The educational problems in France and England are,—in spite of all superficial difference,—so fundamentally alike that those who are engaged in the same kind of effort in the two countries ought not to miss good opportunities of comparing notes.

. ' .

We gather from a recent number of *The Citizen*—the organ of the American Society for the Extension of University Teaching—that critics of University Extension are not lacking even in America. A General Isaac J. Wistar has lately been decrying the movement as one 'in the direction of diffusiveness and superficiality.' He strongly deprecates 'anything that encourages the unlearned to believe that attendance on a few discursive lectures, eked out with skim milk from a half-dozen popular books, is a fair substitute for any real collegiate training.' The gallant General cannot deprecate such a tendency more strongly than we do. But we are entirely unable to agree with our Philadelphian contemporary in finding some excuse for his misconception in the name 'University Extension' itself, and in the fact that 'in England where the movement started, it certainly was meant at first to extend to groups of people outside the Universities very much the same sort of instruction as that given within its walls.' We confess frankly that we prefer the attack to the apology. If University Extension teaching in its highest development means less than this, it means to us nothing.

. ' .

'The lectures,' said Professor Stanton speaking at the London Conference in 1894, 'were not simply to be University Extension lectures in the sense that they are lectures in populous places organized by the Universities, but lectures having something of a University character ... There are certain aspects of a University education which cannot possibly be extended to the provinces, and for which those who are able must always go to the great centres of learning. But there are certain qualities which we felt could be so extended. One of the chief of these was that the populace should be brought into personal relations with and be under the direct personal influence and guidance of teachers of a high degree of culture, in order that education for them might not mean simply the reading of text books, or study under teachers who had had no University training, but under teachers whose methods of study had been formed in the University, who came with a thorough University spirit, and who would communicate some of that University spirit to those who worked under them. Then along with this there was to be thoroughness in our work.' 'Oral teaching of the highest class,' said Mr. James Stuart on the same occasion, 'was what we undertook to give, what we professed to give, and what, when I appealed to the University to act, I asked it to give throughout this country.... We resolved in the University that we would give of our very best to this work.'

. ' .

We in Oxford have always endeavoured to act up to the high ideal set before themselves by these stalwart Cambridge pioneers, and we should account it a grievous blow to the whole movement were the University character of Extension teaching to be minimized or ignored. That the friends of the movement in America are prone to neglect this important truth we do not for an instant suppose. But on a point so vital we can afford no hesitating or ambiguous utterance. The provision of 'college-bred men as teachers' is something ; but in our view it falls far short of the ideal of University Extension

lecturing. We cannot believe that our colleagues in Philadelphia think otherwise, and nothing could be more explicit or more admirable than their declaration that 'the mission of the University Extension teacher is precisely not to lead people to think that there are short cuts to a complete education. It is rather to show them the need of education, its pleasures, and its cost in labour, and to make the undisciplined mind chary of venturing when the trained intelligence goes with difficulty.'

. ' .

The August number of *The Citizen*, published by the American Society for the Extension of University Teaching, contains articles, editorial notes and reviews, and University Extension news. Among the articles is one by Mr. J. T. Taylor of Oldham, which deals with the educational phases of the English Co-operative movement. In the University Extension news and announcements there is comment on the Summer Meetings in England and the United States, and general notes on the progress of University Extension in various parts of the world.

. ' .

We are requested to give prominence to ;the arrangements made for the Co-operative Holidays of the National Home Reading Union, and we do so with pleasure. 'These holidays, so successfully inaugurated in 1893, and carried on with further good results in 1894, will be continued this year—it is hoped on a still more extensive scale. The aim of the 'Holidays' is to provide the best possible recreation of spirit, mind, and body to tired workers of either sex, and of every kind. Four centres have been chosen for resort. Keswick is of course amidst classic ground of inexhaustible charm and interest. There again we are to have the friendly offices of Canon Rawnsley, to whom already we owe a large debt of gratitude. From Barmouth are promised excursions to Cader Idris, Cwmbychan, Harlech Castle, and the Torrent and Precipice Walks. From Portrush, 'The Queen of Ulster,' on a bluff promontory exposed to the full fury of the Atlantic rollers, we shall pay visits to the Giant's Causeway, and a neighbourhood that is proverbially a happy hunting-ground for the geologist, the collector of wierd legend, and the lover of wild coast scenery. Tavistock is a quaint old-world town brought up to date as a health resort for tourists in South Devon, Co-operative Holiday-makers at this centre will be within easy reach of Dartmoor, Exeter, Plymouth, and the Eddystone Lighthouse. Inquiries should be made at once, and bookings made to the address of the Corresponding Secretary for the centre :—Keswick, Miss S. N. Pringle, 113 Summerfield Crescent, Edgbaston, Birmingham ; Portrush, Rev. T. A. Leonard ; Tavistock, Miss Leighton, 10 Wellesley Road, Princes Park, Liverpool ; Barmouth, Mr. J. Hacking, 15 Princess Street, Colne, Lancashire.'

UNIVERSITY EXTENSION COLLEGE, READING.

THE awarding examiners in the Agricultural Examinations held under the authority of the Oxford and Reading Joint Committee have issued the following pass list : Certificate in Agriculture, John Francis Adams ; Dairy Teacher's Certificate, Jane Forster ; Diploma in Agriculture, first year's examination, passed in all subjects, Thomas Edward Gunter, Leyton Price Richards and Charles William Thorp ; passed in all subjects except Biology, Claude Reginald Powell ; passed in all subjects except Chemistry and Physics, Edward Thomas Brown ; passed in Biology and Geology, Eric Dowson ; passed in Geology, Clement Hugh Weston Malet. The following were the examiners :—Professor E. B. Poulton, F.R.S., Professor A. H. Green, F.R.S., Mr. D. A. Gilchrist, B.Sc., Mr. A. F. M. Druce, Mr. W. J. Glasson, M.A., Professor J. W. Axe, Mr. E. Brown, Mr. W. W. Fisher, M.A., and Mr. H. N. Dickson.

The First Experiments in the Extension of University Teaching.

IN the Autumn of 1867 there was established 'the North of England Council for promoting the Higher Education of Women,' its first meetings being held at Dr. Heaton's, Claremont, Leeds, on November 1 and 2 in that year. The primary object of forming this Council was 'to unite the Educational Associations in Manchester, Liverpool, Leeds, Sheffield and Newcastle into a Society for promoting improvements in the Education of Women.' Happening, however, to be founded at a critical time in the history of the movement for improving women's education and to include among its members many persons of great ability and perseverance, the Council came to exert in educational matters an influence which soon extended far beyond any provincial limit. In fact the record of its earlier meetings is almost an epitome of some of the most interesting chapters in our recent educational history. Through the kindness of Miss M. M. Calder of Liverpool, who from June 1870 acted as Hon. Sec. of the Council, I have had an opportunity of studying the reports of its work from 1867 to 1874, and I believe that a short summary of its proceedings will be read with interest by all who know our obligations to the Council for its pioneer work in University Extension.

At the first meeting there were present nine ladies, among whom were Mrs. Butler and Miss A. J. Clough (both at that time resident in Liverpool), and Mr. James Bryce, Mr. F. W. H. Myers and Mr. J. G. Fitch, who could speak to the state of feeling in the Universities of Oxford, Cambridge and London respectively. The first subject for discussion was 'the proposed College for Women,' and a resolution was passed expressing sympathy with the project and willingness to co-operate in any plan for obtaining subscriptions. But the attention of the Council was, at first, chiefly devoted to two objects: (1) the institution of lectures on literary, historical and scientific subjects, and (2) the promotion of examinations for women, with the intention of setting up a carefully chosen standard to be aimed at in their education, and with the further purpose of improving the training of teachers. With regard to the second object, the meeting discussed a plan for University Examinations for teachers and decided to request the voluntary Board, then being formed at Oxford and Cambridge, to institute special examinations for governesses. There followed a debate on the question of registration of teachers, it being ultimately decided, on the motion of Mr. Fitch, that the Council thought it ' premature at present to take any measures for obtaining a Scholastic Registration Act but, as soon as suitable Educational Boards should have been established, would desire to see the principle of registration publicly adopted.' I have gone into these details to show how comprehensive from the first were the deliberations of the North of England Council, but its action in regard to the establishment of lectures is what specially calls for record in these columns. At the same time, it must be remembered that the Council never confined itself to the task of arranging courses of lectures. That work it did with excellent success, but always as part of a larger programme of educational effort. And what made its deliberations so influential and caused so much to spring out of the lectures which it arranged, was the fact that its members always kept a broad policy before them and were resolved to think of the educational problem as a whole.

Accordingly, at its' first as well as at all its later meetings, the Council discussed much besides the details of lecture-organization. One part of these early debates is specially interesting at the present time, when the same controversy has been renewed. Mr. Bryce proposed and Mr. Myers seconded a motion that the Council recommend Miss Davies (whose plan for a College for women was before the meeting) to reconsider that part of her scheme in which she suggested that the examinations for women should be the same as those for men at Oxford and Cambridge. There was so much dissatisfaction in the Universities themselves with these examinations, Mr. Bryce remarked, that he felt it a pity that they should be adopted unconditionally elsewhere.

The lectures under the auspices of the Council had begun in the early Autumn of 1867. Mr. James Stuart was lecturing on the history of Physical Science (the title of the course is given as Astronomy in a later report), at Liverpool, Leeds, Manchester and Sheffield. It was reported that the number of students attending these lectures had risen to nearly six hundred, whilst more than three hundred papers were sent in weekly. In the discussion many points of organization, which have since become familiar to us, made their first appearance—the difficulty of arranging summer courses, the need of keeping up the hard work in connexion with the courses lest they should become merely popular lectures, the preference of one town in the combination for literary rather than for scientific subjects, the importance of having 'taking subjects' until the educational value of the lectures was more generally recognized, and the desirability of forming libraries of books for the use of students attending the lectures.

In February, 1868, the second lecture-session began. Mr. Charles Pearson, Fellow of Oriel College, Oxford, gave in Manchester and Liverpool courses of lectures on early English history, and Mr. Hales, formerly Fellow of Christ's College, Cambridge, delivered courses of lectures on early English literature at Leeds, Sheffield and Bradford. About 650 students are reported as having attended the lectures in these five towns.

At the next meeting (April 15, 1868) a representative of Bradford was admitted to the Council. It was reported from Cambridge that the University was clearly prepared to establish an advanced examination for women ('the Oxford representatives, while warmly sympathizing with the movement, could not feel certain that their University would act promptly, if at all, in this matter'); but that, while Miss Davies was of opinion that 'however excellent special examinations for women might be, they would not be regarded by the public so highly as those which secured an identity of tests and, being regarded as inferior to those of men, would naturally tend to become so,' the Vice-Chancellor of Cambridge, and academic persons generally, were opposed to identity of examinations for men and women. Accordingly, when Miss Clough moved ' that the existing University examinations are little suited to the circumstances of most educated women and that it is therefore desirable that other examinations be instituted which should have special reference to the wants and wishes of women as expressed by themselves,' four voted in support of the resolution and none against it.

At this meeting, three new lecturers were proposed. Mr. Linnaeus Cumming of Trinity College, Cambridge (now a master at Rugby), who offered courses on Botany, Zoology and Physical Geography; Mr. William Kennedy, a Cambridge senior classic, who offered lectures on Greek History; and Mr. Case, Fellow of Brasenose College, Oxford, who would lecture on Moral Philosophy and English or Italian History. Eventually Mr. Cumming lectured in October and November, 1868, on Physical Geography at Birkenhead, Bradford, Leeds and Liverpool, when he had respectively 80, 35, 120 and 180 students, with 15, 10, 40 and 50 weekly papers; Mr. Kennedy lectured during the same month on Greek History at Bowdon and Manchester, with audiences of 65 and 75 students, of whom 12 and 22 wrote weekly papers; while courses on English History were given in November and December by Mr. Archibald Milman at Newcastle, Sheffield and York, to audiences of 40, 65 and 90 persons. In all, in the Autumn of 1868, 750 persons attended the lectures, 259 wrote weekly papers, the courses each consisted of nine weekly lectures (except Mr. Milman's, which were of eight), and 38 certificates were granted (on Mr. Cumming's courses), 25 being of the first class.

In Oct. 1868, the Council met again—a new Oxford member appearing in Mr. A. O. Rutson of Magdalen College. A letter was read from Dr. Jowett, suggesting subjects most suitable for lectures and the order in which those subjects should be introduced so as to form a consecutive course for three years. Finally, after a good deal of discussion a Committee was appointed 'to devise plans for connected courses of lectures, and to consider

2

the possibility of forming permanent groups of towns for the purposes of the lectures. A sub-committee was also formed to seek for persons to deliver courses of lectures, to receive their proposals and to advise the Council in relation to them. The Oxford members of this sub-committee were Mr. Rutson and Professor T. H. Green; while Mr. Markby and Mr. James Stuart represented Cambridge, and Dr. Hodgson and Mr. Fitch, London.

In the early months of 1869, Mr. T. S. Aldis of Trinity College, Cambridge, lectured at Birkenhead, Bowdon, Liverpool and Manchester on the History of Science; Mr. J. W. Hales lectured at Bradford and Leeds on English Literature; Mr. F. W. H. Myers at Manchester on English History, and Mr. L. Cumming at Sheffield and York on Physical Geography. The last two courses were delivered in April, May and June. The aggregate attendance at the nine courses was 682 (Leeds and Liverpool furnishing the largest audiences), 178 weekly papers were sent in, 67 certificates were granted (53 being of the first class), and six of the large majority of the courses comprised eight weekly lectures.

At the Council's meeting on June 11 and 12, 1889 (Oxford being represented by Mr. T. H. Green and Mr. Bryce), steps were taken at the suggestion of Mr. Winterbotham, M.P., to bring before Parliament a memorial asking that there should be applied to the education of girls a reasonable proportion of the existing educational endowments of the country. The petition to Parliament was adopted on the motion of Mr. Bryce by eight votes to four. Co-education of boys and girls was also considered. On the second day the Council discussed the best means of establishing by lecture-courses a three years' curriculum of study. Manchester complained of the broken order of its subjects, Greek History followed by Chemistry and English Literature. Birkenhead on the other hand deplored the monotony of four scientific courses in succession. Liverpool took credit to itself for having had more sequence than other towns. Mr. Bryce and Mrs. Butler thought that one central body should have authority to assign lecturers to all the towns. A Manchester representative, however, pointed out that it was impossible to coerce the towns. Mr. Bryce remarked; 'It seems as if we should aim at working into a permanent College with three or four courses going on at once.' 'Yes,' Mrs. Butler is reported to have replied—'a sort of peripatetic College, but at present our beginnings are necessarily desultory to some extent.' Then followed a long talk about subjects, one speaker feeling that Literature would be too apt to degenerate into mere ear-tickling, unless studied along with Physical Science or Mathematics. Mr. Fitch however contended that the lecturer on Literature might be able to give his discourses 'a serious academic tone.' It was finally resolved to recommend 'a long winter course of severer mental discipline and a light summer course of separate or various lectures to stimulate interest,' and to urge the towns represented on the Council to give to a sub-committee greater powers in the choice and arrangement of lectures. The sub-committee appointed for this purpose were Mrs. Butler, Miss Clough and Miss Gaskell. The following scale of fees was also agreed upon:—

8 or 10 lectures in one town only £60.
8 or 10   „   in two towns £100.
8 or 10   „   in three towns £150.
8 or 10   „   in four towns £200.

At the meeting held at Leeds on June 24, 1870, Miss Clough resigned her office as Secretary, and was cordially thanked 'for her exertions in promoting the cause of education and for continuing for three years as Secretary to further the interest of the Council by her unwearied zeal, perseverance and good temper.' Mrs. Butler, in spite of the stress of other engagements, consented to continue as President for another year. The report of the Lectures-sub-committee showed that in the preceding winter the Manchester centre had had courses on English Literature (100 students) from Professor Nichol, on Chemistry (70 students) from Professor (now Sir Henry) Roscoe, and on English History (25 weekly papers) from Mr. F. W. H. Myers. Two small classes had also been

formed in Manchester—one of 11 students for Mathematics and one of 6 students for French. In Liverpool Mr. James Stuart had given courses on Light and Heat and on Electricity to 150 students. Small classes had also been formed at Liverpool in Latin and Mathematics with moderate success. In Leeds Mr. Aldis gave two courses on Astronomy to 60 students; a class in Physiology had also been attended by over 60 persons. In Bradford Mr. Aldis had also delivered his astronomical course to 70 students. At Bradford there had also been courses by Mr. Louis Miall on Botany, and Professor Henry Morley on English Literature. These were both eminently successful, Professor Morley also lecturing at York and Huddersfield.

The lecture-system had already begun to spread beyond the towns which were actually connected with the North of England Council. Lectures, for example, had been delivered by Professor Nichol at Alderley and Congleton; by Mr. Myers at Southport, Cheltenham, Leamington and Malvern; and by Mr. Cumming at Falmouth and Plymouth. Lectures had also been delivered in Clifton, Birmingham, Coventry, Ipswich, Blackheath, Putney and Winchester.

In the minutes of the meeting of June 23, 1871, the name of Miss M. M. Calder appears for the first time as Hon. Secretary. It was reported that the Council had petitioned for the appointment of women as well as men as inspectors of Elementary Schools. Mr. James Stuart had been asked to write a paper on the question of 'University Extension in regard to higher education in great towns,' and had also given a lecture at several towns in the North of England to make the subject more generally understood. The report about the lectures, which had been given in the winter 1870–71, was very satisfactory. Professor Morley had delivered two courses on English Literature at Southport to classes of 140 ladies. In Manchester the lecturers had been Professor Nichol and Professor Hales, both on Literature. Classes had also been formed in Manchester for the study of Logic, Latin, German, French, Arithmetic, Algebra, Geometry. Geology and Zoology. In Leeds Dr. Clifford Allbutt had given two courses on Physiology, and Professor Seeley one on the English Constitution. In Liverpool the Autumn course had been given by Professor Nichol, and that in the Spring by Mr. H. de Burgh Hollings (of Christ Church, Oxford), both being on English Literature. Certificates were given to the students at the end of both the latter courses. The lectures were reported as flourishing in various parts of London and the country, the system in Clifton having begun 'to assume something of the character of a College.'

At this same meeting of the Council (June 24, 1871), the Council decided to sign a memorial on 'University Extension,' which was about to be sent to Mr. Gladstone and to Oxford and Cambridge. The petition drew attention to 'the increasing desire for the opening out of the Universities to those whose circumstances prevent them from being able to reside there': to the difficulties of maintaining the lectures on a voluntary system: to the necessity of offering permanent employment in order to secure the continued services of first-rate men: and to the fact that 'the societies engaged in carrying out the scheme were in a perpetual state of bankruptcy or nearly so,' but that meanwhile the demand for courses of educational lectures continued to increase and deserved the 'consideration of the Universities as the heads and natural guardians of higher education.' The memorial proceeded to point out that 'almost without exception those who have undertaken such teaching work (in the great towns) were Fellows of Colleges, and urges that 'some privileges should be granted by the Colleges to those non-resident Fellows who might be duly sanctioned to carry on this work. If a man doing such work were permitted, in virtue of it, to retain his Fellowship, the income which he would thus derive, together with the payment made by his provincial pupils' would enable the organizers of the movement 'to secure able men to carry on this great and important work.'

The memorialists contended that 'by the adoption of some such scheme, the Universities, while entirely retaining the management of their own funds, would exercise a wider and more beneficial influence than at present over national education ... and that the method of rendering fellowships tenable on the ground of conducting higher education in large towns was one in every way consonant with the idea of a University.' They therefore begged that 'if a Royal Commission were appointed to investigate into the subject of the tenure of non-resident fellowships, that Commission should be instructed to consider what assistance the Universities could afford to higher education in great towns.'

Mr. Stuart further 'suggested the adoption of some such scheme as this: Let a number of towns club together and arrange with the University for six men to be sent, one to each of six towns and, if each individual man satisfied his individual town, and if he made the scheme there sufficiently successful, let them engage him for a year or two years and, if the scheme was still success-ful, let them agree as a whole to take their lecturers as a permanency. He believed men would come on that condition. The question was a pecuniary one eventually. There was a large number of societies able to guarantee to a lecturer a sum of money. The Society of Equitable Pioneers at Rochdale had said they would guarantee a man £100 a year and they would share him with another town. If places would guarantee in this way, it might be made lucrative, and if successful it might be made to compete against the attraction of the public schools and the Bar, which now drew off the Fellows. He thought that a man would be able to undertake the giving of lectures and lessons in two towns. They might manage to give him £200 or £300 a year, and for that he would have to spend eight months out of the year in those towns. He might manage to give in each town two courses of lectures, and of course to mixed classes if the town desired. He thought he might have night classes at least once a week in each town and morning classes for richer people. The demand for some permanent teaching of that kind had been pressed upon him more by the necessity of supplementing lectures by class teaching than anything else.'

At the meeting of the Council on June 25, 1872, it was announced that memorials had been addressed to the Universities of Oxford and Cambridge, begging them 'to take into consideration the question how assistance might be afforded to the higher education of those classes in great towns who are inevitably debarred from residence at a University.' The Oxford memorial was acknowledged by Dean Liddell, then Vice-Chancellor. From this, and other memorials, resulted the official recognition of the University Extension scheme, first by Cambridge and afterwards by Oxford.

It was announced that in the winter 1871–72 the lectures had continued to be successful. The arrangements had been as follows:—

Leeds:

Mr. James Stuart	Meteorology (5 lectures)	100 students.
Mr. Warr	Constitutional History of U.S.A. (8 lectures)	76 students.

Liverpool:

Same lecturers and subjects		190 students.
		175 students.

Southport:

Professor Hughes	Physical Geography	Well attended.
Mr. Warr	Constitutional History of U.S.A.	

The subject of University Extension was fully discussed. Mr. Stuart believed that greater continuity in the subjects chosen was very desirable. 'A more fixed curriculum would render the education more valuable and induce more persons to take advantage of it as an integral part of their education.' He also urged that 'lectures for the working-classes and for young men engaged in business should be conducted in connexion with those for women. This would make the education cheaper and more ex-tensive. A system of co-operation between towns could, he believed, be best and most efficiently brought about

by the Universities.' Mr. T. H. Green of Balliol 'believed that if the funds of the Colleges at Oxford were properly applied, there would be in the case of several of the Colleges a large sum over, after supplying all the require-ments of the University.' But this was before the days of agricultural depression.

The Council met on June 11 and 12, 1873, at Cambridge, many influential members of the University attending the meetings by invitation. Miss Clough was elected President in place of Mrs. Butler, who had been compelled by ill-health to resign the office held by her 'so ably and efficiently' for seven years. Miss M. M. Calder was re-elected Secretary. The report of the lectures for the winter 1872–3, may be summarized thus :—

Leeds:

Prof. Hales	Shakespeare	135 students.
Miss Peachy	Physiology	135 ,,
Mr. Stanton	Political Economy	40 ,,

Liverpool:

Prof. Morley	Poets of 19th Century	300 ,,
,,	Shakespeare	300 ,,

Southport:

Prof. Henry Morley	Poets of 18th Century	Good attendance.
Prof. Hughes	History of Germany	,,

Leamington:

Seven courses	History of England (2)	,,
	Crusades (1)	,,
	Geology (1)	,,
	English Literature (3)	,,

York:

Prof. Hales	Shakespeare and Milton	90 students.
Miss Peachy	Physiology	103 ,,

Bradford:

Classes for Latin, Mathematics, Physical Geo-graphy, Physiology, and German (no lectures) 80 students.

The Council also considered a series of answers to questions which had been addressed to them by Mr. Stansfield with regard to the education of women. These answers are a valuable summary of the Council's experience in the organization of lectures and classes. Fourteen circuits had been arranged in six years. The best time of the year for lectures had proved to be from Oct. 1 till Easter. The forenoon had generally been found the best for lectures for women. The most suitable days were very different in different places. The lectures had succeeded best in those places where the same day and hour had been constantly adhered to. The lectures had never been oftener than once a week. At Manchester and Rugby the system of lectures had been in great measure supplanted by that of small classes, owing to the fact that the professors at Owens College and the masters at Rugby School were willing to give such instruction. In Liverpool, the order of subjects during the six years had been as follows—two courses having been delivered in each winter—Astronomy, History, Physical Geography, History of Science, Light, Electricity and Magnetism, English Literature, Meteorology, History of United States, Poetry of Nineteenth Century, Shakespeare. These 'seemed fairly to have met the wishes of the ladies.' A good deal depended on 'the power of teaching by the lecturer, which had often given a predilection for certain subjects.' In other towns the list of subjects did not greatly differ from those given at Liverpool. Great stress must be laid on the importance of subordinating examina-tions to teaching.

Mr. Henry Sidgwick (who was not on the Executive Com-mittee of the Council) gave an account of the lectures for women which were being given in Cambridge. It had proved impossible to conduct these lectures on a self-supporting basis. Courses of lectures were being given on seventeen subjects. The circular of the lectures ends as follows: 'Students wishing to reside in Cambridge, while attending the lectures, can be received at Merton Hall.

Apply to Miss A. J. Clough, Merton Hall.' This was the beginning of Newnham College, the success of Merton Hall leading its supporters to form in the following year a company called the 'Newnham Hall Company, Limited,' with the object of building a new Hall for Students with the name Newnham Hall.

Towards the close of the Council's Meeting in June, 1873, there was a sort of conference of local secretaries on University Extension teaching, Mr. Stuart asking for 'advice and information which those present representing various large towns could give, upon several questions of detail, viz., the separation of lectures from classes, the local educational resources, the organization of a curriculum of study extending over two or three years, the possibility of combining various classes of society and the two sexes for educational purposes, and the propriety of alternating the literary and scientific subjects. Miss Lambert of Bradford complained of the desultory nature of lectures, and argued that more class teaching was wanted. Miss Swaine of York said that class feeling had broken down the system of class teaching. 'The ladies did not mind men attending the lectures, but the men did not come, the hour being perhaps unsuitable.' Miss Hewison said that in Newcastle 'the ladies would not unite in classes with the gentlemen.' Miss Wallis of Southport, and Miss Rose of Leamington, said that the work in those towns had been principally carried on by ladies connected with schools.

When the Council met at York on June 24, 1874, the University of Cambridge had fairly started upon its organization of University Extension lectures. We need not, therefore, trace beyond this point the work of the North of England Council in furthering this branch of women's education, though lectures by Mr. Newman, the Rev. W. Cunningham, Professor Seeley, Mr. Sollas, Herr Pauer, Mr. T. Humphry Ward, Professor Henry Morley and Miss Peachy are announced in the report as having been delivered at Bradford, Leeds, Liverpool, Leamington and York on various historical, economic, literary and scientific subjects. The labours of the Council had already achieved success. The establishment of new examinations for women, the foundation of a College for women at Cambridge, the official recognition of University Extension lectures—all these had resulted from its unwearied efforts. But, no less important than these had been another, though less palpable, effort of the Council's undertakings—a gradual change in public opinion towards the whole question of women's education. Rarely has so small a group of workers accomplished so great a work.

M. E. SADLER.

VICTORIA UNIVERSITY EXTENSION LECTURES.

THE annual meeting in furtherance of the Victoria University Extension movement was held on June 29 at the Owens College. The Vice-Chancellor of the Victoria University (Dr. Ward) presided, and amongst those present were the Bishop of Manchester, Principal Bodington (of the Yorkshire College, Leeds), Professor Tout, Professor Boyd Dawkins, Professor Dixon, Professor A. Schuster, Mr. Oliver Elton, Mr. P. J. Hartog, Rev. F. F. Cornish (H. M. Chief Inspector of Schools for the North-West Division of England), and others.

The Vice-Chancellor said that he was one of those who thought Universities were established in the country not only for the purpose of bringing on those students who devoted themselves to regular courses within the University sphere to a definite end, but also to spread and popularize culture and a desire for culture in those parts of the country in which they were placed. He had always held that to be one of the functions for which Universities existed, and whether they did that by writing or by speaking on the part of their members might be a matter of convenience or of use at different times.

The Secretary (Mr. Hartog) presented his annual report, which he prefaced by referring to certain events and changes affecting University Extension as a whole. Last year Professor Tout, who was then secretary and was now chairman of the committee, was enabled to state that their examination regulations and those of the University Extension authorities of Oxford, Cambridge, and London had been brought into harmony. The movement of co-operation between the four Universities had now advanced further. A Consultative Committee of the four Extension secretaries had become permanent, in order, if possible, to preserve an agreement on all important points of policy, while at the same time each University had perfect freedom of action. As an outward sign of the agreement a new *University Extension Journal* was to be published in the autumn under the official sanction of the four Universities. They could not but recognize both the wisdom and the graceful action of the older Universities in the sacrifice which they had made in order to combine and to include their younger sister in the new alliance ; and this spirit had been further illustrated by the cession to them by Oxford of a course at Leeds, one of their three University towns. Mr. Sadler's retirement from the Oxford Secretaryship must also be looked on as an event in the history of the movement to whose success his great capacity, energy and personal influence had contributed so much.

The Bishop of Manchester said the first thing that one felt ought to be noticed in connexion with the University Extension movement was this, that it had finally passed beyond the stage of experiment. So much was evident from the number of its students. A movement must be acknowledged to have obtained a firm footing in the world when it had obtained no fewer than 50,000 students in England alone, and, including the students in other nations, more than 100,000. While he fully recognized the great value of extended courses, he believed that one could hardly exaggerate the importance of short courses to the working class. The working class had obtained for themselves extended opportunities of leisure ; but whether that leisure should be of advantage to them or not would depend upon the manner in which it was improved, and he was quite convinced that it would not be improved as it ought to be unless we elevated their intellectual tastes and interests. It did not at all follow that because these courses were popular, they were therefore superficial or devoid of value. Indeed he could hardly see how they could be that. The persons who gave them were University men with a thorough knowledge of their subject. Furthermore, it was always to be remembered that study of this kind would always be conducted according to the internal method of the Universities, that was to say, it would be given in a complete and systematic manner. It would begin at the beginning. It would also not omit any of those necessary links that bound together the beginning and the end. It would not make leaps and bounds for the purpose of getting to interesting points. He was particularly pleased to find that the Government were trying to constitute some sort of relation between the University movement and the instruction of pupil teachers. That, he thought, was also a matter of such importance that it could scarcely be exaggerated, for the pupil teachers were the persons who were to be the teachers of the future generation ; they were students of great capacity and promise, and he was quite sure that they would obtain from the acquisition of the methods of University teaching the means of making themselves brighter and more attractive teachers. Then also he thought it was very desirable, if possible, that definite relation should be established between the University movement and those technical classes that were under the management of the County Councils. He would conclude as he began, by saying that the movement had become one of permanent value and a great success, and that if only those who ought to be its supporters would rally round and give it that enthusiastic aid which it had a right to look for, it would be able not only to smooth over certain social difficulties, not only to give the working class the power of solving some of those momentous social questions which awaited solution, but it would also be the means of making our national life as a whole larger and sweeter and happier.

LETTERS TO THE EDITOR.

[We do not hold ourselves responsible for the opinions expressed by our correspondents.]

School Boards and University Extension.

SIR,—Mr. E. J. Broadfield, a distinguished member of the Manchester School Board, is reported, in your last number, to have said at the Conference of School-Board Clerks, 'that they had at Manchester endeavoured to introduce their pupil-teachers to University Extension lectures, and had found the young people unprepared to take full advantage of the instruction.' The quotation is accurate in itself, but entirely misleading without the context, as the fuller report in the *School Board Chronicle* makes evident. The speaker was pleading for the wider adoption, and for the improvement (by means, among other things, of Extension lectures) of the system of pupil-teachers' centres, which does not yet, in his opinion, yield the results of which it is capable. Mr. Broadfield writes with regard to this matter (authorizing me at the same time to quote his words), 'I have always been in favour of giving Extension lectures to pupil teachers, and our experience in Manchester has only confirmed my judgement with regard to the innovation.' As a matter of fact 65 out of the 104 Manchester pupil teachers obtained certificates; nine with distinction; and of these latter the examiner, Professor Raleigh, writes: 'All did papers better than I should have dared to hope for.' The results of the course are therefore far from unsatisfactory. At the same time every one will agree with Mr. Broadfield that the work done might and would be better still, if certain obvious defects in our present system of preliminary education were remedied.

I am, Sir,

Obediently yours,

The Victoria University. P. J. HARTOG.

[*** We regret extremely to have misrepresented in any way Mr. Broadfield's views, and gladly publish Mr. Hartog's disclaimer. The report reached us from a most careful and accurate correspondent.—*Ed.*]

.·.

'Qualifying' for Examinations.

DEAR SIR,—There is a question which I should much like to see discussed in the pages of the *Gazette*, if you can spare the space.

Your readers are all aware that in order to sit for the examination on a course of University Extension lectures, it is necessary for a student to attend a certain number of the lectures and to write a certain number of the papers set by the lecturer. I suppose that these conditions were imposed chiefly to ensure that some part of the examinee's knowledge of the subject had been acquired through the medium of University Extension; and also, perhaps, to save the examiner from having to read answers that were utterly ignorant and irrelevant.

But has the fulfilment of these conditions any other value? Is it in any way a test of benefit gained from the lectures?

I know that it is considered by some to have no worth; I have heard it described as 'the·farce of qualifying.' But my own opinion is different: I think that to qualify for the examination (at any rate on courses of ten or twelve lectures) necessitates an amount of continued attention to the subject of the course, and of thought thereon, which cannot be without some good effect as intellectual training or stimulus and for the acquisition of information, even upon those students who have neither brilliant capacity nor special enthusiasm for the subject.

It would, of course, be practically impossible to give any general recognition to such work. Even examinations hardly provide an unimpeachable test; and those who will not or cannot take them must be content with the consciousness of their own deserts.

But I should be greatly interested to learn the views held on this matter by other students who have successfully passed the test of examination—especially by those who have at another time 'qualified' but *not* entered for examination. The opinions of any lecturer who would favour us with his view would also be of much interest.

To define clearly the points on which I desire enlightenment, I would therefore like to ask of your readers the following questions:—1. If, at any centre, a prize were offered for the best record of University Extension work during a certain term of years, would you give any advantage to a student who had qualified for more examinations than he had attended, over another who had obtained the same number of certificates, but had *not* qualified on any course besides those on which he had been examined? 2. In such a competition, what relative merit would you as·ign (or, more precisely, what marks would you give) to (*a*) qualifying without entering for examination, (*b*) satisfying the examiner, (*c*) passing with distinction, (*d*) taking the prize at the examination?

I am, dear Sir,

Yours faithfully,

C.

———

A NORWEGIAN ON UNIVERSITY EXTENSION.

IN the first of two articles on University Extension, published recently in the *Aftenposten*, Hr. Arstal of Christiania gives a short sketch of the movement in England, founded partly on personal observation and partly on information received during a visit to the Oxford Summer Meeting of last year. He traces its gradual progress from the early attempts in the forties, rendered abortive by the difficulty of communication, to the developments of to-day, which, as he remarks, 'stand or fall with our railway system.' While much wins his admiration, the points which impress him most of all are the large aims, the systematic arrangements, and the unity of the associations in England.

The second article is perhaps of more interest to English readers, as in it Hr. Arstal tells the story of University Extension in his own country. The first movement in Norway arose early in the sixties, and took the form of a 'Society for the Enlightenment of the People' (Selskabet for Folkeoplysningens Fremme). This was followed a few years later by the 'Society for Promoting the Welfare of Christiania' (Selskabet for Kristiania Bys Vel), which gave weekly lectures 'for the benefit of the young and old of the working and serving classes.' In 1880 Dr. Nyström opened a 'Workmen's Academy' in Stockholm, and this gave rise to the foundation in 1884 of a similar institution in Christiania. The 'Democratic Lecturers' Association' was started in 1892, and last year the University of Christiania tried the experiment of holding a 'Summer Course for Non-Members of the University,' which, it is hoped, may take place yearly.

Of these institutions only two have a definite educational object. The 'Society for Promoting the Welfare of Christiania' and the 'Democratic Lecturers' Association' concern themselves with various social and political questions, though they make their influence strongly felt in favour of education. The 'Workmen's Academy' and the University's 'Summer Course' are purely educational, and together they form a whole which, so far as it goes, corresponds approximately to University Extension as understood in this country. Their work is at present confined to Christiania, but Hr. Arstal expresses the hope that it may prove possible to extend their sphere of action, and suggests that it might be advisable to take advantage of circumstances which call a large number of people together, such as the fishing season at Lofoten, to deliver courses of lectures on suitable subjects. He looks forward to the development of Norwegian institutions on lines similar to those of University Extension in England, to the disappearance of the isolated lecture in favour of the course, and to the growth of a better understanding between the lecturer and his audience.

A. E. GERRANS.

The Universities and Legislation.

A CORRESPONDENT writes: 'On a previous occasion you have drawn attention to the fact that the Universities stand alone in having no Standing Committee or Association to watch the bearing of legislative or other projects on their work and interests. Every other grade of English education has so organized itself and thus possesses the means of bringing its special knowledge to bear on the public discussion of educational questions. Now, there can be no doubt that within a short time we shall enter upon a period during which the problems involved in the organization of Secondary Education will be widely discussed. During the course of that discussion, which may well extend over a considerable time, public opinion will be formed. Proposals will be made, criticized and amended : questions of curriculum will be mooted ; schemes for the provision of scholarships and for the conduct of examinations will be proposed ; the constitution of educational authorities will be debated ; the ordering of that part of education which falls between the Universities and the public elementary schools, will come under review. In many, I may say in all, these questions the Universities are necessarily concerned. From the secondary schools the Universities draw their students, to them they supply the majority of their teachers. Between the curriculum of secondary schools and the programme of academic studies there must always be an intimate connexion. In any schemes for testing the educational efficiency of secondary schools, the Joint Board and the Local Examinations Delegacy should have much to say. A demand for trained teachers would necessarily involve some action on the part of the Universities.

But we cannot afford to wait until legislation is actually accomplished. What form legislation will take when it comes, must to a large extent depend on previous manifestations of public opinion. During the time therefore in which public opinion is shaping itself, the voice of the Universities should make itself heard. There is a general willingness to listen to their counsel, to be guided by their experience. They enjoy great prestige, which their activity during the last twenty years has greatly increased. But it would be foolish to blind ourselves to the fact that there are also forces hostile to our interests, and that if the University point of view finds no means of organized expression, much that we should deplore will be done in ignorance of a better way. Whilst public opinion is in an impressionable state, whilst it is still ready to admit new factors to its judgement, University experience should be promptly stated, in newspaper discussions and in magazines, as need may arise.

The value of an organization, like that which I propose, is well known to those concerned in municipal affairs. The great municipalities have an association, the secretaries of which constantly watch all bills brought before Parliament and all schemes affecting municipal interests, with the result that Town Clerks and other responsible officials are kept continuously acquainted with any movement in which the interests of their Corporations are concerned. This watchful survey enables the municipalities to take from time to time prompt and effective, though often private, action, and thus to protect themselves from serious, even if unintentional, injury and oversight.

The list of educational associations, formed for the purpose of joint action and defence is already a long one. The Headmasters' Conference includes the representatives of the great public schools : the Headmasters' Association those of the smaller, but in the aggregate not much less important, institutions : the Headmistresses have an influential organization : so also have the Assistant Mistresses as well as the Assistant Masters. The Secretaries of the Technical Instruction Committee of County Councils act in union. So do the Headmasters of organized Science Schools. I have not mentioned the Teachers' Guild, the College of Preceptors and the National Union of Teachers because their names will be familiar to every one. Further, the School Boards have a powerful association, and so have the County Councils, while the School Board Clerks possess an influential society of their own. Thus every section in the educational world has its representative committee except the Universities. And yet the Universities must be affected by whatever is done to organize secondary education. Is it not time therefore that a standing committee was formed to watch educational events from the University point of view ? Such a committee would soon come to enjoy great influence in the period of active discussion into which we are about to enter. It would secure a hearing for University experience and prevent many judgements from going against us by default.'

The National Home Reading Union.

A CORRESPONDENT writes :—

'The Summer Assembly of this society was held at Leamington, during the week ending July 6. An ample *menu* of lectures and excursions was provided for the edification and enjoyment of the members, who numbered about 400, a large proportion being residents of Leamington, Warwick, and the surrounding district. The Assembly was opened with a reception given by the Mayor of Leamington, on Saturday, June 29. Sir Robert Ball gave a lecture upon Comets, in which he introduced an illustration from the Bayeux Tapestry, showing a company of mail-clad warriors intently gazing through a thick castle-wall at a star-shaped object with a ridiculously short tail. This the lecturer claimed to be the earliest known portrayal of a comet. Major Darwin, the Secretary of the Royal Geographical Society, discoursed on the necessity of stimulating travel and research in the less known quarters of the globe, in order to avoid the false steps in our foreign policy, which an ignorance of geography would be certain to entail. Dr. Bridge, the organist of Westminster Abbey, delighted his hearers with an outline of the characteristics of the popular music of Shakespeare's time, illustrated with the aid of a local amateur choir. Mr. Yule Oldham, in his two lectures on the Discovery of America, made a very happy use of the limelight, not only in producing excellent views of certain pre-Columbine maps of the fifteenth century, but in vividly contrasting for the audience the fertile and opulent territories which Columbus and his followers, fired by Marco Polo's descriptions, went in search of with the arid and desolate spot upon which they actually landed. Dr. T. J. Lawrence's and Mr. J. R. Tanner's lectures on the history of the Tudor period drew remarkably large audiences, allowing for the fact that the hour at which they were delivered—9.30 a.m.—is less frequently selected for such functions in inland watering places than in seats of academic learning. Dr. Braunholtz, lecturer in French at Cambridge, struck fresh ground in his discourses on 'The French Stage in Shakespeare's Time' and 'English Heroes in Early French Romance.' The Geology and Botany of the district were discussed in a series of lectures by Mr. J. E. Marr (the Secretary of the Geological Society), and Mr. G. F. Scott Elliot. The excursions included Stratford-on-Avon, Coventry, and Compton Winyates, as well as the nearer antiquities of Warwick, Kenilworth, and Stoneleigh. At Warwick the members of the Assembly were conducted over the castle and grounds, and entertained at afternoon tea, by the Earl and Countess of Warwick. The weather lent its aid to the success of the Assembly by remaining almost continuously fine.'

REPORTS FROM THE CENTRES.

PUCKLECHURCH.—A meeting of the centre was held on Friday evening, May 24, when the accounts for the last session were read and passed : there was a small adverse balance, but this had been considerably reduced during the past year. As no grant is receivable next winter from the County Council, it will be impossible to continue the lectures during the coming year; but it is hoped the centre will keep its organization, so as to be ready for future sessions. Its record of long sustained successful work, and its library of presented books (small though it is), provide a ground for continuance.

A WORKMAN ON THE EDUCATION OF WORKMEN.

THE *Todmorden Advertiser* recently contained an interesting report of an address given to the Cornholme Mutual Improvement Society by Mr. Frederick Rogers, a workman resident in the district, who has intimate and personal acquaintance with the needs of those for whom he spoke. As he has never been an Extension student, his appreciation of the value of its work is that of an observant onlooker.

Mr. Rogers pointed out the advantages which he thought had come to the working classes by the extension of education. It had been a most powerful factor in the raising of the general level of intelligence among them, and in promoting their social and material welfare. Popular education began with the establishment of Sunday schools in Gloucester by Robert Raikes, followed by the establishment of elementary day schools in 1798 by Jos. Lancaster. Having given a quotation from Green's history to show the condition of the working people about the middle of last century, Mr. Rogers proceeded to sketch the various stages in that movement, showing that between 1859 and 1892 there was an increase of something like five millions in the amount granted for elementary education. By Mr. Forster's Education Act the Government acknowledged its responsibility in this matter and made education compulsory. In 1891 that measure received its complement by the passing of the Free Education Act. A commission was now sitting with reference to secondary education, and it must be very gratifying to some in this district to know that a weaver living a few miles from where he stood, and a personal friend of his own, had been selected to give evidence on the subject before that commission. He (the speaker) believed that the ultimate result of these measures would be to so arrange matters that the more promising students among the working classes would be able, on leaving the elementary school, to attend a secondary school and in some cases to pass to the University. Mr. Rogers went on to say that, corresponding with this educational movement, there had been an equally great improvement in the condition of the working classes, socially and materially: wages were higher, they followed their employment under better sanitary conditions, and there had been a multiplication of the conveniences and luxuries of life. He granted that it would be very foolish to assume that the whole of this had been due to educational effort, but said it would be equally foolish to ignore education as one of the factors that had contributed to that progress. The progress of trade unionism, for instance, was due to the spread of education and the consequent increase of intelligence. The spread of education, moreover, had a powerful influence in breaking down the distinctions of birth and rank, narrowness and intolerance gradually disappearing. Mr. Rogers fully recognized the valuable results of the University Extension system in bringing the workers into direct and immediate contact with the trained intelligence of the country, and materially helping to break down the barrier to which he had just alluded. If education had done no more than this, there would have been abundant cause for gratitude, but the political liberties and privileges now enjoyed by the people were largely due thereto. The working class had come to see that these things were not matters for which they were to beg and pray, but rights which belonged to them. Mr. Rogers dwelt further upon the great movement in the direction of technical education and the revised code which gave evening continuation schools, pronouncing the latter admirable in every respect and thoroughly adapted to the various needs of a district like this. Plainly, he concluded, it was to the interest of the working people to see that these facilities were not neglected. He hoped that that society at Cornholme might be a centre of educational influence, educating the life of its own members and conferring a benefit upon the community at large.

SADLER TESTIMONIAL.

List of Subscribers.

Mr. H. Abbott, Severn Street, Birmingham.
Rev. H. G. Alington, Tunbridge Wells.
Miss M. Allen, Penzance.
Miss E. Arnold, Tunbridge Wells.
Mr. C. R. Ashbee, King's College, Cambridge.
Miss A. L. Ashby, Reigate.
Miss E. Ashby, „
Mr. T. E. Ashworth, Todmorden.
Mr. Badger, M.A., New Coll., Oxford.
The Misses Badley, Dudley.
The Rev. Dr. Bailey, Lincoln Coll., Oxford.
Miss F. J. Baker, Reigate.
Miss Bandinel, Bristol.
Miss Banford, Severn Street.
Mrs. Barclay, Reigate.
Miss Barrow, Edgbaston.
Miss M. Basden, W. Brighton.
Miss T. Basden, „
Miss Baumgarten, Reigate.
Miss M. S. Beard, Oxford.
Mrs. Beaumont, Caversham.
Mr. A. Bentley, Severn Street.
Miss E. Blake, Bedford.
Miss E. Bodger, Peterborough.
Miss H. Bogue, Bournemouth.
Mr. E. Booth, Severn Street.
Miss C. G. Borlase, Penzance.
Miss M. B. Borlase, „
Miss J. E. Brailey, Banbury.
Mr. M. Brice, Wells.
Miss M. Briggs, Bournemouth.
Miss Brooke-Hunt, Gloucester.
Mr. R. Warwick Bond, Queen's Coll., Oxford.
Miss Bull, Hereford.
Mr. G. J. Burch, M.A., Oxford.
Mr. A. Burrows, Oxford.
Miss Burt, Cuckfield.
Miss Campbell, Exmouth.
Mr. C. E. Carless, S. St. B.
Mr. G. Carnell, Severn Street.
Rev. J. Estlin Carpenter, M.A., Manchester Coll., Oxford.
Miss E. Carter, Oxford.
Mrs. Carter, Ryde.
Miss G. Carter, „
Miss Casson, Oxford.
Miss Catherford, Norwood.
Miss S. A. Catterick, Margate.
Mrs. Charington, Reigate.
Mrs. Charlesworth, Reigate.
Miss Chatwood, Worsley.
Mr. Cheesman, Exeter.
The Chester U. E. Committee.
Mr. W. M. Childs, B.A., Keble Coll., Oxford.
Mr. J. Churton Collins, M.A., Balliol Coll., Oxford.
Mr. J. Clark, Severn Street.
Mr. A. W. Clayden, M.A., Christ's Coll., Cambridge.
Miss J. Clift, Falmouth.
Mr. Colchester, Ventnor.
Mr. J. J. Colman, Norwich.

Mrs. S. C. Colman, Peterboro.
Miss J. L. Colman, „
Miss K. E. Colman, „
Miss S. K. Cook, New York.
Mrs. Cooke, Ilkley.
Miss Cooke, „
Mr. F. Cooper, Brighton.
Mr. G. H. Cooper, Oxford.
Miss Corin, Whitehaven.
Miss Cowley, Kenilworth.
Miss Cox, Ryde.
Mrs. Crosfield, Reigate.
Miss C. Cross, Ripon.
Miss F. M. Cross, „ .
Mrs. Crumpton, Edgbaston.
Mrs. Cudworth, Reigate.
Miss Culpin, Peterborough.
Miss Dagg, Brighton.
Miss Dale, Ilkley.
Mr. W. Darby, Severn Street.
Mr. A. Davidson, Oxford.
Miss B. K. Davies, Chester.
Mr. J. Davison, Severn Street.
Miss C. R. Day, Tunbridge Wells.
Mr. C. Donaldson, Oxford.
Miss M. H. Downes, B.A., U. E. College, Reading.
Miss A. Drury, Bournemouth.
Mrs. Dymond, Exeter.
Miss Dymond, „
Miss Earle, Reigate.
Miss Eberty, „
Mr. G. Edens, Oxford.
Mrs. L. M. Edwards, Tunbridge Wells.
Miss Edwards, London.
Mr. P. Elford, M.A., St. John's Coll., Oxford.
Miss Elgie, Exeter.
Mrs. G. Elkington, Edgbaston.
Miss Elliott, Oxford.
Mr. O. Elton, Manchester.
Miss M. Everard, Stansfield, Clare.
Mr. W. H. Facer, Severn Street, Birmingham.
Miss Fairbrother, Bournemouth.
Mr. A. Fallows, Oxford.
Mr. J. J. Farrell, Bodmin.
Mr. E. Fawcett, Wells.
Miss Fenning, Reigate.
Mr. Ferguson, Colombo.
Miss Fish, Reigate.
Rev. A. H. Fish, B.A., Chester.
Mr. W. W. Fisher, C. C. C., Oxford.
Dr. A. H. Fison, Willesden Green.
Miss Fletcher, Skipton.
Miss Floyd, Coventry.
Mr. R. Fox, Falmouth.
Mrs. Frankland, Reigate.
Mr. Fretwell, Sutton.
Mr. T. Gibbs, Severn Street, Birmingham.
Mr. H. Gilbert, Severn Street, Birmingham.
Miss Gilmore, Weston.
Miss Goldie, Tunbridge Wells.

Miss Gordon, Malvern.
Mr. A. J. Grant, London.
Mr. Greaves, Bournemouth.
Prof. Green, M.A., Oxford.
Mrs. T. H. Green,   ,,
Miss G. Green,   ,,
Miss K. M. Green, Liverpool.
Miss E. Greenside, Wimbledon.
Miss Greenwood, Burnley.
Mrs. Gribble, Oxford.
Miss Haigh, Reading.
Rev. K. Hake, Bournemouth.
The Misses Hales, Oxford.
Mr. R. Halstead, Hebden Bridge.
Miss M. E. Hargood, Tunbridge Wells.
Miss Harrop, Huddersfield.
Miss D. Harris, Cockermouth.
Miss S. J. Harris,   ,,
Harrogate Students.
Mr. P. J. Hartog, M.A., Victoria University, Manchester.
Miss E. Haughton, Dublin.
Miss Hayward, Reading.
Miss Heap, Rochdale.
Miss M. Heap,   ,,
Mr. R. Heaton, Severn Street, Birmingham.
Hebden Bridge U. E. Committee.
Mr. Hesketh, Reigate.
Mr. W. H. Hills, Ambleside.
Miss F. Hippenstall, Huddersfield.
Mr. J. A. Hobson, M.A., Lincoln Coll., Oxford.
Mrs. Hody, Honiton.
Miss Holley, Bath.
Mr. G. Holloway, Severn Street.
Dr. Holst, Christiania.
Miss Hopkins, Edgbaston.
Mr. E. L. S. Horsburgh, B.A., Queen's Coll., Oxford.
Mrs. Hull, Reigate.
Miss Huntington, Oxford.
Mr. J. L. Hutchison, Wells.
Miss Hyett, Stroud.
Miss Irwin, Clifton.
Miss A. W. Jackson, Ealing.
Mrs. Jackson, Whitehaven.
Miss Jackson,   ,,
Miss Jaffray, Reigate.
Miss Jarvis, London.
Miss F. Jarvis,   ,,
Mr. T. R. Johnson, Peterborough.
Miss V. C. Johnston, Westerham.
Mrs. R. C. Jones, Tunbridge Wells.
Miss E. F. Jones,   ,,
Miss L. F. Jones,   ,,
Mr. A. F. Jones,   ,,
Miss H. E. Justice,   ,,
E. K., Chorlton-cum-Hardy, Manchester.
Mr. W. Kane, Severn Street, Birmingham.
Miss Keele, Torquay.
Miss M. Keene, Halstead.
Miss Kenrick, Edgbaston.
Miss Kett, Bedford.
Miss King, Exeter.
Miss King, Winchester.

Mr. F. Kirkham, U.E. College, Reading.
The Misses Krober, Liverpool.
Miss Lacey, Somerville Coll., Oxford.
Mr. W. Landan, Severn Street.
Madame F.E. Landolphe, Paris.
Miss Leach, Ventnor.
Dr. T. M. Legge, Trinity Coll., Oxford.
Miss Livett, Wells.
Miss Lovell, Exeter.
Rev. E. Luce, Brighton.
Miss A. Lund, Ilkley.
Mr. H. Macgregor, Severn Street, Birmingham.
Mr. H. J. Mackinder, M.A., Ch. Ch., Oxford.
Miss Makin, Rawtenstall.
Miss March, Ashstead.
Mrs. Marlande, Penzance.
Miss F. M. Marlande,   ,,
Mrs. Malone, Reigate.
Miss Martineau, Edgbaston.
Mr. J. A. R. Marriott, M.A., New Coll., Oxford.
Miss Martin, Bakewell.
Miss Mason, Manchester.
Miss Maude, Ilkley.
Mr. J.E. Mawby, Severn Street, Birmingham.
Miss E. M. Maycock, Oxford.
Mr. Maynard, Taunton.
Mr. McLeod, Ryde.
Miss A. McLure, Rugby.
Miss McNiel, Oxford.
Miss Mercer, Ripon.
Miss Mewburn,   ,,
Dr. H. R. Mill, Edinburgh University.
Mr. A. E. Mills, Wells.
Miss Montgomery, Exeter.
Miss Morris, Torquay.
Miss F. Mortlock, Oxford.
Mrs. Croft Murray, Ryde.
Dr. E. Nader, Vienna.
Miss Nash, Bishop-Stortford.
Mr. E. Neal, Severn Street, Birmingham.
Fraulein Nehring, Neston-Stewart, N.B.
Mrs. Newcombe, Winslow.
Miss Nichols, Bournemouth.
Mr. A. J. Nixon, Severn Street, Birmingham.
Miss Noad, Reigate.
Miss Offord, Dover.
Mr. Ogle, Reigate.
Miss Orger, Oxford.
Miss F. Orme, Wells.
Mrs. Overton, Tunbridge Wells.
Mr. C. Owen, Oldham.
Mr. W. E. Owen,   ,,
Mr. J. Owen,   ,,
Mr. W. Palmer, B.Sc., Reading.
Miss I. Parkinson, Grange.
Miss L. A. Parkinson,   ,,
Mr. R. Parry, Reading.
Miss Parsons, Edgbaston.
Miss E. Partridge, King's Lynn.
Miss S. Partridge, Ashstead.
Mr. T. Peace, Severn Street, Birmingham.
Mr. H. Pearce, Severn Street, Birmingham.

Miss Pinn, Exeter.
Miss Pollard, B.Sc., Oxford.
Miss M. E. Porter, Tunbridge Wells.
Mr. Potts, Banbury.
Prof. Poulton, F.R.S., Oxford.
Mr. E. Powell, Chester.
Miss Price, Oxford.
Mr. Pringle, Buckingham.
Miss C. Pullein, Tunbridge Wells.
Miss Punch, Bournemouth.
Mr. T. Read, Brighton.
Rev. the Rector, Exeter College, Oxford.
Miss E. Reece, Edgbaston.
Mons. Rey, B. es Sc., U. E. College, Reading.
Mr. J. H. Rice, Severn Street, Birmingham.
Mr. J. T. Ridley, Bournemouth.
Miss Rigby, Southport,
Mrs. Roffey, Reigate.
Miss Rogers, Bournemouth.
Mr. H. W. Rolfe, M.A., Philadelphia, U. S. A.
Mr. J. H. Rose. M.A., Christ's Coll., Cambridge.
Miss Ross, Penzance.
Mrs. Rothwell, Bury.
Mr. C. Rowley, Manchester.
Miss A. E. Ruegg, Stroud.
Miss G. Ruegg,   ,,
Mr. L. Scarth, M.A., Bournemouth.
Miss Schapps, New York.
Miss A. Scott, Severn Street, Birmingham.
Miss E. Scott, Skipton,
Miss H. Scott,   ,,
Miss M. Scott,   ,,
Mr. T. Sharkey, London.
Miss Sharp, Rugby.
Miss Sharpe, Reigate.
Miss C. Shepherd, Settle.
Miss Sholto, Exeter.
Mr. A. Sidgwick, M.A., C.C.C., Oxford.
Mrs. Sitwell, Chester.
Miss Sitwell,   ,,
Miss Skinner, Stroud.
Miss C. Smith, Ashley Guise, Bedfordshire.
Miss Smithson, Edgbaston.
Miss E. L. Smythe, Truro.
Miss Snowdon, Ilkley.
Mrs. Sonnenschein, Harborne.
Miss Soulsby, Oxford.
Mr. L. Southall, Severn Street, Birmingham.
Mrs. Southall, Edgbaston.
The Misses Southall,   ,,
Miss M. Spencer, Longsight, Manchester.
Miss Steele, Abergavenny.
Mr. Stone, Banbury.
Miss C. E. Strachan, Reading.

Mr. W. H. Sturge, Severn Street, Birmingham.
Miss H. C. Sturton, Croydon.
Mr. H. Sutton, Reading.
Miss Swann, Oxford.
The Tean U. E. Committee.
Miss K. Telfer, Oxford.
Miss Tetley, Wellingborough.
Mr. J. Thomas, Severn Street, Birmingham.
Mrs. Arthur Thompson, Reigate.
Mr. Though, Sheffield.
Miss Timmins, Edgbaston.
Miss P. Timmins,   ,,
Mr. Tregidga, Rawtenstall.
Miss H. N. Trevenen, Tunbridge Wells.
The Thornton U. E. Committee.
Miss Tucker, Southbourn.
Miss Vant, Ripon.
Sir E. Verney, Winslow.
Miss B. Vivian, Camborne.
Miss E. S. Waddell, Manchester.
Dr. Wade, Torquay.
Mr. Wakefield, Taunton.
Miss Walker, Whitehaven.
Miss A. M. Watson, Tunbridge Wells.
Miss J. Webster, London.
Mr. J. Wells, M.A., Wadham College, Oxford.
Mr. E. West, U. E. College, Reading.
Miss N. C. West.
Mr. T. West, Severn Street, Birmingham.
Mr. C. Wharam, Severn Street, Birmingham.
Miss M. W. Whelpton, Oxford.
Miss A. M. Whidbourne, Torquay.
Miss C. M. Whidbourne, Torquay.
Miss White, Brighton.
Miss Widmill, Bournemouth.
Miss Wilson, Whitehaven.
Mr. Carus-Wilson, F.G.S., Parkstone.
Miss M. E. Wilson, Tunbridge Wells.
Mr. T. H. Wilson, Grange-over-Sands.
The Misses Wilson, Edgbaston.
Mr. E. Withey, Severn Street, Birmingham.
Miss Woodhead, Brighton.
Rev. F. H. Woods, St. John's College, Oxford.
Mr. E. Woolaston, Severn Street, Birmingham.
Mr. W. B. Worsfold, M.A., University Coll., Oxford.
Mr. Worthington, Taunton.
Mr. F. H. Wright, U. E. College, Reading.

BOOKS ON OUR TABLE.

MR. ASHBEE has prepared an elaborate and valuable *Table of the Eighteenth Century,* which students of the period will do well to consult. Though dealing primarily with the arts and crafts of the period, the chronological arrangements with dates, historical events and personalities are of general as well as special interest. The Tables are to be had at the Reception Room for 1s. each.

ARRANGEMENTS FOR 1895-6.

Autumn, 1895.

All lectures are at fortnightly intervals except where otherwise stated.

Certificates are awarded on courses of 12 Lectures only.

Centre.	No. of Lectures in Course.	Subject of Course.	Lecturer.	Course begins.	Course (or Half-Course) ends.
UNIVERSITY EXTENSION COLLEGE, READING (evening, weekly)	12	Citizen Education...	A. L. SMITH, M.A. ...	Th. Oct. 3	Dec. 19
ALTRINCHAM (evening) ...	6	Mediaeval England	Rev. W. H. SHAW, M.A.	F. Oct. 11	Dec. 20
ASHTON-UNDER-LYNE (aftern.)	6	Puritan Revolution	,, ,, ...	T. Oct. 8	Dec. 17
BIRMINGHAM, SEVERN STREET (evening)	6	The Reformation to the Revolution	,, ,, ...	T. Sept. 24	Dec. 10
BOLTON (evening)	6	The Reformation to the Revolution	,, ,, ...	Th. Oct. 10	Dec. 19
†BURY (evening)	12	History of Florence and Florentine Art	Rev. W. H. SHAW, M.A. & J. E. PHYTHIAN ...	F. Oct. 4	Dec. 13
CHELTENHAM (afternoon) ...	12	Italian History	{Rev. W. H. SHAW, M.A. & {E.L.S. HORSBURGH, B A.	Th. Oct. 3	Dec. 12
CHELTENHAM (evening) ...	12	Mediaeval England	,, ,, ...	W. Oct. 2	Dec. 11
CIRENCESTER (afternoon) ...	6	History of Florence ...	Rev. W. H. SHAW, M.A.	M. Sept. 30	Dec. 9
GLOUCESTER (evening) ...	6	Mediaeval England	,, ,, ...	M. Sept. 30	Dec. 9
HEBDEN BRIDGE (evening) ...	6	Making of England	,, ,, ...	S. Oct. 12	Dec. 21
KESWICK (evening)	6	Making of England	,, ,, ...	M. Oct. 7	Dec. 16
MALVERN (afternoon) ...	6	History of Florence ...	,, ,, ...	W. Oct. 2	Dec. 11
OLDHAM (evening) ...	6	The Reformation to the Revolution	,, ,, ...	W. Oct. 9	Dec. 18
†OXFORD (evening)	12	Age of Elizabeth	{Rev. W. H. SHAW, M.A. & {E.L.S. HORSBURGH, B.A.	Th. Oct. 3	Dec. 12
SALE (evening)	6	English Social Reformers ...	Rev. W. H. SHAW, M.A.	T. Oct. 8	Dec. 17
†STROUD (afternoon)	12	Puritan Revolution and the Later Stuarts	Rev. W. H. SHAW, M.A. & E. L. S. HORSBURGH, B.A.	T. Oct. 1	Dec. 10
WIGAN (afternoon)	6	History of Venice... ...	Rev. W. H. SHAW, M.A.	W. Sept. 25	Dec. 4
BRIDPORT (evening) ...	6	British Colonies	J. A. R. MARRIOTT, M.A.	T. Oct. 8	Dec. 17
†DORCHESTER (evening) ...	12	Industrial Revolution ...	,, ,, ...	M. Oct. 7	Dec. 16
STRATFORD-ON-AVON (evening)	6	Age of Louis XIV ...	,, ,, ...	M. Sept. 30	Dec. 9
WEYMOUTH (afternoon) ...	6	Not fixed	,, ,, ...	T. Oct. 8	Dec. 17
BARNSLEY (evening) ...	6	Shakespeare	F. S. BOAS, M.A. ...	T. Oct. 8	Dec. 17
†BRIGHTON (St. Michael's Hall) (morning)	12	Shakespeare	,, ,, ...	F. Oct. 4	Dec. 13
ROCHDALE (afternoon) ...	6	Browning	,, ,, ...	W. Oct. 9	Dec. 18
SETTLE (evening)	6	Shakespeare	,, ,, ...	W. Oct. 2	Dec. 11
WAKEFIELD (evening) ...	6	Arnold, Swinburne, and Rossetti	,, ,, ...	T. Oct. 1	Dec. 10
BRADFORD (evening)	6	Eighteenth Century	C. E. MALLET, B.A. ...	Th. Oct. 3	Dec. 12
BRIGHTON (afternoon) ...	6	English Prose Writers ...	,, ,, ...	M. Sept. 30	Dec. 9
NEATH (afternoon) ...	6	The Two Pitts	,, ,, ...	F. Oct. 11	Dec. 20
NEATH (evening)	6	The Stuarts	,, ,, ...	F. Oct. 11	Dec. 20
OTLEY (evening)	6	The French Revolution ...	,, ,, ...	F. Oct. 4	Dec. 13
SWANSEA (afternoon)	6	English Novelists	,, ,, ...	Th. Oct. 10	Dec. 19
†WEST BRIGHTON (afternoon)	12	Age of Elizabeth	,, ,, ...	M. Oct. 7	Dec. 16
†BURGESS HILL (afternoon) ...	12	Shakespeare	Rev. J. G. BAILEY, M.A., LL.D.	Oct. 17	Dec. 12
DEVIZES (evening)	6	In Memoriam	,, ,, ...	Th. Oct. 10	Dec. 19
EASTBOURNE (afternoon) ...	6	Shakespeare	,, ,, ...	W. Oct. 2	Dec. 11
TUNBRIDGE WELLS (afternoon, weekly)	10	Shelley, Keats, Coleridge, and Wordsworth	,, ,, ...	T. Oct. 8	Dec. 10
†WEST BRIGHTON (evening) ...	12	Shakespeare	,, ,, ...	Th. Oct. 17	Dec. 12
†BOURNEMOUTH (afternoon) ...	12	18th & 19th Century Literature ...	E.L.S. HORSBURGH, B.A.	S. Oct. 5	Dec. 14
BOURNEMOUTH (evening) ...	6	Puritan Revolution	,, ,, ...	F. Oct. 4	Dec. 13
CANTERBURY (afternoon) ...	6	Age of Elizabeth	,, ,, ...	T. Oct. 1	Dec. 10
CHESTER (evening)	6	Not fixed	,, ,, ...	W. Oct. 9	Dec. 18
†FOLKESTONE (afternoon) ...	12	Shakespeare	,, ,, ...	M. Sept. 30	Dec. 9
HYDE (evening)	6	French Revolution ...	,, ,, ...	M. Oct. 7	Dec. 16
LYMINGTON (afternoon) ...	6	Age of Elizabeth	,, ,, ...	F. Oct. 4	Dec. 13
*NEWPORT (evening)	12	The Renaissance	,, ,, ...	W. Oct. 2	Dec. 11
†RAMSGATE (afternoon) ...	12	Napoleonic Era	,, ,, ...	S. Sept. 28	Dec. 7
†REIGATE (afternoon)	12	Shakespeare	,, ,, ...	F. Oct. 11	Dec. 20
ROCHESTER (evening)	6	Studies from 18th & 19th Centuries	,, ,, ...	T. Oct. 1	Dec. 10
†RYDE (afternoon)	12	The Renaissance	,, ,, ...	Th. Oct. 3	Dec. 12
ST. HELENS (evening)	6	Not fixed	,, ,, ...	Th. Oct. 10	Dec. 19
†SANDOWN & SHANKLIN (aft.)	12	Not fixed	,, ,, ...	W. Oct. 2	Dec. 11
THORNTON (evening)	6	Industrial and Economic Questions since 1789	,, ,, ...	T. Oct. 8	Dec. 17
†VENTNOR (evening)	12	The Stuart Monarchy	,, ,, ...	Th. Oct. 3	Dec. 12
HALIFAX (evening, weekly) ...	12	Wordsworth	Rev. P. H. WICKSTEED, M.A.	Th. Sept. 26	Dec. 19
HARROGATE (evening, weekly)	12	Dante	,, ,, ...	F. Sept. 27	Dec. 20

† The figures in the second column include lectures to be delivered in the Spring Term, when these courses will be continued.

* Arrangements not yet completed.

Centre.	No. of Lectures in Course.	Subject of Course.	Lecturer.	Course begins.	Course (or Half-Course) ends.
ILKLEY (afternoon, weekly) ...	12	Dante	Rev. P. H. WICKSTEED, M.A.	F. Sept. 27	Dec. 20
RIPON (afternoon, weekly) ...	12	Dante	„ „	W. Sept. 25	Dec. 18
BATH (afternoon)	6	The Work of the Air ...	H. R. MILL, D.Sc. ...	Th. Oct. 10	Dec. 19
BATH (evening)	6	The Work of the Air ...	„ „	Th. Oct. 10	Dec. 19
BEDFORD (evening)	6	Astronomy	A. H. FISON, D.Sc. ...	F. Sept. 27	Dec. 6
CARLISLE (afternoon) ...	6	Astronomy...	„ „ ...	F. Oct. 4	Dec. 13
COCKERMOUTH (evening) ...	6	Astronomy...	„ „ ...	W. Oct. 2	Dec. 11
EDGBASTON (afternoon) ...	6	Astronomy...	„ „ ...	Th. Oct. 10	Dec. 19
GRANGE (evening)	6	Forces of Nature (Light) ...	„ „ ...	Th. Oct. 3	Dec 12
HODDESDON (afternoon, weekly)	12	Astronomy...	„ „ ...	T. Oct. 1	Dec. 17
KENDAL (evening)	6	Forces of Nature (Light) (probably)	„ „ ...	F. Oct. 4	Dec. 13
†STROUD (evening)	12	Forces of Nature	„ „ ...	W. Oct. 9	Dec. 18
WINSLOW (evening)	6	Architecture	F. BOND, M.A. ...	T. Oct. 8	Dec. 17
WELLS (evening)	6	Shakespeare	R. W. BOND, M.A. ...	Th. Sept. 26	Oct 5
WESTON-SUPER-MARE (even.)	6	Shakespeare	„ „ ...	W. Sept. 25	Oct. 4
PETERBOROUGH (evening) ...	6	The English Citizen ...	W. M. CHILDS, B.A. ...	T. Oct. 1	Dec. 10
ASHTON-UNDER-LYNE (even.)	6	The Reformation to the Revolution	W. G. DE BURGH, B.A.	T. Oct. 8	Dec. 17
BANBURY (evening)	6	Astronomy...	R. A. GREGORY, M.A. ...	Th. Sept. 26	Dec. 5
CIRENCESTER (evening) ...	6	Industrial Problems of To-day ...	J. A. HOBSON, M.A. ...	M. Oct. 7	Dec. 16
NEWCASTLE-UNDER-LYME (evening)	6	Industrial Problems of To-day ...	„ „ ...	W. Sept. 25	Dec. 4
TEAN (afternoon)	6	Modern Thinkers upon Life ...	„ „ ...	Th. Sept. 26	Dec. 5
KIDDERMINSTER (afternoon) ...	6	Architecture	J. E. PHYTHIAN ...	W. Oct. 2	Dec. 11
BAKEWELL (evening)	6	South Africa	W. B. WORSFOLD, M.A.	T. Oct. 1	Dec. 10
MATLOCK (afternoon)	6	English Poetry & Fiction since 1851	„ „ ...	W. Oct. 2	Dec. 11
*LOUTH (evening)	6	Hygiene	H. E. NIBLETT, B.A. ...	Not fixed	Not fixed.
CLEVEDON (evening)	6	Hygiene	C. H. WADE, M.A. ...	W. Oct. 9	Dec. 18

Spring, 1896.

Centre.	No. of Lectures in Course.	Subject of Course.	Lecturer.	Course (or Half-Course) begins.	Course ends.
UNIVERSITY EXTENSION COLLEGE, READING (afternoon, weekly)	12	Literature	Not fixed	Not fixed	Not fixed.
„ (evening) ...	6	Astronomy...	A. H. FISON, D.Sc. ...	Th. Jan.16	Mar. 26
BATH (afternoon)	6	Not fixed	J.A.R. MARRIOTT, M.A.	Th. Jan. 23	Apr. 2
BATH (evening)	6	Not fixed	„ „ ...	Th. Jan. 23	Apr. 2
†DORCHESTER (evening) ...	12	Industrial Revolution ...	„ „ ...	Th. Jan. 16	Mar. 26
SWINDON (evening)	6	Not fixed	„ „ ...	W. Jan. 15	Mar. 25
†WEST BRIGHTON (afternoon)	12	Age of Elizabeth	C. E. MALLET, B.A...	M. Jan. 20	Mar. 30
†BURGESS HILL (afternoon) ...	12	Shakespeare	Rev. J. G. BAILEY, M.A., LL.D.	Th. Jan. 30	Apr. 23
†WEST BRIGHTON (evening) ...	12	Shakespeare	„ „ ...	Th. Jan. 30	Apr. 23
†BRIGHTON (St. Michael's Hall) (morning)	12	Milton	F. S. BOAS, M.A. ...	Not fixed	Not fixed.
†BOURNEMOUTH (afternoon) ...	12	18th & 19th Century Literature ...	E.L.S.HORSBURGH,B.A.	S. Feb. 1	Apr. 11
*BRECON (evening)		Not fixed	„ „ ...	T. Jan. 21	Mar. 31
†CHELTENHAM (afternoon) ...	12	Italian History	„ „ ...	Th. Jan. 23	Apr 2
†CHELTENHAM (evening) ...	12	Mediaeval England ...	„ „ ...	W. Jan 22	Apr. 1
*DOVER (evening)		Not fixed	„ „ ...	M. Jan. 27	Apr. 6
†FOLKESTONE (afternoon) ...	12	Shakespeare	„ „ ...	M. Jan. 27	Apr. 6
*NEWPORT (evening)	12	The Renaissance	„ „ ...	W. Jan. 29	Apr. 8
†OXFORD (evening)	12	Age of Elizabeth	„ „ ...	F. Jan. 31	Apr. 10
†RAMSGATE (afternoon) ...	12	Napoleonic Era	„ „ ...	S. Jan. 25	Apr. 4
†REIGATE (afternoon)... ...	12	Shakespeare	„ „ ...	F. Jan. 24	Apr. 3
†RYDE (afternoon)	12	The Renaissance	„ „ ...	Th. Jan. 30	Apr. 9
†SANDOWN & SHANKLIN (aft.)	12	Not fixed	„ „ ...	W. Jan. 29	Apr. 8
†STROUD (afternoon)	12	Later Stuarts	„ „ ...	W. Jan. 22	Apr. 1
†VENTNOR (evening)	12	The Stuart Monarchy ...	„ „ ...	Th. Jan. 30	Apr. 9
LEAMINGTON (evening) ...	6	Astronomy...	A. H. FISON, D.Sc. ...	F. Jan. 17	Mar. 27
†STROUD (evening)	12	Forces of Nature	„ „ ...	W. Jan. 15	Mar. 25
WIRKSWORTH (evening) ...	6	Commerce, Colonization & Empire	K. D. COTES, M.A. ...	Th. Jan. 30	Apr. 9
ABERGAVENNY (afternoon) ...	6	Not fixed	W. G. DE BURGH, B.A.	S. Jan. 18	Mar. 28
HEREFORD (evening)	6	English Exploration & Discovery	„ „ ...	M. Jan. 20	Mar. 30
LEOMINSTER (evening) ...	6	English Exploration & Discovery	„ „ ...	T. Jan. 21	Mar. 31
ROSS (evening)	6	English Exploration & Discovery	„ „ ...	W. Jan. 22	Apr. 1
GLOUCESTER (afternoon) ...	6	Literature	J. A. HOBSON, M.A. ...	Not fixed	Not fixed.
GLOUCESTER (evening) ...	6	Problems of Poverty ...	„ „ ...	Not fixed	Not fixed.
BEDFORD (evening)	6	Architecture	ARNOLD MITCHELL, F.R.I.B.A.	F. Jan. 24	Mar. 13
†BURY (evening)	12	Florentine Art	J. E. PHYTHIAN ...	Not fixed	Not fixed.

† The figures in the second column include the lectures given in the Autumn Term, from which these courses are continued.

* Arrangements not yet completed.

Note.—Application for Courses and all information as to fees, &c., can be obtained from The Secretary, University Extension Office, Examination Schools, Oxford.

OXFORD UNIVERSITY

EXTENSION GAZETTE.

VOL. V. No. 60.]   SEPTEMBER, 1895.   [ONE PENNY.

UNIVERSITY EXTENSION JOURNAL.—NOTICE TO CONTRIBUTORS.

All communications intended for the Editorial Committee of the new 'University Extension Journal' should be addressed, in the case of Oxford centres, to the Secretary, University Extension Delegacy, Oxford.

NOTES AND COMMENTS.

With the issue of the present number the *Oxford University Extension Gazette* comes, in its existing form, to an end. But this means not, as some have too hastily assumed, extinction, but transformation. From the ashes of the existing *Gazette* and the existing *Journal* there will arise in October a new *Journal* designed to further the aims of the University Extension movement in England as a whole.

.·.

The new *Journal* will be published, as we have announced, on the 1st of each month from October to May, and in the middle of July. The annual subscription, which is 2s. 6d. post free, may be paid either to the publishers, Messrs. Archibald Constable & Co., 14 Parliament Street, Westminster, or to the University Extension Office, Oxford.

.·.

Communications intended for the Editorial Board of the new *Journal* should be sent, in the case of Oxford contributors and Oxford centres, to the Secretary to the Delegates, Examination Schools, Oxford.

.·.

The Seventh Summer Meeting is now a thing of the past ; a pleasant memory, as we trust, to all who took part in it, whether as visitors, students, lecturers or organizers. Writing, as we do, before the generous plaudits of the concluding conversazione have faded from our ears, while the impress of hundreds of hearty hand-shakes is still fresh, it is too soon perhaps to attempt to deduce whatever lessons the recent Meeting may have taught, or to insist upon the suggestions it offered. We publish elsewhere a brief Summary of the First Part from a practised pen, and Reports on the more important Classes in Part II. But there are one or two features of the Meeting just concluded which may be mentioned appropriately here.

.·.

The number of visitors attending the Meeting shows a considerable diminution on the figures of 1894, just as those of 1894 showed a considerable falling off as compared with 1892. It seems probable that the high-water mark was reached in the latter year, and it is the deliberate conviction of those who were responsible for the organization of that Meeting, that the large numbers threatened the whole administrative machinery with paralysis. There was certainly no sign of it at the time. But undoubtedly it was the large and unexpected influx of visitors in 1892 which induced the Delegacy to adopt two momentous resolutions : (i) to announce a limit of numbers in 1894, and (ii) to propose a biennial instead of an annual Meeting. Neither resolution has lacked critics, especially among those who had come to regard an annual visit to Oxford as among the highest privileges of their lives,

and it is significant that the number-limit has never since been reached.

.·.

About 650 tickets were issued for the First Part of the Meeting, and about 250 for the Second. Of these visitors not less than 300 were present for the first time—a significant and encouraging feature which should not be ignored. It was probably this large influx of fresh students which caused the Meeting to seem to hang fire to some extent on its earliest days. But the chill (even if it existed outside the over-anxious imagination of the organizers) soon wore off, and the enthusiasm which pervaded the Meeting as a whole was at least equal, if we may trust the testimony of our oldest friends and critics, to that of any that has been held.

.·.

The Summer Meeting is every year assuming in more and more marked degree the character of an international conference on Education. No feature of this Meeting has been more pronounced or more pleasant than the extraordinary number of distinguished foreigners who have attended it. Germany, Norway and France were very largely represented : while Austria, Sweden, Denmark, Turkey, Holland, Belgium and Italy each supplied its quota. From the United States we had, as usual, visitors in large numbers and from all parts ; from New York, Boston, Washington, Philadelphia, New Jersey, Rhode Island, Baltimore, Georgia, Kentucky, South Carolina, Florida and Minnesota. It would be difficult to exaggerate the importance of the gathering even from this single point of view. An interchange of ideas on educational questions among people whose experience has been acquired under circumstances so widely differing, would in itself render the Summer Meeting memorable.

.·.

A large party of students were most hospitably entertained at Worcester College throughout the whole Meeting. The privilege of residence within College walls was very highly appreciated alike by Englishmen and by foreigners. And a wonderfully interesting gathering it was. Professors and Privat Docenten from Germany and Norway ; lecturers from Philadelphia ; operatives from Lancashire ; elementary teachers, mechanics, and architects ! A marvellous medley ; and yet, largely on that account, a true microcosm of University Extension. The warmest thanks alike of the students and of the University Extension Delegacy are due to the Governing Body of Worcester College for their hospitality.

.·.

An opportunity was afforded at the Summer Meeting for hearing several gentlemen who are candidates for appointment as University Extension lecturers. Mr. Hilaire Belloc of Balliol College made an exceptionally brilliant first appearance ; his speech at the Union (of

1

which he was recently President) and his lectures on Eighteenth Century France alike giving promise of excellent work in the future. Mr. Garstang, Fellow of Lincoln College, who lectured on Biology, and Mr. de Selincourt of University College (English Literature) also made very favourable impressions, both upon their audiences and upon the expert critics; while much gratitude was expressed to Mr. R. E. S. Hart, B.A., of Merton College, for the great pains he bestowed upon his class in the Philosophy of Plato. There is no doubt that in many of those who were heard for the first time during the past month the Delegacy will find valuable recruits.

.·.

The aggregate number of lectures delivered was considerably below that of last year. This alteration was due to the feeling widely entertained and expressed by visitors to former Summer Meetings, and it is at least an open question whether the process of reduction should not be carried further. There are few things more exasperating to the average student than conflicting lectures at the same hour. And while it is undeniably wise to encourage students to adhere in the main to one or two sequences of study, it is equally desirable so to arrange the 'Time Table' as to permit the students to attend *all* the lectures on a given subject.

.·.

There was a general feeling of regret that Mr. C. W. Furse was too unwell to fulfil his engagement to lecture on the English Painters of the Eighteenth Century. Music, however, was well represented by Mr. F. Cunningham Woods and his gifted assistants. Miss Carrie Townshend's pianoforte recital, too, was a brilliant success; while the performance of the Jane Austen Comedies by Mrs. H. M. Dowson (Miss Rosina Filippi) and her friends did much to brighten the concluding conversazione of Part I. The concert at the close of Part II was entirely provided by the students themselves, under the able direction of Miss Partridge, a prominent member of the Ladies Committee.

.·.

Special prominence was given in this Meeting, as in the last, to the study of Economics, historical and theoretical. Into his three lectures on the ' English Town in the Eighteenth Century,' Mr. Graham Wallace put much excellent original work; as did Mr. L. L. Price in his lecture on Adam Smith. Sir Robert Edgcumbe's lectures on ' Currency' were models of lucidity. While Mr. Fowle's vigorous discourses on the Poor Law and kindred problems will be remembered as one of the special features of the meeting of 1895. During Part II, Mr. Hobson (of whose restoration to health all our readers will be glad to learn) conducted a series of valuable student-classes in the Development of Economic Theory since the days of Adam Smith.

.·.

By far the most numerously attended of the regular classes in Part II was that on Education. A report of its doings will be found elsewhere; but it ought to be known that the Delegates are hoping to make ' Pedagogy' an even more prominent subject in the next meeting. The excellent papers read by Miss Louch and Miss Welldon on ' Froebel's Principles' and ' Child-study' respectively, are already published, while that of Miss Beale, on the ' Training of Teachers,' will be reprinted from the *Journal of Education.*

.·.

The Conferences arranged during the course of the Meeting, especially the later and less formal ones appear to have been particularly helpful and stimulating. The first was presided over by Sir William Hart-Dyke, M.P., the rest by the Secretary to the Delegates. Among others who took part in them were the Bishop of Hereford; Dr. Roberts; Professor Tout; Mr. Nolen; Mr. Leppington of Leamington; Mr. Leveson Scarth of Bournemouth; Mr. Mackinder; Mr. Shaw; Mr. Wells; and a large number of local secretaries. The words and

general attitude of Sir William Hart-Dyke gave great encouragement to those who look to the State for aid in the development of the University Extension system, while the Bishop of Hereford, in his earnest but temperate speech, insisted strongly that the time had come when the State might fairly recognize the Extension movement by a grant in aid of local contributions. The note thus struck by the Bishop and Sir William Dyke was echoed at several of the later Conferences. On the matter of State Aid more will probably be heard before the year is out.

.·.

Among the questions discussed at the less formal Conferences, the following were perhaps the most prominent, (i) The development of Class Teaching and Tutorial Supervision (on which an admirable paper was read by Mr. Leppington, secretary to the Leamington centre). (ii) The scheme lately issued by the Delegates for the grant of Certificates on Connected Short Courses. (iii) The relations between the different University authorities, and the question of territorial areas. (iv) The development of Travelling Libraries, and (v) State Aid. We much regret that want of space compels us to omit even a resumé of the discussions which took place on these questions; but we share the feeling generally expressed that they are likely to prove of the highest possible utility.

.·.

One of the pleasantest features of the Summer Meeting is the opportunity it affords for the interchange of courtesies between the different bodies engaged in the work of University Extension. This year we had the pleasure of welcoming to our Conference Dr. Roberts of Cambridge, Mr. John Nolen of Philadelphia, and Professor Tout of Victoria. In the lecture-rooms, Cambridge was represented by Dr. Kimmins, Mr. Holman and Mr. Matthew; Bangor, by its Principal, Professor Reichel, and the American Society by the Rev. William Bayard Hale of Boston, U.S.A. The latter was also kind enough to preach at St. Mary's—a sermon memorable even among the memorable sermons of 1895. The other special preachers were the Lord Bishop of Hereford, Canon Gore, the Rev. C. G. Lang, the Rev. C. Hargrove, and the Rev. J. E. Odgers. Mr. Hale's sermon is, we are glad to learn, about to be published.

.·.

Decidedly one of the most enjoyable courses in Part II was that of Mr. Francis Bond on Architecture. The lectures themselves were given on alternate days; the intervening days being occupied by architectural excursions and demonstrations. Most of these illustrations were found in Oxford itself, but on two occasions the class went further afield. Few things in the Meeting were more thoroughly enjoyed than these excursions, the first to Iffley and Dorchester; the second to Stanton Harcourt, South Leigh and Eynsham.

.·.

The Secretary to the Delegates desires to be allowed, through the columns of the *Gazette,* to reiterate his expression of gratitude to all those students who kindly contributed to the very handsome sum presented to him, at the final Conversazione by the ladies of the Reference Committee. This much appreciated gift has been handed over, together with another generous donation received in the course of the Meeting, to the Scholarship Fund for 1897.

SADLER TESTIMONIAL.

Additional Subscribers.

Miss Bellamy, Clifton.

Miss Bellamy, Downs Road. Clapton.

Mr. F. Bond, Lincoln College, Oxford.

Mr. Keyman, Winschoten, Holland.

Mr. C. Maher, Altrincham.

Mr. W. Clarke Robinson, Philadelphia, U.S.A.

Mrs. Williams. U.S.A.

FAREWELL WORDS.

WITH this, the last number of its fifth volume, the *Oxford University Extension Gazette* comes to an end. The years during which it has been published happen to have been years of swift and striking change in the history of English education. In every grade of it, primary, secondary and University, new ideas, new experiments, new acts of the central authority have followed in quick succession. They have been at once the symptoms of a great and striking movement and also the cause of fresh developments of eager enterprise. The religious movement, the social movement and the educational movement are all closely connected with one another; each in turn is affected by and affects the rest; the three can only be fully understood in their mutual relations; all of them are the evidence of a deep and far-reaching change in our national life. Nor is the three-fold movement confined to England alone. In America, and in every country of Western Europe, we see signs of the same currents of thought. In all of them, there is taking place a gradual readjustment of old ideas to new needs and of old institutions to new duties. The work of individuals here and there may have called attention to the strength of the movement, may have somewhat changed the direction of its energy, may in some cases have hastened, in others have checked its advance. But, speaking broadly of it as a whole, the movement is not the result of a few men's work; it is an instinctive movement of public opinion, one of those great waves of tendency which affect great masses of people and sweep men forward with irresistible force.

And therefore, though the primary purpose of this journal has been to record the progress of what has come to be known by the name of University Extension teaching, our columns have contained constant reference to the wider aspects of the educational movement, of which University Extension is a part. As the educational movement became stronger, so at the same time our part of that movement became stronger too. Its relation to other efforts in the field of educational activity became more apparent, and the dependence of our work on the work done by other agencies compelled us more and more to think of education as a whole. Any one who looks through the five volumes of the *Gazette* will see that, step by step, the pursuit of our own aims has led us to understand and to sympathize with the aims of other workers in national education, to consider how our efforts may best be harmonized with theirs, and so to conceive, in common with them, a larger view of what education may accomplish for the good of the State.

During the five years, the work of the County Councils has been enormously increased by the provisions of the Local Taxation (Customs and Excise) Act of 1890. The financial changes brought about by that Act have made it possible to establish two University Extension Colleges, which have already achieved remarkable success. The growth in our work, due to this and other connected circumstances, led to the reconstitution of its academic basis, and the establishment of the new Delegacy for the extension of University teaching. The educational results of the special endowment of technical instruction raised alarms lest English education should suffer by a one-sided development and by the neglect of the literary and historical studies which are necessary parts of a complete training. Experience also proved that technical instruction could not be profitably given except on the basis of a sound secondary education. From this there followed the Secondary Education Bill, the County Council and the School Board gatherings, the Oxford Conference and finally the Royal Commission on Secondary Education. In every stage of this movement, University Extension workers have taken an interest which has become stronger year by year.

But as an educational movement can only be understood in the light of history, we have also attempted to give a complete record of the development of University Extension teaching from its first beginnings to the present time. In this task we have been aided by many of those who bore part in its earlier stages, some of them—such as Lord Arthur Hervey, Professor Henry Morley and Mr. Alfred Robinson—now no more. We have also given prominence to the observations of foreign critics, French, German, Belgian, Scandinavian, and Italian. And, since University Extension (as its name implies) is not confined to sending out lecturers and arranging courses of instruction in a large number of towns, we have noticed month by month the rise of new Universities and the rapid developments of the older ones. Finally, we have always insisted that University Extension is not the work of one University alone, but a common task in which all the Universities are jointly concerned. The success of one branch is the success of all and the interest of all. To our great satisfaction, therefore, there has been during the last few years a steady growth in the co-operation between the different Universities engaged in Extension work, a co-operation which has been greatly furthered by the establishment of the joint committee of the general secretaries and by the decision to unite this and its sister organ in a single journal.

It has come to be generally agreed that the liberal education of adult citizens, men and women, is one of the needs of a modern state. 'Vis consili expers mole ruit sua.' Nor can this education be provided and directed by the State alone. It must take various forms according to the needs of the different localities and of the different types of student. It must rest primarily on local interest and local effort, to which the State can give advice, dignity, stimulus and aid. In its organization and management, the teacher himself must have a large and influential part. For its harmonious development, public education must be viewed as one whole, not as a number of sections each estranged from and often jealous of the rest. The teacher in the elementary school, his colleague in the secondary school and the tutor in the University are all members of one profession, to divide which is to weaken it. And in the great work of national education, the Universities with their ancient traditions and perpetual youth have a duty and an opportunity which grows in importance as public interest in education grows. In a sense, the Universities are the keystone of the arch of national education. 'Nous devons travailler de toutes nos forces' said Albert Dumont at Grenoble nearly twenty years ago, 'à cette étroite solidarité de toutes les formes de l'instruction ... Des études secondaires mal faites donnent aux Facultés des auditeurs mal préparés; des Facultés languissantes rendent difficile le recrutement de l'enseignement secondaire. Les Facultés, les lycées, les collèges préparent, éprouvent les réformes qui améliorent peu à peu l'enseignement primaire, qui en modifient les méthodes et en élèvent le niveau.'

The work of the Universities is twofold—intensive and extensive. They are the shrines of learning, the laboratories of study; they render, as the centres of the highest knowledge and instruction, priceless service to the commonwealth—a service which is needed by no form of government so incessantly as by the democratic. 'Toute république qui perdrait un seul instant le sentiment profond des choses supérieures serait bien près ou d'une apathie; ou des intérêts mesquins qui détruiraient toute dignité; ou de l'anarchie.' On the other hand, and at the same time, it is they and they only who can lead the way in providing for all who are competent to profit by it the liberal education which should be within the reach of every adult citizen. We do not want to overcrowd the Universities with students of mediocre abilities. To do so would be to produce an 'academic proletariate.' But there is no reason, as experience has abundantly proved, why men and women, engaged in daily toil in the home, the office and the factory, should not fully avail themselves of cheap and constant opportunity of acquiring the gist of a liberal education if it is brought within easy reach of their own doors. They need, not what Edward Thring called 'feverish snatching at scraps,' but carefully planned courses of ordered study, so devised as to help any student who will give the pains necessary to all self-education, to fit himself 'to perform justly, skilfully and magnanimously,' all the offices which fall to the lot of the citizen in a modern state. To achieve this aim, the Universities, while centralizing and fostering their own

2

inner centres of the highest teaching, are seeking to decentralize themselves as well, and to multiply the points of what we call Extension teaching. They, like the wise men of Bacon's New Atlantis, 'have circuits or visits of divers principal cities of the kingdom.' And though the profit of all education ultimately rests on the character, the moral earnestness and the industry of the student himself, books alone cannot convey true instruction. The learner needs, as well as books, the stimulus of the teacher's personality, the voice of the living teacher himself. And greatest of all oral teaching is that which carries with it the intangible influence of the living tradition which clings to a great University – 'an Alma Mater' as John Henry Newman wrote, 'knowing her children one by one, not a foundry or a mint or a treadmill.'

S.

THE SEVENTH SUMMER MEETING.

PART I.

As year by year one more recollection of a Summer Meeting at Oxford is added to our store, we naturally ask: How does this Meeting compare with those of former years? in what direction do the signs of growth and development point? And two questions, more than all others, rise to the lips of those who look on the Summer Meeting as a very important feature of a great educational movement. They are, first, Is the educational influence of the Meeting waxing or waning? Is it keeping still abreast of those general improvements in systematic education which have so marked the evolution of University Extension teaching generally? And secondly, Is the Meeting as vigorous and enjoyable as those which first gave such impetus and tone to the whole movement?

On both sides there were, perhaps, some drawbacks to be encountered. Those enthusiastic students of men and manners, above all of national life, who make up the bulk of University Extension students, have always, I think, looked a little askance at the eighteenth century, as one in which glory, and vigour, patriotism, and that almost passionate devotion to deeds of noble adventure which distinguished earlier periods of our history, had given way to sloth and materialism; when the seeds of so much that disturbs our national peace and well-being to-day were sown and watered and took root.

And others knew that whatever the subject of study might be, whatever the lectures might give us, we should miss at every turn the inspiriting presence which in other years, whether as lecturer, as guide at delightful visits to colleges, as the perennial source of wise and statesmanlike counsel at conferences, or as head and director of the whole movement, has made the Oxford Summer Meeting what it was, and what we believe it always will be.

With regard to the subject of the Programme: every student who heard the eighteenth century criticized (sometimes severely) by some lecturers, and defended by others, but illuminated by all, came away feeling that in every department of study, whether on the arts or the scientific side, was matter of burning interest, amply repaying devoted attention.

As usual the lectures in Part I may be roughly classed under the following heads: (i) The History, Literature, and Art of the period; (ii) Economics, including Political Science and Social Reform; (iii) Natural Science; (iv) Theology: with (v) some miscellaneous lectures.

It is impossible to mention more than a few of those who helped to carry out that carefully-arranged scheme of consecutive study which was laid before us during the fortnight, but the following outlines may give some imperfect idea of the shape taken by the courses. The history included a course on William III and the Revolution of 1688, Marlborough, the Diplomacy of Louis XV, and France previous to the Revolution; one on the Scottish History of the period; another on Prussia and Frederick the Great; with lectures on Bolingbroke, Walpole, Pitt, Burke, The English Power in India, Alberoni, Wilberforce and Wesley.

In Literature there were memorable lectures on Addison, Pope, Defoe, and Dr. Johnson, rounded off with the most delightful dramatic illustrations of the comedy of Jane Austen, and in Art, the fascinating musical lectures of Mr. F. C. Woods and his helpers, and a lecture on Garrick by Sir Edward Russell.

When it is understood that among the lecturers in this group of History and Literature were Prof. Lodge, Messrs. Armstrong, A. L. Smith, Hassall, Sidgwick and Augustine Birrell, in addition to many old friends among the University Extension lecturers, some idea may be formed of the educational character and the delights of our studies.

Perhaps no course was followed with keener interest than that on civic history and kindred subjects, which, introduced last year under such excellent auspices by Mr. Graham Wallas, was this year continued by him and the Rev. T. W. Fowle. To the latter our thanks are especially due for the ready kindness with which at such short notice he lengthened his part of the course, the last two lectures of which, though delivered in Part II, must, by a species of reasoning not unfamiliar to students of eighteenth century history, be included in Part I.

One of the greatest possible claims of the Oxford Summer Meeting on the admiration and respect—I use the word advisedly—of the public, is the provision of lectures and teaching on subjects of such vital importance, in such a place as Oxford, rich with memories and historic associations, removed from the tumult of party feeling and strife, and from whence, at so many times in our national story, the stream of social and religious reform in various shapes has flowed. To place such lectures as these, supplemented by and connected with the discussion of the period from almost every other possible point of view, before a large number of persons, most of them with the best half of their lives before them, is in itself a most admirable contribution to public education and public life.

Among the lectures given by those outside the University of Oxford must be mentioned that of Professor Mahaffy, which perhaps was not less enjoyed because the Professor seemed to consider an Extension student both necessarily and rightly a light half-believer of his casual creed, and because that view of our work and ourselves immediately met with an eloquent and indignant repudiation!

In the department of Natural Science, the inaugural lecture of Professor Odling was a source of much pleasure to both scientific and non-scientific students, followed as it was by those of Dr. Kimmins, Dr. Fison, and others of a more technical and practical nature.

Every one interested in the future of University Extension work was glad to meet the latest addition to our list of lecturers, Mr. Hilaire Belloc. In his lectures on Rousseau, on France before the Revolution, in his frank and brilliant criticism of Socialism in the *Merrie England* debate, in his eloquent interpretation of modern political aims and tendencies by the light of French training and inherited ideas, Mr. Belloc showed himself to possess in a marked degree those qualities of imagination, sympathy and verve which are as indispensable as knowledge in Extension lecturing.

A special feature among the College visits was Mr. Wells' series, which gave colour and point to much of the history study. The advantages of visits to places and buildings of historical interest under trained and scientific guidance, in addition to the ordinary methods of studying history, is a subject of which many of us have heard much recently, but which few of us have had any opportunity of realizing except in connexion with Summer Meetings. Mr. Wells' intimate knowledge of Oxford and her history, combined with his happy possession of the true Extension spirit, made these lecture-visits much appreciated by all who were fortunate enough to join the parties.

Sir W. Hart Dyke's address as chairman of the Conference on University Extension and Higher Education was both interesting and significant. Even to those who did not quite agree with him on certain administrative questions, his speech was full of hope for all interested in the higher moral and intellectual training of all classes, by whatever means it may be attained.

At the two succeeding Conferences, hope was again in the ascendant, though most of us were anxious to know what was the experience which had wrought that hope. On which subject we shall be enlightened in due time.

One important effect of this Meeting (and its predecessors) has been to show students how impossible it is to cut history up into fragments, isolated periods, a nd then obtain any grasp of the subject. With each summer's work on successive periods, we feel that each is—over and above its own special value — a preparation and introduction to the study of the next period. It is in the sequence of the teaching of these Summer Meetings and the methodical study which they yearly inaugurate afresh, that much of their worth must always lie. Every year too makes more obvious the care and foresight needed in the arrangements for these lectures, and the enormous amount of work and responsibility involved in carrying them out successfully.

Now as to our second question, let us say at once that though it might be difficult to recapture that first, fine, careless rapture which distinguished the earliest Meetings, when the Oxford we now know and love so well lay still as some unexplored fairy world before so many eager students, yet all the old elements which make for delight, both intellectual and purely social, were there, with the same freshness for the new student, with an additional grace for those who have known them of old. The private and the public hospitality and graciousness of the beloved city have not stopped short at a seventh Summer Meeting, nor have use or custom been suffered to rob them of their well-known charm. It would be a very invidious and thankless task to select names for any praise of mine, but I feel that all Extension students, old or new, would wish to say how much they appreciate the labours of the Secretaries, and to join in the expression of the opinion that this seventh Summer Meeting of 1895 has been one of the most successful from the educational, and enjoyable from the social, point of view that we have ever had.

BEATRICE VIVIAN
(Camborne).

PART II.

IT was rather melancholy to see so many empty chairs when Part II began, and to feel that our numbers were greatly reduced ; but, in reponse to Mr. Horsburgh's words, we settled down quickly to harder and steadier work, with a delightful sense of anticipation. Two early morning lectures introduced us to Literary Society in Athens, and the regular attendance of the same set of students at the Philosophy of Plato indicated a real interest in the subject : quite a fresh avenue of thought was opened to many non-classical students ; and the lectures, increasing in vitality as they drew to a close, have left us with much to think out at home, such as the striking resemblance between some of the ideas of Plato and the Pauline theology.

Another course of lectures was on Political Economy, which was felt to be a very useful sequence to Mr. Graham Wallas's 'English Towns' in Part I. Several students wrote papers on economic questions for the lecturer, and made good use of the books in the reference library. It was not a difficult matter to distinguish the novice from the more proficient student, on the face of the one was an intense frown of eager striving to follow the line of thought, on the face of the other a calm look of satisfaction and enjoyment, which suggests the advisability of reading up such a subject before attending the course of lectures.

The students who took up architecture had a very enjoyable and instructive time, thoroughly enjoying the alternate lectures and excursions, and taking an intelligent interest in the reasons which underlie the beauty of the buildings in Oxford and the neighbourhood, and even taking round stray students themselves, to whom they gave a résumé of what Mr. Bond had taught. Eighteenth century literature drew an interested and appreciative audience, and though a very efficient substitute was

always found, great regret was felt that the lecturer himself was not always well enough to deliver his own lecture.

The ' Progress of Discovery in the Eighteenth Century' and the 'Food Supply of England' were not less attractive than they sound, and we were greatly amused at Mr. Lyde's ' tip' about New Zealand mutton. Food Supply and Discovery are naturally interesting topics to children, and appeal to their sympathies, why is it then that teachers still adhere to the penance of the Geographical text-book and do not give lessons on more interesting lines ?

Professor Wright satisfied our curiosity as to the meaning of Dialect Dictionary, and revealed to us that we are the truly ignorant who condemned the peasant as illiterate because his grammatical construction was not the same as ours ; and when we say a man is ' mouching,' we are using good English and not slang, for we mean ' he is gathering blackberries.' The Debate on the motion that ' the time has come for the House of Lords to be abolished' created no little amusement ; the result was, in favour of the motion 42, against 66. Though there was a special appeal for a speech from some woman-student, there was no response, and for the space of two minutes ' soft whispers circulated round the room.' It is to be regretted that no woman rose to defend a position nor to return a charge, for everybody knows that they have notions on the subject under discussion, and also on the Higher Education of Women. May it be suggested that a few of us learn to speak before 1897, and then rise with the courage of our convictions ?

The students who attended the Conference on Class Teaching will watch with some interest any indications of desire on the part of their centres for this 'intensive Extension work,' and the fact that the Delegates are ready to meet the demand may rouse some latent desire into activity.

We got some delightful little bits from some of the lectures, e. g. ' a bad scrawl is so snug' (Swift), and how many of us will ' make a clean sweep of our spare room mantelpiece ornaments ' when we get home ? in response to the pathetic request of our lecturer on Design.

The three lectures on eighteenth century Ireland aroused great interest, and were invaluable, not only as forming the groundwork for a proper understanding of the question of to-day, but as a lesson in moderation, in the fact that there are two sides to every question, and that in this question both sides are to be pitied. We cannot testify too strongly to Mr. Marriott's justice and impartiality in dealing with so difficult a subject.

Two lecturers, from other Universities, kindly gave us an evening, Mr. Mathew from Cambridge on ' Scott as an eighteenth century historian,' and Mr. Hale, from Massachusetts, on the American Constitution. We have been conscious all the time that we have been living in a higher atmosphere than that of the workaday world to which we are accustomed, and have become a little imbued with the noble spirit of the Extension movement and the high aims of its organizers ; the sermons at St. Mary's on Aug. 18 and 25 gave expression to what we felt but could not have put into words, and deepened our sense of gratitude and responsibility. We do not fear that the pursuit of knowledge will shake our faith, for the Creator is revealing Himself through the created, and we learn to look for God Himself in the history of nations and in the laws of Natural Science.

We were all sorry to say good-bye on Monday night after the conversazione in the East School. The pleasant programme, arranged and carried out by the students themselves, passed only too quickly, and the Summer Meeting is now a thing of the past. We know that ' the first thing a kindness deserves is acceptance, the next is transmission,' and we are leaving Oxford feeling that not only are we more advanced intellectually, but that we have had striking lessons in courtesy and kindness ; and we are going home to work.

RACHEL FAIRBROTHER
(Bournemouth).

REPORTS OF SPECIAL CLASSES AT THE SUMMER MEETING.

I. Geology.

EIGHT names were entered for Geology, but only seven students attended ; these were Miss A. Dakin, W. A. Hoffmann, G. H. Pickles, Ed. Dock, Miss Stephens, Miss A. Heath, T. E. Mole.

There were twelve working days, and these were devoted to lectures, laboratory demonstrations, and more especially to field-work. The scheme of the course was such that just so much theoretical Geology was taught as could be clearly illustrated in the time at my disposal in the country around Oxford. Almost every statement made in lecture was verified in the field or in the Museum. The fine weather enabled us to miss no item of the programme which had been suggested by Professor Green, and the successful issue of the course was materially helped by the willingness of Mr. Haughtin (Professor Green's assistant).

The attendance was as follows :—

*Miss A. Dakin	. . . . .	7 out of 12.
*W. A. Hoffmann	. . . . .	10 „
*G. H. Pickles	. . . . .	11 „
Ed. Dock	. . . . . .	6 „
*Miss Stephens	. . . . .	6 „
Miss Heath	. . . . .	3 „
*T. E. Mole	. . . . . .	12 „

N.B. Except in the case of Miss Heath (who was unable to walk) each attendance means presence at lecture and demonstration or excursion. All who attended showed great earnestness and desire to learn, and I have marked with an asterisk in the foregoing list the names of those who showed special zeal in note-taking and special intelligence in questioning.

On the whole, though the class was small, I am satisfied that a certain amount of accurate knowledge has been assimilated in such a way as to awaken power of observation and reasoning which might otherwise have remained dormant and useless.

G. A. LEBOUR, *Lecturer.*

.·.

The special class in Geology—a somewhat 'hard' subject, containing plenty of nuts to 'crack '—was, in the absence of Professor Green, who was recruiting his health in Norway, taken by Professor G. A. Lebour, F.G.S., in the Geological lecture-room of the Musuem.

The lecture proper, of about an hour's duration, was followed by explanations, the answering of questions on points difficult to novices, and the further elucidation of apparently obscure statements. The greater part of the first three afternoons was spent in demonstrations on, and the examination of, actual geological specimens, in which the microscope played an important and most interesting part. On other days and sometimes during almost the whole day, excursions were conducted by the lecturer, sometimes by rail and sometimes on foot, to Charlbury, Fawler, and Stonesfield ; to Enslow Bridge (on which occasion the party was fortunate in having the very valuable advice and assistance of J. Parker, Esq., of Oxford) ; to Islip ; to Shotover Hill, &c. ; to Cumnor ; to Faringdon, whence good specimens of the far-famed fossil sponges were obtained ; and to Moulsford and Upton, the latter bringing these much-enjoyed and practical excursions to an end. In this way all the secondary rocks, except the trias, the lower lias and the upper chalk have been viewed, the excursions being so arranged as to strictly follow the sequence of the geological beds, so well exposed in the neighbourhood of Oxford. Good representative specimens of the various formations and their respective fossils were easily sought for and obtained, classified and named under the careful and assiduous attention of Professor Lebour, whose patient teaching and lucid explanations of technical terms and phrases cannot be too highly praised, and will certainly be long remembered with gratitude. The students also had the very valuable and courteous aid of Mr. W. F. Haughtin, assistant to Professor Green.

Each lecture was thoroughly well illustrated by specimens from the Museum of the various rocks and fossils under notice.

The class numbered seven, the very stormy weather during the First Part of the Meeting perhaps helping to deter others from joining, though, fortunately for the excursions, the students were favoured by fine weather.

This course of lectures should prove a valuable introduction and incentive to the study of this absorbing subject, so truly educational. Long may the privilege continue, and increasingly may it be appreciated.

THOMAS EDWARD MOLE
(*Chillerton School, Isle of Wight*).

II. Botany.

I HAVE pleasure in transmitting the following short report of my class.

From Aug. 13 to Aug. 26, I delivered a series of daily lectures, each lecture being succeeded by an hour's practical work. The sixteen students who came to the course were very regular in their attendance.

I was more than satisfied with the progress they made in their work, and with the enthusiasm and interest they exhibited in the subject.

I have good reason to believe that the majority of the class will continue their botanical studies elsewhere.

PERCY GROOM, *Lecturer.*

.·.

Mr. Groom's course of lectures on the 'Evolution of Flowering Plants' has been an ideal one. The subject in itself, while one of intense interest to all students of botany, is one of great difficulty and full of pit-falls for the student without direction and guidance. Direction and guidance of the very best we have had from Mr. Groom. He has given us the botany of mountain and moor, field and hedgerow, and his lectures have had the freshness and clearness that only those who love their subject can impart. Dividing the course equally between lectures and practical work, Mr. Groom in the most fascinating manner dealt with the shapes, structure and functions of root, stem, leaf, flower and fruit ; the evidences of evolution, geological and historical in the plant world ; the origin of flowers and the changes they have undergone during past ages ; cross-fertilization and its advantages, self-fertilization with its advantages, and with the relation between insects and flowers. We were thus led to realize the debt we owe to the insect world, which has done so much to make this world so full of beauty for us.

The course ended most suitably with the subject of death and immortality in the plant-world.

The practical work consisted in dissecting and drawing a number of plants, all with some story to tell : of organs lost through disuse, or changed for protection, &c., the plants being those of the way-side and hedges, which one might never suppose had a story to tell.

Mr. Groom has shown us what an immense field of investigation lies near to our hands ; and more important still, he has pointed out the way in which we can investigate it for ourselves. I think I am only echoing the opinion of every member of the class, in saying that while Mr. Groom has taken the utmost pains and care to make every point clear and distinct, we have never had a single dull moment.

J. C. HARRISON (*Scarborough*).

III. Greek Class.

THE amount of work covered in a fortnight was very considerable, being (practically) the grammar up to and including λύω (active and passive), a large number of exercises (70 pages), and about five pages of Xenophon's *Anabasis*. Considering the time available, I consider the work decidedly creditable : most of the candidates have a good hold of the Greek accidence, and the translation was very carefully prepared.

At the same time there were manifest marks of haste :

the grammar, though creditable, was very uncertain, especially in the verbs; and the translation showed that the construction of the Greek was not always understood.

On the whole I think Mr. Gibson and his class may be congratulated on a fortnight of good work.

J. WELLS, M.A.,
Fellow and Tutor of Wadham College.

.·.

The Greek class has been a source of much enjoyment to those who attended it; and I think each one must feel that a very real step forward in knowledge has been made. The work has been most carefully gone through, every difficulty noted and explained by Mr. Gibson, and no pains have been spared in laying a solid foundation on which I expect all of us will endeavour to continue to build. That enthusiasm was excited for the apparently dry subject of Greek Grammar is, I think, proved by the fact that the students, for the most part, attended both classes, and several availed themselves of Mr. Gibson's kind offer to give an extra hour's teaching in the evening. A keen desire to meet again next year and continue the work so begun is, I am sure, the result in the mind of each student who attended the Greek class this year; and we should all wish to express our sincere thanks both to our teacher and to those who made the necessary arrangements for the holding of the class.

MAY E. PARRY.

IV. Education Class.

THE Theory of Education took a prominent place among the subjects reserved for the Second Part of the Summer Meeting. The care which had evidently been bestowed on the arrangement of the course, and the fact that the lectures were diligently attended by many English and foreign teachers, and others interested in education, show, if proof were needed, that special study for the profession of a teacher is becoming recognized as a necessity, and that why and how to teach are felt to be questions of as much importance as what to teach. The Oxford Extension authorities are not behindhand in this any more than in other matters, and the lecturers selected were men and women whose names are well known in the educational world.

The course opened with an introductory paper by Miss Beale of Cheltenham Ladies' College, who dealt with the subject of training, firstly from a philosophical and teleological point of view, and secondly from a practical standpoint, sketching an ideal training college in connexion with a large school and an annexed smaller practising school. The tone of seriousness of purpose and inspiring energy which characterized this lecture, was indeed the key-note to the course that followed. On the second day, a conference on Fröbel's principles was opened by Miss Welldon (Head of the Kindergarten Training Department, Cheltenham Ladies' College), in which she showed herself a thorough mistress of her subject, dealing with the Fröbellian principles rather in the spirit than in the letter, and showing how the Kindergarten system is compatible both with the requirements of the government code, the legitimate demands of parents, and preparation for public school life.

Mrs. Ward, the delegate of the Fröbel Society, took part in the discussion which followed, pointing out that the development of mental power was what Fröbel aimed at especially rather than the learning of useful arts; finally, Miss Welldon was warmly thanked for her paper by Mr. Marriott, on behalf of the University Delegates.

Later in the meeting another informal conference was held, at which students of the Education Class had the opportunity of listening to an exceedingly interesting paper on 'Child-Study,' by Miss Louch. Miss Louch's paper, as well as Miss Welldon's has now, we are glad to learn, been published in pamphlet form [1].

Mr. Cook contributed two lectures on art teaching

[1] The above may be obtained at the University Extension Office, price 3½d. and 2½d. respectively.

in schools. In a manner all his own he demonstrated how art teaching should follow the mental development of the child, how the teacher should himself be taught by his pupil, how the chief use of art is to train in observation, that it is a means of gaining knowledge as well as of expressing it; that the drawing lesson should be in correlation with other studies, and that the object of work with pencil and brush at the school age is not to make pictures but to cultivate the power to make pictures, as well as many other things when the school age is over. Mr. Cook exhibited the unaided work of some of his pupils, which testified to the interest aroused by this ingenious and enthusiastic teacher, who was himself a pupil of Ruskin.

His lectures were followed by a practical address from Mr. Elford on the teaching of science, from the Kindergarten age upwards. The educational and ethical value of science was well demonstrated; a science course was sketched which would cover the school period, a course well calculated to afford training in observation and energy in a high degree. Mr. Elford advocated the making of rough and ready apparatus by the science teacher himself, and gave many suggestions for appliances he had himself devised.

The course concluded with the *pièce de résistance*, a series of six lectures on psychology by Mr. Holman (H. M. I.). In these the lecturer dealt with a wide and difficult subject, compressing, selecting and connecting with great judgement. Pyschology and Herbartian philosophy, coloured with the lecturer's own personality and practical experience, were presented in such a way that the interest of the audience never flagged, and the time allotted for the lecture never seemed long enough. The development of mind in the individual, and of knowledge in the individual and the race, were cleverly sketched; commonplace educational maxims gained a new meaning, and time was found for practical application of the principles discussed.

Students who attended this course carried away with them more than their certificate of attendance; they cannot fail to have gained new ideas, new light on old ideas, suggestions for improved educational methods, and a great impetus to the study of educational problems. The course was only too short; we hope that on another occasion students attending the First Part of the Meeting will have the opportunity of hearing a similar series of lectures.

THE WOMEN LECTURERS' ASSOCIATION AT THE SUMMER MEETING.

THE thanks of the Women Lecturers' Association are again due to the Oxford Delegacy for allowing another informal Conference to be held at this Summer Meeting, as during the one last year, for the purpose of discussing a subject at the University which has already been under consideration in London.

The point was, how to secure a high standard of efficiency for women lecturers, and the following practical resolution, passed by the Conference, seems to offer a solution: ' It is eminently desirable in the cause of education that a Board be established, armed with the highest possible authority to grant certificates to women lecturers.'

The establishment of a Women Lecturers' Institute and Board of Examiners—which shall also be a Board of Management—seems to follow as a natural consequence. Miss Edith Bradley (Managing Director of the Women Lecturers' Association) read the draft scheme of this proposed new development of her Association, and as a whole it was favourably received. Mr. J. Wells (who kindly presided) asserting that in his opinion there was a real need for such a scheme, he also considered that the Women Lecturers' Association might be extremely useful in preparing the way for University Extension. It would be a great help to women lecturers if the suggestion made last year by Mr. Marriott, as to the assistance they might render University Extension by tutorial work could take any definite form.

EDITH BRADLEY.

THE DUKE OF DEVONSHIRE ON UNIVERSITY EXTENSION.

WE are glad to fulfil the promise made in the August *Gazette* of giving some copious extracts from the exceedingly interesting and important speech made by the Lord President of the Council at Exeter.

I am not here as an educational expert; I am not here as professing to know very completely or thoroughly of what has been done in the establishment of this College. If I have any claim to be here at all, it is simply that I happen to have the honour of being Titular head or Chancellor of the University of Cambridge, with which you are connected. As most of you know, that office is a purely honorary one. No Academical duties are connected with it, and the Chancellor has nothing to do with the government of the University, or with the ordering of its studies. If there is any advantage at all in the office of Chancellor, it is that the Chancellor forms a sort of connecting link between the University and the outside world. He is the connecting link between those men who spend more or less retired lives in study and in teaching and the great masses of the people, who are, in reality, whether they know it or not, deeply interested in the operations of the University, which may have wisely contributed to the very great improvement in their intellectual and even in their material condition. Taking this view of the office which I hold, it is natural, since I have held it, that I should have taken more interest in the steps by which the University has in recent years sought to bring itself into more close contact and touch with the outside public, and even in the improvements which it has introduced into its own course of studies. When I refer to the changes which have recently taken place in the University, I may call attention to the fact that it is constantly endeavouring to adapt its teaching more and more to the wants of the masses of the community than to any select body of students.

* * * * *

But the University has done more than extend the circle of instruction within its own walls. It has stepped outside the borders which formerly confined it, and, by means of the University Extension lectures, it has endeavoured to open for the use of the whole community the stores of knowledge it possesses, and to make them available for the benefit of the public generally. The Mayor has referred to the University Extension Syndicate. I believe some of the ablest members of the University of Cambridge are as deeply interested in the success of this enterprise in which we are engaged as in anything which is going on within the limits of their own University itself. They believe this movement has passed beyond the experimental stage, and has proved itself to be a success and of great value in many respects to the country. If I attempt to describe the objects of the University Extension movement I do not know I could do it better than by referring to the words used by the Chancellor of the sister University of Oxford, Lord Salisbury, at a conference last year, in which he described the efforts in which the two Universities are engaged as one for the purpose of utilizing the manufactured article which the Universities produced in such great quantities, namely, the highly-cultivated graduate, to send him forth as a missionary of knowledge to all parts of the country, and thus to extend their influence in quarters where it never in any other way could have reached. As Chancellor of the University of Cambridge, I venture to second him in describing as beneficial the movement which we are bound to wish all success.

* * * * *

Summing up what we have got in the way of higher education, we possess, in the first place, our old Universities; then, our University Colleges; then, our endowed schools; all these extended and developed, as I have attempted to explain to you. These may be called the regular forces of higher education. Then, in addition to the regular forces, we have the Militia and the Volunteers in the shape of the local Science and Art Classes, Technical Classes, University Extension lectures, and examina-

tions. It must be admitted that we have made already tolerably large provision for the supply of the higher educational wants of the country. But if we ask ourselves the question, How has all this provision been organized and ordered? I doubt whether we shall obtain such a satisfactory answer. The greater part of what I have described are voluntary educational agencies, and, while being controlled by local Committees, are more or less under the control of certain central bodies, such as the Science and Art Department in London, or the Syndicates of the Universities of Oxford and Cambridge. In such a condition of things as this we might expect to find, and I believe that we do find, a certain amount of waste of power; a misdirection of effort; in some cases even a certain amount of friction and misunderstanding. If you would imagine, or attempt to imagine, what would be the condition of a school or a College where there was no Head-master or Principal; where there was not even a Council of those who were engaged in the teaching; where every Master or Professor gave his own series of lectures, and started upon his own course without any consultation as to what his fellow-labourers were doing, you can very easily imagine what state of confusion that College or school would soon be in. This is what is taking place at the present moment in a great many of our counties and our municipal boroughs. We have a series of educational agencies with but little common direction, and with little connexion with each other. We have them in the main managed by local Committees, who possess full local knowledge, but who, probably, are not educational experts. We have a certain amount of control from central bodies in the Metropolis or the Universities composed of educational experts, but necessarily not having full knowledge of the opportunities, wants, and requirements of the district. An attempt has been made already by Reading, and an attempt has been made here, to introduce somewhat more of order into this system. And it has been met, so far as I am informed, with the most hopeful of results.

* * * * *

You have in this way secured for Exeter, and over that part of the county of Devonshire which is accessible from Exeter, a College which possesses all the advantages which are possible under the conditions which here exist. This city, although a place of considerable size, is not a centre sufficiently large to be able to possess a University College such as those of Manchester or Bristol. Your population is not large enough; your resources are not adequate to maintain a permanent staff of teachers of sufficient ability to form a complete staff for the permanent teaching of science; but you are able by the assistance of the connexion which is established with the University of Cambridge to supply a circulation of qualified teachers who, under direction, might be able to give you all you require. This, in my opinion, is an experiment of very strong interest, not in the interests of Exeter or Devonshire alone, but of the whole country. I should have been glad if I had seen upon the paper of our proceedings to-day that others who know more of the progress of this experiment were about to address you. I should like to know what are the difficulties and what is the measure of success you have already met with. I daresay something may be heard this evening of financial difficulties. Generally, upon occasions of this kind, something is said upon that question. I believe the demands which this College makes upon the resources of this city and district are not very large. I believe, however, that even for the services of the Principal, upon the attention of whom almost the whole success of the enterprise and experiment depends, the funds are not permanently assured. In this respect, I believe you are somewhat at a disadvantage as compared with the sister College of Reading, where they have the advantage of the Principal who holds a Fellowship of a College in the University of Oxford, which has been created for the sole purpose of enabling its holder to attend to University Extension work. Cambridge, I am sure, would gladly follow the example which has been set by the University of Oxford, did its financial position enable it to do so. But neither the Colleges nor the University of Cambridge are financially prosperous. Their revenues do not enable them to do more than to adequately carry out their own work within their own walls, and, of course, until that is done they cannot undertake further work. But I trust means may yet be found by which the Universities may in the future be enabled to undertake the work outside their own borders, and to carry it on as efficiently as it is within their own borders. I remember at the Conference held last year your energetic Secretary (Miss Montgomery) asked, 'Has the pious founder become extinct?'

* * * * *

I believe that if the necessity were known, there are many who might be disposed to aid in this noble work which has been undertaken by the Universities. And when once the necessity and need is known, financial difficulties will not stand in the way of the Universities completing that which we have so well begun. At all events, I believe that you here in Exeter, with the assistance of some of the public-spirited and influential members of your community, have been the means of initiating an experiment of the highest value and of the greatest importance not only to your own city and county, but to the whole community, and, in that belief, I have had the greatest pleasure, as Chancellor of the University of Cambridge, which takes so deep an interest in the Extension movement, in accepting the invitation to come here to-day and to declare this building open.

PROPOSALS FOR A STUDENTS' MAGAZINE.

AT the recent Summer Meeting of Extension students held in Oxford, a short discussion took place, and a Report was invited, as to the feasibility of starting a Magazine specially devoted to the interests of Extension students. These form a scattered body sprinkled all over the country, having unity of aim but, as yet, little cohesion except what is given them by their individual connexion with local centres or Students Associations. Nevertheless in numbers they abound, and they are for the most part earnest and enthusiastic. If any method could be devised for launching and keeping afloat a Magazine, however modest in size and appearance, which could form a means of intercommunication between these students, which could give heart to their efforts and expression to their ideas, a great development might gradually take place in the whole range of University Extension teaching. The suggested Magazine would cover entirely different ground to that on which the *University Extension Journal* is based. It would be in no sense an official publication, but would be carried on by students in the interests of students, and with especial reference to their literary or lecture needs. It would also enable the lecturers to guide the studies of students between the courses of lectures. Moreover the new regulations for Connected Short Courses will necessitate the preparation of short guides or syllabuses for intermediate work, and a Students' Magazine would be the most effective medium for communications of this nature.

There are two publications (perhaps more) which are in existence at the present moment, the enterprizing precursors and pioneers in this field of work. The Oxford Extension movement is greatly indebted to Mr. Bowman of Gateshead, the Editor of *The Student*, and to Miss Punch, the Editor of the *Bournemouth Students' Association Gazette*, for the efforts they have made, in the north and in the south, to meet the requirements which this Magazine is designed to satisfy. It is quite impossible to over-rate the advantage which has accrued to University Extension through their admirable initiative; and in the discussion to which this paper is intended to give rise their experience, and if possible their co-operation will be most valuable, especially as to points of management and finance.

At the very outset it should be clearly stated that there seems no manner of use in attempting to start and carry on a Magazine, however desirable, and however apparently welcome its early numbers might be, if its circulation is to depend upon the voluntary subscription of here a student and there a student. It will be better not to make the attempt at all than to fail on account of a financial deficit. Unless a guaranteed circulation of some thousands of copies can be assured, constant difficulties will only lead to ultimate and inevitable failure. If, on the other hand, the Magazine can be established as not merely the organ of the students, but as the very sign and evidence that each subscriber is a recognized member of a Students' Association, then the circulation will not only be sufficient, but the character of the publication will be maintained at a high level. By virtue of its distribution to all students it will be a practical power in University Extension.

To this end, the Magazine must be published at a low price. If twelve monthly numbers are produced at one penny each, the sum of one shilling annually could not be felt as a burden by any student, if the payment were added to the ordinary subscription of the nearest Students' Association; especially as there would be value received, and an enhanced feeling of comradeship and membership. In order to bring about this state of things, it would be necessary to form a Federation of Local Students' Associations pledged to fall in with this plan. Any student whose Association declined or did not locally exist, could be requested to join the nearest federated body for the purpose of receiving the Magazine by post through its Hon. Secretary. In this way, by the co-operation of the Associations, the expense and trouble which would otherwise be caused by the central distribution of single copies would be avoided.

The management of such a Magazine would have to be central, although what should be implied by this word is a matter of opinion. That Oxford should operate with Cambridge, London and Victoria is unquestionably proper so far as concerns the official organ of the united Universities, but it is less obviously desirable in the case of a Students Magazine which may owe much of its usefulness, if not its continued existence, to the loyal support of groups of students attached in the main to one University.

There is danger lest individuality be lost in an endeavour to make it general. Moreover as the Magazine, to become useful, must be warmly and continuously supported by the lecturers, the Editors might find it difficult to keep in touch with the staff of all four Universities. Nevertheless on the other side may be urged the increased circulation and enlarged scope, which would have the effect of attracting advertisements.

A combined Magazine must almost necessarily be published in London, whilst the smaller venture would have its headquarters in Oxford, although not at the Examination Schools. This consideration would materially affect the personnel of the editorial staff, as those who could perhaps manage for Oxford alone might be unable to work with London as their base.

The literary material of the paper might consist in part of the best essays written for the lecturers. To be 'recommended for publication' would be a matter of honourable ambition. The lecturers would probably contribute articles by arrangement. Reviews of books, correspondence, questions and answers, prize competitions would, with notes and comments, go far towards making a monthly number which every student would find of direct practical use and interest: whilst the syllabuses of intermediate work, and suggestions for home reading would make it a necessity for all those who were working for the Certificate given for Connected Short Courses.

The present seems a suitable time for ventilating this subject, as University Extension has reached a stage when it requires the co-ordination of all its scattered forces in order to take some forward steps. Progress on various lines and in many directions is imperative if the movement is to have a leading place amongst the agencies which are to be vitalized and stimulated into further efficiency by the impending Report on Secondary Education.

Signed {
KATHLEEN MARTIN (*Bakewell*).
LEVESON SCARTH (*Bournemouth*).
C. E. MALLET (*Staff-Lecturer*).
}

LETTERS TO THE EDITOR.

[*We do not hold ourselves responsible for the opinions expressed by our correspondents.*]

'Qualifying' for Examinations.

DEAR SIR,—In your last number a correspondent invites discussion on 'Qualifying for Examination.' I suppose that by this is understood not only attending a certain number of lectures and writing a certain number of papers set by the lecturer, but also attaining a certain level of excellence, which is denoted by the marks assigned by the lecturer to each paper.

If at any centre a prize were offered for the best record of University Extension work during a term of years, would not the most equitable way of judging the merit of the qualified students be this—to take the total marks gained for paper-work during the successive courses and add to these the marks gained for other successes? When the marks are given numerically, this may easily be done; there is more difficulty, on the students' side, in judging the relative merit of their papers when such marks as 'V.G.' 'A.I.' and so forth, are used by the lecturer. Perhaps, in the latter case, either a numerical value may be assumed for the symbols, or the rank taken by the students ascertained from the lecturer.

I venture to make the above suggestion in reply to your correspondent's first question, but those which relate to the marks given for different grades of success can hardly be answered by a student.

I am, dear Sir,

Yours faithfully,

I. A. C.

.·.

The Summer Meeting.

SIR,—Although an Extension Summer audience presents outwardly few points of difference as compared with any other conference, yet in reality it consists to a large extent of persons who are not only hearing lectures continually, but whose duty it is to be constantly measuring the value of lectures for teaching purposes. This develops in them a critical spirit, but it also creates a grateful quickness to recognize when eminent lecturers are giving forth their very best and not making the dire mistake of under-rating their hearers.

The fact that year by year the art of lecturing to Extension audiences becomes more developed by practice, is, if true, an indication of a growth in the capacity of the students to understand and appreciate good teaching.

Through the quiet work which goes on all over the country it has become possible to treat a century or a subject from the platform with great breadth and vigour, owing to the certainty of an intelligent response on the part of the students. In consequence of these increased capabilities there has been manifested in a high degree this year that sense of touch between lecturer and audience which is of the very essence of collective teaching. In fact it appeared to me to be a chief characteristic of our recent delightful and successful Summer Meeting.

Yours very faithfully,

LEVESON SCARTH.

— — ... —— .— —

LECTURERS' RESERVE FUND.

SUBSCRIPTIONS AND DONATIONS RECEIVED SINCE JAN. 22, 1895.

	£	s.	d.
The Misses Prangley	1	1	0
Miss Bridges	0	10	0
Miss Lee	0	10	0
Miss Bentley	0	10	0
Miss Cooke	0	5	0
Miss Snowdon	0	5	0
Mrs. Reid	0	5	0

Travelling Libraries: their Purpose and Possibilities.

(*By a Local Secretary.*)

ONE of the subjects discussed at the Oxford Summer Meeting this year was the scarcity of books in towns where there were no free libraries. The Travelling Libraries sent down to the centres during the lectures are most useful; but they leave a great gap when books are needed, and they come at a time when reading has to be somewhat specialized for writing the weekly papers, and when there is consequently little opportunity for studying the broader aspects of the subject.

For this reason some Students' Associations have made efforts to form small libraries of their own, and to borrow books from other centres. Where this has been carried out, the students have always found that the work done quietly before the lectures has been far more valuable to them than any reading they could accomplish under pressure of time later on.

The new regulations for granting Certificates on Connected Short Courses, held in sequence and supplemented by intermediate work, bring the difficulties of obtaining books into special prominence this year. A supply of books between the courses will now be imperative for those centres that are undertaking connected courses. The question is, 'Where is this supply of books to come from?'

In certain places, such as Bournemouth, the private benefactor has opened the doors of his library to all Extension students, and after some years experience declares that he has never had cause to regret his generosity; but it is to be feared that the possessors of large libraries will not often follow so good an example, and though much more can doubtless be done locally, by the loan of books, than has yet been tried, yet such loans cannot be depended upon, and must always be considered as supplemental. Something too can be done by Students' Associations making an effort to buy a 'library' for one course of lectures, and lending it out afterwards for a small fee, again buying books with the proceeds. But the time may come when no centre wants to hire that particular set of books, and this source of income fails.

Nevertheless, if centres are to be encouraged to work in sequence they must have books, and failing local supplies, we turn once more to consider whether the circulation of the Travelling Libraries can be made still more effective than it is already.

The present 'Travelling Libraries' are sent out about a fortnight before the course of lectures begins. In most small centres such a library, if sent six months earlier, would be sufficient to supply the students with all the books they need for intermediate work.

We therefore offer the following suggestions for the consideration of the Delegacy:

1. That the libraries be sent out as soon as the subject of the course is fixed.

2. That the books should be allowed to remain in the centres until the following March, or in the case of Spring centres, April.

We know that even such a slight change as this appears to be would not be without difficulties. The sending out of the books would come at the busy season in the Secretary's Office instead of as now at a slack time. There would not, at present, be always enough books to supply both Autumn and Spring centres that were taking the same courses. But we hope the difficulties in the official department may be surmounted, and we are sure that many centres would be more than willing to have rather fewer books during the lectures, if they could keep even twelve for intermediate work. In the meantime we look forward to some substantial aid to our work, whether from the State or from the foundation of University Extension Fellowships, or from the 'Pious Founder,' which will ease the financial strain, and will enable the Delegates, who have already done so much, to do still more in supplying the needs of earnest students.

ARRANGEMENTS FOR 1895-6.

Autumn, 1895.

All lectures are at fortnightly intervals except where otherwise stated.

Certificates are awarded on courses of 12 Lectures only.

Centre.	No. of Lectures in Course.	Subject of Course.	Lecturer.	Course begins.	Course (or Half-Course) ends.
UNIVERSITY EXTENSION COLLEGE, READING (even. weekly)	12	Citizen Education...	A. L. SMITH, M.A. ...	Th. Oct. 3	Dec. 19
ALTRINCHAM (evening) ...	6	Mediaeval England	Rev. W. H. SHAW, M.A.	F. Oct. 11	Dec. 20
ASHTON-UNDER-LYNE (aftern.)	6	Puritan Revolution	,, ,, ...	T. Oct. 8	Dec. 17
BIRMINGHAM, SEVERN STREET (evening)	6	The Reformation to the Revolution	,, ,, ...	T. Sept. 24	Dec. 10
BOLTON (evening)	6	The Reformation to the Revolution	,, ,,	Th. Oct. 10	Dec. 19
†BURY (evening)	12	History of Florence and Florentine Art	Rev. W. H. SHAW, M.A. & J. E. PHYTHIAN ...	F. Oct. 4	Dec. 13
†CHELTENHAM (afternoon) ...	12	Italian History	{Rev. W. H. SHAW, M.A. & E.L.S. HORSBURGH, B A.	Th. Oct. 3	Dec. 12
†CHELTENHAM (evening) ...	12	Mediaeval England	,, ,,	W. Oct. 2	Dec. 11
CIRENCESTER (afternoon) ...	6	History of Florence	Rev. W. H. SHAW, M.A.	M. Sept. 30	Dec. 9
GLOUCESTER (evening) ...	6	Mediaeval England	,, ,,	M. Sept. 30	Dec. 9
HEBDEN BRIDGE (evening) ...	6	Making of England	,, ,,	S. Oct. 12	Dec. 21
KESWICK (evening) ...	6	Making of England	,, ,,	M. Oct. 7	Dec. 16
MALVERN (afternoon) ...	6	History of Florence	,, ,,	W. Oct. 2	Dec. 11
OLDHAM (evening) ...	6	The Reformation to the Revolution	,, ,,	W. Oct. 9	Dec. 18
†OXFORD (evening)	12	Age of Elizabeth	{Rev. W. H. SHAW, M A & E.L.S. HORSBURGH, B.A.	Th. Oct. 3	Dec. 12
SALE (evening)	6	English Social Reformers ...	Rev. W. H. SHAW, M.A.	T. Oct. 8	Dec. 17
†STROUD (afternoon) ...	12	Puritan Revolution and the Later Stuarts	Rev. W. H. SHAW, M.A.& E. L. S. HORSBURGH, B.A.	T. Oct. 1	Dec. 10
WIGAN (afternoon) ...	6	History of Venice... ...	Rev. W. H. SHAW, M.A.	W. Sept. 25	Dec. 4
BRIDPORT (evening)	6	British Colonies	J.A.R. MARRIOTT, M.A.	T. Oct. 8	Dec. 17
†DORCHESTER (evening) ...	12	Industrial Revolution ...	,, ,,	M. Oct. 7	Dec. 16
STRATFORD-ON-AVON (evening)	6	Age of Louis XIV ...	,, ,,	M. Sept. 30	Dec. 9
WEYMOUTH (afternoon) ...	6	English History in 13th century...	,, ,,	T. Oct. 8	Dec. 17
BARNSLEY (evening) ...	6	Shakespeare	F. S. BOAS, M.A. ...	T. Oct. 8	Dec. 17
†BRIGHTON (St. Michael's Hall, morning)	12	Shakespeare and Milton ...	,, ,,	F. Oct. 4	Dec. 13
ROCHDALE (afternoon) ...	6	Browning	,, ,,	W. Oct. 9	Dec. 18
SETTLE (evening) ...	6	Shakespeare	,, ,,	W. Oct. 2	Dec. 11
WAKEFIELD (evening) ...	6	Arnold, Swinburne, and Rossetti	,, ,,	T. Oct. 1	Dec. 10
BRADFORD (evening) ...	6	Eighteenth Century ...	C. E. MALLET, B.A. ...	Th. Oct. 3	Dec. 11
BRIGHTON (afternoon) ...	6	English Prose Writers ...	,, ,,	M. Sept. 30	Dec. 9
MAIDSTONE (afternoon) ...	6	The Two Pitts	,, ,,	T. Oct. 8	Dec. 17
MAIDSTONE (evening) ...	6	The Two Pitts	,, ,,	T. Oct. 8	Dec. 17
NEATH (afternoon) ...	6	The Two Pitts	,, ,,	F. Oct. 11	Dec. 20
NEATH (evening) ...	6	The Stuarts	,, ,,	F. Oct. 11	Dec. 20
OTLEY (evening) ...	6	The French Revolution ...	,, ,,	F. Oct. 4	Dec. 13
SWANSEA (afternoon) ...	6	English Novelists ...	,, ,,	Th. Oct. 10	Dec. 19
†WEST BRIGHTON (afternoon)	12	Age of Elizabeth ...	,, ,,	M. Oct. 7	Dec. 16
†BURGESS HILL (afternoon)	12	Shakespeare	Rev. J. G. BAILEY, M.A., LL.D.	Oct. 17	Dec. 12
DEVIZES (evening) ...	6	In Memoriam	,, ,,	Th. Oct. 10	Dec. 19
EASTBOURNE (afternoon) ...	6	Shakespeare	,, ,,	W. Oct. 2	Dec. 11
TROWBRIDGE		Not fixed	,, ,,	Th. Oct. 10	Dec. 19
TUNBRIDGE WELLS (afternoon, weekly)	10	Shelley, Keats, Coleridge, and Wordsworth	,, ,,	T. Oct. 8	Dec. 10
†WEST BRIGHTON (evening) ...	12	Shakespeare	,, ,,	Th. Oct. 17	Dec. 12
†BOURNEMOUTH (afternoon) ...	12	18th & 19th Century Literature ...	E.L.S. HORSBURGH, B.A.	S. Oct. 5	Dec. 14
BOURNEMOUTH (evening)	6	Puritan Revolution ...	,, ,,	F. Oct. 4	Dec. 13
CANTERBURY (afternoon) ...	6	Age of Elizabeth ...	,, ,,	T. Oct. 1	Dec. 10
CHESTER (evening) ...	6	Not fixed	,, ,,	W. Oct. 9	Dec. 18
†FOLKESTONE (afternoon) ...	12	Shakespeare	,, ,,	M. Sept. 30	Dec. 9
HYDE (evening)	6	French Revolution ...	,, ,,	M. Oct. 7	Dec. 16
LYMINGTON (afternoon) ...	6	Age of Elizabeth ...	,, ,,	F. Oct. 4	Dec. 13
†NEWPORT (evening) ...	12	The Renaissance	,, ,,	W. Oct. 2	Dec. 11
†RAMSGATE (afternoon) ...	12	Napoleonic Era	,, ,,	S. Sept. 28	Dec. 7
†REIGATE (afternoon)... ...	12	Shakespeare	,, ,,	F. Oct. 11	Dec. 20
ROCHESTER (evening)... ...	6	Studies from 18th & 19th Centuries	,, ,,	T. Oct. 1	Dec. 10
†RYDE (afternoon) ...	12	The Renaissance	,, ,,	Th. Oct. 3	Dec. 12
ST. HELENS (evening) ...	6	Epochs from English History ...	,, ,,	Th. Oct. 10	Dec. 19
†SANDOWN & SHANKLIN (aft.)	12	French Revolution ...	,, ,,	W. Oct. 2	Dec. 11
THORNTON (evening) ...	6	Industrial and Economic Questions since 1789	,, ,,	T. Oct. 8	Dec. 17
†VENTNOR (evening) ...	12	The Stuart Monarchy ...	,, ,,	Th. Oct. 3	Dec. 12
HALIFAX (evening, weekly) ...	12	Wordsworth	Rev. P. H. WICKSTEED, M.A.	Th. Sept. 26	Dec. 19
HARROGATE (evening, weekly)	12	Dante	,, ,,	F. Sept. 27	Dec. 20

† The figures in the second column include lectures to be delivered in the Spring Term, when these courses will be continued.

Centre.	No. of Lectures in Course.	Subject of Course.	Lecturer.	Course begins.	Course (or Half-Course) ends.
ILKLEY (afternoon, weekly) ...	12	Dante	Rev. P. H. WICKSTEED, M.A.	F. Sept. 27	Dec. 20
RIPON (afternoon, weekly) ...	12	Dante	„	W. Sept. 25	Dec. 18
BATH (afternoon)	6	The Work of the Air	H. R. MILL, D.Sc. ...	Th. Oct. 10	Dec. 19
BATH (evening)	6	The Work of the Air ...	„ „ ...	Th. Oct. 10	Dec. 19
BEDFORD (evening)	6	Astronomy	A. H. FISON, D.Sc. ...	F. Sept. 27	Dec. 6
†CARLISLE (afternoon) ...	12	Astronomy...	„ „ ...	F. Oct. 4	Dec. 13
COCKERMOUTH (evening) ...	6	Astronomy...	„ „ ...	W. Oct. 2	Dec. 11
EDGBASTON (afternoon) ...	6	Astronomy...	„ „ ...	Th. Oct. 10	Dec. 19
GRANGE (evening)	6	Forces of Nature (Light) ...	„ „ ...	Th. Oct. 3	Dec 12
HODDESDON (afternoon, weekly)	12	Astronomy...	„ „ ...	T. Oct. 1	Dec. 17
KENDAL (evening)	6	Forces of Nature (Light) ...	„ „ ...	F. Oct. 4	Dec. 13
†STROUD (evening)	12	Forces of Nature	„ „ ...	W. Oct. 9	Dec. 18
WINSLOW (evening)	6	Architecture	F. BOND, M.A. ...	T. Oct. 8	Dec. 17
*SOUTHAMPTON (evening) ...	6	Elizabethan Literature, Shakespeare	R. W. BOND, M.A. ...	F. Oct. 11	Dec. 20
WELLS (evening)	6	Shakespeare	„ „ ...	Th. Sept. 26	Oct 5
WESTON-SUPER-MARE (even.)	6	Shakespeare	„ „ ...	W. Sept. 25	Oct. 4
PETERBOROUGH (evening) ..	6	The English Citizen	W. M. CHILDS, B.A. ...	T. Oct. 1	Dec. 10
ASHTON-UNDER-LYNE (even.)	6	The Reformation to the Revolution	W. G. DE BURGH, B.A.	T. Oct. 8	Dec. 17
STAFFORD (afternoon) ...	6	Wordsworth, Coleridge & Scott ...	„ „ ...	W. Oct. 9	Dec. 18
BANBURY (evening)	6	Astronomy...	R. A. GREGORY, M.A.	Th. Sept. 26	Dec. 5
CIRENCESTER (evening) ...	6	Industrial Problems of To-day ...	J. A. HOBSON, M.A. ...	M. Oct. 7	Dec. 16
TEAN (afternoon)	6	Modern Thinkers upon Life ...	„ „ ...	Th. Sept. 26	Dec. 5
KIDDERMINSTER (afternoon)...	6	Architecture	J. E. PHYTHIAN ...	W. Oct. 2	Dec. 11
BAKEWELL (evening) ...	6	South Africa	W. B. WORSFOLD, M.A.	T. Oct. 1	Dec. 10
MATLOCK (afternoon) ...	6	English Poetry & Fiction since 1851	„	W. Oct. 2	Dec. 11
LOUTH (evening)	6	Hygiene	H. E. NIBLETT, B.A.	F. Oct. 4	Dec. 13
CLEVEDON (evening)	6	Hygiene	C. H. WADE, M.A. ...	W. Oct. 9	Dec. 18

Spring, 1896.

Centre.	No. of Lectures in Course.	Subject of Course.	Lecturer.	Course (or Half-Course) begins.	Course ends.
UNIVERSITY EXTENSION COLLEGE, READING (afternoon, weekly)	12	Literature	Rev. J. G. BAILEY, M.A., LL.D.	Not fixed	Not fixed.
„ (evening) ...	6	Astronomy...	A. H. FISON, D.Sc. ...	Th. Jan.16	Mar. 26
BATH (afternoon)	6	Not fixed	J.A.R. MARRIOTT, M.A.	Th. Jan. 23	Apr. 2
BATH (evening)	6	Not fixed	„ „ ...	Th. Jan. 23	Apr. 2
†DORCHESTER (evening) ...	12	Industrial Revolution ...	„ „ ...	Th. Jan. 16	Mar. 26
SWINDON (evening)	6	Not fixed	„ „ ...	W. Jan. 15	Mar. 25
†WEST BRIGHTON (afternoon)	12	Age of Elizabeth	C. E. MALLET, B.A....	M Jan. 20	Mar. 30
†BURGESS HILL (afternoon) ...	12	Shakespeare	Rev. J. G. BAILEY, M.A., LL.D.	Th. Jan. 30	Apr. 23
†WEST BRIGHTON (evening) ...	12	Shakespeare	„ „ ...	Th. Jan. 30	Apr. 23
†BRIGHTON (St. Michael's Hall) (morning)	12	Milton	F. S. BOAS, M.A. ...	Not fixed	Not fixed.
†BOURNEMOUTH (afternoon) ...	12	18th & 19th Century Literature ...	E.L.S.HORSBURGH, B.A.	S. Feb. 1	Apr. 11
*BRECON (evening)	6	Not fixed	„ „ ...	T. Jan. 21	Mar. 31
†CHELTENHAM (afternoon) ...	12	Italian History	„ „ ...	Th. Jan. 23	Apr 2
†CHELTENHAM (evening) ...	12	Mediaeval England	„ „ ...	W. Jan. 22	Apr. 1
DOVER (evening)	6	Not fixed	„ „ ...	M. Jan. 27	Apr. 13
†FOLKESTONE (afternoon) ...	12	Shakespeare	„ „ ...	M. Jan. 27	Apr. 13
†NEWPORT (evening)	12	The Renaissance	„ „ ...	W. Jan. 29	Apr. 8
†OXFORD (evening)	12	Age of Elizabeth	„ „ ...	F. Jan. 31	Apr. 10
†RAMSGATE (afternoon) ...	12	Napoleonic Era	„ „ ...	S. Jan. 25	Apr. 4
†REIGATE (afternoon)... ...	12	Shakespeare	„ „ ...	F. Jan. 24	Apr. 3
†RYDE (afternoon)	12	The Renaissance	„ „ ...	Th. Jan. 30	Apr. 9
†SANDOWN & SHANKLIN (aft.)	12	French Revolution	„ „ ...	W. Jan. 29	Apr. 8
†STROUD (afternoon)	12	Later Stuarts	„ „ ...	W. Jan. 22	Apr. 1
†VENTNOR (evening)	12	The Stuart Monarchy	„ „ ...	Th. Jan. 30	Apr. 9
*CARLISLE (evening)	12	Astronomy...	A. H. FISON, D.Sc. ...	Not fixed	Not fixed.
*HUDDERSFIELD (evening) ...	12	Astronomy...	„ „ ...	Not fixed	Not fixed.
LEAMINGTON (evening) ...	6	Astronomy	„ „ ...	F. Jan. 17	Mar. 27
†STROUD (evening)	12	Forces of Nature	„ „ ...	W. Jan. 15	Mar. 25
WIRKSWORTH (evening) ...	6	Commerce, Colonization & Empire	K. D. COTES, M.A. ...	Th. Jan. 30	Apr. 9
ABERGAVENNY (afternoon) ...	6	English Exploration & Discovery	W. G. DE BURGH, B.A.	S. Jan. 18	Mar. 28
HEREFORD (evening)	6	English Exploration & Discovery	„ „ ...	M. Jan. 20	Mar. 30
LEOMINSTER (evening) ...	6	English Exploration & Discovery	„ „ ...	T. Jan. 21	Mar. 31
ROSS (evening)	6	English Exploration & Discovery	„ „ ...	W. Jan. 22	Apr. 1
GLOUCESTER (afternoon) ...	6	Literature	J. A. HOBSON, M.A. ...	F Jan. 17	Mar. 27
GLOUCESTER (evening) ...	6	Problems of Poverty	„	F Jan. 17	Mar. 27
BEDFORD (evening)	6	Architecture	ARNOLD MITCHELL, F.R.I.B.A.	F. Jan. 24	Mar. 13
†BURY (evening)	12	Florentine Art	J. E. PHYTHIAN ...	Not fixed	Not fixed.
*ANCOATS (evening)	6	Not fixed	H. BELLUC	Not fixed	Not fixed.
*KERSAL (evening, weekly) ...	8	France in the 18th Century ...	„ „ ...	M. Jan. 20	Mar. 9

† The figures in the second column include the lectures given in the Autumn Term, from which these courses are continued.

* Arrangements not yet completed.

Note.—Application for Courses and all information as to fees, &c., can be obtained from The Secretary, University Extension Office, Examination Schools, Oxford.

PUBLISHED MONTHLY}
Vol. V. No. 60 }

SEPTEMBER, 1895

PRICE ONE PENNY
Subscription, including Postage
1s. 6d. per Annum

THE OXFORD
UNIVERSITY EXTENSION
GAZETTE

A MONTHLY RECORD AND MAGAZINE DESIGNED TO FURTHER THE AIMS

OF

UNIVERSITY EXTENSION IN ENGLAND AND WALES

CONTENTS

OXFORD
PUBLISHED BY HORACE HART, AT 116 HIGH STREET
AND AT HIS OFFICE IN THE UNIVERSITY PRESS

LONDON: HENRY FROWDE, OXFORD WAREHOUSE, AMEN CORNER, E.C.

AND AT THE RAILWAY BOOKSTALLS

THE UNIVERSITY EXTENSION JOURNAL.

WITH THE COMMENCEMENT OF THE SESSION 1895-96 THERE WILL APPEAR
A NEW PUBLICATION ENTITLED

THE UNIVERSITY EXTENSION JOURNAL.

THE two magazines hitherto published in the interests of the Movement— viz. the *University Extension Journal* and the *Oxford University Extension Gazette*—will no. longer be continued (the former ceasing with the June issue of this year, the latter with the September issue), and the new JOURNAL will deal with the progress of the work throughout the country. It will be published under the official sanction of the Oxford, Cambridge, London, and Victoria University Extension authorities, and will be conducted by a joint Editorial Committee appointed by these four bodies.

It will appear nine times in the year—viz. from October to May, inclusive, on the first of the month, and in July, this number having special reference to the Summer Meeting of the year. The first number will be published on October 1, 1895.

THE UNIVERSITY EXTENSION JOURNAL

WILL BE PUBLISHED FOR THE PROPRIETORS BY

MESSRS. ARCHIBALD CONSTABLE & CO.,

14 PARLIAMENT STREET, WESTMINSTER, S.W.,

To whom all orders, both individual and trade, should be addressed. The price of each number will be 3*d.* ; post free, 3½*d.* The annual subscription will be 2*s.* 3*d.* ; post free, 2*s.* 6*d.* Secretaries of University Extension centres will be entitled to order packets of not less than a dozen at trade rates, particulars of which may be obtained from the Publishers.

All communications for the Editorial Committee should be addressed to the
Sub-Editor, University Extension Journal Office, Charterhouse, London, E.C. ;
or, to the Secretary of the University Extension authority with which the contributor is associated.

Subscriptions may be paid either to the
SECRETARY, UNIVERSITY EXTENSION OFFICE, OXFORD, or direct to the PUBLISHERS.

**All Advertisements and other business communications
should be addressed to the Publishers.**

Oxford University Extension.

THE FOLLOWING PAPERS CAN BE OBTAINED FROM

The Secretary, University Extension Office, Examination Schools, Oxford.

1. Pamphlet containing list of Delegates, Local Secretaries, Lecturers, &c.; Programme of Courses; Table of Fees; Information as to award of Certificates; Scholarships; Summer Meeting, &c., pp. 68, stitched in cover. Price 6d., post free.
2. Instructions and suggestions for the use of Local Committees and others engaged in the Organization of University Extension Teaching, pp. 35. Third Edition. Price 6d., post free.
3. County Council Scholars at the Oxford Summer Meeting, 1892. Price 6d., post free.
4. Specimen copies of Lecturers' Syllabuses. 6d. each, post free.
5. Suggestions for the formation of Students' Associations. 1d., post free.
6. Regulations and programme of the Home-Reading Circles. 1d., post free.
7. Regulations for class teaching in Languages and Natural Science. 1d., post free.
8. The English Universities and the English People. Report of a Conference on the Extension of University Teaching among Workmen, August 3, 1892. 6d., post free.

BOOKS ON OUR TABLE.

The Earth. An Introduction to the Study of Inorganic Nature. By EVAN W. SMALL, M.A., B.Sc., F.G.S. London, Methuen & Co. (University Extension Series.) Crown 8vo, pp. viii, 220. Price 2s. 6d.

The Life and Duties of a Citizen. By HENRY ELLIOT MALDEN. London, Methuen & Co. (Commercial Series.) Pp. xii, 206. Price 1s. 6d.

Louis XIV and the Zenith of the French Monarchy. By ARTHUR HASSALL, M.A., Student of Christ Church, Oxford.

Visitors to any of the last three Summer Meetings will be glad to learn that Mr. Arthur Hassall's long promised volume on Louis XIV has been lately published by Messrs. Putnam. It forms the latest addition to their well-known 'Heroes of the Nations' series. We regret that we are unable, owing to lack of space, to do more than chronicle its appearance, and to say that the work is not unworthy of Mr. Hassall's reputation as a historical scholar.

Four Years of Novel Reading. Edited, with an Introduction, by Professor R. G. MOULTON, M.A., Ph.D. Boston, U. S. A., D. C. Heath & Co.

The above is an exceedingly dainty volume, published by Messrs. Heath of Boston, U. S. A. It contains a most interesting account of the formation and progress of the 'Backworth Classical Novel-Reading Union' from the facile pen of its Secretary, Mr. John U. Barrow. The account is a wonderfully interesting and suggestive one. To this are added an Introduction by Professor Moulton, to whom the initiation of the experiment was due, and four representative Essays on English Fiction by members of the Union. We warmly commend this charming little volume to members of Students' Associations, and to all who are interested in University Extension developments.

Presented by Messrs. Macmillan & Co.

Rowe, Tennyson's *Lancelot and Elaine.* Hallward and Hill, Lamb's *Essays of Elia.* Balfour Stewart's *Lessons in Elementary Physics.* Webb, *Selections from Cowper's Letters.* Morris, Milton's *Tractate of Education.*

THE OXFORD UNIVERSITY EXTENSION GAZETTE.

Bound Copies of Vol. V.

(OCTOBER, 1894—SEPTEMBER, 1895)

Can now be obtained from

THE PUBLISHER, UNIVERSITY PRESS, OXFORD.

Paper Boards, cloth back, Price 3s. post free.

CLARENDON PRESS LIST.

BOOKS SUITABLE FOR CANDIDATES FOR OXFORD LOCAL EXAMINATIONS, 1896.

THE OXFORD HELPS TO THE STUDY OF THE BIBLE. Comprising Introductions to the several Books, the History and Antiquities of the Jews, the results of Modern Discoveries, and the Natural History of Palestine, with copious Tables, Concordance, and Indices, and a series of Maps. New, Enlarged, and Illustrated Edition. 1s. net; or Large-type Edition, 4s. 6d. net.

OXFORD HELPS TO THE STUDY OF THE BOOK OF COMMON PRAYER. Crown 8vo, 3s. 6d.

NOVUM TESTAMENTUM GRAECE. Ed. LLOYD. 18mo, 3s.

A GREEK TESTAMENT PRIMER. An Easy Grammar and Reading Book. By E. MILLER, M.A. 3s. 6d.

SHAKESPEARE'S HENRY THE FIFTH. Edited by W. ALDIS WRIGHT, D.C.L. 2s.

SHAKESPEARE AS A DRAMATIC ARTIST. By R. G. MOULTON, M.A. Third Edition, Enlarged. 7s. 6d.

MILTON'S POEMS. Edited by R. C. BROWNE. Volume I (including 'Paradise Lost,' Book III). New Edition. 4s.

SCOTT'S LAY OF THE LAST MINSTREL. Edited by W. MINTO, M.A. 2s.

NIEBUHR'S GRIECHISCHE HEROEN-GESCHICHTEN. Edited by EMMA S. BUCHHEIM. Stiff covers, 1s. 6d.

CAESAR.—DE BELLO GALLICO. Edited by C. E. MOBERLY, M.A. Books I, II, 2s.; Books I-III, paper covers, 2s.; Books III-V, 2s. 6d.; Books VI-VIII, 3s. 6d.

LIVY.—BOOK V. Edited by A. R. CLUER, B.A., and P. E. MATHESON, M.A. 2s. 6d.

VIRGIL.—AENEID, BOOKS I—III. Edited by T. L. PAPILLON, M.A., and A. E. HAIGH, M.A. 3s.

HORACE.—THE ODES, &c. Edited by E. C. WICKHAM, D.D. 6s.

XENOPHON.—ANABASIS, BOOK III. With Introduction, Notes, &c. By J. MARSHALL, M.A. 2s. 6d.

VOCABULARY TO THE ANABASIS. By J. MARSHALL, M.A. 1s. 6d.

HOMER.—ODYSSEY, BOOKS VII-XII. Edited by W. W. MERRY, D.D. 3s.

EURIPIDES.—MEDEA. Edited by C. B. HEBERDEN, M.A. 2s.

THE ANCIENT CLASSICAL DRAMA. A Study in Literary Evolution. Intended for Readers in English and in the Original. By R. G. MOULTON, M.A. Crown 8vo, 8s. 6d.

A LATIN PROSE PRIMER. By J. Y. SARGENT, M.A. 2s. 6d.

HINTS AND HELPS FOR LATIN ELEGIACS. By H. LEE-WARNER, M.A. 3s. 6d.

A PRIMER OF GREEK PROSE COMPOSITION. By J. Y. SARGENT, M.A. 3s. 6d.

A SHORT HISTORICAL ENGLISH GRAMMAR. By HENRY SWEET, M.A. 4s. 6d.

A PRIMER OF HISTORICAL ENGLISH GRAMMAR. By HENRY SWEET, M.A. 2s.

GEOGRAPHY OF THE DOMINION OF CANADA AND NEWFOUNDLAND. By W. P. GRESWELL, M.A. 6s.

EUCLID REVISED. Edited by R. C. J. NIXON, M.A. 6s.

Sold separately as follows:—

Book I. 1s.	Books I, II. 1s. 6d.
Books I-IV. 3s.	Books V, VI. 3s.

ELEMENTARY PLANE TRIGONOMETRY. By R. C. J. NIXON, M.A. 7s. 6d.

A CLASS-BOOK OF CHEMISTRY. By W. W. FISHER, M.A. Second Edition. 4s. 6d.

ELEMENTARY MECHANICS OF SOLIDS AND FLUIDS. By A. L. SELBY, M.A. 7s. 6d.

HYDROSTATICS AND ELEMENTARY HYDROKINETICS. By G. M. MINCHIN, M.A. 10s. 6d.

AN ELEMENTARY TREATISE ON HEAT. By BALFOUR STEWART, LL.D., F.R.S. Fifth Edition. 7s. 6d.

AN INTRODUCTION TO THE MATHEMATICAL THEORY OF ELECTRICITY AND MAGNETISM. By W. T. A. EMTAGE, M.A. 7s. 6d.

PRACTICAL WORK IN HEAT, AND PRACTICAL WORK IN PHYSICS. By W. G. WOOLLCOMBE, M.A. Each 3d.

BOOK-KEEPING. By Sir R. G. C. HAMILTON and JOHN BALL. 2s.

BRACHET'S ETYMOLOGICAL DICTIONARY OF THE FRENCH LANGUAGE. Translated by G. W. KITCHIN, D.D. Crown 8vo. 7s. 6d.

A CONCISE ETYMOLOGICAL DICTIONARY OF THE ENGLISH LANGUAGE. By W. W. SKEAT, Litt.D. Crown 8vo, 5s. 6d.

MATHEMATICS AND PHYSICAL SCIENCE, &c.

CLASS-BOOK OF CHEMISTRY. By W. W. FISHER, M.A., F.C.S. Second Edition. Crown 8vo, 4s. 6d.

BOOK-KEEPING. New and Enlarged Edition. By Sir R. G. C. HAMILTON and JOHN BALL. oth, 2s.
Ruled Exercise Books adapted to the above may be had, price 1s. 6d.; also, adapted to the Preliminary Course only, price 4d.

ELEMENTARY MECHANICS OF SOLIDS AND FLUIDS. By A. L. SELBY, M.A. Crown 8vo, 7s. 6d.

EXERCISES IN PRACTICAL CHEMISTRY. Vol. I. Elementary Exercises. By A. G. VERNON HARCOURT, M.A., and H. G. MADAN, M.A. *Fourth Edition.* Crown 8vo, 10s. 6d.

TABLES OF QUALITATIVE ANALYSIS. By H. G. MADAN, M.A. Large 4to, paper covers, 4s. 6d.

FIGURES MADE EASY. A first Arithmetic Book. By LEWIS HENSLEY, M.A. Crown 8vo, 6d. Answers, 1s.

THE SCHOLAR'S ARITHMETIC. 2s. 6d. Answers, 1s. 6d.

THE SCHOLAR'S ALGEBRA. Crown 8vo, 2s. 6d.

GEOGRAPHY FOR SCHOOLS. By ALFRED HUGHES, M.A. Part I. Practical Geography. With Diagrams. Crown 8vo, 2s. 6d.

AN ELEMENTARY TREATISE ON ANALYTICAL GEOMETRY. By W. J. JOHNSTON, M.A. Crown 8vo, 10s. 6d.

AN ELEMENTARY TREATISE ON ELECTRICITY. Edited by WILLIAM GARNETT, M.A. 8vo, 7s. 6d.

PRACTICAL WORK IN HEAT. By W. G. WOOLLCOMBE, M.A., B.Sc. Crown 8vo, 3s.

PRACTICAL WORK IN GENERAL PHYSICS. By the same Author. Crown 8vo, 3s.

ENGLISH.

SHAKESPEARE.—SELECT PLAYS. Extra fcap. 8vo, stiff covers. Edited by W. G. CLARK, M.A., and W. ALDIS WRIGHT, D.C.L.

The Merchant of Venice. 1s.	Macbeth. 1s. 6d.
Richard the Second. 1s. 6d.	Hamlet. 2s.

Edited by W. ALDIS WRIGHT, D.C.L.

The Tempest. 1s. 6d.	Coriolanus. 2s. 6d.
As You Like It. 1s. 6d.	Richard the Third. 2s. 6d.
A Midsummer Night's Dream. 1s. 6d.	Henry the Fifth. 2s.
	King John. 1s. 6d.
Twelfth Night. 1s. 6d.	King Lear. 1s. 6d.
Julius Caesar. 2s.	Henry the Eighth. 2s.
Much Ado about Nothing. 1s. 6d.	

THE STUDENT'S CHAUCER: Being a Complete Edition of his Works. Edited from numerous Manuscripts, with Introduction and Glossary. In One Vol., cloth, 7s. 6d. By the Rev. W. W. SKEAT, Litt.D., Editor of the 'Oxford Chaucer.' Six Vols., £4 16s.; and 'Piers the Plowman,' £1 11s. 6d.

SCOTT.—LADY OF THE LAKE. Edited, with Preface and Notes, by W. MINTO, M.A. Extra fcap. 8vo, 3s. 6d.

SCOTT.—MARMION. Edited, with Introduction and Notes, by T. BAYNE. Extra fcap. 8vo, 3s. 6d.

CONCISE ETYMOLOGICAL DICTIONARY OF THE ENGLISH LANGUAGE. By W. W. SKEAT, Litt.D. Fourth Edition. 5s. 6d.

A PRIMER OF ENGLISH ETYMOLOGY. By the same Author. 1s. 6d.

THE PHILOLOGY OF THE ENGLISH TONGUE. By J. EARLE, M.A. Fifth Edition. 8s 6d.

A MANUAL OF CURRENT SHORTHAND, OR THOGRAPHIC AND PHONETIC. By HENRY SWEET, M.A., Ph.D. Crown 8vo. 4s. 6d.

AN ELEMENTARY ENGLISH GRAMMAR AND EXERCISE BOOK. By O. W. TANCOCK, M.A. Third Edition. Extra fcap. 8vo. 1s. 6d.

AN ENGLISH GRAMMAR AND READING BOOK. For Lower Forms in Classical Schools. By the same Author. Fourth Edition. 3s. 6d.

A Catalogue of the Clarendon Press Publications will be sent post free on application.

LONDON: HENRY FROWDE, CLARENDON PRESS WAREHOUSE.

Printed by HORACE HART, Printer to the University (Controller of the Clarendon Press), at his Office in the Press, in the Parish of St Thomas, and published by him at the Depository, 116 High Street, in the Parish of All Saints, in the City of Oxford.—Tuesday, September 3, 1895.

CPSIA information can be obtained
at www.ICGtesting.com
Printed in the USA
BVHW041401050719
552699BV00006B/28/P